For the last twenty years **Jane and Michael Stern** have chronicled American pop culture in eighteen books, including the bestsellers *Elvis World* and *The Encyclopedia of Bad Taste;* in a nationally syndicated newspaper column, "A Taste of America"; and as reporters at large for *The New Yorker* magazine.

Jane & Michael Stern's

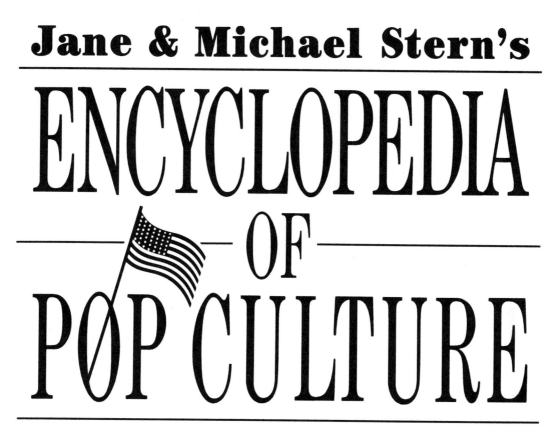

ENCYCLOPEDIA OF POP CULTURE

An A to Z Guide of Who's Who and What's What,
from Aerobics and Bubble Gum to *Valley of the Dolls*
and Moon Unit Zappa

HarperPerennial
A Division of HarperCollinsPublishers

Excerpt from *Mayberry—My Hometown,* by Stephen Spignesi, copyright © 1987. Reprinted by permission of Popular Culture Ink Publishers.

Lyrics from "Louie Louie." Words and Music by Richard Berry. Copyright © 1957 Limax Music, Inc. Copyright Renewed, assigned to Limax Music, Inc., and American Berry Music. International Copyright Secured. All Rights Reserved.

PHOTO CREDITS

Aerobics, Spandex: *The Firm;* Angelyne: *Scott A. Hennig;* Balloons: *Balloon City, USA;* Mr. Blackwell: *Pharos Books;* Dr. Joyce Brothers: *Dr. Joyce Brothers;* Captain Kangaroo, Soap Opera: *CBS Photo Department;* Cheerleading, Davy Crockett, Drive-Ins, Grand Ole Opry, Harley-Davidson, Holiday Inn, Howard Johnson's, Hula Hoops, "I Love Lucy," Jeep, Mickey Mantle, McDonald's, Motown, Mister Rogers: *Preziosi Postcards;* Julia Child: *Paul Child photo;* Crazy Eddie: *East Coast Media;* Credit Cards: *Fleet/Norstar Financial Group Archives;* Cuisinart: *Cuisinarts;* Ann Landers: *Ann Landers;* Arthur Murray: *Arthur Murray, International, Inc.;* "Peanuts": *United Feature Syndicate, Inc.;* Clara Peller, "Saturday Night Live": *TV Collectors;* Nathan Pritikin: *Pritikin Longevity Center;* Remote Control: *Zenith;* "The Simpsons": © *1990 20th Century Fox Film Corp.;* Martha Stewart: © *1991 Elizabeth Zeschin;* Supermarkets: *Food Marketing Institute Archives and the History Factory;* Three Stooges: © *Columbia Pictures Corp., Courtesy of The Three Stooges Fan Club;* Toilet Bowl Cleaner (Automatic): *Block Drug Company;* Wayfarer Sunglasses: *Bausch & Lomb.*

All other photos are from the *Pop Culture Archives.*

FIRST EDITION

DESIGNED BY JOEL AVIROM

LIBRARY OF CONGRESS CATALOGING-IN-PUBLICATION DATA

Stern, Jane.
   Jane & Michael Stern's encyclopedia of pop culture : an A to Z guide of who's who and what's what, from aerobics and bubble gum to Valley of the Dolls and Moon Unit Zappa. — 1st ed.
      p.   cm.
   ISBN 0-06-055343-X — ISBN 0-06-096972-5 (pbk.)
   1. United States—Popular culture—History—20th century.
I. Stern, Michael, 1946–   . II. Title.   III. Title: Jane and Michael Stern's encyclopedia of pop culture.
E169.12.S835   1992
973.9—dc20   92-52546

92 93 94 95 96 DT/RRD 10 9 8 7 6 5 4 3 2 1
92 93 94 95 96 DT/RRD 10 9 8 7 6 5 4 3 2 1 (pbk.)

A c k n o w l e d g m e n t s

For guidance, inspiration, trust, and friendship, we bow in heartfelt thanks to editor Rick Kot. Thanks also to publisher Bill Shinker and agent Binky Urban; to copy editor Patrick Dillon, designer Joel Avirom, and art director Joseph Montebello. We are also grateful to Sheila Gillooly for always being there to help; and, as always and especially, we compliment the investigative work of Sara Palmer, our secret weapon in the front lines of the Dewey Decimal System.

For supplying us with research material and information, we deeply appreciate the contributions of Doodyville scholar Burt Dubrow; Scott A. Hennig in the office of Angelyne; Balloon City, USA; Dr. Joyce Brothers; Julia Child; Bausch & Lomb (Wayfarers); Susan Dumont-Bengsten of Cuisinarts; Ann Landers; Liz Rainey and Mark Henriksen of The Firm (Aerobics); Catherine Horton of Safety 1st (Baby on Board); Eleanor Jacobs (Earth Shoes); Jerry Carroll of East Coast Media (Crazy Eddie); Helen Oakley of Glen Raven Mills (Pantyhose); John I. Taylor of Zenith (Remote Control); Joy Pratt of Keds Corp. (Running Shoes); Diane Dickey of the Kellogg Company (Pop-Tarts); Liz Dolan of Nike (Running Shoes); Dean P. Siegal of Block Drug Co. (Toilet Bowl Cleaner, Automatic); Gary Lassin of the Three Stooges Fan Club; Diane Alpert of TV Collectors of Easton, Mass.; Video Cinema of Georgetown, Conn.; The Tag Sale Shop of Georgetown, Conn.; Mindy Merrell of Dye, Van Mol & Lawrence in Nashville, Tenn.; Beth Buchanan and Barbara van Achterberg of the Bethel Public Library; and Mark and Colleen Pinter (Pop-Tarts, Soap Opera, and more).

Photo credits are on the preceding page.

Contents

Introduction

POP culture is the closest thing America has to a national faith. However different we are, most of us share a common knowledge about subjects as diverse as the Super Bowl, Bruce Springsteen, Cher's tattooed rear end, Oprah's weight problems, "Star Trek," and the Woodstock festival. A few generations ago, to learn about Donald Trump's love life or Roseanne Arnold's childhood sex traumas, you would have had to scour the lowliest gossip magazines; now, such subjects are the stuff of respectable newspapers and prime-time television. Once at the periphery of what seemed to matter, pop culture has become the drumbeat of everyday life. This is nothing less than a major realignment of American culture. Whether it makes you cry or clap your hands with joy, and whether you see it as dismally vulgar or the genuine expression of a robust democracy, pop culture cannot be ignored.

Pop culture *is* American culture. If you doubt it, consider how the rest of the world knows this country. Is it by our ballet, our great painters, or our poet laureate's latest sonnet? Not likely. Nor is America renowned any longer for its industrial might. In the late twentieth century, America's great global image is as a fount of pop culture: Disney World, Madonna, Elvis, James Dean, Levis, rap music, fast food, TV soap operas, and action movies starring Schwarzenegger and Stallone provide—for better and for worse—a new national identity.

America used to be a nation of doers and makers rather than dreamers. It was a land of people proud of their unrivaled assembly lines, vaulting skyscrapers, and waves of amber grain. Today the grain farmer's son, as he toils in the field, likely dreams of playing guitar with a famous rock band; the hardhat's daughter wants to be on the cover of a fashion magazine; and the assembly line worker is madly sending in funny home videos to the TV show that promises to make him an instant star. America has become one big fantasy land, where everyone waits breathlessly for his or her fifteen minutes of fame.

You can look back at pop culture to see just how far we have come in recasting our national character. Think of Frank Capra's *Meet John Doe*, a quintessential 1940s movie, in which Gary Cooper, playing a reluctant everyman, is suddenly thrown into the public eye. His self-effacement is what tagged him as so admirably American: humble, plain, soft-spoken, moral, and ill-at-ease in the spotlight of fame. Now, in contrast, think of the cast of ordinary folks who appear daily on "Oprah!" or "Donahue" or the evening news. Every streetcorner mugger, male stripper, and victim of exploding silicone breasts seems to know exactly which camera to look into, and how to come up with a catchy sound bite. Instead of a blushing Gary Cooper, aghast at finding himself the center of attention, the prevailing philosophy in pop America is that it is better to air one's most personal secrets in public than to live as an unknown.

And so pop culture has become something much more than mere entertainment. It is America's modern mythology, peopled with an ever-changing cast of heroes, devils, and cause célèbres. Being on the cover of a newsmagazine has made a criminal who eats his victims equal in stardom to the President of the United States. The bimbo who slept with the famous man eclipses Mother Teresa in the Q ratings on "Entertainment Tonight." Supermarket tabloids have already influenced two presidential elections, and the more "serious" press has emulated the tabloids by learning to dig up lurid dirt on sex-crime victims.

Our aim in writing an encyclopedia of pop culture has been to preserve and to scrutinize the most important, outrageous, audacious, and symptomatic elements of pop culture as it has evolved since World War II. We believe that it is essential to do so because pop is, by its nature, short-lived. It is not destined to be guarded in museums

or to last for centuries. Some of its most telling manifestations are utterly disposable (lambada, anyone?) and often forgotten (who invented the TV remote control?). A lot of pop culture gets chronicled plenty as it happens, and there is no shortage of information, trivial and scholarly, about such renowned phenomena as Howdy Doody, "I Love Lucy," and Madonna; but despite the prevalence of pop, little effort has heretofore been made to describe the big picture. That is what we set out to do in this book: provide a clear idea of what things mean and how and why each of them has become a significant icon of American mythology.

The strangest thing we realized in researching and writing this book is that, despite the importance of American pop culture both here and around the world, taking it seriously is a relatively new idea. It is only in the last ten or fifteen years that the term *pop culture* has come into common use. A mere four decades ago, such subjects as celebrity, pop music, street fashions, and the like were considered strictly kid stuff, trash for fan magazines, or, at best, sub-rosa stories for reporters with time on their hands.

One thing is certain: Pop is here to stay. That is why we wanted to write an encyclopedia that was a useful reference tool with not only the essential facts about each subject, but also as much lesser-known information as we could find. We wanted to create something deeper than a catalogue of nostalgia, so we strove to offer a perspective of where each entry fits as a facet of America's national character. The goal was to make this book a pop culture literacy guide for a Mickey Mouse world.

To write a truly complete encyclopedia of postwar pop culture would be to create a concordance filled with everything and everybody that mattered outside the world of fine arts, politics, and science for the last forty-five years—in other words, an impossible task, and one whose implications gave us more than a few sleepless nights. We had no scientific formula or readers' survey to determine what ought to be included. We were guided by personal passions and by our own experience as journalists on the pop-culture beat for the last twenty years. We did not include many subjects, such as Barbie dolls and game shows, here because we wrote about them in our previous book *The Encyclopedia of Bad Taste* (Most bad taste is pop culture, but not all pop culture is bad taste). On the other hand, our buddy Elvis Presley appears again despite the fact that we have written about him before, simply because he commands a place in any real pop pantheon.

A few years ago we were halfway around the world in the Canary Islands doing some magazine reporting and as we walked along the dirt street of a little village, people who obviously recognized us as Americans called out to us: "Hello, Michael Jackson; hello, Mickey Mouse." Never did we have a clearer sense that the world has indeed become a global village and that American pop culture is its international language. We hope this book helps you appreciate what an outrageously imaginative country we live in.

AEROBICS

A erobics rewrote the language of sex appeal. This fact was proven by a 1991 broadcast of TV's "Love Connection" on which a male contestant told host Chuck Woolery that he was looking for a sweetheart with less than 10 percent body fat, a pulse rate of sixty or below, and a regular exercise program that included some form of pulmonary conditioning. The show found the lucky guy the girl of his dreams, and she emerged from behind the "Love Connection" partition in a veil of skin-hugging Lurex glory, cross-training sneakers on her feet, and a hot-pink sweat band on her head. She was a vision of cardiovascular preparedness.

The widespread acceptance of aerobics has helped a lot of people get in shape, and its influence on physical culture has been prodigious. But as popular culture, it has gone way beyond hearts and arteries. Its principles and rituals, and the very look of those who do it (or want to convey the impression they do it), have become a kind of modern Holy Writ set to a Top 40 beat.

Going to the gym used to be a rather eccentric obsession for athletes and body builders only. Aerobics made exercise into a popular leisure time activity. What's more, it *changed the shape and size of ideal human bodies.* Long ago, most men yearned to be brawny, and the bigger they were, the more women liked it. Even if a guy's gut hung over his belt, that was socially acceptable just so long as he was massive, which equaled manly. As for women, what mattered on their bodies back in pre-aerobic days was the measure of their bust, the line of their legs, and their general curvaceousness, all of which was about beauty but had nothing to do with vitality.

Susan Harris of The Firm

Consider, if you will, the physiques of Marilyn Monroe and John Wayne in their prime—both considered ideals for their gender. By today's reigning standards, Marilyn was outrageously flabby, maybe 30 percent adipose tissue; Duke, even before he plumped out with age, was a cumbersome side of beef in cowboy boots. Their curves and bulk, respectively, used to be qualities men and women hankered for, for themselves as well as in the opposite sex; but they have now been replaced by aerobic ideals. Today, litheness is testimony to a more sophisticated attitude toward the human form, and men and women alike strive for the aerobic look: sinewy, fat-free, with well-toned but not necessarily huge muscles, and possibly some big, blue popping veins along the arm or up the neck—visible evidence of gangbusters circulation.

The age of aerobics began in 1968 with the publication of Dr. Kenneth H. Cooper's book *Aerobics*. Dr. Cooper, a U.S. Air Force major with a doctorate in exercise physiology, was assigned to develop a special drill for a group of Air Force recruits desperately in need of improvement. They were selected as test patients because they were, in his words, "overweight, over-anxious, chain-smoking slobs." The results? Dr. Cooper said:

> The men who had weight to lose, lost it, or changed fat to muscle.
>
> The smokers quit or cut down. "Don't need it as much any more."
>
> The drinkers found that exercise relieves tensions as much as a Manhattan.
>
> And, in chorus, they exclaimed they felt better, were more relaxed, and were eating less but enjoying it more.

Senator William Proxmire, in the introduction he wrote for Dr. Cooper's book, declared, "There's no doubt about the sheer euphoria that comes from following the Cooper prescription."

Euphoria indeed! Aerobics was boosted by believers as a miracle, and it was certainly the most influential concept in fitness since Yale University football coach Walter Camp formulated the "Daily Dozen" calisthenics in the 1920s. (Camp created his program by watching lions stretching in their cages at the zoo—"hands, hips, head; grind, grate, grasp; crawl, curl, crouch; wave, weave, wing"—and it was popularized via fifteen-minute workout programs on the radio.) Dr. Cooper's idea was simple: aerobics ("a-er-ó-biks," he instructed) was an exercise program designed to stimulate the heart and lungs enough—by jogging, swimming, bicycling, ANY sustained exercise—so the body consumed up to fifty milliliters of oxygen in twelve minutes. Consuming more oxygen increased blood circulation, which made you feel (and *be*) healthier, and prolonged life.

Aerobics and Cooper's sequels, *The New Aerobics* (1970) and *Aerobics Program for Total Well-Being* (1982), as well as the book he wrote with his wife, Millie, *Aerobics for Women* (1972), sold millions of copies. They were easy to understand, and they had a contagiously triumphant attitude. Millie Cooper began her book like this: "I sit here now thinking about what aerobics has done for me in terms of my figure (dress size down to size 8 from size 12), my weight (down 10 to 12 pounds), my energy and sense of well-being, the luxury of eating what I please without worrying about calories, and my freedom from tension and insomnia, and I feel rather smug."

The rise of aerobics as a new regime for millions began in 1971 when Jacki Sorensen, a dancer from Malibu, led the first aerobics dance class of six students in a church basement. Here was a way for people to suck in their daily dose of oxygen and have fun at the same time. Unlike such lonely aerobic activities as running and rowing, aerobic dancing has all the conviviality of a sock hop and a coffee klatch combined: a true bop-till-you-drop gathering of women (maybe some men too) dressed to boogie, with hot music blasting. "Fame," "Gloria," "Beat It," "Totally Hot," and "Boogie Oogie Oogie" have been some of the perennial favorite tunes for aerobic dancing, which has pretty much *become* social dancing for many of its modern devotees. By the mid-1970s, gym floors across the country were rumbling with the thud of students lunging, scissors-kicking, doing buttocks lifts and Rover's Revenge, as well as regularly checking their pulse rate, on their way to good health and happiness.

Aerobics has become a whole culture unto itself in recent years; and thanks especially to diet-and-exercise guru Richard Simmons (see "Infomercials," p. 241), it is now sold not only as a regime for serious fitness buffs, but as a good-time activity for all those who are differently sized (that's the correct term for "fat") and want to have fun "Sweatin' to the Oldies." Anyone can do aerobics at home watching videotapes made by Richard with his hefty friends, or by Raquel Welch, Debbie Reynolds, Hulk Hogan, or, of course, the Godmother of home exercise, Jane Fonda (see p. 181). In addition to dozens of competing videotapes, there are whole catalogues of gear and clothing to affect the aerobics look; and beyond basic running, cycling, swimming, and dancing there are low-impact aerobics (better for the skeleton) and step aerobics (ritualized climbing on and off a single step). The toughest and most effective of all aerobics programs adds weights to the routine and is marketed by a gung-ho company called The Firm, which promises "triple the fat loss" and features men and women with drop-dead gorgeous bodies in their inspirational videotapes. There are now even televised semiprofessional aerobics competitions, similar to the floor exercises in gymnastics contests but with special emphasis on drills that really get the heart pumping.

Even if you don't have an official exercise tape, don't worry. Jacki Sorensen suggested that zealous fitness buffs could fit aerobic behavior into *everything* they do, any time: put on peppy music while cleaning the house and work as fast as possible; become an active cheerleader while watching your favorite sports team on television; try "action cooking," which means doing knee bends, hip swings, and leg lifts while mixing a salad or stir-frying dinner. Even some strip tease artists now base their acts on aerobics routines, peeling off slouch-sock leg warmers and zip-front multitrainer upper body tank tops instead of dinner gloves and seamed stockings.

The greatest impact of aerobics, other than on circulatory systems and ideal body types, has been on fashion. The outfits people wear for aerobic dance classes once would have been taboo in public: too sloppy, or in some cases too revealing. But the new, hyper-oxygenated sense of leisure wear, favored now by lots of fashion-conscious people who might not ever dream of actually exercising, says it's fine to go almost anywhere dressed for the gym. Since 1982, when Jane Fonda started cajoling viewers to "go for the burn" on her *Workout* tape—the best-selling video in history—it has become common to see women and men in malls, restaurants, on trains and planes, and even on "The Love Connection" wearing billowy exercise suits or Supplex thong leotards and Lycra Capri leggings as tight and close-fitting as their skin. Thanks to the rage for aerobics, it is not only socially acceptable and fashionable but downright seductive to look like your day is devoted to stimulating your heart muscle and working up a sweat.

AFROS

The idea of the Afro hairdo, which first got wildly popular in 1968, was to sport a symbol of racial pride. "We decided to stop hating ourselves, trying to look like you, bleaching our hair, straightening our hair," a member of the Afro American Students Union at the University of California told a white reporter from the *New York Times* in 1967. The next year James Brown released a song called "Say It Loud—I'm Black and I'm Proud" and transformed his famous acrylic-smooth waved and curled locks into a spongy diadem of only slightly relaxed black hair without even a twinkle of pomade. "It was like givin' up something for Lent," Brown said about the change of appearance. "It was a real attraction to my business, but I would cut it off for the Movement." Sylvester Stewart, a former disc jockey, got a multiracial act together called Sly and the Family Stone and toured America and England in 1968 wearing an immense Afro and singing about togetherness. Other popularizers included radical Angela Davis, the Jackson 5 (including pre-altered Michael), Marsha Hunt (poster girl for the musical *Hair*), and Jimi Hendrix.

Long hair had been a symbol of rebellion since white juvenile delinquents had perfected duck's-ass haircuts with greasy sidewall fenders in the fifties; but a lesser-known phenomenon had been happening among disaffected black people at the same time. Huey Newton, a founder of the Black Panthers in 1966, recalled some of his friends refusing to process (straighten) their hair back in the 1950s as a gesture to show their unwillingness to "whiten" themselves in any way. Being "natural" and having natural hair was a way to let the world know you enjoyed your racial characteristics, and Malcolm X frequently chided black people with processed hair, telling them they were capitulating to whitey. The look of free-ranging hair, Huey Newton wrote, "caused awe in some people and frightened others." At the same time, Chicago's most notorious South Side African-American street gang, the Blackstone Rangers, began to cultivate what they called the "Ranger bush," a hairdo with a big, unprocessed top and close-cut sides. They said they liked the bush because it helped cushion the blows of police billy clubs.

The Afro became chic as part of a general renaissance of interest in all things African, including the Swahili language and such clothes as dashikis and caftans. Letting your hair grow natural was one thing, and it was a fairly easy thing to do; but when you grew it out long and carefully shaped and curried it into a serious, symmetrical Afro, you created a great crown with a ceremonial quality underscored by all the tending it required with an Afro rake (a wide-tined comb) and spray cans of Afro Sheen to help it stand up straight and shine. In its first few years of general popularity, until about 1970, the big Afro was the preeminent expression of black pride. It was also a symbol of black power, along with a

AFRO AMERICAN LOOK $14⁸⁸

#7—9353
Today's newest idea in stretch wigs and the very latest look is the NEW AFRO-AMERICAN LOOK! Created to blend with the Afro fashions and jewelry this 100% Dynel wig is permanently curled on a lightweight stretch foundation. Jet Black, Off Black, Dark Brown or Mixed Grey. $14⁸⁸

100% REAL DYNEL

raised fist, and it was worn by virtually all militants (and sympathizers) who considered themselves at odds with white culture.

There was, however, a fundamental ambiguity about using so decorative a haircut as a token of rebellion. In its fullest form, it was just too pretty to retain the fearsome mien that militants wanted to affect. Besides, there was no way to keep a distended Afro neat beneath the military-style black berets favored by the Black Panthers. And then it got so popular it lost even its racial integrity.

The cachet of Afros began to evaporate when lots of people who weren't black began to wear them. After long hair, and the defiance it signified, had gotten stylish in the 1960s, white people with curly hair (who could never hope to imitate the Beatles or Sonny and Cher) found the Afro a handy way to express their own countercultural affiliations. Even Bob Dylan, who was known for an uncombed, freewheelin' thatch in his acoustic days, matched his switch to electric guitar and a rock beat with a shapely crown of curly hair and a new, dandified image, which was the inspiration for the famous Milton Glaser poster included in his *Blonde on Blonde* album. Art Garfunkel was another white boy who grew what was soon being called an "Isro," or in the case of non-Jewish white people, an "Anglo." To this day, big curly crowns of unstraightened hair are fairly common among white men and women. But among most blacks, even those proud to have hair that is natural, the immense, radiant Afro has become a slightly embarrassing reminder of the fashion faux pas of the seventies. What happened to it?

As more and more black entertainers, athletes, and fashion-conscious street people adopted Afros, and as their 'fros grew ever higher, neater, and shinier, the big headdress of hair quickly lost all connotations of "naturalness." It turned from the foremost banner of black pride into a distended parody of it. By the late seventies, the only famous black people still sporting full-fledged Afros were parodic stage acts like the various Parliament Funkadelic groups, led by George Clinton, who once performed in leopard skins, carrying a spear, wearing boots shaped like chicken feet, and outfitted with a blond Afro wig five feet in diameter. Afros are now remembered less for their role as a sign of black pride than as the hairdo of ghetto fops in peach-colored jumpsuits, gigantic knit "applejack" caps, and glitterfunk platform-heeled shoes.

At one time in the 1970s the Afro was banned in Africa. In an effort to promote national pride, the government of Tanzania outlawed them because the outsized topiary halos of hair had become an emblem of western cultural colonialism, favored by fashion-conscious members of Tanzania's decadent elite. The privileged classes had adopted Afros as the high style look because the grandiose hairdo seemed so American. No poor African person, and even few working class people in the U.S.A., had the time or the money required to shape, trim, spray, and maintain so decorative a coiffure.

ALAN ALDA

For six years in a row starting in 1979, Alan Alda was the best-liked human being in America. He was rich, successful, happily married, a good father, a sex symbol that women adored and men found nonthreatening, a champion of underdogs and of women's rights—quite simply the nicest famous person since Shirley Temple. "Concerned, considerate, generous" are the adjectives the *New York Times* said fit him best in a 1981 profile titled "A Nice Guy Finishes First." *People* magazine was even more effusive that year, announcing that Alan Alda "has achieved something close to pop cultural sainthood."

His star has dimmed a bit since those giddy days when he replaced John Wayne (p. 551), who died in 1979, in the Q polls as America's favorite personality; but even if Alan Alda is no longer the guy *Ladies' Home Journal* readers most want to have dinner with (as he was in 1985), his unique combination of decency, whimsy, and iconoclasm established an enduring gold standard: along with his daytime-TV soul mate, Phil Donahue (p. 123), Alan Alda defined a new kind of hero for the 1970s and beyond —the Sensitive Man.

The Sensitive Man was a striking contrast to such other male prototypes of the time as Clint Eastwood and Sylvester Stallone (p. 472), who were more traditional American males in that they didn't talk much, preferring to express themselves (on screen, anyway) through action, which was frequently violent. Alan Alda, on screen and off, talked a blue streak. He was a man of words and feelings, not deeds. Describing Jack Burroughs, the character he played in *The Four Seasons*, a movie he scripted, directed, and starred in in 1981, Carey Win-

frey wrote in the *New York Times*, "While totally male, Alda-Burroughs is a man of sensitivity rather than action, more adept in the kitchen than riding a motorcycle or sailing a boat." Alda himself described Jack Burroughs as "satiric of my own character, like the fact that I like to take off on verbal riffs that I find stimulating but other people either have to put up with or decide is charming in order to be my friend."

Other male stars, to prove they were all-man, might tell the press that their hobby was hunting or fishing or race-car driving, or at least working out with weights; but Alda revealed that his favorite thing to do was to sit around with friends and bare souls. As a lad growing up he had felt repressed because boys weren't supposed to giggle or cry and were expected to score with girls, which offended him. But as a grown-up, Alda learned that men didn't have to be

so tough or always prove their manhood; and in the early 1980s he rejoiced: "Times are changing. I'm delighted to feel kinship with more and more men. Men are feeling free to be exactly what they are."

For Alda, being exactly what you are meant only one thing: talking compulsively, which he did in interviews, and his characters did without mercy on television and in the movies. Writing in *Vogue* about *The Four Seasons*, Amy Gross called Alda "a pornographer of emotions" because he held nothing back, allowed no privacy, leading to conversational moments that were more intimate and embarrassing than any explicit sex scene. "Tall, dark, strong, and talkative, able to confront naked emotions armed only with a wisecrack," Gross wrote, "Alda likes to get to the heart of things. In fact, he's compelled to get to the heart of things."

In addition to being ready, willing, and eager to talk about feelings, Alda endeared himself to American women, as well as to men in search of a less macho self-image, by his disarming lack of swagger. "Off the set, his idea of fun is reading *Scientific American* or having a long conversation," the *New York Times* reported, noting also that "more often than not, the unaffected star even does the family grocery shopping." He also frequently cooked the family meals—Chinese stir-fries, low on the food chain, and with no MSG.

Before he starred in the TV show "M*A*S*H" (1972–1983), Alda (son of actor Robert Alda) just as often played a heel as a likable guy. (In the 1970 movie *Jenny*, he marries a vulnerable and pregnant Marlo Thomas in order to avoid the draft, then isn't kind to her.) At first he worried that "M*A*S*H" would be a "thirty-minute commercial for the Army" (he is a pacifist), but he took the role when its creator, Larry Gelbart, agreed to include an operating-room sequence in each episode, thus assuring

Alda the show would expose the ugly side of war. Based on the Robert Altman movie, "M*A*S*H" (from Richard Hooker's book) was exactly what America needed to watch in the 1970s. Ostensibly about the Korean War, it provided a country wearied and shamed by the conflict in Vietnam a once-a-week opportunity for self-flagellation in the form of antimilitary sarcasm. Alda's character, Hawkeye Pierce, who was conceived in the movie as a skirt-chasing, nihilistic smart-ass, was transformed over the course of the TV show into a feministic upholder of human values against the evils of war, against chauvinism (political and sexual), and against medical hubris. By the end of its run (the last episode was the most-watched episode of a series in television history, attracting 125 million viewers) "M*A*S*H" had become a forum of issues and ideas with a liberal perspective on subjects that ranged from personal relationships to social problems; and Alan Alda—the only person ever to win Emmy awards for acting, writing, and directing—had come to thoroughly personify its point of view. Americans liked, respected, and admired him more than any living human being—especially now that John Wayne was not only dead, but considered by many to be an emblem of a bygone kind of masculinity.

Alda's next television venture, a series based on *The Four Seasons*, was a dud, although Marlo Thomas called it "a great try. Nobody's ever really tried before doing a series that explored friendship." His post–"M*A*S*H" movies, including *Sweet Liberty* (1985) and *Betsy's Wedding* (1990), haven't been too successful, either. Letty Cottin Pogrebin, writing in *Ms.* magazine in 1988, blamed his movies' failure on what she called "wimp-bashing," citing negative reviews that criticized him for playing characters who were sincere, dedicated, and life-affirming—all considered undesirable qualities at a time when macho heroes like Rambo were box office kings. She also noted that Alda personally took a lot of heat in the revisionist 1980s because he was happily married and a vocal advocate of women's rights: misogynists hated this paradigm of egalitarian malehood.

Alda himself once attributed his films' problems to the fact that for more than a decade, "M*A*S*H" fans grew to know and love him as Hawkeye Pierce, the television alter-ego that seemed inseparable from his real personality. As much as the characters he has played on screen share some of Hawkeye's much-vaunted tenderness, they aren't Hawkeye. The Sensitive Man Alan Alda seemed to be on TV in the 1970s was just so darn likable that no one really wants to see him be anybody else.

MUHAMMAD ALI

"A fresh breeze ... flamboyant, colorful, cocky, and confident ... the all-American boy ... the natural attraction, everybody's hero." These are the plaudits fight promoter Bill McDonald pitched at Cassius Marcellus Clay on the eve of his first title fight against world heavyweight champion Sonny Liston in February 1964. McDonald was telling Clay all these things not to puff him up but because he was worried—worried that if fight fans found out the truth about the challenger, the whole counterpoise of the match would be ruined, and no one would pay to see it. Liston had been positioned as the bad guy: a scowling felon, a thug, a bully and a brute. His challenger, Clay, gold medal winner at the 1960 Olympics, had been promoted as the nice, clean, polite, patriotic alternative. But this prefight strategy was being jeopardized, McDonald warned, by rumors that Cassius Clay had become a Black Muslim. He demanded the challenger renounce his faith. Clay refused.

Liston went down in six rounds, beaten by finesse, fancy footwork, stinging combinations, and psychological warfare the likes

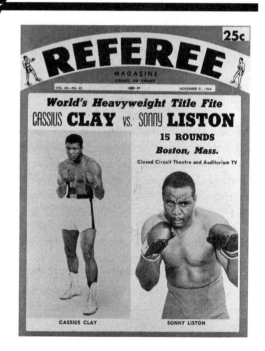

of which boxing had never known. The world had a new heavyweight champion. "I am no longer a slave," Cassius Clay announced the day after he won the title, affirming membership in the Nation of Islam and informing the world that he had taken a new name to symbolize his freedom: he would henceforth be known as Muhammad Ali.

Muhammad Ali became the most famous American on earth. Far beyond the world of boxing, his name came to stand for a new kind of hero who did things his way, according to his own conscience, in defiance of the rules. He was a lightning rod for the 1960s —some have called him the decade's premier antihero—but just as he transcends his sports achievements, he is bigger than the particular issues, including racism and the war in Vietnam, against which he defined himself. Muhammad Ali is a classic; and in some ways, despite his startling originality, he is an immemorial American hero: as full of pride and braggadocio as Yosemite Sam, perpetually young and brash even now as he ages, and a person who, perhaps more than any other celebrity of our time, has felt the absolute freedom to invent himself.

As a showman, he had no peers. Ever since he was a teenage amateur boxer, he developed his ability to attract attention by yelling out at his opponents, "I'm the greatest, I can't be beat!" He explained this strategy in his autobiography, *The Greatest*, by saying, "No one likes a blowhard, an immodest braggart"; so he cultivated his relentless boastfulness to make people *pay attention.* By the time he won his Olympic medal (as a light heavyweight), he was notorious for his gasconade; but it was after he turned pro and went to fight in Las Vegas, in 1961, that he got a lesson from a master—professional wrestler Gorgeous George, whom he remembered crowing to the crowd, "Look at my velvet skin. Look at my pretty hair. If that bum messes up my hair tomorrow night, I'll annihilate him!" Like Gorgeous George, Ali flaunted his vanity—a show-biz tactic previously unheard-of among respectable professional athletes (pro wrestling doesn't count), who were in-

variably expected to be modest and humble. Black athletes, in the tradition of Jackie Robinson, were expected to be even *more* modest and humble, as an implicit sign of their gratitude at being allowed to play. Such compliance was not in Ali's nature. As he prepared for his first title fight with Sonny Liston, he traveled in a bus painted orange, green, red, yellow, and blue; emblazoned across one side: WORLD'S MOST COLORFUL FIGHTER—CASSIUS CLAY. The other side of the bus announced: SONNY LISTON IS GREAT, BUT HE'LL FALL IN EIGHT.

Ali's self-aggrandizing rhymes were outrageous for their unabashed egotism; and although they were uniquely his, they were connected to a long-standing tradition of Afro-American toasts and boasts (see "Rap," p. 411).

The poetry, the predictions stating in which round his opponent would fall, and Ali's generally unruly-seeming (but in fact shrewdly calculated) behavior were more than ways to get attention: They were tactics he used to rattle his foe. It was especially effective in the first fight against Liston, partly because no one had ever seen the full extent of Ali's repertoire before, and also because Liston was terrified of insanity, and Ali knew this. In every other way, Liston was fearless, renowned as a pitiless destroyer; and he threatened to flatten Ali in the first round. So Ali switched strategies and, borrowing a trick from Gorgeous George, made the prefight weigh-in (formerly a drab formality) into the first round, complete with boasts, threats, glares, and a prophecy (correct) of Liston's defeat in six rounds.

Ali's victory and subsequent proclamation of his new name and faith earned him worldwide admiration that few Americans have ever known. The Pope has asked for his autograph; and Russian premier Leonid Brezhnev once instructed an editor at *Izves-*

FLOAT LIKE A BUTTERFLY CHAMP 3 TIMES 1978 STING LIKE A BEE—"ALI"

tia to provide better coverage of his career. In *The Autobiography of Malcolm X*, Malcolm recalled visiting Mecca in 1965 and trying to communicate with the pilgrims who spoke no English. Malcolm had been Ali's mentor, and so the words that came to his mind were "Muhammad Ali Clay—my friend." The listeners misunderstood and thought he was saying that he *was* Muhammad Ali. They lit up "like a Christmas tree," he said, because they liked Ali so much: "Apparently every man, woman and child in the Muslim world had heard how Sonny Liston (who in the Muslim world had the image of a man-eating ogre) had been beaten in Goliath-David fashion by Cassius Clay, who then had told the world that his name was Muhammad Ali and his religion was Islam and Allah had given him his victory." As recently as December 1990, before the shooting war against Iraq started, Ali was able to use his credibility in the Moslem world to win the release of fifteen American hostages being held by Saddam Hussein. When some accused him of becoming a pawn of international politics, one of his companions on the trip said that such issues didn't concern Ali, who "has always shared himself with everybody, unconditionally."

In the beginning of his reign as champion, Ali's new religion was a major issue.

In 1965, after beating Liston a second time (in the first round), he fought one of the nastiest heavyweight fights ever, against Floyd Patterson, who as a matter of principle refused to call Ali by his newly chosen name and had declared that he intended to beat him to keep the title out of Islam's hands. "What's my name?" Ali demanded as he punched Patterson silly for twelve rounds. "What's my name?" Ali's trainer, Angelo Dundee, begged him to knock Patterson out and end his misery; but for Ali, this fight against Patterson, whom he called a "white puppet," was about something more than showmanship. He was in that ring doing battle against all the forces that didn't want him to be the man he was.

He took on his biggest opponent in 1967, outside the ring, when he refused induction in the U.S. Army. He said his religion prohibited him from fighting in a war; but for Ali —as well as for his supporters and his enemies—this was something more than a matter of attaining conscientious objector status. "I ain't got no quarrel with those Vietcong," he said. "They never called me nigger." He was stripped of his championship title and banned from boxing, then sentenced to five years in federal prison for draft evasion. During his appeal and before the verdict was ultimately reversed by the U.S. Supreme Court, Muhammad Ali—exiled from the ring in the prime of his career —became a hero to America's growing antiwar movement, as well as a role model for many, in and out of sports, who were finding that a lot of the issues convulsing the late 1960s demanded his kind of moral fortitude and tough conscience. Baseball great Reggie Jackson called him "king of the athletes." Tennis star Arthur Ashe said, "Ali was fighting for all of us."

Ali began a campaign to win back his championship title. On March 8, 1971, in New York (where posters continued to advertise him as "Cassius Clay, a.k.a. Muhammad Ali"), he met Joe Frazier for the first of three epochal bouts, this one billed as "the Fight of the Century" and deemed by *Ring* magazine "the most hyped fight in boxing history." Ali proclaimed himself "the people's champion," "people" being a somewhat euphemistic term for those outside the establishment. Joe Frazier, on the other hand, was a blue-collar hero, a modest, soft-spoken, Bible-reading Christian whom establishment types found easy to like. Ali called Frazier an Uncle Tom. Frazier called Ali a phony, "using his blackness to get his way." Frazier won a fifteen-round decision, knocking Ali to the mat and handing him his first defeat. All sports writers agreed: no one could have beaten Joe Frazier that night, he was so psyched up for the match. His cornerman Eddie Futch said that while Frazier was normally calm and cool, the pressure of the Ali-Frazier duel had made his man "a machine of destruction."

Three years later, however, Ali returned and beat Frazier; and he beat him again in 1975 in the match known as "the thriller in Manila," for which Ali received a then-record six-million-dollar purse. A lot of people wish he had hung up his gloves in 1974, when he took back the title, from George Foreman, in a match that a then-obscure promoter named Don King managed to stage in Zaire, Africa (where a ringside seat cost $2,492). But Ali seldom did what a lot of people wished; and despite his earlier promises to retire with dignity and his good looks intact, he continued fighting for seven more years. The head blows he took left him suffering pugilistic brain syndrome; the tissue damage combined with a case of Parkinson's disease have now rendered the eloquent dynamo, whose motto was "Float like a butterfly, sting like a bee," a muted still-life of his former self. He did win the title an unprecedented third time, in 1978 from an out-of-shape Leon Spinks, but the final years of Muhammad Ali's career are remembered more for his six brutal losses, especially his penultimate humiliation, at the hands of Larry Holmes (before the final loss, to Trevor Berbick). The Holmes defeat happened in Las Vegas in 1980, when Angelo Dundee finally stopped the fight by throwing in the towel in the thirteenth round as Ali staggered to keep his balance —the first time in his career he could not go the distance. Holmes, the victor, pleaded, "Why did he have to come back?" crying tears for his defeated opponent, who simply did not know when or how to quit.

"ALL IN THE FAMILY"

When "All in the Family" premiered in January 1971, beginning with the sound of a toilet flushing (a television first), CBS put extra phone operators on staff to answer all the angry calls they expected. Almost no one called, and 60 percent of those who did said they liked what they saw. Indeed, not that many people watched; and the show was ranked at a meager fifty-four in the Nielsen ratings. But "All in the Family" built viewership through the summer, via word of mouth and critiques—mostly negative—in the press: "tasteless," decreed the *New York Times;*

Jean Stapleton (Edith Bunker), Sally Struthers
(Gloria Stivic), Rob Reiner (Mike Stivic),
Carroll O'Connor (Archie Bunker)

"boring and predictable," decided *Time;* and Laura Z. Hobson, author of the antiprejudice novel *Gentleman's Agreement,* condemned it for only pretending to be courageous by using such epithets as "hebe" and "spade" rather than the more vicious-sounding "kike" and "nigger." Furthermore, Hobson said that its hero, Archie Bunker, although clearly depicted as a nincompoop and an ignoramus, was nonetheless likable enough to make his racism go down easy.

Neither viewers at home nor the TV industry agreed with the fault finders. "All in the Family" won three Emmys in May, and by the fall it toppled "Marcus Welby, M.D." as the most popular series on the air. It stayed America's number-one show for five years; including its metamorphosis into "Archie Bunker's Place," it enjoyed the second-longest run—twelve years—in situation comedy history (after "The Adventures of Ozzie and Harriet"); and eventually Tom Shales of the Washington *Post* declared it "the most significant and best-written TV series of the decade." Archie Bunker—the first prime-time hero with outspoken political views—became a national institution. (Archie and Edith Bunker's armchairs are now in the collection of the Smithsonian Institution.) The "controversial" nature of the show only added to its ratings at a time when much of America felt the anxiety and titillation of being split into an establishment and a counterculture that seemed intent on destroying each other. As Rick Mitz wrote in *The Great TV Sitcom Book,* " 'All in the Family' gave us permission to laugh, which took some of the pressure off."

It also reflected the freaky fascination many people had at the beginning of the 1970s with blue-collar life, as seen in movies ranging from *Joe* (about a berserk construction worker) to *Kansas City Bomber* (about the déclassé sport of roller derby). Suddenly the lower middle classes, who had been pretty much ignored during the way-out extremisms of the 1960s, were mythologized as the Silent Majority—a force to be cultivated (by Nixon-Agnew, who won a landslide victory in 1972 by appealing to them) or laughed at, as in "All in the Family." Just as so many antiestablishment types yearned to make fun of these blue-collar Blutos, the blue-collar crowd was hungry for a spokesman more sympathetic than Spiro Agnew. Archie Bunker was the man of the hour for both sides.

Liberals loved seeing him spout off, sounding like the worst sort of abusive, narrow-minded bigot; and narrow-minded bigots delighted in seeing one of their own kind validated, in a sense, on prime-time television. The goal of the show was expressed by a disclaimer that CBS added to the beginning of the first episode, when it came on the air following the then very popular "Hee Haw": "The program you are about to see is 'All in the Family.' It seeks to throw a humorous spotlight on our frailties, prejudices, and concerns. By making them a source of laughter, we hope to show, in a mature fashion, just how absurd they are."

Archie Bunker's buffoonish vulgarity was the main butt of the humor, and also a delicious opportunity for all right-thinking viewers to feel good about their own, superior attitudes. The image that ran underneath the show's credits—row houses in Corona, Queens, as seen from a passing car—had a strangely voyeuristic quality, as if the camera were driving through a tacky part of town for kicks; and in fact it can be argued that the popularity of "All in the Family" among middle-class suburbanites had a lot to do with the fact that it gave them an opportunity to make fun of someone who was clearly their social, not to mention intellectual and moral, inferior.

Despite the clear moral thrust against Archie Bunker's narrow-mindedness, he was played with such finesse by Carroll O'Connor that eventually, after many engagingly acted episodes, it grew impossible not to see him as a real, even sympathetic human being. The show was an eloquent forum for statements against prejudice and in favor of tolerance; but in spite of that, Archie Bunker became a national folk hero, or more accurately, a folk antihero. "Move Over, Chairman Mao—Here Comes Archie Bunker!" boasted a paperback book published in 1971 titled *The Wit and Wisdom of Archie Bunker*, filled with his humorously imbecilic ideas about politics, law and order, sex, women's lib, and prejudice.

However dubious Archie Bunker and his opinions, one thing is clear: He was a quintessentially American kind of guy. Oddly, he didn't start that way. The original "All in the Family" was an English television comedy called "Till Death Us Do Part," created in 1965 by Johnny Speight and starring Warren Mitchell as an opinionated, blue-collar dock worker living with a son-in-law who always

gets his goat. Norman Lear, a movie and TV producer who had started his career in comedy back in the 1950s writing material for Dean Martin and Jerry Lewis, bought the U.S. rights to the English show in 1968 and offered the lead role to Mickey Rooney, who turned him down, worrying it was just too offensive to be popular. In 1969 Lear taped two different pilot episodes, now retitled "Those Were the Days" and starring Carroll O'Connor; but ABC, which had the option to air the series, rejected both. The next year Lear sold the show to CBS, which was then struggling to overcome its image as the network of "The Beverly Hillbillies" and "Petticoat Junction"—shows that were immensely popular among viewers in the 1960s but didn't do enough to attract either prestige or money from advertisers (who as a rule don't like rube audiences). Network president Robert Wood was convinced that "All in the Family" was just what CBS needed to develop a more sophisticated image.

In some ways, there was nothing new about this family show that took place in the living room and featured a couple of generations who loved each other but fought a lot. In fact, "All in the Family" harked back to some of television's earliest comedy series. Like "The Life of Riley" and "The Honeymooners," it was about a lower-middle-class urban family; and its hero, like Chester A. Riley and Ralph Kramden, was a slob and a boor whom you couldn't help liking for his ingenuous disposition, however wrong he was. For viewers accustomed to sitcoms of the 1960s, which mostly featured either properly mannered suburban characters ("The Dick Van Dyke Show," "The Brady Bunch," "My Three Sons") or harmless country yokels ("The Andy Griffith Show," "Green Acres"), it seemed daring, almost risqué, to encounter a borough-accented lout like Archie

Bunker, who carried a lunch pail every day to Prendergast Tool and Die Company and was unafraid to mouth off to anyone and everyone with whom he disagreed.

What made "All in the Family" seem revolutionary, and the reason that even today critics bow to it as "the single most influential program in the history of broadcasting" (according to Alex McNeil's *Total Television*), was its focus on contemporary issues. Its characters didn't bicker about going bowling (like the Kramdens) or fixing a leaky faucet (like the Rileys); they fought about all the issues of the day, including race relations, the Vietnam War, the energy crisis, and the Watergate hearings; they debated feminism and whether or not God is dead. The family dynamics were artfully fabricated to provide an ongoing point-counterpoint between Archie and his son-in-law, Mike Stivic (Rob Reiner), known to Archie as "the Meathead," and daughter, Gloria (Sally Struthers), who were as blindly idealistic as he was narrow-minded. Archie's wife, Edith (Jean Stapleton)—whom he usually called "the Dingbat" and frequently advised, "Stifle yourself"—seemed like the show's resident dimwit but could be counted on to provide just enough natural, intuitive wisdom (the kind women, especially mothers, always seem to have on television) to defuse the hostilities between Archie and the kids. Beyond the family, there were neighbors and relatives who served as catalysts for squabbling: the Jeffersons, an African-American family where the father was every bit as dogmatic as Archie; Edith's cousin Maude, a loudmouth liberal who loved taunting Archie; and the Lorenzos, who made Archie furious because they switched traditional sex roles (he cooked; she was a plumber).

In addition to airing funny and clamorous debates about the important issues of the day, "All in the Family" broke ground by building episodes around many personal subjects that had been considered taboo on television, especially in comedies. Edith Bunker went through menopause in one show and got attacked by a rapist in another. ("You smell wonderful," the rapist says. "That's Lemon Pledge," Edith answers.) Gloria (who was also the victim of an attempted rape in one episode) had a miscarriage. Mike had a vasectomy. Archie lost his job.

The basic formula of "All in the Family" —making issues into a source of comedy, and using comedy to explore serious themes—became the familiar refrain of several spin-off shows produced by Norman Lear, including "Maude," "The Jeffersons," "Gloria," and "Good Times" (a spin-off from "Maude"). The effect of this new, heightened sense of purpose on all television programming was profound; and it became almost compulsory for even the silliest sitcoms to appear to deal with relevant issues and contemporary social problems. To be escapist, to present mere fantasy or an idealized picture of life—as had so many family comedies of the 1950s and 1960s—had become anathema. For a lot of people who like to think of television as something greater than America's communal tranquilizer, this development was swell, making the 1970s, which were dominated by "All in the Family" and its progeny, what John Javna in his book *The Best of TV Sitcoms* called "the golden age of sitcoms": "For the first time sitcoms commented intelligently on important issues in American society.... Characters could relate to each other as real human beings did. They did real things—got drunk, divorced, frustrated, depressed. And then (miracle of miracles) at the end, they didn't necessarily solve their problems. The best sitcoms weren't twenty-two minutes to a happy ending anymore."

In addition to this emphasis on important issues, another legacy of "All in the Family" was the predominance of putdown humor in family shows well into the 1980s. The Bunkers and their neighbors and friends, especially the characters in "Maude" and "The Jeffersons," expended so much of their energy humiliating and ridiculing people with whom they disagreed and yelling invective at one another that their raucous hostility began to seem like the TV family norm. By 1984 it was well-nigh heretical when Bill Cosby introduced a television family in which the characters were actually nice to each other (see p. 106).

"AMERICAN BANDSTAND"

Now that popular music, hit movies, and fashion trends are decided mostly by teenage tastes (because teens spend money so generously), it seems practically medieval when you look back at American culture of the 1950s and see teenagers treated as a small and peculiar subculture, separate and distinct from the adult world. Their musical likes, their heroes, and the way they talked and dressed and combed their hair were theirs and theirs alone, and most adults hardly even wanted to know about it. That is probably one reason many people who grew up in the fifties have such rosy memories of it, contrasted to the more homogeneous culture of today. Even if they were not necessarily truly happy days, most pre-Beatles teens can remember the rude delight of feeling part of an exhilarating little world apart where they could wallow in their taste for charm bracelets and pointy-toed shoes, Bobby Rydell and Shelley Fabares, slow dancing and music with a beat you could dance to.

The place where it all came together, the first network series devoted to teens and rock and roll, was "American Bandstand." Well before the brief popularity of "Shindig" (1964–66) and "Hullabaloo" (1965–66), and

a quarter-century before MTV (p. 344) systematized the selling of pop music (and attitude) via television, "Bandstand" was a teens-only musical oasis on a programming schedule filled with such adult series as "Dragnet," "The Life of Riley," and "Arthur Godfrey Time." It lasted well into the 1980s, by which time grown-ups were dressing in blue jeans and paying serious attention to the likes of Madonna; but when it began, it was for teens only; and it heralded the arrival of a new generation eager to embrace a pop culture of its own.

It started as a local show on WFIL-TV in Philadelphia, called "Bandstand," hosted by deejay Bob Horn on a set designed to look like the kind of record shop where you could come in and hear a song you were interested in buying. Horn spun platters and kids danced, but in 1956 he got a lot of bad publicity when he was caught driving drunk, so he was replaced by WFIL radio's Dick Clark, a personality who then hosted a show for teens and adults featuring a mix of popular music and old standards. Clark later remembered arriving on the "Bandstand" set "with only a foggy notion of what the kids, the music, and the show were really about," confessing to one record promoter, "I don't understand this music." Clark caught on quick, rounded up advertisers ("Teens have nine billion dollars a year to spend," he told *Time*), and on August 5, 1957, "American Bandstand" went national on ABC—still the same simple formula of records, dancing, and a set of bleachers for schmoozing between songs. Every fave teen act came to know it as a hitmaker (except Elvis and Ricky Nelson, who never appeared); it helped launch Simon and Garfunkel (then known as Tom and Jerry), Frankie Avalon, and Chubby Checker; and it virtually invented Fabian and Bobby Rydell.

The unique charm of "Bandstand" was due neither to the stars it attracted nor to the charisma of Dick Clark, but rather to the fact that it gave teens at home an opportunity to share time with peers who were anything but TV stars. It was a slice of South Philadelphia teenage life in the raw. Regular Bandstanders Myrna Horowitz, Carmen Jimenez, Carol Scaldeferri, and Denny Dziena dressed as if they had just come from school (they had), the girls in sweater sets or Peter Pan blouses with circle pins and back-belted saddle shoes with rolled socks, the boys in tight pants and winklepicker

shoes. At four o'clock they took center stage and did the greatest after-school job any kid could imagine. They did the Pony and the Stroll and slow-danced and drank Pepsi and played rate-a-record: "I give it an eighty-nine—it's got a good beat and you can dance to it." "Bandstand" kids had it made. They were professional teenagers. As a nation of their peers watched, they flirted, broke up and got back together, and danced all afternoon. For millions of viewers living at home under parental rule, their lives— presided over by benign and distinctly nonparental Dick Clark—was a vision of teenage bliss.

Dick Clark's little world had all the usual cast of characters of every society of young people in the heyday of American teens: the popular beauties, the playboys, the lonely souls. Although the roster of kids changed, there were some who left indelible impressions. Carol Scaldeferri was known as the "Bandstand" cover girl because of her aspirations to be a model. She was famous for precision dancing and a meticulous wardrobe. Jimmy Peatross was the fastest dancer on the show. Jimmy went through partners like popcorn, exhausting girls with his lightning-fast jitterbug.

The soul of "Bandstand" society was its couples, the most famous of which were Bob and Justine. Justine Carrelli first appeared in 1956. Bob (Robert Harry Clayton) was a viewer who fell in love with the beautiful blonde and came from his home in Wilmington, Delaware, to Forty-sixth and Market in Philadelphia (the "Bandstand" studio) to meet her. He was a good dancer, and he was cute...but Justine wanted nothing to do with him. She was going steady with Tex Conners. But Bob's persistence paid off, and soon he cut in. Viewers swooned as Bob and Justine's passion grew stronger, day by day, dance by dance. Then, after two years of public going-steady and after more dreamy looks and sweaty dances than anyone could remember, Bob and Justine split up. No explanation; but everyone, including Dick Clark, looked a little sad to see them on the dance floor side by side, but now with different partners.

In August 1963, "American Bandstand" moved from weekdays to Saturday afternoons. The next year, 1964, the Beatles came to America; and in the spring Dick Clark took the show out of Philadelphia to Los Angeles, where it was easier to book talent and to branch out and produce other television shows. Since then, Clark has built upon his affable image to create an entertainment empire, starting with "Dick Clark's World of Talent" in 1959 and moving on up to "TV's Bloopers & Practical Jokes" in 1984. Now he is probably most famous less for anything he ever actually did, including "American Bandstand," than for the fact that he has stayed so amazingly young-looking. He remained the host of "Bandstand" for the rest of its life, until it went off the air in 1989. Popular as it was until its final years (it was ABC's longest-running series until 1987 when it went into syndication), the switch to Los Angeles and to Saturday afternoons signified a major change of character. The unvarnished magic of the early 1960s, of watching South Philly teens act like teens when school got out, was left behind in the old neighborhood. "American Bandstand"—and the rock-and-roll music it showcased—became big-time show business.

ANGELYNE

"I am famous for doing nothing," Angelyne once said, but show business's oddest love goddess was too modest. She is famous, so to speak, for her billboards, which she has leased in and about Hollywood, as well as in New York and London, since 1981 to promote her career as a sex symbol. Her most famous display was actually the entire side of a building at the corner of Hollywood and Vine, where a ten-story tall likeness of Angelyne gazed down through wraparound sunglasses over and across her bosoms at passing cars for over three years. It is possible you've never heard of Angelyne and have never seen one of her billboards; and we're the first to admit that there are plenty of celebrities who have done greater things than she. But we are obliged to include Angelyne in this

pop-culture pantheon. It's not for what she has done; Angelyne is here for what she, more than anyone, signifies: raw fame, unsullied by any known talent, charm, or accomplishments. Angelyne is a true icon of modern celebrity: a human being who has made herself a giant-size image of renown. All her billboards display her tremendous bust line and puckered lips but contain no written information other than her name, in pink, and the number to call if you want to hire her.

Hire her to do what? That's hard to say, because as Angelyne herself has declared, "I really don't want to be famous for being an actress. Anybody can do that. I just want to be famous for the magic I possess." Whatever her talents and skills as an actress, model, singer, writer, or genetic scientist (all of which she has claimed to be at one time or another), they have nothing to do with Angelyne's great, unchallenged achievement: She has made herself known. Angelyne's press release, printed on hot-pink paper, describes her as "a visual phenomenon, a living icon, Hollywood billboard queen, the new Love Goddess of the future! For those who come to Hollywood in hopes of catching a glimpse of some celebrity, an Angelyne sighting is an unforgettable experience. Driving through the streets of Hollywood in her famous pink Corvette, greeting her fans, Angelyne personifies the glamour and magic that is still Hollywood."

Actually, even if you aren't lucky enough to experience an Angelyne sighting in the flesh or see one of her billboards, you may have seen her in the movies. She says she has appeared, briefly, in five, including *L.A. Story*, in which she has a nonspeaking role as a restaurant patron whose breasts begin to jiggle during an earthquake. (However we must admit that when we saw that movie, we somehow neglected to detect her performance.) And she has had two sandwiches named for her at the Beverly Hills Diner (whitefish and the broiled hamburger patty). She claims to have appeared in print and on television over two hundred and fifty times. She made a record in Europe called "Animal Attraction" and a music video called "My List," and she has written a script called *Angelyne: The Movie*, which "chronicles the adventures of a Sex Goddess in Hollywood and beyond" and begins with a scene in which she places her bust print in wet pink cement. She does not reveal her real name, although it is known that she was born in Idaho and that she is around forty years old.

Angelyne is an idealist, she says, explaining that her ten-year campaign to show her bosoms to the citizens of Hollywood is an effort to make the world a more feminine place. Her long-range goals, according to a recent article in the Los Angeles *Times*, are to one day star as Juliet in *Romeo and Juliet* and to build her own scientific research laboratory. She described her unique star quality as "an inner magic that people can relate to and worship at the same time."

When last interviewed by the *Times*, Angelyne impressed writer Al Martinez as "a caricature, rather than a real person... wearing outfits too preposterous to be enticing for a persona too obvious to be ignored." While he was rattled by Angelyne's fuchsia makeup, hip-swinging walk, wild bouffant hair, and zebra-striped mini-dress, he managed to keep his wits about him and precisely summarize Angelyne's significance: "a perfect metaphor for those who strive with limited talent and staggering ingenuity to be seen."

ANSWERING MACHINES

Most technological gizmos seem extraordinary for a while, then either go away because nobody needs them (electric knives) or blend into the world of things we take for granted (remote control TV). No one is amazed or troubled anymore—as people once were—by the implications of a horseless carriage, a transistor radio, a Cuisinart food processor, or a personal computer. But isn't it strange how answering machines, which are over a quarter-century old, still make a lot of people act so funny?

Some callers are rendered speechless. For many, refusing to leave a message on the tape is a gesture of principle: They consider answering machines to be a symbol that the world is becoming less personal. If you are this type of staunch "people person," you might just refuse to talk to a machine, or possibly leave a Bronx cheer rather than a message; and maybe you will even scold the machine's owner when you finally talk to him or her: How dare they install a robot voice in their place and expect any sensitive-souled human being to exchange words with it! Then, too, there is old-fashioned stage fright. Few other occasions in life call upon you to sum up your thoughts and express them clearly and concisely—for the record. "The caller feels ambushed," Lance Morrow wrote in a *Time* essay in 1984, "like one who has suddenly learned he is being bugged. He becomes more responsible for his words. They are not going to vanish into air. They can be replayed again and again, like the videotape of a fumble. The machine subtly puts the caller on the defensive, thus reversing the usual telephone psychology, in which the caller is the aggressor, breaking in on another's silence."

If talking *to* a machine makes some callers seem rude or foolish, programming one has become a veritable amateur night of merry self-expression that would otherwise have no venue in everyday life. Apparently, many normally reserved answering-machine owners believe they have an entertainer inside them who deserves to come out and spend a little moment in the spotlight. For the length of time it takes to deliver their message, they can take advantage of something that is rare even for professional actors: a captive audience, which sits waiting patiently and politely for a beep. And while it waits, it has the privilege of listening to whatever humorous shtick the answering-machine owner has programmed.

Sometimes the routines try to be cute. You hear recordings of newborn babies gurgling or slurring tots who can barely speak trying to tell you what to do at the sound of the beep. Funny sound effects can be added, such as kazoo whistles or dog barks, or musical passages ranging from Renaissance madrigals to the opening notes of Beethoven's Fifth Symphony to James

Brown yelling "Yow!" Personally recorded singing recitals are popular also, especially around the holidays, when fractured Christmas carols can serve as messages. Then there are jokes: "You have reached Salman Rushdie. I am not home, and I have no intention of telling you where I am, but leave a message anyway." Or the ever-popular "I am not home, but because of all the robberies around here lately I am out buying shells for my shotgun. Leave a message or come on down: I'll be waiting!"

How to Make Your Code-A-Phone Talk Funny, written by Rick Campbell, suggests thematic messages. A plumber might put some gurgling noises on his tape and ask people to leave a message at the sound of the flush. A lawyer might tell callers to plead whether they are innocent or guilty. For a person in love who suspects his sweetheart will be calling, Mr. Campbell advises leaving these words on the outgoing tape: "When I can't see you or touch you the world seems a barren and colorless place. The petals fall from the roses of my heart. High-flying birds cry out." After this message, presumably, one leaves a seagull's shriek in lieu of an ordinary beep. However, Mr. Campbell does not suggest what will likely happen if a colleague from work or your estranged spouse, rather than your lover, calls and listens to you poetize about flowers and birds. Nor does he say what the appropriate response should be if you are the caller and you intrude upon so lyrical a message.

For people who crave to be funny but can neither write nor perform their own routines, imaginative merchandisers market all kinds of messages with other people's amusing voices on them. You can have Humphrey Bogart, W. C. Fields, or Mae West answer your telephone; a while ago, one inventive company was selling a Rich-ard Nixon–voiced recording that said, "I promise not to erase the tape."

According to *Miss Manners' Guide for the Turn-of-the-Millennium*, all such shenanigans are rude: "The best joke in the world would be tedious to anyone who called more than once, and Miss Manners has not noticed a high standard of humor in this particular medium." As for people who call and leave messages expressing anger at being forced to talk to a machine, she wrote, "Miss Manners is tired of hearing that you hate it," and explained that it has done a perfectly fine job (in this one respect) of replacing the butler, one of whose duties was to protect his employer from the unexpected public. She decreed that it was correct to screen calls using a machine, just as it is acceptable to hang up on one if you don't choose to talk to it.

To our knowledge, the one answering-machine protocol on which Miss Manners has not yet issued a ruling is the situation of arriving home with a guest: Do you discreetly turn off the machine and wait until you can hear your messages in private, or do you play your messages with the guest in earshot, risking the embarrassment of sharing whatever intimacies your friends and admirers have left on your tape? Furthermore, may you leave your answering machine turned on while you are entertaining visitors? If you do, and someone calls and begins to deliver a message you don't want your guests to hear, is it polite to drop your drink and canapé and sprint over to the machine in hopes of intercepting it?

In the beginning, when *Time* called answering machines "mildly Buck Rogers" (1965), the niceties of their operation could hardly be imagined. In fact, they were praised precisely because they seemed to promise the elimination of the telephone rudeness associated with answering services, living human beings who sometimes forgot messages, missed calls, or were curt with callers. The first personal models were available in the early 1960s only as rental units ($25 per month) from AT&T. Then in 1965 a company called Robosonics started selling them for $400 to $700, the top-of-the-line model boasting six hours of available message space. These earliest machines were pitched at businesses that needed a way to get customers' messages even if nobody was minding the store. They were especially popular among meat wholesalers, whose retail customers could call and place the next day's order late at night, when all the butchers were home asleep. Late in 1965, the RSVP company began marketing a machine that allowed its owner to call in from anywhere and change the outgoing message. *Time* noted that instead of using an answering machine, lawyer Melvin Belli had equipped his office with a futuristic "call diverter." This device allowed Mr. Belli to switch incoming calls from his office to wherever he happened to be at any time of the day. Since the caller didn't know that the call was being switched, *Time* imagined that this machine "should prove a boon to wayward husbands or junior executives who have slipped out for a quick pick-me-up."

By the early 1980s, answering machines had shed their somewhat eccentric image and become, like Cuisinarts and BMWs, axiomatic gadgets for the home of career-minded young professionals: God forbid they should miss an important call from one of their business associates. According to *The Official Young Aspiring Professional's Fast Track Handbook*, published in 1984 (before "yuppie" became the commonly accepted word for these sorts of people), "the phone answering machine is an essential accoutrement for the YAP household, [en-suring] your round-the-clock availability." The *Handbook* also advised that a new outgoing message every day was a wonderful way to "show callers how clever you are." As for the *The Yuppie Handbook* (1984), it listed answering machines right up there with the Walkman, the cordless phone, and the electronic toy collection as one of the essential ingredients of any careerist's "media room."

In 1985, IBM started selling an alternative to the answering machine, known as the Phone Slave, which used the power of a personal computer to actually carry on primitive conversations with callers: ask questions, deliver messages, maintain a database of who has called. Phone Slaves themselves never got popular, but one of their progeny, voice mail, is well on its way to replacing answering machines—in businesses and soon in private homes, where families use it to deliver and collect elaborate messages for each person in the house. So now, instead of complaining about talking to a gadget, technology's eternal victims find themselves abused by voice mail's required number-punching (to wend one's way through the system) as well as the pleasant music that can be programmed to play while they are waiting to get through. Computerized voice mail almost never makes a mistake and nearly eliminates the need for all person-to-person conversations. It has been installed at the Vatican ("press 1 to hear a message recorded by the Pope") and in doctors' offices ("press 9 if you are having an emergency"), and it seems to be well on its way to making answering machines—with their crude message tapes, vulgar beeps, and mechanical failings—seem almost human.

ROSEANNE ARNOLD

Roseanne Barr (who has since become Roseanne Arnold) appeared on more magazine covers in one year (1989) than any other person in recorded (by *Advertising Age*) history. The woman whom one writer described as "the second coming of feminism" and another called "Donna Reed fattened up for veal" rose from obscurity to become the star of a number-one-rated television sitcom, favorite punching bag of the supermarket tabloids, exalted symbol of working-class womanhood, and inspiration for one of the memorable modern newspaper headlines, in the *New York Post:* BARR-F! At the height of her notoriety, when the President of the United States called her "disgraceful" and *Esquire* magazine named her one of the "Women We Love" because "Roseanne knows who she is," she took stock of her career: "As long as I bitch and get paid for it, I'm the luckiest person in the world."

Prior to her starring in ABC's "Roseanne," she had honed her stand-up comedy routine in the early 1980s in a biker bar and a punk bar in Denver, where she was loved, then in a comedy club where her act was criticized by the proprietor as too "down to earth." In her autobiography, *Roseanne: My Life as a Woman,* she recalled the time a drunken woman in the audience heckled her for not being feminine enough. "Suck my dick," she said to the woman. Presenting herself as a cynical "domestic goddess" fed up with her menial role as a housewife, she swore, made fun of men, used bad grammar, and generally thumbed her nose at all the standards of prettiness and politeness that are applied especially to women. "I had found my voice," she wrote. "No longer wishing to speak in academic language, or even in a feminist language, because it all seemed dead to me, I began to speak as a working-class woman.... This was the language that all the women on the street spoke."

Roseanne had always had a take-charge charisma: as a child, playmates knew her as "Bossy"; in Denver, before becoming a comedian, she gave (in her words) "seminars on racism, classism, anti-Semitism, pornography, and taking power"—all of which she turned into what she called "a brand new thing I call funny womanness." The principle of her funny womanness was to offend her audience. "The bigger comedy is, the more outrageous it gets, the more you can get away with saying," she wrote. "People will laugh and think you're an asshole if they want to, but you're still sayin' it."

Competing against a field of sixteen men, she won the Denver Laugh-Off, went to Los Angeles, and almost immediately debuted on "The Tonight Show." Her own show went on the air in the fall of 1988. The huge and immediate success of "Roseanne" was especially stunning because it knocked "The Cosby Show" out of first place (in the 1989–90 season). "Cosby" had been golden and untouchable, number one since 1985— a warm, friendly program populated with polite, middle-class people. Since "Ozzie and Harriet" and "Father Knows Best," that had been a surefire formula for TV sitcom success. Roseanne owed more to Norman Lear (see p. 11) than Ozzie Nelson; it was anything but polite and middle-class. Although in the beginning there were reportedly cataclysmic fights between Roseanne (who wanted to make the episodes angrier and more issue-oriented) and the writers (who wanted to go for more conventional family comedy), the programs that got on the air were definitely different, if for no other reason than the fact that Mom and Pop in this family were morbidly obese— latter-day Honeymooners with two Ralph Kramdens instead of one. Roseanne and her TV husband were lunch-pail laborers who worried about making ends meet and who drank beer and ate Chee•tos. (Monitors of sex-role stereotyping expressed delight because in this family, the husband was the warm, fuzzy, friendly one.) A publicist for the AFL-CIO declared, "Roseanne does a great job of capturing what a working mother is all about. She connects with reality by showing glamour is lost real soon." *Time* called the show "an honest portrayal of blue-collar family life," with observations that "teach us a lesson."

Not everyone found "Roseanne" so *real.* Television journalist Ron Powers said that it only pretended to raise serious issues (unemployment, child care)—it always defused them and made viewers wind up feeling comfortable and cozy just like any other TV sitcom, and yet smug about their brush with the show's phony social awareness. He found an "essential neutralizing falsity" in the characters' cute grins and Roseanne's "tele-moppet" children and the bland happy endings. In the *National Review*, Jim Atkinson accused Roseanne of reverse sexism; and in the *New York Times*, Ann Taylor Fleming, who couldn't bring herself to like Roseanne, wondered, "Was I just being squeamish, a goody-two-shoes suburban feminist who was used to her icons being chic and sugar-coated instead of this gum-chewing, male-bashing, or at least male-baiting, working class mama with a bad mouth?"

By early 1990, "Roseanne," the show, was scarcely an issue anymore. Roseanne herself had become, in the words of the *Wall Street Journal*, "the human tabloid." There isn't space in this encyclopedia to enumerate all the overly publicized battles with her show's writers and producers (who got fired at her behest), her feud with Arsenio Hall (she accused him of being Jim Nabors's homosexual lover), her fistfights with paparazzi, her headline-making love affair— including vicious fights—and subsequent marriage to Tom Arnold (they got matching tattoos and went on a mooning binge), her battle royal with the *National Enquirer* and its ilk, who have branded her a spoiled bitch and whom she has called "the tabloid assholes," and her sensational front-page revelations that she was sexually abused as a child. Suffice it to say that the unifying theme of everything she does is that Roseanne is a woman who insists on being herself, even—no, especially—if that means flipping the bird at the whole wide world. That absolute, unwavering, and downright pugnacious conviction is why her television fans adore her, even if her motion picture career to date, in *She-Devil,* and as a child's voice in *Look Who's Talking Too,* has been a conspicuous bust. When

Entertainment Weekly listed her at number four among the top entertainers of 1991 (alongside a photo that showed her getting her back tattooed), it explained its admiration: "Amid carefully packaged celebrities, Roseanne is an endangered species: She says what she wants, when she wants, how she wants."

One particular incident does deserve recounting in this regard: Roseanne's interpretation of "The Star Spangled Banner" before the second game of a San Diego Padres double-header on July 25, 1990. Never known for her lovely voice, she was asked to sing the national anthem by Tom Werner, who is not only one of the producers of "Roseanne" but also general partner of the Padres: It would be good publicity all around. When she began to sing, the fans started hooting and hissing: They felt that her screeching, off-key voice was a purposeful sign of disrespect. Later, she said that it was simply the best she could do, especially considering the feedback from the sound system in the ball park. By the end of the song, a crowd of thirty thousand angry patriots was bellowing with anger, so Roseanne did what all good comedians do when they are being heckled: She shot them a zinger. She grabbed her crotch, just like male baseball players are always doing, and she spat, just like any repulsive guy.

Later, Roseanne held a press conference to assure everyone she didn't mean to make fun of the national anthem; still, the next night the Padres brought in the Marine Band to do it properly. Roseanne sang the song better a few days later on Sally Jessy Raphael's talk show, and she broke into public tears on "Into the Night" when a viewer called in and said he intended to kill her. Her show's ratings dropped (but only temporarily) and sponsors withdrew (but not for long), and despite her remorse, Roseanne couldn't help sending one of her famous barbs towards the people who were so upset: "If this is the worst thing they ever heard, they've had it really easy."

ASTRONAUTS

As a job, being an astronaut is still hugely impressive, as distinguished as almost any earthbound vocation. But there was a time when astronauts were more than merely impressive: They were living gods, twentieth-century conquistadors on their way to master the universe. They were the men of the hour at a time when it seemed that the sky was no longer the limit for a human race capable of doing anything it set its mind to.

The fantastic dream of space travel, a pop-culture staple going back at least to George Méliès' outlandish movie, *A Trip to the Moon* (1902), was a growing obsession in the UFO-haunted 1950s. Space was the new frontier, and the exploration of the cosmos (like the exploration of the New World three centuries before) was understood by most Americans to be a totally good and honorable thing to do. Until only recently, planting the flag beyond the horizon has

been considered a symbol of humankind's ever brighter future; so when NASA introduced the first seven astronauts at a Washington, DC press conference on April 9, 1959, it truly seemed like tomorrow was at hand and they were its deliverers. *Time* called them "the architects of man's expansion"; *Life* called them "daring and courageous . . . cool and resourceful . . . physically strong [with] nerves of steel [and] devoid of emotional flaws." It is almost impossible today to fully recollect the immense hope they embodied, and the admiration they inspired, when they were presented to the world.

Their job, called Project Mercury, was not only to begin the conquest of space; it was to eradicate a major inferiority complex the U.S. was suffering. The Russians had beaten us to the heavens, launching satellites called *Sputnik* and *Sputnik II* (the latter carrying Laika the dog) in 1957, then sent a man, Yuri Gagarin, on a round-trip, round-the-world space flight on April 12, 1961. Their rockets were huge and powerful, while ours, in comparison, were limp little wieners that blew up on the launch pad or popped off and belly flopped into the ocean. It was *SO* humiliating: WE WERE LOSING THE SPACE RACE! And the space race, between the Kremlin and what was then known as the free world, was not only

about science and technology. It was a metaphor for the great global struggle of our way of life against theirs. The mandate of the astronauts was to become the first FREE MEN in space, and in doing so, to restore the manly confidence of the U.S.A. In response to Gagarin's pioneering voyage around the earth, President Kennedy one-upped the Reds and announced, in April, "We are going to the moon," proclaiming "a new age of exploration" and describing the space program as "a great new American enterprise."

The men chosen to lead this campaign were selected by the National Aeronautics and Space Administration (started in 1958, just months after *Sputnik*'s launch) from a pool of 508 military test pilots. The name "astronaut," coined by NASA, was meant to suggest the voyaging Argonauts of Greek mythology, as well as the postwar aeronauts (such as Air Force Lt. Col. David G. Simons) who had tested the limits of ascent in helium balloons that soared to over 100,000 feet above the earth. The pilots were given an unprecedented barrage of tests, including these written questions documented in *The Astronauts* (1960):

Analogies

LAUGH: (a. joke, b. cry, c. grin, d. humor) :: JOY: SORROW
VACUUM TUBE: THYRATRON :: CONTINUOUS:
(a. alternating, b. regular, c. discrete, d. diminishing)

True or False

Sometimes I feel like cursing _____ TRUE ____ FALSE ____
Strangers keep trying to hurt me _____ TRUE ____ FALSE ____

Incomplete Sentences

I am sorry that _____

I can never _____

I hope _____

Because earthlings could hardly imagine what superhuman strength was needed to conquer space, the astronauts' physical drills were arduous beyond all logic. Since the early 1950s, Americans had thrilled to scenes in movie newsreels that showed test pilots getting their faces stretched out of shape like a rubber Halloween mask by G-forces while accelerating on rocket sleds, or floating around in the cargo compartments of airplanes that were able to simulate weightlessness for a minute or two. But such amusement-park antics were nothing compared to what potential astronauts had to endure. *Man into Space*, written in 1961, described their ordeals as "a bewildering nightmare of gadgets and instruments of torture," including rides in a chest-crushing centrifuge (during which they were required to solve complex math and engineering problems), gnawingly tedious isolation tests, stress tests (in which they were given an impossible amount of illogical tasks to perform), sleep deprivation tests, tests in which they were jolted from hours of absolute silence by blasts of noise strong enough (in the words of one attendant doctor) "to shake, jar, and then vibrate their entire bodies," and space suit survival tests in which they had to swelter inside their famous silver double-walled garments (which cost $80,000) in a 280-degree heat chamber and wear them while parachuting from an airplane into water (where they then had to float for hours).

All would-be rocket jockeys discovered to be glory hogs or hotdoggers were weeded out, as was anyone who complained, even a little bit, during the tests. Requirements also included being less than 5'11" and under 180 pounds (to fit in the cramped space capsule), under forty years old, and—of course—male. The chosen ones were, in a sense, the most normal guys in America: short-haired, well-groomed WASP family men without discernible psychological quirks. They were, in the word of one flight surgeon who helped select them, "SUPERNORMAL," and their strangely superhuman way of speaking to mission command (which Americans overheard during live space broadcasts) entered the language as a kind of robot-speak suitable for anyone who wants to seem astronautlike—meaning unflappable, efficient, and supremely competent: "A-OK" for okay, "affirmative" for yes, "check" to indicate a necessary task has been performed, "copy" to mean something is understood. (Also, the word "glitch," meaning an unexpected and inexplicable malfunction, was coined by the astronauts to describe the original Mercury space capsules' tendency to signal an emergency when none actually existed.)

Benedictions of the original astronauts in *Life* magazine (to which they sold their exclusive story) were almost as adoring as fan magazine panegyrics to the Beatles. Story after story sang of their excellent character —not only of the heroic qualities they shared, but of every one's unique persona. Just as each of the four lads from Liverpool had his own distinctive and adorable sense of style, each astronaut had at least one endearing personality trait that set him apart. According to the editor of *We Seven*, a book written by the astronauts with the help of *Life* in 1962, these traits were:

Alan Shepard: "bright-eyed and articulate"
Gus Grissom: "warm, friendly, and extremely thoughtful"
John Glenn: "sternly self-disciplined and almost ascetic in his pursuit of perfection"
Scott Carpenter: "an intense, pensive, and sensitive young man"
Deke Slayton: "taciturn and somewhat shy"
Wally Schirra: "the only one who does not wear his hair either close-cropped or in a crew cut . . . the most naturally jovial and outgoing man on the team"
Gordon Cooper: "a twangy, sardonic sense of humor"

These guys were America's last pure heroes, and their unsullied, government-approved goodness made them stars (albeit humble, modest, and unaffected stars).

In their wake, astronauts saturated pop culture, along with almost anything even vaguely related to space travel, from freeze-dried food (which they ate) to silver windbreakers inspired by their suits (see also "Tang," p. 505). G.I. Joe (p. 193) could be outfitted in space duds and stuffed inside a floating space capsule, complete with life raft and oar; and Barbie got a "Miss Astronaut" outfit of metallic silver fabric, gold buckles, zip boots, and white plastic helmet, plus an American flag. (Ken got his own similar "Mr. Astronaut" ensemble.) Television's "I Dream of Jeannie" (1965–70) featured Larry Hagman as an astronaut who had aborted his mission and parachuted to earth on an uninhabited Pacific island. Before he was rescued and brought back home to Florida, he uncorked a bottle containing a genie named Jeannie (Barbara Eden), who became his close friend (platonic until 1969, when they were married), and the source of weekly silly adventures based on her jealousy of other women and his attempt to conceal her magic powers from NASA. There was even a pop singing group who named themselves "the Astronauts" for no apparent reason other than astronauts were out-of-this-world cool (these boys were from Denver and they sang surf songs); "Telstar," an instrumental by the Tornadoes, named for the first communications satellite, sold five million copies in 1962; and David Bowie first made himself known with a song called "Space Oddity" (1969, inspired by Stanley Kubrick's movie, *2001: A Space Odyssey*), in which Bowie assumes the role of astronaut who decides not to come back to earth.

America's astronauts accomplished their mission. They won the space race. Starting with Alan Shepard's first Project Mercury ride, a fifteen-minute, 115-mile high suborbital shot into the stratosphere above the Atlantic Ocean on May 5, 1961, then to projects Gemini and Apollo, our guys licked the Russians. It was a breathtaking come-from-behind story, and even in the beginning when the Russians were still ahead of us (making longer trips, with more men and heavier payloads), the sterling character of the astronauts made America proud. As John Dille, writing for *Life*, put it after John Glenn (now a U.S. Senator) became the first American to orbit the earth in February 1962—*after* the Russians had done so—"Glenn's mission was a much more daring and honest gamble. For Glenn was the representative of a free and open society." *Newsweek* reported that Glenn's accomplishment "lifted the self-doubt that had plagued the United States since *Sputnik*. Gone was the nagging suspicion that the American economic and political system was somehow inadequate." Fêted with the kind of ticker-tape parade generally reserved for victorious generals, Glenn became the personification of all the hope, promise, goodness, and moral enlightenment that space travel (by free men) represented. One fifteen-year-old fan was quoted as saying, "Glenn's an astronaut, and a baseball player ain't nothing."

The climax of the space race came at 10:56 P.M., Eastern Daylight Time, on Sunday, July 20, 1969, when Neil Armstrong became the first human to walk on the moon. As he hopped from the ladder of the LM (lunar module) to the powdery surface of the moon, he said, "That's one small step for a man, one giant leap for mankind." According to George Plimpton, who researched this famous proclamation for *Esquire*, Armstrong made up the words on the spot, amazing people at Mission Control (who considered him a matter-of-fact guy incapable of such a profound construction [and who also knew that the distance between the bottom of the ladder and the surface of the moon was in fact quite a long jump, not a small step]). Plimpton also reassured posterity that Armstrong did indeed say "a man," not merely "man," as most people heard, but that the *a* was lost in transmission.

The lunar landing was, by any measure, a great moment in history—seen on TV by six hundred million people around the world and honored by the Ohio Dairymen's Association with a sculpture of astronaut Armstrong made from nine hundred pounds of butter. That Sunday night huge TV screens were set up in New York's Central Park, where crowds watched and ate free blue cheese as Neil Armstrong and Buzz Aldrin bobbed along the lunar surface (at one-sixth normal gravity) with a buoyant gait reminiscent of Howdy Doody's, and then planted an American flag—their historic walk subtitled with this astonishing caption: LIVE FROM THE SURFACE OF THE MOON. Hotel magnate Barron Hilton revealed plans for the Lunar Hilton, to be built underneath the surface of the moon; and Pan Am (which was then the great, globe-girdling carrier) announced that it had accepted 90,000 civilian reservations for tickets to the moon, to be used for travel just as soon as regular round-trip service was begun.

Reaction to the moon landing was mostly ecstatic. President Richard Nixon (who spoke to Armstrong and Aldrin as they stood on the moon and he sat at his desk in the Oval Office) called the voyage "The greatest week in the history of the world since creation"; and Gina Lollobrigida said, "Nothing in show business will ever top what I saw on television today." But not everyone perceived it as wonderful. Artist Pablo Picasso said, "It means nothing to me . . . I don't care." And Rev. Jesse Jackson complained, "We can send men to the moon [but] we can't get foodstuffs across town to starving folks in teeming ghettos."

Alas, the glorious achievements of the Mercury Seven and the astronauts who followed them in the 1960s happened at a time when many eyes began to turn away from the hope and promise of outer space towards more compelling anxieties here on earth. The month after Neil Armstrong landed on the moon, Charles Manson (p. 299) sent his deranged minions out to begin "Helter Skelter"—what he believed would be an apocalyptic civil war. Helter Skelter didn't happen, but Manson's crimes had undeniable portent as the symbolic demise of many 1960s convictions. By the summer of 1969, the grandiose can-do optimism that energized the beginning of what some dubbed "the space age" ten years before had been eclipsed by cynical melancholy—not just because of Manson and a counterculture gone sour, but because of racial conflict, the Vietnam war, political assassinations, and a sense of sinister social decay. The splendor of the astronauts' triumphs stood in sharp contrast to an overriding disillusionment with so many noble national ideals—including, for many Americans, those once embodied by the space program. Even *The Right Stuff* (1979), Tom Wolfe's bestselling book about the pioneers of the space program, focused almost entirely on their personal derring-do (the meaning of "the right stuff"), with little regard for the patriotic and philosophical righteousness that once defined them.

Since 1981 and the introduction of the space shuttle—a reusable vehicle that serves as a sort of rocket-powered delivery van to cart scientific projects, commercial satellites, and military gear into orbit—a lot of the remaining glamour has gone out of space. The reckless test pilots and intrepid early astronauts of *The Right Stuff* now seem like distant history, and except for Sally Ride, the first American woman astronaut in 1983 (who was cheered in the song, "Ride, Sally Ride"), and Christa McAuliffe, the New Hampshire schoolteacher who perished in the explosion of the *Challenger* in January 1986 (a catastrophe that turned many remaining space fans, especially among the press, into cynics), most modern space travelers are anonymous. "These days few people learn the names of astronauts," Marvin Minsky wrote in *Ad Astra*, the magazine of the National Space Society, in 1991. "Today it is robots like R2-D2 [from *Star Wars*] and HAL [from *2001: A Space Odyssey*] that are 'in.' " Mr. Minsky believes the diminution of the human role in space flight is a very good thing, contending that artificial intelligence is far better suited to explore the universe than sluggish human brains, and that robots don't require the stifling safety standards needed when living astronauts are on board.

Stunning evidence of just how irrelevant astronauts can seem occurred in the early months of 1992, when Soviet cosmonaut Sergei Krikalev was nearly forgotten out on *Mir*, the Soviet space station. Krikalev had been shot into space by the U.S.S.R. in May 1991; but after he began what was supposed to be a five-month stay, the Soviet Union fell apart, and the Baikonur space center from which he left the earth was nationalized by the newly independent Republic of Kazakhstan. When it came time to bring him down, the Kazakhs noticed they had no engineers who could replace him; besides, they were busy with the more pressing earthbound task of creating their nation. So they simply left him out in orbit. A cargo rocket was sent up with food and a sheaf of autumn leaves to remind him of home; but poor Comrade Krikalev continued to circle the earth sixteen times every day with basically nothing to do but tinker with things that needed repair on *Mir*. Sometimes he talked on the radio with his wife and members of the skeleton crew left at the space control center; on occasion he was able to see his two-year-old daughter via television hookup; but few people, either in the former Soviet Union or in the U.S.A., paid his dilemma any mind. Krikalev was finally brought back down in March, still wearing the uniform of the U.S.S.R., which no longer existed. The space race was over for sure.

AVON LADIES

"Ding-dong, Avon calling!" was to midcentury America what "Have a nice day!" has been to recent times. If you lived behind a door with a bell, you could expect to hear it firsthand. On television and radio, stand-up comedians based routines on it. A branch of mutant knock-knock jokes was created, all of which began with "Ding-dong" and usually followed with a ribald punch line about the Avon Lady. "Ding-dong, Avon calling!" was the trademark of women selling Avon cosmetics door-to-door, and it helped make them the best-known sales force in the history of peddling. First heard in television advertisements broadcast in 1954, the Avon Lady's

Avon headquarters

call has become part of American folklore.

The first Avon Lady was a man: David H. McConnell of New York. When Mr. McConnell started selling books for the Union Publishing Company in 1878, itinerant peddlers were considered suspicious characters, with a reputation for knavery inherited from the likes of Connecticut's nutmeg salesmen, who pawned off whittled wooden nutmegs as real. "No respectable sales manager considered for a moment the possibility of a house-to-house campaign," wrote Alfred Fuller, the original Fuller Brush Man, in his autobiography, *A Foot in the Door* (see p. 188). "To do so was the kiss of death, because of the peddler's reputation." In order to get his customers—nearly all of whom were women—to like him, Mr. McConnell began offering free bottles of perfume if they would listen to his spiel.

McConnell bought the book company in 1883, but soon realized that people were more interested in perfume than in Shakespeare. So he created five different fragrances—Violet, White Rose, Heliotrope, Lily-of-the-Valley, and Hyacinth—that in his words had "as fine an odor as some of the old and tried perfumes," and established the exotic-named California Perfume Company in a one-room office on Chambers Street in New York. McConnell hired Mrs. P. F. E. Albee of Winchester, New Hampshire, who had sold books for him, to establish the door-to-door selling strategy. "In her hands I placed the first sample case, or outfit, in the perfume business," McConnell recalled in a memoir he wrote in 1903, in which he anointed her "Mother of the California Perfume Company."

Mrs. Albee believed that housewives would be more likely to trust other women, so she created an all-female sales force; and to assure customers that her ladies weren't like other peddlers, the company instituted a money-back guarantee. In 1897, Mrs. Albee fielded twelve women to sell eighteen fragrances; by the next year, five thousand were going door to door, selling not only perfume but Sweet Sixteen Face Powder, Rose Lip Pomade, headache cures, cologne, shoe cleaner, furniture polish, spot remover, moth-proofer, food flavoring, cookbooks, shaving soap, and tooth-cleansing tablets. McConnell introduced a new line of products in 1929, called Avon in honor of Shakespeare; and in 1939, to reflect its national dominion and expanded product line, the California Perfume Company changed its name to Avon Products, Inc.

In 1936, when Avon received the *Good Housekeeping* Seal of Approval, it began advertising for the first time since 1906. The first ads (which ran in *Good Housekeeping*) asked, "What does 'shopping the Avon way' mean to you?" and answered: "Selecting beauty preparations, toilet articles, exquisite perfumes and household aids in the comfort and convenience of your home. It means dealing with a friendly Avon representative—a trained, carefully chosen, responsible person, living in your own neighborhood." That same year, America got divided into Avon territories, each one covered by a representative overseen by a manager. "No Door Unopened . . . No Bell Unrung" later became a motto used by managers to encourage representatives to call on new customers.

Some interesting firsts and facts:

- Avon introduced the first musk perfume to America in 1906.
- During World War II, Avon supplied American forces with insect repellent and gas-mask canisters.
- In 1975 Avon—the world's largest manufacturer and distributor of cosmetics and fragrances—became the world's largest jewelry manufacturer, known for its "look of real" line of Precious Pretenders.
- There are one-and-a-half million Avon Ladies (and two thousand Avon Men); Avon is the world's biggest employer of women.
- The Avon catalogue is one of the ten most-circulated magazines in America, requiring two million, eight hundred thousand pounds of paper every month.
- Every three weeks Avon representatives call on two-thirds of all the households in Mexico.
- Avon ladies are now at work selling door-to-door in Hungary, Germany, Russia, China, all of Western Europe, Malaysia (where, to please Islamic customers, products are certified alcohol-free), Thailand (where high humidity has made fragrant talcs the best-selling product), Nigeria where skin softener and jewelry sell best), and Japan (where women spend more on skin care and makeup than anywhere else in the world).
- In 1990 Avon introduced its first celebrity scent, Undeniable by Billy Dee Williams, available as perfume, talc, skin softener, and cologne and after shave for men.
- The *Avon Times*, the world's largest monthly publication about Avon memorabilia, lists the following books for *serious* collectors: *Avon Bottles by Any Other Name* (other brands they have made and distributed), *President's Club Jewelry* (awards given to representatives), *Avon's Congratulations—Awards, Gifts and*

Prizes (similar to *President's Club Jewelry* but focusing on plates, china, silver, and spoons), and *Avon's Award Bottles, Gifts and Prizes* (similar to *Avon's Congratulations* but with more award bottles).

- Bud Hestin, author of *Avon Bottle Collector's Encyclopedia*, says, "I think the Avon collecting hobby is the best hobby around today. Avon collecting is for all ages, both young and old. It's a hobby for the entire family." As of 1988, Mr. Hestin had sold 620,000 copies of his book.

Avon has more than five hundred products in its current catalogue. It has peddled videotapes of Patrick Swayze showing viewers *How to Do Dirty Dancing;* after-shave decanters shaped like Winnebago motor homes; combination shoehorn/lint removers; collectible porcelain bells; battery-powered Home Fragrancers, which spritz the air with Nursery Soft, Fresh Lemonade, Herbal Garden, or Clean Air scents; personalizable ceramic coffee mugs (complete with permanent marker); and the Endangered Species Mini Beer Stein collection. Who buys this stuff? According to the *Wall Street Journal*, the typical Avon customer is "the woman who does her work at home maintaining a household, caring for a family, watching Oprah Winfrey on television, worrying along with Ms. Winfrey about her weight, getting a little blue, and actually looking forward to a visit from the Avon Lady."

Avon's most peculiar success in recent years has been a bit of an embarrassment to the company, for whom a tasteful image has always been of paramount concern. Skin-So-Soft, "the beauty treatment for dry skin," sold as lotion, bath oil, body cream, talc, and as individually wrapped after-bath towelettes, has become one of the most exciting underground products since LSD in the sixties. Avon markets it strictly as a dry skin treatment, with all the soft-focus, dainty presentation that so personal a product deserves; but many people buy it because they know it as the ultimate weapon against insects. In fact, it repels mosquitoes so well that the U.S. Army has issued Skin-So-Soft to troops in infested areas (an event Avon doesn't like to talk about); nudist camps reek of it; and flea market hucksters, who buy it by the carton and sell it quite outside authorized channels of Avon distribution (without a money-back guarantee, and with no "Ding-dong, Avon calling!" to their customers), frequently accompany their jugs of the gray-market skin softener with crudely mimeographed tip sheets that list as many as a hundred different uses for the miracle emulsion *beyond* bug repelling.

A bulletin of hints we acquired at a flea market in Illinois in 1991 includes:

- It removes gum from carpet, hair, and skin.
- It removes "ring around the collar."
- It removes Liquid Nail paneling glue.
- It's a wood cleaner.
- It's a massage oil.
- It cleans heavy grease and oil from Ultrasuede.
- It cleans vinyl surfaces inside your car and removes cigarette smoke odor.
- Sponge it around doors and windows to keep crawling bugs out.
- Lubricate pipe joints and fittings that don't slip together as easily as they used to.
- Two glass bowls stuck together? Drizzle a little SSS down the sides and they'll come apart easily.

BABY ON BOARD

Cars are an excellent way to express yourself. A vehicle alone says a lot about its driver (sexy, safe, cute, sporty, drab, well-maintained, or a falling-apart wreck); and beyond its intrinsic qualities, it supplies an abundance of free advertising space to announce to all who pass (or get passed) the beliefs, moods, and favorite things of its occupant. Until 1984, the main means of written communication on cars were little window decals (to exhibit where you had been), bumper stickers (to proclaim your affiliations), and vanity license plates (to show you were someone special). But then Michael Lerner of Newton, Massachusetts, devised a new way of exhibiting your real self to the world. Michael Lerner invented the BABY ON BOARD sign.

Actually, the idea belonged to Mr. Lerner's friend Tony Pintsopoulos; but in 1984, when Mr. Pintsopoulos came to him for advice about marketing a little (five-by-five-inch) yellow square, like a highway Caution

Variation on a theme

sign, to hang in the window of a car and warn everyone around that they should drive extra carefully because there was a baby inside the car, it was Lerner who marketed the hell out of it. "Kids place their trust in grown-ups," he told *People*. "It is for us to add to their well-being." Lerner, a thirtysomething unmarried entrepreneur who had already gotten rich in real estate, explained, "We're in the business of child safety"; and he formed Safety 1st to market the signs. By mid-1986, he had grossed millions selling them for two dollars apiece, at first mostly to proud, conscientious, first-time moms and dads who delighted in trumpeting their parenthood to the world.

Babies were only the beginning. "The yellow fever began with Baby on Board and caught on," *Life* magazine declared in its end-of-1986 summary issue, which featured a two-page photo spread of spin-off signs announcing SECRETARY ON BOARD, SKIER ON BOARD, GENIUS ON BOARD, TWINS ON BOARD, FITNESS FANATIC ON BOARD, 36-24-36 ON BOARD, ATTACK DOG ON BOARD, and COWBOY ON BOARD, as well as one that said BEAM ME UP, SCOTTY. Michael Lerner was not amused. In fact, he thought he was being ripped off; and he was especially peeved that his high-minded concept had been twisted into a joke. Safety 1st, which is still in business selling all manner of things to safeguard children (stove knob covers, window locks, lead test kits), tried to trademark the concept, but it was too late.

There was no stopping the little yellow signs, which, as much as power ties (also usually yellow) and overpriced German sports sedans, perfectly expressed the boastful, self-righteous egotism of the mid-1980s. The purpose of the sign, after all, was to alert others on the road that they were in the vicinity of a vehicle with occupants who expected to get special attention. You didn't have to be a spoiled yuppie to appreciate

this message; and you certainly didn't actually have to have a human baby on board. By 1987, one company in California was offering over a hundred five-by-five-inch yellow "Fun Signs" aimed specifically at pet owners (BULLDOG ON BOARD, MY CAT LOVES ME, even I LOVE HORSES), a hundred "Heart Fun Signs" (from I ♥ ADAM to I ♥ WAYNE as well as I ♥ WHAT'S HIS NAME and I ♥ BOYS—but strangely, no I ♥ GIRLS), plus 282 miscellaneous Fun Signs, including I BRAKE FOR BEER, NOBODY ON BOARD, DAMN I'M GOOD, PROUD TO BE ME, ATTACK CAT ON BOARD, JESUS ON BOARD, WHO CARES WHO'S ON BOARD? and EX-HUSBAND IN TRUNK.

Although they are still available in some truck stops and novelty stores, yellow signs are a fad that's passed; and in 1991 we had a devil of a time locating a classic BABY ON BOARD. In fact, the signs were outlawed in some areas (including New York) as safety *hazards* that reduce vision and may actually increase the chance of accidents. The genre of automobile appliqué that BABY ON BOARD pioneered remains a varied and innovative field, and includes wiggling plush cats with suction cup feet to stick on the insides of windows, as well as tails and hindquarters of small beasts to affix to trunk lids and gas tank doors so the hapless animals appear to have been trapped and squashed there.

BALLOONS

Formerly the innocent, Crayola-colored playthings of childhood, balloons have become the new way to mark almost any occasion including a funeral, for people of every age. They appear at weddings and dog shows, tag sales and bar mitzvahs; they are colored boudoir pink or high-tech silver and shaped like Disney characters or sex organs; and they are branded with slogans ranging from OVER THE HILL to EAT MY SHORTS. People who love balloons see them as a guileless way to bring joy into people's lives. Balloonophobes say they are vulgar— a glaring emblem of cheap, unnatural, ersatz beauty (compared to, say, lovely bouquets of flowers). No doubt about it: balloons have become a class issue.

Three years ago at a wedding reception in the San Francisco Bay area we witnessed a stand-off between the mother of the groom, who had brought hundreds of shiny heart-shaped Mylar balloons to decorate the ceiling of the rented banquet hall, and the bride's family's caterer, Berkeley's best-known chic restaurant, which prepared to leave the premises when a helium tank was wheeled in to fill up the balloons. The foodies announced that their house policy was to never serve their well-bred comestibles in any place hung with such lowbrow decorations. (The dispute was resolved when it was agreed that the balloons would be floated only on one far side of the hall, where people in the food service area would not be exposed to them while they selected their meal from the elegant buffet.)

Environmental activists don't like balloons either, because, they say, balloons turn into unsightly litter and, worse, wild animals eat their deflated remains and die. This was not something anyone was con-

cerned about until 1985, when a dead whale washed up on the New Jersey shore and the Marine Mammal Stranding Center found the remains of a Mylar balloon in its stomach. Two years later, when Susan and Peter Hibbard of Toms River, New Jersey, found another balloon in the stomach of a dead leatherback sea turtle, they founded the Balloon Alert Project, which has led a campaign to prevent mass releases of balloons at outdoor sporting events, political rallies, store openings, and the like. Four states have passed laws restricting balloon releases. "Children don't want anyone to buy balloons anymore," lamented Philip Levin, president of Balloon City, U.S.A., a wholesaler in Harrisburg, Pennsylvania, who said it was young people who had convinced state legislators to ban them. "Crying children say we're killing hundreds of animals."

At the Indianapolis 500 race (which has released balloons every year since 1946), Brownie Scout Troop 245, from the town of Muncie, campaigned to ban balloons in 1991; but their efforts were countered by lobbyists from the balloon industry, who convinced the Speedway to proceed. Declaring that "our studies have indicated little evidence that balloons released into the atmosphere here in Indianapolis have caused animals to die," they sent thirty thousand red, white, and blue balloons up into the Indiana sky.

Lex Latex, a comic-book character created by Balloon City, U.S.A. to fight for balloons' rights, noted in a recently published comic book, 'We all mourn the unnecessary death of wildlife, but our grief shouldn't lead us to jump to conclusions." Mr. Latex, a talking balloon who resembles a water-filled condom with stick limbs and Mickey Mouse–gloved hands, explained that balloons "are a safe and beautiful way to celebrate the American spirit"; and his friend, the clown without a name, reminds readers that "many people all over the world support their families on money they make from balloons." At the end of the comic, after all the kids and grown-ups are convinced to buy lots of balloons, Latex vanishes. "Hey, where'd he go?!" one child asks. "Probably back to nature already," another answers.

The balloon industry says that helium-filled latex balloons generally go five miles up into the air before they burst; then their shreds decay in about a year—faster than oak leaves and wood chips. As for dead animals, Lex Latex argued that the famous balloon-blocked dead whale was actually suffering from pneumonia and had been wounded from a shark attack and battered against a fishing pier in stormy water: the foil balloon in its stomach might have been mere coincidence. Balloon boosters do warn people to never release a helium balloon with anything attached to it that an animal might swallow; and they advise never to launch Mylar balloons, which don't decay.

Not so long ago, balloons were a nearly universal sign of delight with no class or environmental implications. Chinese acrobats used them to decorate their balance sticks as early as 200 B.C.; hot air balloons first ascended in the seventeenth century; and ever since French scientist J. A. Charles discovered hydrogen in 1783 (and filled featherweight taffeta orbs with it), children have loved balloons for their gravity-defying powers. Vulcanized rubber balloons were introduced in the U.S. in the middle of the last century, and they were almost immediately adopted by political parties for rallies where their release and inevitable ascension seemed such a good metaphor for winning. Not only have balloons stood for childlike fun and victory, they also are a convenient symbol of a kind of whimsical freedom, as displayed in the tragicomic French film parable *The Red Balloon* (1955), about a lonely lad whose balloon friend accompanies him everywhere, nearly perishes of deflatus, then lifts him into the sky.

Even before dead animals were found with balloon remains inside them, the naive image of balloons had begun to erode. At fault: Andy Warhol, who in the 1960s sometimes used balloons to decorate his "Factory" studio (anything but a childlike place) and who even included a *silver* balloon in his first book, *Andy Warhol's Index (Book)* in 1967. In short course, like so many pop-art affectations (Mylar wallpaper, supergraphic interior decor), Warhol's metallic balloons floated down the status ladder to become the overmerchandised regalia of what must be called the avant garde manqué. Like unicorns and rainbows, balloons lost a lot of their magic through overexposure. Once a curious kind of pennant for adults with a wacky attitude towards life, they are now a common sight on suburban streets, attached to mailboxes as flags for party guests or to let passers-by know where the tag sale is, then for weeks after that, as sad, slowly deflating reminders of an event long past.

As balloons have become overly familiar signs of prefab uniqueness, manufacturers have made great strides in enhancing the traditional opaque, ovoid latex gasbag. They invented Mylar balloons in the shape of animals, hearts, and letters of the alphabet, micro-Mylars (excellent for balloon arches around the altar at a wedding), and opaque sculptural balloons inside clear round ones. A heretofore unknown profession evolved —that of "balloon artist," who uses balloons to make six-foot-tall wedding hearts, palm trees, pink gorillas, and hula bears for parties or for surprise home deliveries.

BASEBALL CAPS

"Baseball caps are the new T-shirts," the *New York Times* announced in 1991, describing the progress of billed caps "from home plate to fashion plate." Originally designed about a hundred years ago (no one knows exactly when or by whom), the soft, head-hugging beanies with a bill that sticks out only in front were needed so that baseball players—outfielders in particular—could keep the sun out of their eyes and their hat firmly planted on their head, but suffer minimal interference from a brim.

For many years, the only people who dared wear a baseball cap off the field were children—little boys or tomboys in particular—because the rules of fashion allowed tykes to be informal, and it was considered rather adorable to see one sporting a part of his baseball uniform around town. For any adult other than a ball player on duty to wear one in public was a sign that he or she was deranged or delinquent, a derelict unable to afford a decent hat, or, most likely of all, dim-witted. Grown men wore dignified homburgs or fedoras; women favored fashionable feminine millinery. Times have changed now, and adorability is a quality sought by many adults who aren't necessarily suffering from arrested mental development. And because the concept of proper street wear vanished long ago, plenty of grown people have eagerly donned baseball caps as a sign of their youthfulness, exuberance, and fun-loving personality.

It was the ascent of long hair for men and of the bouffant for women in the 1960s that signaled the end of traditional hat styles. Hairdressers replaced milliners as

the arbiters of head fashion, and hat sales went to hell. Hip guys occasionally wore Beatles caps (derived from Greek fishermen's wear), and cowboys continued to wear Stetsons; but most men's and women's heads were left out in the cold. Then a curious thing began to happen in the 1970s. Some time after Ed "Big Daddy" Roth started marketing hot-rod T-shirts to surfers and the car culture (in the mid-1960s), and Budweiser discovered how much party-hearty collegians wanted to wear a Bud-logo T-shirt (in 1975), seed and feed distributors and tractor manufacturers took a cue from these savvy shirt-makers and began to give their customers something even more useful: a cap that would keep the sun out of a farmer's eyes. Known as "cat hats" (after the Caterpillar tractor company, which gave away more than anybody else) or "gimme caps" (because they were free for the asking), the cheaply made, one-size-fits-all billed caps became a favorite fashion not only among farmers and outdoor laborers, who needed them, but also among large numbers of pickup-driving good ol' boys, who welcomed headgear that allied them with a manly country lifestyle but was free of the pomp and the cowboy-dude implications of a ten-gallon hat.

In the 1980s baseball caps expanded from being an essential component of redneck chic to street fashion at all but the truly fashionable levels of society. They appeared as components of fast-food employee uniforms, as part of the ensemble of many rap musicians (generally worn with the bill out to the side or facing backwards), as leisure wear for yuppie dads and moms and their infants, and as advertising vehicles for untold numbers of products, celebrities, rock tours, motion pictures, tourist attractions, and even favorite baseball teams. Some of the significant landmarks in baseball caps' ubiquity include:

- Tom Selleck wore a Detroit Tigers cap on his hit TV show, "Magnum, P.I."
- Madonna was photographed wearing a baseball cap while jogging in Central Park. Early in her career, when she flaunted the hip-hop name Boy Toy, she wore a baseball cap with the word BOY spelled out in mirrored letters on the crown.
- Grandmixer DST, of the Infinity Rappers, wore a fur baseball cap when the pioneering rap group was featured in the New York City Rap Tour of 1982. The style was carried on by Human Beat Box of the Fat Boys, Flavor Flav and Chuck D. of Public Enemy, and Afrika Baby Bambaataa and Sammy B. Manhattan of the Jungle Brothers.
- Billy Crystal, playing a cuddly urban dude in the movie *City Slickers*, wore a New York Yankees cap. The semiology of his attire was explained by Dr. Stuart Ewen, professor of media studies at New York University, as a "new-man image," meaning the wearer is goofy and lovable but no less masculine.
- Spike Lee, originally known for wearing a vintage Brooklyn Dodgers cap, helped popularize caps as advertisements for whatever movie he was currently producing or promoting. Now virtually every Hollywood movie gives out caps with the name of the movie on it—to the crew, to stars for wearing on talk-show publicity junkets, and to street people of all kinds, few of whom seem to have any qualms about becoming walking billboards.
- John Goodman made a baseball cap part of his regular indoor and outdoor attire as the blue-collar husband on "Roseanne."
- Candice Bergen frequently wears a baseball cap, with a place for a ponytail out the back, on "Murphy Brown": she's one of the guys.

Over five hundred million baseball caps are sold or given away in America every year, half of them made in China and the Orient and dumped cheaply in the U.S. market, according to the Headgear Institute of

America. Susan Tildesley, the institute's director, explained the caps' appeal by pointing out that they are cheap and unisex and come in every material, some with built-in ponytails for bald men or people who have to keep their hair short for work but want to sprout some when they go out at night. Many people collect caps and don't even wear them, taking advantage of their festive colors and advertising motifs to use them as cheap decoration on rec-room walls or on the back ledges of automobiles. One other reason for the caps' popularity, Ms. Tildesley pointed out, is concern about cancer. "Don't forget the ozone layer," she said. "Fear of the sun plays a big part in this."

THE BEACH BOYS

For a few years in the 1960s, the Beach Boys and Motown seemed to be the only two musical forces that stood between the American pop charts and the British Invasion. The Beatles appropriated Top 40 music, and in their wake came the Rolling Stones, the Dave Clark Five, Herman's Hermits, Gerry and the Pacemakers, and countless now long-forgotten Merseybeat bands, as well as hundreds of homegrown performers who tried desperately to look and sound and act English, or at least like the four famously successful lads from Liverpool. Meanwhile, the Beach Boys looked and acted like guys from California and sang about good waves, fast engines, girls with tans, and summer vacation.

That is what makes the Beach Boys so outstandingly American. They created poetry out of such unpoetic stuff as power-shifting in a triple-carbureted Little Deuce Coupe or cutting class to hit the beach. Their lyrics were an ode not merely to the sport of surfing but to the joy of the surfing life, including all the wave rider's favorite spots to shoot the pier, the glory of sun-bleached blond hair on boys and girls, the proper car in which to carry one's board (a woody), and the state of California as teen Mecca.

If God is in the details, the Beach Boys were divine, for so many of their best songs enumerate the fine points of this life with obsessive ecstasy and are rich with technical minutiae that convey—better than any abstract poesy—the exultation of riding waves or simply spending a summer catching rays by day and dancing by the moonlight. Much has been said about the acuity of their surf songs; but their car songs were every bit as alluring, and probably the most persuasive argument ever made on behalf of America's love affair with big engines and hot wheels. No one else delineated car culture as convincingly as they did (with the aid of disc jockey and auto enthusiast Roger

Al Jardine, Dennis Wilson, Carl Wilson,
Brian Wilson, Mike Love

Christian, who helped write lyrics), in songs such as "Cherry, Cherry Coupe," "Car Crazy Cutie," "Little Deuce Coupe," "Shut Down," and "A Young Man's Gone," which was one of the most poignant of the car-death songs, about James Dean's crash in a speeding Porsche.

They began as a high school quintet when surfing music was already locally popular—but only as instrumentals by the likes of Dick Dale (and the Deltones), whose genius, it was said, was that he captured the *feel* of the ocean in his twanging guitar and thumping drums. That wasn't quite enough for the Wilson brothers—Dennis, who was himself a surfer, Brian (who was afraid of the water), and Carl. They believed they could become a successful singing group if they had an angle. Their angle would be surfing, and they wrote a song with lyrics that described the surfing life. Along with a cousin, Mike Love, and their friend Al Jardine, they recorded "Surfin' " in the summer of 1961. When it was released as a single on December 8, it became a local hit. KFWB radio played it once an hour, and it eventually got onto *Billboard*'s national Hot 100 song list. They began performing with a repertoire of exactly three songs; but they practiced hard and developed a nice, all-American reputation on the West Coast. They went national in 1962 with "Surfin' Safari."

The Beach Boys found themselves at the vanguard of a trend that began to sweep the country. Surfing, beach parties, summer sun, fast cars, and California: these were the joys of a life that millions of Americans longed to savor. By 1964, when the Beach Boys' "I Get Around" became their first number one hit (on July 4), the notion of fun at the beach (and on the drag strip) was a national obsession (see "Beach Party Movies," p. 40). But that was also the year America discovered the Beatles; and, alas, it is the Beach Boys' fate in nearly all chroni-

cles of rock and roll to serve as an opening act to the more "important" musical trends that followed them. "The success of these Beach Boys' hits provided advance warning of the message that was to be hammered home so forcefully by the British groups," Charlie Gillett wrote in *The Sound of the City*. Critic Dave Marsh described their work as possessing an "inkling of rebellion [which] was never more than implicit," in contrast to the bold and admirable rebelliousness of the British acts who came next.

Hot as they were in the mid-1960s, with such songs as "California Girls" (1965), "Help Me, Rhonda" (1965), and "Good Vibrations" (1966), the Beach Boys were twice killed as culture heroes—not only by the Brits but by the rise of hippies, who had little use for the wholesome fun and well-crafted musicianship that their sensuous harmonies had come to symbolize. The Monterey International Pop Festival in June 1967 put the stake in their heart. The Beach Boys were invited to headline and originally accepted the invitation, but Brian Wilson (who had already suffered a nervous breakdown en route to Australia in 1964) got to worrying: "All those people from England who play acid rock," he said—"if the audience is coming to the concert to see them, they're going to hate us." The Beach Boys backed out and Otis Redding took their place. The music at Monterey defined the new, more exotic, and even occasionally subversive sound of the sixties: Ravi Shankar, the Who, the Byrds; blues, folk rock, hard rock, and the L.A.-based "California sound" of the Mamas and the Papas, but nary a surfer song. During his hot-lick set on Sunday night, Jimi Hendrix paused while playing "Third from the Sun" on his fuzz-tone Rickenbacker (an apocalyptic change from the surf sound's reverberating Stratocaster) and sneered to the audience, "You heard the last of surfing music!"

Of course the Beach Boys didn't just evaporate after Monterey Pop, although they were shut out of the top ten between 1966 and 1976. Like so many other late-sixties pop music acts, they got psychedelic and pretentious for a while; and Brian Wilson, who was now confined to home because of mental problems, developed a reputation as an artist on the verge of greatness, although the album supposed to prove it, *Smile*, got released only in unremarkable bits and pieces, then as *Smiley Smile*. Some critics consider their album *Pet Sounds* (1966) every bit as creative as the Beatles' *Sgt. Pepper* (which it predated by a year), but its harmonic audacity had little appeal to Beach Boys fans, who mostly liked them because they were fun to listen to, not because they were innovative musicians. *Pet Sounds* was their first conspicuous commercial failure.

Touring without Brian, whose reclusiveness only added to his mystique as a genius, the remnant Beach Boys became a good-times oldies act in the seventies and eighties, offering nostalgic memories to aging baby boomers who once looked good in bathing suits. Meanwhile, a darker side of the Beach Boys has emerged, shadowing their legend with ugly stories of severe drug use and awful mistreatment by the Wilsons' abusive father (who may have permanently deafened young Brian in one ear with a childhood beating); and Brian, who has gained and lost hundreds of pounds, has been accused by the others of being in thrall to a Svengali headshrinker. Nonetheless, Brian resurfaces periodically from his strange psychological condition to reclaim his title as pop prodigy. Whatever the group's destiny, however weird Brian gets, and regardless of aficionados' convincing claims for them as truly great and important American artists, the Beach Boys' place in the archives of pop culture is well-ensconced: in the Hall of the 1960s, where they stand as symbols of a sunnier America on the verge of cataclysmic social change.

BEACH PARTY MOVIES

"When 10,000 biceps go around 5,000 bikinis, you *know* what's going to happen." In case you don't know what's going to happen, the poster for *Muscle Beach Party*, the first sequel to *Beach Party*, went on to enumerate: "Surf and Sun, Music, Lovin', and Beach Time FUN!" No sex, no pregnancy, no drugs, no drinking, no illness, no hard work, no cloudy days or lonely nights, no parents, and very few adults were also part of the formula for beach party movies, which were the culmi-

nation of that branch of motion picture art known as teen exploitation cinema.

There were five fundamental beach party movies, all made quickly and cheaply between 1963 and 1965 by American International Pictures (AIP): *Beach Party, Muscle Beach Party, Bikini Beach, Beach Blanket Bingo*, and *How to Stuff a Wild Bikini;* and there were two corollary AIP films, *Pajama Party* and *Ski Party*, as well as several dozen lower-budget imitations, such as *Horror of Party Beach, Daytona Beach Weekend* ("60,000 Fun-Hungry Kids Blow Off Steam!"), and *The Girls on the Beach.* "We simply cannot believe," the *New York Times* observed, "that teenagers buy such junk. It's for morons!" But for a few years —until 1966, when a harsher kind of rock and roll got popular, and teen movies metamorphosed into "youth movies," featuring drugs, protest, and freer sex—teenagers flocked to pictures filled with the antics of happy, wholesome beach bunnies and beach boys enjoying innocent pleasures and living a carefree life that seemed like endless summer.

Ironically, *Beach Party*, the first of the genre, was conceived by AIP as a story about dope-smoking juvenile delinquents— bad kids out for trouble. That's pretty much the formula AIP had used since it started in the teen exploitation business in 1956 with such pictures as *Dragstrip Girl, Motorcycle Girl, The Cat Girl, Island of Prehistoric Women*, and *Invasion of the Saucer Men.* Every few years there was a new theme that AIP (and other production companies) tended to milk for all it was worth: beatniks, girls in prison, teenage monsters, high school rebels. Big studios had done well with *Gidget, Where the Boys Are*, and *Blue Hawaii* (the latter starring Elvis), all of which took place mostly on the beach, and AIP believed that beaches and teens could be the next winning formula.

When they gave the script of *Beach Party* to director William Asher (of television's "I Love Lucy"), he changed it totally, declaring that audiences were "bored with juvenile delinquency" and eager to see some nice, clean sex appeal on the screen. Instead of the usual wild-youth-on-the-rampage story, Asher made a movie about likable kids who wanted nothing but respectable fun. For the lead roles he cast ex-Mouseketeer Annette Funicello (still under contract to Walt Disney, who insisted she keep her navel covered) and ex-teen idol Frankie Avalon, whose songs "Venus" and "Why" had both risen to number one in 1959 and who had played the male ingenue in *Guns of the Timberland* and *The Alamo.* To populate the sands around Frankie and Annette, Asher recruited dozens of tan young bodies and also a campy bunch of nonparental adults, including Harvey Lembeck as ho-dad motorcyclist Eric Von Zipper and Bob Cummings as an anthropologist named Mr. Pigbristle, who is writing a book about the mating habits of California teenagers. Dick Dale and the Deltones—the original surfer band—provided genuine surf music.

As might be expected, critics were not kind. The *Times* called the cast "the dullest bunch ever" and said that Dick Dale and the Deltones "look like praying mantises"; *Time* magazine said, "As a study of primitive behavior patterns, *Beach Party* is more unoriginal than aboriginal." But theater owners loved it. As one of them said about the second sequel, *Bikini Beach*, "Here is a picture that the young folks will go to see and it will make any theater money. All theaters should play AIP pictures. They have made many films that have kept small-town theaters in business."

Beach Party came out in the summer of 1963, the same summer Jan and Dean's "Surf City" reached the top of the *Billboard* pop chart. Beach party movies and surf music hit their peak at the same time—a last gasp of vernacular Americana before pop culture was swamped by the British Invasion, then bent out of shape by psychedelia. The plots may have been silly or nonexistent, but many beach party movies, including the four AIP sequels (all directed by William Asher) featured some extraordinary music, even beyond the surfing sound: *Muscle Beach Party* introduced "Little Stevie Wonder," who also sang "Fingertips" in *Bikini Beach* (a spoof of English singers, with Frankie Avalon playing both an American beach boy and a mod pop star); Paramount's *Beach Ball* featured the Supremes, the Four Seasons, the Righteous Brothers, the Hondells, and the Walker Brothers.

Even when they were released, beach party movies looked anachronistic. The winds of change were sweeping fast across the country, not only on the music charts. In the summer of 1964, Ken Kesey and his Merry Pranksters hit the road to dole out LSD, and Carol Doda began dancing topless at the Condor Club in San Francisco. At the same time, Frankie Avalon was being tortured in *Muscle Beach Party* by having to decide between his infatuation with a beautiful Italian countess and his true love for Dee Dee, played by Annette Funicello wearing some of the largest and most modest two-piece swimsuits in fashion history. In a society that seemed to suddenly explode everywhere with audacious challenges to convention, beach party movies were an oasis of old values, populated by kids who behaved. "They're what I want my son to be at their age," William Asher said.

Compared to the calamitous events that shook the world after John Kennedy's assassination in 1963, including a civil rights war starting in the South and body counts beginning to come in from Vietnam, the hijinks in these happy musicals were ridiculously dreamy. That was exactly why beach party movies succeeded when they did: for many Americans—young people as well as adults—the cultural maelstrom of the sixties was terribly anxiety-provoking. Beach party movies showed a safe world untouched by moral skepticism and war. It wasn't only teens who found happiness watching Frankie, Annette, and friends: theater surveys showed that adults made up an inordinately large percentage of their audience, possibly because these blithe movies already had the appeal of nostalgia. Annette Funicello reminded one interviewer that there were still plenty of kids who were morally virtuous, kids whose "big dream was to come out to Malibu Beach and to surf and dance on the sand, and to have weenie roasts every night." Beach party movies, Annette explained, "showed you that you could have fun without using vulgar language and without explicit sex scenes." Unlike the sixties, all beach party movies ended happily.

In 1987 the genre was reprised with *Back to the Beach*, a high-gloss production starring Frankie and Annette as parents and resurrecting Dick Dale and the Deltones, with appearances by professional nostalgia kindlers Jerry Mathers and Tony Dow (Beaver and Wally Cleaver from "Leave It to Beaver"), Bob Denver (Maynard G. Krebs from "The Many Loves of Dobie Gillis"), and Ed Byrnes (Kookie from "77 Sunset Strip"). Like a high school reunion, *Back to the Beach* was fascinating and yet strangely unsatisfying: confirmation that you cannot go home again, but with the irresistible morbid allure of seeing how symbols of eternal youth manifest the ravages of time.

BEATLES

Pop doctrine sees the early 1960s as the dark ages of rock and roll. The commonly accepted view of the era is that the rebellion and insolence of mid-1950s music had been tamped down and repressed or stolen by big business, and that pop had fallen into the hands of venal grown-ups who castrated it and sold the resulting harmless musical pap to gullible teens. This official history makes short shrift of the fact that in the early 1960s Motown was beginning to percolate, that the street-sound New York girl groups produced by Phil Spector were discovering their declamatory powers, that surf music and folk music were bursting with yet-unrealized creative exuberance, that James Brown, Sam Cooke, and Jackie Wilson were all performing and recording some of the best soul music of their lives, and that even Elvis came back from the army and cut one of his finest albums (*Elvis Is Back*) in 1960. But the Dark Ages concept is necessary to rock dogma because it helps position the Beatles as the renaissance. "They may not be responsible for everything, but nearly everything that comes after would be impossible without them," wrote Tim Riley in *Tell Me Why.*

It wasn't just their cataclysmic influence on music that has made the Beatles into pop historians' favorite symbol of rebirth, liberation, enlightenment, and invention. The Beatles were the embodiment of 1960s iconoclasm of all kinds, including their long hair and sartorial bravura, their endorsement of drugs as a means of finding deeper truth, and their dabbling in several then-current brands of mystical wisdom from the East. Most important, they signify the official transmutation of pop culture from mere fun

Clockwise: **Paul McCartney, George Harrison, Ringo Starr, John Lennon**

into something that a lot of people began to analyze in a thoughtful—and frequently pretentious—light. Earnest critics of such things like to say that the Beatles turned rock and roll music into something "legitimate." And just as they deserve the lion's share of credit (or should we also say blame?) for making rock and roll seem like Art with a capital A, it was the Beatles, more than anyone else, who injected the audacity of youth straight into the cultural mainstream. "They changed rock, which changed the culture, which changed us," Jeff Greenfield eulogized for the *New York Times Magazine* in 1975.

In the beginning, they were kid stuff; and they were nothing but cute. When "I Want to Hold Your Hand" was released on December 26, 1963, the number one hit on the pop chart was "Dominique," an adorable ditty by Soeur Sourire, the Singing Nun; and to many who first heard about these wisecracking lads from Liverpool with their mushroom haircuts and matching slim-cut, lapel-less jackets, it was possible to believe they were just another musical novelty—a live-action Alvin and the Chipmunks for the 1960s; and exactly the kind of meaningless, merry fun that America needed in the grim aftermath of the November 1963 Kennedy assassination. They were already huge hits in England (even the Queen Mother liked them), and when they came to the States to appear on "The Ed Sullivan Show" in February 1964, press coverage focused less on their musical prowess than on their breezy attitude, their mop tops, their mod clothes, and most of all, their amazing effect on young girls, who cried and wailed and tried to get close enough to the handsome quartet to tear off a piece of their flesh.

If they were a fad, it was soon apparent that it was a fad of unprecedented dimension. By April 1964, the Beatles held all five of the top spots on the *Billboard* Hot 100 list ("Can't Buy Me Love," "Twist and Shout," "She Loves You," "I Want to Hold Your Hand," "Please Please Me"), and their "yeah, yeah, yeah" chorus from "She Loves You" had become a national refrain. Bob Dylan remembered hearing them constantly on the car radio while driving cross-country that spring: "I kept it to myself that I really dug them. Everybody else thought they were just for the teenyboppers, that they were gonna pass right away. But it was obvious to me that they had staying power. I knew they were pointing the direction where music had to go."

Although they had in fact been carefully groomed and packaged for stardom by manger Brian Epstein (who nixed their greasy hair and the sullen, beat image from which they devised their name, *Beat*les), John Lennon, Paul McCartney, George Harrison, and Ringo Starr dazzled the press and their public with the fun-loving spontaneity they ex-

uded. They seemed to be their own men, and they constantly made it clear on stage and off that no one pulled their strings. They weren't quite dangerous (not yet, anyway), because they were such merry fellows; but they were completely unpredictable. They seemed to burst with creativity at every minute, and they were entertaining in ways that pop musicians had never been, a fact they proved with barrages of clever, ad-libbed quips during press conferences. And although much of their early music owed a debt to American rhythm and blues, the fresh-faced enthusiasm they brought to their performances— bobbing their heads up and down and howling with pleasure—made their versions of previously recorded tunes like Chuck Berry's "Roll Over Beethoven" and Little Richard's "Long Tall Sally" seem brand-new, and made their own driving compositions, such as "I Saw Her Standing There," so absolutely infectious that it soon became possible to believe that they were indeed the harbingers of a new attitude towards music and towards life itself.

The Beatles paved the way for a mammoth "British Invasion" of singing groups as long-lasting as the Rolling Stones and as silly as Freddie and the Dreamers. U.S. ROCKS AND REELS FROM BEATLES INVASION, *Billboard* headlined, declaring that "Great Britain hasn't been so influential on American affairs since 1775." Their success spelled doom for surf music (see "Beach Boys," p. 38), folk music, and many developing girl groups, and (temporarily) eclipsed soul singers and rock and roll originals who could never hope to pawn themselves off as mod Liverpudlians. Little Richard, the Beatles' idol (and a huge hit when he toured England), remembered being reduced to playing "dumps, snake holes, rat holes, and pig pens" in the Beatles' wake. "Things had changed. There were all these English groups," he wrote in *The Life and Times of Little Richard.* "They just overshadowed my thing." Some American performers, however, did manage to create (or re-create) themselves in the image of the almighty Brits, including the Beau Brummels (from San Francisco), Sam the Sham and the Pharaohs ("Look! They've Gone British!" proclaimed a 1965 press release), and the Sir Douglas Quintet, from San Antonio, who managed to echo the Beatles' "yeah, yeah, yeah!" by adding a series of "hey, hey!" yelps to their hard-rocking Tex-Mex song "She's About a Mover." Beatles imitators were everywhere, from the shrewdly packaged Monkees (p. 329) to such quick-buck sensations as the Liverpools ("the down-beat quartet with the down-sweep hair-set") and the Liverpool Mop Tops ("four young men who have adopted the style of BEATLING, the hottest craze in show business").

Such oddities aside, the Beatles' effect on the music *business* (never mind aesthetic issues) was monumental. Since Elvis Presley, it had been a cash cow, but a lot had changed in the eight years since Elvis's manager, Colonel Tom Parker, used to personally walk up and down the aisle at concerts and hawk phony autographed pictures of the King for a buck apiece. The unparalleled adoration they roused and the hundreds of singing groups who imitated them or were simply inspired by their art or their success helped do something more than revitalize rock and roll. The Beatles made rock and roll permanent, global, and nearly ubiquitous. Their success, more than anybody else's, helped transform what had begun as an eccentric business into an industry that encompassed not only music but merchandise galore.

Abetted by Mary Quant's miniskirt, James Bond movies, Carnaby Street clothiers, and a *Time* cover story that declared London "the city of the decade," they also helped make England the center of the swinging world in the prehippie 1960s; they were rewarded for their achievement by Queen Elizabeth II, who bestowed upon all four of them the MBE—Membership in the Order of the British Empire. "We thought getting the MBE was as funny as everybody else thought it was," John Lennon later said, revealing that he and the boys had run into a palace washroom before their investiture and smoked a joint. But not everyone thought it was funny, and some war heroes returned their medals in protest that such an honor had been awarded to what one naval veteran described as "a gang of nincompoops."

Meanwhile, the Beatles were busy proving to a majority of the civilized world they were anything but nincompoops. The teen heartthrobs conquered the movie business with *A Hard Day's Night* (1964), a whimsical semidocumentary, and *Help!* (1965), a luxuriant evocation of mod London, for which they won praise as latter-day Marx Brothers. Both films were directed by Richard Lester, who had cut his teeth making television commercials; and both can be seen as feature-length sales pitches for the Beatles as nothing less than the greatest product in history. Then the foursome began to release records that went beyond the vivacious, sometimes tender songs about love that first made them famous. In such compositions as "Eleanor Rigby," "Nowhere Man," and "Paperback Writer," they sang about interesting characters with literary lyrics and created provocative, ambiguous sets of circumstances far outside the usual arena of rock melodramas. At a time when "relevance" was exalted, junior professors began using Beatles songs as texts in poetry and literature classes! Like Bob Dylan (p. 159), who came to the pop charts from the folk scene, the Beatles were learning to infuse their lyrics with messages and social commentary and, sometimes, a real subversive temperament. All this helped transform them in their maturing public's eyes from lovable moptops into the inevitable leaders of the burgeoning youth revolution. Their music itself took on weight, too, as the Beatles immersed themselves in orientalism and struggled to push the outside of the envelope of conventional pop sound: George played a sitar (very hip) in "Norwegian Wood"; and their album *Revolver* was rich with tricky mystic riffs and misterioso reverberations created in the studio. "The Beatles were no longer teen angels," said *Rock of Ages: The Rolling Stone History of Rock and Roll*, "but electronic Pied Pipers of psychedelicism."

The Beatles grew unhappy touring in cute matching outfits, performing their songs for screaming little girls who didn't really listen to all the important lyrics and sophisticated glissandos they worked so hard to create. So they quit the road, Paul explaining that studio recordings were "our most important form of communication," and applied their prodigious energies to creative sessions where they made music as no one before them ever had. The culmination of their efforts and the peak of the Beatles' authority over pop culture was *Sgt. Pepper's Lonely Hearts Club Band* (1967), a concept album from first song to last (the conceit being they are an old-time music-hall band singing songs about contemporary English life), a landmark in its use of sonic montages, tape loops, and multitrack recording, and a psychedelic mind-voyager's delight, loaded with sly and secret references to getting high.

Sgt. Pepper was a challenge to virtually all performers who had designs on the pop market: top it, match it, challenge listeners' expectations, subvert traditional forms, or become history. Innovation became pop's

god. But the Beatles' audacity turned out to be a mixed blessing. Groovy as they proved they could be, in the wash of their sitar and polymorphous tonality came hundreds of psychedelic "experiments" by everyone from the Rolling Stones (*Their Satanic Majesties Request*) to the Marketts (a former surf-music band, who released *Sunpower*, described on the liner as "for the 'now' generation!") and a little-known group called the Mustang, whose *Organ Freakout!* featured the quasi-religious "Joshua Got Busted" and promised that "when the Mustang mounts the Hammond Organ and the 'amps' start cookin', look out, baby: IT'S AN ORGAN FREAKOUT."

The most profound effect of *Sgt. Pepper*, beyond its own technical and aesthetic innovations and trippy messages, was that it certified rock music, which had once belonged to happy-go-lucky kids, as a consequential and potentially profound aspect of modern life. For the first time, rock critics (a job that hadn't really existed until the Beatles came along) began talking about a whole album as a work of art, not just a collection of songs. "Scholarly articles probe the relationship between the Beatles and the *nouvelle vague* films of Jean-Luc Godard," *Time* gasped, noting that in "chic circles," not liking the Beatles meant you were uncultured. To this day, the intellectual gymnastics that peaked with *Sgt. Pepper* not only have caused rock and roll to be perceived as important; they have also encouraged untold numbers of other recording artists to take themselves seriously, whether or not their talent demands it. One has to wonder, for example, if the world really is a better place because Bob Thiele and his Sunflower Singers, accompanied by television's Steve Allen, recorded "Here Comes Sgt. Pepper" on an album called *Do the Love*, which features Mr. Thiele on the cover in an old-time band uniform like the ones worn by the Beatles on their *Sgt. Pepper* cover and promises its listeners a "right-now aura."

Critics tripped over themselves rushing to praise *Sgt. Pepper*. Writing in *Partisan Review*, Richard Poirier declared, "The Beatles now exist not merely as a phenomenon of entertainment but as a force of historical consequence." Peter Scrag in *Saturday Review* said, "Among all the works of commentary and protest produced by and for the so-called new generation in the English-speaking West, none have turned out to be wittier or more revealing." Kenneth Tynan announced that the album was "a decisive moment in the history of Western Civilization."

However, not all of Western Civilization was pleased that the Beatles—arguably the four most influential men of the decade—had become the leaders of the youth revolution. Their rebellious and iconoclastic approach to music, as well as their candid approval of drug use, their long hair and flamboyant clothes and well-honed attitude of witty insubordination, were all reasons that many fans and social critics fairly worshiped them; but they were also causes for some people to become convinced that they were pure evil. Ever since John Lennon told an interviewer in 1966 that the Beatles were more popular than Jesus Christ and that rock and roll might very likely outlast Christianity, there were belligerent groups of tradition-clad Americans, especially in the South, who wanted them banned because they were undermining morality. In South Carolina, the Ku Klux Klan put a Beatles record on a wooden cross and set it on fire; in Birmingham, Alabama, radio station WAQY broadcast announcements every hour urging listeners to turn in their Beatles records and souvenirs for a great community bonfire; and the Grand Wizard of the Ku Klux Klan exhorted, "Get out there, you teenagers, and cut off your Beatle-style long hair. Join those at the bonfires and throw your locks into the fire! Burn, burn, burn everything that is Beatle!"

Their drug references in particular got people riled up. Art Linkletter, whose daughter Diane jumped out a window because of an LSD trip, called them "leading missionaries of the acid society." In his book *The Marxist Minstrels*, David A. Noebel, a Colorado clergyman, lamented that "the drug world of the Beatles progresses unrelentingly. John can emerge from his pad and tell our youth to 'turn off your mind, relax, and float downstream' [as he did in the song 'Tomorrow Never Knows']. ...And sound engineers are still trying to reproduce the *Sgt. Pepper* effects for pot smoking." Similarly, Bob Larson's *Hippies, Hindus and Rock & Roll* worried, "If the Beatles are going to pray to Hindu gods, invite demon spirits to enter and control their bodies, and encourage America's youth to do likewise, where might it all lead?"

Loony as such anti-Beatles sentiments may sound, they were exactly echoed by radical White Panther leader John Sinclair, who adored the Beatles, in his 1972 celebration of the counterculture, *Guitar Army:*

> It seems obvious to me that the *Sgt. Pepper* phenomenon was, along with Tim Leary and LSD, the major observable influence on the "youth revolution" as it exploded onto the scene as a mass movement. I mean when the Beatles came out with mustaches and beards and beatnik long hair, smoking dope and coming on like weirdo acid freaks [*sic*], playing and singing songs about acid and getting high and scenes on the sofa with a sister or two, it was a real bombshell that was dropped into the ruins of western civilization, and its effects were enormous. ...It effectively legitimized

the hippie dope scene for the popular media and consequently played an indispensable role in bringing about the hugest change in a generation's consciousness in human history.

In his Beatles biography, *Shout!*, Philip Norman described the arrival of *Sgt. Pepper* as one of the truly memorable moments of the 1960s, right up there with Kennedy's assassination and the moon landing. Its dominion, he wrote, was total:

> It encompassed the most avant-garde and most cautious; both fan and foe alike. The wildest acid freak, listening in his mental garret to "Lucy in the Sky with Diamonds," could not doubt that his mind had been blown to undreamed realms of psychedelic fancy. Nervous old ladies, listening to "When I'm Sixty-Four" in their front parlors, would never be frightened of pop music again.

Norman also quotes LSD proponent Timothy Leary's ecstasy upon hearing the new album: "I declare that the Beatles are mutants. Prototypes of evolutionary agents sent by God with a mysterious power to create a new species—a young race of laughing freemen.... They are the wisest, holiest, most effective avatars the human race has ever produced."

The Beatles went on to record many more hit records, including "Hey Jude" (their most successful single ever) and the albums *The Beatles* (known as the "White Album") and *Abbey Road;* they also made the conspicuously unsuccessful *Magical Mystery Tour* for television. But after their stunning trajectory from "I Want to Hold Your Hand" to *Sgt. Pepper*, there were simply no more heights to scale. The Beatles became hippies and temporary followers of the Maharishi Mahesh Yogi, then new-age entrepreneurs when they formed the Apple Corps (which Paul said was their attempt to create "a kind of Western Communism"); and they sang "All You Need Is Love," an anthem for flower children, in a worldwide satellite broadcast. But by the end of the decade, the Beatles were no longer at the culture's cutting edge. As John Swenson noted in *The New Rolling Stone Record Guide*, "the group's much-lamented decision to call it quits as the 1970s began was entirely appropriate; the collected work does not leave you with the impression that there were unfinished statements."

It can be argued that Timothy Leary's consecration of the Beatles as another order of being was almost right; that they *did* help create something new—if not a new species of humanity, then certainly a whole new set of vistas for popular culture. The world mourned when the most influential band in history broke up in 1970 to go their separate ways. Each of them remained in the spotlight, but no matter what they went on to accomplish as individuals, each is destined to be first and always a former Beatle. As Beatles, their effect on pop culture—in and out of music—has not dimmed as the decades have passed, as evidenced by the booming market in Beatles collectibles and memorabilia. With the possible exception of Elvis (and this is debatable), no other persons or products in the baby boom era have had as dramatic an impact on the sound and look of everyday life as they.

One of the most curious aspects of Beatlemania, starting in 1969 and lingering even beyond John Lennon's murder by a crazed fan in 1980, is the persistence of folklore about Paul McCartney having died. KIDS' NEW MACABRE GAME: IS PAUL MCCARTNEY DEAD? *Variety* headlined in October 1969, saying that the story had recently begun in the East (no one knows exactly how), then spread "like wildfire across the country." John Lennon called it "a rumor invented by a jackass as perpetuated by an out-of-work grave digger," and McCartney himself denied his demise for *Life* magazine; but by the end of the 1960s, the Beatles' own trippy lyrics and enigmatic double entendres had injected occult meaning into everything they said and sang, encouraging their more deranged followers to discover strange and frequently morbid messages in their work —Charles Manson (see p. 299) found his own mayhem manifesto in their song "Helter Skelter." Many Beatlemaniacs came to believe that if you could crack the riddle of mysterious numbers that appeared on the album jackets (the license plates on *Abbey Road*, the pointing fingers on *Sgt. Pepper*), you wound up with a phone number, and if you dialed that number, you got a free plane ticket to Pepperland, a Beatle paradise (was dead Paul there?) from which visitors never returned. Back in the mid-1970s, the *Journal of Popular Culture* itemized these pieces of "evidence" from then-current Paul McCartney necrology:

- If you grease *Abbey Road* up with petroleum jelly, Paul's face will disappear.
- In the *Magical Mystery Tour* album, the accompanying booklet shows the three other Beatles with red carnations. Significantly, Paul is wearing a black one.
- According to the University of Michigan *Daily*, *walrus* is Greek for *corpse*. [Paul sings "I am the walrus."]
- If you play "Revolution No. 9" backwards, you hear the lyric "turn me on, dead man"; and Paul's last name has nine letters in it. Also, the area of the White Album between the songs "I'm So Tired" and "Blackbird" contains the words "Paul is dead. Miss him. Miss him. Miss him."

One school of thought, according to the *Journal of Popular Culture*, was that Paul was not actually deceased but only spiritually or socially out of commission, or per-

haps in a permanently vegetative state induced by too many drugs. But as late as October 1991, the Toronto arts tabloid *Eye* quoted a local cab driver who was still absolutely convinced that Paul had passed away twenty years before:

> I remember the night they announced he died, for me it was like the night the *Challenger* blew up. He was replaced by a guy from Ontario. You know how on the *Abbey Road* album cover it says OPP on his sleeve?: Ontario Provincial Police. [One can also read his sleeve as OPD, short for "Ontario Police Department," or possibly "Officially Pronounced Dead."] This guy had won a Paul McCartney look-alike and personality contest and had a girlfriend in art school called Linda Eastman. Nixon had Paul killed because he was afraid of Paul's power over the youth of America.

The *Eye*'s reporter, Mary-Lou Zeitoun, attended a Paul McCartney press conference (which he staged on behalf of his 1991 documentary film, *Get Back*) and concluded afterward: "There was little to indicate whether or not Paul is indeed really dead."

BEATNIKS

Dig: In the 1950s there were these crazy cats so bugged by Squaresville that they split the cornball organization-man rat race and got with a far-out groove. They were hip to funky poetry and they pounded piccolo bongo drums, they got their kicks being cool and they almost never cracked a smile. These holy barbarians were so gone, so wigged out, that San Francisco *Chronicle* columnist Herb Caen was inspired to take the Russians' name for the ultimate way-out space voyager of 1957—*Sputnik*, the first earth satellite—and apply its diminutive suffix to them. They called themselves beats, they dug anything that really *sent* them, and there was nothing that had been sent farther out than *Sputnik;* moreover, they tended to brood like stereotypical Russians, and they were at least a little bit subversive. So "beatnik," which included all these notions, plus a touch of disrespect, had a compelling ring. Caen's word turned out to be one of the great neologisms of our time.

Beatniks saturated pop culture starting in 1959. They became *the* image of nonconformity—prototypical malcontents whose manners, lingo, and attitude have helped define nearly every kind of social rebel for more than thirty years, including motorcyclists, folkniks, the Beatles (whose name was a way of saying they, too, were beat [p. 43]), hippies (p. 212), and all the way to postmodern punks. In the spring of 1992, Madonna (p. 296) announced that her next album would be full of what she called "beatnik-style poetry."

The original beatniks of San Francisco and Venice (California), Greenwich Village, and the Left Bank of Paris dressed mostly in somber black; they favored turtlenecks

M. Stern as a beatnik, 1959

or sloppy sweatshirts, dungarees or corduroys, and berets for their heads. They wore sandals because sandals were freer than lace-up shoes, and they hid their eyes behind sunglasses—to help protect them from the onslaught of the sun (they were nocturnal types), from offensively bright advertising billboards (they were antimaterialists), and possibly from the flash of the atomic blast they always worried about. Men sometimes wore boat-neck fisherman's shirts, and if they simply had to wear a tie, it was a nubby-textured one, with a dark, unpressed shirt (maybe a chambray work shirt); they grew goatees and didn't comb their hair. Chicks let their hair grow long and straight; they sported dangling hoop earrings and abstract ethnic jewelry that jangled when they moved; they wore black scoop-neck leotards and ballet slippers, the ultimate goal being an out-of-this-world appearance similar to that of Vampira, Hollywood's semiprofessional ghoul (see "James Dean," p. 128).

Whatever they wore, the one thing all beatniks had in common was their attitude: they were morose, slightly wayward egghead types who were not merely annoyed by the square world but totally bored by it.

They may have been agitated by the sterile two-cars-in-every-suburban-garage mentality around them, but instead of hollering or demonstrating or creating a surreal counter-culture like hippies did a few years later, they assiduously cultivated ennui and a posture of unimpressed insouciance. For example, instead of clapping loudly to show approval of a poet's reading in a coffee-house, they coolly snapped their fingers. The kind of art they liked went against the grain of neat-and-tidy culture: they appreciated abstract painting, non-sequitur verse, atonal jazz, anything that didn't fit a square's idea of correctness and harmony. They wanted no part of the straight world, so they resented any pressure to get a job or to conform. Most of all, they relished being different.

It is urgent here to distinguish between beatniks, who were a charismatic media image through the mid-1960s, and the beats, who preceded them as a genuine literary movement. Although the beats provided the original inspiration for beatnik style, they loathed the popularization and exploitation of their life, and especially the cleverness of the term "beatnik." "All hipsters hate the word," Jack Kerouac wrote in 1958, lamenting that what had begun for him and his peers as a truly spiritual approach to life and art had become a faddish affectation. "It's an insulting term," Allen Ginsberg complained in a letter to the *Chronicle* pleading that they not refer to him as a beatnik. Long before the funny, Russkie-sounding word was coined, Kerouac, Ginsberg, Kenneth Rexroth, Lawrence Ferlinghetti, et al. liked to refer to themselves as "beats," or sometimes "beatsters" (like hipster), because of three different implications of the word "beat": first, they dug the jazz beat; second, they felt beat (as in crushed) by the square world; and most especially, they shared what Kerouac called "beatitude"—gained

in their spiritual quest (via poetry, painting, even peyote) for true kicks in the existential void. These beatific litterateurs were iconoclasts who were troubled not only by button-down shirts and pious America's obsession with bread (money) and status seeking but by the empty-headedness of rock and roll, which they considered to be as vapid as a hula hoop. "Beat" was a word with nearly religious meaning for these mind voyagers as they tried to define a creative life in a square world they believed to be repressed, insensitive, impersonal, and cluttered with Pepsodent jingles and IBM ("Do not bend, fold, staple, or mutilate") punch cards.

When they were discovered by the public towards the end of the 1950s, starting with an explosive series of articles in 1958 by June Muller in the San Francisco *Examiner* about the weird ways of the shaggy denizens of North Beach, the earnest beats became an unwilling news story. Muller focused on their delinquency: They caroused along the street (their "faceless jungle of nothingness") at four in the morning; they drank too much, smoked reefer, cohabited with Negroes (whom they called spades), and were flagrantly promiscuous. What a juicy exposé all this made, and it was elaborated by reporters (frequently crime reporters) in newspapers from California to New York. Soon after Herb Caen invented the word "beatnik" to describe the occupants of what he called "the bearded byways of North Beach," Gray Line bus tours was offering sightseeing trips past authentic beatnik pads and coffeehouses (a practice reprised in 1967 when beatniks were eclipsed by hippies and the buses ran through Haight-Ashbury).

As portrayed in movies, on television, and in scandalous novels, beatniks had little of the serious literary intent of the original beats. They were simply fallen angels out looking for kicks, and they became fair game for all manner of caricature and parody, from *Mad* magazine to dozens of sitcom episodes built around encounters with bereted, poorly groomed nonconformists whose beatnikness was frequently nothing more than an excuse for not getting a decent job.

Most pop-culture beatniks were silly sorts of characters played for laughs, foremost among them the amiable, bongo-patting lazybones Maynard G. Krebs (Bob Denver) of television's "The Many Loves of Dobie Gillis" (1959–63). Even Mister Ed, television's talking horse, joined a band of beatniks in one episode, titled "Ed the Beachcomber" (1962), during which the eloquent equine declared, "I'm real down. Beat. Like depressed, neglected, rejected, befuddled, bemuddled." Nancy Nalven, author of *The Famous Mister Ed*, documented other episodes in which Ed was heard saying, "Wow, dig that crazy transmitter," "This pad's gonna be jumpin' tonight, daddy-o!" and "For every swinger you crush, another hep cat will pick up the bongos." Some of the most ridiculous beatniks appeared as finger-snapping coffeehouse patrons in the movie *Visit to a Small Planet* (1959) from a Gore Vidal stage play, about a space alien (Jerry Lewis) who digs their way-out attitude because it's so much like life on his faraway planet; they, in turn, think he's a gas. At one point, one of their number recites these screeched, staccato fragments of a poem: "O video/O rideo/Mop-mop!" In an episode of "The Dick Van Dyke Show" Carl Reiner played a beatnik artist, complete with goatee, commissioned by Laura Petrie (Mary Tyler Moore) to paint her portrait. Being a real beat, he isn't satisfied painting her superficial appearance, so he imagines the real Laura (and paints her) in the nude, causing no end of trouble for the poor woman from Squaresville.

Not all contemporary images of beatniks were so amusing or benign. Because of their unconventional attitudes about sex, they were also ripe for portrayal as dangerous psychopaths in such exploitation movies as *The Beatniks* (1959), the poster for which exclaimed, "Their password was mutiny against society!"; *Beat Girl* (1960), which promised "wild parties in back street sin cellars"; and *Daddy-"O"* (1959), which dared viewers to "Meet the 'Beat': Daring to live, daring to love!" The most lurid of all beatnik exploitation pictures was *The Beat Generation* (1959), which described its subject as "sullen rebels and defiant chicks searching for a life of their own! The pads, the jazz, the dives, those frantic, 'way-out' parties beyond belief!" The novelization of the movie, written by its producer, Albert Zugsmith, described beatniks at a "beach pad party" as including

men who exulted in being feminine, women who flaunted their masculinity [who all] had in common their creed: The world is full of dinglebodies. The crumbumbs who go to work, eat, sleep —and just vegetate. All dinglebodies were walking dead who didn't *go*. But the elect vibrated with the beat. Laws were passed for them to flout. Social taboos existed for them to reject. The past was hoary with laughs and lies. The future promised H-bombs or hideous mediocrity. There was only now. To learn the beat you had to suck the last drop of juice from the present.

One of the chicks at the party, "a youngish woman with a mane of long hair spilling over her sweater," recited a poem:

The spittle of this morning's smile
Splashed like a resounding wave
Upon the you-and-me bit we dug
And digging deeper together we found
  nothingness.

Because they flaunted a fashionable intellectualism and had connections to real art and literature, beatniks also provoked much serious study. *The Real Bohemia*, a sober examination of their culture written in 1961 by Francis J. Rigney (a psychiatrist) and L. Douglas Smith (a psychologist), began with a glossary of the new Bohemians' language. Most of the terms are now so familiar they need no definition, including to "bug," to "dig," a "drag," "funky" ("from Old French, *funicle*, meaning terrible; today it means 'that happy-sad feeling' according to some jazz musicians"), the "fuzz," a "gas," a "hang-up," a "pad," to "scarf" ("from a French chef, Scarfannelli"), to "shack up," to "turn on to," and "what's happening?" ("the equivalent of *hello*"). The glossary features a special subset of beatnik words used by the drug takers among them (there were plenty, the authors note), including "dealer," to "OD," and "strung out." Most of this language entered the mainstream via hippies, who were a lot like beatniks with lobotomies. (Hippies were forever looking to "blow their minds," an expression *not* included in any beatnik glossaries.)

The Real Bohemia includes some fascinating notes on nuances of meaning in beatnik speech, in particular their use of the words "hip," "man," and "like." "Hep is no longer used AT ALL," the authors advise, explaining that one who is truly hip is referred to as "down." Unhip people are "nowhere." "When one member of this community says 'I'm hip,' the person spoken to is, for practical purposes, also 'hip.'" As for "man" and "like," they are, the authors say, essentially untranslatable. "Man" is a kind of honorific form of address, generally reserved for fellow beatniks only. One of their number is quoted as saying, "A high honor for a chick is to call her 'man.' It means you're on an even level of rapport." "Like" was used to provide cadence to a sentence, as a kind of spoken ditto or exclamation mark. The authors give this example: "'Like man, I dig you' can be translated as 'Mister, I understand you; *indeed* I understand you.'" They speculate that "like" also provided beatnik speech a certain spiritual quality, "conveying to the listener the eagerness of the speaker to indicate that he really means what he is saying, even though mere words are inadequate." Curiously, this most mystical of all beatnik words is the one that has most thoroughly permeated street talk in the last three decades (see "Valley Girls," p. 546), providing just about everybody's casual chatter with a dash of, like, beatnik spirituality.

CHUCK BERRY

Chuck Berry created rock and roll. There were others who had a lot to do with making it popular, including Bill Haley and Elvis, and disc jockey Alan Freed, and lots of lesser-known songwriters. But Chuck Berry gave it its heart and soul. He wrote the seminal songs, set the beat, established the fast peal of an electric guitar as its cadence, and conceived the duck walk— progenitor of a thousand similarly mischievous stage moves elaborated by everyone from Mick Jagger to Hammer. More than

any of these particular achievements, Chuck Berry formulated the essential attitude of rock by combining the sexuality of rhythm and blues with a jolt of country-style fun. His greatest songs—including "Maybellene," "Roll Over Beethoven," "Reelin' and Rockin," "Nadine," "Johnny B. Goode," and "Brown Eyed Handsome Man" —are reckless and romantic, and have the boastful energy of a rollicking American folk tale.

Despite his universally acknowledged achievements, which put him securely in the pop-culture pantheon, it is hard not to look at Chuck Berry's career and see a man who took a bum rap, who never really got what he deserved. Rock's most influential songwriter and one of its greatest performers has had only one certified million-selling number-one hit song (and it was, ironically, the most trivial he ever recorded—"My Ding-a-Ling," in 1972), and in the great, golden early years of rock, between 1956

and 1960, only four of his songs made the national top ten.

Worst of all was the morals charge that nearly ruined him. After a dragged-out trial that began in 1959, Chuck Berry went to prison in 1962 for violating the Mann Act by taking a fourteen-year-old girl across state lines for immoral purposes. He had brought her from Texas to work as a hat-check girl in his St. Louis club. Berry's lawyer argued that she had been a prostitute and went with his client willingly; and Berry explained he had hired her only because she spoke Spanish and he wanted to learn the language in order to write some Spanish songs. But regardless of the facts, it is likely that no legal argument could have gotten him off the hook, because Chuck Berry was a rock and roll singer—a sexy, successful one. In the early 1960s that was evidence enough to assure the world he was immoral (similar disgrace had awaited Jerry Lee Lewis when he married a thirteen-year-old third cousin); plus Berry was a cocky black man. So it was decided he should pay his debt to society by spending two years in a federal penitentiary.

Until the trial, Chuck Berry had been riding high. A former cosmetician and graduate of St. Louis's Poro School of Beauty Culture, he was brought to Chess Records in Chicago in 1955 by Muddy Waters. He came with a song called "Ida Red," actually an old country-western fiddle tune that he had rewritten into a boogie-woogie novelty song about a guy in a V-8 Ford chasing after a woman in a Cadillac Coupe de Ville. After he renamed it to honor his beauty-culture background (or, according to one interview he gave, in remembrance of a cow named Maybellene he knew during his Missouri boyhood), "Maybellene" went on to become a big crossover hit, followed by "Roll Over Beethoven," "Too Much Monkey Business," and "No Money Down." These songs were very different from traditional blues in their high-flying rhythm as well as in lyrics that sang of triumph and fun rather than despair and escape. Chuck Berry sang like he was on top of the world; and by 1959 he was. He had his own nightclub in St. Louis, and he and his family were living in a mansion.

When he got out of prison in 1964, his family was gone. Rock and roll had changed; the Beach Boys had "borrowed" Berry's "Sweet Little Sixteen" melody and made it "Surfin' USA" (for which he was later compensated); and the Beatles and the Rolling Stones were about to conquer the world—singing a lot of cover versions of Chuck Berry songs! The 1960s was a bad decade for Chuck Berry. He had been a founding father of rock and roll, but so many of those who learned from him started veering towards sophisticated (or pretentious) lyrics and mind-blowing riffs and ragas. Audiences who fell into rapture over the intellectual complexity of the Beatles' *Sgt. Pepper* or the obfuscation of Dylan's "Positively 4th Street" found it all too easy to look upon such clear and simple (and superb) 1960s Berry songs as "Nadine" and "Promised Land" as shallow. One thing Chuck Berry was not was psychedelic.

Once known as a happy-go-lucky performer, Berry became notorious for his evil temper and for his absolutely rigid concert demands: if you wanted Chuck Berry to perform, you were required to pay him *per song*, with an extra fee demanded if you wanted him to do the duck walk. The quality of the shows depended entirely on how much Berry got paid; and if the promoter was a cheapskate, unwilling to fund a stellar performance, Berry sometimes got booed off the stage by dissatisfied crowds. This businesslike attitude did not endear him to a generation of rock fans who liked to see performers as family and concerts as communal love fests (see "Grateful Dead," p. 198).

It wasn't until 1972, when he began performing in Las Vegas, that Chuck Berry regained the national renown he had enjoyed in the 1950s, and then some; he has since been inducted into the Rock and Roll Hall of Fame and is universally recognized for his greatness. In 1986, for his sixtieth birthday, he teamed up with the Rolling Stones' Keith Richards for a televised concert called "Chuck Berry: Hail! Hail! Rock 'n' Roll," which concluded with his arrival on stage in a red Cadillac as he sang his 1957 hit "School Days." And when *Voyager I* was sent into outer space in 1977 in hopes that some aliens would find it, it contained a copper phonograph record with greetings in a hundred languages, Bach's Brandenburg Concerto No. 2, and Chuck Berry singing "Johnny B. Goode."

BIKER MOVIES

The first biker movie was *The Wild One* in 1954, inspired by a 1951 short story in *Harper's* magazine called "The Cyclists' Raid." The story itself was based on a real rumble that took place back in 1947, when several hundred bikers terrorized the little California town of Hollister, an event that was documented in July of that year by *Life* magazine, which featured a cover portrait of a repulsive man sitting on his motorcycle swilling beer. (See also "Harley-Davidson," p. 205.) What's interesting about the picture is that the man looks nothing at all like the sensitive, tempestuous biker outlaw that Marlon Brando played in the movie. He is a bleary slob in white trousers (not jeans) and a windbreaker (not a leather jacket), and he is lumpish and middle-aged (not sexy and young).

By the early fifties, the Hell's Angels had been established in California, but bikers were still a rare, weird phenomenon—a "new breed," in the words of producer Stanley Kramer, who spent three weeks along with Method actor Marlon Brando actually hanging out among motorcycle nomads to gather material for the movie. Their research yielded what was to become the seminal biker-film exchange:

"What are you rebelling against?"

"Whaddya got?"

Although some film critics have noted that biker movies are like westerns on motorcycles instead of horses, *The Wild One* established some fundamental differences. Biker movies are always more about outlaws than good guys, and whereas the fun in most westerns is to see the good guys win, the appeal of all biker movies, beginning with *The Wild One*, has been seeing depredation, pillage, and sacrilege . . . until the last few minutes, when the bikers get punished. "Somewhere along the way we went off the track," Marlon Brando said. "Instead of finding out why young people tend to bunch into groups that seek expression in violence, all we did was show the violence." Unlike westerns, which tend to be about the bringing of civilization to a wild land, biker movies are about the demolition of culture and civility. Aside from these thematic differences, the big thing that makes biker movies different from westerns is that by now, westerns—even new ones—look like classics, and some of the great ones are motion picture art; biker movies—even the ones that try to be arty—always have the titillating look of cheap exploitation. A study commissioned by the AMA (that's the American Motorcycle Association) in 1987 showed that there have been some seventy biker pictures since *The Wild One*, virtually all of them exploitative portraits of bikers as villains.

The Wild One purported to be socially responsible, and even included a message superimposed over the last shot in the film to assure viewers that all the bad bikers got properly punished; but its energy came from the hyped-up chopper jockeys, not the dull, sniveling townsfolk. Kramer originally wanted to call his movie *Hot Blood* and release it with posters that featured "HOT!" branded onto Marlon Brando's forehead. Columbia thought that approach was just too lewd, so the movie got renamed, and the new posters coyly hinted, "That *Streetcar*

Marlon Brando in *The Wild One*

Man Has a New Desire!" (referring to Brando's previous sexy role, as Stanley Kowalski in *A Streetcar Named Desire*). Even with *The Wild One*'s tacked-on, law-abiding message and supposedly cooler title, Columbia Pictures was worried that the film would cause riots. It did not; but Brando's surly mumble, his sideburns, his leather outfit and hobnail boots established style and standards for punks and bikers that have never faded, in movies and beyond.

Throughout the fifties, bikers appeared as nasty guys in juvenile-delinquent pictures, including *Motorcycle Gang* (1957), *Dragstrip Riot* (1958), and *The Hot Angel* (1958), but there was nothing particularly "bikerly" about those movies' scooter trash; they were simply wicked ruffians who happened to go around on motorcycles. In the mid-sixties, once again real bikers were in the news and became the catalyst for a motion picture. After a notorious gang-rape case in 1964, "the biker menace" made the cover of the *Saturday Evening Post*, and Hunter Thompson, after riding with them, immortalized what he called "the human zoo on wheels" in his book *Hell's Angels*. By 1965, a reckless year when America began to crave counterculture heroes who knew how to stick their thumb in the eye of the establishment, bikers were hot. As Stanley Kramer had done a decade before, Roger Corman looked at *Life* magazine and got inspired. *Life* showed a picture of a "biker funeral," attended by a gang in full regalia. The funeral became the centerpiece of Corman's 1966 movie, *The Wild Angels*.

George Chakiris was originally cast in the lead role of *The Wild Angels*, but he couldn't (or wouldn't) do his own riding; so he was replaced by Peter Fonda, who rode alongside Nancy Sinatra in front of a pack of genuine Hell's Angels. With little more than a hundred lines of dialogue in the entire script, the film was a bonanza of drunken orgies, gang rapes, and biker wars, ending with a church funeral that turns into a wild party. The cast of genuine gang members gave *The Wild Angels* an aura of reality (production assistant Peter Bogdanovich got the shit beat out of him during filming); and although critics stomped on it ("an ugly piece of trash": *Newsweek*), it made lots of money and became an art-house favorite (shown at the Cannes and Venice film festivals, by invitation) for its cinematic, rather than dialogue-laden, storytelling. In fact, it was the panache of *The Wild Angels* that first alerted many film connoisseurs to the talents of Roger Corman, who had been making low-budget action movies since the mid-fifties and had earned a small cult following with a series of Poe-inspired horror movies.

In the next three years, two dozen biker films were made, each built around approximately eighty minutes of senseless violence and ten minutes (or less) of amends. *Hell's Angels on Wheels* featured Jack Nicholson as a rebellious dude named Poet who admires and joins the gang because he sees them as free spirits (but learns differently in the end). In *Born Losers*, Tom Laughlin first created the character of Billy Jack, a half-breed Vietnam veteran who in this film takes on a bad biker gang almost single-handed. *She-Devils on Wheels*, made by B-movie king Herschell Gordon Lewis, was about a female gang called the Man-Eaters (their theme song: "We are the Hellcats that nobody likes/Maneaters on motorbikes"). *The Savage Seven* pitted bikers against a tribe of Native Americans; in *Angels from Hell*, a returning Vietnam vet forms an outlaw biker gang to combat the corrupt establishment police; in *Chrome and Hot Leather*, a former Green Beret joins up with his buddies on bikes to savage a bad biker gang that raped and murdered his girlfriend. Some other noteworthy names include

Hell's Belles (a remake of *Winchester '73*), *The Hellcats* ("Leather on the Outside . . . All Woman on the Inside!"), and *Satan's Sadists* (Russ Tamblyn as Charles Manson on a motorbike).

Most of these movies were so déclassé that even aficionados of exploitation films now disdain them. Alan Betrock, author of *The I Was A Teenage Juvenile Delinquent Rock 'N' Roll Horror Beach Party Movie Book*, wrote of biker films, "To my mind they don't really fit into the category of teen exploitation movies." Why not? "The films did not really examine an aspect of teenage culture." Betrock explains that the target audience for biker films was a male in his twenties rather than his teens, living in the South or Midwest, "where it seemed that

sado-masochism on film had a rather large following."

Cheap, sensationalistic movies about motorcycle gangs continued being made into the early seventies, and there were even a few mutant biker movies after that (George Romero's *Knightriders* in 1981 and *Timerider* in 1985); but the genre had pretty much lost its juice by 1969, when *Easy Rider* (see p. 172) recast bikers as mellow dudes on wheels—peace-loving hippies who wanted only to be free to do their own thing. "A Man Went Looking for America, and Couldn't Find It Anywhere," *Easy Rider* advertisements said. Quite a change from Marlon Brando in *The Wild One*, whom the original posters described as a man "Driven Too Far by His Own Hot Blood!"

MR. BLACKWELL

M r. Blackwell created the worst-dressed list. (We are talking about Mr. *Richard* Blackwell; the other famous Blackwell, Earl, maintains the "Celebrity Register" and is no relation.) Before Mr. Blackwell, there were dozens of nice-tempered annual fashion honor rolls, published by various manufacturers, clothiers, and publicists primarily as a means of getting good press for their products and clients. In 1960, as an alternative to publicist Eleanor Lambert's International Best Dressed List, an innocuous puff-piece selection of good-looking ladies, Mr. Blackwell drew up a list of the ten worst female fashion criminals for *American Weekly* magazine. "As a designer, I found that the overpampered, overpuffed, overperfumed, overpublicized and overdressed ladies of the silver screen

knew as much about fashion as King Kong," he recalled. "And I said so."

Not beholden to any product or movie studio, Blackwell (his friends never use the "Mr.") had a real knack for saying delightfully nasty things about important people. In 1960 most of the respectable press was still circumspect in its handling of stars and dignitaries, so his audacious criticism of even pillars of propriety came as an impudent (and exhilarating) shock. Anne Baxter's hair, he wrote, "looks as if someone ran a brush through it, then said, 'Oh, the hell with it.'" Princess Margaret reminded him of "a grand revival of *Charlie's Aunt* with a rock 'n' roll beat." Lucille Ball was a "Halloween trick without the treat." And Elizabeth Taylor in tight clothes looked to him "like a chain of link sausages."

Blackwell had no intention of making his list an annual event, but it was such a sensation that he has been doing it ever since, never at a loss for new material or for malignant words to describe them. "Who could believe a Cher? An Elizabeth Taylor? A Barbra Streisand? A Madonna?" he asked in the introduction to his book, *Mr. Blackwell's Worst: 30 Years of Fashion Fiascos.* "Only a fashion masochist experiencing a dreadful fever dream under a full moon, that's for sure, which proves you can be famous, rich, powerful, talented, and gorgeous—and still look like something the cat refuses to drag in."

What kind of man invents a worst-dressed list? A fifth-grade dropout who appeared in Dead End Kids films as a character named Ears (because they "stood out like taxi doors," he says), Blackwell (né Richard Sylvan Selzer) was given his name by Howard Hughes, who thought he was so handsome he could be a romantic leading man. He never made it as an actor, although

he has continued throughout his life to maintain and improve his appearance by numerous plastic-surgery procedures, including jowl, cheek, and chin lifts, ear reduction, eye narrowing, and a pioneering three-quart liposuction that reallocated the fat from his love handles to his buttocks. "The most wonderful thing in the world is our bodies," he once said.

After his acting career fizzled, Blackwell became a personal manager, but according to one account, he soon realized that the clothes he supplied his clients attracted more attention than their talents; so he began Mr. Blackwell Designs in 1957. "Thoroughly entertaining fashion fantasies" is how he described his work for clients, the most famous of which have been such vintage Hollywood glamour queens as Loretta Young, Jane Russell, and Jane Wyman.

Worst lists are now a staple of popular culture; and they have become ever more enjoyable and necessary-seeming to provide a fitting balance for all the puffery that passes for news and information on TV and in the press. In a culture that provides such a wide berth for swelled egos, pretense, and exhibitionism, worst lists are a welcome opportunity to deflate all the hype—cleverly, and sometimes downright meanly. Tabloids feature weekly photos of overexposed celebrities' fashion boners ("Would You Be Caught Dead In This Outfit?"); nearly every movie reviewer has a worst-picture list at the end of the year, usually featuring the most bloated Hollywood turkeys; and embarrassing faux pas in fields from high fashion to belles lettres are regularly honored by such magazines as *People* and *Entertainment Weekly*. It would be wrong to credit Mr. Blackwell as the direct inspiration for all of these best-of-the-worst phenomena; on the other hand, it is only fair to say that he was a pioneer of this unique kind of cultural criticism—the first arbiter of taste to celebrate the joy to be mined from abysmal failure rather than conventional success.

For more than thirty years, Mr. Blackwell has maintained his status as supreme judge of fashion blunders, thanks not merely to his list but to the poisonous commentary that accompanies it. ("Barbra Streisand: she looks like a masculine Bride of Frankenstein." . . . "Queen Elizabeth: God save the mothballs!" . . . "Shirley Temple: from 'The Good Ship Lollipop' to the *Titanic*, nonstop!") Indeed, Blackwell's list has become such an institution that some women clamor to be on it (apparently because there's no such thing as bad publicity); and

he says that one year Lynn Redgrave demanded to know why he had dropped her, insisting, "I haven't improved any." Mr. Blackwell attributes the list's popularity to his willingness to be honest. "Every woman is saying in private what I dare to say out loud," he said. And because he specializes in going after self-important and generally disliked celebrities ("Seeing Nancy Reagan in knickers is cause for laughter. It's either that, or lose your mind completely"), his every-January presentation of the world's Worst-Dressed Women has become the one moment of the fashion year relished even by people who don't care about fashion.

BOBBY SOCKS

"Everybody's talking about bobby socks and the bobby-socks brigade," the *New York Times* announced in the spring of 1944, just after Frank Sinatra (see p. 450) left Tommy Dorsey's band to become a regular performer on radio's "Your Hit Parade." The bobby-socks brigade had a lot of adults worried, and not just because they cried and fainted when the Moonlight Swoonatra sang. Their hys-

terical reaction was only one symptom of a troubling phenomenon that was starting to take shape in America; bobby socks were their badge. Girls who wore them were part of an apparently growing subculture that didn't want to play by the old rules of fashion or behavior. "The police are 'taking steps' and sociologists and defenders of the home are calling meetings," the *Times* said, "but no one seems to know exactly what a bobby sock is and where it gets its name."

Bobby socks were anklets, almost always white, differing from ladies' half-socks only in the fact that they were purchased by teenage girls to become part of a livery that signified what was fast becoming one of America's most worried-over problems: adolescent rebellion. The otherwise innocent anklets, when worn with blue jeans and flapping shirttails, or as part of a big-band "beat feet" ensemble with little bells on the laces of saddle shoes, or with dog collars

[B]
THE ANKLET
25¢

[A]
NAILHEAD
PUMPS $2.29

ALSO OTHER
COMBINATIONS
$3.00 VALUE!

and ID bracelets strapped around the ankle, were one of the earliest ways modern teenagers set themselves apart from traditional adult society. Refined girls wore nylons; or if they did wear socks, they kept them pulled up neat, high around the ankle. Bobby-soxers liked to wear them sloppy and wrinkled, and folded over low to expose the ankle: while not exactly insurrectionary, it was a style that flouted propriety.

If the origin of the name remains a mystery, bobby socks' beginnings are clear. They were first worn in the mid-1930s in southern California by young, devil-may-care fashion pioneers who considered hosiery too formal for sunny patio parties, and even for Friday-night jitterbugging to the sound of big bands. The Montgomery Ward catalog began to feature pastel half-socks called Hollywoods—"the anklet color craze started by the stars." When the war put a halt to sales of nylon stockings, as well as of garters and girdles (these required Malayan rubber, which had fallen into Japanese hands), women had no choice but to wear socks. And when thousands of them went to work in pants and overalls, anklets were a natural. By the end of the war, well over three hundred million pairs of anklets were being sold every year.

Whatever the logical reasons for their increasing popularity, bobby socks—like slacks—represented a significant challenge to accepted notions of feminine style. To wear them when you didn't need to could be seen as a gesture of defiance; and by the mid-1940s, when people started worrying about the bobby-socks brigade and Frank Sinatra's disturbing effect on young girls, bobby socks were part of the uniform of wayward runaways in wartime boom towns, and loose-morals types known as "victory girls." Their disrepute only augmented their appeal to many relatively virtuous young girls in high school and college

who were eager to rebel (if only a little), and they soon became part of nearly every teenager's wardrobe. By the early 1950s, they were even listed in the staid Montgomery Ward catalog as "Bobby Socks—the teen-agers' favorite."

Bobby socks were one of the first articles of clothing to work their way *up* in status, setting a pattern increasingly evident in postwar fashion. Blue jeans, T-shirts, leather jackets, and Madonna's underwear all first appeared as fairly vulgar street wear and then, because of their youthful panache, rose to middle-class acceptability (if not high fashion). Phil Spector even named a singing group after them in the early 1960s —Bob B. Soxx and the Blue Jeans, who, led by Darlene Love, sang a novelty revival of "Zip-A-Dee-Doo-Dah."

In fact, bobby socks got so popular as a postwar teen icon that a little later, when baby boomers started entering their teens, eager to distance themselves from grown-ups, bobby socks (or any white socks) became emblematic not of someone who was appealingly rebellious and hip but an out-of-it nerd with fashion ties to an older, out-of-date generation. "In the 60s and 70s you wouldn't be caught dead in white socks," Michael Jackson wrote in his autobiography, *Moonwalk.* "It was too square to even consider—for most people." But not for Michael, who bravely wore white socks on stage and in music videos and declared, "Now it's cool again."

"BONANZA"

I n the 1960s, a decade that tested values of togetherness and tradition, the Ponderosa ranch, where "Bonanza" took place, became America's foremost symbol of home and hearth. On the air from 1959 to 1973, and number one in the Nielsen ratings from 1964 to 1967, "Bonanza" touched on many serious subjects—some, such as prejudice or pacifism, with contemporary implications—but it had just one eternal theme: the strength and unity to be drawn from family life.

Strangely, the Ponderosa was not occupied by anything like a traditional family. Its main inhabitants were four strapping men —Ben Cartwright (Lorne Greene) and his sons, Adam (Pernell Roberts), Hoss (Dan Blocker), and Little Joe (Michael Landon) —plus a Chinese houseboy named Hop Sing (Victor Sen Yung). Each of the Cartwright boys had had a different mother, all of whom had died. Adam, the mature, introspective one, had been born in New En-

gland when Ben was a ship's chandler. When his mother passed on (of an unspecified illness), she had told Ben to follow his dream and go west, which he did. Hoss, the huge, friendly, not-too-bright one, was born on a wagon train heading towards Nevada from Missouri, after which his mother, a Norwegian woman named Inger, was killed by Indians. And Little Joe, the impulsive, romantic one, was born after his father had established the ranch in Virginia City; but then his mother, a southern belle, had died too, when her horse stepped in a hole and threw her.

In the first couple of seasons, the boys' variant inherited personalities made them quarrel frequently; but viewers weren't much interested in a family drama that pitted son against son, especially because the plots accentuated all their unpleasant qualities—Adam's Yankee priggishness, Hoss's Scandinavian stubbornness, Little Joe's southern recklessness—and Ben's sorry inability to cope with single fatherhood. Ratings were not good. In 1961 a strategic change was made: "Bonanza" was moved from Saturday to Sunday at nine P.M., which is usually considered an hour when whole families are most likely to watch television together. And the focus of the plots shifted. The boys learned to forget their differences; they were now best buddies, one for all and all for one. Banded together, the Cartwright clan became the fair-fighting champions of each week's underdog (frequently a celebrity guest star); and "Bonanza" became a huge ratings hit.

Perhaps the show's greatest charm was its size. It seemed big in the way a six-passenger Chevrolet sedan was big: a family-size bulwark of strength, with down-to-earth appeal for traditionalists. Everything about it was expansive, from the fast-driving twang of its catchy theme music, written by Jay Livingston and Ray Evans, which played over an image of a blazing map of Nevada, to gorgeous photography, not only of mountains and prairies but of ranch interiors that were lit with the kind of complex visual refinement normally seen only in feature films. ("Bonanza" was the first western televised in color.) The guys themselves were extraordinarily big, especially Ben and Hoss; and their ranch was a vast, prosperous thousand acres of prime western scenery.

"Bonanza" was such a hit that all the Cartwrights went into an RCA recording studio and made an album in 1964: *Ponderosa Party Time*, featuring their renditions of such happy, whole-fam-damily classics as "Skip to My Lou" and "Miss Cindy," as well as the inspirational song "The Place Where I Worship (Is the Wide Open Spaces)." The album sold so well that RCA issued a second, "Welcome to the Ponderosa," and Lorne Greene recorded a single on his own. Greene, who at the beginning of his career was an announcer for the Canadian Broadcasting Company, where he was known to listeners as "the Voice of Doom" for his resonating baritone delivery of bad news, had never sought to be a recording artist. But he recalled that when he read a poem called "Ringo," about a sheriff who saves the life of a gunslinger, he got chills and felt it ought to be put on record. He declaimed the words with a dramatic musical accompaniment; and in December 1964 "Ringo" reached number one on the pop charts, displacing the defiant teenage dirge "Leader of the Pack" by the Shangri-Las. (One other interesting fact, which we learned from *The Billboard Book of Number One Hits:* Lorne

Greene invented the backwards stopwatch, for announcers who have to keep track of how much time they have left.)

There was a failed attempt to revive "Bonanza" in the mid-1980s with the production of a feature-length TV movie called *Bonanza: The Next Generation.* Lorne Greene was scheduled to reprise his old role, but when he died in 1987, John Ireland took the part of the family patriarch. He was introduced as Ben Cartwright's brother, a former sea captain who stupidly lets miners and oil speculators ravage the Ponderosa—until they are stopped by the returning sons of Little Joe and Hoss. In fact, none of the original cast members appeared in the TV movie. Dan Blocker had already died; Michael Landon, who had gone on to "Little House on the Prairie," was busy with "Highway to Heaven" (although his son, Michael Landon, Jr., did have a part, as did Lorne Greene's daughter Gillian); and Pernell Roberts simply wasn't interested. Roberts had walked off the original "Bonanza" at its peak in 1965, damning it as "junk TV" and describing its treatment of the Cartwrights as an untoward glorification of rich landowners.

BOOMERANG FORMICA

As much as tail fins on cars and the atomic-molecule motif (a nucleus surrounded by orbiting electrons), the boomerang is one of the prime signs of modern life as it was fashioned in the 1950s. On the countertops of diners and of family dinettes, little images of boomerangs signaled a forward-looking point of view, defiantly different from old, dowdy motifs such as cabbage roses or Grecian urns. Now, boomerang Formica is as nostalgic as doo-wop music and Brylcreemed hair, a reminder of an optimistic time when the future was sleek, curved, and speedy.

Formica itself goes way back, to 1913, when it was created by an engineer named Dan O'Conor, who named it (and started the Formica Corporation) because he thought its heat-resistant properties would make it a good substitute *for mica*, which was used as insulation in electric motors. Some ten years later the Formica Corporation began making decorative panels from its miracle plastic laminate, which could be fashioned to resemble almost any other hard material. They made wood-grain fronts and fascias for some of the earliest console radios, mar-

ble-textured counters for soda fountains, and even a black-onyx-look Formica for knickknacks and art deco furniture. Formica became so popular that wood kitchen tables and even enameled metal ones began to look terribly passé. During World War II, Formica's fortunes boomed. It was made into a material called "Pregwood" for airplane propeller blades; and when the *Queen Mary* was fitted as a troop transport, Formica was used throughout because it was so tough.

After the war, a Formica Corporation film called *The Formica Story* boasted that a force of company research men "has been busy every day seeking new ways to improve Formica and its uses, not only for industry and industrial designers but for homes." The single great moment occurred in 1950, as Americans were poised to move into the suburbs and surround themselves with convenient, modern kitchens, when Brook Stevens Associates designed the Skylark pattern—a series of similar (but not identical) thin-lined boomerang-shaped outlines in one, two, or three colors, overlapping each other on a plain Formica surface. The design was finessed four years later by Nettie Hart of Raymond Loewy Associates, and the result was the ultra-stylish pattern that, as much as push buttons and rocket shapes, defined consumer taste in the fifties.

Boomerangs were one of the most exalted shapes of the era, suggesting supersonic airplane wings, wind tunnels, and—most important of all—modernity. (Consider McDonald's golden arches, created in 1948; each of them is a parabolic curve that could almost be a boomerang.) Boomerang patterns on anything were considered as modern as tomorrow; on Formica, the manmade miracle plastic, well, it was simply an epiphany of jet-age design. The truly inspired thing about Skylark Formica is that it was not made to look like artificial wood or stone or even linoleum. It was Formica, and darn proud of it! Its dancing boomerangs celebrated the triumph of manmade plastic over anything nature had to offer. That ingenuous attitude is why Skylark-pattern Formica today has become such an amusing emblem of times gone by.

"THE BRADY BUNCH"

It never got high ratings and was dismissed by critics as contrived, annoying, or at best harmless, but "The Brady Bunch" endured five years on the air (1969–74), spun off into "The Brady Kids" (a Saturday morning cartoon, 1972–74), "The Brady Bunch Hour" (an indescribably strange variety show in 1977), "The Brady Brides" (a short-lived series in 1981), and "The Bradys" (now *three* generations of family fun, 1990), and has continued to enjoy a long syndicated afterlife.

It has become a renowned video oddity —adored, abhorred, and one of the most irrepressible shows of all time. It was born in a TV era best remembered for such groundbreaking series as "All in the Family" and "Laugh-In" (see pp. 11, 272). But even in its original five years on ABC, it was an extraordinarily square half-hour, a contrast not only to vanguard television but to the iconoclasm that permeated so much pop culture at the time. Its resolute triviality was especially shocking because it looked so doggone contemporary: set in what was purported to be modern-day California, it was about a family of lively young nowsters who dressed in flowery jumpers, billowy mod shirts, and burnt-orange bell bottoms; the entire cast, even the adults, spoke sanitized street jargon that included such hip

Top: Ann B. Davis (Alice), Barry Williams (Greg), Robert Reed (Mike), Eve Plumb (Jan); *center:* Christopher Knight (Peter), Florence Henderson (Carol), Maureen McCormick (Marcia); *bottom:* Susan Olsen (Cindy), Michael Lookinland (Bobby)

words as "groovy" and "outtasight." Despite this shimmer of Aquarian sensibility, "The Brady Bunch" was utterly out of synch with life on earth as it was then, is now, or ever has been. Therein lies its bizarre allure.

In case you are too young or too high-brow to recall, or have blocked it from your memory, the Brady Bunch was a wholesome blended family of a single woman (Florence Henderson, never precisely identified as a widow or a divorcée) and her three very lovely girls (Maureen McCormick, Eve Plumb, and Susan Olsen), a widower (Robert Reed) with three boys (Barry Williams, Christopher Knight, Michael Lookinland), plus a harried housekeeper named Alice (Ann B. Davis), a dog named Tiger, a mouse named Myron, a pair of rabbits named Romeo and Juliet, and a parakeet without a name. They lived in a big ranch house on Clinton Avenue in an unspecified suburb; Mom and Dad were shown together, sometimes even smooching, in a double bed (a TV sitcom first!); and some scenes took place in a most peculiar bathroom that had a tub and a sink but no toilet, because the toilet had been removed so as not to offend the viewing audience.

As a public service, we shall now name all the Brady family members. This is information you need to know if you ever find yourself a member of a hostage negotiating team dealing with a crazed criminal who refuses to surrender unless someone on the team names every single Brady—*as actually happened at the Deer Island House of Correction in Massachusetts in 1990.* So, in the interest of justice and law enforcement, here they are, along with thumbnail dossiers:

Mike Brady (Dad): architect, council master for the Frontier Scouts. His biggest familial concern: the kids just won't stay off the telephone.

Carol Brady (Mom): PTA member, former twist contest winner, with no profession but many hobbies, including sculpture, photography, and trying to get an article published in a women's magazine.

Marcia (oldest daughter): senior class president, head of the Davy (the Monkee) Jones Fan Club.

Greg (oldest boy): good student, baseball player, surfer, the most mod dresser of all the Bradys, and a budding ladies' man who likes to play the field and sometimes finds himself with two dates for one night (yikes!).

Jan (middle girl): has the blondest hair of all the Bradys. She once wore a brunet wig to try to establish her own identity because, as the middle child, she is the most insecure.

Peter (middle boy): idolizes Greg and in later seasons follows his older brother's skirt-chasing ways. He learned to box so he could beat up Buddy Hinton, the series' perpetual bully, who was making fun of youngest sister Cindy's lisp.

Cindy (youngest girl): the cutest Brady, with pigtails; frequently carries a Kitty Karry-All doll as her familiar.

Bobby (youngest boy): shares, with Cindy, the world record for continuous teeter-tottering.

Oliver (the nephew): not a charter member of the Brady Bunch. Oliver is Carol's cousin, introduced in the last season when Bobby and Cindy had become too old to say cute things the way they used to.

Alice (the housekeeper): With all those kids to serve, a house to clean, and meals to cook, Alice was constantly working, her role in the family described in a *New Yorker* article about the show as "the perennial outsider," a situation that only accentuates her natural inferiority complex. Even on "The Brady Bunch Reunion," broadcast in 1990, she spends most of her time in the background of scenes, sweeping, dusting, and eavesdropping on Brady family conversations.

If you doubt the lasting impact of these terminally vacuous characters, consider what must surely be one of the oddest dramaturgical phenomena of recent times—the success of a stage show called *The Real Live Brady Bunch*. It opened in 1990 and was produced by the Metraform Theater group of Chicago, previously known for such provocative works as *That Darned Antichrist* and *Coed Prison Sluts*. Line for line, gesture for gesture, the actors—all adults—performed a different complete episode of "The Brady Bunch" every week for fourteen months. Theatergoers were delighted, and frequently called out favorite lines in unison with the actors, and their applause, giggles, and groans of embarrassed recognition were accompanied by a canned laugh track, just like on the show. When *The Real Live Brady Bunch* moved to the Village Gate in New York, *Time* magazine wondered whether the production was "either a tribute to a classic piece of TV kitsch or the End of Theater As We Know It."

To understand why "The Brady Bunch" maintains its queer fascination, you have to see it. Synopses and descriptions and theatrical homages do not convey the power of the TV show's awesome blandness any more than a psychiatrist's notes can really reveal the visceral grip of a patient's dementia. Partly because it was shot with a single camera (like a movie) instead of three (like an ordinary sitcom), it contains a ferocious number of close-ups and curiously angled shots, and its lighting, instead of being soft and vaguely mottled (as is usually the case when three cameras are used) is direct, piercingly focused, and virtually without shadows. This makes the colors—a ghastly palette of early-1970s earth tones—seem so intense that they appear to have swallowed up all the usual primary hues. The Brady world is an apparition of heightened reality in which the standard spectrum has shifted shockingly to one of harvest gold and avocado green, burnt sienna, tangerine, mocha, happy-face saffron, chartreuse, and Easter-egg pastels. These colors combine with crystalline imagery to create a visual experience that isn't just unreal, it is *surreal*—as bright as a dream or a stupefying hallucination.

Beyond the visual punch, there are equally uncompromising dramatic principles at work. The show was created and produced by Sherwood Schwartz, who also wrote the words of the theme song, originally performed by the Peppermint Trolley Company (then by the Brady kids themselves), and who had honed the art of perfect inanity in his first hit series, "Gilligan's Island" (1964–67). In "The Brady Bunch," he went beyond mere inanity and created a vehicle so bland, so trite, so achingly synthetic that it now plays—exactly as it was originally written—as theater of the absurd.

The disquieting sense of aberrant being that saturates "The Brady Bunch" comes also from hammering monotony—the sameness and predictability of the plots—as well as from the mundane life lessons the kids learn (about getting braces for their teeth or not reading other people's diaries). And the corker in nearly every show, the moment when the proceedings are almost guaranteed to send you into a state of hysteria, delirium, or possibly a coma, is the scene in which parental units Mike and Carol, separately or together, issue homilies designed to teach their bunch how to be normal. Andrew Edelstein and Frank Lovece, authors of *The Brady Bunch Book*, noted these words of wisdom, delivered by Mom and Dad to the kids in various episodes:

- "There's an old saying: You can't take a step forward with two feet on the ground."
- "Find out what you do best and then do your best with it."

- "Money and fame are very important things, but sometimes there are other things that are more important—like people!"
- "No one has ever solved a problem by crawling into a hole."

Ultimately, what makes "The Brady Bunch" an unavoidable classic in the pop pantheon of truly bizarre Americana is the dissociative behavior of the characters, who all resemble human beings but behave like relatives of Barbie Doll—always happy, good, nice, pretty, and plastic. To watch them interrelate is like finding yourself in an episode of "The Twilight Zone" in which everything appears perfectly normal... until you begin to realize that in the Brady world, normalcy is the weirdest, craziest condition of all.

DR. JOYCE BROTHERS

D r. Joyce Brothers invented mass-media psychology. Before her there were sob sisters of the air and a few religious guys like Norman Vincent Peale who generally advised their suffering correspondents to buck up or perhaps offered them a soft shoulder to cry on. Dr. Brothers did those things and more: she explained behavior; she prescribed strategies for coping; she enumerated scientific studies and helped people understand why they (and others) did what they did. What's more, she embellished her authoritative advice with a dash of fun, plenty of sympathy, and a good measure of wholesome sex appeal. A press release issued by her agent said, "She looks like Loretta Young, walks like Marilyn Monroe, and talks like Dr. Freud." Seymour Krim pointed out back in 1980 that she was probably the only practicing psychologist with an active show business agent.

Now, of course, there is an abundance of shrinks in show business. In Dr. Joyce Brothers's wake, TV studios have filled up with penitents and sufferers revealing everything about their private lives, and therapists of every stripe, including professional counselors, semiprofessional ex-

perts, and too many talk-show hosts to count, all of whom help explain to the viewing audience why the sufferers do what they do and what it means. It is now so common to psychologize about behavior on radio and television that the practice of amateur analysis has become almost invisible; we practically guarantee that if you tune in to a talk show—*any* talk show, even one about politics or gardening—you will hear the participants cogitating about motivation, repression, desire, ego fulfillment, masturbatory fantasies, and a dozen other such things that used to be considered the province of mental health specialists.

Freudianism and dilettante brain therapeutics have been popularized on and off since the teens and twenties, but they had a real renaissance in the 1950s as many people began to worry deeply about the perils of conformity and to develop an affinity for maverick behavior, as evidenced by beatniks, folksingers, teen rebels, and juvenile delinquents. Cute eccentrics were especially prized, a fact Mrs. Joyce Brothers (then a student of experimental psychology at Columbia University, where she wrote a thesis about "The Conditioned Salivary Response in Human Subjects") noticed when "The $64,000 Question" went on the air in June 1955. This pace-setting big-bucks show loved oddball contestants. Among its first winners were a Staten Island policeman who was a student of Shakespeare and a Bronx shoemaker who knew all about opera. Mrs. Brothers—petite, blond, and shapely—presented herself to the producers as an expert in, of all things, boxing. In fact, she knew nothing about the manly art; but she was a quick study, and the way she figured it, there were only a limited number of facts to learn. So she learned them all by memorizing the *Ring Encyclopedia*, and in December she became only the second person (after a Marine captain who was an expert gourmet cook) to go all the way to the top and win $64,000. She stunned the audience of what was by then the most popular television show in America by knowing what a *cestus* was (the glove worn by ancient Roman pugilists), then breezing through a sixteen-part answer to a final question that had been concocted by a team of sportswriters who, she now maintains, had been instructed to stump her because the producers had begun to worry that a doctoral candidate was too elitist a type of person to carry off the top prize.

Three years later, when a grand jury investigated the rigging of quiz shows, Dr. Brothers was one of the few celebrated winners who did not admit to cheating. In fact, she answered six grueling hours of questions about the fight game just to prove to the jury that she really did know her stuff.

By the end of the 1950s, Brothers had her degree and was hosting a thirty-minute afternoon advice show on WRCA-TV, writing a newspaper column, and co-hosting NBC-TV's "Sports Showcase." She went on to write several books, including *Ten Days to a Successful Memory*, *What Every Woman Should Know About Marriage*, *How to Get What You Want Out of Life*, and most recently, *The Successful Woman: How You Can Have a Career, a Husband and a Family—and Not Feel Guilty About It;* but it is for her media appearances that people know Joyce Brothers best. As familiar a video visitor as Orson Bean, Hildegarde, and Charo once were, she has long been one of the most popular all-around guests on talk shows ("The Tonight Show"), variety shows ("Sha Na Na"), and dramas ("One Life to Live," in which she played herself), always good for a little bit of amusing advice-giving or, with Johnny Carson, some slightly risqué repartee. Her own television shows over the years have included "Consult Dr. Brothers," "Tell Me, Dr. Brothers," "Appointment with Dr. Brothers," and "Living Easy with Dr. Joyce Brothers," the latter branching out from the problem-solving format to include celebrity interviews, fashion tips, cooking demonstrations, and Dr. Brothers's own advice on home decoration. She has also made frequent guest appearances on "Captain Kangaroo" (see p. 80), and she was a pinch-hit panelist on "The Gong Show" for four years starting in 1976.

Dr. Brothers loves being in the spotlight, although there are some things she will not do. Early in her career, after demonstrating the utmost composure under the pressure of "The $64,000 Question" as well as its sequel, "The $64,000 Challenge" (where she won again), she turned down the opportunity to have an antiperspirant soap named after her.

As a media psychologist, she described herself as "kind of a middleman between the viewer and psychological literature"; and one of her trademarks is that rather than merely offer her opinion, she frequently accompanies advice and counsel by fascinating statistics, apparently tackling human dilemmas with the scholarly diligence she used to win her quiz show cash. For example, these are some of the interesting facts and studies she has cited, as discovered by Seymour Krim and published in his book *What's This Cat's Story* and by Henry Allen writing in the Washington *Post:*

- Studies show that sweat prepares animals to cope with danger.
- Men think about sex every other minute. Women think about it once every ten minutes.
- A male gorilla's genitals are teensy.
- There is a study that was done in another country which indicates that sometimes the stress of children, family, husband, career is changing the endocrine balance and women are developing chest hair.
- They are teaching men to cry to grow chest hair.
- Medically speaking, there is no such thing as a nervous breakdown.
- Studies show if you're the kind of person who makes others uneasy, people will like you better if you do something clumsy like spill your drink, trip over the rug, enter a room with a smudge on your face.

JAMES BROWN

James Brown was born dead. In a shack in the pine woods of South Carolina, his mother delivered a boy on May 3, 1933, but the baby was still. They slapped it and stroked it and, getting no response, gave up hope and laid it aside. The boy's aunt Minnie would not accept this. She picked up the baby, rubbed its back, and blew air into its mouth. The baby began to breathe, then to move. And for the rest of his life, James Joe Brown, Jr., has done an extremely convincing job of showing everybody that he is very much alive.

Of all the high-powered performers since the 1950s, he is the most superpowered of all, blasting an unequaled 114 songs onto the R&B charts and known at various times in his career as "Mr. Dynamite," "the Hardest-Working Man in Show Business," "His Bad Self," and "The Minister of the New New Super Heavy Funk." No one else has ever moved so fast and furious on stage. To have witnessed him perform at his peak in the mid-1960s is to have seen Terpsichore in stovepipe pants. He spun, pinwheeled, boogalooed, bled, sweated, cried, collapsed, and raised himself up again. He worked audiences into a frenzy and left them crying out his name. His was a show that was more than music, more than rhythm. James Brown set himself forth as an element of nature. Once in the 1980s he announced that he had invented "Nuclear Soul" but was waiting to confer with the leaders of

the world's superpowers before he dared unleash it to the public.

He does not read a note of music, and *Rolling Stone* once described his voice as "somewhere between a murder-bent chicken hawk and the screech of subway wheels," but his impact on modern music is immeasurable: in rhythm, choreography, showmanship, and most of all, in an audacious, fearless attitude that he devised and has perfected through the years. "James Brown is magic," Michael Jackson said. "He's got a kind of freedom. I crave it. Every day." John Leland, writing in *Newsweek*, said, "There's an argument to be made that James Brown is the most important musical force of our time. . . . He tore down popular music and rebuilt it around rhythms and grooves rather than melodies." Beyond the authority of his musicianship and ripsnorting performances, James Brown has established an indisputable dominion as one of the major forces of popular culture, similar to the status that Picasso enjoyed in art. Once called "Soul Brother Number One," he has now become "the Godfather of Soul."

He started performing in church as a boy in Augusta, Georgia (where he went to live when he was six), with a group called the Ever Ready Gospel Singers, who in their spare time imitated rhythm and blues artists like the Dominoes (led by Clyde McPhatter), the Orioles, and the Five Royales. "I stayed on top of all the latest dances," Brown recalled in his autobiography: "the slop, the funky chicken (even before it was called the funky chicken), the alligator, the camel walk. . . . I developed my own camel walk so that it would eventually become the James Brown." When they began performing in clubs, the Ever Readys decided they needed a new name—something that "captured what we had been trying for in our music since our first rehearsal." Inspired by a local group they liked called the Torches, "we became the Flames, full of fire and romance," later amplified to the Famous Flames. One night they opened for Little Richard (who wasn't yet famous himself). Little Richard was so impressed, and so worried they would upstage him, he stopped their show in the middle. "You're the onliest man I've seen who has everything," Brown recalls Little Richard telling him that night.

In 1956, James Brown and the Famous Flames recorded "Please, Please, Please" above the objections of studio engineers who declared, "It's a stupid song. It's got only one word in it." It became a million seller, number one on the R&B charts and a big hit in England . . . although it was ignored by most white American disc jockeys, who were busy worrying about the Caucasians-only battle between Elvis Presley and Pat Boone for American teenage hearts. More big hits followed, still ghettoized, and by the early 1960s James Brown, virtually unknown by the white record-buying public, was the hottest black singer in America. His album *Live at the Apollo* stayed on the charts for sixty-six weeks in 1962–63. He toured constantly and perfected his act.

No one else put on a show like James Brown and the Famous Flames. As he described it, "Back then a lot of the groups were pretty, performing with top hats and canes and singing mellow, close harmony stuff. You didn't see too many groups like us, dancing all over the place, cutting flips, slinging sweat, and singing real raw." He arrived on stage with the highest, most elaborately waved and sculpted conked hair in show business, wearing one of his five hundred brightly colored ripcord suits. By the end of the show the suit was shredded from his skids across the boards, soaked and heavy with his sweat, torn away from his chest so he could breathe, and his hair was hanging loose and low. At the end of every show—during which he would usually lose eight or nine pounds, and after which he sometimes required intravenous glucose—he collapsed with exhaustion as the crowd watched. Starting in 1964, Brown made his exhaustion part of the act. As he finished the last song of his set, "Please, Please, Please," he dropped to his knees in a state of total collapse. One of the Flames came and wrapped a velvet cape over his shoulders to escort the beaten man off stage, but before he could be taken away he threw off the cape—re-energized by the throb of the music still playing—and returned with his last shred of strength for an encore. Then he fell to the floor again, got wrapped in the cape again, walked away again, and staggered back to the microphone again for yet another encore. And again and again. The cape routine, Brown said, he learned by watching Gorgeous George, the wrestler, on television.

A lot of white people learned about James Brown because of his performance in the *T.A.M.I.* [*Teenage Awards Music International*] *Show*, filmed for television but also shown in theaters in 1965. It was a concert film with a truly extraordinary and eclectic cast of musicians that included Chuck Berry, Bo Diddley, the Supremes, Marvin Gaye, Smokey Robinson and the Miracles, Lesley Gore, Jan and Dean (who emceed), and the Rolling Stones. The Stones, who were just becoming teen faves at the time, were scheduled to be the climax of the show, right after James Brown and the Famous Flames. During the dress rehearsal, when Mick Jagger saw the act that was supposed to precede him, he begged producer Steve Binder for an earlier spot in the lineup: *no one* could possibly follow James Brown. He was at his peak for that show, and he did countless encores and the full cape routine during "Night Train." When Mick Jagger finally came on to do the finale, he hopped a little on one foot, furiously shook his maracas, and tried to put some fast moves into his act, but he looked like a frightened schoolboy compared with James Brown, the hot-footed, rhythm-crazed "Sex Machine" (another one of his monikers).

Because he was such an astounding performer, James Brown's energy sometimes obscured the unique perspective of his hit songs. Long before rap got popular, he was speechifying about life on the street—real life, from "Hot Pants (She Got to Use What She Got to Get What She Wants)" to "Say It Loud—I'm Black and I'm Proud." Even when the subject became the stuff of a more traditional ballad, as in "Try Me" and "It's a Man's World," he declaimed the story with so much emotion that it gave new meaning to the concept of soul music. "I'm not a rock 'n' roll singer," he said. Actually, he is more a poet than any kind of singer, and his songs are like ragged-seeming street verse set to music and shouted out—the antithesis of the simple-sexy-sad formula typical of so many hummable Top 40 ditties. A James Brown song is personal, eccentric, sometimes ranting and raving, always connected to vernacular life, and always uniquely his. That helps explain why no performer has ever done a memorable cover version of one of his hits (although Sinead O'Connor, George Michael, and Fine Young Cannibals have tried). To hear another singer do "Cold Sweat" or "Licking Stick" is a little like hearing a Redd Foxx party album as performed by Bill Cosby.

Like his music, James Brown's well-publicized personal life has always been unconventional and astonishing. Early in his career, he was a major force in integrating concert halls throughout the South. His song "Don't Be a Drop Out" endeared him to Vice-President Hubert Humphrey in the late 1960s—a friendship that lasted until Humphrey's death. And although he cut his famous hair into an Afro (see p. 4) "for the movement," some black militants labeled him an Uncle Tom for attending a White House dinner in 1968, then going to Vietnam to entertain the troops and singing "America Is My Home." He got death threats because his bass player was a Caucasian. And when he endorsed Richard Nixon for President in 1972, his concerts were picketed.

Although in 1986 he won a Grammy award and hit the top ten with "Living in America" (the theme from the movie *Rocky IV*), James Brown had a very hard time in the 1980s. The Internal Revenue Service put a lien on his house in 1985. Police were repeatedly called to his ranch to settle domestic disputes. On one occasion, he shot holes in Adrienne's mink coat and in her mattress and put three thousand dollars' worth of bullet holes in her clothes. Another time, Adrienne was arrested for setting fire to their New Hampshire motel room (with Brown in it). In May, Adrienne called police to come settle a domestic dispute. James Brown eluded the cops, sped away in his car, then assaulted an officer and was caught carrying the drug PCP. The court

sentenced him to perform a benefit concert. He sang "I Feel Good" to an audience of 381 people and 7,119 empty seats.

In September things got really bad. Toting a shotgun, he busted into an insurance seminar in a building where he had an office and accused the assembled salesmen of using his bathroom without permission. When the police were called, James Brown leapt into his pickup truck and led them on yet another chase, this one for a half hour of high-speed driving in and out of South Carolina, until his tires were shot out and he crashed into a ditch. The arresting officers said he was incoherent and drenched with sweat when they pulled him from the car; when he was booked, he began to dance frenetically.

James Brown scarcely contested the charges against him. "Being a hero and a legend like Martin Luther King, it would have been detrimental to the community here," he explained. "It was a sacrifice. I'm like Kennedy—it's not what your country can do for you, it's what you can do for your country." In December he was sentenced to prison for six years, shortly after which he became a cause célèbre and subject of the song "Free James Brown." The Reverend Al Sharpton, the New York activist, whose hair is styled in waves and billows as a homage to Brown, called the sentence "total castration and castigation."

Brown served just over two years, during which his wife, a former hair stylist, visited him in prison every weekend to attend to his coiffure and bring him Lysol to sanitize his cell (he is a fanatic about cleanliness). While incarcerated, he learned to cook and served breakfast in the prison cafeteria and directed the chapel choir, then did community service among old ladies in rest homes and counseled young people about the evil of drugs. He was released on February 27, 1991, and two days later he flew to Los Angeles to have eyebrows tattooed on his forehead (his natural ones had fallen out from too much boxing as a youth) and eye liner tattooed on his lower lids. In May Polydor released *Star Time*—a colossal seventy-one-song boxed set of James Brown classics going back to 1956 that *Newsweek* called "as good as pop music gets."

Adrienne Brown recanted her stories about James being mean to her and welcomed him home. Earlier, she had been ar-rested at the Augusta airport for possessing PCP (hidden in her bra), and had offered a unique plea, which the court did not accept. Adrienne argued that she was entitled to diplomatic immunity: two years earlier Representative D. Douglas Barnard of Georgia had officiated over James Brown Appreciation Day, during which the U.S. congress-man proclaimed James Brown to be America's Number-One Ambassador of Soul.

"BUT WAIT, THERE'S MORE!"

If you watched much television in the 1970s, it is likely your brain has been branded by a few compelling scenes. Remember steak knives sawing through tin cans and roofing nails to prove the blades' strength? Remember the karate master trying to chop a tomato in half with his hand

and mashing tomato pulp against the cutting board? Remember a large striped bass baked into a birthday cake? These were some of the astonishing visual images concocted to sell such products as Ginsu knives ("Isn't that a clever cleaver?"), stainless steel bowls ("It can turn a birthday cake into a fish cake"), and Miracle Slicers and Dusters. One company created all of them: Dial Media, which first took to the airwaves in 1975 selling Miracle Painters (the roller that didn't splatter) with fast-talking spots on late-night TV that promised to solve all your painting problems for $19.95.

Dial's genius was to find (or create) products that had charismatic television appeal. For example, in a retail store a set of kitchen knives can only sit on a shelf looking drab. On TV, knives can be a thrill if you see them work. Dial came up with truly ingenious ways to demonstrate their sharpness, toughness, and usefulness, but that's not all: they completely reconceived the product to fit a spellbinding sales pitch. The knives they sold (still being marketed today as "Ginsu 2000") were originally brought to Dial by a salesman who simply billed his product as the knife that never needed sharpening. Arthur Schiff, creative vice-president of Dial Media, described it as "just a knife. A *nice* knife, but just a knife." Schiff devised a karate-oriented advertising theme and invented the Japanese-sounding name "Ginsu." ("There *is* a similar Japanese word, for 'sharp,'" he once told *TV Guide.* "Kinda eerie, huh?") Ginsu ads showed a frustrated karate warrior shattering bricks with a chop of his hand, but then fuming because his chop wasn't nearly as effective as a Ginsu knife when applied to a tomato. Later ads for Ginsu II showed the same wretched fellow kicking his bare foot into a watermelon, spewing pulp and seeds, after which a Ginsu knife cut another melon into lovely, tidy segments.

Such goofy-seeming presentations, which became Dial's trademark, were in fact an astute homage to Ronco's Ron Popeil, the original direct-market TV auteur, who pitched the Veg-O-Matic, Popiel Pocket Fisherman, and Mr. Dentist using a classic hard-sell formula: show a problem, then sell the solution. In the case of Ginsu advertisements, the "problem" presented at the be-ginning of the ad was rendered as an attention-grabbing joke: nobody in the viewing audience, it is safe to assume, was distraught because they could not slice a watermelon using karate kicks. Nonetheless, Ginsu knives were the solution. Probably the best-remembered such inversion of genre expectations was Dial's ad for Armourcote nonstick pans, which began with a raw egg being cracked over a diamond. "It's the world's hardest surface," the announcer hollered, *"but you can't cook on it!"*

Dial Media's off-the-wall presentations added a level of hip, crafty badinage to direct-response television ads, but their greatest contribution to the field was not an intellectual one, it was visceral: the giveaways. If you bought ten Ginsu knives, you got ten more free . . . plus a cleaver . . . plus two paring knives . . . plus a bread knife . . . plus a fish knife . . . plus a bunch of teaspoons. The bonuses kept on coming, and just when you thought you knew everything your $19.95 would buy, the announcer threw in something else. The words he used —"But wait, there's more!"—became a Dial trademark, and possibly the single best-known line in the history of television. "I invented it," Arthur Schiff once boasted. "'But wait, there's more' is mine."

CABBAGE PATCH DOLLS

"They were grabbing at each other, pushing and shoving. It got ugly," said a department store manager in West Virginia after five thousand shoppers rioted in late November 1983 because they could not get enough Cabbage Patch dolls. In a store in Pennsylvania, a woman suffered a broken leg in the push to get to the toy counter, where the toy department manager swung a baseball bat for protection. Arms were broken in Dallas; shoppers were trampled and hospitalized in Miami. A hoax

was perpetrated in Milwaukee, where doll-crazed customers showed up at County Stadium in below-zero weather with catchers' mitts and credit cards because they believed Cabbage Patch Kids were about to parachute out of a B-29 bomber. Twenty thousand counterfeit Kids were seized by customs agents in New York. When executives from Coleco, the company that manufactured Cabbage Patch Kids, traveled to appear on talk shows, they had to carry their dolls in brown paper bags, lest they be mugged by passersby eager to get their hands on one.

A year after the riots, *Esquire* magazine declared Cabbage Patch Kids "perhaps the greatest success story in the long history of dolls." Bigger than pet rocks or hula hoops, they were a fad and a marketing phenomenon that seemed to gather strength by going up against the prevailing winds of pop culture. At the height of a decade crazed by high-tech, boinging electronic gadgets, Cabbage Patch Kids did nothing but sit still and look dumb. In a narcissistic era that worshiped at the altar of supermodel beauty and superficial glamour, they were unashamedly homely. Sophisticated young urban professionals were supposed to be setting all the trends, while these kids, fresh from the cabbage patch, were aggressively

homespun and unprofessional. No one could really explain their near-deification (although psychologists, ministers, children's rights activists, and toy manufacturers tried to do so, ad nauseam); but whatever its reasons, once the Cabbage Patch craze took off, its dimensions were staggering.

A Texas orthodontist devised a way to outfit them with metal braces, using Super Glue. A New Jersey man started a summer camp for them; it cost thirty dollars for four weeks, and the doll was sent home with a photo of itself with its bunkmates and a camp T-shirt. *The New Yorker* reported on a woman who gave a party for thirty girls and their dolls, at which they played Put the Pacifier in the Mouth of the Cabbage Patch Kid instead of Pin the Tail on the Donkey. There were stunt marriages and funerals, beauty pageants, and even psychological doll counseling available for Cabbage Patch Kids whose owners wanted to change their names (each doll came from the factory already christened). *The Nation* magazine used Cabbage Patch Kids as the occasion for a sarcastic story about fundamentalism, announcing that "the Reverend Jerry Falwell said that the dolls were blasphemous caricatures. 'According to Holy Scripture,' he said, 'only Adam and Eve had no navels. The hand of atheistic Communism is apparent.' " (A funny story, but the writer was wrong: Cabbage Patch Kids *do* have navels.)

The man who invented them was a cowboy-hatted Georgian named Xavier Roberts, described in his authorized biography ("a moving story of an artist with a dream" titled *Fantasy*, with a cover picture of a Kid sitting among stacks of money) as "a loner who spent many hours by his mother's side as she quilted and made crafts for which the Appalachian region is so famous." In 1977, Roberts began to make soft-sculpture, polyester-filled dolls with pudgy cloth faces and beady, close-set eyes. The dolls, which he called the Little People, won prizes in crafts shows, and the next year he formed a company to sell them. No, correct that: not to *sell* them but to *offer them for adoption.* He established the Babyland General Hospital in a former maternity clinic in the town of Cleveland, Georgia. It was a factory, gift shop, and distribution center, but it still looked just like a maternity ward, and Roberts conceived a set of humanizing rules for selling his wares. They included:

- *Doll:* Little people are most certainly *not* dolls.
- *For Sale:* You cannot buy a Little Person any more than you can buy love or affection. They are, however, available for adoption to good homes.
- *Shop or Store:* Little People Babies are unavailable in any mere shop or store. They are, though, waiting to be adopted at all Official Adoption Agencies or Placement Centers.
- *Customers:* There are no customers, only prospective adoptive parents interested in providing good and loving homes for all Little People.
- *Place Where Little People Are Made:* Little People Babies are "born" in the magical cabbage patch.

Each original Little Person was unique and signed by Xavier Roberts, and they were issued in limited editions. They were bought mostly by adult mothers and grandmothers, and by doll collectors at crafts shows for prices of about a hundred dollars apiece. By August 1979, Roberts' company, Original Appalachian Artworks, had a staff of fifty-six "doctors" and "nurses" (all employees, including traveling salespeople, wore white uniforms). One of the first people to be widely seen with a Little Person doll was Georgian Amy Carter, daughter of the President of the United States. The dolls' burgeoning success was noted by the

Chicago *Tribune* in a story on what it called the "polyester baby boom."

By 1983, a quarter-million Little People had been sold (some original-edition, handmade dolls are now worth over five thousand dollars), and Xavier Roberts decided he needed the market muscle of a big national toy distributor. After being rejected by Mattel, Fisher-Price, Ideal, and Tamy, he made a deal with Coleco, which began turning out twenty-five-dollar, vinyl-face models (each one guaranteed to be unique) in Hong Kong. They started advertising the dolls in June 1983, mostly on Saturday-morning television children's shows—although it is now believed that most early decisions to buy a Cabbage Patch Kid were made by adults who thought them adorable. In October, pregnant *Today* show host Jane Pauley, America's favorite mother-to-be, spent five cozy minutes of air time with Cabbage Patch Kids. All the women's magazines had pictures of Cabbage Patch Kids along with articles that suggested they would make good Christmas presents. The rush was on.

Coleco chartered planes to bring in two hundred thousand dolls every week, but they could not keep up with the demand. By Christmas, supplies were so short that the consumer affairs department of Nassau County, New York, accused Coleco of "harassing" children by advertising dolls that were not available. Coleco eventually suspended all advertising because they were getting so much free publicity. "We don't need to spend the money," said a company spokesperson. A billion dollars' worth of Cabbage Patch Kids and accessories were sold in the first year after Coleco introduced them. That was 10 percent of the entire toy industry's business.

The next year, Xavier Roberts announced, "The Kids'll be my base, but I'm lookin' to do more in-depth things." Such as? "I want to market my cowboy hats and my boots under my own name. I want to design houses, clothes, and cars for people. I want to create a legend. I want to build fairy tales. Discover Cinderellas." He was reported to be planning Cabbage Patch Park on four hundred acres of woodland near the original Babyland General Hospital, and a second theme park in Colorado, each offering guests a sense of "what it's like to live in Cabbage Patch Land."

Cabbage Patch Land was not to be. "From Cabbage to Briar Patch," headlined *Newsweek* in 1988, when Coleco Industries went bankrupt after Kid sales plummeted.

The next year, Hasbro (maker of G.I. Joe) bought the rights to Cabbage Patch Kids and have since tried to bring them back to life. Outfitted in brighter clothes and nineties hairstyles, the new Kids were declared by a toy industry analyst to be "a plus for Hasbro, but not crucial one way or the other." As for Xavier Roberts, he followed the Cabbage Patch Kids with a considerably less successful concept, the Koosas. Koosas were soft-sculpture pets, but like the Kids, each one was different and, according to Mr. Roberts, each "combined the most lovable features of cats and dogs."

CALIFORNIA DIP

California dip—dry onion soup mix combined with sour cream—is democracy on a potato chip: Serve yourself, no servants are required. It is a pop-culture icon of the utmost ease, and also the preeminent symbol of a new style of socializing that took hold in the 1950s— the casual, middle-class cocktail party. When it was invented in 1954, convenience cooking seemed to most people, even to some who fancied themselves gourmets, the last word in modern living. Eliminating drudgery was the way of the future, and the American way to do this was to combine packets, cans, and boxes of ingredients right from the supermarket shelf and, presto chango, create something swell to eat. What a contrast this style of cooking was to old grandmotherly kinds of food preparation that required dragging about town to a butcher and a baker, then sweating in a kitchen pounding dough and stirring pots of things like some old pioneer woman. Zip open a packet of dehydrated onion soup, pop a pint of sour cream, stir them together, and *voilà:* California dip, ready to serve and eat.

It was the ideal hors d'oeuvre for suburban hosts and hostesses, who relished all kinds of new, informal ways of entertaining —on the patio, in the family room, around an electric skillet full of sukiyaki or a bubbling fondue pot. The fun of being casual

was that everybody helped themselves; it was so sociable! As Poppy Cannon wrote in her *Can-Opener Cookbook* (1951), "We suggest your party guests do most of the work right at the party—and have a fine time doing it!" California dip was especially inspired in this regard because it required no utensils, no plates, no napkins. Guests could hold a highball in one hand and shovel up a gob of dip with the other, using nothing other than a sturdy corrugated potato chip (see p. 397) as an edible implement.

The name itself suggested easy living: From California dip to the more recent California cuisine, the name of the golden state has always been our country's modifier for foods that are casual and yet have panache. As a matter of fact, it was a housewife in California who first concocted the dried soup and sour cream dish, then suggested it to Lipton, which named it after her home state.

California dip was a watershed moment for dry onion soup. Campbell's had been touting the multiple uses of canned soups in casseroles and sauces for decades ("Helps for the Hostess," a brochure from the 1920s, suggests such delectables as "Spaghetti à la Campbell" and fish steaks with "Indian Sauce" made from tomato soup); but dry soup could be used in untold numbers of new ways: as a spicy and salty addition to meat loaf, as a dry rub for pot roast, and even as a flavoring in bread dough. It grew so immensely popular as a mix-in for sour cream that Lipton now sells it as "Lipton Recipe Soup Mix—for Soup, Recipes & California Dip."

An even bigger beneficiary of California dip's popularity was sour cream. Virtually no early-fifties cookbooks mention using sour cream in appetizer dips, or in anything else for that matter. Even *Sour Cream Cookery*, published in 1947, denigrates its star ingredient as a member of "the fermented milk tribe," but says that it is good to use anyway because it is healthful, exotic, and a thrifty way to utilize spoiled cream. The idea of it being chic was then preposterous: like yogurt, sour cream was considered quite odd, and even possibly un-American. California dip made sour cream, formerly a dairy product with health-nut and ethnic-food connotations, into a staple of modern American suburban cookery. Only after the popularization of California dip did America's epicures and not-so-epicurean home cooks popularize beef Stroganoff, sour cream Jell-O molds, and sour cream cheese cake.

The American Dairy Association got busy promoting sour cream as fashionable, as can be seen in a rousing late-fifties pamphlet titled "The Gourmet Touch to Everyday Cooking." Included are recipes galore for dips, as well as for "stroganoff pizza," "oeufs benedict nouveau with mock hollondaise [sic]," and "peanut butter freeze" (sugar, peanut butter, and sour cream hardened in ice trays). The pamphlet begins with these encouraging words—"Dairy sour cream can make everyday cooking as exciting as the exotic cuisine of world famous chefs"—then moves on to a recipe for "deviled dip" (sour cream, pickle relish, mustard, and horseradish) served in a hollowed-out Bermuda onion.

Here is the classic recipe for California dip:

1 packet dry onion soup mix
2 cups sour cream
Combine. Serve.

"CAPTAIN KANGAROO"

Bob Keeshan, who has played Captain Kangaroo on television for over thirty-five years, once received a complaint from a mother. (The letter was sent in 1961, and as far as we have been able to determine, it was the only time any criticism was leveled by a parent in the history of the program.) The protestor griped that the character of Captain Kangaroo—soft-spoken, tender-spirited, kindly, patient, loving, avuncular, reassuring, moral, calm, sensitive, and cherubic—was "too gentle" and "ignored the fact that violence was part of life."

All good and normal parents love Captain Kangaroo. In a world of children's programming brimful of savage cartoons, hyperthyroid hosts of inane tot-gang screamfests, and venal advertisements for squirt guns, toy hand grenades, and white sugar, he has been a beacon of virtue and warmth. From eight to nine in the morning on CBS, starting October 3, 1955 (the same day "The Mickey Mouse Club" premiered in

the afternoon on ABC), he presided over a privileged hour when television actually seemed moral. "We don't really think of it as a show, but we do think of it as a *visit*," Bob Keeshan said. "We have always tried to serve our audience. We respect them, and we respect their intelligence, and their potential good taste, and we program accordingly.... So we've always had the support of thinking parents."

Each episode of the original "Captain Kangaroo" had a theme—voting in a democracy, how to tell time, home safety—illuminated by the Captain, who wore a motorman's uniform and was named for the pouchlike pockets of his coat, which were always filled with fun surprises. The Captain frequently explained things by having conversations with an unsophisticated farmer named Mr. Green Jeans (played by Hugh "Lumpy" Brannum), the show's resident expert on the natural world, which included a steady procession of live animals. The Captain and Mr. Green Jeans were the only full-time human inhabitants of a place called Treasure House, whose residents also included a philosophical puppet named Bunny Rabbit (his problem: he was addicted to carrots), a grandfather clock that spoke in rhymes, and a giant-size Mr. Moose, who told "knock-knock" jokes, as well as occasional visits from the perpetually inquisitive Miss Frog and a scholarly fowl known as Word Bird. There was a regular nonviolent cartoon series called "Tom Terrific," about a boy with magical powers and his cowardly pet, Manfred the Wonder Dog; and there were frequent sessions in which the Captain read from a book (with classical background music) or showed children how to make totem poles out of old magazines and bulletin boards out of shirt cardboard.

One of the distinguishing features of Treasure House was that no children lived there. Instead of performing in full cry to a rollicking grandstand filled with hysterical moppets, the Captain spoke softly and intimately with his viewers (who generally ranged in age from three to nine), providing actual food for thought. A typical riddle, for example, asked, "What invention permits you to see through a brick building?" The answer: "A window."

After "Captain Kangaroo" was on the air three months, *Newsweek* praised its "quiet, nonaggressive, diffident approach," which it suggested might be Bob Keeshan's reaction to "five years of pandemonium" while working in "that heroic school of hard knocks, seltzer-squirting, and childish hysteria, the 'Howdy Doody' show" (see p. 232). Keeshan had begun in television as the helper who gave out prizes to kids on "Howdy Doody" when it went on the air in 1947. At first he wore the uniform of an NBC page (his job since being discharged from the Marines in 1946); but in March 1948 the page uniform was deemed too stuffy and it was replaced by a clown suit. Keeshan took the name Clarabell and quickly became one of the most beloved (albeit incorrigibly mischievous) characters in Doodyville. During his first year as Clarabell, Keeshan got no salary. "Every day Bob Smith (Buffalo Bob) would slip me a five-dollar bill," he recalled. He finally left the show in 1952 (although the Clarabell character continued) because he wanted more money.

Keeshan was unemployed for a year and about to become a life insurance salesman when he took the job of Corny the Clown on a noontime show on ABC in New York called "Time for Fun." Corny sat on a park bench with a cocker spaniel and talked to kids between cartoons; and he was a hit.

"Corny the Clown convinced me that a gentle, intimate approach to children could succeed," Keeshan wrote in his autobiography, *Growing Up Happy*. Soon he began hosting a one-man morning show, also on New York's WABC, called "Tinker's Workshop," where he was able to abolish the cartoons he hated (because they were violent, mean, and racist) and—playing a jovial Alpine toymaker—just *talk* to children. He told stories, fed puppies and kittens, and gave kids do-it-yourself crafts advice.

"Tinker's Workshop" got better ratings in New York than NBC's "Today" and CBS's "Morning Show" (then starring Jack Paar) combined. CBS hired Keeshan to replace one hour of "The Morning Show" with "Captain Kangaroo." It did so well nationally that rumors suddenly abounded that NBC was about to revamp "Today" as a kids' program; eventually, all that happened was that J. Fred Muggs, the "Today" chimpanzee, had his role on the show expanded.

Children liked Captain Kangaroo; and "thinking" parents liked that their kids liked it. The first Peabody Award (of two, plus six Emmys and three Gabriels, which are for children's shows) given to the show, in 1958, declared it "the only genuine children's program left on television—certainly the only one which puts the welfare of the children ahead of that of the sponsor; which instructs children in safety, in ethics, in health."

Everybody venerated "Captain Kangaroo" (except Buffalo Bob Smith, who said "there were people on ['Howdy Doody'] who had more talent in their pinkies than he has in his present two-hundred-plus pounds"); but network television doesn't run on reverence, and CBS executives threatened to dump the show since 1957. The big problem: Despite good ratings (about six million kids a day) Bob Keeshan wouldn't accept lucrative advertisements for products he thought were bad (war toys, junk food) or allow cast members to endorse things. Revenues were low, and CBS lost a million dollars a year on "Captain Kangaroo." In the seventies, as the morning hours became more coveted, CBS's Dick Salant told Keeshan that he wanted the time slot for the news department, but so far he had resisted taking it because "I don't dare put myself onto the firing line against the mothers of America."

The power of the Captain's prestige ran out in the fall of 1981, when his show was reduced to a half hour and moved to a seven A.M. time slot in order to make way for an expanded "CBS Morning News," in hopes that adult programming would help the network catch up with "Today" and "Good Morning America." (It did not.) In January 1982 it was bumped back to six-thirty. The new time was Siberia; only half of CBS affiliates carried the show, and soon it was gone. "CBS's New Year's resolution must have been to behave like Scrooge," lamented Peggy Charren, president of Action for Children's Television, who called the move a "dishonorable discharge."

As for Bob Keeshan, he declared, "They can take me off the air, but I'm not ready to call it quits." Although well enough fixed to retire on the millions he made in three decades on the network, Keeshan went right back to "Captain Kangaroo," now broadcast on public television stations, and also spends time trying to promote quality children's programming by lecturing and testifying as an expert witness before Congress. His last big network television appearance was in 1985 as host of a CBS evening special (for grown-ups) that featured a cartoon in which a forlorn little boy searches for the solution to the show's title—"How to Be a Man"—by opening doors marked "Men." All he finds is people yelling and fighting.

JOHNNY CARSON

His name is Johnny. Not Jonathan or John or Jack—Johnny. It's the name of a boy, a nice boy from a small town in farm country in the heart of America. And that is who Johnny Carson is, even in his sixties, and even though he is one of the most powerful men in television and has been through more than his fair share of wives (three of them, curiously, named Joanne, Joanna, and Jody) and is notoriously tough in business deals and painfully secluded in his private life. Until his retirement from "The Tonight Show" in May 1992, fifteen million people every night basked in the tender glow of their television set around midnight so they could drift off in the comfort of the nice boy's cheerful averageness. Polite, clean-cut, energetic, a good sport, and slick as polished chrome, with a midwestern face you knew you could trust and a mischievous—but never actually mean—sense of humor, Johnny Carson is the most purely American character in popular culture since Mark Twain invented Tom Sawyer.

As successful as most of this country's media superstars are in other countries, Johnny Carson—the highest-paid, longest-lasting performer in the history of television —has never translated well outside his na-

tive land. Other people just don't get him. Even in England, where they speak (almost) the same language as we, there was little interest in "The Tonight Show Starring Johnny Carson" when it was tested there. The problem was not that so much of the program, especially Johnny Carson's opening monologue, deals with topical issues of interest only to Americans; the problem was that to really understand Johnny Carson you have to be fluent in American life. You have to be up on water-cooler humor at the office and familiar with the doings of the Kennedys (see p. 256) and the Simpsons (see p. 447). You have to know the nuances of advertisements for breakfast cereal and the current height of skirt hems and depth of blouse cleavages; you have to at least instinctively understand that Johnny Carson's ongoing character "Carnac the Magnificent" is a parody of such early TV psychics as Criswell (who, like Carnac, used to hold an envelope to his forehead and divine its contents). And you must realize that the Carnac parody isn't even supposed to be a good one: its fun, you understand, comes from how amateurish it all is—see Johnny Carson giggle as he does it!—and from the kick of watching a grown man on national television behave like a naughty little boy. There are levels of irony

at work here that require viewers be completely comfortable in the culture Johnny plays with. Most important, to really understand Johnny Carson, you have to realize that the subject of Johnny Carson's show is not Carnac or the Kennedys or the Simpsons or anything else he is talking about or spoofing; it is always, invariably, *Johnny Carson*—the wide-eyed, bedazzled, but unflappable Nebraska boy who finds himself with great delight and even a little bit of awe on network television.

He is the great reactor; and it was always the nuance and innuendo in his reactions that were the essence of his success and made his "Tonight Show" an inexorable television phenomenon. He ad-libbed, paused, lifted his eyebrows, tapped his pencil, cocked a double take, spread an elfin smile, and fired off a laugh with the precision of a Marine drill team—never, never ever, losing control over the theme of his presence, which was nothing less than a performance art piece that could be titled *Life in These United States as Seen by Johnny Carson*. Whether he was reacting to astronomer Carl Sagan, a monkey brought by Joan Embry from the San Diego Zoo, Madonna, Hubert Humphrey, or Charo, whoever was sitting on the chair across from Johnny's desk—whether they were deep-dish or dopey, a celebrity or an unknown eccentric—what made their appearance on "The Tonight Show" unique was not them but the way Johnny Carson received them. Johnny established the appropriate response, and for many new guests (especially new comedians, including once-unknowns Joan Rivers, Robert Klein, and Roseanne Arnold) who pleased him, conspicuous success with Johnny Carson—his approval—could launch a career. His predictable and therefore reassuring reaction to his guests, as well as to bandleader Doc Severinsen's notably loud wardrobe, to Ed

McMahon's pseudo-pontificating, even to his own (sometimes purposely bad) jokes, made Johnny Carson a stand-in for all normal Americans and a barometer of American taste.

Johnny Carson was not just a talk show host. He *is* pop culture, a creature of the video age whose taste, values, and attitudes have uncannily reflected this country's prevailing worries and delights for the last thirty years. Just as it is not possible to imagine Johnny Carson's elusive charm making him a huge success in any other medium, there is no way to envision what television would have been like without his having defined the talk show. More than any other human being since Philo T. Farnsworth (who invented TV), he established the fundamental personality of the medium as it developed in the U.S.A.—primarily as a source of reassurance and tranquility, and a way to help viewers get to sleep. *People* magazine reported that he has been called "the Sominex of the masses" and "history's most effective contraceptive."

His career began when, as a teenager in Norfolk, Nebraska, he created a magic act for birthday parties called "The Great Carsoni." He developed skills as a ventriloquist while serving in the Navy, wrote a senior thesis about comedy at the University of Nebraska, worked in local radio and TV in the late 1940s, then went to Los Angeles in 1950, where his low-budget skit-comedy show, "Carson's Cellar," won the attention of network programmers. His first big national exposure came when Red Skelton, whose live TV variety show he was writing for, knocked himself unconscious during a dress rehearsal. With only hours to prepare, Johnny went out and delivered a monologue. He brought the house down, and soon got his own network show, "Earn Your Vacation," a quiz brought over from radio on which contestants won trips to the des-

tination of their choice. In 1957 he took over for Edgar Bergen as host of "Do You Trust Your Wife?" which, its title amended to "Who Do You Trust?" became television's highest-rated daytime show. (Later on, a grammatical correction further amended the show's title to "Whom Do You Trust?")

"The Tonight Show" had been on the NBC schedule since 1954, when Steve Allen established its enduring basic format, but with a somewhat greater emphasis on music than in the incarnations that followed. Allen left the show in January 1957 to concentrate on his Sunday-evening variety show (which ran in competition with "The Ed Sullivan Show"); and after an ill-starred six months during which a replacement called "Tonight: America After Dark" floundered without a host, Jack Paar took the helm and made "The Tonight Show" a hot property again. Paar, who was more an earnest conversationalist than a comedian, was known for his temper, his petulance, his feuds with other actors and the network, and his unpredictability (he actually walked off in the middle of the show one time in 1960 when he became infuriated that network censors wouldn't let him tell a joke about a toilet). When he left for good in 1962, it was in a cloud of hostility generated by a flag-waving show he did at the Berlin Wall.

The difference between volatile Jack Paar and glacier-cool Johnny Carson was dramatic, although buffered by a six-month interim of guest hosts, including Soupy Sales, Groucho Marx, and Arlene Francis. After Carson took over on October 1, 1962 (bringing along Ed McMahon, his sidekick from "Whom Do You Trust?"), ratings drifted for a while, then began to improve. By 1972, when the show moved from New York to Los Angeles, Johnny was unquestioned king of the night, which he remained until his retirement.

There have been plenty of people named Johnny in the public eye since 1962, but to nearly everyone conversant with the culture of this land, "Johnny" means, first and foremost, Johnny Carson. He was (and is) an institution, so much a part of our folklore that Stephen King (p. 261) built one of the scariest scenes in *The Shining* around the moment when the demented hero, named John, announces his presence in a ghoulish imitation of Ed McMahon's traditional introduction, "Heeeere's Johnny!" Until the debut of "The Arsenio Hall Show" in 1989 (which attracted mostly new, young viewers who previously hadn't watched late-night TV), Johnny Carson was renowned for being immune to ratings challenges from competing shows. Among those who went up against him on other networks but failed to make a dent were Merv Griffin, Dick Cavett, Joey Bishop, Alan Thicke, Joan Rivers, and Pat Sajak.

His invulnerability hints at another side of his appeal, which had as much to do with strength as with charm. Likable and genial as he was in his role as host, Johnny Carson's iron will was never really far from sight, even when he was being very entertaining on camera; and one of the reasons he became so popular was his notorious toughness. People always used to relish stories about how he played hardball with the network, getting paid mammoth amounts of money for minimal work (one estimate put his NBC salary at $2380.95 per minute of air time). As he hosted his show, you didn't have to be an insider to notice how he managed its progress with precision so seamless that it never looked brutal. But it could be. Johnny was famous for being pathologically unfriendly when the camera was off; and even when it was on, it was never very difficult to pick up on the moment-by-moment calculations he made to keep the show rolling along without a hitch. Johnny

decided who among his guests would be allowed to sit on the couch and chat, and he decided how long they would do so. He cut to a commercial when a guest was dull or offensive; and when the show returned, the guest was gone. (Just in case, a three-foot-long pair of industrial bolt cutters was always kept just off stage to help remove any guest who decided to handcuff himself to Johnny's desk.) His own mime-perfect control of his facial reactions always let the audience know when they could laugh with or sometimes *at*, a guest; and he even let you know when you were allowed to laugh at his own mistakes or bad jokes—and when you were not allowed to do so. Always, just beneath the impish smile and crinkle of his laughing eyes, Johnny Carson was a man who had what most of us would like to have but don't: total control and power.

What was so amazing about Johnny Carson as a performer was that he simultaneously projected his absolute authority and a merry, uninhibited sense of humor. He made it look so easy to be him that it was quite possible to take for granted the rigid control he held over himself and the show: he looked simply like a guy having a swell time with some interesting people, kibbitzing with his old friends Ed and Doc as well as such regular guests as Steve Lawrence and Eydie Gormé, Don Rickles, Burt Reynolds, and Suzanne Pleshette, and letting viewers feel like they were free to join the party. He was, in more ways than one, television's perfect host.

Formalized as the show eventually became, it was also in some ways TV at its most intimate. (This feeling may have been partly due to the fact that so many people watched it in bed as they drifted off to sleep.) Highlights of "Tonight Show" history are by no means *important* moments in broadcasting like the moon landing or the

Persian Gulf War, but a lot of viewers recall them with the kind of familiarity inspired by a family photo album. In his book *Total Television*, Alex McNeil enumerated some of the on-camera incidents that stand out as special in "Tonight Show" history, including:

- The demonstration of tomahawk throwing in which a cardboard dummy got the hatchet in his crotch, provoking possibly the longest moment of sustained audience laughter in television history (1964).
- The on-camera wedding of singer Tiny Tim to Victoria Budinger (known as Miss Vicky) on December 17, 1969.
- The time in 1973 when Johnny jokingly referred to a toilet-paper shortage, and supermarkets around the country found their supplies picked clean within twenty-four hours.

There are highlights galore (offered to viewers periodically in "Tonight Show" retrospectives on NBC), as well as some fairly dramatic off-camera incidents, such as Johnny's banishing of Joan Rivers when she started her own short-lived late-night show on the Fox network; but such moments are not really all that decisive in assessing the importance of Johnny's reign. He became America's benign addiction not for out-standing or remarkable events, nor for any particularly interesting guests (he had well over twenty thousand of them in his career), but for all the hallowed rituals of the show. These include his pantomimed golf swing into a commercial at the conclusion of the monologue and the bit of repartee in which Johnny coaxed the audience to ask him a question such as "How hot is it?" or "How busty was she?" so he could deliver one of his patented punch lines, constructed around an embellished hyperbole, that begins "It was *so* hot. . . ." The original intent, as well as all of the spontaneous humor of such comedic strategies, was long ago lost in the mists of time, but such rites were the backbone of Johnny Carson's career as host of "The Tonight Show." When you tuned in to watch him, you knew Johnny would be the same as he always was, never shocking or disturbing, never ruffled or upset (except once: on July 17, 1991, when he told the audience about the accidental death of his son Rick). Johnny was America's favorite television personality because you could count on him; he became a member of the family, someone who was always good to be with and with whom you didn't mind sharing the bedroom. The laughter he evoked was the reassuring kind —warm, comfortable, and familiar.

CB RADIO

W hat is "the most powerful communications medium available to ordinary people"? According to a man called "Ink Slinger" (a.k.a. Larry Adcock), author of the 1977 book *Not for Truckers Only*, it is the Citizens Band radio, an electronic transmitter for motor vehicles (also available for homes) that was about the size of an eight-track tape player, with a microphone and speaker that allowed the owner to talk to other CBers within a ten-mile radius. For a few years in the mid-seventies,

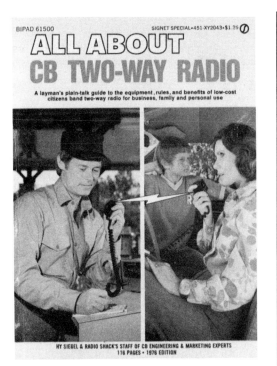

CB radio was—according to a 1975 story in *Time* magazine—"the fastest-growing communications medium since the Bell telephone."

A half a million people every month were applying to the FCC for a CB license (a mere legal formality, since anyone could buy and install and use one). CBs were credited with keeping sleepy drivers awake, saving motorists who ran out of gas in deadly blizzards, helping lost families find their way, relieving lonely people's depressions, and speeding the flow of interstate commerce. "I have seen no major accidents on the highway involving CB-equipped vehicles," one enthusiast from Union, Maine, wrote to *Harper's Weekly* in 1976. "But I have seen countless accidents avoided because of advance warnings on the CB." Some ratchet-jaws (CB users' name for themselves) were predicting that soon telephones would be obsolete: after all, Ma Bell charged per minute; CB time was free. Best of all, thanks to the dramatic proliferation of the CB radio, America seemed to be turning into a great big neighborly country once again. The booster from Maine declared:

> In a sea of negativism, the CB is the one place where total strangers are cooperating for the common good. I have been all over the country . . . and I'll tell you, what's going on out there is the first really positive social expression I have seen on a major scale in this country in almost fifteen years. Suspicion, mistrust, and negativism have swept through us like a plague strewing alienated paranoiacs in its wake. Nobody trusts anybody any more—except on the CB where everybody trusts everybody.

The thrill of CB was that it was the voice of the people, and when you talked on it you were tuning in to a network of comrades free of government restriction. You could say what you wanted; and even if Smokey (the police) could listen in, he might never find you, because the CB possessed the most wonderful and most American quality—mobility. Despite the technicality of an FCC license, CB seemed deliciously exempt from authority; and that quality was amplified by the fact that no one ever used his real name when broadcasting. Everybody went by a "handle," which provided not only anonymity but the chance to invent yourself all over again . . . creatively, wishfully, ironically, however you liked. An accountant from Oshkosh could become the High Plains Drifter, and a grandmother from St. Pete was free to be Hot Pants; and the highways (and airways) were crowded with Dallas Cowboys, Roadrunners, and Convoy Queens. Megaphone Mouth, a CBer out of Arkansas, gave this advice for selecting a handle: "Try to step outside yourself a little bit and think of yourself as some friend you know. Then, if you were to make fun of your friend, what would you call him?"

To understand the tremendous appeal of going by a goofy nickname, it is necessary to understand that an awful lot of Americans in the mid-1970s were feeling oppressed by a big, impersonal, unfriendly, and apparently corrupt government. "My posterior pants pocket is hauling around eighteen different numbers by which a batch of bureaucrats know me," Ink Slinger wrote. "But on the CB, well, that's a different story." On the CB, everybody knew everybody else as "good buddy." It provided a friendliness and instant warmth that were conspicuously missing in what Jim Pollman, writing in *Icons of America*, described as "a huge, bland, pedestrian nation of clones [where] the CB has partly reversed the loss of community, and helped generate a rebirth of regionalism—a CB regionalism, the electronic drawl, a new language rooted in Southern wrappings."

After an incomprehensible Southeast Asian war that ended with depressing ambiguity, and the revelations of the Watergate scandal, and a crippling oil crisis in 1973–74 that led to the federal imposition of a fifty-five-mile-per-hour speed limit, the CB radio provided motorists a little opportunity to make some rules for themselves and to outwit the government . . . and that felt mighty good. For all the fine and upstanding things one could do with a CB radio, its basic purpose for most people was to avoid getting caught speeding. By listening to drivers up ahead along the road, you could almost always make yourself aware of "Kodiaks with Kodaks" (police, a.k.a. Smokey the Bear, using radar), "Tijuana taxis" (local police cars), and even "Smokeys with ears" (police using their own CB radios) early enough to avoid apprehension.

The exhilaration of communicating via CB radio inspired an early (1977) Jonathan Demme movie called *Citizens Band* (the name of which was changed to *Handle with Care* when studio executives worried some viewers would think it was a musical because of the word "band"), in which a dozen strangers' stories are interwoven on the air in a kind of global-village vision of what the CB meant. The outlaw kick of it was best rendered in a novelty song called "Convoy," spoken entirely in CB jargon, about a trucker with the handle "Rubber Duck" who leads a speeding formation of eighteen-wheelers across the country, outwitting police all the way. "Convoy" so infuriated Iowa state officials with its anarchic theme that they pressured Des Moines' WHO into banning the song (temporarily); but it hit number one on the *Billboard* chart in January 1976. Its co-writer and singer, C. W. McCall, actually an Omaha advertising executive named Bill Fries, explained that he wasn't suggesting anyone use the CB to break the law. " 'Convoy' is a metaphor," he said. "Any trucker knows that. And any CBer knows that."

Truckers were the ones who first brought CB radios to the public's attention, during a strike in late 1973 that followed the huge jump in fuel prices, gas rationing, and the new double-nickel speed limit. Citizens Band had been around since the FCC created Class D service in 1958, and was used mostly by farmers and ham radio operators; but by the time of the strike, a lot of truckers had installed CB radios to let each other know where they could get gas and where the police were lurking. When strike leaders were interviewed on the national news, they went by their handles—Swamp Fox, Steel Bender, Lone Coyote—rather than their names. It was exciting to see these rugged guys do what so many ordinary citizens wanted to do: thumb their noses at the government and ride the highways with impunity. Truckers became heroes—independent individualists, the last American cowboys—and when their strike ended, there were a lot of folks who wanted to be like them, at least a little bit. To share in the truckers' world, all they had to do was get a CB radio, invent a handle, and start jawjacking.

For four-wheelers (people in cars), much of the fun of the CB radio was tuning into an elaborate highway subculture that had been evolving for years. Truckers had their own way of talking (mostly with a Texas-Oklahoma drawl); and their rambling life had a quirky idiosyncrasy that they expressed in a fully developed slang almost like another language, but an easy one to understand and even to invent. Like astronauts, motor mouths used code for everything. Yes was "affirmative"; no was "negative," "negatory," or "suppository"; to speed was to "let the hammer down"; every state and city had its own CB name (Rhode Island = Mini, Milwaukee = Brew Town, Reno = Split City); and there were even sets of underground number codes, including the profane eights ("eight-one" means "You're shitting me," "eight-seven" means "This place sucks") and the sexual nines ("nine-eleven" means "Let's meet at the motel," "nine-twenty" means "bend over and grease up"). Sign-offs for the end of conversations, which truckers had originated as creative ways of saying goodbye when they parted at truck stops, grew baroque as CB slang evolved: "Keep your nose between the ditches and the Smokeys off your britches, sunny side up and the rubber side down."

And as millions of people installed CB radios in their cars, the airwaves filled up with channel hogs, truck-stop hookers advertising their wares, and, worst of all, rookie mush-mouths looking for directions to the nearest family campground who didn't quite fathom the clever, inventive spirit of CB communication. "It helps to think of the CB as a cocktail party," Ink Slinger suggested before offering these adroit opening lines for beginners:

- "I'm looking for someone who can tell me how that sky's going to treat us for sure." (This means "What's the weather?")
- "I'm looking to talk to a friendly soul on this fine day."
- "Say, this is Little Miss Muffet here. Any truckers out there like to talk at me to pass some time?" (Says Mr. Slinger: "My only caution here is that you must be a good sport.")

America's infatuation with truckers and their freewheelin' life did not last into the yuppie era, nor did the antiestablishment titillation of talking on the CB radio. Some of the once arcane lingo is now commonly known—"Smokey" (police), "10-4" (message received), "beaver" (woman). But the mischievous thrill of communicating with a network of unseen strangers has moved from cars and trucks into people's homes, where outlaws of the ether do it via modem and personal computer, some using programs designed to simulate CB radios. Vehicular CBs are still around and used by many professional drivers, but they now seem more like a curious slice of life left over from the post-Watergate 1970s than like the successor to the telephone.

CHEERLEADING

What ballet is to Russia and flamenco dancing is to Spain, cheerleading is to the U.S. of A.: it's the shared dance that stirs our passion, inspires us to public rapture, and makes us proud to be Americans. It's corny, fresh, loud, and energetic; and it's very, very sexy but very, very, *very* virginal.

Nowadays there are nearly as many male cheerleaders as there are female; but that wasn't always the case. The earliest known cheerleading crews, about a century ago, were single-sex: men only. At Harvard, they were makeshift squads of injured players or off-duty substitutes; the University of California used junior professors to stir up enthusiasm among the spectators. Among the first colleges to elect an official "Yell Marshal" was the University of Minnesota, where he led people in the stands to shout in unison: "Rah-rah-rah, Ski-u-ma, Minn-so-ta." Another popular early cheer, documented in Barbara Egbert's authoritative book, *Cheerleading and Songleading:* "Rah, rah, rah, sis boom yah."

Until World War II, the All-America Cheering Squad, a group of seven selected every Christmas week by Gamma Sigma, the national college cheerleaders' fraternity (a nine-hundred-member organization whose insignia was a shield with two crossed microphones), was limited to men only. The All-Americans were selected based on three criteria:

1. The cheering section's reaction.
2. Good judgment in choosing just the right moment to lead a cheer.
3. Acrobatic skill, including a talent for cartwheels, handstands, synchronized tumbling, the Nelson Arch (a back flip), and the

formidable Ritter Span (an elaborate back flip, invented in 1937 at the University of Michigan, in which the cheerleader leaps up, twists into a horizontal arc, bounces onto his hands, flips backwards, and lands standing at attention).

As more women went to college, they too became cheerleaders, and by the late 1940s every college and nearly every high school had a squad—many of them coeds chosen because they had qualities practically guaranteed to boost the spirit of their classmates: they were pretty, peppy, and popular. The golden age of cheerleading was the 1950s, when such spectacular teams as the Rangerettes of Kilgore, Texas, thrust their close-order drill into halftime and the Illinettes of Champaign, Illinois, began high-stepping and twirling their pompons to crowds' delight.

Because its purpose is to create a positive attitude, cheerleading has enjoyed respect as a paragon of goodness. Despite their short skirts, bare legs, and exposed panties (in the prepantyhose era), and despite even the semisexual innuendo of some of their classic routines, female cheerleaders have customarily been considered the epitome of chaste femininity. One cynic described them as "locked inside a bulletproof sugar coating of overdone, over-made-up, over hairsprayed, ultra-exaggerated, nicey-nicey wholesomeness." But to those less hostile towards the notion of a little peek-a-boo sexuality, cheerleaders have always been symbols of American girlhood at its cutest. They are expected to be happy, up-beat maidens with a perpetual smile and bounce in their step, and a comely figure, too: up-and-coming pillars of polite society. "Cheerleading instills a lot of moral responsibility," said Lawrence "Herkie" Herkimer, president of the National Cheerleaders Association (NCA), which sponsors the National Cheerleading Championship in Dallas every year. "The girls are on pedestals, and once they get there they don't want to risk falling off."

Herkie probably did more than anyone else to transform cheerleading from a mere extracurricular activity for pep rallies into a national institution. He was a cheerleader himself (four years in high school, three years at Southern Methodist University, one year at the University of Illinois); he founded the NCA, which now supplies the nation with over $25 million worth of uniforms, megaphones, and crepe decorations every year; and he invented the modern pompon (or, as most now call it, pom pom) by attaching strands of multicolored crepe to wooden sticks. Editor of *The Megaphone* and author of *Champion Cheers* and *Pep Rally Skits and Stunts*, Herkie has catalogued such regulation stunts as the Thigh Stand (two girls facing in the same direction, the one in front standing on the thighs of the one in back, as the girl in back holds the front girl by the waist) and the Extra Point Kick (two people form a goal post and another "kicks" someone through). There is even a cheerleader's jump named after him, the Herkie, in which a girl kicks one leg straight out in front and the other leg back and bent while punching one arm high in the air and placing the other against her waist with the elbow thrust out like a wing.

One of the momentous events in modern cheerleading history was the introduction of *professional* cheerleaders by the Dallas Cowboys in 1972. The Cowboys had formerly used high school girls; and the new squad—seven scantily clad, full-figured women—tested the limits of what had always been implied in cheerleaders' routines. They were hot—so hot that they became the inspiration for the very successful porno film *Debbie Does Dallas*—and soon National Football League teams in other cities hired their own hootchie-cootchie dancers to get the men in the crowd steamed up (and to keep them glued to their TVs during halftime).

The heightened sexuality of the new breed of professional cheerleaders got a lot of people steamed up, but not always in a good way. Strangely, the complainers were not the traditional Bible-thumping moralists, who generally approved because the girls were in the wholesome cheerleading tradition. No, those who objected said they were worrying not so much about sexuality but about hypocrisy. Molly Ivens, writing for the *Progressive*, arched her eyebrows over the allegedly clean-cut image of the Dallas Cowboy Cheerleaders (they visit nursing homes, they won't do beer commercials, they don't perform where alcoholic beverages are served) and wrote, "There's no denying that what those girls do is dress up in costumes that would do credit to a strip-tease artiste and then prance about in front of hundreds of people shaking their bums and jiggling their tits."

Lately sexuality has become an issue on campus as well as with professional teams. Similar reproaches were leveled in 1990 at the Illinettes, whose pompon performances were singled out by the University of Illinois Campus Task Force on Sexual Assault, Abuse, and Violence as "one of the activities that project women as sexual objects." Squad captain Pam Withers objected, saying that the Illinettes are role models on campus and that they considered cheerleading a serious sport.

For some people, it is more than a sport. In 1991 Wanda Webb Holloway of Channelview, Texas, was convicted on a charge of murder for hire. Mrs. Holloway wanted Verna Heath and her eighth-grade daughter, Amber, dead because Amber had made the cheerleading squad at Channelview Junior High School two years in a row, whereas Mrs. Holloway's daughter, Shanna, had been rejected. Now that the two rival girls were on their way to high school, Mrs. Holloway figured that if she bumped off Amber, or at least Amber's mother, Shanna would practically be guaranteed a spot on the Falcons'

cheerleading squad. Police caught Mrs. Holloway before her hit man could do away with Amber or her mom, and the cheerleading tryouts went on as scheduled. Once again, Amber made the squad and Shanna didn't. Mrs. Holloway, now known as "the Pompom Mom," was sentenced to fifteen years in prison.

Despite such rare examples of the lust to cheer getting out of hand, and despite the recent focus on cheerleaders' untoward sexuality, cheerleading maintains its image in many people's minds as a bastion of old-fashioned values about sex and womanhood. In a *New York Times* column in 1988 called "Three Cheers for My Daughter," Kathleen Cushman admitted that when her high-school-age daughter, "born in the summer of love," told her she was becoming a cheerleader, she panicked. It was so conventional! So square! So unfeministic! Still, after observing her girl's routine, which Ms. Cushman saw as "Dionysian, ritualistic, bizarre—a wild concatenation of female passions, a screaming, ritualized celebration of sex and power," she concluded that cheerleading might be, in fact, a worthy activity. Because of it, her daughter had "seen the face of the god, drunk the wine of female power and known its rites."

CHEEZ WHIZ

One thing about which we Americans are proudest and also most embarrassed is our talent for making synthetic pleasures. Movies, theme parks, television: all provide amazing imitations of natural experiences. When it comes to food, no other country on earth has devised so

many wonderful and elaborate methods for altering, emulating, and improving upon basic ingredients. From TV dinners to Fizzies (tablets that make water into soda pop), spray-on cheese to Pop Tarts, our kitchen shelves are a bonanza of things designed to improve upon nature. Of all these

products, few are as beloved, or as emblematic of American ingenuity, as Cheez Whiz. In fact, Cheez Whiz was specifically created to eliminate the defects of ordinary cheese.

The problem faced by Kraft laboratory technicians when they began working on a pasteurized, emulsified, homogenized cheese food product in 1951 was that cheese clumps. When it melts, it can separate; it can disintegrate into ugly, oily wads of dairyfat glop that no one wants to eat. Welsh rarebit was still a popular dish at the time, and it required melting cheese, so Kraft's men in white coats determined to design a perpetually stable cheese for the rarebit trade.

What they invented was something greater than rarebit fodder. They created Cheez Whiz, a solution for everything from old-fashioned rarebit to modern quickie nachos grandes. As of July 1, 1953, the day Cheez Whiz went on sale across the nation, the clumping problem was history. In the tradition of Velveeta, which Kraft had introduced in the 1930s as a new product better than plain cheese (because "nutritive value" was added by scientists), Whiz improves on anything a cow and dairy farmer could produce. So long as the cap is on the jar, it can be stored endlessly; it melts on contact with hot food, thus eliminating the need for grat-

ing; and it is as smooth as a baby's bottom. Instead of being just one monotonous kind of cheese, it is "cheese food," containing American mozzarella, Muenster, and Gouda as well as the tastes of mustard, salt, and Worcestershire sauce, the preservative powers of sorbic acid, and the distinctive school-bus-orange hue of food dye #A001M.

When it was test-marketed in 1952, housewives reported 1,304 uses for it, including spooning it into hot macaroni, mixing it with vegetables (as a way of getting children to eat broccoli), dolloping it warm on frankfurters, and spreading it on crackers. They also liked the glass jar it came in (eight- or sixteen-ounce size), which could be reused for jelly or even as an emergency drinking glass.

Microwave ovens have made Cheez Whiz even more convenient. Bombarded by electromagnetic energy for a few minutes, the stuff in the jar slackens into a fluid custard usable as hot cheese sauce—without a single pot or pan getting soiled. Gourmets despise it (they don't like any processed cheese); but there are certain junk foods that cannot properly be made without it. For instance, cheese fries to accompany a Philadelphia steak sandwich demand the silky-smooth texture of warm, runny Cheez Whiz. For pouring in a baked potato (as served in mall food courts), it is de rigueur. And Louis Lunch in New Haven, Connecticut, where the hamburger was invented nearly a hundred years ago and where the finicky kitchen allows no ketchup on the premises, uses only Cheez Whiz, smeared on white toast, to make its cheeseburgers.

CHER

S he's a miracle: For over a quarter-century now, Cher has changed constantly but remained the same. Every year, every time her picture appears on the cover of a supermarket tabloid, whenever she goes on tour to sing or takes a role acting in a movie, she looks different: new hair, new clothes, new cheeks (top and bottom), new bosoms, new nose, newly bonded teeth, newly lustrous skin. And yet she is ceaselessly, unmistakably, and immutably Cher, the gypsy tramp, the motorcycle mama, chronically underdressed, doing-her-own-thing sovereign of trash glamour to generations of teenage (and older) fans. Whatever is the most brazen look of the time, from 1965 to the present day, you can

count on Cher to sport it. Some people think of Madonna (see p. 296) as the star who first gleefully elevated the principle of self-adoration into a form of performance art and made a mint by dressing naughty in public; but Madonna wasn't yet ten years old when Cher, alongside her first husband, Sonny Bono, became famous as a fashion outlaw.

When Sonny met Cherilyn Sarkisian LaPierre in the early sixties, she was an aspiring singer; he was a backup musician for Phil Spector. Using the name Bonnie Jo Mason, Cher recorded a single for Spector: "Ringo, I Love You." It was a flop; but when Cher and Sonny teamed up for their first duet, "Baby Don't Go," the mixture of their voices was well-nigh perfect: a sinewy whine (his) and a fulminating boom (hers). They married in 1964 and formed an act called Caesar and Cleo, which went nowhere until they reclaimed the names Sonny and Cher and recorded Sonny's composition "I Got You Babe"—a vainglorious tale in which the singers wail about how they are rebuked and scorned by straight-laced people because they look so odd, but they don't care because they have each other's love. It looked and sounded like their autobiography, and it became one of the essential anthems of the love generation, who, like Sonny and Cher, were proud to look freakish.

The song, in its lyrics' relentless self-absorption about its singers' hair and clothes and precious feelings for each other, foreshadowed what was to become the guiding principle of Cherdom: vanity as art. At the time of Sonny and Cher's first success, it was their style much more than their singing that critics and fans noticed.

Cher (with Sonny)

"Kids identify with them," explained a Los Angeles radio program director to account for their success. "Cher has acne. Sonny wears Eskimo boots." *Newsweek* quipped in 1965 that in less than a year they had "risen from rags to custom-made rags—bell-bottom corduroys, green suede vests, red, black, and white striped shirts." *Look* called them "the latest in Pop music and Op fashion...soulmates of America's teenagers." And *16* magazine proclaimed them "outasite and groovy," promising that their first movie together, *Good Times*, would have "jungle scenes, cowboy scenes, spy scenes, knock-out cars and clothes, and fantastic new Sonny and Cher tunes galore. Hey babee—like don't miss it!"

Cher's appeal was that of a sullen teen who was mod and out-of-sight and head over heels in love with Sonny, but who also projected a distinctly ethnic quality, although exactly *which* ethnic group she favored was never clear. Even before cosmetic surgery, she had big cheekbones; and these, combined with the hump in her nose and a long shock of dark, straight hair, made her an ideal goddess for a counterculture that reviled anything white-bread American. She played the part to the hilt, accenting her dark eyes with monochromatic rings of eye shadow and dressing in such native duds as Indian doeskin tunics, headbands, and Masai warrior braids. The ethnic aura stayed with her until the eighties, and many of her solo hits traded on it: "Gypsies, Tramps and Thieves" (1971), "Half-Breed" (1973), and "Dark Lady" (1974).

Part of Cher's mystique in the early days was that she didn't talk much. Sonny was the blabby one. According to George Barris, their car customizer, Cher was "quieter, less outgoing, but extremely perceptive, a person whose words mean more because there aren't many of them." He contrasted the duo by noting that Sonny was the modder one and "loved high-powered cars more than anything else on earth," whereas Cher was an intellectual who preferred classic Rolls-Royces that were beautifully tasteful and rich-looking. He summarized: "You could compare them to an excellent modern painter and an old master." Cher was the old master.

Sonny and Cher were famous for being kicked out of hotels all over the world because of the way they looked. At a black-tie benefit in Hollywood in 1966, with Britain's Princess Margaret in attendance, Sonny outfitted himself in a yellow turtleneck and pirate's clothes; Cher arrived in a yellow-and-white striped suede top and bell-bottom trousers with cavalry stripes. Wherever they went, they turned heads, especially after acquiring a matched set of Ford Mustangs—*his* in gold with bobcat-fur interior, *hers* in hot pink with ermine insides—which they drove around Hollywood in tandem. As psychedelic fashions proliferated in the late sixties, however, Sonny and Cher's folk-rock fuzziness was eclipsed by even more flamboyant rock-and-rollers; and their big bell-bottoms and patchwork appearance became common on city streets. "There's no sense trying to shock people with the way you dress," Cher lamented in 1968. "They don't shock easily anymore."

Television provided a new source of fashion audacity. For the Second Age of Cher, following the Sullen Hippie era, she was reborn as a Sardonic Siren. After a few years of relative obscurity at the end of the sixties, the couple came back in 1971 with a TV show called "The Sonny and Cher Comedy Hour," which featured easy-to-listen-to rock music and amusing banter between Sonny, who was always a little simpleminded, but enthusiastic, and Cher, who spent the program making amusing deadpan wisecracks at his expense. Leaving her hippie wardrobe behind, Cher was outfitted every week in spectacular outfits designed by movie costumer Bob Mackie. She appeared as an Aztec princess, a Vegas show girl beneath a twenty-pound headdress, a vamp from a silent movie—costumes that were sometimes so elaborate she could barely walk. "Each week audiences waited for the newest witty extravagance in cloth to appear on the most-photographed female singer of the decade," Mablen Jones wrote in *Getting It On*, noting also that when Cher wore Bob Mackie outfits offstage as well as on-, she turned every public appearance into a "modeling session joyously received by every press photographer." The zenith of this phase of Cher's career was her 1974 see-through gown with only a few silver beads to hide her nipples and pudendum. It established a bare-all tradition that Cher has maintained at nearly every Academy Awards ceremony since.

Their TV show was a big success (the top-rated variety show of the 1973–74 season); but as *Movie Stars* magazine revealed in a May 1974 article titled "How Cher Plays Wife to Two Men at the Same Time!," Sonny and Cher's marriage was on the rocks. The problem (according to *Movie Stars*): Sonny still saw her as a "feisty childwoman." Her new love, record executive David Geffen, treated her as an "elegant woman." Sonny and Cher broke up and their TV show ended in 1974; but after each tried a solo show (with little success), they got back together, on camera only, for the sake of the ratings. Then the Third Age of Cher began. Cher the Free Spirit.

No longer Sonny's smart-mouth partner, liberated Cher took rock star Gregg Allman as a husband in 1977, about the time the new TV show fizzled and her singing career seemed to be going nowhere. After that, Cher's well-publicized liaisons with the likes of actor Val Kilmer, rock-and-rollers

Gene Simmons and Richie Sambora and "bagel boy" Rob Camilletti have had the flavor of a princess selecting ripe male concubines. The men in her life, like the wardrobe, seem to have been selected as reflections of her whim of the moment, which frequently defies propriety and convention. "Cher is a very passionate woman who needs to have a man in her life," the *National Enquirer* quoted an "insider" as saying in a 1991 article headlined CELIBATE CHER! THE SECRET IS OUT: "I HAVEN'T HAD SEX FOR 10 MONTHS."

Regardless of what the tabloids say, it seems safe to say that Cher relishes projecting the image of a woman who makes her own rules. She once called herself "an X-rated Cinderella," and when you look into her world, it does seem to have the monomaniacal purpose of a fairy tale in which every person and thing exists to illuminate its star. It is impossible to say whether this perfect egocentricity is her design, or if she simply has such an interesting personality that all else around her pales. "Somebody's got to do it," she explained to *Us* magazine. "It's a dirty job, being ridiculous, but I'll do it." One measure of the reach of her ridiculousness: when surveyed about their knowledge of current events a few years ago, some American high school students described "Chernobyl" as Cher's full name. The fact is that whatever she wears (and whichever parts of her body it shows) and whoever she is with, Cher radiates *something* mighty powerful, and she is guaranteed to attract more attention than anyone else on earth . . . except, now, Madonna.

In some respects, Cher is *still* better than Madonna, even though she is older and it is harder to be attractively slutty once you are in your forties, and Madonna sells far more records. For one thing, Cher gets effusively praised by movie critics for performances in such thinking-person's pictures as *Silk-*

wood, *Mask*, *The Witches of Eastwick*, and *Moonstruck* (for which she won a Best Actress Academy Award), whereas Madonna's movies are a joke. She was elected Woman of the Year by Harvard's Hasty Pudding Club in 1985, and three years later she introduced her own fragrance ("Uninhibited")—neither achievement matched by anything Madonna has done so far. Writing in the *New York Times Magazine*, Bruce Weber observed that "Cher's identity as a famous person has been complicated by the burgeoning acceptance of her screen talent"; and it is because of her work in "serious" motion pictures that Cher has won a reputation as a person of some real intelligence (despite her wardrobe), offering her philosophy to no less than Barbara Walters on TV. Madonna, on the other hand, gets herself in big trouble when she tries to talk. Also, Cher has lots of tattoos and Madonna has none.

CHEWING GUM

E mily Post didn't even mention chewing gum in *Etiquette* until the early 1940s, when the first edition of her set of cultivated commandments was already two decades old. Most books about social graces don't have to cover the subject: all polite readers know that gum chewing is a repulsive habit indulged in only by the lowest elements of society—hash slingers, gangsters and their molls, dead-end kids. The issue was, however, tackled head-on in *Manners for Millions*, a no-holds-barred guide to proper behavior written in 1932. This book is different from all other etiquette guides in that it was directed not at middle-class people who wanted to climb the social ladder but at slobs who didn't have a clue and needed remedial instruction in civilized conduct. "Chewing gum! Ugh! How can anyone indulge in this vulgar habit?" *Manners for Millions* ejaculated, advising that "no person of refinement would so violate the rules of politeness," and cautioning those who nonetheless were compelled to chew:

- Never make a noise (smacking, snapping) as you chew.
- Never twirl the gum around in the mouth, folding it over the tip of the tongue as you chew.
- Never pull the gum out in long strings.
- Never park your gum any place that another is likely, or is obliged, to touch it with his fingers.
- Never take gum from another person's mouth.

In the early forties, about the time chewing gum first appeared in *Etiquette* (which even in its current edition says, "It is hard to understand why so many otherwise attractive people totally destroy their appearance by chewing gum like a cow chewing cud"), Lily Haxworth Wallace's *The New American Etiquette* deigned to admit that "to attempt to stop the practice of chewing gum in public is like trying to hold back the tide with a toy shovel and pail." Ms. Wallace expressed her firm opinion that there was nothing wrong with chewing when driving a long distance in a car or strolling across a

Beech-Nut GUM

Everywhere it goes the assurance of Beech-Nut for fine flavor goes with it

PEPPERMINT FLAVORED CHEWING GUM ALWAYS REFRESHING BEECH-NUT GUM

Those who take active part in sport, as well as those who just watch, enjoy the refreshing flavor of BEECH-NUT GUM.

field (alone) in the country. She deemed chewing proper on an airliner (where you were also allowed to yawn) and while swimming, so long as the gum wad was properly disposed of—preferably by swallowing it.

Psychiatrists have called chewing gum oral masturbation; dentists have claimed that it rots teeth; food writer Waverley Root said its popularity betrayed Americans' defective diet because we chew it in lieu of eating nutritious food; it has been accused of causing intestinal blockage (if swallowed), wrinkled faces, and premature death (by exhausting the salivary glands). Despite its disreputable character, Americans chew about two and a half billion dollars' worth of gum per year, and although it is now surely an international practice (Japan's Let's Chew More Gum Association was inaugurated in 1962 by a Shinto priest's prayer to the "Great Spirit of the Chewing Gum"), it was in the U.S.A. that what is in fact an ancient habit was advanced and improved by moving from spruce-tree sap to wax and rubber to chicle to the current basic ingredients—butadiene-styrene, polyvinyl acetate, and petroleum wax. American soldiers have always been issued gum with K rations and in survival kits, and the call "Any gum, chum?" greeted American troops in World War II wherever they went. Like chocolate bars and stockings, chewing gum used to be one of those pleasures our boys had and everybody else wanted.

Spruce gum had been an Indian chaw for centuries when a down-east seaman named John Curtis began making and selling batches of "State of Maine Pure Spruce Gum" in 1848. It cost a penny for two mouthfuls, and became popular enough around the country for Mark Twain to include a scene in *The Adventures of Tom Sawyer* in which Tom and Becky pass the same piece back and forth. Still made in Maine, spruce gum is dour stuff and hard to chew—not at all like modern gums, which are softer and as sweet as candy. Gum as we know it began in 1869 when a patent was issued to an Ohio dentist, William Semple, for an "Improved Chewing Gum" made of rubber and dentifrices. Semple did nothing with his patent; but that same year, an inventor named Thomas Adams, Jr., went to Staten Island, where he met with the exiled Mexican general Antonio López de Santa

Anna, "butcher of the Alamo," who had come to the U.S. with a quarter-ton of chicle (sap from Mexican sapodilla trees) in hopes of forming a partnership with a gringo rubber maker and creating artificial rubber. The plan was a bust, and Santa Anna eventually was allowed to return home, where he died; but Mr. Adams, to recoup some of the money he lost in the synthetic rubber scheme, rolled his surplus chicle into little balls (unflavored) and began marketing them in 1871 as "Adams' New York Chewing Gum—Snapping and Stretching" in a two-hundred-ball box with a picture of City Hall on the front. Soon he added sassafras flavoring, then anise (creating Black Jack, which is still made), and then tutti-frutti, which he sold as gum balls from vending machines throughout the city.

By 1890, when William Wrigley, Jr., introduced Vassar chewing gum (named to appeal to highfalutin chewers), there were a hundred brands of gum on the market, and gum barons were getting rich. Vassar wasn't a success, but Wrigley's Juicy Fruit and Spearmint brands, first marketed in 1893, were big hits because of their flavor, which was subtler than overpowering rival gums'. In 1899, when America's six largest gum makers asked Wrigley to join them in a chewing gum trust, Wrigley refused and went his own way . . . and never looked back. His first leap towards dominating the market was during the recession of 1907. While other gum makers cut back production, Wrigley said "People chew harder when they are sad" and bought a million and a half dollars' worth of advertising. Business tripled, and since then it has been a truism that gum sales go up in hard times.

Wrigley was a tireless advertiser and promoter. In 1915, he sent four free sticks of gum to every person listed in a U.S. phone book. He was the first distributor to place gum next to restaurant cash registers (be-cause it "aids digestion"). He regularly sent sticks of gum to two-year-olds on their birthdays to get them in the habit. Wrigley died in 1932, but his son and grandson have continued his relentless sales policies. During World War II, Wrigley advertisements recommended five sticks of gum per day for every war worker ("Factory tests show how chewing gum helps men feel better, work better") and described "monotony, fatigue, false thirst, and nervous tension" as agents of the enemy—all of which could be vanquished by chewing gum.

Wrigley was caught off-guard by Trident (sugarless gum) in the 1970s, but introduced Extra sugarless in 1984, which is now the top-selling sugarless brand. A *Wall Street Journal* article about the company in 1991 marveled at its ability to dominate the market using "advertising campaigns with themes that have been around since Eisenhower"—in particular, the Doublemint Twins, a corny series that shows happy lookalikes who chew and click their packs together. The article stated that the most difficult job a gum marketer has is overcoming the social stigma that is still attached to people who chew. Experts pointed out that "chewing and popping are a major statement in some circles" (the *wrong* circles, Miss Post would have insisted!) and that gum makes its chewer feel tough and rebellious. A recent Wrigley's ad campaign, titled "Piece of America," showed otherwise proper citizens chewing wads in public.

Here are some interesting gum facts, gathered from Robert Hendrickson's comprehensive *The Great American Chewing Gum Book:*

- If all the gum chewed in America each year were laid end to end, it would be a stick five million miles long.
- Bubble gum was perfected in 1928 by Walter Diemer, who dyed it pink because it was the only color food dye he had on hand at

the time. It was called Dubble Bubble and was far more successful than its inferior predecessor, Blibber Blubber, which clung fiercely to skin when a bubble burst.

- The first bubble gum baseball cards (preceded by tobacco cards) were introduced by Topps in 1951. Other stars of gum cards have included Davy Crockett, Elvis Presley, the Kennedy family, the Munsters, the Green Berets, famous anticommunists, and General Norman Schwarzkopf.

- To remove gum stuck on clothing, rub it with an ice cube until it hardens; then scrape it off with a knife. To remove bubble gum stuck on nose, lips, chin, or cheek, chew more gum, then pull the wad from your mouth, press it hard against the stuck gum, and yank.

JULIA CHILD

Before Julia Child, almost nobody cooked for fun. Preparing food was a chore, and the gourmet way of life was an indulgence reserved for a tiny number of sophisticates and eccentrics. As the best-known chef on television for the last thirty years, Julia Child, more than anyone else, is responsible for food preparation and connoisseurship turning into a national leisure-time passion. She has elevated the aspirations of American home cooks and inspired untold numbers of women and men to try their hand at coq au vin and to dare whip up a towering soufflé. Even many television viewers who have never seriously watched her to learn about cooking have an affection for Julia because of her zany, vivacious manner in the kitchen, where she sometimes goofs while demonstrating recipes, but always makes cooking look like fun.

Her first book, *Mastering the Art of French Cooking*, which she wrote with Louisette Bertholle and Simone Beck after years of living in France and studying its cuisine, was published in 1961. It was a landmark event: here at last was a set of hands-on lessons that demystified French

cooking and put it within reach of any diligent reader. It was not a typical early-1960s cookbook for suburban moms who needed jiffy recipes and easy, cheap, low-cal answers to their kitchen problems; in fact

Julia was successful partly because she didn't address readers as harried den mothers but provided them instead a breather from the rat race of convenience food and short-cut recipes. With her as their guide, adventurous pleasure-seekers learned to cook for the sheer joy to be found in the act of cooking, and for the satisfaction of eating something truly special that they had crafted all by themselves.

Julia came on the scene at a time when a lot of restless members of the swelling middle class were hungry for more sophistication in their lives. After eight years of old, homespun Ike and Mamie Eisenhower as the national First Couple, the young, glamorous Kennedys provided a welcome touch of continental savoir faire. In fact, Jackie wowed even the hard-to-please French when she visited them (she spoke their language fluently), and she hired the *très soigné* René Verdon to cook in the White House. At the same time, international travel, once the privilege of the wealthy few, was becoming a real possibility for many; and as people ventured overseas, they tasted international cuisine. For those who came back and yearned to continue the adventures of their newly cultivated cosmopolitan palate in the home kitchen, Julia Child was a revelation.

Although her book was a bestseller, it was on television that she became an icon of popular culture. As "The French Chef," starting on Boston's educational channel, WGBH, in 1962 (followed by "Julia Child and Company" in 1978–79 and "Dinner at Julia's" in 1983), she has shown her viewers that anyone can cook fine food if he puts his mind to it. She doesn't just give one-two-three lessons, as had so many of the early television chefs who preceded her. Nor does she have anything like an actorly inflection when she breathlessly exclaims her way through a demonstration. If she trusses a turkey, she does it with a panache that would be the envy of any game show host; she rhapsodizes about the turkey's thighs, she pats it like a favorite pet, she swoons when she first catches sight of it coming out of the oven—she has a ball!

And she is anything but fussy, the way gourmets used to be. When she cooks, she sticks her fingers in the sauce to taste it, she licks the spoon, she sometimes drops things and tosses them right into the stew pot, and she relishes her sips of wine (actually, a mixture of water and Gravy Master). "Julia is so spontaneous, freewheeling, relaxed, and utterly real," Betty Fussell wrote in *Masters of American Cookery*, "that many Americans are convinced she is either loony or drunk." She is neither, but she sounds awkward and looks clumsy . . . and that is her charm. Good as she is in the kitchen, she appears to have none of the spit-and-polish precision of a pro, and so even amateurs in her audience are encouraged that they can do it, too.

Julia Child has transformed cooking into entertainment, and became the inspiration for one of Dan Aykroyd's funniest bits on "Saturday Night Live" (playing Julia, he cut off his thumb and bled to death without missing a beat) as well as for a musical play in 1991 called *Bon Appétit!*, in which Jean Stapleton sang in Julia's voice while she whipped egg whites and presided over a race between a hand beater and a mixing machine. Following Julia's engaging example, it long ago became fashionable to invite guests into the kitchen to watch or even to help in a meal's preparation. Her gusto became a model for virtually all the television chefs who have come after her, although none has ever seemed as disarmingly candid as she. Once, when some viewers accused her of being too sloppy as she cooked, she responded, "They're prissy people, and to hell with them."

COLLECTORS ART

ollectors Art of Dundee, Illinois, is a traveling exhibition of paintings for sale, probably on its way to a motel or hotel near you. If Collectors Art isn't coming, maybe one of its competitors, like Starving Artists, Art Riot, Art Warehouse, or Nudes in Oil, will.

You don't have to read *Art News* to know they are coming. Just keep your eye on your television set, and towards the end of the week before the opening of one of these shows, advertisements begin to trumpet the glad tidings. An announcer so enthusiastic he sounds on the verge of a stroke imparts the amazing news that genuine oil paintings —created by actual living artists, on bona fide canvas, in wood frames, and ready to be hung on a wall for all to see—will be on display for the weekend at the local Marriott or Holiday Inn. These are not odd-lot pictures, remnants, or artists' rejects. They are factory-fresh works of art, direct from artists' studios. The truly marvelous thing is that they are sold for unbelievably low prices—dollar-figures that always end, in the time-honored tradition of bargain salesmanship, in 95, or 98, or 99 cents. The season for the shows lasts from autumn through about March, and most major television markets have three or four shows each year. (There are none in summer because trucking the paintings between motels that time of year becomes a problem: heat can cause canvas to buckle, frames to warp, or paint to soften and melt.

You have seen the paintings these companies sell on display in motel rooms, dentists' offices, and foyers of businesses that want to look genteel. They depict crashing surf, weathered barns, apple-cheeked moppets, sad or funny clowns, and grizzle-

cheeked sea captains. Each painting is done by hand; but in many instances the differences between them are slight. The artists who produce them do the same subject over and over again in different sizes and colors, which makes it easy for customers to choose just the right shade of sunset to match the living room couch or drapes.

Unlike a lot of art sold in important galleries or displayed in museums, Collectors Art paintings do not appear to have sprung from the tortured brow of some exquisitely creative soul. They are not original or iconoclastic; and they do not make good investments. They exist for the most basic reason, to make the person who looks at them happy. Some fans have told us that they like going to the shows even if they don't buy something, because looking at the paintings reminds them of their summer vacation or maybe a dream. In one way, Collectors Art is the purest kind of pop culture, because, simply, it is culture that is popular.

The paintings are customarily exhibited in a large meeting room in a hotel, where hundreds of them are piled up. The cheapest ones, some under ten dollars, are heaped on circular tables in the center of the room: they are devoted to smaller subjects like wishing wells, or rosebuds. At a far end of the room are stacks of larger paintings for a hundred dollars or less; and in one specially designated area, Collectors Art shows the cream of the crop—the biggest paintings with the most detail in elaborate frames, some approaching a thousand dollars. These will be complicated scenes that took someone a lot of time and effort to paint: great effulgent bouquets of flowers with little gerbils crouched around the vase; a bucolic farm scene with a milkmaid in a disco shag haircut resting contemplatively against a tree trunk; a bearded frontiersman in a fringed buckskin shirt standing in front of a snow-capped mountain wearing a hat made out of an eviscerated animal whose legs hang limply over the man's ears; a winter landscape with ducks flying to the left or the right—take your pick, whichever fits the flow of space in your home.

Although most customers buy the less expensive works of art, everyone who comes to a Collectors Art exhibit likes to look at the top-of-the-line pieces, many of which aspire to a style reminiscent of a recognized master. The soft pastel ones bring to mind Monet; street scenes with dancing lights suggest Utrillo; a *Last Supper* is done in the classical manner of Leonardo, except that Christ and his table mates have a strangely twentieth-century aspect to their faces and blow-dried hair, like nice-looking men you might expect to see any Sunday buying auto accessories at Sears. The low-end paintings of clowns leaning on lampposts and sad puppies come with no such complex cultural baggage.

When Collectors Art came to our town, we spoke to Jan Johnson, who has been with the company and traveling with its shows for many years. Mrs. Johnson, a hearty midwestern woman with a booming voice who traveled thirty-three thousand miles last year selling art in hotels coast to coast, explained that preferences in art vary in different parts of the country. Fairfield County, Connecticut, was not a good place to sell that picture of the mountain man with the dead animal on his head that we were admiring. "In the East, it's lighthouses, covered bridges, ducks, and anything old English. In Pittsburgh and Philadelphia, portraits are popular. In the Midwest, they like red barns. In the West, Indian is big—so is the frontier." She explained that people's taste is always changing. "Owls are out this year [1991], clowns are back, and winter is in."

Like so many art gallery proprietors, Mrs. Johnson is subject to the whims and caprices of her buyers, and we watched her solve the problems of befuddled Collectors Art patrons. Like Heloise, she had a practical hint for everyone. A man worried that the landscape painting in his den was getting baggy was advised to mist it lightly with a spray bottle and it would snap right back. For a white frame that had gotten nicked, Mrs. Johnson prescribed a dab of white shoe polish. One despondent customer wanted to know if there was something that could be done about a canvas with a bullet hole in it. Most complaints came from people who bought a painting, took it home, and decided they didn't like it. This was a problem easy to solve, because Collectors Art exchanges any painting that doesn't look right over the couch. "You can't do that at K-Mart!" Mrs. Johnson said with delight.

Mrs. Johnson is convinced that there is nothing quite like an oil painting, because oils change almost magically when they are put in the right light. To demonstrate this phenomenon, she frequently takes a painting that a customer is considering for purchase into a special curtained-off booth in the center of the room, where incandescent lights bathe it in a warm glow. Marveling at the transformation, she announces, "Oil painting is like nothing else—you put it on the wall and it's alive!"

About the only thing Mrs. Johnson doesn't like about the paintings is the way some of the artists sign them. "You'd think they were all doctors," she sighed, trying to decipher the name of a painter represented by a high-priced, three-by-four-foot canvas

of a flock of shriveled-looking parrots frolicking on the branches of a fruiting tree. The artist, whatever-his-name-is, paints the same parrots all the time and signs every painting. Despite the maddening illegibility of his signature, Mrs. Johnson explained that it was important that every painting have one: it signifies genuine art, not something made by a machine.

CORVETTE

Sex, power, youth, fun: They are what you get when you buy a Corvette. A Vette, as its friends like to call it, is the only truly made-in-America sports car; and as such, it is pop culture's supreme symbol of automotive thrills. It promises adventure (Martin Milner and George Maharis drove one around the country on television's "Route 66"); it's a sign of ever-ready masculinity (Ted Danson owns one on "Cheers"); it's got womanly sex appeal, too (Angelyne [see p. 17] pilots a hot-pink one around Hollywood); and it can lick almost anything on the road: "Gotta be cool now!"

rejoice the Beach Boys in "Shut Down," a song about a fuel-injected Corvette that leaves a Super Stock Dodge in the dust. Along with Cadillacs (see *The Encyclopedia of Bad Taste*) and Harley-Davidsons (see p. 205), the Corvette is one of the enduring superstars of America's highways. "Years ago this land knew cars that were fabricated out of sheer excitement," proclaimed a Corvette advertisement in 1955. "Magnificent cars that uttered flame and rolling thunder from exhaust pipes as big around as your forearm, and came towering down through the summer dust of the American roads like the Day of Judgement."

The Corvette was conceived by Harley Earl (see p. 167) as competition for the growing number of imported sports cars—MGs, Jaguars, Nash-Healys—all of which were small, speedy, somewhat inconvenient (they had stick shift), and a great blast of open-air fun. He thought a domestic version could be made to sell cheaply, for under two thousand dollars, and would appeal to young suburbanites as a second car, for leisure-time driving or commuting.

In 1953 at the Motorama, General Motors' annual display of dazzling, impossibly futuristic vehicles (known as dream cars), onlookers were wowed by one billed as the EX-122, a swoopy, low-slung little speedster with wire-mesh headlight screens, bucket seats, and rust-free fiberglass body. In June of that year, the EX-122 went on sale—as the Corvette. It was an unprecedented marketing strategy: Motorama cars were only supposed to hint at the wonders of tomorrow; to actually sell one, virtually unchanged from its Motorama specifications, was a near-miracle to America's future-hungry car buyers. "You don't have to 'just look' at this dream car," said early Corvette advertisements. *"YOU CAN OWN IT NOW!"*

This first Corvette was, in fact, a dud—sluggish and sloppy, with an anemic six-cylinder engine and a two-speed Powerglide automatic transmission, the same transmission used in family sedans and station wagons. There were no roll-up windows, just plastic side curtains, and the body wasn't even made of steel: Glass-reinforced polyester resins had been used, partly because they saved time and tooling costs, and also because the glass fiber material seemed so modernistic. In the first year of production, 1953, just over three hundred Corvettes were built.

Many fastidious sports car fans snubbed the Corvette, partly because they were convinced that nothing really sporty could be manufactured by the American automobile industry (whose idea of jaunty fun was a two-ton Buick bulgemobile) and partly because of that boring six-cylinder engine and —the coup de grace—its automatic transmission. (All ardent car enthusiasts, even today, are supposed to like to shift for themselves; automatics are considered the sissies' way of changing gears.) Also, in the 1950s each car manufacturer had a very well-defined image, and Chevrolet's was as a producer of sedate family cars, not necessarily fun ones. A 1951 Chevy advertisement (showing a station wagon) boasted

that the product was "American as cider in the fall, reliable as the good earth, familiar as a roadside stand: that's Chevrolet, America's favorite car."

A V-8 engine was offered as an option in the 1955 Corvette, boosting the zero-to-sixty time from a drowsy 11 seconds to a peppy 8.7. There were now also roll-up windows and a choice of colors, but there was still that automatic transmission. The 1955 Corvette sold a mere seven hundred copies, and those few people who bought one sometimes knew it by a now long-gone diminutive nickname, a Corvie. A Corvie was cute, but with the notable exception of the Volkswagen Beetle, cuteness has never been a top priority among American car buyers. "We really didn't know what we wanted," recalled Chevrolet's chief engineer, Ed Cole. "We had no real feeling of the market. Was Corvette for the boulevard driver or the sports car tiger?" It is a question that has never been answered fully. For its whole life, Corvette has appealed equally to adult show-offs and hot-rodding grease monkeys; it has served admirably both as a street-cruiser sex symbol going 20 miles per hour in the parking lot of a drive-in and as a serious sports car for rallies, race tracks, and drag strips.

On the verge of death, Corvette was resuscitated in 1956 with a new, more modern body style and a close-ratio, floor-mounted stickshift, as well as an optional V-8, high-lift cam engine with two four-barrel carburetors. Zero-to-sixty time had dropped to 7.3 seconds. The new Corvette was a screamer . . . and a commercial success at last. The next year, fuel injection was offered, lowering its zero-to-sixty run to a blazing 5.7 seconds, and giving the hot-optioned 1957 model a top speed of 132 miles per hour. In succeeding years, available power went up, up, up (to a staggering 460 horsepower, more than most Mack trucks, in 1970); and the sprightly little Corvie roadster metamorphosed into the dangerous-looking Sting Ray (1963, based on a dream car called the Mako Shark), then into the musclebound Vettes of the 1970s.

Nearly forty years old, today's Corvette has managed to avoid the corporate senescence that befell the Thunderbird (its rival in the beginning) and the homogenized look of the modern Mustang. It remains in a class by itself, not just because it is America's sports car but because it is the only high-performance ride with true proletarian, rather than snob, appeal. It *is* expensive—the top-of-the-line ZR-1 costs nearly seventy thou—but the Corvette's aura is not a matter of price. Its raw power and unsurpassed agility have made it the standard-bearer of American automotive machismo. Case in point: Bruce Springsteen can afford any car he wants, but what does the impeccably masculine blue-collar hero prefer? His 1958 convertible Corvette.

There are plenty of fast, hot, two-seater vehicles in the world—Ferraris, Porsches, etc.—but their glamour is mostly as toys for the rich and egotistical; and coveted though they may be, none has the brawny, breezy, down-home charisma of a top-down Corvette—preferably white with lipstick-red interior, and with Chuck Berry blasting on the radio as the highway winds ahead and the phone poles tick by like pickets in an endless fence.

"THE COSBY SHOW"

Early in 1984 comedian Bill Cosby surveyed the shows on TV and was dismayed by what he saw: "car chases and breasts and characters yelling at each other and saying 'Yowie!' " All the situation comedies, he said, "get their laughs by using euphemisms for sexual parts of the body," and nearly every one was posited on ugly conflicts among the generations. Laughs that weren't about boobs and butts were harvested from barrages of mean-minded one-liners that were the legacy of the put-down humor developed in "All in the Family" (see p. 11) and its spin-offs and imitators.

Cosby decided to do something different. "I proposed a situation comedy based on my personal experience as a husband, as a parent." He originally came up with an idea for a show about a family in which the father was a chauffeur and the mother was a carpenter; but his real-life wife, Camille, vetoed the idea, saying the world already knew Bill Cosby as a college-educated, middle-class kind of guy. Instead, he made the man an obstetrician ("I wanted to be able to talk to women who were about to give birth and make them feel comfortable") and the woman a lawyer (as a role model that would "aid the female going into the future . . . in her job, in her life as a mother, a wife, and a woman").

NBC executives were uncertain about "The Cosby Show" when it premiered in the fall of 1984. Although it was a situation comedy about an African-American family, it had none of the ethnic humor and street lingo that characterized previous black sit-

Top: Malcolm-Jamal Warner (Theo),
Lisa Bonet (Denise);
middle: Keshia Knight Pulliam (Rudy),
Bill Cosby (Heathcliff Huxtable), Phylicia Rashad
(Clair Huxtable); *bottom:* Tempestt Bledsoe (Vanessa)

coms such as "The Jeffersons," "Good Times," and "Sanford and Son." Aside from not adopting the TV formulas of how non-Caucasian families were supposed to behave, "The Cosby Show" wasn't like *any* other half-hour comedy then on the air. It had no wisecracking teens, no idiot adults to be laughingstocks, no sexy bimbos or lewd double entendres, and—most shocking of all—no hysterical gag lines suitable for cranking up the laugh track.

Cosby had won three Emmy awards for his role in the sophisticated espionage spoof "I Spy" (1965–68) and had done very well as a stand-up comic but had enjoyed only small success with "The Bill Cosby Show" (1969–71), "The New Bill Cosby Show" (1972–73), and "Cos" (1976). Brandon Tartikoff, NBC's entertainment president, believed the new show could work if it gave its star and producer the chance to develop the subject that made his stand-up comedy monologues so funny as well as insightful—parenthood. (Cosby is a certified expert in this field, having earned a doctor of education degree at Amherst College with a thesis titled "An Integration of the Visual Media Via 'Fat Albert and the Cosby Kids' [a Saturday morning cartoon series he developed] into the Elementary School Curriculum as a Teaching Aid and Vehicle to Achieve Increased Learning.")

By the middle of the 1984–85 season, "The Cosby Show"—broadcast in competition with the immensely popular "Magnum, P.I."—had become the number-one-rated program on the air, a position it held until the end of the decade, helping to lift NBC from last place to first among the networks and to establish Bill Cosby as the holder of the highest Q rating (the measure of how well liked a celebrity is) in history. *Esquire* called him "the decade's antidote to sleaze and cynicism, the self-appointed ombudsman of American morality, the Great Black Father of his country."

The Huxtable family of "The Cosby Show" were not, as the show implied, just normal people; they were considerably better than normal, verging on flawless: Mom, Dad, and kids, along with plenty of friends and, in the last years of the show, some extended family. They all looked nice and clean and healthy; they spoke politely and with respect for each other and the rest of the human race; and although each child was outspoken, they all deferred to their parents, who knew best. Most of the problems they encountered were the kind of little daily-life issues that may have tested their patience but never their faith, and they frequently solved these problems by engaging in a courteous and sometimes witty discussion among themselves, for which there was always enough time and willing energy. There were no financial problems, nor were there worries about child care; and their lovely brownstone home on a safe street in Brooklyn, although always full of life and healthy activity, was never messy.

In some superficial ways "The Cosby Show" was very much a product of the 1980s: a materialist's prime-time fantasy about the good life, as signified by the Huxtable family's fashion-plate clothing (including Dad's thousand-dollar sweaters), well-furnished home, and financial security. But beyond these obvious trappings of success, the soul of the show—and the reason viewers adored it—was that it set forth more enduring standards of behavior, described this way by *People* magazine: "Love each other, join together in families and in neighborhoods, have children and teach them the value of discipline, hard work, and mutual respect. It's an old-fashioned vision, but also profound and healing. It creates a common ground, a timeless island of shared humanity." Such values were at the heart of television's first two popular sitcoms back in 1949, "The Goldbergs," which was about a Jewish family in the Bronx who loved each other very much, and "Mama," about a close-knit Norwegian family in San Francisco. "The Cosby Show," like these ancient predecessors, and like the successful family sitcoms of the 1950s ("Leave It to Beaver," "Father Knows Best," etc.), was a fantasy of family life, with little of the taboo-shattering relevancies and disturbing real-life dilemmas that made such 1970s shows as "All in the Family" and "M*A*S*H" seem so important (and, occasionally, self-important). Its overwhelming warmth and whimsy made it easy to give short shrift to the fact that serious issues were indeed dealt with in many episodes—from dyslexia to apartheid—but the fact remained that spending a half-hour with the family on "The Cosby Show" guaranteed millions of viewers a weekly dose of friendship, family, and brotherhood by the time the credits rolled.

For some socially conscious critics, who believe television should be a forum for debate and dissent (as on "Maude," say, or "L.A. Law"), the upbeat idealism of "The Cosby Show" was politically incorrect, and it was especially wrong to present the Huxtables as comfortable and middle-class. Writing in the *New York Times*, Henry Louis Gates, Jr., worried that the conspicuous success of this family ("the most nobly idealized blacks in the history of entertainment") implied that social conditions in the real world were just fine and "reassuringly threw the blame for black poverty back onto the impoverished." Critic Mark Crispin Miller complained that the show gave the misleading impression that blacks were free to enjoy life like white people do, "and there are no hard feelings, none at all, now that the old injustice has been so easily rectified."

On the other hand, David Cuthbert of the New Orleans *Times-Picayune* wrote, "Sure, it is glossy and very upscale and very idealized. But in some ways, that's better than something more downbeat or realistic. It fulfills one of TV's roles, which is to give us something to aspire to." Coretta Scott King, writing in *TV Guide* in April 1992 as "The Cosby Show" was about to go off the air, offered a similar perspective:

> At a time when American families have been disintegrating at an alarming rate, Bill and his excellent cast and staff have taught viewers so much about the importance of strong, caring parents, about the values of honesty and openness.... We owe him our thanks, not only for the laughter and enjoyment, but also for demonstrating the educational potential of prime-time television, for caring about and contributing to our children's

moral development, and for showing us how our families can thrive with harmony and love.

In the same farewell-to-Cosby issue of *TV Guide*, critic Jeff Jarvis admitted that he was never very happy with the preachy tone the show sometimes used, but there was no denying the goodness of its influence—in reviving the sitcom and virtually saving NBC, and in exalting the family. "[Cosby] made family life look like so much fun," Jarvis wrote, "I decided to have one. Hail, Cosby."

HOWARD COSELL

In 1978 *TV Guide* conducted a survey that showed that "Monday Night Football" announcer Howard Cosell was the most popular broadcaster in all of sports. The same poll also revealed that Howard Cosell was the most *un*popular broadcaster in sports. In a 1989 *Sports Illustrated* "Point After" column called "Yearning for Howard," Franz Lidz recalled him as "the know-it-all who drove you nuts with his long-winded pronouncements," but then went on to praise him as an embodiment of journalistic integrity. Whatever else people have to say about "His Royal Heinous," everyone agrees that Howard Cosell—the man ridiculed with more zeal than any other twentieth-century American besides Richard Nixon and Dan Quayle—rewrote the rules of sports broadcasting.

No other announcer has ever had such influence and notoriety, even—especially—among people who aren't fans. A fan, after all, is mostly interested in the game or the match: He or she wants to know what's the score, who's got the ball—what, precisely, is happening. Howard Cosell rarely spoke about such trifling things. When he announced a fight or a football game, he told you about the psychological idiosyncrasies of the participants, the political implica-

tions of the contest, the moral nuances of the rivalry, and the aesthetic dimensions of the strategy. In doing so, he reached beyond fans and made sports seem like a human drama, one of interest to a lot of people who didn't care to listen to the fine points of a 4–3 defense.

Sports fans, especially sports writers who were sports fans, really resented him for it. He took what was theirs—the bar-room arguments, the dearly held opinions, the mostly male rituals of banter during an athletic contest, and all the implicit and metaphorical meanings of sport—and made them explicit, open and available to the public at large. Until Cosell, the man in the announcer's booth was thought of as a neutral kind of guy, a sort of news broadcaster, not an impassioned commentator. Personal opinion was taboo, as were humor, speculation, excuses, and analysis. Most important, sportscasters were not expected to say anything bad about the players or the game. Negativity was considered unsportsmanlike; it was an announcer's job to be a self-effacing Pollyanna and to support all the players (maybe the hometown ones a bit more), to always say what a good, fine job they were doing, and to remind the audience what an excellent and upstanding event they were observing.

Not Cosell. In a stentorian voice that sounded like Paul Harvey delivering a Bronx cheer, Cosell proclaimed that football "has become an utter bore . . . like a form of Chinese water torture." He said that baseball was "an artistic and aesthetic mess." He called the Indianapolis 500 "a blood event embodying the two principal characteristics of our time: swiftness and violence." He described bantamweight boxer Mark Pacheco's losing record as "a thing of sadness." He praised Muhammad Ali (see p. 8) because "he'd let you ride the sharp curves and walk the dark alleys of his psyche." Describing his own work on "Monday Night Football," he asserted that his contribution was to "rescue the viewers from being bored to tears with an endless stream of nonsensical football jargon." And he criticized his fellow broadcasters as a "jockocracy" not up to the challenge of real sports journalism: "Can you ever imagine these two ex-jocks [Terry Bradshaw and Harvey Martin, two former pro football

players hired by CBS] reporting on sensitive, complex issues such as drug abuse, antitrust legislation, and racial discrimination? They are simply not equipped to handle the job."

Cosell made himself and his penchant for exaggerated and frequently outrageous commentary an unavoidable part of the event. He was an entertainer, and he knew it. (His one foray beyond sports, however, as host of ABC's variety show "Saturday Night Live with Howard Cosell" in 1975–76 was a flop—despite the duet of "Anything You Can Do" he sang with Barbara Walters.) "Isn't it absolutely incredible what wondrous verbiage flows from my mouth?" he once observed, only half kidding. "We weren't watching the Ali-Spinks fight," Tom Shales of the Washington *Post* wrote in a column he addressed to Cosell in 1978. "We were watching you watch the Ali-Spinks fight. The sound of your voice was virtually visual. . . . It was a transmogrification into a personal and intimate form, a manageable, living-room form, of the roaring crowd that filled the Super Dome." In the 1970s, thanks in large part to Howard Cosell, *watching* a sports event on television at home or in a bar became at least as hallowed a ritual as being at it in person.

Cosell started as a broadcaster in the 1950s when he hosted a radio show on which Little League ball players interviewed major leaguers. The Little League was one of his clients in a successful New York legal practice, but Cosell decided he liked radio work more than the law ("I was restricted by the rules of evidentiary procedure") and went south with a thirty-pound tape recorder to get interviews during baseball spring training. Soon he had his own radio show on ABC and was known in particular for his coverage of boxing, sitting ringside with Rocky Marciano, who he said taught him "the inside" of the sport. He listened to trainer Cus D'Amato, whom he called "a reporter's dream" for his Freudian lectures on boxing and boxers, and soon Cosell began to focus his attention as a broadcaster and interviewer on the boxers themselves: Floyd Patterson, "who carried his emotional baggage like a huge stone on his shoulders," and Muhammad Ali, "a symphony of metaphors and rhymes."

Ali didn't need Cosell, and Cosell didn't need Ali, but they were perfect broadcast partners, in interviews as well as pre- and postfight commentaries. Both men were charismatic blowhards, and Cosell found in Ali a never-ending fount of material that he could use to expound about boxing, sports, society, and life in general. When Ali refused to be inducted into the Army, Cosell came to his defense, calling the government "inhuman" and declaring that he had been drafted only because he was black and boastful—resulting in a hail of hate mail to ABC demanding they remove the "nigger-loving Jew bastard" from the air. Although Cosell's pontifications frequently seemed to be far out of proportion to the triviality of the subject he was covering, Ali was a man clearly worthy of embellished analysis—in Cosell's words, "a figure transcendental to sports." As Robert Lipsyte described the relationship in the *New York Times*, Cosell "helped raise the consciousness of the country by giving clear, fair electronic voice to Muhammad Ali as charmer, hustler, religionist, superstar, and the illegitimate target of politicians."

Cosell also made enemies defending Tommie Smith, an American sprinter who raised his fist in a black power salute at the 1968 Olympic Games, but it wasn't until the debut of "Monday Night Football" in 1970 that he became the man television viewers most loved to hate. As one of three announcers in the booth (along with Frank Gifford and Don Meredith), Cosell tried to humanize the game. "It was up to me to interact with the millions of women and casual fans who were tuning in and get a reaction out of them." He definitely got his reaction: After the first several games, Howard Cosell was being talked about more than football, and mail ran nine-to-one against his adjective-laden prose and the windy, free-form digressions with his partners, which sometimes seemed to drift into a kind of men's-club banter utterly oblivious to the game being played on the field. Angry as many viewers may have been, they tuned in to "Monday Night Football" in record numbers, and complaining about Howard Cosell became as much a national obsession as the game.

The transformation of sports into big-time show business was not Howard Cosell's fault, but he was there as it happened, and his penchant for dramatization helped it happen by opening boxing and football up to audiences beyond the usual Joe Sixpack fans. This was a development about which Cosell, as well as his critics, had deeply ambivalent feelings. At the same time that he was responsible for making advertising minutes on "Monday Night Football" so valuable, he was decrying the commercialization of sports. "The paradox about Howard is that he's the guy who stands outside the tent at the carnival, shouting: 'Step right in and look at the naked girls,'" Robert Lipsyte observed. "But when you get inside, Howard's in there, too, saying, 'Hey, you should be ashamed to be in here.'"

Eventually, the tension between his love of sports as (in his words) "surcease from the daily travail of life" and his instinct to puff mere athletic contests into (his words again) "drama on its grandest scale" caused Howard Cosell to quit. He gave up on boxing in 1982 when he decided that it was crooked, rigged, and brutal; and the next year he left "Monday Night Football," declaring himself fed up with the sport and with "the inane blathering of [the] ex-jocks" with whom he shared the broadcast booth. Two years later, in a brutal book called *I Never Played the Game,* Cosell announced: "I am convinced that sports are out of whack in the American society; that the emphasis ... distorts the real values of life; ... that the world of sports today is an ever-spinning spiral of deceit, immorality, absence of ethics, and defiance of the public interest."

Although Cosell has no regular forum on the air anymore, he has continued to proclaim his opinions, most recently in a book called *What's Wrong with Sports* (1991), which covers such subjects as Pete Rose's lack of character, urine tests to check athletes for drug use, the unhealthy relationship of commercial television to the National Football League, and illegal sports gambling. "I believe in all the clichés," Cosell said while promoting the book. "I am a sports fan."

CRAZY EDDIE

In order to sell more stereo equipment, Brooklyn shopkeeper Eddie Antar declared himself insane in 1972. His idea was to make customers believe that they could make out like bandits if they came to his store on Kings Highway in Brooklyn and took advantage of his mental disability, which always caused him to price merchandise ridiculously low.

Antar had already failed at his first stereo store, called Sights and Sounds, which had opened in 1969 and lasted less than a year. He blamed its collapse on lackadaisical merchandising. When he opened his second store he took a more aggressive tack and named it after himself—Crazy Eddie. Crazy Eddie had a sales policy that the staff knew as "nail 'em at the door": Antar lay in wait by the exit, and if a browser seemed about to leave without having bought anything, he leapt forth to block the way, berating and badgering the customer to turn around and make a purchase. It was a "stand-up-and-scream business," one associate recalled.

Jerry Carroll

To let people know he was crazy, Eddie Antar bought time on local radio. One night he heard disc jockey Jerry Carroll, known as Doctor Jerry, read one of his commercials with maniacal enthusiasm. Crazy Eddie was so impressed by Doctor Jerry's impersonation of a madman that he hired him to become his spokesman in a television advertising campaign that made history: the loudest, most grating, most hysterical, highest-pitched ads ever broadcast. There were dozens of variations of the same spot: Doctor Jerry began calmly, recounting the bargains—always "brand-name merchandise" sold at 30, 40, 50, 60 percent off the list price—and as he talked he became unhinged with discount frenzy, concluding the commercial by gesticulating rabidly towards the camera and ranting about the insanity of Crazy Eddie's prices.

With demented Doctor Jerry as its figurehead, Crazy Eddie expanded like crazy in the roaring 1980s, when sales of VCRs and answering machines skyrocketed. According to one former store manager, the success was based on bait-and-switch tactics. By 1985 there were forty-three Crazy Eddie stores in the Northeast, and Jerry Carroll had become, in *Forbes*'s words, "an advertising institution by appearing to require institutionalization." But the manic thrill didn't last. Crazy Eddie stores collapsed in a scandal-riddled heap in 1989 (sharehold-

ers accused Mr. Antar of engineering "what may be the largest securities fraud in history"), by which time Jerry Carroll had started his own advertising firm, called East Coast Media, for which he became the sane voice of St. John's University and Intel computer chips.

It was an inspired advertising formula while it lasted, and the campaign was so successful that other would-be pixilated stereo equipment merchandisers hired fast-talking loonies to go on TV and babble, too. But no one else captivated the viewing public like Crazy Eddie's man, Doctor Jerry, who clutched at the camera as if he wanted to strangle it. Many viewers assumed Doctor Jerry *was* Crazy Eddie. Dan Aykroyd based one of his best "Saturday Night Live" characters on the shrieking pitchman, and at one point a poll found that "insane" Jerry Carroll was more recognizable than New York City's mayor, Ed Koch.

CREDIT CARDS

"I felt I was worthless, absolute garbage. I locked myself in my bedroom, crouched in a corner, and seriously contemplated suicide." Jean Reilly pulled herself back from the brink when she found the courage to cut all her credit cards in half and to begin making payments to the twenty-eight different card issuers who were hounding her to pay for the thousands of dollars' worth of things she had charged. In a 1988 *People* magazine article that called her "a recovering addict, hooked not on heroin but plastic," Ms. Reilly described her rush towards emotional and financial ruin: a five-year spending spree in search of the good-

life highs experienced by buying designer clothes, eating in gourmet restaurants, and going on hot-air balloon vacations—all classic symptoms of credit card abuse. Finally, when her cards were tapped out, she lamented, "The American dream is no longer a reality for me."

No question: For some people, buying lots of wonderful things and extraordinary experiences *is* the American dream; and although credit cards are now a global phenomenon, their extravagant use was born and bred in the U.S.A. The thrill of acquisition they facilitate, and their power to indulge, *now*, and worry about the consequences at a more convenient time, have become qualities that the rest of the world surely considers to be as American as Cadillacs (low monthly payments) and Walt Disney World (American Express, Carte Blanche, Diners Club, Discover, enRoute, MasterCard, and Visa accepted). They are so much a part of daily life for all but underclass Americans that few who regularly use them consider the privilege they imply. (Advertising by credit card companies does frequently dwell on the worldwide respect and admiration that is tendered cardholders.) To brandish a credit card is to exercise authority: You get what you want by merely signing your name, never having to soil your hands touching the same money poor people touch.

What a capitalistic horror modern credit cards would seem to the Massachusetts dreamer who coined the term in 1888! Edward Bellamy, the utopian author of *Looking Backward*, envisaged America in the year 2000 as a cooperative commonwealth in which each citizen carried a piece of pasteboard with his "share of the annual product of the nation" inscribed on it. Cash was obsolete, as was gold; there were no monthly bills; and everyone got just what

he needed by merely presenting his card. Bellamy's visionary "credit card" made socialism work.

But that's not the way things happened when the first real credit cards were given out early in the century by such swank hotels as the Ritz and the Waldorf, as well as by Western Union, to notable patrons as a signal to the staff to give preferential service and prompt attention. Cards were strictly for VIPs, as was the Traveletter System of credit, begun in 1894, which allowed executives to charge lodging expenses. In 1922 Filene's department store of Boston issued three-by-five-inch cards to its choice clientele; and in 1924 General Petroleum of California issued a card to employees and select customers, who could use their "metal money" to buy gas and pay for repairs. In the late thirties, airlines and railroads introduced company charge cards, but it was not until after World War II that credit companies entered the picture and cards usable at different businesses were issued.

The use-it-everywhere concept was formulated by Frank McNamara, operator of a small loan company in New York, who one night in 1950 found himself short of cash when a restaurant check arrived. After the embarrassing incident, known in the credit card business as the First Supper, McNamara had an idea. He convinced twenty-eight New York night spots and restaurants to accept a card instead of cash, and also convinced them to tender him a fee for doing so! In return, he covered any expenses incurred at the restaurant by people who were members of the "Diners Club" to whom he sent out his cards. The next year, the Franklin National Bank of New York issued a card that worked the same way, but also listed the amount of funds available to the cardholder; in 1958 American Express joined the buy-now-pay-later game.

Ten years after its founding, the Diners Club issued a press release that succinctly explained the psychological reason for credit cards' burgeoning success: "To charge is to attain a status and this has been an age of status. The businessman is striving for success and to have automatic credit wherever one goes has become a symbol of success." In his book *Buy Now, Pay Later* (1961), Hillel Black further explained, "In a society where spending is becoming the ultimate value . . . only the needy carry cash."

"The credit card is the modern Lamp of Aladdin," declared Dr. Ernest Dichter of the Institute of Motivational Research in 1960. Dr. Dichter believed that the popularization of credit cards was a significant milestone in the transformation of the very character of America, from a puritanical culture to a hedonistic one. Simply put, "We are getting our pleasures, our purchases, our entertainment, before we've actually earned them." To Martin Meyer, author of *Credit Cardsmanship—How You Can Win Big in the Credit Card Game* (1971), the spread of credit cards was a downright patriotic turn of events, resulting in what he called "today's democracy of affluence." He wrote, "You want all the fine things that America can produce, and all the fine services that America can offer, and you just don't have the free cash with which to buy them." Credit cards to the rescue! Mr. Meyer compared them to electric power: "Take the system away and the nation's stores black out. But keep the power flowing and the nation prospers. And so do you—in continued employment, in higher wages, in more money with which to make more credit purchases and re-charge the economy to greater prosperity."

The bank card era began in earnest in 1965 with the Bank of America's Bank-Americard, which was backed by a consortium of banks able to exchange funds across the country, thus giving the card national appeal; the next year, Interbank, supported by a different group of banks, issued its first Interbank card. In 1967 Interbank changed its name to Master Charge (originally, the orange and tan one); and in 1977, because some banks around the world didn't want to be associated with anything called the Bank of *America*, Bank-Americard was renamed Visa (originally, the blue, white, and gold one).

By the sixties credit cards were being made of crisp, clean plastic instead of cumbersome metal or unsightly cardboard, which, like money, got frayed and dirty; and, until forbidden to do so by the Fair Credit Billing Act of 1974, banks mailed unsolicited cards to just about any adult with a name and post box. When self-pampering and indulgence became a way of life in the Me Decade, credit cards provided wondrous opportunities for people to gratify heretofore unattainable wishes, from buying high-tech stereo gear to traveling through twenty-one European countries in twenty days. The power of plastic had become a national obsession by 1973, when a California financial planner named Walter Cavanagh began amassing all the credit cards he could get, eventually obtaining the world's largest collection—over twelve hundred—and a million and a half dollars' worth of credit. "I can charge ice cream in Texas or a house on the East Coast," he boasted.

By the roaring eighties, nearly every American—not just preferred customers— had a credit card, so it became crucial once again to provide show-offs with a distinctive mark of their superior status. Gold cards and even more exclusive platinum cards, for which people pay additional yearly fees, provide their holders such privileges as medical assistance, legal referrals, and huge credit limits, as well as the recurrent excitement of impressing clerks, dinner guests, and bystanders when it comes time to pay a bill. The newest innovation in the credit card business is "Custom Mark" cards, issued by a bank card company but specially designed with the logo of a trade organization, fraternal group, charity, or product name on the card, so the user is reminded of his favorite thing whenever the card is used. Credit industry figures reveal that most people are delighted to pay interest rates well above those charged by generic cards if they can get a custom credit card decorated with endangered animals or Martin Luther King, Jr.'s or Elvis Presley's face.

Few people with credit cards don't abuse them. Surveys have shown that consumers spend 23 percent more when they use credit cards instead of paying cash; and credit card customers in restaurants eat twice as much. In some situations, such as renting a car or checking into a hotel, cash is no longer honored because it is only worth its face value. On the other hand, a credit card gives the recipient access to nearly limitless amounts of money from the user (if they trash their hotel room, damages can be billed to the card); and as for credit card users, they also get access to more money than they probably ought to have, plus all the honor and respect that money can buy.

DAVY CROCKETT

Davy Crockett claimed to have personally killed 105 grizzly bears in a span of nine months during the early 1820s, and to have shot, knifed, and wrestled to death more wildcats than he could count, but his accomplishments in animal mortality are nothing compared to the number of raccoons who gave up their lives in 1955 so American children could wear Davy Crockett caps made from their skins. The wholesale price of raccoon tails quadrupled (from two cents to eight apiece); trappers crowded the woods looking for more, and under a headline that read A CRISIS IN COONSKIN, *Life* magazine warned that the situation had come to a question of "which will be exhausted first: the supply of raccoons or the parents who have to buy the caps."

The catalyst for the coonskin craze was "Disneyland" (the television program),

Davy Crockett
Hurls a Comet across
The Pages of History

which in December 1954, its first season on the air, broadcast the original episode of a three-part show about Davy Crockett —arguably, the prototypical television miniseries. "Davy Crockett, Indian Fighter," starring Fess Parker wearing buckskin duds and a cap made out of a dead raccoon, complete with tail dangling down the back, was followed in January by "Davy Crockett Goes to Congress" and in February by "Davy Crockett at the Alamo"; and even though Davy died at the Alamo, the series was so successful that Disney made two more episodes to run the next season, "Davy Crockett's Keelboat Race" and "Davy Crockett and the River Pirates."

The homespun he-man became a fad of truly unprecedented dimensions. Slinky and Silly Putty, Hopalong Cassidy and Howdy Doody had already shown that the postwar generation of kids had a voracious hunger for fun and games; but no one, not even Walt Disney, anticipated a marketing phenomenon on the scale of Davy Crockett, who captivated American boys—and girls —like no one and nothing in history before him. In his wake there would be other, even bigger cash-producing comets, from Hula Hoops and the Beatles to Bart Simpson and Teenage Mutant Ninja Turtles, but Davy Crockett was the first demonstration of the staggering buying power that could be wielded by children when they were whipped into a frenzy of gotta-have-it-now avidity. With preternatural foresight, financial columnist Sylvia Porter noted the buying craze and worried that "we're creating a nation of spenders from infancy."

Some three thousand different Davy Crockett souvenirs were eventually produced, including toy flintlock rifles and plastic powder horns (which some children filled with their mother's face powder), bath towels "the kids will beg to take a bath with" (according to advertisements), and lunch boxes and girls' panties imprinted with Fess Parker's face. By April 1955 there were sixteen different versions of the TV show's theme song on record, as well as a "Davy Crockett Mambo" and a cautionary ballad by Fess Parker and Buddy Ebsen, who played his sidekick in the series, called "Be Sure You're Right," which they re-

corded in response to a schoolteacher's plea for something that would help calm her students down from their Davy Crockett dementia. Coonskin caps, with snap-on tails, were the most conspicuous symbol of kids' infatuation; when fresh pelts ran out, manufacturers started buying up all the used raccoon coats they could find and cutting them up to make caps; and in major American cities in the spring of '55 it was not uncommon for every clothing store to be completely sold out.

Davy Crockett had been a part of American folklore since his death in 1836. Even when he was alive, Crockett cultivated his image as a backwoods ace, spinning tall tales of his own derring-do fighting grizzly bears and Creek Indians while serving as a scout for Andrew Jackson, and bragging that he could "grin like a hyena until the bark would curl off a gum log." Crockett contended he didn't even have to kill a bear if he didn't want to; he could just scare it away by baring his teeth. All this self-promotion helped define a new kind of American hero: the frontier fighter who was crafty, rugged, outspoken, and no one's fool —able to wrestle any beast to the ground and drink any man under the table. When he ran for Congress in 1827, he boasted to his constituents-to-be, "They accuse me of being a drunkard. It's a lie, for whisky can't make me drunk."

When America became infatuated with Davy Crockett in 1955, Crockett's hillbilly manner provided antirural intellectuals some delicious material for debunking the "King of the Wild Frontier" (as he was called in the TV show's theme song). John Fischer of *Harper's* tried to convince readers that "Davy Crockett was never king of anything, except maybe the Tennessee Tall Tales and Bourbon Samplers' Association," describing him as "a juvenile delinquent who ran away from home at the age of thirteen," and saying that "when he claimed that he had shot 105 bear in nine months, his fellow tipplers refused to believe a word of it on the sensible ground that Davy couldn't count that high." In the New York *Post* Murray Kempton said Crockett was a man "who would bear any hardship to escape a routine day's work"; and other cynics contended that it was Crockett himself, in his fabulous (and fabricated) autobiography, as well as some highly fictionalized posthumous accounts, known as Davy Crockett *Almanac*s, published in the 1840s and 1850s, that had puffed up a drunken, philandering, cowardly absentee congressman into a national hero.

Naturally Disney smoothed all the rough edges off its own version of Davy Crockett and put him on a pedestal. As portrayed by six-foot-five Fess Parker, his buckskin clothes were clean, as were his speech and manners; and unlike the real Davy, he didn't tell the citizens of Tennessee to go to hell when he lost his last run for Congress. In the TV show he went to help defend the Alamo for the sake of freedom, but some historians have suggested that he and the dozen men who accompanied him from Tennessee came looking for cheap land and

the opportunity to get rich quick in Texas. Disney also perpetuated the myth that Davy died in battle in the baptistry of the Alamo after killing dozens of Mexican attackers. In fact, he was one of only seven men who survived the fight. He was brought to General Santa Anna, who had him tortured (eyewitness accounts say Davy didn't so much as complain), then shot.

The Davy Crockett fad was dead by the end of 1955, when Davy Crockett T-shirts, which had been selling for $1.29 in the spring, were reduced to thirty-nine cents for quick clearance, and suddenly there was a surplus of coonskin caps in every store. "Kids are more fickle than women," grieved the National Retail Dry Goods Association. However, just when raccoons might have been thinking it was safe to wander carefree in the woods again, another coonskin craze took off. In 1957, American women went wild for vintage raccoon coats from the 1920s. When it was discovered that most of the old coats—an estimated two million —had been cut up and made into Davy Crockett caps two years earlier, the hunt for fresh skins was on once again. "There are still plenty of raccoons to be trapped," *Life* announced in September.

CUISINART

There was nothing intrinsically revolutionary about the Cuisinart food processor when Carl Sontheimer, a fifty-three-year-old inventor of electronic gizmos and a passionate amateur cook, brought it to the American market at the Housewares Show in Chicago in 1973. It sliced, it diced, it pureed just like dozens of

Chop-O-Matics, Veg-O-Matics, and Wonda-Graters that had beguiled cooks since the 1930s. But it did all those things more efficiently than its forebears, and furthermore, it had the weight, pedigree, and price of a professional cooking apparatus. Prior to the Cuisinart, most "miracle" kitchen appliances were looked upon by gourmets as

rather silly American toys—more befitting the gadgetry of a *Popular Mechanics* type of kitchen tinkerer than the essential *batterie de cuisine* of a serious gastronome.

Gourmet magazine proclaimed the Cuisinart "phenomenal," describing not only all the impressive recipes it facilitated but also its admirable lineage. It had been invented in France in 1963 by Pierre Verdun and sold strictly to professional French chefs as the Robot-Coupe. Carl Sontheimer had discovered it at a French cookery show in 1971 while he was looking around for a new career (he was considering high-tech burglar alarms). He signed a distribution deal with Robot-Coupe and adapted their machine for home use, but in no way diminished its formidable presence on a kitchen counter. His original Cuisinart food processor weighed a hefty twelve pounds and came with six or eight different blades that did the work of dozens of tools and took the drudgery out of everything from kneading dough to tearing leaves of lettuce. It took some time to learn to use, and was an effort to clean, and

it was best suited to preparing large quantities of difficult-to-mix foodstuffs (gazpacho, pureed vegetables) rather than such trivial and rudimentary things as tuna salad or pancake batter. It was a solid, serious machine with the priceless cachet of genuine French cuisine, which was still considered by most 1970s gourmets to be the last word in sophistication.

The timing of its appearance in the American marketplace could not have been more perfect. Just as *Gourmet* was singing its praises and Craig Claiborne was declaring it the greatest food invention since toothpicks, a new subculture was taking shape in America: the foodies. Foodies were different from most earlier gourmets, for whom an appreciation of gastronomy was simply one of life's many sensual pleasures, along with art, music, and travel. Foodies just about worshiped food. They made chefs into celebrities. They evaluated restaurants as seriously as critics appraised art. They doted over exotic ingredients and arcane recipes from around America and the world. And in their homes and apartments they constructed extravagant kitchens that were temples to their passion. Nothing served so well as the altar in a foodie's kitchen temple than a massive Cuisinart.

In the first few years of its existence, owning a Cuisinart was a sign of serious culinary intention. Unlike a microwave oven (p. 316), which signaled sloth, or an electric knife, which only meant you were a sucker for any kind of contraption, a Cuisinart was the emblem of someone who cooked the way the men in white toques cooked: seriously, in big batches. By Christmas, 1975, the demand for Cuisinarts was so high that department stores and gourmet shops (the only places you could buy one) were selling empty Cuisinart boxes—to be redeemed for a machine as soon as the factories, in France and Japan, could produce enough of them. The Cuisinart's efficiency and the surgical sharpness of its blades even inspired a small branch of gastronomic sick humor, e.g.: What's green and goes a hundred miles an hour? A frog in a Cuisinart.

The rage for fancy home cooking soon spread beyond hard-core foodies. In fact, for a while starting in the late 1970s, serious gastronomy was such a big social trend that professional-looking kitchens became one of the era's great interior-decor status symbols, the way high-tech recreation rooms had been a few years earlier. Even people who could barely boil an egg installed great Viking ranges and batteries of copper bowls and Sub-Zero refrigerators to show that they were at the vanguard of chic; and many cooks who seldom put together anything more complicated than a grilled cheese sandwich bought a Cuisinart because it had begun to seem as essential to modern life as an electric can opener. And Cuisinart—a brand name so dominant that it assumed generic meaning in most people's minds—turned into a preeminent symbol of early-1980s conspicuous consumerism, right up there with such other extravagant totems of success as BMW and Gucci.

Soon Cuisinart had competition from other, cheaper food processors, but it held its status by maintaining its position as the priciest and best-made food processor of all. In fact, when other companies cut prices and sold their imitation Cuisinarts at K-Mart, Cuisinart countered by introducing more deluxe and more expensive models, including one that cost six hundred dollars and was named by *Forbes* "the ultimate kitchen status symbol." This was a marketing strategy that could succeed only in the high-flying, free-spending early 1980s. In 1985, when Sunbeam came out with a sixty-dollar miniature food processor called

Oskar (an acronym for Outstanding Superior Kitchen All-Rounder), Carl Sontheimer sneered at it as a gimmick, a "gumball machine." But the tide had turned: Two million Oskars were sold the first two years it was on the market; and since then Presto has come out with the fabulously successful Salad Shooter, and nearly a dozen other companies are now marketing small, cheap appliances that can do just about anything a Cuisinart can do. In 1989 Cuisinarts, Inc. filed for bankruptcy.

Food processors, large and small, are a familiar presence in many kitchens (although surveys have shown that well over half of them do nothing but gather dust). Whatever its actual value to a home cook, the food processor's role as the dominant symbol of yuppie food fetishism has left it with a slightly embarrassing reputation as a sign of profligacy and self-indulgence, especially now that old-fashioned values and traditional cooking skills are back in fashion. In his book *Simple Cooking* (1987), John Thorne mused about the "mindless, frantic gnawing" of the blades of a food processor, which for him was only a sign of people's alienation from their natural appetites and from the hands-on pleasures of cutting, slicing, and grating food. Similarly, Laurie Colwin, in her book *Home Cooking* (1988), celebrated what she called the "low-tech" kitchen life and the honest pleasures of knives, a grater, a blender, a strainer, and a wooden pestle. "Most things are frills," she wrote about such appliances as the microwave oven and the food processor. "It is perfectly possible to cook well with very little. Most of the world cooks over fire without any gadgets at all."

"DALLAS"

The most successful prime-time soap opera in TV history, "Dallas" wallowed in the villainy of the filthy rich. When J. R. Ewing (Larry Hagman), its central character, was shot at the end of the 1979–80 season, curiosity about who did it made "Who Shot J.R.?," the fifth episode of the subsequent season, the highest-rated show in television history, until it was beaten by the last episode of "M*A*S*H" (see p. 6) in 1983. (The answer to this burning national question was such a precious secret—in fact, the producers themselves didn't know who shot J.R. when they scripted the assassination attempt—that five alternate endings were actually put on film, thus preventing any of the actors or crew from revealing the truth, and the chosen one was

**Linda Gray (Sue Ellen Ewing)
and Larry Hagman (John Ross Ewing)**

delivered to CBS on the morning of the broadcast, November 21.) "Oil, love, lust, and greed" are the qualities that *Soap Opera Digest* singled out to explain what made "Dallas" such a charismatic phenomenon and J. R. Ewing such a culture hero in America as well as nearly every civilized nation on earth . . . with the conspicuous exception of Japan, for whom he was simply too much a cheater and a maverick to be admired.

You could probably chart the adoration of "Dallas," which hit its peak when three out of four television viewers watched "Who Shot J.R.?" and stayed high through the mid-1980s, exactly parallel to a graph of Reagan-era infatuation with big business and billionaires. (See also "Donald Trump," p. 529.) Created by David Jacobs as a five-week pilot in the spring of 1978, the show returned on the fall schedule, mushroomed in popularity, and spanned the next decade. By the time it went off the air in 1991, America's exhilaration with the trappings of material success was fading fast. "Is this the end for TV's prime time soaps?" *TV Guide* wondered at the beginning of the 1987–88 season, calling it "an anti–soap opera, less about emotional needs than corporate needs" and noting that "The Cosby Show," a quiet paean to home and humanity (see p. 106), had knocked "Dallas" and all its high-finance, glitz-and-glitter progeny out of the Nielsen top ten.

It was known not merely for its episode-to-episode continuing story line but for notorious season-to-season cliffhangers. The last show in the spring always ended with a huge, unsettled question, the answer to which was revealed only in the fall. At the end of the 1978–79 season, J. R. Ewing's wife, Sue Ellen (Linda Gray), a pregnant alcoholic, escaped from the sanitarium to which J.R. had committed her and drove herself right into a car crash: Would she survive? After "Who Shot J.R.?" (it was Sue Ellen's younger sister, Kristin [Mary Crosby], who was carrying J.R.'s baby), audiences were left at the end of subsequent seasons wondering if Cliff (J.R.'s sister-in-law's older brother [Ken Kercheval]) had really committed suicide; if the Ewings would escape their burning mansion, Southfork; whose body was floating in the Southfork swimming pool; and—once again—who shot J.R., in 1984. (This time, it was revealed in the fall that it wasn't really J.R. who had been shot in the previous season's climax; it was his younger brother Bobby [Patrick Duffy], who happened to be sitting in J.R.'s chair, and he had only been wounded.)

The original basic tension of "Dallas" came from the rivalry between the Ewings and the Barneses (clan patriarchs Jock Ewing and Digger Barnes had once been partners in the oil fields), which was ignited when young Bobby Ewing married Pam Barnes (Victoria Principal) in the original five-week pilot run of the show. But aside from the murderous family feud, the real fun came from watching the supremely dysfunctional interaction among the Ewings themselves. J.R. was one of television's most exquisitely contemptible philanderers, who drove his wife to drink and to her own parade of paramours; and when he wasn't playing around (and sometimes when he was), he was busy scheming to screw his own brothers both personally and in business, double-cross his friends, and lock up his wife in a mental institution. And he always did it with a twinkle in his eye and a smug smile. Slick as the oil that made him rich, J.R. was a character audiences just loved to hate; and in some truly perverse

way, he was a role model for an era in which money lust, corporate greed, and the will to win at any cost were celebrated ingredients of real-life success.

In retrospect "Dallas" made its fatal miscalculation at the start of the 1986–87 season. Before this, it seemed the show's writers could do no wrong. No treachery was too heinous, no plot twist too convoluted to shake audiences from their devotion to the tube on Friday night (people planned dinner parties around it). But a sacred trust was broken when, in the first show of the season, Bobby Ewing turned up whistling in the shower. At the end of the 1984–85 season, he had been killed off (while saving his wife from a hit-and-run accident) because Patrick Duffy wanted to leave the show. So all through the 1985–86 season, the characters in "Dallas" behaved as if he was dead. J.R. shed great crocodile tears at his funeral. But ratings slipped; Duffy was convinced to return to the show; and in the fall of 1986, when Pam found him in the shower, she realized, much to her—and the audience's—amazement, that the 1985–86 season had all been a dream. "The return of Bobby Ewing from the grave to the shower damaged the credibility of prime time soaps," said Los Angeles *Herald-Examiner* TV critic Rick DuBrow. "Audiences really distrusted cliffhangers after that. It was just so absurd that they felt they were being had."

But it wasn't just the plot manipulations and overhyped suspense that were killing off "Dallas" audiences. Favorite cast members were leaving: The year after Bobby was resuscitated, Victoria Principal exited the show (for good); and in 1989 Linda Gray left, too. By the last season, Larry Hagman and Ken Kercheval were the only performers still remaining from the beginning. And beyond these logistical problems, "Dallas" had become thematically moribund. A big, self-indulgent soap opera about the wonderment of cash and commerce had begun to look like an unpleasant relic of a selfish time in American history that an awful lot of TV viewers really wanted to forget. When

"Dallas" finally went off the air, number forty-three in the ratings, the top-ranked show was "Roseanne"—a comedy about a working-class family who have a hard time making ends meet.

DAYTIME TALK SHOWS:
Phil, Oprah, Sally, and Geraldo

"What we do," Phil Donahue once said, "is provide on daytime TV a relief from the soaps and game shows." It may be quite a stretch for those who delight in the daily doings of Phil, Oprah, Sally, or Geraldo (all so familiar that first names only suffice) to think of what America's Big Four daytime talk show hosts do that's a "relief" from the make-believe melodrama of the soaps or the inanity of game shows. Yes, we'll agree that they are a relief in the sense that it is always nice to see people whose problems are worse than yours; and more often than not the guests on these shows have problems you and I won't likely be worrying about soon, such

as "Women in Love with Serial Killers" and "Custody Battle over Frozen Sperm." But does it really make sense to think of shows about "Teenage Strippers and Their Mothers" (Phil, 12/16/91), "Sisters Abused by Family Members" (Sally, 12/11/91), "Mothers and Fathers Who Kill" (Oprah, 1/15/92), or "Unspeakable Murders" (Geraldo, 12/4/91) as a *relief* for any human being trying to maintain sanity in this world? To put it plainly, most of the programming on these talk shows is, by any humanistic standard, very, very upsetting. One could even argue that what they do is almost exactly what the soaps and game shows do—tell lurid melodramas and rouse studio audiences (as well as viewers) to a state of frenzy—but they do it even more effectively because they are *real*.

This kind of reality programming—showing actual people having unscripted discussions—has been part of TV since its beginnings; and, of course, such pillars of programming as "The Tonight Show" and "Meet the Press" are based mostly on the fine arts of conversation and interrogation. From gentle-tempered Mike Douglas and jolly Merv Griffin, to gossipy Virginia Graham and warm-hearted Dinah Shore, to earnest intellectual David Susskind, to such ferocious verbal warriors as Joe Pyne and Alan Burke (see "Tabloid TV," p. 501), television has always had a surfeit of extempore chatter; but when Phil Donahue went national in 1970, it was the beginning of a new era in talk shows. Donahue was broadcast during the day, to an audience that was overwhelmingly housewives (about 90 percent women)—a programming niche generally owned by either the soaps or the game shows, or by totally lighthearted (and usually featherbrained) talk shows that dealt with issues no more serious than how to make a tuna noodle casserole or new techniques in leg waxing.

Phil Donahue was different because he dealt with topics that were philosophical, intellectual, political, controversial, and almost always *important*. This, of course, is what he meant when he said his show was a relief from ordinary daytime programming. Women at home who yearned for intellectual stimulation and challenge could turn to Phil and find it. " 'I'm thirty-four years old and stagnating,' " Phil imagined his typical viewer saying to herself. "In Dayton and Des Moines and San Diego [they] are wondering sadly, 'Hey, wait a minute, do I have to spend the rest of my life putting Downy in the rinse cycle?' " Gary Deeb, TV critic for the Chicago *Tribune*, once wrote of Phil, "His daily program reduces the Mervs and Mikes and Dinahs to the level of Tupperware parties." Phil wasn't just the housewife's friend; he was her teacher, guide, and sometimes her gadfly. Writing in *Esquire*, William Brashler observed, "More women are educated—about sex, morals, trends, and personalities—by Donahue than by any other person—man or woman —in the land."

Phil Donahue's first guest when he went on the air with a local television show in Dayton, Ohio, in 1967 was chosen because Phil knew she would generate controversy among his studio audience (and ratings from viewers at home): Madalyn Murray O'Hair, the atheist who got prayer kicked out of public schools. She was followed in a procession of issue-oriented shows by the likes of Ralph Nader, Gloria Steinem, Betty Ford (talking about her addictions), Nazis and Ku Klux Klansmen, black separatists, homosexual priests, lesbian nuns, and widows whose husbands had committed suicide. Not everything Phil did, even in the beginning, was socially or politically consequential. He hosted astrologers and pet trainers; celebrities hawking their latest movie, book, or record; Frederick of Hollywood; Siamese twins attached at the head; and an eight-foot-tall woman. But even with the oddest people and most peripheral topics, Phil always seemed to probe deeper than sensationalism. What did it feel like, he asked the fourteen-hundred-pound twin sisters, to go shopping and find nothing that fits?

Erma Bombeck explained his appeal: "He's every wife's replacement for the husband who doesn't talk to her. They've always got Phil who will listen and take them seriously." Phil really did bring his viewers into the action. Unlike nearly all prior talk shows, which presented a tableau of people having a discussion that we in TV Land were privileged to observe, Phil seemed to depend on his audience to keep the show lively. Using the (then novel) phone-in technique he had developed on his mid-1960s Dayton radio show, "Conversation Piece," he invited viewers to place calls to his guests, ask questions, and offer their own observations about the topic at hand. And he raced among the studio audience wielding his microphone with a purposefulness and curiosity that truly made people feel as if they were a necessary part of Phil's encounter group, not just detached observers.

Phil cares about all issues, but women's issues especially. (He is an active feminist and member of the National Organization for Women.) And in the early 1970s, as the women's movement grew and his syndicated show spread to markets throughout the country, he became (along with Alan Alda [see p. 6]) one of the foremost symbols of what was being called "the new male." The new male wasn't macho; he wasn't afraid to show his emotions; he liked to talk about his feelings and to share a whole lot more than just sex with women. Phil was not himself emotionally incontinent (Jack Paar was TV's most conspicuous crybaby; and even Geraldo Rivera, in his early days, shed more tears than Phil ever did), but as the conductor of his hour-long show, he was a master at bringing out other people's emotions and baring, if not his soul, then at least his very sincere thoughts. His telegenic sensibility always mined feelings out of issues. First Lady Rosalynn Carter was practically in tears when he put her on the spot about her husband's firing of feminist Bella Abzug from the National Advisory Committee for Women; and he got nearly the whole audience to weep when he interviewed Fletcher and Debbie Miller, the adoptive parents who were ordered by a court to give away their twenty-two-month-old daughter.

In another life, Phil might have been a doctor. In the course of hosting countless shows about every medical and psychological condition known to man, he has become so up-to-date with biotechnical terms that sometimes his guests—even Tula, the beautiful British sex change—have no idea what he is talking about when he discusses the details of their medical circumstances. Beyond women's issues and medical conditions, Phil's strong suit is politics, and he takes much pleasure in sharing his stage with Russian spokesman Vladimir Pozner,

who, like Phil, is a great champion of understanding through dialogue. In recent years Phil has done some notoriously lewd shows —strippers with huge breasts, "Lesbo À Go-Go," women's fashions for men (that's the one on which he wore a skirt)—but he does them with an almost engaging grin-and-bear-it attitude. "Hey, it's out there," he says, "so it should be talked about." But beneath this disingenuous apology there is a good Catholic boy who knows he's being naughty and would very much like to be more high-minded than his salacious competition.

Phil was unchallenged king of issue-oriented daytime talk shows until 1986, when Oprah Winfrey licked him. "The Oprah Winfrey Show," which spun out of "AM Chicago," had twice as many viewers as Phil within months of its going into syndication. Oprah wasn't so much a teacher or a provocateur as Phil had been when he started. If Phil's gift was to make almost anything seem important, Oprah's was to make everything personal. She became daytime TV's open-armed friend, who frequently (in the beginning, especially) cried right along with her guests, hugged members of the audience, and could be counted on, at moments of great excitement, to slip into her down-home Afro-American patois for a disarming, "Girl, do tell!" Audiences have learned everything there is to know about Oprah: about her relationship with boyfriend Stedman Graham; about how she was sexually abused as a child; about her famous on-the-air diet (at the conclusion of which she wheeled a wagon loaded with sixty-seven pounds of animal fat onto the stage) and how she put the weight right back on; about her Elvis-sized generosity towards her best friend, Gayle King, and her staff. She even created a stunning show that personalized racial tension when she did an on-location broadcast from all-white Forsyth County, Georgia, during which a member of the Committee to Keep Forsyth County White actually said the word "nigger" to her.

Oprah's concern with making her show very personal brought a new level of what might charitably be called intimacy to the talk show formula. Whereas Phil had done plenty of programs about matters of private behavior and sexual identity, they almost always related to public issues (should priests marry?). When Oprah plumbed similar material, she seemed less interested in the greater sociological picture than in the cleansing act of *sharing* for its own sake. Her approach not only got great ratings, it established intimacy as one of the fundamental tenets of daytime talk. The ability to share and reveal one's heart and soul—and on some occasions, such as her buck-naked panel of nudists, one's body—has always been Oprah's Holy Grail. On her stage, being honest and open is set forth as one of life's greatest achievements (and as a solution to most of life's problems), and some of her most admired shows have featured people talking candidly (and without prurience) about their own personal experiences with adultery, impotence, the pain of aging, racism, and infertility.

Frequently, though, the intimacy of "Oprah" tends to be more immodest than it is informative. "Does Sexual Size Matter?" an early program wondered; when she did one called "Ask the Porn Stars," she inquired of one of her guests, "Don't you ever get sore?"; when she interviewed a woman who had had sex with seven different priests, she asked, "What did you do when the first one pulled his pants down?"; and on a show about sex surrogates, she had one woman describe—in gynecological detail—how the surrogate had used his finger to bring her to the first orgasm she had ever had. Oprah pioneered the concept of doing shows without apparent shame or embarrassment with panels of people who all share one humiliating or eccentric quality: high school nerds, conceited men, women who have had affairs with their spouses' siblings, men addicted to masturbation. Such highly focused themes have since become popular among all the major daytime talk shows.

"I am Betty Crocker," Sally Jessy Raphael once said to describe her on-the-air personality. And it's true: She is a mature, not-quite-matronly woman who seems reasonable, almost as square as Dear Abby, but who happens to find herself surrounded by an astonishing number of freaks and weirdos. Sally's world is one of grandma strippers, nude evangelists, satanic murderers, and flight attendants who are members of the "Mile High Club" (the entrance requirement for which is to have had sex on a commercial airline flight). When we wrote *The Encyclopedia of Bad Taste* back in 1990, it was Sally who had us on her show —for a full hour devoted to Elvis impersonators, tacky souvenirs, mile-high bouffants, and a fashion show of the most hideous clothing of the last quarter-century.

"We've been accused of showing women who used to be men, of focusing on nudists and terrorists and wives who shot their husbands," Sally's producer, Burt Dubrow, told *Newsweek*. "But I don't agree. We just do subjects we feel will compel people to watch." Where Phil or Oprah might be quick to throw up their hands and go toe-to-toe with a really obnoxious guest, Sally is almost always respectful (with the notable exception of the time African-American writer Shaharazade Ali said white people shouldn't be allowed to adopt black babies, which made Sally fume). She speaks in a measured tone (derived from her earlier work on radio), and she tries, really tries, to understand all the strange things that come her way. This explains the appropriateness of her trademark big red glasses, which always cause her to look a little bemused. But make no mistake: Sally is in control; her soft manner is just a way of bringing people out. And she always takes extra care when there are children on her panel of guests, sometimes asking that they be escorted off the stage when something like cannibalism or ritual dismemberment is about to be discussed.

When Geraldo Rivera came to the daytime talk show format in 1987 after a series of wildly successful syndicated TV specials (see "Tabloid TV," p. 501), he pushed the envelope of bad taste beyond what any of his competitors had dared do. He fomented a major fistfight on a 1988 show about "Teen Hatemongers" that resulted in his getting a broken nose, courtesy of the White Aryan Resistance; and he brought his exclamatory sensibility to shows that ripped the lid off doctors who abuse their patients, explored the world of women boxers, exposed the cover-up at Chappaquiddick, told the truth about teen sex, and took viewers inside a topless donut shop in Florida. There seemed to be no limit to what Geraldo would do; but then in 1990 he told *TV Guide* that he was going to become more sober in his selection of themes, explaining, "I'm embarrassing myself." The new, chaste Geraldo has covered such topics as cannibal murders, how modern groupies deal with the threat of AIDS, and how much Ted Kennedy drank the night William Kennedy Smith allegedly committed rape.

A former lawyer, Geraldo can sometimes cross-examine guests as if they were unfriendly witnesses; but no one, not even Oprah, gets as sympathetic as he does to real underdogs, or as involved in subjects that really move him. When doing a show that explored what it was like to be overweight, he hung sixty pounds of sandbags all over himself and even had prosthetic fat cheeks added to his face so he could feel the burden of obesity. He has frequently dressed to suit the subject of the day, giving up his usual dapper suit and tie for a turtleneck if a guest is a hip individual, rolled-up sleeves for some blue-collar subjects, and a tight-fitting T-shirt if male sex appeal is the issue. The consummate professional, he sometimes is so moved he is rendered speechless. Last year before he showed a home videotape made by a teenager preparing to commit suicide, he tried to warn viewers that what they were about to see was mighty grim; but midway through his injunction, he choked up and looked with pleading eyes into the camera, silenced for a moment before he could say "Roll it."

With four major talk shows gobbling up twenty topics every week, and perhaps a dozen other, lesser-known nationally syndicated shows in need of interesting things to talk about, one has to wonder if a time will soon come when absolutely everything has been discussed. Already some of the shows have been stung by a serious shortage of good guests. Alex McNeil reported in *Total Television* that one man who appeared on "Sally Jessy Raphael" as an impotent husband was caught moonlighting on "Geraldo" as a middle-aged virgin, and an individual on an "Oprah" panel of "Women Who Hate Sex" had also made an appearance on Sally's show as a sex-for-hire surrogate.

JAMES DEAN

He was beautiful, he was gifted, and he was young. His career lasted less than five years, and he starred in only three movies—*East of Eden, Rebel Without a Cause,* and *Giant*—and when he crashed and died in a speeding car at age twenty-four, on September 30, 1955, he wasn't very famous. James Dean has since gone on to become one of the gods of popular culture.

Mostly he is known for his attitude. Sullen, painfully vulnerable, tormented by a world that offended him and also by internal desolation, he smoldered as an actor with such heat that the plots of his movies seemed to melt into nothingness around him. Not only in the movies but in nearly every photograph taken of him off the set, candids as well as studio shots, he radiated anguish and impudence. He was tough but tender, brooding but clownish, and defiantly sloppy in looks and behavior—second only to Marlon Brando in his fame as a mumbler. Most striking of all was the way this lonesome midwestern farm boy, whose mother died when he was nine and who had been raised by an aunt and uncle, seemed to pity and loathe himself. (His coroner noted a "constellation of keratoid scars" on his torso, acquired in the days when he was known as "the Human Ashtray" in East Hollywood's best-known leather bar.)

He did not originate the pose of the doomed misfit. James Dean's reputation as an insolent angel was built on an image that was already a teen paradigm in the early 1950s, developed by untold numbers of anonymous hoods as well as by a host of young New York "Method actors" and even by Tony Curtis as an Amboy Duke in the gang film *City Across the River* (1949). But it was Dean, better than anybody else, who

Rebel without a cause

honed that image into a timeless icon of swaggering yet somehow sympathetic impertinence. In jeans and white T-shirt, with his long hair fashioned into an audacious wave (but always unkempt), a cigarette dangling from his mouth, and a chip precariously perched on his shoulder, he epitomized youthful unruliness so absolutely that generations of angry teens (and older mavericks) in America, England, Japan, and around the world have mimicked the James Dean style even if they don't know who James Dean was.

He was famous for not fitting in. He arrived at fancy dinner parties wearing a rumpled sweatshirt. He once walked through the lobby of a grand hotel with long pieces of breakfast pastries dangling from his nostrils. Asked why he hadn't passed his army physical, he explained, "I kissed the medic."

When starlet Pier Angeli, with whom he was supposedly smitten, got married to Vic Damone, he sat outside the church on his motorcycle, gunning the engine to drown out the sound of the wedding bells. "In New York [where he began his career as an actor] his outré behavior had been cute," wrote Warren Newton Beath in *The Death of James Dean*. But in Hollywood "it was said that he had graduated from method school obnoxiousness to exhibitionism."

Most Hollywood stars respectfully kowtowed to gossip columnist Hedda Hopper, who could make or break their careers. In her memoir, *The Whole Truth and Nothing But*, she described her first impression of Dean, at the Warner Bros. commissary:

> The latest genius sauntered in, dressed like a bum, and slouched down in silence at a table away from mine. He hooked another chair with his toe, dragged it close enough to put his feet up, while he watched me from the corner of his eye. Then he stood up to inspect the framed photographs of Warner stars that covered the wall by his head. He chose one of them [Humphrey Bogart], spat in its eye, wiped off his spittle with a handkerchief, then like a ravenous hyena, started to gulp the food that had been served him.

Hedda wrote a column condemning James Dean as "another dirty shirttail actor" from New York (she already loathed Marlon Brando), but when she beheld his work in *East of Eden*, she was converted. "I couldn't remember ever having seen a young man with such power," she wrote; and the next time she interviewed him, at her home, James Dean told her that he had purposely acted like a slob to see if she had guts enough to write the truth about him. This made Hedda love him even more. And when he spontaneously did the "To be or not to be" soliloquy from *Hamlet* for her, standing on the rug in her living room and smoking a cigarette, she became his champion forever. When he died, she said, "I loved that boy and I always will," and she begged the Motion Picture Academy to award him a special, extra-large granite Oscar to serve as his headstone. The Academy refused.

James Dean ascended into teenage Valhalla almost as soon as he was buried. Only one of his movies *(East of Eden)* had been released. The second, *Rebel Without a Cause*, premiered three days after his car wreck. The coincidence was uncanny. As subscribers to the *Daily Press* in Paso Robles, California (where the crash had occurred), were reading about the "speed-loving young man" who had been killed that weekend in "one of the most terrific crashes of two cars in the county's record," James Dean, playing a speed-loving juvenile delinquent, was drag-racing with other teens on movie screens across the country. *Rebel Without a Cause* was quintessential James Dean; it gave him the opportunity to fully exhibit his hot blood as well as a futile yearning for tenderness (which female fans in particular craved to give him). The combination of his screen charisma and his violent death was potent; and what followed was, in Kenneth Anger's words, "the greatest wave of posthumous worship in Hollywood history."

A year after James Dean died, he was being sent eight thousand fan letters a week. At the premiere of *Giant*, when he first appeared on the screen, one girl stood up in the audience and cried, "Come back, Jimmy, I love you. We're waiting for you!" *I, James Dean*, a book written in the first person, describing his life, death, and afterlife, became a bestseller. *James Dean Returns!*, supposedly dictated to a dime-store sales clerk by the undead Dean, announced, "I am not dead. Those who believe I am not dead are right." There were tribute records and special television showings of some of the early video dramas he had acted in; and *Photoplay* readers voted him number one in the actor popularity poll—the first time a dead person had ever taken top honors. There were reports of some young fans so disconsolate about losing him that they committed suicide, leaving behind notes explaining that Jimmy was calling them. Dozens of fans began to make regular pilgrimages to Griffith Planetarium (one of the key scenes in *Rebel Without a Cause* had been filmed there), where they wandered aimlessly and called out his name; and some gathered at the Warner Bros. gate, certain they would spot James Dean alive—although horribly disfigured by the accident—if they waited there long enough. Since 1955 his gravestone in Fairmont, Indiana, has been replaced many times because souvenir hunters keep chipping away pieces of it for luck. On Highway 46, where the fatal accident occurred, a multimillionaire real estate tycoon from Japan named Seita Onishi erected a chrome cenotaph in 1981, followed by two tablets, a bronze fallen sparrow, and a thirty-six-foot-tall limestone bust. Today, in the parking lot of the Jack Ranch Cafe at the junction of routes 46 and 41, there is a stainless steel monument on which Dean is honored with quotations from Gide and Saint-Exupery.

The weirdest thing that happened after James Dean died was the time he walked into Googie's Coffee Shop. Just weeks after the crash, swathed in bandages, with his familiar mussed hair sticking out from the top of the gauze and horn-rimmed glasses planted where his face would be, he limped into the cafe, which had been a favorite haunt of his when he was alive. Actually, it turned out that the walking accident victim wasn't really James Dean. It was just a young kid who had been dressed to look like a bandaged Dean by one of Dean's former friends, Vampira—the tall, voluptuous, raven-haired ghoul who hosted horror movies late Saturday nights on a Los Angeles television station. Vampira thought it would be a funny stunt to make James Dean return from the grave. Dean would have enjoyed it, certainly, because one of the things the two of them had shared when he was alive was a delight in the macabre.

James Dean loved death. Many Dean cultists who have gone to scour the crash site and have pored over police photos and highway patrol reports are convinced he didn't even apply the brakes when he saw the calamity begin to happen (an oncoming car turning left across his lane): There is evidence he sailed right into sure annihilation, looking for the great beyond. Earlier, he had had himself photographed in a coffin (and sometimes slept in one at his home in Sherman Oaks). There were pictures he had posed for with a noose around his neck, and standing next to a tombstone he found that read DEAN. And he often used to wonder out loud what it would be like to rot in a grave. Vampira, who was part beatnik and part witch, as well as Hollywood's foremost symbol of death and sex when he arrived in town, was irresistible to him. Dressed in a tattered black shroud that clung to an hourglass figure, wearing fingernail polish that she called "hemorrhage red," she signed "epitaphs, not autographs," and had a pet spider named Rollo. There are some who believe that his short friendship with Vampira is what did him in. In November 1954, as his star was beginning to rise, he publicly spurned her, telling Hedda Hopper, "I do not date cartoons." According to David Dalton in *James Dean: The Mutant King*, Vampira retaliated by putting a curse on him, and that was the beginning of his end.

But the truth is that James Dean didn't need any help finding his own personal hex.

As a member of the Malecfarum Coven, a Hollywood witch cult of long standing, he frequently announced to fellow Satanists that he would soon cross the Styx, and intended to do so in a quick, exciting way. "Jimmy really believed in this stuff," Sal Mineo told *After Dark* in a 1966 interview. "He had some sort of odd idea that since Natalie [Wood] and I were getting close to him [they were his co-stars in *Rebel Without a Cause*], we would be cursed, too . . . [and] all die violent deaths." (They all did, eventually.) The day after his crash, the *New York Times* ran a story headlined, FRIENDS TELL OF STAR'S DEATH WISH.

One member of Dean's coven told Ron Smith, author of "The Car, the Star—and the Curse That Linked Them" in *The Robb Report*, that Dean came back from the dead to announce that there was an evil spell on his Porsche. When it went on tour in 1957 as "James Dean's Last Sports Car" (twenty-five cents per look at the twisted remains), it rolled off its display and crushed one spectator (a fifteen-year-old who was dressed exactly like Dean in *Rebel Without a Cause*) and twice fell out of the trailer truck carrying it from town to town, killing two more people. On another occasion, in New Orleans, it inexplicably broke into eleven pieces. Also, a race car driver who

bought the still usable two rear tires off Dean's wreck was killed two days after installing them on his own car; another driver, who had salvaged Dean's transmission, was killed when he lost control of his vehicle during a race; and a third driver, who had gotten engine parts from Dean's Porsche, crashed into a tree and nearly died. George Barris, the Hollywood car customizer who put the death car on tour, told Ron Smith, "Ever since I started having anything to do with the car I had felt bad vibes coming from it. It was bizarre."

In 1960, James Dean's Porsche was put into a boxcar on a train to make the trip from Florida to Los Angeles. The boxcar was sealed, and Pinkerton detectives were posted to guard it all the way. When it arrived in Los Angeles, still sealed, the boxcar was empty. The wreckage of the cursed Porsche had vanished, and no one has seen it since. You can, however, buy an exact replica of it as it was before the crash—a "Vintage 550 Spyder," manufactured in Texas by Blue Ray G.T. Engineering. Blue Ray advertisements assure prospective customers, "The Spirit of James Dean Lives On!" No doubt this sentiment would greatly please James Dean, who once said, "To me, the only success, the only greatness, is immortality."

"DEAR ABBY"; "DEAR ANN LANDERS"

Abigail Van Buren (née Pauline Esther "Popo" Friedman) and Ann Landers (née Esther Pauline "Eppie" Friedman) have had a famous fight or two since they were born seventeen minutes apart in Sioux City, Iowa, on Independence Day, 1918, but they have also been as close to one another as a mirror image, and as inti-

Ann

Abby

mate as only identical twins can be. They double-dated in high school, sharing a single purse; they co-authored a gossip column, titled "Campus Rats," for the Morningside College newspaper; they shared a marriage ceremony in 1939 (to two different, unrelated men) and set off on their honeymoons in tandem; and within months after the 1955 death of Ruth Crowley, author of the Chicago *Sun-Times'* advice column, "Dear Ann Landers," they both started advice columns of their own: Eppie as Ruth Crowley's replacement in Chicago, and Popo at the San Francisco *Chronicle* as Abigail Van Buren—a name she chose from the Old Testament ("Blessed are thou, and blessed is thy advice, O Abigail") and from America's eighth president, Martin Van Buren, which Popo said she liked because of the "aristocratic old-family ring."

Much ado has been made of the rivalry between the two advice columnists (for eight years after they started their columns, they refused to speak to each other), but Abby says the stories of their disaffection aren't really true, blaming them on a press

that relishes bad news, and Ann doesn't like to talk about it, saying simply, "I was the first one to go into this work." Their relationship over the years hasn't all been catcalling and snubs: When Ann's husband, Jules Lederer (founder of Budget Rent-a-Car), left her for another woman in 1975, Abby rushed to Chicago from her Bel-Air home to comfort Ann in her grief. ("The lady with all the answers does not know the answers to this one," Ann said in her column on July 2, revealing to the world that her marriage was on the rocks.) The next year the two sisters went together to their high school class's fortieth reunion, and hugged and air-kissed each other in public to show their mutual affection. According to the (unauthorized) dual biography, *Dear Ann, Dear Abby*, classmates observed that the twins seemed to have had identical plastic surgery on their faces and buttocks.

Neither of the sisters denies that there was bad blood, at least at the beginning of their careers. For a few weeks after Eppie wrote her first "Dear Ann Landers" column on October 16, 1955, she sent some of her readers' letters to Popo in San Francisco, who helped her answer them. Whether it was a matter of simple twin-sisterly camaraderie or—as one news service put it when this bit of history was dredged up many years later—a case of Abby "ghost writing" the Ann Landers column, the practice stopped as soon as Ann's editors found out about it. They forbade her to send letters outside the office, and suddenly, as Abby put it, "the ball was over." She had relished helping Ann dispense wisdom to the lovelorn, and knew she was good at it; so she went to the *Chronicle*, where they happened to be looking for someone just like the hot new advice columnist at the Chicago *Sun-Times*. Popo didn't tell them she was Ann Landers's twin sister when she invented her highfalutin name and started her own column on January 9, 1956.

Ann learned about "Dear Abby" as a fait accompli. "I guess it's all right," she allowed her sister, "as long as you're not syndicated outside San Francisco." Within months, however, Abby was in the New York *Mirror*, proclaimed by *Time* "the fastest rising star in the business," and featured on Edward R. Murrow's "Person to Person." Ann countered with an appearance on "What's My Line?" Then Abby struck the coup de grace: She offered "Dear Abby" to the Sioux City *Journal*, the twins' hometown newspaper, in perpetuity and at a reduced rate . . . but only if the *Journal* agreed to never run "Dear Ann Landers." Ann's fury was intensified by the fact that Abby owned her column—she *was* "Dear Abby," and has always enjoyed introducing herself as such—and could write exactly what she pleased, whereas Ann (who in fact hates to be called Ann Landers) was at that time merely working as a hired gun, her column subject to the whims of her editors. Since then, Eppie has become sole proprietor of the name Ann Landers, and when she left the *Sun-*

Times a few years ago, she took the name with her. (Her replacement, curiously, was two people, one of whom was Ruth Crowley's daughter Diane, who began writing "Dear Diane"; the other was Jeffrey Zaslow, who gave his advice in a column called "All That Zazz.")

However they really feel about each other, the fact is that Abigail Van Buren and Ann Landers dominate the advice column business, and have for nearly forty years. The competition between them has helped ensure this supremacy, not only because it has generated lots of publicity but also because it has allowed the two of them— whose attitudes, opinions, and writing style are basically as identical as their nasal cornbelt twangs and their asymmetrical shellacked hairdos with a side flip-up on the right (Abby) or the left (Ann)—to absolutely define what being an advice columnist is all about. (Before them, the big name in daily advice was Dorothy Dix, whose 1940s column, "Dorothy Dix Talks," had a readership of sixty million.) Until the ascendance of Miss Manners in the late 1970s, whose directions are more focused on etiquette, they had no real rivals other than each other. As Abby recalled about their simultaneous 1950s rise to glory in her book *The Best of Dear Abby*, "Nearly every city had two newspapers, and when Abby went into one, Ann went into the other." John McMeel, head of Universal Press Syndicate, which distributes "Dear Abby" (the most widely syndicated column in the world), put it this way: "Between Ann and Abby, the market is taken."

What is it about Abby and Ann that has made them so popular, other than the opportunity their columns provide to eavesdrop on other people's problems? *Time* magazine described Ann Landers's appeal as a mixture of liberal politics (antigun, antinuke, proabortion) and conservative morals (she doesn't like drinking, drugs, profane language, or casual sex). Both Ann and Abby are squares and proud of it, but hardheaded enough to tackle even kinky problems with aplomb (and usually a leavening rejoinder). They are the quintessential symbols of conventional wisdom, and their advice is sought because they represent normalcy. But of course Ann and Abby have made their living by devoting their attention to deviation—ranging from hanging toilet paper so it comes off the top of the roll rather than down along the wall (which Ann says is normal) to rape and incest. They have confronted decades' worth of changing social standards and are famous for their implacable jauntiness when dealing with such touchy modern issues as animal rights (Ann's against them; similarly, Abby says she likes people better than animals) and homosexuality (Abby says "God made gays just as surely as He made straights. And all His children are entitled to live and love in dignity, without shame or guilt"; Ann, on the other hand, has called homosexuality a "personality disorder"). In his book *Dear Ann Landers* David Grossvogel chronicled the changing standards in Ann's column by noting these linguistic breakthroughs:

1962: "Make out" became acceptable to describe intimacy, but the word "sex" was still taboo.
1964: "Menopause," formerly called "that time of life," first appeared.
1965: "Breast" and "syphilis" were used.
1970s: "Incest," "rape," and "gay" made their appearance.
1979: "Condoms" were discussed by name instead of vaguely, as "protection."
1980: A letter was printed from a woman who wrote to complain of her husband's "premature ejaculation."

When they started in the 1950s, both Abby and Ann were bulwarks of conventional behavior and traditional values. Even into the 1960s they held their guns against the tides of moral slackening ("Hippies disgust me," Abby once said; "A fellow with a full head of waves and curls is out of order," declared Ann), but by the 1970s even these two straight arrows began to bend. Abby pronounced it okay for unmarried couples to live together. Ann stopped telling unhappily married people to maintain a happy facade for the sake of the children. Ann used her column to conduct a survey of teenage sex habits. Abby asked readers to tell her if they had ever been unfaithful to their spouses (she got over two hundred thousand replies, only a quarter of whom said yes). Both women came out for the Equal Rights Amendment; and their stand in favor of abortion rights has made them targets of the prolife lobby. "There are a lot of problems in the world," said the director of the Conservative Caucus Foundation. "Ann and Abby are one of them." Curiously, Abby's and Ann's (relatively) controversial positions on important political issues haven't engendered nearly as much contention as their pronouncements about trivial ones: the toilet paper debate, the sex surveys, a column about how to peel an onion without crying, and—perhaps most notorious of all —the Great Meat Loaf Disaster of 1970, when Ann Landers printed her favorite recipe and got about a hundred thousand letters from readers who didn't like it.

One of the reasons people enjoy reading Abby and Ann is the names they provide their anonymous correspondents, reminiscent of the days when Emily Post gave lessons in etiquette by creating little dramas starring such symbolically named characters as Mrs. Toplofty and Miss Not-From-Much. Some of the people who have solicited Abby's advice are:

- Worn Out in Alabama (Her husband wants too much sex.)
- Disappointed in Bismarck (Her husband gave her a cemetery plot instead of a sewing machine for their forty-fifth wedding anniversary.)
- Wants to Be Spanked ("I have tried spanking myself with a wooden spoon but it wasn't very effective.")
- Born Again in Connecticut (She lost 126 pounds at Overeaters Anonymous.)

And Ann has responded to letters from:

- Long-Suffering Top Banana (She is worried that she'll lose her boyfriend because she always beats him at bowling.)
- Adrift Without Answers (Her daughter wears miniskirts and irons her hair: "We just don't know where to draw the line!")
- Hard-Boiled Harry (He won't give up his seat on the bus to anybody, not even a pregnant woman.)
- Vino La Difference (Does wine improve sex?)

As writers, Abby and Ann share a style that is blunt, full of wisecracks, occasionally sanctimonious, and always clever unless the topic is one of the biggies, such as teen pregnancy, AIDS, or drug use. Abby advised one reader, "A bad habit never disappears miraculously; it's an undo-it-yourself project." Ann Landers frequently suggested a delightful penalty for dealing with people (including herself) who deserved to be castigated, but not too sternly. Her prescribed punishment: "Forty lashes with a wet noodle." Even serious issues sometimes get a capricious reply. In her very first column, Ann told a woman who had fallen in love with a philandering delivery boy, "What this man is delivering to your home sounds like baloney." To a woman who wrote that she could not stop her husband's unwanted sexual advances and believed that men ought to have sex only after they ask their wives' permission, Ann replied, "I think such a request will turn up an awful lot of men who suddenly have no lead in their pencils." To a woman whose husband told her that scratches on his back came from a feather in a motel mattress, Abby advised, "It's unlikely that the scratches came from a feather. It was probably the whole chick." Abby explained the enduring success of the sisters' relentlessly saucy style to *Editor & Publisher:* "People like something that's cute and flip. It might be the only laugh they get all day."

DEEP THROAT

Although it was temporarily banned by a New York City judge after it opened at the New Mature World Theater in 1972, *Deep Throat* has been seen by more human beings than any other hard-core sex movie, eventually earning possibly as much as half a billion dollars. (The exact gross is unknown, owing to the covert role of organized crime in the picture's unorthodox distribution.) If any one event could be said to signify the fullest flowering of the sexual revolution before its consequences and its very nature started looking dire, it was the immense popularity of this sixty-two-minute film among respectable and otherwise conventional citizens. For a short

Linda Lovelace

while in the 1970s, *Deep Throat* seemed to announce that virtually all barriers of propriety were gone, at least from cinema, and that explicit sex acts might well become as common an occurrence in movies as kissing. "Hard core grows fashionable," the *New York Times Magazine* headlined, calling the phenomenon "porno chic."

In some respects *Deep Throat* was a cut above the ordinary ten-minute stag films that used to be viewed in private, mostly by bunches of guys at basement "smokers" or fraternity parties. It was shot in Eastmancolor, using full-size 35mm film, with actual cinematic lighting instead of motel-room lamps, and with performers who spoke some lines of dialogue—synch sound!—between their sex scenes. There were also several nonsex scenes that developed characters with vaguely human personality traits. The movie even had something like a plot, and a silly sense of humor that resembled wit; its performers were fairly nice-looking people who seemed to be enjoying themselves. It had theme music with specially written words ("Deep throat, deeper than deep...") and a melody that one re-

viewer described as "sprightly and haunting." It looked and sounded pretty much like a real movie, with credits (mostly pseudonyms) superimposed over live action scenes at the beginning and a—pardon the expression—grand climax of sorts at the end.

Despite its respectable trappings and contemporary claims by *Deep Throat* supporters that it signaled the arrival of sex films as motion picture art, the gist of the movie was pretty basic porno fare, consisting of jumbo genitalia filling the screen during all the important scenes. The plot is this: The heroine, announced at the beginning with the title "Introducing Linda Lovelace as Herself," discovers that her clitoris is located in her throat. So Miss Lovelace sets out to find satisfaction by performing fellatio on men with extra-large penises, which she can fully engulf by opening her esophagus like a sword swallower (hence the movie's title). She also gets boffed in the butt once or twice and shaves the stubble off her nude-look pudendum. The prosecutor in the New York obscenity trial enumerated fifteen sex acts in the film, including seven of fellatio and four of cunnilingus.

Deep Throat was not the first almost-feature-length porn flick to attract the attention of film critics; one named *Mona*, about a girl with a really big mouth, preceded it into New York theaters by a few months and was hailed by some avant-garde types as the harbinger of a new era of permissiveness. But *Deep Throat* was closed down (temporarily) by the cops, and so it became a cause célèbre among champions of free speech, sexual libertines, and freethinkers who honestly believed that dirty movies ought to be part of the cultural mix in a sophisticated society. Eventually the United States Supreme Court issued the 1973 decision that replaced "redeeming social value" with "community standards" as a measure of acceptability; but meanwhile, *Deep Throat* made a lot of friends, and "celebrities, diplomats, critics, businessmen, women alone, and dating couples" were all spotted watching the movie by the *New York Times*. Among those who were reported to have enjoyed it were Johnny Carson, Mike Nichols, Sandy Dennis, and "the in-crowd from Elaine's." Truman Capote told the *Times* he thought Linda Lovelace was "charming."

Ms. Lovelace (née Linda Boreman) became an international celebrity; and several bargain-basement, ten-minute movies she had made earlier—featuring her having sex with a dog, a foot, and a fist as well as peeing on another woman—became the most popular loops at peep shows all over America. She gave interviews to the press (including not only *Screw* magazine and *Playboy* but the *New York Daily News*) in which she described, in graphic detail, just how much she relished performing all kinds of kinky sex with all kinds of people, animals, and inanimate objects. She went to the Cannes Film Festival (in a see-through dress) and tried to parlay her success into a real acting career in the R-rated *Linda Lovelace for President*. But *Deep Throat* was to be her one and only hit. In 1980 she disavowed it. In her autobiography *Ordeal* she revealed that she hadn't really enjoyed all the supposedly freewheeling sex: Her manager had forced her to perform in the films, keeping her captive for years, beating her and threatening to shoot her if she disobeyed; he then forced her to say she had liked it. By the time the sequel to the best-selling *Ordeal* was published, *Out of Bondage* (1986), with an introduction by Gloria Steinem, Linda Lovelace had become a spokesperson (as Linda Marchiano) for Women Against Pornography and had testified before Congress about the evils of the dirty-movie business.

Deep Throat's director, Gerard Damiano, went on to make *The Devil in Miss Jones*, a feature-length adult film starring "Georgina Spelvin," and the Mitchell Brothers of San Francisco made *Behind the Green Door*, a rape fantasy starring Marilyn Chambers, a former model who had once appeared on the Ivory Snow soap box tenderly nuzzling a toddler. In 1973, box office receipts for *The Devil in Miss Jones* and *Deep Throat* ranked six and eleven, respectively, among all films released in the U.S., according to *Variety*. *Deep Throat* heralded what was probably the most permissive era in Hollywood movie history, and some libertines were predicting that hardcore sex would soon be an ingredient of mainstream movies. However, by the end of the 1970s, most Hollywood movies got considerably cleaner as the sexual revolution began to seem like something less than its original billing as America's psychosocial millennium. The home video market is now where nearly everybody who wants to see a dirty movie goes to get one (for viewing in private, as in the old days). Even the title *Deep Throat*, adopted as a code name by the mysterious government employee who spilled the beans on Watergate to Washington *Post* reporters Woodward and Bernstein, is now more evocative of government scandal than of fellatio.

DEODORANT

T he art of making oneself fresh and lovely would seem to be more a matter of personal hygiene than of pop culture; but because body odor is such a source of anxiety, and because that anxiety has been exploited with gusto by companies with deodorant to sell, B.O. has become as popular a dilemma as obesity, and its many formidable adversaries, from Mum and Hush to Yodora and Brut, are folkloric heroes who have helped millions of people to get dates, clinch the big sale, and have friends. Smelling bad is one of America's most terrifying public nightmares, depicted in cautionary advertisements now for nearly a century; and the armaments, strategy, and secret code words employed in this nation's relentless battle against it are fine examples of popular culture's ability to make even sweat into an adventure.

"B.O."—an oblique term for "body odor"—was first employed in 1919 in advertisements by Odo-Ro-No, a deodorant cream for women's armpits (known henceforth, in the exquisitely euphemistic parlance of the trade, as "underarms"). It was the watershed moment in deodorant history, because previously all the ads gingerly circumlocuted the issue and spoke only about achieving daintiness and sweetness. Odo-Ro-No ads, which challenged readers to take the "Armhole Odor Test" (sniff the armhole of their blouses), said flatly that smelling bad was a social disgrace and that something simply had to be done about it if one wanted to be a success in life. These advertisements continued for decades, into radio and then television, usually built around a little theater-of-cruelty production in which a distressing social situation was going bad: A girl sits by the sidelines at a dance as all the boys keep far away from her and whisper to each other about her alarming smell; a businessman is rejected by a customer whose sour face and wrinkled nose reveal the real reason the repulsive salesman couldn't clinch the deal. In the depths of their despair, the unlucky skunks are visited by a deep, ominous, disembodied voice that intrudes, like God from above, and shouts "B.O.!" at them, and the offending parties look appropriately embarrassed and chastened.

For millennia, we humans have been repelled by the way we smell and have invented ways to disguise or eliminate the odor; but the science of staying fresh and lovely didn't begin until just over a hundred years ago, when sweat glands were discovered. Before that, the only ways to not be offensive were to bathe and to veil the offending stench with perfume. Soon after it was learned that sweat was the culprit—especially under the arms, where there is an abundance of apocrine glands—scientists learned that zinc would retard sweating; and in 1888 Mum antiperspirant was introduced. It was an oily cream that contained zinc, and was soon improved upon by a brand named Everdry (1902), which supplemented the zinc with aluminum chloride so the cream would dry.

All early deodorant advertising was aimed at women, for whom it was apparently more important to be dainty, sweet, fresh, and delightful-smelling. Producing equal measures of anxiety and hope, advertisements told women that if they didn't use deodorant, they wouldn't be loved; and if they did use it, they would be happy. For Veto, a cream marketed by Colgate, the enemy was referred to as "underarm 'O,'" and the operative word was "lovely," as indicated in this advertisement from the 1940s: "Your loveliness is doubly safe. Veto guards your loveliness night and day and it keeps you lovely. Always creamy and smooth and lovely to use!"

The era of real deodorant awareness started in the late 1940s, when more and more people began to consider themselves members of the middle class. To many newly affluent citizens, body odor was a shameful mark of proletarianism, completely out of place in a refined home. Even the home itself was now thought to need deodorant, in the form of Airwick, which had been invented by Guy Paschal in the late 1930s, tested at the Lion House of the Bronx Zoo (where it completely eradicated the offensive odor of the jungle cats), and

made available to consumers, in Mr. Paschal's words, as "a valuable contribution to public welfare." Airwick Industries, which now sells rug and room deodorizers, deodorizers for small places (cupboards, closets), and Binaca to deodorize breath, recently noted that its original air freshener, created by Mr. Paschal in a "quest for clean, fresh aromas," predated Earth Day, and the ensuing concern about clean air, by a quarter-century.

Back in the 1950s, dutiful consumers were taught to believe that they could make their lives good by getting new products; and in this golden age of purchasing power, personal deodorant was one of the products that seemed to just keep getting better all the time. Scientific progress was an axiom of life; and although the essential working ingredients in deodorant have never really changed since zinc was discovered to be effective (to this day, no one knows exactly why), B.O.-battling companies found a nearly infinite number of ways to improve the packaging. "Cosmetic science goes loping ahead each year," *Mademoiselle* rhapsodized in an article called "That Certain Air—It's Freshness" in 1955, explaining that new formulations made deodorant easier, more pleasant to use, more comfortable, and therefore—because you could slather on more of it—more effective.

Formerly available only in jars or tubes, deodorant was repackaged as a spray bottle ("keeps you sweet and dainty, and won't harm clothes!"), purse-size cream stick ("contains new 'anti-immunity' factor so you can re-apply it all day long"), liquid deodorant cologne ("head to toe protection"), dry stick ("goes on dry and speedy!"), roll-on bottle ("The future is here, now—under your arms"), and an aerosol can ("for the whole family"). Recent concerns about the earth's ozone layer have inspired the development of spray cans without fluorocarbons. One of the popular ways to apply deodorant these days is while one washes, by using soap with built-in deodorant (although some studies suggest that they are only temporary solutions and actually encourage the efflorescence of bad smells).

One major result of deodorant's becoming as necessary as toothpaste has been the disappearance of blunt anti-B.O. advertising. You don't want to tell a customer directly that he reeks; you only want to get him a little nervous about it and suggest how sweet he can be and how confident he can feel. Starting in the 1950s with ads that showed classical statuary with upraised arms and spoke about "the mature man" and "the mature woman" (a theme parodied hilariously by *Mad* magazine, among others), deodorant advertising has returned to an age of extraordinary euphemisms. Long gone are the echoing supernatural voices proclaiming anxious people's offensive smell and scenes in which the pitiful stinkers are caused to suffer for their sin. Instead, deodorants are pitched by showing a person walking through fields of flowers or raising his arm in class (with no sweaty stains on his shirt) or crowding into a small car, or—in what is truly a stroke of euphemious genius—demonstrating dryness by rolling a deodorant onto someone's inoffensive forearm rather than onto an unsightly armpit.

The art of speaking allegorically about the problem was perfected in the late 1960s when deodorant manufacturers began to realize that by concentrating on underarms they had been neglecting all the rest of the human body, which, although it doesn't have as many apocrine glands to produce sweat, is capable of producing at least as much anxiety. The best known of these products was, and still is, feminine hygiene spray (see *The Encyclopedia of Bad Taste*), for which advertisers invented whole new

levels of extenuative delirium. In the early 1970s the National Association of Broadcasters issued the following guidelines for feminine hygiene spray commercials:

> Sexual themes and connotations should be avoided. Men should not appear except in an assemblage of people in which there is no association of a particular man (e.g. boyfriend, escort, fiancé) with a particular woman. Copy referring to loving relationships, being a big girl or physically mature (in a sexual context), or language such as "I no longer sleep with dolls" or "you are the very air he breathes" would not be accepted.

In keeping with this directive, FDS advertisements said, "Having a female body doesn't make you feminine," and asked, "Could you be the last woman to be using just one deodorant?"

Just as there are folk tales about a perpetual light bulb and a car that runs on water (both of which, the stories go, were squelched by manufacturers with bulbs and gasoline to sell), it has long been rumored that drug companies have perfected a way to eliminate body odor altogether, but that the discovery has been kept under wraps so manufacturers can sell more deodorant. *Newsweek* investigated one such product in 1942. Called OD-30 because it supposedly eliminated all odor in thirty seconds—by simply oxidizing all bacteria before they assailed one's nose—the product was found to be effective in combating a skunk's spray and stench bombs as well as fried fish and cabbage, and was even useful as a mouthwash to combat onion breath. But for body odor OD-30 was useless, because it combated only the emanated odor, not the source, and so would have to be reapplied constantly. Also, *Newsweek* cautioned, it destroyed pleasant smells, too, thus neutralizing perfume.

Eight years later, the De Pree Company of Holland, Michigan, announced a product it felt would revolutionize the deodorant industry: a chlorophyll tablet called Nullo. Within one hour after you swallowed your Nullo, nothing about you smelled anymore. You still sweated, but the chlorophyll in your system eliminated all odors: from underarms, feet, mouth, and what were then known as "private parts." A month's supply of Nullo sold for $1.25; and although it did not in any way minimize America's love affair with deodorants, *Time* magazine reported that veterinarians had discovered that Nullo was a wonderful way to improve the social life of elderly dogs with objectionable breath and smelly hides.

DIRTY HARRY

Critics loathed him as much as audiences cheered him; and to this day, more than twenty years after the release of the movie *Dirty Harry* (1971), its hero, police inspector Harry Callahan (Clint Eastwood), endures as one of modern cinema's most inflammatory characters. In the original film, as well as in its sequels, *Magnum Force* (1973), *The Enforcer* (1976), *Sudden Impact* (1983), and *The Dead Pool* (1988), he is a law enforcement officer who bends or sometimes breaks the rules in order to see justice—his kind of justice—done. Known for his Smith & Wesson Model 29 .44 magnum revolver with an extravagant 8⅜-inch barrel, Dirty Harry hates lily-livered politicians, permissive judges, and all the little, stupid legal punctilios that allow criminals to run rampant. He is a symbol of righteous wrath in a make-believe movie world where there is never any ambiguity about who, exactly, is the scum of society; and he is endowed with the power to do what seldom happens in real life: catch the bad guys, make them cry uncle, then kill them.

In the original *Dirty Harry* the bad guy is exquisitely bad: a raving psychotic serial killer named Scorpio (played by Andy Robinson in the performance of a lifetime) who stalks San Francisco dispatching gay men, blacks, and women, all the while whining with self-pity and cackling with glee. Based on a real, unsolved case known as the Zodiac Murders, the John Milius script (originally meant for Frank Sinatra or John Wayne, who both turned it down because they considered Harry too sleazy) depicts Scorpio as a pseudo-hippie who is clever enough to manipulate the law to his own advantage, at one point hiring someone to beat him up (he loves pain) so he can claim that Dirty Harry did it. When it is decided that his rights have been violated because Dirty Harry broke down his door, shot him in the leg, and made him confess, the gutless weasels in charge at City Hall let Scorpio go free. "The law's crazy," Dirty Harry declares; and when Scorpio kidnaps a whole busload of children, Harry makes it his business to save the children, then become judge, jury, and executioner so he can rid the world of this trash.

Although set in modern America, the story had the stubborn purpose and clarity of a classic cowboy movie. Director Don

Clint Eastwood as Dirty Harry Callahan

dispensing "man with no name" from his Sergio Leone spaghetti westerns, such as *The Good, the Bad, and the Ugly* (1966), Siegel fashioned *Dirty Harry* into a moral parable of crime and retribution. In the Leone movies, Eastwood had always played the good guy, but with a nature every bit as brutal as the villains'; and in fact, some of *Dirty Harry*'s more intelligent critics (there have been a few, including Jay Cocks of *Time*) have pointed out that in some ways, Harry and Scorpio were two sides of the same coin: both obeying a higher law, both attracted to violence, and fascinated in a nearly fetishistic way by each other. As in the Old West, vigilante action was made to seem justifiable and necessary, however ugly, because the law wasn't doing what it was supposed to do.

Dirty Harry gave people a chance to root for a right-minded hero, and to enjoy seeing criminals get what they deserve. This was a formula many Americans, fed up with countercultural attacks against the establishment, were ready and eager to embrace in 1971, and in sequels that lasted well into the Reagan years. In fact, Ronald Reagan himself once took a cue from the character of Dirty Harry, who in *Sudden Impact* dared criminals with itchy trigger fingers by saying, "Go ahead—make my day!" An old hand at theatrical effect, Reagan used those exact words, his veto poised like Dirty Harry's .44, to challenge Congress to put a tax increase on his desk; and it became an occasion for anti-Reagan editorial writers across the land to bemoan the President's cinematic view of the world. Reagan, like Dirty Harry, was frequently accused of oversimplifying complex moral issues; and indeed, it can be argued that his unshaded moral perspective is why he was so popular. It certainly explains the popularity of Dirty Harry, who gave audiences the satisfaction of seeing justice done with the kind of final-

Siegel, an action ace with a penchant for antisocial characters driven by unknown demons (Steve McQueen in *Hell is For Heroes* [1962], Lee Marvin in *The Killers* [1964], nearly everyone in *Invasion of the Body Snatchers* [1956]), made Harry Callahan into a presence as potent as a force of nature. Building on the persona that Eastwood had developed as a pitiless, justice-

ity that, alas, does not happen anywhere other than in the mythological world of pop culture.

Many high-minded reviewers were disturbed by the political implications of *Dirty Harry*. Roger Greenspun of the *New York Times* described its might-makes-right appeal as "hard-hat sentiment"; *Variety* called it "a glorification of police and criminal brutality"; Pauline Kael came right out and called it "deeply immoral," an expression of the "fascist potential" of Nixon-era law-and-order ideals. *Newsweek* compared it to the "hatreds, angers, and frustrations that find their political echoes in the speeches of extreme right-wing politicians." As for Clint Eastwood, he thought that such caviling was taking it all far too seriously. "When I go to the movies," he said, "it's to have a few laughs and a couple of beers afterward. I don't worry about social injustice." Nonetheless, Iain Johnstone reported in his book *Clint Eastwood: The Man with No Name* that the Philippine police force requested a print of *Dirty Harry* "for training purposes" and that after the movie's release Clint Eastwood was frequently asked to address police groups about law enforcement issues (he refused).

What especially upset the critics when *Dirty Harry* played to packed theaters was that audiences didn't just enjoy it: They *cheered* Dirty Harry when he ground his shoe into Scorpio's wounded leg and made the annoying little maniac scream for mercy; they roared with glee when he plugged fleeing criminals from a hundred yards away; and they exulted at the end of a gunfight when, getting a felon in the sights of his mighty six-shooter, instead of reading him his rights according to the Miranda decision, Harry drew a bead and gave this speech:

> I know what you're thinking: Did he fire six shots or only five? Well, to tell the truth, I kind of forgot myself in all this excitement. But being that this is a .44 magnum, the most powerful handgun in the world, and will blow your head *clean off*, there's only one question you should ask yourself: Do I feel lucky? Well, do you, punk?

Commentators often noted that *Dirty Harry* played especially well to audiences composed of lower-class, disenfranchised inner-city people—society's most powerless, and those most frequently victimized by crime—who delighted in seeing justice meted out the old-fashioned, all-American way: swiftly and decisively from the barrel of a gun.

DISNEY WORLD

Disney is to fun what Velveeta is to cheese: pasteurized, processed, smooth, neat, bland, square, loved by children, and a world-renowned symbol of America's corporate genius. Walt Disney World, the company's theme park environment in Florida, is the biggest block of cheese ever packaged.

When it opened in Florida on October 1, 1971, five years after Walt Disney died, it didn't extend much beyond the Magic Kingdom, which was a lot like Disneyland in Cal-

Walt Disney

ifornia, but more deluxe (it had thirty-six audio-animatronic Presidents instead of only one; its Cinderella's castle was twice as big; live Spanish moss rather than vinyl leaves grew on the Swiss Family Robinson's tree). There was a natural lake as well as a Disney-made Seven Seas Lagoon, and there were two hotels, including the (then) strikingly modern A-shaped Contemporary Resort, where a futuristic monorail actually *came right into the lobby* to pick up visitors and take them to the park.

Since then, Disney World has grown to become the most commercially successful tourist attraction on earth, a travelers' destination with drawing power surpassed only by Mecca and the Vatican. Walt Disney would not have been surprised by its eminence, for he intended Disney World to be important and influential. In fact, he envisioned it as a biosphere-like model world that would literally be under glass. Epcot—

his acronym for *E*xperimental *P*rototype *C*ommunity *of* *T*omorrow—was originally designed to be a portion of Disney World built under a huge dome so everything, including weather, could be controlled. He described it as a "living blueprint of the future"—an experiment in social regulation where genuine human beings would actually live and work and play and go to school and maybe even get born (but not die) in a completely computer-coordinated environment with no crime, no litter, and no pets. It didn't quite pan out that way, but the Disney designers, known as "Imagineers," who did build Epcot, which opened in 1982 and is now one of three Disney World theme parks (also including the Disney-MGM Studios, which opened in 1989), did their mentor proud. Epcot's Future World is a "community" of corporate-sponsored exhibits that show the amazing technology that will soon make our lives better; and its World Showcase boasts about a dozen international pavilions that feature re-creations of familiar landmarks from around the world, stores that market souvenirs designed to evoke pleasant thoughts of other countries, and cafes that sell sanitary foreign food. *Time* recently quoted one happy visitor to the World Showcase as saying, "Probably it's much cleaner here than some of those countries you would go to."

Disney World is about twenty miles outside Orlando, a city in central Florida whose main claims to fame before 1971 were Gatorland and lovely groves of orange trees. Since 1960, the population has quadrupled and the orange groves have been cut down, and every supermarket in the downtown area has been shuttered (not profitable enough, the *Wall Street Journal* reported). Orlando has sprouted more motel and hotel rooms (76,300) than New York City. It has become the vacation objective for families from around the world, with untold numbers of fast-food franchises, discount outlets, shops selling Elvis-headed lamps and seashell ashtrays, and a magnet for the biggest concentration of mobile home communities in the country. And it has become home base to, among others, Tammy Faye Bakker (after husband Jim went to jail), the Maharishi Mahesh Yogi (who is building a theme park of his own, called Vedaland), and convicted financial scam artist Glenn Turner, who encouraged his followers to sing—to the tune of the anthem from television's "Mickey Mouse Club":

Now's the time to say goodbye to all
  our poverty.
M-A-K–I-N-G M-O-N-E-Y.

The commotion and crudity that have come to Orlando in the wake of Disney World's success make driving into Disney World all the more fantastic, because once you get through the traffic jams and inside Epcot or the Magic Kingdom, chaos is not allowed. Everything is well ordered, and nothing is out of place. There are no unsightly strip malls with Day-Glo signs hawking water beds and fanny packs, and there are no traffic jams, because everybody walks or takes the monorail or a boat. There *are* lines—there are almost always lines, for every attraction—but they are orderly lines, and waiting politely until it's your turn is part of the Disney World experience, part of what makes it seem so businesslike and well run.

The main reason Walt Disney came to Orlando was that he didn't like what had happened all around Disneyland after it opened in Anaheim, California, on July 17, 1955. Almost as soon as the crowds started flooding to his first park, which was situated on a mere two hundred acres, it was surrounded by other people's businesses—hotels, hash houses, souvenir stores, and enterprises that were unsightly and not in keeping with the Disney image; and worse, they were making a half a billion dollars every year on Disneyland's coattails. "We lost control of the environment," said one Disney executive in 1971, explaining why Walt Disney had bought forty-three square miles in Florida for his second theme park. This parcel of land, twice the size of Manhattan, was declared by the state of Florida to be a special taxing region, authorized to establish its own fire department and building codes, and exempted from paying impact fees on new construction. In some ways, Disney World is a sovereign place. "They could build a nuclear plant out there, and there'd be nothing we could do about it," an Orange County commissioner told *Time* in 1991.

Only that kind of extreme control has allowed Walt Disney World to become a place where order reigns and flawless experiences are guaranteed—a hygienic environment that makes most people, children especially, ecstatically happy . . . but causes some others, who are appalled by the relentless orthodoxy, to weep with despair. In *Esquire* Max Apple wrote, "At the end of every line, the lifelike idols leer, lights flash, and a droll informative recording turns the adventure into a learning experience that can be captured by a snapshot and encapsulated by a souvenir." Apple compared Disney's vision of the world to Franz Kafka's (both obsessed with the smallness of humans in an overwhelming universe), called the experience "ultimately empty," and bemoaned the loss of funky, unpredictable amusement parks.

The transformation of organized fun from old-fashioned nickel-and-dime thrill rides into big-dollar family vacations was Walt Disney's greatest achievement, beyond the cartoons on which his empire was founded, and beyond his award-winning nature movies and the "Wonderful World of

Disney" television show. He reconceived amusement parks (or as Popeye used to call them, "abusement parks") into what he liked to call a "themed entertainment experience." Just before Disneyland opened in 1955, *Newsweek* did a cover story called "A Wonderful World—Growing Impact of the Disney Art," which described the new park as "a big, though quite calculated, risk" because Walt Disney was ignoring a trend: "In the last few years Coney Island and Luna Parks from coast to coast have been darkening their strings of Mazda bulbs, shuttering their merry-go-rounds, and draining their 'Old Mills' and 'Tunnels of Love.' In all this time, however, Disney kept stubbornly in mind his plan for the most fantastic park of them all."

There would be no Tunnels of Love at Disneyland—too sexy! There would be no freak shows or sideshow barkers or hootchie-cootchie girls or bump-'em cars, and no drunken sailors on weekend leave. No litter, no pickpockets to look out for, no flimflam artists dealing three-card monte. Like his television show, which went on the air only a year before the park opened and was originally named "Disneyland," this park would be an artfully arranged simulation of wholesome Americana. Disneyland was a place for children (and adults) to *live* their fantasies. Instead of knocking milk bottles off a shelf to win a plush animal or gawking at bearded ladies, guests—never, ever called "customers"—enjoyed the thrill of actually being in something like a movie, or having something close to an actual experience. Among Disneyland's early featured attractions were a trip in an airborne galleon over Never-Never Land, where a pirate hiding behind a big skull threw Ping-Pong balls at passengers, an Alice in Wonderland Walk-Thru, and a child-size medieval torture chamber (all in fun!).

The basic idea at Disneyland, amplified and improved at Walt Disney World, is to create nostalgia for the past (on the happy little Main Street, which is built five-eighths normal size so it seems more toylike) and excitement about the future (Epcot) and get away from the present and all the mundane, unpleasant things about it. The Magic Kingdom is famous for its grid of underground passageways that allow materiel to be brought to the fantasy environments without guests having to see delivery vans, which would spoil the illusion. These corridors are also used by cast members—people who work at Disney World are never called "employees"—to appear at their attraction without having to mingle with guests.

What impresses everybody about Walt Disney World is how efficiently it works. Few things in the non-Disney World are so flawless, especially few things that use such elaborate social engineering. But it does work—because of Disney's absolute control. (Once, when it was suggested to Walt Disney that he run for mayor of Los Angeles, he responded, "Why should I run for mayor when I am already king?") In fact, Disney World works so well that some have suggested it really has served as an "urban laboratory" and a model for the renewal of American cities, as seen in such "theme" environments as New York's South Street Seaport, Baltimore's Harbor Place, and Boston's Faneuil Hall—all of which have been attempts to revive decrepit neighborhoods by making them fantasy environments very much like the themed experiences Disney World provides.

Disney's effect on urban planning was duly noted by a *Time* cover story in 1991 called "Fantasy's Reality," which hinged on the irony that the community of Orlando was imitating Disney World as a model for its stupendous growth, and that Disney World is in many ways itself an imitation of what a community like Orlando might have been years before the arrival of Disney World. The line between Disney Imagineers and the rest of the world has been thoroughly muddied in recent years by the company's phenomenal growth, which includes a building boom of hotels, offices, and resorts designed by most of the important postmodern architects in the world. Of course postmodernism, known for its kitschy nostalgia and a cartoonish approach to design, is itself extremely Disneyesque to begin with, so when designer Michael Graves (whom one critic called "the Ralph Lauren of architecture") creates such goofy-looking, hilariously ostentatious hotels as the Dolphin and the Swan for Disney World, or when Robert A. M. Stern builds a nineteenth-century New England seaside resort, complete with a scenic shipwreck outside the windows, it's a bit like it would be if Andy Warhol had designed a new soup can for Campbell's: a confusing and provocative conjunction of art, kitsch, and commerce.

Michael Eisner, who now runs Disney, explained that when he hired important architects to work for the company, he felt as free to monkey with their work as any studio executive does when dealing with someone who makes movies. "I know how to make creative people see that something is not as good as they can do," he said. *Time* reported that he has personally overseen such decisions as light fixtures, paint colors, and masonry textures on each building project. "We're Disney. We've got to have the biggest, the best, the most tasteful," Mr. Eisner declared, also announcing that the 1990s will be "the Disney decade." To this end, there are plans afoot to create new Disney environments in California and Kansas

City. With Tokyo Disneyland already a big success and Euro Disneyland, just east of Paris, freshly opened in the spring of 1992, Edward Ball, writing in the *Village Voice*, warned, "The slow drip of the Disney serum into the social body has increased to a stream."

There are many reasons for Disney World's success; not the least of them is that it is so clean. One carelessly tossed corn dog stick could ruin the effect of colonial-era Liberty Square. Every morning before the park opens, each blob of spit-out bubble gum is scraped off the sidewalks; and throughout the day, if you drop a piece of litter anywhere at Disney World, it is likely to be gone within moments, stealthily evacuated by a cast member dressed as Pluto or Donald Duck.

For a lot of people, the Disney fantasy world works, which is why a family of four happily parts with over four hundred dollars for tickets that allow them the privilege of spending four days in the Disney World habitat. "It brings you back to a moral, clean time that today we've lost," one guest told *Time* magazine. Another asked, "Do you see anyone jumping on your car and wanting to clean your windshield—and when you say no, they get abusive?"

To ensure that the clean, wholesome fantasy is sustained, everybody who visits Walt Disney World must wear a shirt and shoes at all times (although nude-look shorts and vulgar T-shirts are, apparently, allowed). Cast members, also known as hosts and hostesses, must conform to rigid standards of dress, grooming, and personal hygiene which, when brought to bear upon applicants at Euro Disneyland in 1991, caused French Communists to rise up and protest an "attack on individual liberty." In the newspaper *Le Figaro*, which published an entire special supplement filled with vitriol against the new theme park, one intellectual declared, "I wish with all my heart that rebels would set fire to Disneyland." When a French musician learned he would have to cut off his ponytail to audition to work there, he walked away, telling the *New York Times*, "Some people will turn themselves into a pumpkin to work at Euro Disneyland. But not me." Some of the rules, published in an employees' guide called "The Disney Look," are as follows:

- As a condition of employment with Walt Disney Attractions, you are responsible for maintaining an appropriate weight and size.
- [Men's] hair should be neatly cut and tapered so it does not cover any part of your ears. (Putting your hair behind your ears is not acceptable.) Hairstyles termed "natural" or "Afro" are acceptable, provided they are neatly packed. Women's hair cannot be frosted or streaked, and must be one uniform "natural color."
- Mustaches and beards are not permitted.
- Medical verification from a doctor is needed if a wig or hairpiece is to be worn.

- The use of a heavy after-shave cologne should be discouraged. A light cologne, however, is acceptable.
- Dark red, frosted, gold, or silver-toned nail polishes are not considered part of the "Disney look." Fingernails should not extend more than one-fourth of an inch beyond the fingertips [for women].
- Women are required to wear appropriate undergarments.
- Neither men nor women are allowed to expose any tattoos.
- A single earring, no more than ¾-inch in diameter, in each ear is acceptable [for women only].
- All employees are expected to arrive at work fresh and clean each day.

Walt Disney was a stickler for such rules, but he himself favored loud sports jackets, and he frequently wore moccasins instead of lace-up shoes. He liked to have a strong cocktail at the end of the day, and when he got angry at employees, he swore. And he wore a mustache. He never would have been allowed to work at Walt Disney World.

DISPOSABLE DIAPERS

Not many articles of clothing become a provocative social issue, let alone an ethical bellwether with devotees and detractors. Usually it happens when a garment is considered too risqué or somehow rebellious: miniskirts, zoot suits, bobby socks. Who would have thought, back when topless bathing suits were getting everybody riled up, that in the 1990s the civilized world would find itself in an uproar about babies' diapers? From potty to pop culture, they have now become emblematic attire that, every bit as much as a black leather jacket or a white-frilled tuxedo, tell the world what kind of person you think you (and your baby) are.

No one seemed to worry about the five billion pounds of paper-and-plastic nappies that are carted to America's landfills every year until the late 1980s, when anti-disposable-diaper sentiment blossomed as part of the Green consumer movement. By early 1990, Pampers' manufacturer, Procter & Gamble, was facing what one reporter called "the company's biggest public-relations challenge since the early 1980s, when its Rely tampons were linked to toxic shock syndrome." Disposable diapers were being accused of no less than suffocating the earth, threatening the health of garbage collectors, and leaching dangerous bacteria into ground water. The company countered by pointing out that diapers were "only" 2 percent of landfills' solid waste, and that laundering a reusable one creates ten times as much water pollution as manufacturing a disposable. An executive in charge of Procter & Gamble's worldwide paper operations exalted Pampers as "one of the greatest new products of the postwar era."

No one questions disposables' superior ability to keep babies dry. Since 1985 and the introduction of Super Pampers, which contained a newly formulated gel capable of retaining more than eighty times its weight in liquid, throwaway diapers have been far and away more absorbent than cotton reusables—a fact proven in a Procter &

Gamble–commissioned medical survey called "Etiology of Diaper Dermatitis." To critics who pooh-pooh such studies, superior absorbency is more a convenience for parents than a boon for babies, and diapers are a moral issue beyond convenience: "The first lesson a child learns is that when you make a mess, you throw it in the garbage and it goes away," objected Patricia Greenstreet, a lawyer and former nurse in Seattle. "That message is fundamentally wrong."

Diapers have become an issue bigger than baby poop. In fact, they have become a symbol of cultural affiliation as revealing as the cotton-versus-polyester question. The unspoken aspect of the quarrel is the way it crystallizes the class hostilities that emerged towards the end of the eighties. For many working people who have no time (and less money) to fuss with diaper pins, pails, and services, disposables are a godsend. They are quick and easy; and their superabsorbency allows for fewer changes. For parents who can afford to hire nannies to do the work or to take their own time and dote on baby's needs, there is something honorable and good about the extra effort old-fashioned diapers require—like baking your own honest loaf of whole-grain peasant bread. As for Pampers users, they tend to see cotton-diaper people as elitist yuppie snobs.

When first sold in America, by Johnson & Johnson in the late forties, disposable diapers were a product aimed at the leisure class, marketed as a time saver for modern families on vacation. They were called Chux, and they were based on a paper-and-plastic, use-once-and-chuck-it design developed in Sweden after World War II. Disposables' breakthrough to popular acceptance came in 1961 when, after five years of market research, Procter & Gamble began selling Pampers with an ad campaign that suggested they be used all the time in lieu of cotton diapers. "Cloth diapers bunched up, did not keep the babies dry enough, and required plastic pants which could irritate the baby's tender skin," P&G reported in a brochure called "Consumer Choice." Original Pampers still required diaper pins, and at first they were prohibitively expensive (about forty cents apiece in today's currency); but Procter & Gamble was eventually able to raise its volume and drop the price to about six cents, and by the mid-sixties sales were soaring. Tape fasteners hit the market in 1968 on Kimbies, made by Kimberly-Clark, which was also the company, ten years later, to introduce contoured diapers with elastic legs: Huggies.

In France (where ninety-eight out of a hundred diaper changes now involve throwaways), a 1985 invention called the Babylodie made life for toddlers' parents even easier. Placed inside the diaper next to baby's bottom, the little plastic Babylodie burst forth with a microchip rendition of "When the Saints Go Marching In" at the first sign of wetness, thus eliminating the need to check for a wet bottom. (Some parents worried that Babylodie might cause babies to pee deliberately to hear music;

others were concerned about untoward Pavlovian reactions to music later in life.) Superabsorbency became an issue in the mid-eighties, about the same time slimmer and trimmer disposable dydees were developed; and the latest improvements include gender-specific models and reusable, all-cotton diapers with Velcro tabs and a form-fitting shape just like disposables.

Life becomes ever more convenient for parents willing to use throwaways, especially now that diapers have entered what the *New York Times* called "the smart weapon phase" when Procter & Gamble introduced ultra-absorbent curly cellulose disposables in June 1992. But some states and localities have begun to consider (and in some cases, have enacted) laws banning or taxing diapers that don't quickly decompose. According to a recent article in the *New York Times Magazine*, "Not since the automobile begat the suburb has a product so essential to the American lifestyle become so maligned as a symbol of pollution and waste. The disposable diaper," the *Times* declared, "is suddenly the environmental bad boy of the nineties."

"DRAGNET"

No other television show in history has been the inspiration for as much parody and caricature as "Dragnet." The bizarre behavior of its main character, Joe Friday; its memorable theme music; its Spartan narrative form; its insistence that everything it showed was true; and its absolute morality have made it a cultural landmark with a strange but irresistible charisma.

Its roots go back to "Pat Novak for Hire," a private-eye adventure broadcast on local radio in San Francisco for twenty-eight weeks in 1946. Pat Novak was a gumshoe with a wisecrack for every situation, a chip on his shoulder, a hip flask in his jacket, a snub-nose .38 in his holster, and a roving eye for any shapely pair of gams. He was played by Jack Webb, a World War II flyboy who had already made a local name for himself starring in an antibigotry radio series called "One out of Seven." Webb hadn't aimed for a career in broadcasting—before the war he had gone to USC on an art scholarship—but the success of "Pat Novak" had made him, in his words, "everybody's hotcake"; and when he moved to Los Angeles, he got radio roles as gangsters, cops, and burglars, as well as private eyes named Johnny Madero and Jeff Regan, all of whom shared Pat Novak's inclination for adroit dialogue, violent action, and steamy sex. He also got a bit part in *Sunset Boulevard* (1950) and a choice little role as a paraplegic in *The Men* (1950).

One day in 1948, while he was playing the part of a police lieutenant in the movie *He Walked by Night*, Webb found himself cornered by the picture's technical advisor, a Los Angeles cop named Marty Wynn, who gave him an earful. "Why don't you do a show about *real* cops?" Wynn asked. Webb pointed out that there were already such shows on the radio: "Gangbusters" and "True Detective Mysteries," for example. But Jones told Webb that cops-and-robbers

Jack Webb as Sergeant Joe Friday

adventures like that were only comic-book versions of real police work, which was much more interesting, and their heroes were unrealistic supermen rather than human beings faced with the formidable task of keeping the peace. He said he could arrange for Webb to have access to the files of the Los Angeles Police Department, so he could use real cases as the basis of a lifelike series. The idea, Webb later recalled, "began gnawing a little hole in my mind," and soon a title popped up: "Dragnet." He described how he conceived the show's hero:

> I sketched out the details on the lead character, a quiet, conservative, dedicated policeman who, as in real life, was just one little cog in a great enforcement machine. I wanted him to be the steady, plodding kind of cop the public never really understood or appreciated or ever heard about. I wanted him to be . . . the image of 50,000 real peace officers who do their work without the help of beautiful, mysterious blondes, hefty swigs from an ever-present bottle, and handy automatics thrust into their belts or hidden in their socks.

Webb named him Joe Friday because he wanted a name that "had no connotations at all: He could be Jewish or Greek or English or anything. He could be all men to all people in their living rooms."

Despite radio executives' reservations about a police show in which you rarely heard a gunshot, a scream, or a fistfight, "Dragnet" went on the air on June 3, 1949, with Jack Webb playing Sergeant Friday, a by-the-rules law officer who solved cases the old-fashioned way—by pounding the pavement, conducting interviews, and piecing together shreds of evidence. At first the show's ratings were weak, but audiences grew intrigued by the opportunity to eavesdrop on real police work, to hear cops talk about a suspect's "MO" or a "211 in progress," and to listen in not on gory crimes being committed but on the painstaking and inexorable details of a cop's routine. By the fall, it had become a national addiction, and soon after that, the nation's number-one-rated radio show. "Dragnet" lasted seven years on the radio; and when Webb took it to television in 1951, it was a smash hit. By 1953 "Dragnet" was number two in the TV ratings, topped only by "I Love Lucy," and had won the first of its three Emmy awards.

The show featured Barton Yarborough as Ben Romero, Friday's deadpan partner, for three episodes; but Yarborough died of a sudden heart attack, and in the fourth episode Friday explained his absence by including a line revealing that his partner had suffered cardiac arrest. Off camera, Webb told the press, "I thought it only right that he should go the same way in our make-believe world." The role of Friday's foil was eventually taken over by Ben Alexander, playing Officer Frank Smith, a character with a touch of whimsy that contrasted with Friday's rule-book disposition.

Whereas the radio show had sounded as spare as a documentary, beginning every week with the line "My name is Friday— I'm a cop," television's "Dragnet" began with theme music. And what music it was! Called the "Dragnet March" and also "Danger Ahead," it was written for the program by Walter Schumann and featured a staccato four-note introduction—dum-de-dum-dum—that soon became the most famous four notes since the opening of Beethoven's Fifth Symphony, and an enduring symbol of police justice on the march. As a single, the "Dragnet March" actually became a top ten song, performed on "Your Hit Parade," and Webb recalled that its ubiquity "eventually had me putting square pegs into round holes: College bands from coast to coast

played it at football games every time the referee marched off penalty yardage." Those first four notes of the theme eventually grew so familiar that Webb once received a fan letter addressed simply, "Dum-de-dum-dum, Hollywood."

Critics adored "Dragnet" for its realism, about which Webb was a fanatic. On one occasion he actually gathered up cigarette butts from police headquarters to use in the ashtrays on his set, because he felt that it was important to have cigarettes that really looked like they had been smoked to the nub by low-paid cops, then stubbed out with a policeman's forceful self-assurance. In 1952, when "Dragnet" returned for its second season, *Time* raved that it "has become the best of the TV crime shows by tossing overboard TV clichés from incendiary blondes and comic stooges to roaring gunfights and simple-Simon detection." *Variety* called the first TV episode, titled "The Human Bomb," about a criminal who threatened to blow up the Los Angeles City Hall unless his brother was released from jail, "taut, suspenseful, hard-hitting, masterfully constructed, and a king-size contribution to the medium." At the height of its popularity, "Dragnet" boasted thirty-eight million viewers a week; by the end of the 1950s, Friday had become a lieutenant and Officer Smith had earned his sergeant's badge. Webb was proud of the show's reliance on police work rather than melodrama: In the first sixty episodes, only fifteen gunshots were fired, and there were just three fights.

"Dragnet" was also a television landmark. Before it, every successful series had been comedy or variety, or such lowbrow stuff as pro wrestling and bowling for dollars. There had been some dramatic anthologies, including "Philco TV Playhouse," but they were mostly telecast theatrical plays, and there had been plenty of action-packed shoot-'em-ups. But "Dragnet" was a genuine original: the first thinking man's drama, complete with such realistic touches as voice-over narration (by Webb) that gave exact time and weather reports as crimes were solved, and a coda at the end of every show that revealed what punishment the criminal received, as well as a disclaimer by the announcer (George Fenneman in later years) reassuring viewers that although the story they had just seen was true, the names had been changed "to protect the innocent."

"Dragnet" stayed on the air until 1959 (and was then revived for four more years in 1967), and during that time an astounding number of its contrivances and catch phrases became American folklore, from the inspired monotony of details in the voice-over narration to the sweaty-handed stamping of "Mark VII" (the name of Webb's production company) into stone, and especially Friday's refrain to witnesses: "Just the facts, ma'am."

It was Jack Webb himself, playing Joe Friday, who became the show's most enduring pop culture icon. There has never been another character on TV or in the movies at once so completely tedious and yet so enthralling. The original concept of a cog in a law-enforcement machine, whom Webb described as "a neutral character," remained unwavering for the life of the show, at least in its first version in the 1950s. "He has no religion, he's had no childhood, no educational background, no war record, no personal side at all," Webb said, and that is the way he played him—as an android without flaws, quirks, or humor. Webb never had any illusions about his acting talents (he much preferred the roles of producer and director—not only of "Dragnet" but of such subsequent shows as "Adam-12" and "Project UFO" and of several feature films in which he starred, including *Pete Kelly's Blues* and *-30-*); and yet his relentlessly la-

conic portrayal of the inscrutable Joe Friday bewitched the viewing public. In some way, his blankness made him like a Rorshach test, and Joe Friday fans had to wonder: Was his magnificent repression (and his complete lack of personal life) the result of some awful trauma years ago, or was it a way of coping with the demands of his job as a cop?

When "Dragnet" returned, as "Dragnet 1967," the extremism of Joe Friday's character became a leitmotif, occasionally even a source of humor. His new partner, Officer Bill Gannon, played by Harry Morgan, frequently needled Joe Friday about the sparseness of his personal life as a bachelor, and on one fascinating occasion even invited him home to supper to show him how nice domesticity could be. (Friday reciprocated in another episode, in which he entertained Gannon and his wife in his bachelor pad and cooked steaks for them on a hibachi grill.) Jack Webb continued to play Joe Friday as the stiffest man in show business; but the temper of the times—and "Dragnet" scripts—had changed by the late 1960s, and in episodes about student protest, drug use, long hair, and radicalism there were moments when Friday could no longer contain his pent-up feelings. The officer who was once content only to record and analyze the facts frequently delivered long, indignant lectures to miscreants and wayward youths, and once, when a dope-smoking couple accidentally let their baby drown in the bathtub, he was actually driven to tamper with evidence: At the end of the episode, he is so infuriated that he crushes the couple's bag of marijuana in his fist, crumbling it to smithereens in a big, climactic close-up.

"Dragnet" reflected Jack Webb's moral convictions, as well as his sledgehammer film style (also especially evident in *The D.I.*, an entire film acted and shot with the cadence of a close-order Marine drill); but lackluster Joe Friday was *not* an accurate reflection of Jack Webb. A jazz fanatic, a weekend painter, an accomplished cook, Webb was a passionate man whose four wives included the sultry star Julie London and Jackie Loughery, Miss U.S.A. of 1952. Unlike the taciturn Friday, he was a compulsive talker. "I don't even have a psychiatrist," he once wrote in an article called "The Facts About Me" for the *Saturday Evening Post.* "A psychiatrist would be wasting his time asking me to talk it out. I already talk too much. I have to sit on my head to keep my mouth shut." Also unlike Friday, Webb had a mischievous sense of humor. One time, when making a guest appearance on "The Ed Sullivan Show" in a comedy bit in which he was supposed to be in New York hunting for a beauty to play a role in the show, he told Ed, "I'm looking for a three-eleven-W." Webb later recalled, "The audience got nothing out of the phrase, but my police friends all over Los Angeles had a laugh. 311-W is police code meaning a case of exposure which is endangering the public morals."

Webb was a workaholic who estimated that he walked twenty-five miles a day while working at the studio as an actor, producer, director, writer, and editor. His talents even included singing, and he once cut an album called *You're My Girl: Romantic Reflections by Jack Webb*, in which he almost croons—actually enunciates—poetic verses from love songs, accompanied by an orchestra puffing out notes of swollen passion. By 1973 he was producing five different television series at one time. But it was "Dragnet" by which everyone remembered Jack Webb when he died of a heart attack in 1982 at age sixty-two. Sergeant Friday's famous badge, number 714, was encased in a block of Lucite and put on display at the police academy in Los Angeles, and at L.A.P.D. headquarters flags were flown at half-staff to mark his passing.

DRIVE-INS
(Restaurants, Movies, etc.)

Cars are nice to sit in—so nice that getting out of one and leaving it behind while you go about your business can seem like more trouble than it's worth. For contented motorists who would rather stay behind the wheel, America's auto-smitten landscape has offered up movies, hamburger joints, dry cleaners, banks, liquor stores, groceries, copy centers, stock brokerages, vaccination clinics, and even churches that don't require any effort greater than reaching for your wallet and rolling down the window. Now that conscientious citizens have learned to frown on the profligate use of cars as wasting energy, such automotive fetishism is pretty much out of favor, vanishing, or extinct (with the exception of drive-through fast food restaurants), but there was a time when commanding a set of wheels provided endless, devil-may-care opportunities to live it up by driving in.

"People with cars are so lazy they don't want to get out of them to go eat," declared J. G. Kirby, a candy and tobacco wholesaler, to explain the new kind of restaurant he

At Sivils Drive In
Dallas, Texas

opened on the highway between Dallas and Fort Worth in September 1921. Kirby's Pig Stand sold nothing but barbecued pork (its motto: "Eat a Pig Sandwich") and it had no tables and chairs; it was the first restaurant designed to serve people sitting in their cars. The same year, E. W. Ingram began serving five-cent hamburgers from a truck stop in Wichita, Kansas, that he called White Castle. He sold the tiny steamed burgers by the sack, and it was not unusual for customers who couldn't find a seat at his counter to eat outside, sitting in their car or on their running board. Two years later, Roy Allen and Frank Wright, who had recently opened successful root beer stands (called A & W) in Lodi, California, and Houston, debuted three more stands in Sacramento, one of them offering "tray boy" service—aproned waiters in white caps who carried root beer out to customers in cars. By the early 1930s there were more than sixty Pig Stands, not only in Texas and the Southwest but from New York to California; and there were almost two hundred A & W's, mostly in the West and Midwest, nearly all featuring tray boy (and soon tray girl) service. In Normal, Illinois, in 1934, A. H. "Gus" Belt began a chain of Steak 'n' Shakes that featured "four-way service" allowing customers to sit at a counter, occupy a table, "takhomasak" (carry out a bagful), or—the latest craze—eat in their car.

Bill Marriott, an A & W franchise operator in Washington, D.C., wasn't happy selling only cold root beer, so in 1927 he expanded his soda stand into a tiny restaurant with a counter, tables, and chairs. He called it the Hot Shoppe because it served spicy chili con carne and hot tamales, as well as beef cut by a carving chef who stood over the roast and sliced as a fan blew its aromas out to the sidewalk and attracted customers. The formula was a success, and more Hot Shoppes were built throughout the East, many of them featuring in-car service by a staff that came to be known as the Marriott "running boys." (When Bill and Paul Marriott realized that some drive-in customers at their Fourteenth Street Bridge Hot Shoppe arrived in taxis on their way to nearby Hoover Field and ordered food to go, the Marriotts began delivering meals to the airport, and in 1937, directly to DC-3's—the beginning of "In-Flite" service.) It wasn't long before tray boys, tray girls, and running boys all came to be known by a single name, carhop, because they took customers' orders after hopping onto the car's running board.

When Mr. and Mrs. J. D. Sivils decided to close their restaurant in downtown Houston and open Sivils Drive-In out in the prairie in 1939, they took the carhop concept to a new level of showmanship. Their tray girls, selected on the basis of "good figure, a high school education, health card, and come-hither personality," became famous for their scanty satin majorette costumes and high white boots, as well as for the way they patrolled the parking lot in military cadence, marching to the rhythm of music blasted by loudspeakers. Mrs. Sivils coached her platoon of a hundred girls in diction, posture, and deportment; she established rigid rules about exactly how trays should be carried (at ear level, on one hand); and she meted out proper punishment (napkin-folding duty) for such infractions as touching a patron or carrying a tray too low. Carhops memorized the menu, were instructed to laugh at customers' jokes, and were paid nothing, but frequently made as much as five dollars a day in tips.

Drive-in restaurants were everywhere in America by 1940, but they were at their best and most numerous in California. "Everything about the state favored drive-ins," Philip Langdon observed in *Orange Roofs, Golden Arches*, "the mild climate that permitted year-round operation, the dispersed cities and suburbs, the widespread reliance on automobiles, the willingness to experiment." California had A & W's, Pig Stands, and Hot Shoppes as well as its own drive-in chains—Stan's, Simon's, Pig 'n Whistle, Carpenter's—and innumerable one-of-a-kind tamale shops shaped like tamales, chili parlors shaped like bowls of chili, and drive-ins in the form of pigs, pumpkins, igloos, kegs, and frankfurters. Most of the early California drive-ins, Langdon points out, were circular shapes, which made them look streamlined and modern and also encouraged cars to pull up all around them. That made life easier for carhops (who didn't have to walk so far) and also gave customers a nice sense of rubbing bumpers (not shoulders) with fellow diners, something akin to animals gathering around a favorite watering hole. "Nobody was really ever in a hurry about leaving," Mike Anson recalled in a *Motor Trend* article about the 'Wich Stand drive-in in Los Angeles. "We were all there to look at other guys' cars, nurse our malts as long as possible, talk to girls, and find out who was racing whom later that night."

A landmark in the drive-in's gastronomic progress occurred in California in 1936 when Robert C. Wian, Jr., proprietor of a Glendale diner called Bob's Pantry, looked across his ten-stool counter at the hungry members of a local band who pleaded with him for a meal that was really satisfying. Wian invented the double-decker hamburger. He called it a Big Boy—a deluxe, fully dressed behemoth on a triple-decker bun that soon became the featured attraction at Bob's Big Boy drive-ins throughout the state, then the nation.

In 1940, four years after the invention of the Big Boy, the future of drive-ins looked brilliant, especially in California, so Mac and Dick McDonald gave up trying to run their movie theater in Glendora and decided to open a drive-in hamburger shop in San Bernardino instead. Fourteen years later, when Ray Kroc bought the right to franchise McDonalds nationwide, there were already about a dozen outlets in the West (see "McDonald's," p. 310). The fifties became a golden era for drive-ins (movies *and* restaurants). By this time the term had come to include not only restaurants with carhops but any self-service stand at which customers could eat in their cars: Dairy Queen (based on a formula for semifrozen ice cream invented in Illinois in 1938); Carvel; Tastee-Freez; Dog 'n' Suds; Sonic Burgers; Burger Chef; and, of course, Burger King, which first opened in 1953 in Jacksonville, Florida, after Keith G. Kramer, owner of Keith's Drive-In in Daytona Beach, went to San Bernardino and observed the success of the McDonald brothers. (Thus it can be —and has been—argued that Burger King in some way predates Ray Kroc's campaign with McDonald's, although it does not predate the McDonald brothers' "Speedee service" concept, which had been in place since 1948.)

Self-service fast-food restaurants, although still known as drive-ins, were much more efficient than classic drive-ins with carhops. Not only were fewer employees needed; on the average, customers at self-service restaurants came and went in about ten minutes. At a drive-in, where there was more interaction with human beings, the average visit took twice as much time.

In a foreshadowing of things to come, many drive-ins of the fifties supplemented carhops with electronic ordering systems as a way to speed up service. Each car slot had a microphone and speaker to communicate with an order taker in the restaurant, thus eliminating the carhop's first trip out to take an order. "The rage of the fifties," according to Philip Langdon, these systems went by such futuristic names as Auto-Dine, Dine-A-Mike, Dine-A-Com, Electro-Hop, Orda-phone, Fone-A-Chef, and Servus-Fone. One called Aut-O-Hop boasted of its exclusive "AMG" (Automatic Message Greeting), which didn't only take orders; it greeted customers with a customized message, suggesting what they ought to eat, then, when it was time for the tray to be removed, thanked them with a prerecorded message and sent them on their way. In the mid-1970s drive-through service was popularized, which featured drive-by speaker systems at which customers communicated with an order taker inside the restaurant before driving around the building to retrieve their feed.

During the 1960s a lot of people were suddenly horrified by urban sprawl, ugly billboards, and highway strips of fast-food restaurants. In *God's Own Junkyard* (1964) Peter Blake wrote, "In America today, no citizen (except for an occasional hermit) has a chance to see anything but hideousness—all around him, day in and day out." Cars took the blame for spawning the unsightly mess, and car culture, including drive-ins, was transformed from what it had been in the thirties and even more so in the fifties—a sign of American civilization's progress—into a badge of shame. "By the latter half of the sixties," Philip Langdon wrote, "the uproar against drive-ins re-

sounded throughout the land." They were blamed for being intrinsically ugly—garish concrete-and-neon founts of roadside litter —and also as breeding grounds for teenage mischief. A 1966 article in *Drive-In Restaurant* magazine suggested that operators try to beautify their establishment by adding trees and flowers, and perhaps thorny bushes "in a favorite place where teenagers loiter on foot."

In 1964, the same year *God's Own Junkyard* was published, the last Bob's Big Boy drive-in was built. Bob Wian had decided that coffee shops and family restaurants were the future of fast food. By the eighties, the few real drive-ins that remained (the ones with carhop service) had become places for middle-aged people to congregate (preferably in vintage convertibles), listen to golden oldies, and feel nostalgic for the days when cars were nothing but good, clean fun.

There is no more evocative symbol of America's now-tarnished love affair with automobiles than the drive-in movie. The first one opened on June 6, 1933, alongside Admiral Wilson Boulevard in Camden, New Jersey. It had parking places instead of seats and an outdoor screen that customers looked at from their cars while they listened to sound from speakers planted underneath each parking place. Its creator, a chemical manufacturer named Richard Hollingshead, Jr., had experimented by projecting movies in his driveway for friends and family, and he believed that he had found a winning formula to reattract people to the movies and away from all the roadside miniature golf they had been playing. He would combine the two things Americans loved best: movies and their automobiles. He erected a forty-foot screen in a field with parking for four hundred cars.

Motion Picture Herald was very specific in April 1944 when it stated the appeal of drive-in theaters, enumerating the following reasons for their bright postwar future:

1. The joy of being released from gasoline rationing.
2. The availability of all-beef hot dogs.
3. Resumption of normal restrictions upon the amorous impulses of youth.
4. Need for fresh air after years of propaganda.

Drive-in theaters were a uniquely social way of watching movies that provided a sense of community as well as the special privacy of being safe in one's own vehicle. Families could come to drive-ins with the kids in their pajamas, Mom in curlers, Dad in his undershirt, and nobody would mind. Unlike a normal theater, where you sat surrounded by other patrons, you could be entirely anonymous if you wanted to be: That's why Jimmy Cagney and his gang hid out at a drive-in in the 1949 gangster picture *White Heat.* Carloads of teenagers could come to the drive-in and smooch or otherwise cavort without being bothered by an usher. And yet for all the privacy it allowed, there was something communal about going to the drive-in, a sense of sharing the fun with others, honking at sappy love scenes or stupid-looking monsters, or maybe sitting beside your car in lawn chairs as if you were at an evening community picnic. (One theater in Vermont actually offered a "motel section" for patrons, where they could drive in, rent a room, and watch the movie from a picture window alongside their bed!)

Sometimes theater owners used the uniquely public nature of the experience to add special zing to the evening's merriment. During showings of low-budget horror movies that played the drive-in circuit in the fifties, ghouls, mummies, vampires, or werewolves employed by the management stalked among the rows of cars, popping up at windows during tense moments to terrify the occupants . . . and frequently got Cokes and boxes of popcorn dumped on their heads.

Between 1945 and 1955, the number of drive-in movie theaters in America rose from three hundred to more than four thousand at the same time the number of regular movie houses started to decline. The *New York Times Magazine* made note of this phenomenon in the summer of 1955 in an article titled "The Family 'Drives In' ": "The drive-in theater, once scorned as odd, even disreputable—the movies were always very old and very bad, the audiences not always solely interested in the movies—has become solid and respectable. . . . [Drive-ins] attract millions of car-borne families, show first-run films, often ahead of Broadway, and serve the community somewhat as a social center." The article was accompanied by photos that showed wholesome children romping on the jungle gym at the Bay Shore–Sunrise Drive-In Theater and families lining up at the cafeteria to have dinner during a forty-minute intermission.

In the 1970s energy crises drained the fun out of car cruising, and rising real estate values rendered drive-in movie theaters inefficiently big for the profits they made. Their time was up, and they became, like Saturday serials and dish night, objects of moviegoers' nostalgia. In April 1988 in New York City the American Classics Drive-In began offering customers the opportunity to watch movies inside a big Eleventh Avenue warehouse with a screen, from seats in thirty-six permanently parked convertibles. The movies shown were campy ones from the fifties. *New York* magazine called it "the last word in silly nostalgia." Just last year, redneck movie critic Joe Bob Briggs observed that some drive-ins that had closed in the eighties were reopening because so many young couples were having babies and needed a way to go to the movies without having to pay for a babysitter. He called what was happening "a little drive-in renaissance." Still, less than a thousand remain; and the last one in New Jersey, where drive-in movies were invented, was razed in 1991 to make way for a mall with a twelve-screen multiplex. Its final features were *The Girl Can't Help It*, starring Jayne Mansfield, and *The Fly*, starring Vincent Price.

There are very few kinds of business that have not offered drive-in service. One of the best-known modern ones is Robert Schuller's church in Garden Grove, California, with its own radio signal for drive-in parishioners and a view of Disneyland's Matterhorn in the distance. Reverend Schuller once called it a "twenty-two-acre shopping center for God" and described its advantages as "accessibility, service, visibility, possibility thinking, and excess parking."

In the seventies, Alvin Verrette, a funeral director in New Roads, Louisiana, opened a drive-in funeral parlor in which the embalmed corpse of the deceased was displayed behind a five-by-seven-foot glass window adjacent to a driveway by the side of the building. Just outside the window, at a level comfortable for drivers, a register was set upon a podium for those who wanted to sign in.

A few years ago, Mr. Verrette's formula was brought up to date at Gatling's Funeral Home in Chicago. Gatling's offers "Drive Thru Visitation" but has solved the problem of being able to show only one corpse at a time. If you are a mourner, you drive up to a speakerphone similar to the Electro-Hop of the fifties and push a button to request service. The mortician at the other end of the line asks whose remains you want to see. You give a name, sign a register, and the disembodied voice tells you to proceed a few feet forward to the viewing area. As you are inching forward, the person with whom you have just spoken presses the proper buttons on a control panel, so as you reach the viewing place the designated cadaver's head appears, in a live, closed-circuit broadcast direct from its chapel, on a twenty-five-inch color television. The picture lasts only three seconds, but there is another button you can press—and keep pressing—to see the dead person again, as many times as you wish. It is possible to look for hours, but established drive-in etiquette would seem to limit last respects to a reasonably quick once-over if there is a long line of cars waiting their turn.

BOB DYLAN

Bob Dylan is one of pop culture's best-known icons of insubordination. In the 1960s he pioneered a look and attitude of rebelliousness that included not only rumpled work clothes and messy hair but a gaunt appearance and insolent style that became the way millions of young people announced their defiance of the establishment. His uncanny, grating (but somehow compelling) voice was *the* voice of protest at a time when it seemed that protesters really would change the world. He started as a folksinger but went on to influence all of popular music as thoroughly

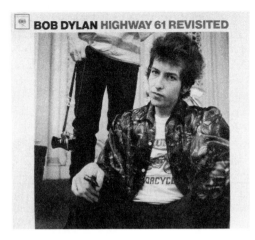

BOB DYLAN HIGHWAY 61 REVISITED

as the Beatles. Before him, most serious-minded people thought of pop songs as meaningless and moronic; after him rock and roll has been considered by many to be the true (and sometimes even profound) voice of the disaffected.

Dylan's first big impact was as the writer of "Blowin' in the Wind," which Peter, Paul and Mary recorded and released as a single in 1963. It sold more than three hundred thousand copies in two weeks—faster than any previous record in Warner Bros.' history. It was immediately adopted as the freedom song of the civil rights movement, and suddenly everybody with a conscience seemed to know the name Bob Dylan. At the Newport Folk Festival in July, Peter, Paul and Mary introduced their rendition of "Blowin' in the Wind" by saying it "was written by the most important folk artist in America today." And later, when Dylan himself got onstage to sing it, the audience went wild with adulation and joy. Dylan was joined by Joan Baez singing harmony, then folk eminence Pete Seeger, then Theodore Bikel, and the Freedom Singers. The crowd was overwhelmed by the power of the song and the solidarity of its singers; and they demanded an encore. All the performers

joined hands and sang "We Shall Over-come." It was the epiphany of the folk music movement in the 1960s.

Dylan's rise to fame had been fast. Less than a year before his Newport triumph, in a *Time* cover story about the folk revival, John McPhee devoted one short paragraph to the "promising young hobo [who] dresses in sheepskin and a black corduroy Huck Finn cap, which covers only a small part of his long, tumbling hair." Born Robert Zimmerman and raised in Hibbing, Minnesota, he had come to New York in 1961 at the age of nineteen, embellishing his conventional middle-class childhood with tales of carnival roustabouting, life in an orphanage, and hard-knock adventure on the open road.

"Dylan was constantly inventing himself," recalled fellow folksinger Ric Von Schmidt. His high school yearbook listed his goal as "to join Little Richard"; but in Dinkytown, Minneapolis's Bohemia, he hung around a coffee shop called the Ten O'Clock Scholar and sang folk songs made popular by Pete Seeger, the Kingston Trio, and Harry Belafonte. His date for the junior prom in high school said, "We were so different from all these other gung ho, goody-goody kids and we just didn't fit in. We just wandered around by ourselves. I went home crying."

Dylan went east, where he got close to Woody Guthrie, who was by then incapacitated in a New Jersey hospital with Huntington's disease. In September 1961 he was discovered singing at Gerdes Folk City, a Greenwich Village coffee house, by *New York Times* critic Robert Shelton. The Greenbriar Boys were the show's headliners, but the *Times* reviewer was awed by Dylan—"one of the most distinctive stylists to play in a Manhattan cabaret in months... bursting at the seams with talent." Ed Sullivan rejected him, and his image was still so unformed that there were some people in the folk scene who thought he maybe should team up with another unknown singer, Barbra Streisand, to sing duets; but John Hammond of Columbia records signed him to cut an album solo. It was called *Bob Dylan* and contained only two original songs, "Talking New York" and "Song to Woody," among a group of traditional blues and country ballads. The album came out in February 1962, and it was pretty much a dud, selling a mere five thousand copies through the summer. Few outside the hard-core folk scene in New York knew about him, but those who became aware of Bob Dylan in the course of the next year began to feel a powerful sense of destiny.

If you weren't there to discover it for yourself in the spring or summer of 1963, it is simply impossible to convey the marvelous impact of the music of his second album, *The Freewheelin' Bob Dylan.* It was a vision of apocalypse and redemption all in one. Its wrath ("Masters of War"), its wit ("I Shall Be Free"), its buoyancy ("Honey, Just Allow Me One More Chance"), its delicacy ("Blowin' in the Wind") displayed a range of feeling that put Dylan the singer in a class by himself. The scope of its lyrics was audacious, too—from the ordeal of James Meredith in "Oxford Town" and nuclear annihilation in "A Hard Rain's A-Gonna Fall" to the introspective poetry of "Bob Dylan's Dream."

What was most impressive as the world began to learn about Bob Dylan in 1963 was how he sounded so prescient. He sang in his enigmatic way not about yesterday's issues but about where we all seemed to be headed. In his next album, *The Times They Are A-Changin'*, Dylan solidified his position as oracle with the title song, and he furthered his image as seismograph of the emerging protest movement with "The Lonesome Death of Hattie Carroll" and "Only a Pawn in Their Game." "It's spooky, really it is," a New York folknik told Dylan biographer Anthony Scaduto. "The kid was more than a genius. He was a reincarnation of *all* the folk geniuses there ever were."

Time made fun of him in May 1963, describing him as "faintly ridiculous" because of his citybilly idiosyncrasies and a voice that "sounds as if it were drifting over the walls of a tuberculosis sanitarium." *Time* made fun of his fans, too, who "have an unhappy tendency to drop their g's when praisin' him—but only because they cannot resist imitatin' him." The mockery demonstrated exactly what Dylan was singing about in "The Times They Are A-Changin' ": an unbreachable and ever-growing rift between *his* kind of people—the young, restless, angry ones—and the writers and critics and old people who could not fathom what was happening. The battle lines of the sixties were being drawn.

It was not only stuffed shirts from the established media who were bothered by Dylan's affectations and eccentricities. Serious doubts were beginning to float through the folksinging community about this new folk hero. The old timers loved "Blowin' in the Wind" and "North Country Blues"—such ballads were what folksinging was all about. But what were they to make of "Boots of Spanish Leather" and "One Too Many Mornings" on *The Times They Are A-Changin'*? These were introspective art songs about Bob Dylan's private dreams and demons, with no references whatsoever to significant public issues. Then, too, they were bothered by Bob Dylan's fans: *fans*, not serious aficionados —squealy fourteen-year-old girls who came to Dylan's concert at Town Hall in 1963 and behaved as if he were Elvis Presley.

At the Newport Folk Festival in 1964, Bob Dylan got up and sang... *love songs!* Not one antiwar or antisegregation song in his whole set! A good portion of the audience, many of them rapt Bob Dylan fans to begin with, and many of them much younger than Newport audiences in previous years, were enthralled by the new, intimate Dylan. He, like a handful of pioneering mid-decade mind voyagers (whose leaders included Ken Kesey, Timothy Leary, and Allen Ginsberg), was exploring subjects such as consciousness, values, and freedom that had less to do with public issues than with a very personal kind of radicalization. "I don't want to write *for* people any more. You know—be a spokesman," Dylan told Nat Hentoff in a 1964 *New Yorker* profile. "From now on I want to write from inside me." His next album, *Another Side of Bob Dylan*, released in 1964, was entirely personal—about liberation and freedom as strictly private things. The album's central song, "My Back Pages," proclaimed the end of all the old slogans and old ways of protesting. Instead of offering answers, Dylan deliberately turned away from the problems and looked deep inside himself.

While this radical twist disenchanted many of the old-guard folk community, the newly hip Dylan was embraced by a seething audience in need of a spiritual leader: the youth movement. "He's all of us," *Time* quoted one young fan in 1965. "He's all the things we always felt but could never eloquently express." Dylan sang for vast numbers of alienated, confused, groping people who were beginning to feel stunned by a torrent of events they could not comprehend: hideous violence in the South; riots and conflagration in the cities in the North; tens of thousands of American boys suddenly getting drafted to fight in a war that no one could explain. Politely singing "We

Shall Overcome" or "Blowin' in the Wind" just didn't cut it anymore. For many who felt disillusioned and confused, Dylan's kaleidoscopic absurdism seemed to say it all.

Although conventional wisdom says he abandoned folksinging, what Dylan did was simply abandon the formula of folk music as didactic treatises—the itemized protest songs, the black-and-white morality, the mannerly guitar. "All these labor people, rich suburban cats telling their kids not to buy Bob Dylan records," he said. "All they want is songs from the thirties, union hall songs. 'Which Side Are You On?' That's such a waste. I mean, which side can you *be* on?" What Dylan did was to carry folk music from what it had been—good-time songs sung by the likes of the Kingston Trio, political tracts, or obscure old ballads no one cared about—into an idiom that meant something to real folks, the modern language of rock and roll.

It wasn't only his music that changed. Dylan created a new look for himself, a counterculture style that was imitated by thousands of people who now considered him an idol. He lost all the baby fat in evidence on his first two album covers, abandoned the shaggy ramblin'-man look, and assumed the countenance of a pained and scrawny ascetic. "He generated visions of a young man on a death trip," Anthony Scaduto wrote. "His bones stuck out, and his skin—the color of sour milk—appeared to be stretched to the ripping point."

In May 1965 Dylan recorded his first top ten single, "Like a Rolling Stone" (which reached number two in September). Riding a rippling organ riff and a throbbing bass guitar, Dylan spits out a cryptic diatribe saturated with vengefulness towards some unnamed loser who once believed herself safe from life's existential horrors. That six-minute song (cut into two parts to fit the three-minute format allotted by Top 40 radio stations) defined a new kind of music, known as folk-rock, and opened the doors of pop to lyrics with substance and artists who believed they had something serious to say.

By July 1965, when he was hooted off the stage at the Newport Folk Festival because he used an *electric* guitar (verboten among conservative folkniks), Dylan had created a new idiom and had left traditional folksinging far behind. Now a self-styled rock-and-roll outlaw who, along with the Beatles, seemed to be defining not just music but an entirely new world culture, Dylan released one of the first double albums (*Blonde on Blonde*) and teamed with the Hawks, later known as the Band, and soon became what Robert Santelli in *Sixties Rock* calls "untouchable as a force in American rock." Dylan's career was drastically interrupted by a motorcycle accident in 1966 that put him out of commission until he returned in 1968 with yet another entirely new persona—country balladeer, whose album *John Wesley Harding* was described by Dave Marsh as "intensely religious" and "lovely."

In the last quarter-century, Bob Dylan has metamorphosed many times—changing religions, performing in white clown makeup, performing his old songs with mean detachment, occasionally behaving—in one critic's words—"like a Vegas lounge singer . . . a ghastly reincarnation of Ed Sullivan," and writing lyrics about subjects that range from the love of Jesus Christ to the trumped-up criminal charges against boxer Rubin "Hurricane" Carter and the death of gangster Joey Gallo. There have even been some conspicuously awkward (but interesting) movie roles, as a cowboy in Peckinpah's *Pat Garrett and Billy the Kid* (1973), as a Dylan-like performer in *Renaldo and Clara* (1978), and as a cloddish sculptor in Dennis Hopper's *Backtrack* (1990), all of

which followed his finest film performance—as himself—in the pioneering rock documentary, *Don't Look Back* (1967).

For some critics, it has been sad to see Bob Dylan be anything less than the genius and leader of a generation, as he once seemed: On one staggeringly ironic occasion, while touring some of the less lucrative venues on the rock circuit, he performed one of his golden-oldie protest songs, "Masters of War," for the cadets at West Point. But it hasn't all been like that. In 1988 he teamed with George Harrison, Tom Petty, and the late Roy Orbison to sing as a group called the Traveling Wilburys. That same year he was inducted into the Rock and Roll Hall of Fame. At the ceremony in New York he sang "Like a Rolling Stone," backed by Mick Jagger, Bruce Springsteen, and Mary Wilson, with George Harrison, Jeff Beck, John Fogerty, Neil Young, and Les Paul playing their guitars.

"DYNASTY"

We set out to create the ultimate American fantasy family . . . Rich, powerful, glamorous, living in Denver. . . . It would own mega-corporations. A football team. Horses. Airplanes. Limousines and fine motor cars. . . . The men would buy and sell empires. . . . The women would be extraordinarily beautiful and they would wear the prettiest clothes imaginable.

—Esther Shapiro, co-creator of "Dynasty"

Of the several evening serials that followed in the wake of "Dallas" (see p. 121), each trying to trump the extravagance of life at the Ewings' Southfork ranch and to show billionaires who were even filthier rich, more prodigal, and more treacherous than J.R. and his clan, ABC's "Dynasty," created and written by Esther and Richard Shapiro (known previously for such issue-oriented TV movies as *Sarah T: Portrait of a Teenage Alcoholic*), was the soap with the most: the most expensive jewelry and clothing, the most ravenous scenery chewing by its actors. It also had the most ludicrous plot twists, with the exception of its own spin-off, "The Colbys," which concluded its two-season run in 1987 with the abduction of Fallon Colby (née Carrington) by a flying saucer. Fallon later reappeared on "Dynasty," where she had been presumed dead for some time since her abduction.

The dramaturgical extremism whirled ferociously into never-never land, energized by some of the nastiest cat fights ever shown on TV—between Alexis Morell Carrington Colby (Joan Collins) and Krystle Jennings Carrington (Linda Evans) and featuring perpetual seduction schemes (usu-

ally by Alexis), an especially dastardly kidnapping plot (Krystle was nabbed and "replaced" by a lookalike, also played by Linda Evans), plenty of bribery and extortion, and (in 1985) an end-of-season massacre of nearly the entire cast by terrorists in the Eastern European kingdom of Moldavia. Viewers had so much fun watching these campy goings-on and gaping at the characters' ostentatious lifestyles that "Dynasty" rose to number one in the ratings in its third season (1984–85) and managed to wangle extracurricular guest appearances from such fans as former President Gerald Ford and his wife, Betty, and Henry Kissinger.

Audiences didn't really take it all that seriously; and how could they, considering the side-splitting histrionics of Joan Collins, who truly made an art of overacting? As

John Forsythe (Blake Carrington) and *top:* Linda Evans (Krystle Carrington), Joan Collins (Alexis Carrington Colby), Emma Samms (Fallon Carrington Colby); *bottom:* Pamela Bellwood (Claudia Blaisdel Carrington), Heather Locklear (Sammy Jo Dean Carrington)

expressed by her flaring nostrils, arched brows over dilated eyes, and heaving chest, being evil was life's most exhilarating game. Playing the former wife of Blake Carrington (John Forsythe) with plummy grandiloquence, Collins feasted on her character as a diabolical empire destroyer with a heart of stone and a taste for gold (and diamonds and designer gowns) and a sexual appetite that had doomed a long trail of captains and kings. She was a flamboyant bitch that audiences relished hating but also envied and admired. After all, as described in *Dynasty: The Authorized Biography of the Carringtons*, she was "a world class woman totally in control of her life, who never goes anywhere without being the center of attention . . . a jet-setter with important connections in government, society, finance, and fashion . . . also a talented painter . . . an arbiter of taste wherever she goes. She brands everything she touches with her distinctive signature . . . including men." Alexis was every bit as wicked as J. R. Ewing of "Dallas," but with the added attraction of the show's extravagant wardrobe allowance. In soap opera, as in professional wrestling, it is the villain who makes for an interesting show —the more extreme the villainy, the more exciting the drama—and Alexis was the heart and soul of "Dynasty."

Krystle wasn't rich and upper-class; and therefore she was good and pure—which is why Blake married her in the first episode (and why thousands of new parents named their daughters Krystle in the 1980s). She knew that real happiness wasn't found by exercising greed and wanton lust, although she often worried that maybe she had married too high, considering her background as Blake's humble, working-class secretary. In *The Authorized Biography of the Carringtons* Krystle was described like this: "a tender, loving, feminine woman—a passionate romantic living the life of every girl's dream, but bringing to it common sense, compassion, and cachet. She is a truly beautiful human being."

Everybody else on the show, however, had some very serious personality disorders. Blake, the head of the Carrington clan, was a hugely successful businessman, but he was so driven he neglected his personal life and almost (until he met Krystle) missed out on happiness. Even with Krystle to help him get his priorities straight, his life was a major mess. The troubled man found himself on trial for manslaughter—with his own ex-wife, Alexis, on the witness stand testifying against him; suddenly strapped for cash, he had to trade away 45 percent interest in his football team; he was blinded by a mobster's bomb; he discovered that Krystle's earlier divorce wasn't legal (not her fault!); he got hoodwinked out of a hundred million dollars; and he couldn't communicate worth a damn with his kids.

And the kids: Oh, boy, did they have problems! Steven (Al Corley, then Jack Coleman—the cast change explained by "plastic surgery") couldn't figure out his sexual identity, and that really irked his homophobic dad. And Fallon (Pamela Sue Martin, then Emma Samms) had everything a girl could want—looks, charm, money— but she was bored with life and did naughty things like going skinny-dipping in the family pool and smoking marijuana during Krystle's first formal dinner party. She also inherited Alexis's sexual voracity, and she had affairs with psychiatrist Nick Toscanni and a Brazilian millionaire. Fallon was paralyzed from the waist down when she was hit by a drunken driver; but one day she was lying by the pool and saw her infant son (by her ex-husband, Jeff [John James]) toddle towards the pool, about to fall in and drown. Maternal love surged through her lower body and she leapt up, able to walk again, and saved the little boy.

"Dynasty" presented its calamity-plagued characters as the epitome of class. Unlike the cowboy vulgarians of "Dallas," the Carringtons were glamorous and sophisticated, having frequent occasion to dress in tuxedos and evening gowns and eye-popping suites of jewels as they drank Perrier-Jouet and exchanged rapier-witted insults. It was an image of rich people that audiences relished because it provided an opportunity to see the awful, corrosive effect of great wealth. You could watch "Dynasty" and feel all the envy that other people's money tends to inspire, but then when you saw how miserable they were, you felt a whole lot better about not being a billionaire.

The inevitable reversal of fortune for "Dynasty" (from number one in the ratings in 1984 to number seven in 1985 to twenty-four in 1986) came after the "Moldavian massacre," which was the grand finale of the 1984–85 season (the year Rock Hudson had made his final TV appearance). With all the cast gathered in the European kingdom for the spectacular wedding of Alexis's daughter Amanda (Catherine Oxenberg) to Prince Michael (an event that was designed to pave the way, the following season, for Alexis to become queen), Moldavian revolutionaries mowed them all down. However, the scene turned out to be less a cliffhanger than an over-the-cliff turn of events. With everyone apparently dead, what suspense was there other than disillusioning speculation about how the show's writers would weasel themselves out of the situation? ("Dallas" hadn't yet introduced the it-was-only-a-dream strategy.) Furthermore, the unforeseen massacre upset a lot of viewers who had come to expect only a polite measure of violence among the diamonds and silk that were the main reason to watch the Carringtons' shenanigans. The wedding had been anticipated by fans as a true pageant of glamour and magnificence; it was so eagerly awaited that some people actually planned their own real-life weddings to coincide with the one they expected to watch on TV. So when it ended in bloodshed, a lot of fans weren't happy, and Matt Roush of *USA Today* cited the awful spectacle as the beginning of the end of prime-time-soap-opera success.

In the next season's opening episode, it turned out that all of the principals had been lucky enough to dodge the machine gun bullets. This was an explanation that was true to the outrageous plot twists that had characterized "Dynasty" from the beginning, but nonetheless hard for fans to enjoy—for the simple reason that it was too easy. It wasn't a clever turn of events but simply a deus ex machina, and it seemed, like Bobby Ewing's dreamed death in "Dallas" later on, a sign of disrespect for viewers. Similarly, there was something a little too pat when the beloved Krystle was replaced by her evil lookalike. Furthermore, Joan Collins, fighting about her salary with the producers, was absent from the early episodes in 1985. She returned, but Alexis never did become Queen of Moldavia; and the melodrama never regained the panache of the early years.

When "Dynasty" finally ended its run in May 1989, it ranked fifty-seventh in the ratings. "The suspense isn't killing us anymore," *TV Guide* said in an article that began wistfully—"Remember the days when nighttime soaps *really* were fun?"—and recalled that wonderful season of 1982–83, when not only did Southfork burst into flames and threaten to incinerate the Ewings of "Dallas" but Alexis and Krystle were caught together in a horrific cabin fire on "Dynasty" (deliberately set, of course), from which they both emerged more beautiful than ever, their skin refreshed and rosy thanks to the heat of the conflagration.

HARLEY EARL

Nobody else has affected the look of American material culture as much as Harley Earl. Most people who know his name at all know him as the man who invented tail fins, which he first planted on 1948 Cadillacs. But fins are only the most conspicuous example of the great man's life work of transforming automobiles into possessions that Americans could love and lust for. He was the first to use chrome; he created two-tone paint jobs, pillarless hardtops, quadruple headlights, and wraparound windshields; and he oversaw the design of the original Corvette (as well as the Corvair, which Ralph Nader was to call "one of the greatest acts of industrial irresponsibility in the present century"). His unwavering goal was to make cars lower, longer, wider, and flashier every year, so that buyers were always tantalized and the thrill of driving was always renewed.

In addition to his automotive accomplishments, Harley Earl also changed the shape of American life in these ways:

- He invented tail fins for carpet sweepers.
- He was the first to put food in spray-on aerosol cans. (He told Nabisco to sell cookie dough that way; instead, they used it for spray-on cheese.)
- He pioneered the use of orange Naugahyde on chairs and couches.
- He designed the nylon net playpen for toddlers.
- He designed Fig Newtons.
- He advocated corrugated potato chips as an engineering advance over unruffled ones.
- He designed roll-on deodorant.

Earl's job, as he saw it, was to inspire, then fulfill, fantasies. When asked to describe the purpose of his automobile designs, he never talked about such things as ergonomics or engineering. He said of his ideal car, "Every time you get in it, it's a relief . . . a little vacation for a while." Unlike so many elite industrial designers who have tried through the years to "educate" American consumers to the supremacy of the modernistic less-is-more aesthetic, Earl had no use for the sparse niceties of international modernism and the cult of good taste. He liked flash and glamour; he wallowed in elaborate sculptural effects, the baroquer the better. His gaudy, sensuous ideals, rendered in bosomy bumpers, bulging fenders, and gaping air scoops on cars with such names as Eldorado Biarritz Coupé, thrilled more than fifty million people who bought what he designed during Detroit's golden age. His was an era when it was perfectly acceptable to love a vehicle not for any practical reasons but because it was poetry in chrome and steel—clunky poetry, maybe, but poetry nonetheless. To this day, there isn't a product you can name that is more deliriously, outrageously, and maybe embarrassingly American than a mid-fifties Detroit car designed by Harley Earl.

He came from Hollywood, where he was born in 1893, the son of a coach maker who served wealthy ranchers and growers (before there was a motion picture business and before there were cars). Earl worked with his father in the teens, customizing cars for movie stars, including one for Tom Mix that had a real leather saddle attached to the roof for open-air riding. At the time, Henry Ford's mass-produced Model T, supplied to all customers in generic black, dominated the market; Earl's designs—with sculpted sheet metal in bright colors—were strictly for the ostentatious nouveau riche. His work caught the eye of Lawrence P. Fisher, president of Cadillac, which was part of the new conglomerate called General Motors. Fisher hired Earl as a design consultant to give Cadillacs the custom-built look; and in 1919 Earl moved to Detroit to work for GM, where in 1927 he was made head of a newly formed department: Art and Color. Two years before, GM had devised the notion of an annual model change in order to stimulate sales, and by 1927, the year the Model T went out of production and the Art and Color section was begun, the destiny of the American automobile had been set. Harley Earl became its Zeus. "Never in the history of Western industrial civilization has one man had such an authoritarian influence over a world of values," wrote Stephen Bayley in *Harley Earl and the American Dream Machine.*

Earl began by eliminating stodgy running boards and creating built-in (rather than bolt-on) trunks, then formulated a design ideal that combined aerodynamic streamlining with rococo embellishments. As chief stylist, he had the job of creating a unique visual identity to evoke the separate status niche held by each of General Motors' divisions—Chevrolet, Pontiac, Buick, Oldsmobile, Cadillac. Chevrolets were basic family cars. Pontiacs were sportier, one level up. Oldsmobiles were sedate, for professional people. Buicks had a touch of class and power. And Cadillac was the King of the Road. But that was only the beginning. Within each division, there were three or four different model levels, each with its separate cachet and unique position on the status ladder. A well-educated consumer knew that a Coupe de Ville, although a Cadillac, was the lowest-level Caddy; an Eldorado was the top-of-the-line, except for the Eldorado Biarritz or Brougham, which were higher still (in 1957 the latter came with an Arpège atomizer built into the dashboard, stocked with Lanvin perfume). Stephen Bayley called these "levels of differentiation which would have pleased the most pedantic medieval scholastic," but they were a crucial part of Harley Earl's plan to encourage consumers to believe there was a car exactly right for them, and when the car buyer got a raise or better job, there was an even *better* model waiting.

By the time America's buying frenzy hit full stride in the Populuxe era after World War II, Harley Earl's giddy designs helped make Motor City products a paragon of the materialistic enthusiasms of a growing consumer society. As the country's interstate highways were built, his huge chrome cruisers—introduced with fanfare and drama each year at GM's traveling Motorama—became the predominating symbol of how American life was getting bigger, better, and faster all the time. Each year's model change meant *progress;* and to entice the public about what lay in store for them, he built prototypical "dream cars"—rocket-ship-shaped vehicles with vague resemblances to those available in showrooms.

Eventually, some of the features and styling fillips on the dream cars found their way onto production vehicles, and so each year's new-car buyer felt that he or she was getting a car that had been brushed with the magic of the future.

In fact, Earl was known to actually drive one of his dream cars around Detroit, astonishing other guests at his Grosse Pointe country club and pedestrians along downtown streets as he rocketed past them in the one designated "LeSabre" (after the Air Force's F-86 LeSabre fighter jet), which one automotive writer described as having an "exceptional phallic jelly-mold appearance." This one-of-a-kind, two-seater convertible, built in 1951, had pointy "Dagmar bumpers" (named for the resemblance to a busty starlet, and soon grafted onto Cadillacs), big fins, and a moisture-activated top that closed automatically at the first hint of rain. Earl was so proud of his LeSabre he had a second one built and sent it to General Dwight Eisenhower to use as his personal vehicle around Paris when he served as NATO commander in 1951 and 1952. Although the LeSabre never went into production, its name and many of its styling features (but not its raindrop-activated roof) found their way onto mass-produced Buicks.

None of the automobiles Harley Earl built was important for any engineering, performance, or safety innovation. Styling —a term unknown in the auto business before him—was their triumph. Earl defined good automotive styling as a vehicle that looked fast, heavy, plush, and futuristic. His two greatest masterpieces—the '53 Buick Skylark and the '59 Cadillac—share a brutish majesty that has long since vanished from the highways. The Caddy in particular, with its grinning chrome grille, heavy-lidded quadruple headlights, moon-rocket brake lights, and outlandish tail fins sharp enough to fillet passers-by, marks the absolute extreme of American design delirium . . . and the beginning of the end of Detroit's control of the car market.

Earl retired in 1959, the year tail fins reached their maximum height, and the year before the big three automakers all introduced their first compact cars. He died in 1969. "What was it? A car or an airplane or a rocket ship?" asked Paul C. Wilson in his book *Chrome Dreams* about Harley Earl's crowning achievement, the 1959 Cadillac. "From being a gentle stimulant to pleasurable daydreams, the jetpods, fins, and so forth began to seem like an affront to the motorist's intelligence."

Intelligence? Harley Earl never sought to appeal to buyers' intelligence; he preferred to kindle passions. His cars were designed to inspire desire, build egos, and make ownership feel satisfying and exciting—like sex, but practical as well as patriotic. In 1956 *The Consumer's Guide* declared Harley Earl's Chevrolet Bel-Air—designed with clusters of chrome, two-tone paint and upholstery to match, torpedo-shaped knobs arrayed on the dashboard, and a rocket-ship hood ornament—to be "the architecture of the American psyche made visible."

EARTH SHOES

Shoes got huge in the 1970s. Only a decade earlier, all trendy ones were small —svelte stiletto heels, pointy tiptoes, narrow continental winklepickers—the idea being to minimize the apparent size of the foot. Ballroom slippers or wing-tips, pumps or flats: almost all postwar shoes were designed to suggest that their wearer was a lithe, refined sort rather than a steel-toed workman or a country clodhopper in need of heavy-duty foot coverings. However, by the time men's ties had grown four inches wide (even wider than their side-burns), and bell-bottom pants were taking pants legs to flabbergasting extremes, shoes began to swell, too.

There were tall platforms with thick heels and giant soles that made anyone look like he (or she) was walking with a great cinder block attached to each shoe; there were running shoes (see p. 430) with gobs of padding and insulation all around the uppers and fat shock-absorbing rubber down below; and there were Earth Shoes, with their toe box fanned out as wide as a bear paw and bulky corrugated soles that looked like emergency flotation devices—low at the heel, but with a clump of rubber up front.

"Earth" was the registered trademark of Kalso Systemet, Inc., the only company that could legally sell genuine Earth Shoes, but for a while in the mid-1970s, every major shoe manufacturer was turning out similar footwear that caused pedestrians to rock and waddle like ducks. The *New York Times* fashion page reported on a traditional white wedding at which bride and groom both wore matching Earth Shoes. *Time* noted they were being worn by actors Tony Curtis and James Coburn and Olym-

pian Mark Spitz, and quoted one Malibu housewife as saying that since she got a pair of Earth Shoes, her corkie platforms were "just taking up room in the closet." Kalso Systemet, which began as a single shop on East Seventeenth Street in New York City, had become a multimillion-dollar business by 1976, and there were 135 Earth Shoe stores around the country.

Earth Shoes' first American champions, Ellie and Raymond Jacobs of New York, discovered the cloddish clogs during a family vacation through Europe in 1969. "Everywhere we went, I kept buying shoes," Ellie recalled, explaining that her back was killing her—so much that it was ruining their trip. Finally, in Copenhagen, they came upon a little shop where all the shoes were very ugly... and very orthopedic-looking. Although none of the clerks spoke English, the Jacobses noticed that several of the customers were American travelers—students, outdoor types, health food aficionados— who made a special point of coming to this store to buy shoes whenever they were in Europe because its shoes were so extraordinary.

They had been designed by a yoga enthusiast and former American couturier named Anne Kalsø, who originally conceived them by looking at footprints in the Brazilian earth. For years Ms. Kalsø had devoted her life to better posture; and it was her belief that the Indians of Brazil had excellent posture because for generations they had walked by sinking their heels down into soft terrain, thus forcing them to suck in their stomachs and stand straight. Modern men and women, who walk on concrete and asphalt most of the time, cannot do as the Indians do; but if they had a shoe that let their heels sink down low and allowed their toes to spread nice and wide every time they took a step, they, too, could enjoy perfect posture and all the salubrious benefits it brings. Kalsø made her first shoe in 1957 and spent years taking five-hundred-mile hikes to perfect it.

Sure enough, the shoes Ellie Jacobs bought in Copenhagen cured her bad back, and suddenly she and her husband, who had previously made some independent films and worked in the art world, saw their future: They would bring the weird, wonderful shoes to America. Ms. Kalsø, who had already turned down several American entrepreneurs who wanted to handle her shoes, demanded to know the Jacobses' birth dates so she could scrutinize their astrological charts. Apparently, their signs were excellent, because they were given exclusive U.S. rights—with the provision that the shoes be sold only in a small shop on a small street, with no advertising, so people could discover them when the karma was right. The Jacobs knew exactly where to sell them: in the shop below their apartment on East 17th Street, where the rents were cheap and many neighbors were nature-loving types who would appreciate the shoe. As their store's opening day approached, the Jacobs had a brainstorm. They would open for business on April 1, 1970—Earth Day—and they would name the shoes Earth Shoes. "All those kids who were demon-

strating in Union Square came by, saw us, and we were swamped," Ellie said.

Technically known as a "negative heel shoe," Earth Shoes did wonders for people with corns and bunions because they were so roomy. They offered relief from the pain of hammer toes and from calluses on the balls of the foot. Some converts said that Earth Shoes had increased their circulation and helped them quit smoking. *Time* praised them as "far less dangerous than platforms, which have caused countless sprains and fractures."

Not everybody fell in love with Earth Shoes. Tests at the California College of Podiatric Medicine showed that most people who put them on experienced severe pain and cramping for the first two weeks, but that eventually many symptoms caused by tight shoes were alleviated. However, anybody with flat feet, high arches, or shortened calf muscles (caused by wearing high heels) could expect nothing but agony from a negative heel shoe. Jennifer Yoels, a teacher of the Mensendieck System of Correct Body Movement and Posture in New York, said unequivocally, "This shoe will cripple everyone who wears it."

Despite such controversy, the issue with Earth Shoes never really was an orthopedic one. It wasn't even about comfort, although that's what most enthusiastic wearers spoke about. Earth Shoes were one of the most visible totems of a newly formulating way of life that proclaimed the supremacy of all things natural and earthy as opposed to artificial things that were stiff and constraining. As the New Age dawned, wide and homely was definitely groovier than slim and sleek. Like wild, long hair, Earth Shoes became a way of announcing your cultural allegiances.

You didn't just go to any ordinary shoe store to get them. You went to an Earth Shoe store, franchised by the Jacobses (who paid Anne Kalsø a royalty on every pair sold), who made it their business to transform the shoe-buying experience into a groovy happening. Each store featured nice hanging plants and natural-color paint and Scandinavian-looking wood decor, as well as trained Earth Shoe salespersons, who, at company expense, had taken a course in transcendental meditation to get mellow. When you selected a pair, you took it home in a rough-textured burlap bag rather than a squared-off box, perhaps accompanied by a pair of nonwhite Earth Socks to match. "Most of our shop owners, as well as customers, are into things like yoga and vegetarian eating," explained Ellie Jacobs. "You know, there's a crazy mystique about Anne Kalsø and the shoes."

With much regret, Mrs. Jacobs told us that it was the special nature of Earth Shoe stores that led to the shoes' demise. By 1976, when a hundred different manufacturers were flooding the market with false, cheap imitations, some Earth Shoe store proprietors—who had gotten rich selling the original Danish bluchers—rebelled against the strict rules that had been laid down by Anne Kalsø. They wanted to do their own thing, maybe even expand and sell other brands of shoes. "They were not your conventional store owner," Ellie Jacobs recalled. "They were flower children —honest, leftover hippies." But they were also rebellious like hippies, and their dissidence quickly brought the Earth Shoe business to its knees. In June 1977, Kalso Systemet filed for bankruptcy; and although some imitators continued in the market for many years, the real McCoy was history.

Today Anne Kalsø, in her eighties, is in seclusion in Denmark; and her son, who holds the patent to the shoes, seems to have no interest in exploiting it. After the stores bit the dust, Eleanor and Raymond Jacobs went back to photography and art, and they still live in their same apartment in the now-chic Union Square neighborhood, above the original Earth Shoe shop. Mrs. Jacobs hinted that a conspiracy of some sort had put an end to her once-thriving business, but she would not reveal any details. All the facts will come out, she assured us, when she completes her book about the rise and fall of the Earth Shoe empire.

EASY RIDER

No other movie released in the last fifty years has captured a moment's mood in America as perfectly as did *Easy Rider* in 1969. Here was the end of the sixties precisely realized in a parable about two guys on motorcycles. They start off with a stash of drugs, travel across the country meeting back-to-nature longhairs, an old-fashioned cowboy, and Louisiana whores, then get shot to death by leering rednecks. Their picaresque journey is a lament for the fading ideals of hippie culture and expresses the growing polarity between an uptight establishment and the paranoid remnants of the love generation.

Easy Rider never says exactly who its two travelers are—"Captain America" (Peter Fonda, the film's producer) and "Billy the Kid" (Dennis Hopper, the director) are their only names—and it gives no

information about their pasts, but it is clear from the beginning of their journey, which they start by throwing away their watches, that they are archetypal wanderers in search of America's soul. What they find is an unnerving sense of decay and disintegration. "We blew it," Captain America declares towards the end, when their quest yields only a feeling of post–Mardi Gras desolation. Peter Fonda called it "a story of escape, my own protest against all the hypocrisy of the current American scene."

Although cheaply made, it is a strikingly handsome movie (Paul Schrader called it "counterculture paranoia elevated to a level of superficial Hollywood glossiness"). The New Mexico scenery (filmed by Laszlo Kovacs) is breathtaking—majestic and pure. The fast ride in the wind along the highway is inspiring, and intensified by what was, in 1969, a novel soundtrack—contemporary rock songs (a concept pioneered by Kenneth Anger's underground biker movie, *Scorpio Rising*, then used by Mike Nichols in *The Graduate*). The counterculture characters the two riders meet, including Jack Nicholson as a town pariah, all have beautiful ideals even if, as in the hippie commune, they seem hopelessly naive. But there is something terribly wrong in the America experienced by Captain and Billy: The "straight" citizens they encounter along

the way hate them. They are not allowed in motels; people in small-town cafes make fun of them; they are jailed; and eventually they are killed—all because they look different. "This used to be a fine country," Jack Nicholson says (while inhaling marijuana) shortly before he is beaten to death by evil rubes. "What went wrong?"

Easy Rider confirmed what a lot of young, self-pitying dope smokers had begun to believe about America: The establishment was out to get them. The effect of the last scene in *Easy Rider*, in which the heroes are shot for no good reason, was similar to the murder of Marion Crane (Janet Leigh) in Hitchcock's *Psycho*. Just as lots of people thought twice about going behind a plastic shower curtain after 1960, for years after *Easy Rider* small-town America was considered dangerous by people who took the deaths of Billy and Captain America to heart. They believed that to leave the city was to risk one's life in a savage land filled with gun-toting hillbillies and Bible-thumping bigots.

Easy Rider, made on a minuscule $400,000 budget, earned over $60 million, outgrossing pictures such as *Paint Your Wagon* and *Dr. Dolittle* that had cost twenty or thirty times as much to produce. It seemed to signal a new era of filmmaking—the end of bloated studio productions with high-priced stars and overbaked plots, and the beginning of movies as groovy, youth-serving, antiestablishment expressions of real feelings, the way rock and roll still seemed in the sixties. Dennis Hopper and Peter Fonda became of-the-people culture heroes, and *Time* magazine declared their tragicomic epic "the little film that killed the big film."

Old Hollywood was stumped by *Easy Rider*. "Nobody at the studios understood it," said a Universal Pictures executive in the book *The Fifty Worst Films of All Time*.

"Hopper was just a funny-looking guy sitting around smoking dope. But a lot of the studio moguls got it into their minds that there must be a trend emerging—a trend which they couldn't fathom themselves—the trend of the drug-oriented, experimental, youth-market picture." Dozens of cheaply made pictures with portentous themes about the meaning of America, made by inexperienced pothead directors, were commissioned in hopes of duplicating *Easy Rider*'s success; and all failed. Dennis Hopper was given carte blanche by Universal Studios to work his magic once again, so he took a cast and crew and a multimillion-dollar budget to Peru (supposedly because he had heard that there were some especially potent psychedelic mushrooms there) and made *The Last Movie*, a Piran-dellian allegory about the destruction of innocence. According to film critic Roger Ebert, it was "a wasteland of cinematic wreckage"; the Los Angeles *Times* described it as "inchoate, amateurish, self-indulgent, tedious, superficial, unfocused, dismally disappointing, and depressing."

Time's death knell for slickly made big-budget movies had been premature. Only one year after *Easy Rider* seemed to change the nature of the motion picture business and herald the coming of a new kind of thought-provoking, poetic cinema of real human dimensions and with serious moral and social concerns, the smash success at theaters all across America was Ross Hunter's *Airport*, with an all-star cast and a turgid plot, spawning sequels galore for years to come.

WERNER ERHARD

"Perhaps the first American guru" is how *Los Angeles* magazine described Werner Erhard, founder of est (erhard seminars training, always lowercased): "a salesman who turned spiritualist, a clever craftsman who understood how to combine pop philosophies, Eastern religions, and the Puritan work ethic into an effective way to motivate people." He drew his charisma from all manner of mental mumbo jumbo, and learned how to speak effectively by listening to futurist R. Buckminster Fuller, who made every pause seem pregnant with a question aimed at the listener. He studied Zen, Silva Mind Control, Mind Dynamics, and Dale Carnegie, and is said to have gone through five levels of Scientology. He sold Fords at a dealership run by Lee Iacocca. And he had been through two names already (Jack Rosenberg, then Jack Frost) when, as Werner Erhard in 1971, he had a revelation while driving along a California highway in his second wife's black Mustang.

The revelation was est, and for the next fourteen years he imparted his wisdom to others in group marathon sessions that were supposed to help people—in est terms—"disappear all their old tapes" and get rid of the bad beliefs and barriers by which they lived their stinking lives, and to begin anew. An estimated seven hundred thousand followers have paid between $250 and $625 each for starter lessons in self-reconstruction, at est sessions and at those of est's successor, the Forum; and untold millions of their friends and acquaintances have received Mr. Erhard's wisdom second-hand, via graduates who became true believers.

The original "transforming experience" that est promised customarily took place in a hotel banquet room or other such disorienting institutional environment and lasted the better part of a weekend, during which recruits were berated and abused by seminar leaders, who took the role of drill sergeants, the idea being to break down all resistance. "Your life doesn't work!" they screamed at confused and uncomfortable enlistees, who were provided barf bags but not allowed to eat, drink, look at a clock, or go to the bathroom for hours on end. ("People often avoid things by getting hungry or going to the bathroom," Erhard explained.) During the session, members of the group were instructed to take their fingers off the "repress button" and share their fears, weaknesses, flaws, and vices with everybody else in the room, after which they all lay down on the floor and writhed and screamed and moaned until their nemeses were mustered out.

It was a hypnotic blend of psychological claptrap, group-encounter mass hysteria, and religious epiphany; and at the end of the session, as at the end of boot camp or a fraternity initiation, many customers felt that they had developed a fresh new way of seeing the world around them. They were ready to do what est converts delighted in doing, which was to *take responsibility* for their lives because they had gotten—in est terms—*it*. "It" was a vaguely existential concept that meant understanding that there was no logic or purpose to the universe, and therefore each person is the architect of his or her own life.

An est seminar gave its participants a key for explaining everything and justifying just about anything. The radical personal re-

alignment it encouraged was expressed not only in how people thought and behaved when they left the seminar, but in the very vocabulary they suddenly acquired. Here are some of the words and phrases always used by trainers in seminars, then incorporated into proselytes' conversations as a way of demonstrating that they had gotten "it" (from the 1976 book *est: 4 Days to Make Your Life Work*):

- *acknowledge:* "A means of recognizing an individual or a point of view. ('I acknowledge what you have just said.')"
- *asshole:* "A tenet of est. The training is based on the fact that all trainees are assholes, i.e., machines or tubes. One gives up his asshole status when one gives up his 'acts' or social self."
- *for sure:* "That's correct. Certainly. Of course."
- *space:* "Something you have inside of you" *or* "allowing for observations . . . [as in] 'giving an individual space.'"
- *try:* "A nonword. You either do or you don't. Trying keeps the individual from experiencing."
- *yama yama:* "Blah, blah. Etc., etc. It usually indicates meaningless conversation."

Some of these est words have become part of everyday speech for a lot of people, but just as it is fruitless to try to short-cut psychoanalysis, merely knowing some of est's extensive jargon cannot in any way impart the sense of fanatic exhilaration true believers felt after a weekend seminar. Ex-Yippie Jerry Rubin called it a force "stronger than marijuana"; a Harvard Business School professor, who had served as est president for six years, described his involvement as "like being in love"; William Greene, the est alumnus and devoted apostle who wrote *est: 4 Days to Make Your Life Work*, crowed, "When you get *it*, you've got it made!"

The power of "it" wasn't just that it made a person feel good about himself. By focusing followers' attention entirely on individual fulfillment, est encouraged people to disengage themselves from any hang-ups they felt coming from outside institutions, such as the law or morality or religion. As Andrew J. Edelstein and Kevin McDonough put it in their book *The Seventies*, "est provided many a polyester-clad salesman with a quasi-mystical sense of cut-throat chutspa [sic] that Dale Carnegie never could." est seemed to say that it was okay to be greedy and selfish, which for many people was a great relief from the burdensome social consciousness of the sixties.

Tom Wolfe used a scene in an est seminar as the beginning of the essay in which he coined the term "Me Decade," and that is how est is now known: as the epitome of the seventies' obsession with that wonderful discovery known as the Self. In an era uncommonly blessed with primal screamers, transcendental meditators, astral projectionists, Moonies, Perfect Masters, Scientologists, joggers, fanatical dieters, and a level of self-absorption comparable to a black hole in space, est was probably the most influential of all the flimflam that went by the name of "the Human Potential Movement." By 1984, when Erhard devised a yuppified update of est called the Forum (focusing more on achievement than on self-realization), his company-controlled est centers around the country were taking in an estimated $36 million per year.

Erhard has always tended to avoid newspaper and magazine interviews (but does occasionally appear on television, where he believes he can make his point without being edited). In recent years he has faced lawsuits claiming fraud, wrongful death (a man suffered a stroke during training), and psychological damage; charges by former disciples that he and his staff use violence to enforce obedience and insist that Erhard be referred to as "Source"; and a "60 Minutes" segment in which one of his daughters accused him of incest. (Erhard's lawyer presented the results of a lie-detector test that he says proves Erhard did not molest, rape, or abuse any of his children.)

In 1991 Erhard sold most of his assets, but some of his former associates said it was only a dodge to avoid creditors, and that the people who "bought" his possessions (which included his clothes, his art, and his wine collection) are under his control. Despite legal problems over the years, and despite being branded as the leader of a destructive cult by the Cult Awareness Network, which claims his seminars use mind-control techniques and coerce people to keep coming back to (and paying for) refresher seminars, Werner Erhard has gathered many distinguished followers, including John Denver, Valerie Harper, Raul Julia, Diana Ross, and Yoko Ono. Werner Erhard and Associates—the umbrella company for all his nonprofit, tax-exempt projects, including the Educational Network, the Breakthrough Foundation, the Mastery Foundation, the Werner Erhard Foundation, the Holiday Project, and the Hunger Project —has boasted that it was graduates of est or the Forum who thought up the slogans "Commitment, Integrity, Vision" for Shearson Lehman and "Master the Possibilities" for MasterCard.

E.T.

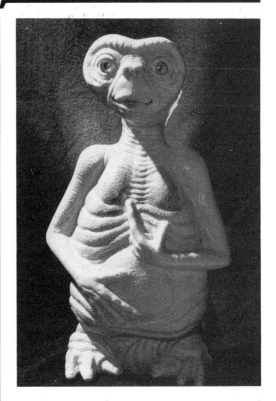

E.T. was a three-foot-tall, turtle-faced creature from another planet who enchanted America more than any human being, including Ronald Reagan, in the 1980s. As created in the movie, *E.T. The Extra-Terrestrial*, written by Melissa Mathison and directed by Steven Spielberg, he was a gentle, long-fingered alien with eyes as big as those of a child in a Keane painting, who found himself accidentally marooned on earth in a typical southern California suburb. He gets befriended by a ten-year-old lad, then the lad's little sister and older brother and their friends, who all try to keep him from being captured by the mean adult earthlings who want to get their greedy hands on the extraterrestrial so they can perform unkind experiments. Then, through a combination of the children's help and his own wizardly powers, E.T. manages to leave the earth in a farewell scene as joyful and tear-jerking as Snow White bidding her melancholy adieu to the seven dwarfs. This thrilling, sentimental, humorous, and morally ballasted plot helped make E.T. the most famous nonhuman movie star since Mickey Mouse.

Originally rejected in screenplay form by the Disney studio, which was then busy trying to refashion its image as a maker of films for grown-ups, *E.T.* is now the top-grossing movie ever made, having hauled in nearly a billion dollars in rentals as well as about two billion in spin-off products. Its cash-producing power has become capitalist folklore: Sales of Reese's Pieces (the chocolate-and-peanut-flavored candy E.T. ate with gusto in the movie) went through the roof as children everywhere imitated their furrow-skinned movie hero; Neil Diamond sang "Turn on your Heartlight" in cel-ebration of E.T.'s recuperative powers, and his fans started bringing pocket flashlights to his concerts so they could turn them on and thus replicate E.T.'s resurrection scene in the movie; phone companies all across the country used E.T.'s words "Phone home" in advertising copy to encourage earthlings to do as the forlorn alien did in the movie; and within three months of the movie's release, Steven Spielberg was reported to be personally earning one million dollars a day from box-office receipts. In its inimitably succinct way, *Variety* summed up the movie's commercial clout—"*E.T.* Equals B.O." ("B.O." is Varietese for box office)—and its review deemed it "the best Disney film Disney never made," giving it credit for not merely buoying Universal Studios, but actually saving all of Hollywood.

Conceived by Spielberg in 1980 while he was filming *Raiders of the Lost Ark* in the Tunisian desert, E.T. was thought of by the young director as a kind of fantasy friend—just the sort of magic pal a lonely person longs for. His physiognomy was kept top secret all during the production of the movie, which took place on a closed set; and even when *E.T.* was released, it was the alien's finger, but never his face, that was featured in advertisements. Spielberg felt so warmly towards the little creature (as well as towards his commercial potential as a movie star) he didn't want the cute-reptilian countenance stolen and used as a character in a quickie TV movie.

To be enchanted by this movie, as it seemed nearly all Americans were in the summer of 1982, was to believe in a teddy bear from outer space and a cosmos full of wonderments and goodness. Unlike so many aliens in countless sci-fi movies before it, E.T. was not evil or omnipotent and he didn't want to steal anything from earth. He wanted only to go home. He was lost, lonely, and lovable. And the story of his attempt to get back where he belongs involves a minimum of dazzling technology and a lot of heart and soul. For all its modern suburban setting and its sophisticated special effects, *E.T.* has the charm of an old-fashioned fairy tale about the freedom and innocence of youth triumphing over the greed and small-mindedness of adults (the scientists and military types who want to trap the creature). This rousing morality play proved irresistible to a nation that craved spiritual reassurance in a jaded era when ugly materialism seemed to reign supreme. After Steven Spielberg personally screened the movie in the White House, he reported that "Nancy Reagan was crying toward the end and the President looked like a ten-year-old kid."

The overwhelming charm of *E.T.* had a lot to do with the fact that it was told from a child's wide-eyed point of view. From the first brutal scene, in which lumbering grown-ups in huge four-wheel-drive vehicles scare away the spaceship (stranding E.T.), nearly all the story's adults are bad guys (even the school science teacher, who wants the class to dissect living frogs); and most of the film is shot from a camera angle about three feet off the ground. "I *am* a kid," Spielberg told *Newsweek*, explaining that he believed children to be intrinsically honest, and *E.T.* to be a paean to their willingness to believe in magic and miracles. In fact, the film took this point of view so vehemently, and its adults are so universally awful (except the little boy's mom, who is merely indifferent), that censors in Sweden banned children under eleven years old from seeing it, lest their minds be poisoned against their parents.

The creature that so beguiled America and the world was actually two different remote-controlled puppets, plus a hollow body suit occupied by dwarfs or, for the well-remembered drunk scene, by a small twelve-year-old boy born without legs. For close-ups, a mime's hands were used; and their characteristic trembling was created by having the mime drink lots of strong coffee every day before filming. E.T.'s big eyes, Spielberg told the press, were inspired by a composite photograph of Ernest Hemingway, Carl Sandburg, and Albert Einstein; E.T.'s actual designer, puppetmaker Carlo Rambaldi, said the eyes were those of his Himalayan cat. The stubby galactic refugee also had a cute, gurgly voice supplied collectively by a sixty-five-year-old elocution teacher with dentures, a shrieking otter, and actress Debra Winger.

He was haglike, and he could be rowdy, but you had to have a heart of stone to not feel warmly towards this creature who was meek and mild and achingly homesick. "What we relate to in E.T.," Spielberg explained, "is not what he looks like from the outside but the goodness inside him." Although in some ways he was at the mercy of humans, he was also superhuman and able not only to fly but also, like a divine being, to come back from the dead. He was innocent but wise, a healer with a heart of love. Indeed, the movie *E.T.* was described by *People* as a holy parable, "a flagrant but enchanting popcult parody of the Second Coming."

Religious implications aside, *E.T.* truly was some kind of spiritual revelation for many who saw it. Like the ugly but enchanting Cabbage Patch Dolls (see p. 75), which got spectacularly popular the following year, this movie's rousing success signified the return of love and cuteness to popular culture. Cuteness has had a fluctuating history since the 1950s, when Walt Disney defined it with such heartwarming visions as Peter Pan and Tinkerbell in his animated 1953 movie, the fresh-faced kids of "The Mickey Mouse Club" on TV, and *The Shaggy Dog* of 1959, which transformed sheepdogs into icons of cute for at least the next de-cade. After Disney's heyday, cuteness peaked once again in the early to mid-1960s, but with a madcap and irreverent twist, as evidenced by such symbols of adorability as the mop-top pre–*Sgt. Pepper* Beatles, the Singing Nun and the Flying Nun, and Charles Schultz's "Peanuts" book *Happiness Is a Warm Puppy*, published in 1962.

By the time the Beatles turned serious, however, it felt as though the 1960s had thoroughly run out of perky naiveté, and cute things were getting trampled by the coarse excess of post-Aquarian pop culture (see, for example, "All in the Family," p. 11). It is possible to see the aftermath of the fun-seeking 1960s as a massive hangover with a nasty disco throb—an era in which the notion of cute was scorned, mocked, or simply ignored while feelings of sarcasm and guile saturated all of popular culture, from funny stuff like TV's "Saturday Night Live" (see p. 434) to the apotheosis of synthetic disco couture. As *Esquire* put it, *E.T.* "reminded a generation bombarded by cynicism that you can go home again." Seeing it for the first time, according to *The Hollywood Reporter Book of Box Office Hits*, was "like your first taste of ice cream in the summer, the first time you saw the vast ocean, or the first ray of sunshine after a three-day downpour."

FANNY PACKS

"I don't see how people get along without some little satchel," Truman Capote said back in 1969. Mr. Capote was a purse pioneer, never going anywhere without his handbag; and although Sammy Davis, Jr., Elliott Gould, and a few other male fashion daredevils joined him back in the 1960s—carrying suede "stash bags" for their marijuana, toting full-fledged shoulder-strap purses designed by Gucci and Rudi Gernreich as part of the unisex trend, or sporting avant-garde Leatherette shirts with

built-in clutches—most guys have felt a little reticent about toting a pocketbook. But now there is a way. Guys and gals alike have an all-new fashion friend: the fanny pack.

A fanny pack, also known as a belt bag, isn't exactly a purse; it's more a pouch. And you don't carry it; you wear it, strapped to your belt, hanging down over a hip or straight out in front or around back. Fanny packs, which the *New York Times* named "this summer's hit" in 1988 and *Adweek* magazine named one of the hottest products of that year, are an active person's godsend—not only for men, who can now, finally, without shame or embarrassment, tote a satchel for their knickknacks, but for many women, too, who enjoy the fact that a fanny pack relieves them of the burden of something hung on their shoulders and leaves their hands free. When you wear a fanny pack, you can push through crowds more easily; you can change a baby's diaper (and tote a spare!) without having to find a place to put a cumbersome purse; you can buy lots of little souvenirs and eat hot dogs and cotton candy by the double fistful; you can use one hand to hold the camcorder to your eye and the other to give directions to the people you are taking pictures of.

No one can say who invented them, but it is believed fanny packs were first developed in the 1960s for ski patrolmen who needed their hands free but had to carry first-aid supplies. They became popular among bicyclists, whose tight-fitting shorts have no pockets, as well as among hikers and photographers, birdwatchers, fishermen, and river rafters; and by the early 1980s they began making their appearance in American vacation spots, mostly on the waists of pickpocket-wary tourists from northern Europe, who wore them with thick-soled sandals, strap undershirts, and shorts as part of a stripped-to-bare-essentials look. (In Norway, the name for a fanny pack is *rumptaske.*) Originally available through camping-equipment suppliers, now sold mostly by street vendors, fanny packs grew popular among all sorts of pedestrians, travelers, and beachgoers who realized the advantages of having an attached receptacle.

Fanny packs are made in all colors, in materials that range from expensive Vuitton-like fabric and suede to the cheesiest vinyl, in sizes nearly as big as a suitcase or as small as a wallet. Most people wear only one, but on a recent trip to the Southwest we noticed a few people (men and women) packing them by the pair, like a couple of jumbo buttock holsters draped back over each cheek. There are inflatable watertight ones, expandable ones that become full-size rucksacks, long-distance ones with built-in water bottles, miniature front-loaders with scarcely room for a pack of cigarettes, and the basic football-size pouch made of nylon (so you can slide it easily on your belt from back to front), with a zippered top (quick access) and miscellaneous zippered compartments on the sides.

Fanny packs are especially fun because they make any day's activity feel like a jaunty outing. At Walt Disney World and Opryland and theme parks and shoppers' paradises around the nation and the world, whole families tramp together wearing pouches on their waists: big, dignified ballistic nylon ones for Mom and Dad, cute little Day-Glo Bart Simpson or Mutant Ninja Turtles ones for kids. Like a rediscovered vestigial marsupium, the fanny pack has changed the look of the human race (or at least that part of the human race who favor extempore fashions) more than any other garment since exhibitionistic T-shirts.

JANE FONDA

Jane Fonda learned her craft at the Actors Studio in New York, where Lee Strasberg taught Method acting. A Method actor gets inside a role—believes it, lives it, digs deep into personal experience to summon up feelings and "sense memories" that allow him or her to *become* a character completely and unequivocally. For Jane, her experience at the Actors Studio was "like a light bulb going on . . . as if the roof had come off my life." As an actress, she has used this training to make movie characters come alive: when filming *They Shoot Horses, Don't They?* she became depressed and lonely just like the heroine she played; after making *Agnes of God*, set in a nunnery, she said she had "returned to a sense of the importance of a Greater Power in my own life."

If by nature and training Ms. Fonda is a sensitive membrane able to become absorbed in and transformed by a role, that is also the leitmotif of her personal life, which even more than her considerable accomplishments as an actress has made Jane Fonda into a pop-culture cause célèbre. From sex kitten to feminist fitness guru, from America's "Miss Army Recruiting of 1962" to Radio Hanoi's antiwar propagandist in 1972, from socialist revolutionary to business mogul, Jane Fonda has spent over half a century Method-acting real-life roles that embrace, reflect, and embody the social and political climate around her. These are

some of the things she has fought for: the Black Panthers, American Indians, army deserters, Cesar Chavez, children of veterans suffering birth defects that might have been caused by Agent Orange, George McGovern, renters' rights, and the environment.

These are some of the things she has spoken out against: nuclear power, the U.S. Army, Richard Nixon, big business, ageism, and sexism.

In the course of her lifelong performance, she has won two Academy Awards, three Golden Globes, and an Emmy; she made the bestselling exercise video ever;

she has been condemned for "treasonable actions" by the Veterans of Foreign Wars (and she has apologized on prime-time television for what she said in Hanoi); and she has amassed a personal fortune that *Forbes* magazine estimated at well over $50 million.

Why does Jane Fonda get her fans and foes so riled up? A lot of other well-known people have adopted self-righteous beliefs and changed their minds and not made the impact she has made; but the difference is that Jane has always done everything publicly, completely, dramatically, and without any apparent doubts. According to Christopher Anderson, author of the unauthorized biography *Citizen Jane*, it has all been a lifelong yearning for attention and for control, spurred by the remoteness of her father, the actor Henry Fonda. As a child, she and her brother, Peter, smoked cigarettes until they became sick; they played with matches; Jane bit her nails and got chubby. At the age of sixteen in 1954, she learned to control her weight by throwing up, then spent what she called "twenty-three years of agony" binging on junk food and vomiting as a way of keeping herself lean and lovely.

In the late 1950s Jane became a model who was known for her all-American attitude, her "curvaceous, high-breasted figure" (according to the Associated Press), and a brain. She announced that she had no intention of devoting herself to a career, preferring what she called a "normal existence" of being a wife, mother, and homemaker. Plans for normalcy were scuttled when she married French director Roger Vadim, the discoverer (and former husband) of Brigitte Bardot and well-known maker of peek-a-boo French "art films." To promote *Circle of Love*, the first picture she made with him, the DeMille Theater in New York erected an eight-story billboard that showed her lying on her stomach in bed with her buttocks exposed. For *The Game Is Over*, Vadim convinced her to take off all her clothes (pictures were filched for *Playboy*, which Jane sued for running them). "I counted seven full-face bare-breast shots of Fonda," Rex Reed announced; and although *The Game Is Over* didn't do much business in the United States, it was a big hit in Europe. While Vadim's movies—including the extraordinarily titillating *Barbarella*—were making her a sex goddess overseas, Americans were getting to know and like Jane as a kookie, wholesome ingenue in such movies as *Barefoot in the Park* and *Any Wednesday* and also as a sex object in *The Chapman Report* and *Walk on the Wild Side*. So it came as a shock to a lot of blasé moviegoers when this vampy sex kitten suddenly got both serious (as an actress) and political (as a radical) at the end of the 1960s.

For the role of Gloria in *They Shoot Horses, Don't They?* (1969) Jane deglamorized herself by cutting off her hair and immersed herself in the depressing role of a down-on-her-luck participant in a grueling 1930s dance marathon. She threw up even more than usual to develop an especially gaunt look for the part, and her performance was rich with the high level of sweat, angst, and exhaustion that wins awards (a Golden Globe) and accolades from critics, who began announcing Jane Fonda's arrival as a serious actress.

On her way from London to Los Angeles for the press screening of *They Shoot Horses, Don't They?* Jane picked up a copy of *Ramparts* magazine with a story about some American Indians who had seized Alcatraz and were claiming it as theirs. The idea of red power, in her words, "blew my mind"; so she had her press agent call the editors of the magazine and tell them that she wanted to get involved with the New

Left. On March 8, 1970, she participated in her first protest march—on Fort Lawson in Seattle, where she and some 150 native Americans informed Richard Nixon, whom they called the Great White Father, that they wanted to reclaim the fort as Indian land. At the press conference that followed her arrest (the first of many) for trespassing, she announced her intention of going to *all* U.S. Army bases in hopes of convincing soldiers of the evil of their government's policies. Many Indians were upset about being lumped into Jane's protest program; but Jane was compelled to shift her attention to the big picture, which included the struggle against the war in Vietnam and the Black Panthers (whom her future husband Tom Hayden praised as "America's Vietcong"). She set off on a cross-country tour to spread her views. On "The Dick Cavett Show," she stepped on stage, gave a clenched-fist power-to-the-people salute to the audience, and began to rail against American imperialism. She had fully embraced the role of revolutionary. J. Edgar Hoover opened an FBI file on her, labeled "Jane Fonda: Anarchist."

After filming *Klute* in 1970 (for which she won a Best Actress Oscar the following year), Jane Fonda decided to devote herself to stopping the war in Vietnam and fighting against what she called "ethnocentric white American male chauvinists." She dropped Roger Vadim (who told the press that being her husband was like "babysitting for Lenin") and took up with SDS leader Tom Hayden, who later recalled their falling in love while looking at a slide show of the history of Vietnam. "We decided . . . to hurl our personal relationship into the center of public life," Hayden wrote in his autobiography, *Reunion*, describing their relationship like "a remake of *Beauty and the Beast*" (later on they were known in the press as "the Mork and Mindy of the New

Left"). Jane renounced all her worldly possessions and took up with Hayden in what her father lamented to *McCall's* was "a shack" in Venice, California.

The image everyone remembers best from Jane's radical adventures is a scene in Hanoi of her wearing a military helmet, seated aboard a North Vietnamese anti-aircraft gun that is presumably aimed at American pilots up above. Once again she had transformed herself, this time from an antiwar activist (a position she shared with millions of Americans) to the world's most outspoken and militant enemy of the American war effort. She spent two weeks in North Vietnam in 1972, during which she made radio broadcasts to U.S. troops telling them they were killers and war criminals and pleading with them to disobey their orders to fight. Despite her apology, many years later, for being "thoughtless and careless," many Americans—particularly POWs who were tortured for not joining her in anti-American photo opportunities—have never forgiven her, and to this day you can still see bumper stickers condemning "Hanoi Jane" as a traitor.

Fury about Jane's radical enthusiasms notwithstanding, it was easy for her to get back into the mainstream when the war was over because so many people had ambiguous feelings about that conflict. She won her second Oscar for *Coming Home* (1978), a movie about healing after Vietnam; and the following year she took up her next big cause: physical fitness. By the late 1970s, getting into shape was a national obsession, and Jane embraced it with all the zeal she had found for revolution ten years earlier. She had come to realize that bulimia was not a good way to stay in shape, so she stopped vomiting, gave up red meat, and began to exercise with a passion. The Jane Fonda Workout Studio opened in 1979 in Beverly Hills; and its combination of strenuous calisthenics ("Go for the burn!" Jane exhorted) and celebrity stardust made it a huge success. The studio begat the multi-million seller *Jane Fonda's Workout Book* (1982) as well as *The Jane Fonda Workout* video (both of which have sired dozens of profitable sequels) and Jane Fonda's ActiveWear clothes (a failure).

By the end of the 1980s Jane Fonda had unrenounced her vows of poverty and was making fortunes as the dominant name in female body toning. Her role as health and fitness queen was especially satisfying to many aging baby boomers because she was over fifty years old and still looked great in leotards. She condemned America's obsession with youthful beauty and physical perfection, but has never publicly admitted to having plastic surgery on her eyes (1986) and implants put in her breasts (1987).

After a brutal, mud-slinging divorce from Tom Hayden in 1989 (she reportedly threatened to destroy his political career by exposing his past drug use; he hired private eyes to ferret out her real worth), Jane married capitalist tycoon Ted Turner in December 1991, deciding that big business might not be so bad after all if you considered it "an art form," as is done in Hollywood. *People* called their coupling "a mythical movieland romance . . . Hanoi Jane and Captain Outrageous . . . an almost unsurpassable standard for power liaisons." In the weeks before her marriage, she appeared frequently on television in an infomercial for *Jane Fonda's Lower Body Workout* (step aerobics); and her next venture is reported to be financial-advice and money-management videos for working women of the 1990s.

FRISBEE

P laying Frisbee is nice—noncompetitive, nonviolent, nonaggressive, and kind of pretty. Anyone can do it, at his own level and at his own speed. Even dogs —unleashed, of course, and preferably wearing a sporty-looking bandana rather than a collar—enjoy it. "There were no boundaries and no officials," George Leonard reminisced about Frisbee playing in *Esquire* in a memoir of the sixties. "The measure was not some arbitrary boundary, net, or goal, nor was it the judgement of some official, but rather your own potential." Is it any wonder that Frisbees became a national fad during the Summer of Love (1967), when so many young Americans went looking for alternative kinds of fun?

Actually, there *are* ways to use a Frisbee in competition (based on accuracy, distance, maximum time aloft) and in rigidly organized group sports (including one called Ultimate Frisbee, which *Sports Illustrated* described as requiring "the quickness of a basketball point guard, the finesse of a hockey center, the blocking techniques of a football guard, and the reactions of a soccer goalie"), and there are national contests to measure players' skills, but the joy of Frisbee for most people is gaily tossing the plastic disc into the air and watching it sail, soar, and float gently into a partner's hands. The special thrill of a Frisbee, unlike a ball, is that its flight can be guided by the clever use of wrist motions when it is tossed, and

The Frisbie Pie Factory

its saucer shape allows a leisurely, even poetic trajectory that seems so much more peaceful than a hardball slamming into a mitt.

Frisbee playing probably goes back to 1920, when students at Yale University were first observed tossing thin metal pie tins back and forth to each other across the New Haven Green. The tins came from the Frisbie Bakery of Bridgeport, and the students used to yell out "Frisbie!" when they hurled the tins in the air; the game remained popular, but strictly local, for decades. The alternative story of Frisbee's origins is set in Nebraska, where five undergraduates from Middlebury College in Vermont are supposed to have had a flat tire while driving cross-country. As two of them fixed the flat, another found a pie tin in a cornfield, threw it in the air, and—for reasons lost in the mists of time—yelled "Frisbie!" A statue on the Middlebury campus commemorates the occasion: It shows a dog leaping in the air grabbing a Frisbee in its jaws.

Whatever its origins, it wasn't until the fifties that Frisbie tossing inspired a product. In 1956, two years before it introduced the Hula Hoop, the Wham-O company of California became intrigued by the possibilities of a gimmick designed and marketed by an inventor named Walter Frederick Morrison. It was a saucer, which he originally made of tin, that could be thrown in the air in such a way that it seemed to hover and float. Nearly anything airborne was fascinating to toy buyers of the fifties, and saucer-shaped things, with their connotations of space flight and men from other planets, were especially appealing. Wham-O signed up Morrison, and in January 1957 they introduced a plastic version of what the inventor had called Morrison's Flyin' Saucer, changing its name to Pluto Platter.

Flyin' Saucers and Pluto Platters got popular on southern California beaches, but not many other places; and like the Hula-Hoop, they seemed like a short-lived fad. After the launch of *Sputnik I* in 1957 and the *real* manned space flights that followed, the whole mystique of flying saucers and the planet Pluto suddenly seemed very passé. In 1959, after an executive from Wham-O got wind of the game played by Yalies (or Middlebury students), the outer-space name was dropped and a new one trademarked: Frisbee.

Still, it was not until 1967, when the International Frisbee Association was founded (lifetime dues: one dollar) "to promote rapport among all Frisbee enthusiasts," that Frisbees started to become a national craze. No gathering in any public park that summer was complete without at least one Frisbee flying overhead; and the next year Wham-O rented the Hollywood Bowl and staged a Frisbee tournament, giving a boost to the idea of Frisbee tossing as a sport. Their popularity has not waned since. They are now available in dozens of colors (including glow-in-the-dark models for evening play) and larger "professional" sizes, and there are pet-shop variants manufactured with outlines of bones in the plastic, made of extra-tough, ham-flavored material guaranteed to withstand dog bites.

Serious Frisbee connoisseurs can throw sidearm, overhand, or backhand; they can catch the Frisbee behind their back, with a single finger (and keep it spinning!), or between their legs. The basic directions, as printed on the Pluto Platter, are unchanging:

Flat Flip Flies Straight
Tilted Flip Curves—Experiment!
Play Catch
Invent Games!

FROZEN FOOD

The idea of eating frozen food is as much pop culture as it is cuisine because it stands for an especially popular ideal: the American way, the convenient, instant-satisfaction road to happiness. Snobs scoff and say frozen food is inferior to fresh, and maybe it is; but a freezer full of TV dinners, sticks of fish and bricks of vegetables, mysterious leftovers, and heat-'n'-eat home-style pop-'em pastries is in fact a whole lot more American than a made-from-scratch apple pie.

"How is it possible to cook and serve your guests splendiferous food and still have the energy left to *be* at the party?" asked Helen Quat, a Long Island hostess and author of *The Wonderful World of Freezer Cooking* (1964). Mrs. Quat answered her question by telling readers that she had figured out a way to cook entire meals the day after she sent out invitations to dinner. Then, the day before her guests arrived, she defrosted everything. Her *Wonderful World* contained recipes for deep-freeze party food that ranged from clam broth puffs to duck sauced with orange juice and currant jelly.

Of course Mrs. Quat was not alone in her discovery of frozen food. She was one of many eager housewives and hostesses of the 1950s and 1960s who were delighted by the new freedom it allowed. Six years before *The Wonderful World of Freezer Cooking*, Craig Claiborne had written that "1958 is loaded with promise—especially for cooks on the run," and went on to laud packaged frozen foods "with a so-called Continental touch that can be heated and brought to the table within minutes—to the awe and delight of guests with educated palates."

The process of quick-freezing food so it doesn't spoil was invented—actually, stumbled upon—by Clarence Birdseye, a United States government surveyor in Labrador in

1911. Mr. Birdseye, who had trained as a naturalist and had earlier made a living collecting frogs and rats for the New York Zoological Society, watched Eskimos freeze their fish in the arctic air, then keep them for weeks before cooking and eating them. He tasted for himself that things frozen in the dead of winter, when the air was coldest, were better than slow-frozen food, and realized that the faster that fresh food could be turned into a solid piece of ice, the more of its flavor was preserved. Ten years later he received a patent for quick-freezing food (mostly cabbage and fish) using brine, ice, and an electric fan. But when restaurants refused to buy his catch, suggesting that freezing removed vitamins (vitamins were the big health-food craze of the 1920s), Birdseye Seafoods went broke. He tried again, starting the General Seafoods Corporation in Gloucester, Massachusetts, which became part of General Foods in 1929.

General Foods thrived (Jell-O was but one of its successful brands), but frozen food went nowhere, for the simple reason that no one—neither supermarkets nor homeowners—had a freezer, so what was the point? The demand for it was limited to a tiny market—mostly luxury items such as lobster tails for gourmets. However, that changed suddenly when Japan conquered Southeast Asia at the beginning of World War II and the major source of tin for cans was cut off. Americans had to figure out how to get vegetables. Victory gardens were one possibility—if you had the skill and space and if the season was right—but for those Americans who didn't have time or inclination to tend a garden, frozen food offered an alternative.

"You've dreamed it! You've hoped for it! And maybe you thought the day would never come! But here it is—a glorious fact today, for now you can buy honest-to-goodness, farm-fresh foods the year 'round!" So began the *Birds Eye Cookbook* (Mr. Birdseye's name was split to create the brand), published in 1941 and subtitled "A Miracle Comes to the Kitchen." The book features recipes including "Succotash with Frizzled Ham" and "Seafood à la Newburg," and also plenty of reassurances about all the vitamins retained in "frosted food," as well as lessons in how frosted food is *modern* (hence, good) whereas fresh food is old-fashioned and wastes time. The book shows families relishing meals prepared in a mere twenty minutes (children even love Birds Eye spinach!) and promises "a whole new food world" devoid of menu-planning worries and the anxiety of buying fresh food and never knowing if it will taste exactly the same as it did last week. "Every package, every ounce of Birds Eye Foods you serve is the same unvarying quality."

Miraculous as frozen food seemed in the early forties (production tripled between 1942 and 1946), it wasn't until after the war that it became really popular—when grocery stores got freezers (in many cases, rented to them by General Foods) and Americans began enthusiastically outfitting their postwar kitchens. "Frozen food and the suburbs grew up together," *Look* magazine observed in a 1967 "Report on Suburbia," rejoicing in the fact that America's housewives could now serve complex meals simply by moving boxes of things from their freezer to the oven, then to the table, thus enjoying the supreme luxury of "paying manufacturers and machines to shell their peas, shuck corn, look up recipes, shop for ingredients, mix, bake and wash up the pans." Convenience was exalted: "Now the complete meal comes frozen in several nationalities and two or three courses, at a saving of huge hunks of time when the family plans an evening of bowling or double-feature movie watching. It feeds children and baby sitter on the parents' night out, and it saves father's life when he is unexpectedly left to play nursemaid." Unlike previous generations of housewives, who were taught to disdain convenience food as a sign of sloth, "the young bride of today," *Look* advised, "regards the contents of the frozen-food cabinet (along with the dishwasher and electric can opener) as her birthright; [and] expediency replaces expertise in the kitchen." The lesson to be learned from suburbia's infatuation with such frozen treats as tuna pie, Bavarian cabbage, garlic snails, and kosher Salisbury steak was that "this country is apt to greet new recipes and new products with more freedom than is displayed in 'the old countries.' Americans are perhaps the world's most adventurous eaters."

To a growing number of back-to-basics gourmets of the 1970s, whose ranks mounted in opposition to the boom in convenience cookery, frozen food was considered the enemy of good taste—"the dirty little secret of American luxury dining," according to John and Karen Hess in their exposé of awful eating habits, *The Taste of America* (1977). The Hesses scorned the proliferation of frozen food as "vandalism" of the American palate, and a perfect symbol of our taste buds going down the drain. Today, although gourmet guru Wolfgang Puck is happy to market heat-and-eat pizzas from the freezer case of your (upscale) grocer, serious gastronomes continue to shun almost anything frozen in favor of anything fresh. But for most of the rest of us, frozen food is a fact of life, now all the more convenient thanks to microwave ovens (p. 316) that reduce or, in the case of some ready-to-zap meals, totally eliminate the most arduous and time-consuming aspect of eating things from the freezer—defrosting them. As Ellen Stern (no relation to us, but a nice person nonetheless) rhapsodized in a recent company report for H. J. Heinz (maker of such iced items as Ore-Ida potatoes, Steak-umms, and Weight Watchers entrees):

> Wherever, whenever one of us dines
> . . . It's ever so likely we dine upon
>   Heinz.
> We open a package and lo! It's a meal.
> But let's not forget that it started out
>   real.

FULLER BRUSH MAN

"The poets have neglected them, and even housewives take them for granted," grieved Alfred C. Fuller in his 1960 autobiography, *A Foot in the Door.* "Odes and lyrics have been written to cats and mice, but none to the brooms and brushes which are employed by even the most primitive peoples." Mr. Fuller knew about brushes' ignominy from personal experience. When, in 1904 at the age of nineteen, he told his parents, with whom he had come to Boston from Nova Scotia, that he intended to have a career in brushes, his father was dubious, and his mother was so adamant that she quoted Scripture to dissuade him. "You, Alfred dear, have had a warning," she said, referring to the fact that Alfred's brother Dwight had died of tuberculosis contracted as a result of inhaling dust while manufacturing brushes. Dwight's

Howard Fuller, Alfred's son

death, she said, was the "Word of the Lord," telling Alfred to stay out of the brush business.

He tried to get jobs doing other things. He worked as a groom in Boston, in which capacity he at least got to use a curry comb, but he was a failure. Then he realized: *Dwight's death was indeed a warning, but his mother had misinterpreted it.* It was a warning, he wrote, "that *when* I entered the brush business, I must guard against the dust." What better way to breathe fresh air than to walk from door to door, *selling* brushes? One day in January 1905, Alfred Fuller set out for Roxbury with a sample case full of brushes from the factory where his brother had worked, and because he genuinely loved brushes so much and loved to show what they could do, he sold six dollars' worth. "With lilting step I turned homeward," he wrote. "I had found myself."

Inspired as he was by the product, Fuller knew that selling anything door to door was a struggle because of peddlers' shady repu-tations as con men—not to mention the two principal hazards, rainy days and dogs. (Actually, rainy days are good for selling, Fuller realized, because more women are home; as for dog bites, "such incidents create a sympathetic atmosphere and often gain admission to the house.") Fuller learned to say "I'll step in" rather than ask "May I come in?" He overcame the stigma of the peddler by focusing less on talking and more on showing what a brush could do. He developed demonstrations for everything. "I washed babies with a back brush, swept stairs, cleaned radiators and milk bottles, dusted floors—anything that would prove the worth of what I had to sell."

As he demonstrated, he developed new ideas for heretofore unheard-of brushes—a spittoon brush, for example—but his employer wasn't interested. So the next year he established his own Fuller Brush Company in Hartford, Connecticut, and, despite the omen of his brother's death, began manufacturing brushes with new designs that he knew he could sell: contoured bath brushes; a knuckle brush to clean grime from workingmen's hands; a two-sided clothes whisk; a scratchless carpet sweeper. Business boomed, and soon Fuller hired minions to carry on his crusade to bring better brushes to America. "Edison gave us the electric light, and Marconi gave us the wireless," comedian Fred Allen once said on his radio show. "And Fuller gave us the brush."

Fuller encouraged his sales force to think of themselves as dealers, not salesmen. In 1922 the *Saturday Evening Post* called them Fuller Brush Men, and the term stuck as the relentless door-to-door army became something of a national obsession in the 1920s, when—faced with competition from the newly invented vacuum cleaner—Fuller's product line expanded to include not only all kinds of brushes and household cleaning products but bobbed-hair trainer and complexion energizer for bachelor girls in the business world. The Brush Men's persistence became the stuff of folklore; their how-to sales brochure included these responses to rejection:

- *Objection:* Times are hard.
  Answer: So is housework, but it has to be done, good times and bad.
- *Objection:* I have no money.
  Answer: I want to save you money.
- *Objection:* My husband would scream if I bought that.
  Answer: I'm sure, Mrs. Brown, that your husband would compliment you on your good judgment.
- *Objection:* Just don't show me any brushes.
  Answer: I want to show you a new face powder that is tailor-made for your lovely skin tones.

Of all techniques, the most important one was to never stop talking, even as an order was written, because a customer could use the silence to say "no."

One Fuller Brush Man is still legendary as the twentieth century's premier door-to-door salesman: Albert E. Teetsel, known as "Fine and Dandy Al," founder of the Fine and Dandy Club, an elite cadre of the most successful Fuller Brush dealers, who pledged to be bright, cheerful, and happy at all times and thus spread the Fine and Dandy spirit. Teetsel, who always introduced himself to customers by saying, "I'm fine and dandy, how are you?" began as a dealer in Poughkeepsie but soon moved to New York City, where he became known for a gaudy diamond pinky ring, loud neckties, and a "Smile King" contest he invented for his customers: The wife who took the happiest-looking photo of her husband setting off to work with a Fine and Dandy Smile on his face won a hundred dollars.

By the time Fine and Dandy Al died in 1945, Fuller Brush Men were as well-known as Avon Ladies (see p. 29); and in fact, in 1948, Fuller began hiring Fullerettes—Fuller Brush Women—to sell cosmetics, perfume, and sachets. That same year, Red Skelton starred with Janet Blair in a movie called *The Fuller Brush Man,* and two years later Lucille Ball was featured in the sequel, *The Fuller Brush Girl.* Alfred Fuller died in 1973 at age eighty-eight.

Today's Fuller Brush catalog contains over two hundred items, only a small number of them brushes; and in 1992, the company officially abandoned its time-honored door-to-door sales strategy. Al Terrasi, who was profiled in *Yankee* magazine in 1988 when he celebrated his fiftieth year as a Fuller Brush Man, confessed that in recent years he had done most of his business by telephone, but still enjoyed walks through neighborhoods making cold calls on potential customers. As for how long he expected to continue selling, he said, "There's no limit. As long as you can get around, fine and dandy!"

ED GEIN

Cannibalism has been popular lately, not only at the movies (*Silence of the Lambs*) but in life: Jeffrey Dahmer, "the Butcher of Milwaukee," is thought to have eaten the better part of at least eleven people, and serial killer Ted Bundy reportedly did a lot of chewing on his victims, even if he didn't swallow. The granddaddy of these fictional and real-life ghouls was Ed Gein.

Gein, who died at age seventy-seven in 1984 at the Mendota Mental Health Institute in Wisconsin, was a bachelor all his life. He lived alone in a primitive farmhouse (no plumbing or electricity) outside the small town of Plainfield, where he made a living doing odd jobs for neighbors. When he was arrested at the dinner table on the first day of deer hunting season in November 1957, police found a human heart simmering in a saucepan on his stove, apparently to accompany his supper of pork chops, macaroni and cheese, pickles, coffee, and cookies.

Gein had a shoebox containing nine salted vulvas, a bowl of noses, skulls on the posts of his bed, and a headless corpse, drained of blood and with its genitalia and internal organs removed, trussed and hanging in a summer kitchen, apparently so it could age like steak. Investigators also found face masks made from skin stripped away from people's heads and a tanned front of a woman's torso with a belt made of nipples so the torso could be worn like a Halloween costume. There were lampshades of human skin and furniture of bones and rotting flesh, and there was litter everywhere. One man from the crime lab was horrified by the mess, which he called "a state of shambles."

A single part of Ed Gein's house, however, was neat as a pin: the bedroom that had been his mother's. He had sealed it after her death, years before, and it was exactly as she left it, except for a thick coating of dust that had gathered in the absence of any life. Sound familiar? Ed Gein, whose story shocked the nation, was the man Robert Bloch used as the inspiration for his novel *Psycho.* Like the Norman Bates character that Bloch created (and Tony Perkins immortalized in Alfred Hitchcock's movie), Ed Gein had a thing about his mother. She had spent her life warning little Eddie about slutty women who wore makeup and short skirts, and who would all be killed on Judgment Day when another great flood would wash away their sins. Eddie was an obedient boy, so he learned to hate other women, and after his father died in 1940 and his older brother died (mysteriously) in 1944, life was finally just the way he liked it: He was alone with his mother. Then Ed Gein's mother did a very bad thing: She died, too (in a hospital, after a stroke). The distraught

Eddie remembered the family medical guide (in which the pictures of women's anatomy, police later found, had nearly decomposed from years of Ed's attention) and the slogan on its front: YOU CAN DO NOTHING TO BRING THE DEAD TO LIFE, BUT YOU CAN DO MUCH TO SAVE THE LIVING. Eddie didn't believe it.

In fact, he wasn't certain that his mother really *was* dead. He heard her voice and saw her face all the time, and soon he devised a plan to bring her back to him. What Ed Gein did was to kill women who looked like her, then remove their faces, breasts, and vaginas, strap the body parts on himself, and dance around outside his house at night by the light of the moon. When he couldn't find a live one, he scoured the obituary notices in the newspaper, then went to the cemetery and dug up a recently buried body, had sex with it, and usually sawed off the head and took it home. No one knows how many women he killed, but at least a dozen graves, including the one adjacent to his mother's, had been robbed in the thirteen years since Mrs. Gein had died.

The 647 citizens of Plainfield were horrified when they found out about Gein's deeds; some of his neighbors were especially unsettled when they recalled how soft-spoken little Ed, who seemed a trifle weird but harmless, used to bring them packages of funny-tasting venison when he came to babysit their children. "I've never shot a deer," he had said while under psychiatric observation. For years after his grisly crimes were exposed, local doctors reported an inordinate number of psychosomatic stomachaches in Plainfield.

After he was declared mentally incompetent and was locked up at the Wisconsin Central State Hospital for the Criminally Insane, full-time guards had to be posted around his house to keep out teenagers who wanted to have beer parties there, and in

March 1958, on the eve of his estate auction, when it was rumored that an interested party was going to buy the property and turn it into a tourist attraction called the House of Horror, a mysterious fire occurred, and Ed Gein's house, along with all its contents, burned to the ground. One bargain-hunting entrepreneur did buy Gein's 1949 maroon Ford for $760, and for years afterward it appeared at county fairs in the heartland as THE CAR THAT HAULED THE DEAD FROM THEIR GRAVES.

Gein entered the annals of pop culture not only because he was the original Norman Bates but because his story was so horrific that it initiated a vein of grim humor in Wisconsin—and to a lesser degree, around the country—that lasted well into the 1960s. "The joking was so common that it could be considered a mass repetition compulsion," observed psychiatrist Dr. George Arndt when he investigated the new kind of sick joke going around, known as a Geiner, the only real precedents for which were Lizzie Borden jokes of the 1890s (and many of which were reprised in 1991 as Jeffrey Dahmer jokes). These are some of the Geiners Dr. Arndt catalogued:

- As he said to some late-arriving guests, "Sorry you weren't a little earlier. Everybody's eaten."
- What did Gein give his girl for Valentine's Day? A box of farmer fannies.
- Why did his girlfriend stop going with him? Because he was such a cut-up.
- Why did the Defense Department call on Gein? To ship arms to Vietnam.
- They never could keep him in jail. He'd just draw a picture of a woman on the wall and eat his way out.

For years after Gein was locked up, zany people in the upper Midwest used to ask for an "Ed Gein beer" when they bellied up to the bar in a tavern. A Gein beer was one that had a lot of body but no head.

G.I. JOE

Listen up: G.I. Joe was not a doll! Never, ever did the company that manufactured him allow that sissy term to be applied to its plastic twelve-inch macho dogface. He was an "action soldier" or "America's Movable Fighting Man," and he was a rugged one at that, with a scar on the right cheek of his face (which was drawn from a composite of twenty winners of the Congressional Medal of Honor) and a tattoo (well, actually a copyright mark) on his butt.

Before G.I. Joe, there were no dolls for boys, except for a small cadre of manly figurines used by child psychiatrists to help their patients act out boyhood traumas. Joe was conceived in 1964 by Hassenfeld Bros., Inc. (later called Hasbro), a toy company in Newport, Rhode Island, that had seen Mattel's Barbie rake in millions of dollars since she was introduced in 1959. Barbie's appeal to toymakers was that she was bought practically nude by kids who then spent years' worth of allowances buying her clothes and accessories. The same concept was adopted for G.I. Joe: to create a soldier who needed uniforms, weapons, and vehicles; bandages, crutches, and medicine; comrades and enemies; and even (for a short time in 1967) a G.I. Joe Nurse to take care of him when he was wounded.

Joe was fully jointed, with twenty-one moving parts, so he could be bent into a crouch, a full salute, or a fetal position, or made to look like his hands were trying to stop the flow of blood from his gut. His hair was painted on his head and came in four colors (black, brown, blond, red); his eyes were blue or brown; and he was sold in the uniforms of the Army, the Navy, the Air Force, and the Marine Corps. Starting in

1965, there was a black G.I. Joe (available only in the North) and a G.I. Joe Green Beret. Also in Joe's family were "Action Soldiers of the World," which were basically Joes with slightly smaller, unscarred heads in the uniforms of Germany, Japan, Russia, England, France, and Australia, each of them equipped with a counterintelligence manual. By 1967 there was talking Joe: Yank his dog tag and he shouted "Medic, get that stretcher!" and seven other battlefield exclamations. The accessories, like those for Barbie, were endless, and included a bazooka that propelled plastic shells nearly ten yards, a flame thrower that shot water, karate uniforms (complete with break-apart bricks), and eventually even a space capsule and astronaut suit.

Within three years of his introduction, G.I. Joe had become the single best-selling toy among America's five-to-twelve-year-olds, bought not only by boys but by girls, who, according to the *New York Times*, were "smitten with the snappy Annapolis and West Point models." Some parents were reported to be upset by the sight of their twelve-year-old boys dressing and undressing a doll, but Norman Westland, a Michigan psychiatrist, reassured them (and Hasbro) by observing that Joe was "a virile, masculine figure. Boys never dwell on the word 'doll.' The say, 'Hey, look at my G.I. Joe.' " Nearly a half a million children had paid fifty cents to join the G.I. Joe Fan Club by 1967, but as the war in Vietnam became a divisive issue at home, G.I. Joe's military bearing quickly turned into a liability.

Anti-war-toy groups singled out Joe as an example of what was wrong with America: He showed children that violence was fun. "If we're going to have toys that teach our children about war, why not have them *really* true to life?" asked an Ohio Mom Against G.I. Joe. "Why not have a G.I. Joe who bleeds when his body is punctured by shrapnel, or screams when any of his twenty-one movable parts are blown off, or vomits at the smell of burning flesh after a napalm attack?"

G.I. Joe was changed, but not into a bleeding, screaming, vomiting basket case. America's Movable *Fighting* Man became America's Movable *Adventure* Man, now available with all manner of demilitarized accessories, including underwater gear for treasure hunting, safari outfits for bagging Siberian white tigers, mountain-climbing equipment, bomb-disposal tools, even a

trench coat and attaché case for secret-agent work. The term "war" was replaced in the *Command Post News* (the fan club bulletin) by "action adventure." At this time, G.I. Joe also got lifelike flocked hair and a neatly trimmed beard.

In 1974, a G.I. Joe variant named Atomic Man (a.k.a. Mike Power) was introduced. He had a left leg and right arm that were see-through plastic, with metal pins instead of bones; he had a Kung Fu grip and an atomic arm that spun like a helicopter rotor; and he had a hole in his head that permitted kids to peer out through his clear right eye. Two years later, Joe got shortened to eight inches, but had a bigger name to compensate—Super Joe. And in 1982 he was shrunk even more, down to an itty-bitty three inches. The idea behind the pipsqueak figurines was that they supposedly fought (and were sold) as a "Mobile Strike Force" that depended on teamwork rather than on individual bravado like the original G.I. Joe. Nowadays, little G.I. Joe is a thriving business, marketed as "a Real American Hero," and stars in videotapes, comics, and games; but among collectors, only large-size Joe is in demand.

GRAND OLE OPRY

Nashville is the capital of country music in America, and the Grand Ole Opry is its heart and soul. All the sentimental ballads, glittering show-biz finery, and hillbilly hokum that make country music different than the pop mainstream can be found on the stage of the Opry. But the Grand Ole Opry isn't only about music; it has helped define "country" as a lifestyle

as well as a music style, and most of the people who have journeyed from all over America (and the world) to bask in its values for the last six decades have come with the joy and purpose of pilgrims, because the Grand Ole Opry feels like their spiritual home.

It began on November 28, 1925, when WSM radio of Nashville broadcast an hour

of classical music from New York hosted by New York Philharmonic conductor Walter Damrosch. Dr. Damrosch apologized to listeners for one of the compositions they heard—a modernistic piece that attempted to be the musical equivalent of a speeding locomotive. "There is no room for realism in serious music," the conductor declared. The next show scheduled to go on the air, broadcast live from WSM's Studio A in Nashville, began with a steamboat whistle and harmonica blues by DeFord Bailey (who could perfectly evoke a locomotive with his mouth harp), then went on to feature three hours of old-time fiddle music by Uncle Jimmy Thompson, guitar pickin', minstrel comedians, more fiddlers, foot stompers, and backwoods yodelers. The announcer, George D. Hay, began the program by responding to Dr. Damrosch: "From here on out for the next three hours we will present *nothing but realism.* It will be down to earth for the earthy." He said, "For the past hour we have been listening to music taken largely from grand opera, but from now on we will present the Grand Ole Opry."

"The Grand Ole Opry," as the show was called from that moment on, was not the first barn-dance radio show on the air, but by the 1930s, when the WSM signal had grown from one thousand to fifty thousand watts, it had become the flagship of the country sound. Most of the early acts were either storytellers or instrumentalists with fiddles, banjos, and guitars—such groups as

the Fruit Jar Drinkers, the Possum Hunters, and the Dixie Clodhoppers. Nearly all of them dressed in bib overalls and played the role of bumpkin to a farcical hilt even when, as Bob Cornfield points out in his book *Just Country,* "these whimsical names were a cover for the finest musicians." When Roy Acuff joined the Opry troupe in 1937 (performers auditioned to become "members" of the Opry), the spotlight of the show shifted from instrumental groups to vocalists, and from bluegrass (which always remained part of the repertoire) to the style of white man's blues that was then known vaguely as folk music and only later got named "country." Opry members have included almost every big name in country, including Ernest Tubb, Loretta Lynn, Dolly Parton, Marty Robbins, Hank Snow, Johnny Cash (fired for kicking out the footlights when he performed all doped up), and, of course, Hank Williams (also fired; see p. 562). Comedians have always been a staple of the Opry, too, from Jam Up and Honey (minstrels in the early days) to Opry doyenne Minnie Pearl, the Duke of Paducah (Whitey Ford), and Jim Varney (now known as Ernest, but first famous for calling the name of his inadvertent victim, "Verne!").

Aside from its stable of performers, one thing that makes the Grand Ole Opry unique is that it has always been a real place. Those who listened to it with religious devotion every weekend knew they could make the journey to Nashville and actually be there, side by side with other country fans, and close to the performers that they loved. When it first went on the air, the Opry was conceived strictly as a radio show, and only a handful of local curiosity seekers came to see it broadcast live. But as the program grew more popular on the airwaves, visiting it in person became a ritual. In 1943, the year Grand Ole Opry broadcasts first went national, *Newsweek* reported that "Uncle Jimmy [Thompson] has since died, but every Saturday night for seventeen years mountaineers and their wives and children have streamed down from the hills on foot, wagon, or jalopy to Nashville to listen to the folk-music festival."

The show had moved to the Hillsboro Theater in the late twenties, then to a series of music halls, and finally, in 1943, to Nashville's downtown Ryman Auditorium. It was at Ryman that the Grand Ole Opry became an American institution. Built in 1891 as a venue for an evangelist named Sam Jones, and originally known as the Gospel Tabernacle, Ryman was a big hall with wooden bench seats and an "1897 Confederate Gallery" balcony that had been installed to accommodate a huge Confederate veterans' reunion. Shows were put on twice a week, and as much as fans loved the place, it was actually a brutal venue for performers and listeners alike. In the summer, temperatures inside surpassed 120 degrees; teams of nurses were kept on duty to revive people who passed out, and included among the backstage crew were employees whose only job was to mop the faces of performers.

By the late 1960s, executives at WSM were getting worried that the old hall might simply fall apart. Program director Elmer Alley, who was in charge of broadcasts from the Opry, hated the rickety place because it was a technical nightmare, especially unsuited for the television shows that had been made there since 1955. At the time, the Opry was merely a two-night-a-week event, but Alley believed it could be made into more. He and WSM president Irving Waugh conceived not just a new, modern auditorium but a whole Grand Ole Opry environment. "Put it on a piece of property that somehow typifies the Tennessee countryside," Alley suggested. "Make it part of a theme park. Have it offer live entertainment, with all kinds of music and dancing."

So Opryland was born. In 1971 the Grand Ole Opry moved to a new, acoustically sophisticated auditorium far from Ryman and downtown Nashville, where it became the centerpiece of a four-hundred-acre theme park and a magnet that helps fill the biggest hotel in the western hemisphere. In addition to the 4,400-seat music hall, which is equipped with all the most modern sound and lighting equipment for television broadcasts, Opryland features a Wild Grizzly river rapids ride and the Chaos roller coaster, as well as nonstop singing and dancing shows throughout the park, including not only country music but rock and roll, jazz, Dixieland, folk, and golden oldies.

The move out to air-conditioned Opryland from decrepit, old, but country-simple Ryman was lamented by a few country-music purists (a *New Yorker* reporter sent to cover the opening of the new music hall was so upset by the betrayal of Ryman that he stayed in his hotel room and listened to the first broadcast from the new Opry on the radio), but few of country music's fans are purists, and today three million of them come to visit Opryland each year.

GRANOLA

In our lifetime, granola began as a counterculture icon—a foodstuff consisting of grains, nuts, coconut oil, and sometimes dried fruit with brown sweetener (as opposed to white sugar) that you ate instead of Kellogg's Corn Flakes or Post Toasties. For many years it was considered as much an emblem of defiance as long hair and men's earrings. To eat granola was to resist the establishment. Now, of course, long hair is no big deal, lots of regular guys have earrings, and Kellogg's and Post both offer their own variations of granola. No one thinks of it as countercultural anymore; indeed, few people remember what a 1960s kind of thing it once seemed to be.

It is indeed a legacy of the sixties, but unlike psychedelic rock music and go-go boots, it comes from an earlier sixties, exactly one century prior. Although it was repopularized by hippies some thirty years ago, granola was invented in the 1860s by one of America's early health nuts, James Caleb Jackson. Dr. Jackson, originator of the Glen Haven Water Cure (drink forty glasses per day) and follower of Sylvester Graham's strict antimeat regimen, decided that the patients at his Our Home on the Hillside sanitarium in Dansville, New York, needed something more than a diet of water and Graham crackers. So he baked thin sheets of moistened Graham flour, crumbled them into bits, then baked them again, creating rock-hard little nuggets he called Granula. Granula was supposed to be prepared by filling a glass one-third full, then topping it with milk and leaving it in an icebox overnight. In the morning, the sodden Granula was eaten alongside a cup of Dr. Jackson's Somo, a grain-based coffee substitute.

Jackson's Our Home Granula Company advertised extensively, and the crunchy particles became the first processed health food sold in America, and the first breakfast cereal as well. Some years later, John Harvey Kellogg, who was operating a sanitarium of his own in Battle Creek, Michigan, added cornmeal and oats to the formula and began marketing his own Granula . . . until Dr. Jackson sued him. Kellogg changed the name of the product to Granola, and by the turn of the century there were over forty different companies marketing similar breakfast cereals that promised good health to people who ate them.

Originally proposed by food faddists, whose programs also frequently included such radical ideas as abstinence, celibacy, and women's suffrage, breakfast cereal was well entrenched in the mainstream American diet by 1965, when long-forgotten granola was resurrected, once again as counterculture food. This time its proponent was Layton Gentry, whom *Time* called "Johnny Granola Seed" for having introduced Crunchy Granola, an all-in-one, genuinely nutritious, dry, portable meal perfectly suited to vagabonds, hippies living in communes and on the street, and any groovy character too stoned to cook. Writing for the *Liberation New Service* in 1969, Ita Jones recommended homemade granola, customarily baked on cookie sheets, to revolutionaries because it could be made in quantities big enough to feed a guerrilla army; because it didn't spoil, it was perfectly suited for sit-ins, demonstrations, and "occupying buildings for a length of time."

As a symbol of hippie values, granola was ridiculed by the *Wall Street Journal* in 1972, which ran a headline asking, "What Tastes Terrible and Doubles in Sales Every 60 Days?," describing it as "something a horse might be fond of . . . about as chewy as leather—and not quite as tasty." Nonetheless, like so many antiestablishment affectations, it soon got co-opted by big business. Its connotations of naturalness and health made it an irresistible product for self-absorbed baby-boom consumers of the seventies and eighties, who soon found store shelves stocked with such granoloid cereals as Nature Valley, 100% Natural, Country Morning, Alpen, and Heartland, not to mention granola bars and clusters infused with honey and coated with chocolate.

"Is there a good reason to choose a health bar over other candy bars?" asked *Glamour* magazine in 1982 in an article that examined the nutritional value of such granola-loaded "health bars" as Joan's Natural Honey Bran Carob Bar and Jack LaLanne's Honey Coconut Bar, and found the allegedly healthful ones approximately as nutritious, and as fattening, as a Three Musketeers or Milky Way.

GRATEFUL DEAD

Nobody likes the Grateful Dead except people who *really* like the Grateful Dead. It is hard to find a pop music critic with much good to say on behalf of this rock-and-roll band that has been a force, or at least a major presence, in American culture for nearly thirty years ("virtually worthless," Dave Marsh decided). But it is easy to find their fans. Just look on automobile bumpers, the sides of vans, high school notebooks, T-shirts, and tattooed arms in any urban park in the Western world, and it is likely you will see the familiar red, white, and blue insignia of eight-tooth skulls and skeletons, sometimes accompanied by roses or a lightning bolt with thirteen points, with or without the words "Grateful Dead," that signifies one's rapture with the band—a condition known as Deadheadedness.

Serious Deadheads think of themselves less as fans than as family, and they would be no more interested in critiquing the band than you would be in critiquing your grandmother. They love the Dead for the simple, indisputable reason that listening to the

band makes them feel good. One of the Dead's concert songs is Buddy Holly's "Not Fade Away." When they sing it, usually towards the end of a show, their audience shouts the chorus—"Not fade away!"—back and forth with the band in a transcendental moment of mutual communion. There are some Deadhead esotericists who believe that the universe is a mind, and that all the things that happen in it are like little electrical sparks, or possibly quarks; so when magic, tripped-out moments like that happen at a concert, it is like a beautiful thought occurring in a mellow mind.

The Dead are a band that looks comfortable when they play: There are no tight spandex pants, no eye-aching strobe lights and histrionic special effects, and no leaping around the stage like agitated junkies. "We're musicians, not performers," said lead guitarist Jerry Garcia. The music they make, which was once the cutting edge of the San Francisco sound when San Francisco was hip Mecca, is now more like a

relic, treasured by fans for its rarity, condemned by critics for its hoariness. Their style and the communal scene around them and their repertoire have changed so little that they are often denounced by critics for not being innovative enough. (After all, if it weren't for innovation, critics would have nothing to write about, which may be why one complained that the Dead offer "facile reminiscence to an audience with no memory of its own.") But John Barlow, one of the Dead's lyricists, answered reproaches about their being stuck in the 1960s in *Rolling Stone* a few years ago: "These are soulless times now, and I don't see anything wrong with people who want to fix themselves on times that were a lot more enriching."

One reason fans love them so much is that the Grateful Dead are not for sale. They began as a community band, and that is what they have stayed—providing maximum music, up to six hours per concert, for minimum ticket prices. They are famous for not making lucrative deals with record companies, never playing on behalf of a political candidate ("Who's that cool, really?" Jerry Garcia asked *Playboy* magazine), and for allowing fans to freely tape-record their concerts (some Deadheads have archives of thousands of such tapes). In fact, through most of the 1980s they avoided studio recording altogether. Their preference has always been making music on the spot, improvising like jazz performers, jamming and enjoying it: a strategy Jon Pareles of the *New York Times* called "a marketing expert's nightmare." More than any other important rock group, they have maintained enough control over their concerts' tickets, at least half of which are sold directly via a Dead mail-order system, to eliminate the most awful forms of ticket scalping.

The appeal of the Grateful Dead goes beyond the kind of calculable qualities most critics are accustomed to measuring. More important than the body of music they have created is the thriving subculture that has grown up around them. Ever since rock and roll took its place as the core of the psychedelic scene in the 1960s, the Dead's unique status has been as the focus for a tremendous sense of communion; they are the hosts of a road party that never seems to end. "The Dead and their audience practically form their own self-sufficient fellowship," Mikal Gilmore wrote in *Rolling Stone*, noting how they thrive in a world of their own outside the conventions of hypercommercialized rock.

Dozens of self-published magazines are devoted only to obsessing about the doings of the Dead; the best-known is *Golden Road*, which described the scene around the band as "an oasis in the desert of American lameness." Computer operators can communicate with a Dead database and Dead bulletin board and exchange gossip and discuss philosophical issues. A small Dead-only publisher in Hanover, New Hampshire, periodically updates a book called *Deadbase: The Complete Guide to Grateful Dead Song Lists*, which includes lists of every word ever mentioned in every Grateful Dead song. For example, in the category "Emotions" the list begins:

Afraid (8)
Anger (1)
Angry (1)
Angry-O (1)
Chills (1)
Cried (4)
Cry (15)
Fear (7)
Happy (6)

Et cetera.

It is common for Deadheads to drive or hitchhike across the country for months at a time, to be present at as many perfor-

mances as possible—usually about seventy or eighty a year. One report estimated that there is a core group of about a thousand who attend every concert, everywhere. They support themselves by setting up shop outside the stadium or concert hall and selling crafts, jewelry, and drugs; panhandling; or supplying the greater world of Deadheads with front-line information about the scene. Deadheads are known to blithely arrive at concerts without tickets because they believe in miracles, and even if they don't get in, it's always a party outside any place the Dead perform. To be a Deadhead is to feel part of a great tribe of good heads all grooving on the same peaceful wavelength, the way it felt for a lot of flower children back when the vibes were good, the punch was spiked with acid, everybody got naked and made love in the sun, and the Grateful Dead began to play.

They started in 1964 in San Francisco as Mother McCree's Uptown Jug Champions, then in 1965 became the Warlocks, who, fueled by massive amounts of high-quality LSD and bankrolled by Augustus Owsley, the famous LSD manufacturer (when LSD was still legal), created a kind of chaotic blues-folk-rock music held together by the sheer volume and complexity of its electronic web. You had to *be there* (and preferably be on acid, too) to feel it, and for many of those who were, it was a religious experience. Starting late in 1965 and running through most of 1966, the Dead hung out with Ken Kesey and went along for his "acid tests" up and down the West Coast, where thousands of people had their minds blown by LSD snuck into the punch or ice cream, then danced and hallucinated and made love as the Grateful Dead played so loud they cracked open people's skulls. Their rambling, throbbing, anything-goes sets were labeled "psychedelic rock" because their chaos and energy were supposed to help stimulate hallucinations, or at least simulate the experience of dropping acid. "They are experts in the art and science of showing people another world, or a temporary altering (raising) of world consciousness," Patrick Cann wrote in the *New York Times*, adding that unlike the mean and nasty Rolling Stones, the Dead "have always used their power *carefully*, to spread positive energy."

They changed their names to the Grateful Dead one day when, stoned out of their minds, they saw the words in a dictionary and liked them. (The Grateful Dead is supposedly a series of folk tales in which a dead man takes a lute and plenty of wine with him on his journey to the netherworld.) Jerry Garcia said a lot of people objected to the name at first because it frightened them—which was fine with the Dead, who thought it was good to upset people's consciousness. "It was kind of creepy," Garcia explained. "It was too weird." In 1966 they moved to what would become the most famous address in Haight-Ashbury—710 Ashbury, a communal house that was the very nucleus of hippie life, a place to get high, read the *Oracle*, hang out with the likes of Janis Joplin, Mouse the poster artist, and a free spirit named Mountain Girl (whose baby may have been the first ever to be named Sunshine). By this time, Jerry Garcia, in his signature Uncle Sam hat, was known as Captain Trips; he and vocalist Pigpen McKernan, known for his corpulence, long mustache, and Indian headband, were already well-known counterculture fashion pioneers.

The Grateful Dead were there at all the cool places and for all the sacred moments of the hippie era: at La Honda with the Merry Pranksters; in the Panhandle giving free concerts as the Diggers (street theater provocateurs) gave away free food; at the Fillmore and the Avalon ballrooms; at the Psychedelic Shop (the first head shop); at the famous Human Be-In; in London with America's Hell's Angels in 1968; at Monterey Pop in 1967, and at Woodstock in 1969. *The Grateful Dead Family Album* describes a "Free City Party" late in the 1960s, at which the Dead played for six full hours while their audience took LSD and all wound up on the floor making love to one another: "Sex, drugs, and rock and roll—perhaps the most outrageous event in the history of rock."

When Haight-Ashbury fizzled after 1967, the Grateful Dead hit the road. And for the last twenty years, with very little change (Pigpen died in 1973—"apparently from natural causes," said the coroner, but everyone knows he drank himself to death), they have continued in that mode. The remarkable and ever-growing Deadhead phenomenon began in 1971 with a "Dead Freaks Unite" campaign, started by the band, to gather a mailing list of the people who liked them. The list was their eliminate-the-middle-man way to do business and alert fans to upcoming concerts, and to receive "feedback." One such piece of feedback was reprinted in *The Grateful Dead Family Album*, and included these musings:

> If I don't hear the Grateful Dead at least once a day I go into withdrawals. Will you come play our softball team? Have you sold out? Whoever wants to be born must first destroy a world. The egg is the world. Their music is hair. We know each other. Remember, the truth hurts! . . . It's impossible to ask any more of any musicians than what you've given us. Release more singles. I love you.

Starting in the late 1980s, the good vibes began to spread beyond the core community of Deadheads. They had their first top ten song, "Touch of Grey," in 1987, and although they have never hit number one on the charts, their ability to sell out concerts has grown tremendously over the last five years as more and more people have become enamored of the 1960s. In 1991, the Dead, whose oldest members, *Time* reported, "will soon be eligible for senior-citizen discounts," were certified by *Amusement Business* magazine to be top-grossing touring band of the year, selling out seventy-six of seventy-nine shows.

The Dead have risen from their status as a fringe group of love-generation leftovers and have turned into a bona fide American institution. Just last year, Mickey Hart, Dead drummer since 1968, "donned a business suit" (according to *USA Today*) to testify before the U.S. Senate Special Committee on Aging, advocating the use of music to make old people feel good. Hart said that rhythm was like the seasons, migrating animals, and the cycle of life and death—natural, and therefore excellent. Just like many other rock musicians, the Dead have done a benefit to save the South American rain forest (after which Jerry Garcia insisted that the money not go to a bureaucracy but be used "close to the bone, grass roots, low scale"). And their role as perfectly acceptable culture heroes was finally secured several years ago when Ben and Jerry, those two shaggy, lovable ice cream entrepreneurs from Vermont, named one of their tastiest flavors "Cherry Garcia" in honor of old Captain Trips, and more recently they began packaging the luxurious stuff in "Peace Pops," a percentage of the profits of which are guaranteed to go to good causes.

Not all people see Deadheads with fondness. Although the Dead themselves are now avuncular and harmless in most people's eyes, their popularity has caused many parents and local authorities to start worrying about the community of peace-loving Deadheads who hang onto them. It seems that some municipalities where the Grateful

Dead perform are not necessarily happy to welcome thousands of vagabonds camping in their streets and supplying their high-school kids with LSD whenever the Dead party comes to town. The Grateful Dead themselves have taken to issuing advisories pleading with their fans not to deal drugs at concerts, and have even performed some "kamikaze shows," concerts given on very short notice so that ticket sales are tilted more towards local people than to the roving camp followers who cause the trouble. (Normally, only about 20 percent of ticket sales to a Grateful Dead concert are to people from the local community; the rest of the tickets are bought by the Deadhead caravan.)

Even Deadheads themselves are worried about their band's newfound popularity. In 1987 *Golden Road* published an article by Blair Jackson called "Will Success Spoil the Grateful Dead?" in which Jackson agonized about "a whole new generation of fans who perhaps have no previous connection with either the culture or values of the Dead community." Jackson recalled that overexposure and overpopulation is what killed the beautiful Haight-Ashbury scene after the Summer of Love, and worried that the same thing could happen to the "fragile flower" of the Grateful Dead and its extended family. Still, comfort could be found in the fact that the Dead's new widespread acceptance wasn't based on their selling out to middle-of-the-road values or packaging themselves as nostalgia. "No," Jackson wrote, "the Dead are still singing about the arms race, sleazy small-time operators, existential angst, and perseverance. The imagery is still mandalas, the tarot, skeletons, eyeballs, and the long guns of war."

HÄAGEN-DAZS

I ce cream has always meant more than itself. During World War II, it was regularly listed as the one food that K-rationed soldiers longed for the most, because it was such a symbol of happy times, of a single soda shared by two people in love, of carefree summer-day double-dip cones, of pie à la mode, birthdays, and the Fourth of July. To some degree, ice cream still has all those connotations, but now it has another meaning, too. Ice cream has become a status symbol—an odd turn of events that occurred in 1960, when Häagen-Dazs was invented.

"Häagen-Dazs" means nothing in Danish or in any other language. In fact, there isn't even an umlaut in Danish. Häagen-Dazs was simply a made-up name for ice cream that was originally manufactured in the Bronx (after that, in New Jersey) by a Polish immigrant named Reuben Mattus, who chose the name and put a map of Scandinavia, with an arrow pointing towards Copenhagen, on the carton because he believed that Denmark was a country that nearly everybody liked. At the time Danish modern design was the height of good taste.

After learning the ropes in the family ice cream business in the thirties and forties, a time when Brooklyn and the Bronx boasted many independent ice cream companies, Mattus saw big corporations begin to squeeze little ice cream makers out of the marketplace. National manufacturers could make and sell the product more cheaply, and worse than that, they frequently concocted deals with supermarket chains to exclude little brands from grocers' freezers. Mattus realized he could not compete against the big boys' low-priced, low-grade half-gallons of mass-produced ice cream. In-

stead, he figured that there might be a "Danish modern" segment of the market: people willing to pay extra for dainty little pints of high-quality, high-tone ice cream with a gourmet prestige. At the time, this was a kind of ice cream no big company thought profitable.

Two years before Julia Child began cooking on television, there were already growing numbers of Americans who were eager to be connoisseurs of fine cuisine. They traveled to educate their palates; they ate in "continental" restaurants; and many of them learned to disdain American food, especially American food that was mass-marketed, inferior tasting, and also embarrassingly jejune. Ice cream, for instance: It was juvenile, the sure sign of an unsophisticated palate, and it was—let's be frank—rather plebeian. But not Mr. Mattus's Häagen-Dazs: It was rich (16 percent butterfat, compared with ten for most other brands), it was expensive (50 percent more than big brands), and it was stylish in its elegant pint container (no clunky half-gallons!) with its lace doily motif and the map of Scandinavia on top. "Unwary buyers of this costly marvel," *Time* teased, "could have been forgiven for assuming that they were getting Prince Hamlet's own recipe from the court at Elsinore." In the beginning there were but three flavors: chocolate, vanilla, and coffee.

Häagen-Dazs was eventually followed into the marketplace by more European-named brands, including Alpen Zauber (from Brooklyn, but "inspired by the Swiss commitment to excellence") and Frusen Glädjé (manufactured in Utica, New York, but by a company that had actually bothered to incorporate in Sweden), then by local-sounding Steve's (from Boston), Dove Bars (from Chicago), and Ben & Jerry's (from Vermont). High-priced gourmet ice cream (known in the trade as "superpremium") became one of the fundamental foodstuffs of the delirious yuppie years; it even made the cover of *Time* in 1981 in an article that proclaimed:

> The great underground truth of our society—a republic in which three-fourths of the males and every female over the age of nine are chained to the Scarsdale Diet, the Beverly Hills Diet, or perhaps by now a starvation routine concocted in some other overfed suburb whose inhabitants are rumored to be of ectoplasmic skinniness—is that more and more of us are now strung out on heavy cream, egg yolks, pure vanilla and—yes, oh yes—hot fudge topping with whipped cream, jimmies and walnuts.

What a weird development! Ice cream, formerly the most unpretentious of good-time foods—a favorite of soldier boys away from home and a special treat for kids who got their tonsils taken out—had been made over into a rich and sinful frolic for self-indulgent baby boomers. Chris Chase, author of *The Great American Waistline*, admitted that she sometimes ate six fancy ice cream bars in a day. "I know it's disgusting," she said in 1981, "but I don't care anymore. And besides, it's a lot cheaper than whisky or cocaine." And Gael Greene, *New York* magazine's "Insatiable Critic," bubbled, "For me, it's not the least bit excessive to rank the quality ice cream explosion with the sexual revolution, the women's movement, and peace for our time." Häagen-Dazs's vice-president of marketing described ice cream as "the one luxury everyone can afford." One clever advertisement, entitled "The Four Food Groups," showed portraits of caviar, an artichoke, a brioche, and a pint of Häagen-Dazs.

By the time Pillsbury bought Häagen-Dazs in 1983, the superpremium market was abounding, and the elegant Danish-modern image that Reuben Mattus had created had begun to seem out of date. Häagen-Dazs was facing serious competition from equally rich and equally expensive brands of ice cream that catered to the new foodies' yearning for novelty rather than good taste. Steve's offered ice cream with Mix-ins (broken-up candy and cookies); Ben & Jerry's was selling millions of dollars' worth of such amusingly named flavors as Dastardly Mash and White Russian. To keep up, Häagen-Dazs added unconventional flavors (vanilla Swiss almond, peanut butter vanilla, etc.) and new concepts (Sorbet & Cream, "special additions" of candy and nuts, and, recently, frozen yogurt); they even put out ice cream bars to compete with Dove. But they got a big black eye in the mid-eighties when Ben and Jerry charged that they were coercing distributors to not sell Ben & Jerry's ice cream—precisely the bullying strategy that had encouraged Reuben Mattus to invent Häagen-Dazs in the first place.

This time, though, Häagen-Dazs was the big guy; Ben and Jerry cleverly positioned their brand as the friendly little ice cream from the country, and they took out advertisements in *Rolling Stone* magazine describing themselves as "two Vermont hippies." They mounted an anti-Häagen-Dazs campaign with the theme "What's the Doughboy Afraid Of?" on bumper stickers, T-shirts, and pints of their ice cream. The matter was settled out of court, but Ben and Jerry succeeded in establishing their product as a high-quality, of-the-people ice cream, whereas Häagen-Dazs was made to look like the snobby spawn of an evil corporate giant. It was a brilliant marketing strategy that is now part of American corporate folklore...as is Reuben Mattus's creation of the superpremium ice cream market nearly thirty years before. Ben & Jerry's supermarket sales in the United States now equal half of Häagen-Dazs' (which are something over $100 million); but meanwhile Häagen-Dazs, whose parent, Pillsbury, was swallowed by Britain's Grand Metropolitan PLC in 1989, has been profitably exploiting a taste for superpremium ice cream in Britain, France, Germany, and Japan. Late in 1991 *Business Week* reported that Häagen-Dazs executives anticipate annual global sales of a billion dollars by 1995, only half of that in the United States. All around the world, by the way, the bestselling flavors continue to be vanilla, chocolate, and strawberry.

HARLEY-DAVIDSON

Harley-Davidsons are motorbikes with balls. Listen to a bunch of them thunder into a parking lot and make the earth shake beneath your feet. If ever a machine was macho, it's a stud-and-leather-trimmed, V-twin-powered, shotgun dual-exhaust Harley, known to those who love it as a hog.

There isn't another product of any kind that enjoys such ferocious brand loyalty. Harley riders wear Harley T-shirts and buy Harley booties for their babies and get themselves (and their family) tattooed with the company insignia, an eagle perched atop the Harley crest. They join clubs for Harley owners; if they're women, they can

join the Ladies of Harley—"the group that put the 'move' in the women's movement," whose recruitment spiel says, "I am woman, hear me roar." They scoff at streamlined Japanese bikes, which they call "rice grinders," and they are proud to tell you that Harley-Davidson is the only motorcycle made in America, made by union men and women, in Milwaukee, the beer city.

It is the ultimate blue-collar, working-class, big-bicep American thing. It is not for sissies or softies or the kind of guys who worry too much about the laws of aerodynamics. If you ride a Harley, you tell the world you like the wind (and maybe bugs, too) slamming in your face. You like to ride with the rumble of a heavy, throbbing power plant between your legs. You didn't buy your bike because the specs told you which brand is more efficient; you bought it based on gut feeling. You bought a Harley because it is a bike with soul, an American soul. "Nothing like America, on an American motorcycle," Harley advertising says. But that's not all. If we say there is something almost religious about a Harley's appeal, you might accuse us of hyperbole, so allow us to quote from a brochure we recently acquired at a biker rally. It is entitled "Jesus the Biker," and it is published by the Sons of God Motorcycle Club: "The government didn't like Him. . . . He hung around people like you and me, not the goody-two-shoes Pharisees. Yes, if Jesus were on this earth in the flesh He would be next to you on His Harley telling you He loved you."

The First Harley-Davidson was built in 1901 by William Harley and the Davidson brothers—William, Walter, and Arthur—in the Davidsons' backyard. They were bicyclists (a common enthusiasm for the late nineteenth century), and their goal was to take the effort out of riding, so they, like some other experimental bicyclists at the time (including the Wright brothers), began

to think about a motorized boost. They clipped a motor on a bike, using a tomato-can carburetor to fuel an engine that developed enough power to move the vehicle up to twenty-five miles per hour on a level surface, but not uphill: For that, pedaling was required. They designed a bigger frame and engine, and in 1903 they produced their first real motorcycles, to which a name was given—"Silent Grey Fellow," to suggest what a nice (and well-muffled) companion it would make on a long, lonesome road. Production increased, and starting in 1907 Harleys were sold to the postal service, the phone company, and law officers; they have been the favored police motorcycle ever since. Harleys earned decorations for serving as scout and messenger vehicles during both world wars; but then, in the late forties, they got into big trouble when motorcycles started getting associated with all kinds of characters on the wrong side of the law and of propriety: Hell's Angels (formed in 1950), juvenile delinquents, sexual fetishists.

On July 21, 1947, *Life* featured a biker on its cover: drunk, swilling beer, sitting on a stripped-down Harley-Davidson. He was identified as one of some five hundred outlaw motorcyclists who had invaded the town of Hollister, California, and wreaked havoc—peeing in the street, exposing themselves, and breaking bottles. Law-abiding Harley riders protested the magazine's coverage, saying it didn't tell about all the *nice* motorcycle riders on the roads; but as Harry V. Sucher wrote in his company history, *Harley-Davidson: The Milwaukee Marvel*, "The incident unfortunately labeled the H-D as the outlaw motorcycle of choice."

Regardless of that one particular event, motorcycles simply did not fit the commonly held ideals of the postwar period. In an era crazed by modernity, and by streamlined-looking vehicles that were as much like rocket ships as technology allowed, a big, unwieldy two-wheeler with fringed saddle bags seemed like an antique, long past its time. At a moment when so many people sought status in their chosen means of transportation, there was none to be found in the putts ridden by cops, gangbangers, and mechanics who couldn't afford to buy a car. What today is sold as motorcycles' charm—they make going someplace a visceral experience—is exactly what most mush-suspension cars of the 1950s promised to eradicate. In 1953, when Indian Motorcycles of Massachusetts went out of production, Harley-Davidson stood as the lone survivor among America's motorcycle manufacturers, of which there had been at least three hundred over the years.

Harley-Davidsons remained a symbol of antisocial behavior, relished by so many of the people who rode them for their ability to upset squares. When Japanese bikes started getting popular in the 1970s, the imports seemed to take the high road. The earliest Honda advertisements, in 1959, promised, "You meet the nicest people on a Honda"—a claim Harley couldn't, and probably wouldn't, want to make. The Japanese manufacturers appealed to an upscale market, selling their overhead cams and modernistic design and reliability, while Harley stubbornly stuck to antiquated push rods and plenty of chrome. So what if a bike broke down a lot? Any real Harley kind of guy knew how to fix it.

Harleys remain *the* ride of choice among all bikers with any outlaw airs, but a lot of vintage leather boys are getting old. (A recent *Cycle World* survey showed the average age of all motorcycle buyers to be thirty-six.) Being a tough character on a Harley has become an image that, if not one hundred percent respectable, has a certain nice patina of tradition. The old-time Harley boys, who may now have graduated from being grease monkeys to operating their own gas stations or hand-tooled leather shops, have become "outlaws" like Willie Nelson is an outlaw—self-proclaimed free spirits who like to thumb their noses at middle-class propriety, at least on weekends, but not to seriously break the law. Most of them are vociferously patriotic, and therefore the Harley, which is made in America and (like them) is big and loud and impolite and has a past as a badass, fits the image perfectly.

But in recent years a perturbing trend has begun to erode the Harley-Davidson cachet. In the eighties, in order to pull itself back from the brink of bankruptcy, the Harley-Davidson company went after the yuppie market. They improved quality control and fit-and-finish; they sponsored an alternative, law-abiding motorcycle club, called H.O.G. (for Harley Owners' Group), and raised half a million dollars for Jerry's Kids; they encouraged dealers to restyle their showrooms (most of which used to have all the atmosphere of a pool hall) into "designer stores" with motorcycle-fashion clothing displayed on mannequins, tidy jewelry cases, and flashy neon lighting. They even sponsored a Harley fashion night at Bloomingdale's. They took out ads in biker magazines that said, "Ride with your headlight on and watch out for the other person. Always wear a helmet, proper eyewear, and protective clothing."

Today, one out of three people who buy a Harley is a white-collar worker; 60 percent have attended college. "Harley's motorcycles may be getting *too* fashionable," worried the *Wall Street Journal*, noting that "Harleys are the bike of choice in Hollywood" and reporting on a "gang" of advertising executives in Chicago who ride Harleys on the weekend and call themselves the Rolex Rangers. Writing in *GQ* in 1990, Trish Deitch Rohrer told of a new crowd hanging out in Malibu known around L.A. as the RUBs, meaning Rich Urban Bikers. One of them explained to Ms. Rohrer that "the $30,000 [cost of a tricked-out Harley] might be a lot less in the long run than seeing a psychiatrist every couple of days. ...It's like Zen, in a way." That same year the editor of *Motor Cycle International* said, "I describe the new buyer as 'Atilla the Stockbroker.' He's a guy past the first blush of youth who is professionally well heeled and wants a slightly rougher image."

Image is what Harley-Davidson has become; and today, when one thinks of guys who ride them, it isn't necessarily rampaging young thugs who come to mind. It is older people with a sporty attitude. Even venerable Malcolm Forbes rode one (as did his pal Liz Taylor, whom he supplied with a Sportster in her favorite purple). Jay Leno and Gary Busey ride them, and Gary nearly killed himself on one in 1988 (after which he campaigned *against* mandatory-helmet laws, then saw the light and campaigned *for* them). Mickey Rourke rides a Harley; so does just about every other unshaven guy who would like to let the world know he's a real man, not a wimp. Cathy Moriarty rides a Harley, too, although she was careful to point out to *Interview* magazine, "I am not a biker chick, and I am not a motorcycle mama."

Is what happened to blue jeans happening to Harley-Davidsons? Are the superheavyweight bikes turning from symbols of working-class rebellion and virility into fashion accessories? Willie G. Davidson, grandson of one of the company's founders and vice-president in charge of styling (and a real biker who wears black leather and has a bird's-nest beard), recently said that making motorcycles was "almost like being in the fashion business."And sure enough, the latest Harley-Davidson catalog—for clothing and accessories, *not* motorbikes—

includes such merchandise as a ceramic piggy bank shaped like a gas tank, a beach towel imprinted with the image of a Harley-Davidson stock certificate, a Harley novelty telephone, a vinyl Harley welcome mat, boxer shorts with pictures of motorcycles on them, Harley-Davidson cologne and after-shave, and—can you believe this?—*removable* tattoos. The catalog also includes an application for a chrome-colored Harley-Davidson Visa card.

Did Marlon Brando in *The Wild One* carry a credit card? Of course not; but then, neither did he ride a Harley. The bad boy Brando personified—Johnny, the Black Rebel—hit town on a Triumph Speed Twin.

HELL'S ANGELS

Not just thugs on motorcycles, not weekend warriors or yuppies on Harleys, Hell's Angels are men who devote themselves to the art of living repulsively; they are the original outlaw bikers, a club of some thirty chapters around the country and about a thousand members, who have been called everything from crude scooter jockeys to the new Mafia. Of all the archetypes in America's well-populated gallery of bad guys—which includes trigger-happy cowpokes, ruthless gangsters, big-shot drug runners, knife-wielding juvenile delinquents, and a wide assortment of nitwit mass murderers—they are the only ones who have invented a sporting club devoted to perfecting their unique brand of psycho-fascist vileness; they have relished, cultivated, and defended their status as mean sons-of-bitches at the bottom rung of the social ladder.

To be a Hell's Angel is to spit in the eye of society. It means being grimy and talking dirty; drinking too much cheap beer and whiskey and probably taking drugs; abusing women (and men, too); and doing it all with extra pleasure knowing how odious you seem to all the tax-paying citizens in the world.

The philosophy of the motorcycle outlaw was formulated out of the unsettled ether at society's fringes after World War II. It combined a good measure of juvenile-delinquent impudence with the rage of restless veterans who felt they couldn't get a break, expressed in a new form of antisocial behavior: the bikers' run, the point of which was to drink yourself silly, break windows, hassle squares, and ride with the wind in your face. None of this was original behavior: There were plenty of outlaws in the Old West who behaved similarly, but Hell's Angels had roaring motorcycles between their legs, as well as a hysterical press and Hollywood B-movie-makers to mythologize their deeds.

Because they have always indulged in the farthest reaches of taboo behavior, frequently going over the line even of countercultural propriety (like machine-gunning bunches of their rivals), Hell's Angels are genuinely dangerous, and therefore a never-ending fount of style and attitude among non-Angels who crave to look naughty and flip the bird at everyone in sight. They weren't the first band of motorcycle outlaws—before them, in the late 1940s, there were the Booze Fighters, the Winos, Satan's Sinners, Satan's Daughters, and the Galloping Gooses—but in the forty-plus years since the founding of their club in the small town of Fontana (near San Bernardino), California, the Hell's Angels have become the definitive badasses of the road, their name as evocative of bikerdom as "Band-Aid" is of adhesive bandages. The Hell's Angels' axiomatic state of mind—feeling sorry for yourself but proud to be a loner—has inspired all manner of misfit, from mildly rebellious teenage punks to blithering psychotic murderers (including, for a while,

Charles Manson), to adopt their airs and colors.

Consider, for example, their contributions to fashion. Hell's Angels were the first modern men to flaunt earrings, then nose rings. They, along with pedestrian punks in urban alleyways, popularized leather jackets as a sign of rebellion against a society in which men were supposed to wear baggy suits. The sleeveless denim vest, still a favorite among many young toughs, was first devised in the mid-1950s by Angels who used them to display their colors on top of —or in lieu of—the traditional leather. It used to be that people threw out their blue jeans or made rags of them when they got pale or tattered. Angels wore their jeans to shreds, a style adopted by hippies that has gone in and out of street fashion ever since. Long hair? They were growing it, as well as beards and mustaches, well before the Beatles. Iron crosses and Nazi insignias? They're the ones from whom heavy metal got the idea. Even the bikes they ride—their big Harley hogs—have become one of the most familiar fashion accessories among Hollywood brats and middle-age executives in search of youthful kicks (see p. 205).

Hell's Angels have assumed a strange kind of romantic status not only as lifestyle pioneers but as homegrown individualists. Hunter Thompson called them "as uniquely American as jazz." Like jazz, they are difficult to define exactly, but this is less because they are slippery and more because the world around them has changed so much. In fact, one of the most remarkable things about Hell's Angels is how rigidly consistent they are. What other subculture in this country has maintained such an inviolable style and attitude during the social upheavals of the last half-century? Although they have remained at least as loyal to their ideals as the DAR is to the flag, their role in the changing fantasies and fears of pop cul-

ture has gone through many permutations. Amazingly, considering they are basically nothing more than a bunch of meatheads on motorcycles, at various times in Hell's Angels history they have been held forth as ready symbols of:

- Freedom
- Rebellion
- Machismo
- Cowardice
- Hipness
- Innocence
- Depravity
- Honesty
- Sex
- Homosexuality
- Heterosexuality
- Brotherhood
- Hate.

Their one truly brilliant moment in the sun was the 1960s, when many rebellious flower children tried to adulate them as Free Men, and it seemed to some hippies that the Hell's Angels really ought to be their spiritual allies. This was fine with the Angels, because it meant they got good hippie drugs and hippie chicks. Their taboo psychosexual mystique was exploited in many Hollywood biker films (see p. 55) and even in the English *Girl on a Motorcycle* (1968), in which Marianne Faithfull declares, "My black motorcycle devil makes love beautifully!" Hunter Thompson started writing about them in *The Nation* in 1965, using a delicious mixture of fear, loathing, and fascination to chronicle their peculiar rise to the status of culture heroes—a situation that confused the Angels, who spent so much time and effort offending people. But the Angels were also delighted, because one of their enduring beliefs—left over from the juvenile-delinquent scare of the 1950s—has been that they are "misunderstood." At last they were getting some respect—from hippies, from Allen Ginsberg (who called them "the Angelic Barbarians"), from philosophical commentators, who compared them to the likes of the Texas Rangers and the great frontier cowboys—a rare breed of unfettered American malehood.

They didn't last long on the counterculture pedestal, because, as always, they didn't play by the rules. Sure, it was fine to party with hippies and even mouth some of the going palaver about doing one's own thing and fighting the uptight establishment; but if there was one thing Angels couldn't go along with it was all the love-and-peace hooey. "Love" was fine if it meant sex, but "love" meaning you shouldn't kick the teeth out of your enemy was anathema to Hell's Angels, for whom fighting was a fundamental tenet of life.

Some of the original Hell's Angels in the 1950s had actually been kind of hip and left-wing in a peculiar sort of way. Hunter Thompson told about a guy named Frank, the Angels' San Francisco chapter president (who set the style for earrings and nose rings), who, when hassled by the police, used to go to the ACLU for protection. In the 1960s, Hell's Angels president Sonny Barger wouldn't have dreamt of seeking help from what he was certain was a pinko-commie organization. Therein lay their basic problem as counterculture heroes: Whereas most of the counterculture had liberal attitudes and middle-class values, most of the Angels were low-class men with fascist values. They beat up demonstrators during antiwar protests, volunteered for special combat duty in Vietnam (the U.S. government was not interested), killed one spectator at the Rolling Stones' notorious Altamont concert (an event which many consider the symbolic end of the Woodstock Nation), and preferred all the wrong kinds of drugs (heroin, speed, and beer instead of pot, LSD, and chablis). By the 1970s, the Hell's Angels had become like Charles Manson: an ugly reminder of what was wrong with the love generation.

The Angels bobbed back up into the news in the mid-1980s when the FBI's "Operation Roughrider," a fifty-city dragnet, busted hundreds of them for drug running. This was not the kind of street-corner reefer sales in which Angels (and so many others) had indulged in the 1960s. This was large-scale organized crime that, according to the FBI, involved extortion, money laundering, contract murders, and racketeering in cahoots with the Genovese family. Like many other professional criminals, the Angels were said to be diversifying into quasi-legitimate businesses, such as catering. According to *Time*, they had built up "a highly sophisticated crime network, amassing tax shelters, high-priced lawyers, and an arsenal of antitank rockets, Claymore mines, and M-60 machine guns." Sonny Barger, once their president, said the charges were a smear campaign by the government.

Despite their troubles, the Hell's Angels keep on keepin' on, and every year at the big biker rally in Sturgis, South Dakota, you'll see clusters of them—older now, but every bit as repulsive—swigging their beer, showing off sagging tattoos, giving the finger to everybody with a camera, engaging in all manner of illegal (or at least improper) behavior, feeling perpetually oppressed, abused, and miserable, yet proud to be one of the American road's elite, an Angel from Hell among normal men.

HIPPIES

Hippies were the last American innocents, and at a time when the alternative—being square—seemed so hammeringly drab, their wide-eyed charm was almost irresistible. They seemed like the nicest counterculture ever: smiling, dancing holy fools who believed in a beautiful world of universal peace where everyone was free to do his or her own thing. They were dreamers who felt they had discovered love, and that love could cure all that ailed the human race. It was an idea at least as old as Christianity, but hippies managed to make it their own. (Indeed, many a hippie male fashioned himself after the familiar image of Jesus Christ: bearded, wearing sandals and a long, white robe.) Their kind of love wasn't only spiritual; hippies liked sex, too, and their sex was billed as free of hang-ups, mind games, and untoward consequences. What's more, the drugs preferred by these self-proclaimed flower children were touted even by many straights as totally nonthreatening, and possibly good for you. So here was a group of people who got high, made love, and danced to groovy music: sex, drugs, and rock and roll put together in a way that promised nothing but pure pleasure. Is it any wonder that by the end of the 1960s long hair—their hallmark—sprouted on city streets from New York's East Village to Golden Gate Park?

Hippies first made the news in 1965 when reporter Michael Fallon of the *San Francisco Examiner* wrote a series of articles about a different kind of Bohemia that had developed in the Haight-Ashbury section of the city. The new hipsters he wrote about, using the somewhat derogatory, or at least diminutive, label applied by some old-style beats—hippies—were post-Beatles characters who yearned to set themselves apart from their beatnik forebears. They dug hot rock and roll more than cool jazz, and they liked to dance all night a whole lot more than they liked to listen to cerebral poetry in glum coffee houses. Defying the customary drab and ascetic counterculture uniform of basic black, they sported foppish thrift-shop mod clothes in wild paisley colors and let their hair grow long and wild. Many of them called themselves acidheads, in honor of acid, a.k.a. LSD, the new mind-expanding drug that had been circulating since Ken Kesey first tried it as part of a hospital experiment in 1960. Most impor-

tant of all, they differentiated themselves from previous cranky countercultures by their unequivocal embrace of happiness.

For rebellious young people who had been raised in a land of plenty and had grown weary of the consumer binge that had motivated pop culture since the 1950s, one of the most appealing aspects of hippie life was that it was antimaterialistic. Many of them lived on the fringe and feasted on the rubble of straight society. They got leftover food from wholesale butchers and old clothes from other hippies and Salvation Army stores. Two weeks after the hippie social-service group called the Diggers opened their "Free Store" on East Tenth Street in New York in 1967, they had already recycled a pair of crutches, a box of kittens, five working television sets, a motorcycle, a shaving kit (who needs it!), and boxes full of old shoes, jeans, and T-shirts. The store's only rule was No Stealing, but that was easy, because all the merchandise was free. Salespeople were known as "life actors"; and if anyone asked to see the manager, he or she was told, "You are the manager." Stew was given out every afternoon at four in Tompkins Square Park.

In an uptight world, it was a gas to declare yourself a freak! "If you can't blow minds," a proprietor of the Free Store told a reporter from *The New Yorker* magazine, "you can't be righteous." Don McNeil wrote an article for the *Village Voice* describing how one group of hippies went about their chosen task of blowing minds: "The Suckmobile, a vehicle which could only belong to the Group Image, hurtles down Second Avenue, ablaze with STP stickers. A stoplight interferes. Group Image Freaks, as members of the tribe are affectionately known, pour out of the back of the truck to dance in the intersection. The light turns green, they jump back in, and the Suckmobile goes off and away."

New York's downtown street scene was as crowded with hippies as the better-publicized Haight-Ashbury. The scene was described by UPI writer Aline Mosby in 1966 as "the most swinging Bohemian quarter anyplace in the world." Mosby saw

women wearing sacky shirts of Indian or African prints, sandals or boots, leather pouch bags, and angular silver "modern" jewelry. The hippie girls and their imitators from Connecticut and other plush suburbs can be spotted in pea jackets or ancient military tunics, tight trousers, long "schoolboy" scarves, high boots, beads, bells, and long, dangling hair, and it is often impossible to tell one sex of the species from the other. Some males wear handlebar mustaches, usually false. Hippies shun bathtubs and combs but are fond of marijuana cigarettes and sugar cubes soaked in LSD.

The sensational account goes on to describe available East Village entertainment, which ranged from discussion groups of people relating their sexual experiences in detail to an underground film called *Kansas City Gork.*

The greatest curiosity about hippie life for most outsiders was sex. Hippies, many a reporter drooled, got plenty. *Playboy* magazine (see p. 388) took its readers to Young Ideas, a commune in California, where a photo essay told all about a commune dweller named Nancy: "tall and blonde, with a voluptuous figure, which she exhibits as often as possible." Nancy had a problem —the kind of problem that *Playboy* readers sincerely wanted to help solve. "She's on a heavy fuck trip," a commune member explained. "When she is looking for satisfaction, it is impossible to ignore her constant display of flesh. Getting caught with her in the kitchen is an exercise in grope therapy. She hits mercilessly with her breasts, her behind, her thighs." Poor Nancy. Like all good hippies, all she wanted to do was love everybody, but *Playboy* told the sad story of how she went to the supermarket and some old townie made a citizen's arrest. Nancy got thrown in jail. The charge: indecent behavior. The town wasn't hip enough to dig Nancy's see-through blouse.

Just in case the reader didn't get the message, *Playboy* asked the Young Ideas commune leader, Guru Jim Brewster, "Do you have group sex?" "How can we avoid it?" Guru Jim responded. Accompanying photos showed the communalists lying by a creek, standing in a field of grain, and in bed— buck naked, most of them, except for beads, headbands, and mandalas.

It wasn't only for carnal reasons that squares sometimes tried to play a little footsie with the flower children. Some did it in the empathic spirit of John Howard Griffin, author of *Black Like Me*, who had darkened his skin and experienced life as a person of color. During the summer of '67, widely advertised as the "Summer of Love," virtually every magazine in America sent a reporter to San Francisco to write the story in the New Journalism I-was-a-hippie-for-a-week fashion. The Washington *Post* assigned Nicholas Von Hoffman to live with hippies for the whole summer, after which he wrote *We Are the People Our Parents Warned Us Against*. When Herb Caen (the columnist responsible for labeling beatniks the previous decade) decided to check out the scene, he described his ritual preparation: "In the interest of basic research, I put on my eight-button double-breasted Brioni jacket, a pair of tight pants and my fruit boots and went out to the Drogstore [*sic*] on Haight St., looking more odd than Mod. The pants were so tight I could inhale only, a situation not devoutly to be desired in the Drogstore." No one mistook Mr. Caen for a hippie.

Lewis Yablonsky, a sociology professor, gave his all researching a book called *The Hippie Trip*. "I am not yet sure," he reported when he was done, "that I have gone through what the hippies call 'heavy changes.'" But the professor did smoke a marijuana cigarette while visiting the pad of one of his guides; he puffed on a banana cigarette at the Banana Be-In; and in the name of sociology, he and his wife took an acid trip ("We blended with the unity and beauty of our world"). Yablonsky visited a hippie commune called Strawberry Fields, where he witnessed what he called the "social fallout" of the "mechanical-man, robot, plastic-world bomb." He dug it; but then he freaked out. After visiting the pad of a newly formed New York tribe called the Rising Sun, where he met a "drooling spastic" hippie and a Bowery alcoholic hippie, Yablonsky suddenly had a panic attack, or what he called "a strong motivation to leave the East Village scene immediately." Although he concluded his trip by saying "Some of my best friends were and are hippies," Professor Yablonsky was powerfully relieved to abandon his quest in the hippie world and return to his role as a "rather 'hip' professor."

For certain establishment types, too hopelessly square to become even a tourist in the hippie world, there were still good reasons to put themselves in the love children's sandals for a while. Writing in the *New York Times Magazine*, June Bingham (identified as the "biographer of Reinhold Niebuhr and U Thant") patiently suggested that many hippie judgments were worth consideration:

- The fact that boys and girls look alike and all call themselves "man" signals that they aren't hung up on sex stereotypes.
- With the exception of their need for a stereo, they are not materialistic.

- If they feel in the mood they will neglect all appointments to marvel at the sight of an onion. [This is a good tendency, the author asserts, in a society ruled by Organization Men.]
- Instead of phony polite small talk, they prefer discussion of Birth and Death, Creation and Destruction. Very real.

Although Ms. Bingham believed the hippies were raising profound questions, she didn't much like their answers. She railed against what she called "the hippie-demic" of drugs, the hippie's "paucity of mental furniture," his self-involvement, his aversion to work, and his abysmal ignorance of Reinhold Niebuhr's distinction between "moral man and immoral society." She concluded with these reassuring tips for square parents trying to deal with a hippie child.

> Don't take LSD with your child; but you must learn, as the young say, to "hang easy."
>
> It will take about two years for hippies to emerge from the danger zone. Then these visible, audible and sometimes smellable rebels will get on with normal life.

Ms. Bingham was right. A majority of hippies eventually cut their hair and got on with normal life. The joy of the Summer of Love quickly turned sour because of overexposure in the press, bad drugs, and the inevitable corruption of psychedelic ideals. Many of the barefoot pilgrims to San Francisco realized how cold it can be on the streets at night, and they saw evil vibes rain down. "It wasn't long before the dream fell apart," said David Smith, founder of the Haight-Ashbury Free Medical Clinic. "By late 1967 many of the original flower children had moved out of the Haight and started the commune movement, and by 1968 the professional heroin and speed dealers had moved into the turf." The *New York Times* proclaimed the end of the hippie scene under a headline that read LOVE IS DEAD. Ron Thelin, proprietor of the Psychedelic Shop, a landmark in the days when the Haight first began to percolate, summed it up: "There was this door that was blown open by God, and light shone in on the world, huge amounts of light, at first blinding; and then a vision of the beautiful world started to be realized, and for about a year and a half the world felt it was really true."

As balmy as such palaver seems today, it is astonishing how deeply hippie culture permeated the mainstream. Consider *The Hippy's Handbook—How to Live on Love*, written by Ruth Bronsteen and published in September 1967, which explained to its readers exactly how to become a flower child. Some of its advice now seems quaint or ludicrous. For example, it contained:

- A movie guide that suggested how to analyze a film in hippie terms. A sample review of Naomi Levine's underground film *Yes* was offered: "Fields and freedom, lovers and friends shown with anti-negative visuals of a naked man riding bare-back on a horse in the sunshine. A statement of life where nothing is wrong as long as it does not harm or endanger anyone else."
- Tips on "How to Get High When Your Stash Is Empty": "Nutmeg: two teaspoons swallowed straight. The high lasts only a few minutes. . . . Lettuce: blend at high speed until reduced to a pulp. The milky residue is poured off and drunk."
- A hippie budget, including "eighty cents a week for incense to cover the smell of pot and three dollars a month to buy new love beads."

Silly stuff, and amusingly archaic; but the one part of *The Hippy's Handbook* that seems shockingly current is the glossary. Most twenty-five-year-old vocabularies are intriguing because the words are so cryptic. Hippie talk is just the opposite. Once an outlaw jargon, nearly all hippie words are now familiar and inoffensive. Some terms still have an air of unruliness—to "freak out" or "blow your mind," for instance—but everybody understands them. Hippie language was sponged up by a generation eager to embrace eccentricity and risk.

To say something is a "bummer" or a "rip-off," to get annoyed by a "hassle," to say you are "into" anything, or simply to utter "Oh, wow" (allegedly Timothy Leary's first expression after his first LSD experience) is to use words that two decades ago would have pegged you as a stoned freak. Here are some of the other terms listed in *The Hippy's Handbook* as new; saying them, the reader is assured, lets the world know you are a flower child:

> *BAG:* Someone's "bit" or "thing." A deep, practically obsessive involvement, as in "He's in a Beatles bag." Or "Papa's got a brand-new bag"

> *BEAUTIFUL:* an all-purpose term of approval. Can also be used as an exclamation

> *BLOW YOUR MIND:* to be totally overwhelmed by a new perception

> *FREAK:* a complimentary term for a person who wears flowers, beads, etc.; it often appears in the term "beautiful freak"

> *GROOVY:* fine, excellent, beautiful, terrific

> *OUT OF SIGHT:* wonderful, fabulous, great

> *RAPPING:* talking rapidly and compulsively while high on amphetamine

> *SCENE:* where it's happening

> *SUPER:* intensifies word to which it is attached; i.e. a super mini skirt is a micro skirt

> *THING:* someone's true nature; as in "Turn on to your own thing"

> *ZAP:* to present something in an indelibly memorable way so as to produce a change: "Zap the world with love."

HOLIDAY INN

"Everyone who has traveled has a favorite Holiday Inn," wrote Ruth Malone in her book *Cooking the Holiday Inn Way*, which was published and reprinted throughout the sixties and seventies. One thing is certain: Everyone who has traveled on the roads of America has seen plenty of Holiday Inns. There are well over a thousand of them—at interstate highway exits, in small towns and downtowns—and there are hundreds more around the world, too. "The Nation's Innkeeper," as the company likes to be known, was the world's largest motel chain almost immediately after it started up, in Memphis, Tennessee, in 1952. In the beginning it had no competition. Holiday Inn was the first.

Actually, Holiday Inn wasn't *quite* the first. Starting in Kentucky in the 1930s, the nation had half a dozen Wigwam Villages, which offered guest units shaped like tee-pees; there were a few Treadway Inns in the East; and back in the twenties, when cross-country automobile travel was a luxury, there had been a chain of expensive, colonial-style inns, built by a gas company, aimed at the swank motor trade. (The term "mo-tel" was coined in 1925 by an inn-

Your host from coast to coast

keeper in San Luis Obispo, California, who wanted to attract people in cars.) By the early fifties, however, there were no national motel brands; and most motor courts and roadside cabins had developed a horrible reputation as flophouses occupied by—in the words of a sensationalistic 1940s paperback called *Teen-Age Vice*—"college town prostitutes and professional young hitchhikers of both sexes, out to fulfill their desire to see what is on the other side of the fence." A motel was where you went for an illicit liaison; it was where stripper Candy Barr made her famous stag film, *Smart Aleck;* it was where gangsters hid out and dead bodies were discovered. Nice people, when they traveled, hoped to stay in nice hotels.

Everything changed in the fifties. Forty thousand miles of interstate highway were built. Dinah Shore serenaded Americans every week to "see the U.S.A. in your Chevrolet." One man who decided to take his family on an automobile vacation in the summer of 1951 was Kemmons Wilson, a Memphis entrepreneur and real estate developer who was the country's biggest distributor of Wurlitzer jukeboxes. The Wilson family had a lousy time, mostly because they hated the seedy tourists courts where they stayed, especially one motel near Washington, D.C., that charged not only six dollars for Mr. and Mrs. Wilson but two dollars more for each of their five children. The

next day, Mr. Wilson bought a tape measure and a note pad, and he spent the rest of the vacation measuring motel rooms and devising the ideal basic living unit for travelers. "I decided to build a motel that had all the things we missed," he said. His place would not be encumbered with luxurious appointments like those in a ritzy city hotel, but it would offer such basic amenities as a television, a telephone, a swimming pool, and a playground for children, plus a do-it-yourself "coffee host" in every room; it would be reasonably priced (kids under twelve stay for free!); and most important of all, it would be clean and polite enough to satisfy a churchgoing American family. All Holiday Inns offered a chaplain on call; maids were instructed to open each room's Bible to a different page every day.

What would Kemmons Wilson's motel look like? That didn't matter. The building wasn't what drivers saw; the *sign* was the important thing. So Wilson hired a man named Eddie Bluestein to design a big green, orange, and yellow billboard that lit up and leaned out towards the road, capped with a twinkling star and an arrow pointing inwards, with marquee space down below to welcome guests with a fun slogan such as KILROY WAS HERE, WHY DON'T YOU STOP, TOO? WE WORK FAST AND ACCURAT, or WELCOME, GEORGIA SHERIFFS CONVENTION. When it came time to choose a name for his wholesome new motel, Kemmons Wilson thought of one of his favorite wholesome movies, *Holiday Inn*, about a hostelry open only on holidays, in which Bing Crosby croons "White Christmas." Within two years there were four identical Holiday Inns in Memphis; and in 1954, the same year Ray Kroc made his deal with the McDonald brothers, Wilson decided to franchise. It was an idea whose time had come.

All around America, as downtowns disintegrated and their hotels started falling into disrepair, strips outside of town prospered. It's a chicken-or-the-egg question whether the strips caused urban decay or were merely a response to it, but either way, the blossoming of postwar car culture was the source of change. All the earliest McDonald's were built for people in cars, as were malls, and every Holiday Inn (over half of which were adjacent to highway exits). When some old hotels got so down-at-the-heels that the Kiwanis and even the Optimists didn't want to meet there anymore, Holiday Inn (and, starting in 1957, Marriott, then Ramada) was out on the strip to serve them—with clean meeting rooms, banquet halls, and deluxe continental restaurants suitable for such activities as conventions, club functions, and weddings. The Holiday Inn formula was so successful that in 1964 the company began producing "Holiday Inn Compacts"—prefab rooms manufactured just like house trailers, designed to be fastened together in bunches of thirty-two, thus providing instant installation in any location. By the 1970s, Holiday Inns were hosting about two hundred thousand customers every night and blatantly advertising

what had made them so successful from the beginning: "No Surprises."

In 1979, Kemmons Wilson (then age seventy-six) had a massive heart attack and retired. He dabbled in various businesses, including cemeteries, health clubs, and nacho chips, then in 1988 began a new chain of budget motels, called Wilson Inns, which he opened adjacent to more expensive places (such as Holiday Inns) to lure their customers with his lower prices. Like the original concept, Wilson's new idealized motel room was basic but with some pleasant amenities, in this case a small refrigerator in every room and free popcorn twenty-four hours a day. "Innkeepers Beware," said *Business Week* magazine, "Kemmons Wilson is checking in again." As of 1991, there were thirty Wilson Inns in Memphis and the South.

In 1989, after the Holiday Corporation of Memphis fought off a takeover bid by Donald Trump, it sold all fourteen hundred North American Holiday Inns to Bass PLC, a British pub-and-brewery conglomerate. *Business Week* noted the sale under a headline that read, "Holiday Inn checks out."

HOME VIDEO

When Hugh Hefner bought a videotape outfit for the Playboy mansion in the early 1960s and installed it in his bedroom, it cost ten thousand dollars; to make sure it worked properly, he hired a live-in, round-the-clock Ampex engineer. How many people today, when attempting to tape something with their home video recorder, wouldn't love to have Hef's engineer on hand to master the baffling multi-

tude of date, time, channel, and tape speed choices! Although a lot of us have trouble with any video feat more advanced than playing tapes from the rental store, the fact is that home video is as essential an element of modern life as a blow-dryer or a microwave oven.

Think of it: When you wanted to see a movie in prevideo days, you actually had to go out in public, to a theater, and sit up straight in a chair, surrounded by other people . . . or hope that it would appear on TV's "Late Show." If there was a particular movie you wanted to see, you had to see it when it came around or it might be gone for years, or forever. To see pornography, you had to sneak off to a nasty theater in a bad part of town or to a sleazy stag party. Now, the whole world of motion pictures is your oyster. Just about any movie you want to see— old or new, clean or dirty—is available for a nightly rental fee, and you can watch it whenever you choose, sitting in your favorite lounge chair, close to your own home refrigerator. Some cinéastes lament home video because it reduces the grandeur of motion pictures to the same smaller-than-life scale as "Family Feud" and "Mighty Mouse," but for folks who aren't so finicky, such aesthetic diminishment is a small price to pay for video's supreme convenience.

Before videotape, there were movies and there was live TV, and to record a television show, you essentially had to point a movie camera at a screen and photograph it (a process known as kinescoping). On November 11, 1951, Bing Crosby Enterprises demonstrated a system it had developed (at Bing's behest) that could record sixteen minutes of picture as well as sound on a reel of tape that sped through a recording machine at a hundred inches per second. The picture was barely visible—it rolled and flickered, and there were ghosts—but in the next few years, Crosby Enterprises, as well as engineers in Britain and Japan and at California's Ampex company, improved it. In 1956 CBS began using an Ampex Quad video recording machine to tape the "Evening News" as it was broadcast live in New York; they then ran the tape three hours later on the West Coast. The Ampex machines were huge, and their tape was two inches wide, on big reels. That same year RCA introduced a downsized "See-Hear" home video system, but the quality was awful; the big machine weighed a hundred pounds; and no one (without his own live-in engineer) could figure out how it worked. Besides, who, other than a gadget-hound, would have any use for home video?

"Are You Ready for Home VTR?" asked the cover story of a magazine called *Tape Recording* in 1967, above a picture of a gentleman in a jacket and tie aiming a camera at a woman with a bouffant hairdo, while in the background a tiny television screen displays the image of her face that he is taping. The story inside explained that VTR was an acronym for "video tape recording," and it predicted the VTR might soon become nearly as popular as reel-to-reel hi-fi audio tapes. Elvis bought a home taping outfit the next year, and he sometimes taped football games that were broadcast during the day when he slept; but mostly the damn thing never worked.

In the late 1960s Sony developed the Portapak, which was barely portable (the camera alone weighed twenty-five pounds) but did allow television stations with well-muscled crews to begin taping things, as well as broadcasting, from far-flung locations. One of the first dramatic uses of live Portapak broadcasting was the Republican National Convention in 1972. Sony soon managed to put the Portapak tape into a quick-change cassette—an advance that finally made video user-friendly enough for people intimidated by the high-tech skills required by tape on reels.

In September 1967 the *New York Times* announced, "Soon you'll collect TV reels, like LPs," and three years later CBS held a momentous demonstration at the Pierre Hotel in New York: their EVR (electronic video recording) system, which caused the assembled press to applaud when they saw the beautiful color picture it produced. "The implications and possible applications are staggering," the *Times'* Jack Gould wrote. Because of technical difficulties producing the electronic cartridges, however, EVR was a flop, as were HoloTapes, PREVS (prerecorded electronic video systems), Cartrivision, and SelectaVision—all of which were touted as the home video system of the future, and none of which survived.

The true beginning of the modern video age was 1975, when Sony introduced its Betamax, a combination cassette video recorder and television set. It was cumbersome, and there were no prerecorded tapes to rent yet, and the first model cost $2300. The first "portable" tape deck, which came out the next year, weighed forty-five pounds and was lampooned as a "$1300 toy" by *Fortune* magazine. Nonetheless, using a nationwide ad campaign that told people they could record shows while they were at work or record one show while they watched another, Sony finally hit on the answer to popularizing VCRs (that's an acronym for "video cassette recorder"): convincing customers that owning one was a way to control time. A Betamax made its owner the master, rather than the slave, of television programming. By the beginning of 1977, surveys showed that half the people in America knew what a Betamax was and what it did; in fact, the trade name "Betamax" almost immediately became a generic term for all home videotape machines.

In 1976 the Victor Company of Japan (JVC) introduced a different-format tape cassette, called VHS, for Video Home System. The player-recorder was smaller and cheaper than the Betamax, and it could re-cord not just one hour, like Beta, but two hours (hence, a feature-length movie) on a single tape. Through the eighties, Beta and VHS competed for customers. The results of the competition (other than Beta's eventual slow death) were fast advances in technology: remote control (1977); automatic tape changers (1979); mini-VHS (1982); hi-fi Beta (1983); cheap, play-only portables (1984). Early VCR ads had recommended, "Get Involved With Your Television Set," and by the mid-eighties most Americans had.

The main reason millions of VCRs were bought was not to record television programs but to play prerecorded movies. In the beginning, most motion picture business executives were terrified by home video recorders (as their predecessors had been by television), because they saw them as yet another reason for people not to go out to theaters, as well as an easy opportunity for unscrupulous entrepreneurs to pirate films. Although studios have long sought to add a "piracy tax" to the cost of VCRs to recompense them for illegal copies, they have now learned to love home video. Indeed, videotape rentals and sales for home viewing are how most movies earn profits; and for film buffs as well as people with children who need regular entertaining, the opportunity to *purchase* favorite movies to see over and over again in "home theater" comfort (perhaps on projection TVs with Dolby surround-sound) is mouthwatering . . . especially when, as was the case with Disney's *Fantasia* in 1991, the product is sold with the added psychological allure customarily used to hawk collectible souvenir plates, coins, and liquor decanters—that it will be on the market for a limited time only, then withdrawn forever.

Until 1977 there were no legal videotapes of movies. That summer a Michigander named Andre Blay started a company called

Magnetic Video, which leased the rights to tapes of fifty movies owned by Fox, including such crowd pleasers as *Hello, Dolly!*, *Patton*, *The Sound of Music*, and *Beneath the Planet of the Apes*. With no place to distribute his tapes, Blay launched the Video Club of America to sell them by mail for fifty dollars a copy. The club was so successful that Fox turned around and bought it from him a year after he started it—for $7.2 million in cash.

One of Magnetic Video's best customers was a guy named George Atkinson, who ran a little shop in Los Angeles that rented 8mm projectors and old cartoons to people for kiddie parties. Mr. Atkinson bought *all* fifty Fox titles, in both VHS and Beta format, started a "video rental club" with a fifty-dollar annual membership fee and began renting out the videotaped movies for ten dollars a day. Business was so good that in the spring of 1978, Atkinson opened another store in Pasadena, then began franchising. In the words of *Fast Forward*, James Lardner's history of the VCR in America, "Over the next few years the VCR and the prerecorded videocassette set hearts on fire in entrepreneurial beasts all over the land. Americans from every imaginable walk of life . . . became the proud proprietors of Video Castles, Connections, Corners, Hutches, Huts, Palaces, Patches, Places, Shacks, Sheds, Sources, Spots, and Stations."

In January 1990 *Video Review* magazine declared VCRs "truly historic for having emancipated viewers from TV programmers. Only with VCRs have viewers been liberated to watch virtually anything, whether available on prerecorded cassette, cable, satellite, or broadcast TV, at any time during the day or night." Untroubled by the fact that virtually all VCRs are manufactured in Japan, *Video Review* concluded that home recording had special meaning to

our kind of free people: "The phenomenon appeals almost spiritually to Americans' instinct for independence."

Home video recording of television programming (which the Supreme Court finally said was legal in 1984) and playing professionally made movies are only two of the ways home video has given Americans a newfound sense of independence about how we entertain ourselves. The other way is that it has made everyone feel free to be a bit of a moviemaker—by using a video camera, known as a camcorder. The first really practical home camera, hardly bigger than a tape cassette and known as a Handycam, was introduced by Sony in 1985. Today an estimated fourteen million Americans make their own home videos—of children's parties, family vacations, and newsworthy events they are lucky enough to stumble on: tornadoes, traffic accidents, and law officers misbehaving (the latter now known as "police videos," the most notorious of which was the beating of Rodney King in Los Angeles in 1991).

The thing to wonder about the millions of hours of tapes people make is: Does anybody really watch them? At least old-fashioned vacation slide shows required that the lights be turned off, so viewers could doze discreetly in peace. Videos are shown on TV, usually in a well-lit room, so there is really no escape from that two-hour tape of "Teaching Billy How to Throw a Frisbee" or "It's Graduation Day!" (which has, one hopes, been enhanced by the addition of music by a video store, which can supply such appropriate moods as "Memories," "Watching Johnny Grow," or "Pleasant Valley Sunday"). According to a recent article in *Time*, the real effect of the camcorder has been "the world's greatest collection of truly awful videotapes—a vast library of raw footage even more droning and banal than the reality it purports to document."

The *New York Times* quoted one avid videographer who had captured hours of tape showing his five-year-old son jumping off a baby grand piano: "You want to save the moment even if it's a dull moment."

Videotape is so popular that plain still cameras seem almost to have become a thing of the past at such tourist attractions as Disney World and Opryland and at family picnics and conventions. Now people bring their camcorders, and walk around with the big, high-tech things attached to one eye while they direct their family in its view. Many use ultra-compact 8mm machines no bigger than an old Brownie; but then, too, there are serious gadgeteers with rolling luggage carts loaded with ten thousand dollars' worth of video equipment, including the amazing gyroscopic Steadicam, which smooths out annoying wobbles and makes camera movements look like they were done with a Chapman crane from Hollywood.

Even if they are fuzzy and dumb, home videotapes apparently mesmerize people— so much so that they became the basis of the phenomenal surprise hit of the 1989–90 television season, "America's Funniest Home Videos," a program that consists mostly of comical tapes sent in by amateurs who have caught their loved ones, their neighbors, or total strangers in humiliating situations. A show devoted exclusively to home pet videos followed but was roundly criticized by animal lovers because some eager videographers seemed to be brutalizing their pets in order to make the tapes funnier. Now all blooper and practical-joke programming (one of television's enduring mainstays) depends on the immediacy of videotape. Recently there have even been dramatic shows, such as Fox's "Cops" and "Yearbook," that use purposely amateurish video techniques to give their material the rough look of a tape you or I might make.

This *video verité* approach makes the action in the shows more credible and therefore more exciting.

One kind of picture taking profoundly affected by the advent of the home video age is wedding photography. Now, instead of having a photographer take still pictures, which have begun to seem formal and old-fashioned, many people hire a crew to make a videotape. If a picture may be worth a thousand words, a really swank wedding video will render you speechless. It isn't just a taped record of a wedding, the way home movies used to be; it is a production that sometimes features hosts from local news or talk shows doing voice-over or on-camera interviews, panel discussions about the blessed couple (like on "Oprah") among the bridesmaids and groomsmen, candid scenes of the bride getting dressed, perhaps even months' worth of advance taping—fabulously interesting stuff like the groom renting his tuxedo, hiring the white stretch limo, or consulting with the caterer. Of course the tape will include the ceremony (we have attended a wedding where the ceremony had to be performed a second time because the videotape crew had technical problems), interviews with all the important participants, and superimposed titles, soft-focus romantic scenes, and slo-mo effects. Wedding videos with high production values dub in the couple's favorite music and add pictures, films, or videotapes from their past for a nostalgic touch. A standard wedding tape runs two hours, but deluxe ones can go as long as six. According to our 1991 *Bride's Guide*, "Videotape lets you capture your special day, with all of its emotion, and relive it whenever you like, for the rest of your life."

An unusual source of home videotapes was reported in 1991 by the *New York Times*, which ran a story headlined NEW IN HOME ENTERTAINMENT: VIDEO OF YOUR LATEST

SURGERY. It told about a Long Island woman who invited guests to her home to see a laparoscoped (inside the body) videotape of her recent operation, featuring her gallbladder in color, magnified sixteen times, accompanied by the surgeons' commentary as they cut into her abdominal cavity. Also included were views of her liver and its bile and a climactic scene in which the woman's tissue was cauterized and her body began to smoke. According to the *Times* story, invited guests munched on potato chips as the gallbladder was cut away, and gave the video a unanimous "thumbs up" when it was over.

One compelling attraction of home video is that, like Polaroid photography, no one else ever needs to see the tape. It is as private as you want it to be, which has led some people to actually tape the birth of their baby, then, presumably, offer the child an opportunity to watch his or her nativity some years later. Actors Bruce Willis and Demi Moore reportedly used three cameras when their second child was born, in order to capture the blessed event from every angle. Sometimes, however, the privacy is only imagined. Actor Rob Lowe was practically ruined when the videotape he made, carousing with underage girls in Atlanta, was made public. And recently two men in Danbury, Connecticut, were charged with rape when police looked at a tape they had made of themselves molesting a woman.

Home video's intimacy has made bedroom videotaping into a kinky new hobby for exhibitionistic couples who record themselves having sex, then rent the tapes to home viewers who snub traditional porno movies in favor of the greater realism of watching their neighbors go at it. There are even some psychologists who suggest that couples make sex tapes as a way to spice up their marriage. They do warn, however, that for the insecure patient, seeing oneself and one's spouse copulate, without benefit of gauzy lighting, makeup, clever editing, and special effects, might also result in a paralyzing emotional trauma.

"THE HONEYMOONERS"

When "Roseanne" became the number-one-rated prime-time show at the end of the 1980s, it seemed weird, because proletarian people had nearly disappeared from television. But the blue-collar home is a classic sitcom milieu (see "All in the Family," p. 11), and in the medium's formative era, the travails of the working classes were a great source of fun in such shows as "The Goldbergs" (Jake was a tailor), "Amos and Andy" (Amos was a cab driver), and "The Life of Riley" (Riley was a riveter). The most fondly remembered of all these lunch-pail laborers is Ralph Kramden, who made sixty-two dollars per week working as a bus driver and lived in a shabby two-room flat at 328 Chauncey Street in Brooklyn.

Ralph was created by Jackie Gleason—TV's original Riley back in 1949—and his show, "The Honeymooners," was not actually a scheduled sitcom in its first run. It was aired beginning in 1950 as part of "Cavalcade of Stars," a variety hour on the now-

Jackie Gleason (Ralph Kramden),
Audrey Meadows (Alice Kramden),
Art Carney (Ed Norton), Joyce Randolph
(Trixie Norton)

long-dead DuMont Network. Gleason created many of his memorable characters on the program, including the unbearably rich Reginald Van Gleason III, sympathetic Joe the Bartender, and obnoxious Charley the Loudmouth. One short sketch on the show was about a guy named Ralph Kramden, his wife, Alice (then played by Pert Kelton), and a policeman (Art Carney). The original title was to be "The Beast," showing how the shrewd, long-suffering wife puts her abusive, big-mouthed husband in his place. But Gleason, who invented most of his own dialogue and produced the show, wanted to give the husband a sympathetic emotional hunger beneath his lumpishness and to show how much the couple really loved each other. So the sketch was renamed "The Honeymooners," and Ralph became a paper-tiger blowhard who lashed out with his tongue but then imploded.

"The Honeymooners" was so well liked that it became a regular, twice-a-month feature on "The Jackie Gleason Show" when Gleason moved to CBS in 1952. Following a monologue by Gleason, production numbers by the June Taylor Dancers, and assorted other comedy skits, "The Honey-

mooners" frequently closed the show. In its new venue, the cast had changed. Art Carney became Ralph's friend, Raccoon Lodge brother, and neighbor, sewer worker Ed Norton (always dressed in T-shirt, vest, and rumpled hat). The original Alice, Pert Kelton, took ill, and in one of TV's fabled moments Audrey Meadows (whom Gleason had rejected for the part as too glamorous) hired a photographer to shoot her first thing in the morning, without makeup, to prove she could be frumpy, and she got the part. Joyce Randolph played Trixie, Norton's wife (who was sometimes referred to as a former burlesque queen). By 1954 "The Honeymooners" was the featured attraction of "The Jackie Gleason Show," with some episodes lasting nearly the full hour. During the 1955–56 season, thirty-nine half-hour segments were filmed as they were performed, Saturday night at 8:30, before a live audience; and these episodes, in syndication ever since, are how many television viewers have since come to know and love the show.

Gleason said he based his blustery character on men he remembered from his youth in Brooklyn (where he, like Ralph, lived on Chauncey Street), and although his talents as a performer extended well beyond Ralph Kramden, there was an uncanny correspondence between the actor (who was famous for his limitless ego as well as for a sentimental heart) and his role. Kramden was one of television's fundamental creations: a little man, a nobody, with an oversize body stuffed into his driver's uniform and extravagant dreams of glory percolating behind his great, popping eyes. Perpetually frustrated by his lot in life, he jumped at any harebrained opportunity to get ahead (including an appearance on a quiz show called "The $99,000 Answer" and schemes to sell glow-in-the-dark shoe polish and diet pizza), and he always wound up putting himself behind the eight ball (as when he developed KranMar Mystery Appetizer, then served it to his boss, only to realize, too late, it was dog food). When his wife, Alice, or his friend Norton got in his way, he fumed, he ranted, he yelled, and he threatened with such immortal (and never carried-out) warnings as "One of these days —POW, right in the kisser!," "Alice, you're askin' for a knuckle sandwich," and "Bang, zoom, right to the moon!" And when they scorned him or made fun of his girth, he turned sarcastic, launching a flesh-shaking "Har-de-har-har!" towards his tormentors. When things didn't work out as he planned (when he wasn't named Raccoon of the Year at his lodge, or when he wrenched his back because he snuck off to bowl the night before his company physical), he was humbled and contrite, sometimes moaning vociferously, "I got a *big* mouth," and he always ended the show by telling Alice, "Baby, you're the greatest."

The fundamental premise of "The Honeymooners" was the strength of the relationship between Ralph and Alice (children never did figure in the situation, except in one reunion episode, filmed in 1966, in which the Kramdens attempt to adopt a baby), but the enduring appeal of the program has a lot to do with the friendship between Ralph Kramden and Ed Norton. As a sewer worker, Norton was one of the few human beings that Ralph, a uniformed bus driver, felt he could look down on, and Norton's dunderheaded way of talking seemed to reinforce that belief ("You're the stupidest man I ever knew!" Ralph erupted on more than one occasion). However, to Ralph's eternal dismay, Norton was always, somehow, outmaneuvering or outsmarting, or at least annoying, him. The very sound of "Hiya there, Ralphie boy" seemed to put the easily miffed Kramden on edge, and when Norton headed for the Kramdens' icebox to

help himself, or prepared to write something with a pencil by flailing his hands and arms with elaborate and ostentatious limbering-up exercises, Ralph would once again be pushed over the edge of exasperation and explode, "WILL YOU CUT THAT OUT!"

In addition to the thirty-nine shows that many devout "Honeymooners" fans know by heart (there is actually a club called RALPH—the Royal Association for the Longevity and Preservation of "The Honeymooners"), hundreds of other episodes of the show were made over the years, including many in the 1960s with Alice played by Sue Ann Langdon or Sheila MacRae. In 1966, the Kramdens and the Nortons even went to Europe together; and there were two reunion specials, in 1976 and 1978. In the 1980s, seventy-five more of the early performances with the original cast were put together as "the lost episodes," and they have been broadcast on cable TV and are available on videotape.

Jackie Gleason had a spectacular showbusiness career. He was an acclaimed actor —especially in *The Hustler* (1961), for which he got an Academy Award nomination—and composed innumerable albums of mood music (as well as the theme song of "The Honeymooners"). But when he died in 1987, it was as the irrepressible Brooklyn bus driver that he was best remembered. Several newspapers ran his obituary under the headline RALPH KRAMDEN DIES.

HOT DOGS

Hot dogs are fun food. Although it is possible that some people actually sit down at the dinner table and eat them with knife and fork, accompanied by a mature burgundy, it seems safe to say that the vast majority of tube steaks are consumed out of hand in the most unceremonious settings: at picnics and ballparks, in airports and on city streets. Just as beef Wellington and lobster thermidor epitomize a certain kind of haute cuisine, hot dogs are the quintessence of pop cuisine, American style. As a nation, we eat enough of them every year that if you laid them all end to end (including foot-longs), you'd make three round trips from the earth to the moon. In fact, weenies did go to the moon —carried by Apollo astronauts who didn't want to leave earth without them.

Despite the hot dog's popularity, there is absolutely no agreement among Americans about what constitutes a great and proper one. Consider this amazing fact: There is no significant national chain of hot dog stands.

There are hamburger places and pizzerias and fried-chicken joints galore—the same from coast to coast. But when it comes to hot dogs, Americans refuse to standardize. We are a nation that likes our franks local and eccentric: split and grilled at the Connecticut shoreline; all-beef and "dragged through the garden" (of condiments) in Chicago; porky and beer-boiled in Milwaukee; topped with stewed onions on the streets of Manhattan or with Pink's sloppy chili in Los Angeles. Upstate New York favors fiery sauce atop porcine red hots that get blackened on a charcoal grill; in Rochester and Syracuse the dogs of choice are *white* hots rather than red. Rhode Island, one of the strangest branches of frankdom, is home of "New York System" wieners—itty-bitty piglets in baby rolls, sold by the dozen under blankets of spicy chili sauce. Connoisseurs there order batches of "wieners up the arm," meaning the server lines them up, wrist to shoulder, so he can quickly apply the condiments. Experienced New York System customers, however, avoid the wiener nearest the dog man's armpit.

A hundred years ago, sausages were a popular American food, especially among communities of German immigrants, who favored tubular delicacies such as the tiny links from Vienna known as wienerwursts (wieners for short) as well as sturdier five-inch sausages with culinary roots in Frankfurt (frankfurters), but the hot dog as most of us know and love it—nestled inside a bun and smothered with mustard, relish, and God-knows-what-else—was still waiting to be born.

Some gastronomic historians contend that it came into this world as a clever way to prevent pilferage. In the beginning, according to this tale, there was Antoine Feuchtwanger, a sausage vendor at the St. Louis World's Fair of 1904. With each link sold, he lent the customer a glove to hold it. The glove kept grease off fingers, and it allowed him to sell the sausage piping hot. One problem: Souvenir-greedy fairgoers were always walking off with his gloves. So Feuchtwanger convinced his brother-in-law (who happened to be a baker) to make him elongated mini-loaves of bread. He sliced the bread down the middle and began selling sausages-in-bread as a package deal. Not only were his worries about stolen gloves over; customers loved the idea because the buns kept the sausages from dripping onto their clothes.

So began the age of the hot dog.

...Unless you believe the other story about the hot dog's birth, which attributes the great moment to a fellow named Charles Feltman, a German pie man who sold his pies from a pushcart along the then-rustic byways of Coney Island in the late 1800s. When a nearby restaurant began serving hot sandwiches for lunch, Feltman got nervous he would lose business. Doggedly, he decided to compete from his pie wagon. There wasn't much room to cook anything elaborate on the roving cart, so he fixed up a small charcoal stove and a pot of water. He boiled frankfurters and sold them two at a time, nestled inside rolls so that customers could eat a hot, cheap lunch standing up.

Feltman's invention was so successful that he soon opened a fancy restaurant of his own, abandoning the pushcart and cheap prices, selling sausages-in-buns as his specialty. A few decades later, in 1916, Coney Island had become a high-toned resort spa, and among its up-and-coming entertainers were a sausage-loving duo named Eddie Cantor and Jimmy Durante. Their problem was that they couldn't afford Feltman's ten-cent sausages. So they convinced a Feltman restaurant employee named Nathan Handwerker to open his own frankfurter emporium, and sell sausages in buns at half price, a nickel each. So began Nathan's of Coney Island...according to amateur historian Murray Handwerker, Nathan's son.

Whichever story one believes about the origin of the sausage-in-a-bun concept, there is little doubt about when and how the hot dog got its name. This chapter in hot-dog history begins in April 1900 at the Polo Grounds in New York. It was opening day of the baseball season, and it was *cold*. Harry Stevens, head of catering, knew he would have a hard time selling ice cream and soda pop. He wanted to give customers something that would warm them up and that would be easy to eat in the bleachers, as well as easy to vend throughout the ballpark. So he equipped his men with thermal boxes. He went out and bought a bunch of the long, skinny links popularly known as dachshund sausages and stuffed them into warm buns. He instructed all his vendors to deal their sausage sandwiches with this cry: "They're red hot. Get your dachshund sausages while they're red hot!" His idea was an immediate success: ballparks and hot dogs have been wed ever since. But they still didn't have their name. The christening came about in 1903, when T. A. Dorgan, a San Francisco sports cartoonist, moved to New York and began working for the *Evening Journal*. Dorgan was so amused by the way Harry Stevens sold sausages at the ballpark that he used to draw cartoons lampooning Stevens's vendors and their peculiar cry. In order to make his cartoons easy to read, he labeled the sausages "red hot *dogs*" instead of dachshunds and drew pictures showing miniature pooches nestled in rolls, barking at each other.

Dorgan's joke went over *too* well. Sausages had long been a suspect food, even before Upton Sinclair wrote *The Jungle*, describing the repulsive parts of animals that went into processed packaged meats. A hundred years before the sausage was popularized in Coney Island, Britons were calling them "mystery bags" and "bow-wows." In the mid-1860s, the Whiffenpoofs of Yale used to serenade in jest:

Bologna sausage is very good
And many of them I see;
Oh where, oh where is my little dog gone?
I guess they make 'em of he!

By 1913, it had become such a widely held folk belief that hot dogs might actually contain dog flesh that the Coney Island Chamber of Commerce forbade the use of the term "hot dog" on signs or menus. Instead, the immensely popular boardwalk snacks were referred to as "Coney Islands" —a still-thriving nickname all across the U.S.A. Well into modern times, hot dogs have retained their shady reputation. "There's a damn good reason we should never sell hot dogs," McDonald's president Ray Kroc declared before he died in 1984. "There's no telling what's inside a hot dog's skin."

The mystery of hot dog ingredients only made them more popular among college students, beachgoers, baseball fans, and fun-loving eaters of every type. Long ago, vendors became known as "dog men" and sausage carts as "dog wagons." And the term "hot dog" has wafted through the American vocabulary for nearly a century —first as an exclamation of overwhelming delight ("hot dog!"), then as a description of a blatant show-off. Relief pitcher Darold Knowles once said, "There isn't enough mustard in the world to cover Reggie Jackson." Actually, it's not so terrible to be called a hot dog—at least it means you're good. No one, however, likes to be called a weenie.

Strangely, despite its ignominious reputation as mystery meat with little nutritional value, the humble hot dog is a dish that we Americans have long been proud to call our own. Its lack of airs makes it the ideal democratic food, and for many years all campaigning politicians have sought to be photographed eating one, in order to prove they are ordinary folks rather than the type of snob who dines on caviar and filet mignon. In 1942, as World War II was getting into high gear and patriotic citizens were busy trying to figure out ways to eat lower on the food chain, Louise Owen wrote an ode to "The Friendly Frankfurter" for *American Cookery* magazine. Here are the first two verses:

The gentle frank all red and white
I love it with all my soul.
It gives me meat with all its might
To eat upon a roll.
It's tasty, toasted—
It's racy, roasted—
It's full of iron and phosphorus;
It's the favorite ration
Of all our nation—
And mustard is the sauce for us!

The frank's the friend of every man,
Proud, modest, shy or snooty.
Its curve is pure American,
And full of eating beauty!
Thanks, thanks
For excellent franks
That are practically always digestible;
The dickens
With chickens,
Or steaks on planks—
The frankfurter's my comestible!

HOWARD JOHNSON'S

Before McDonald's and its burger brethren ruled the road, Howard Johnson's was America's best-known place to eat. It was the original symbol of franchised highway cuisine—the same from coast to coast, as well as from year to year, the only variation being an occasional change in the famous repertoire of twenty-eight ice cream flavors.

Predictability was the key to HoJo's success, as it was to Holiday Inn's (see p. 216). For generations of travelers wary about disreputable roadside diners and indigestible truck-stop grub, the familiar orange roofs were a beacon of civility as well as of disease-free, dependable food. HoJo's colonial cupola was reminiscent of a steeple in an old New England town, and its nursery-rhyme logo, a weathervane of Simple Simon and the Pieman (repeated in the entryway and on some early menus), reassured motorists that they had found a wholesome place where the entire family could eat decently and cheaply, with the extra pleasure of ice cream and candy to take out and enjoy for miles. "Even with cars whizzing past and nearby buildings looking scruffy," Philip Langdon noted in *Orange Roofs, Golden Arches*, "a Howard Johnson's looked solidly and properly planted."

Inside the restaurant hung a patriarchal portrait of the sober Mr. Johnson himself, looking like a stern Ivy League university president or a judge. As trustworthy as Betty Crocker but with the added distinction that he was a real person who had realized the American dream, Howard Johnson became a seal of approval that America found easy to depend on. He truly was a stickler for propriety and detail: His uniformed waitresses were not allowed to chew gum or tap their pencils on their order pads; he made every franchisee keep a daily log of all transactions; and he sent undercover employees to pretend they were customers, then report back to him at headquarters.

Most important, Johnson insisted that the food always be prepared and served in exactly the same way, so that a deluxe hamburger plate in Maine was identical to one in Florida. Orders of baked beans were served in a little Yankee-style bean pot; fried clams came in a paper cup with tartar sauce on the side of the metal serving plate; the hot dog (known, with a subtle dash of Boston Brahmin hauteur, as a "frankfort") was scored with a knife exactly six times before being inserted in its distinctively shaped, toasted, overbuttered bun, which was itself inserted in a white cardboard boat; the manual of standard operations even specified that each cup of coffee was to be poured to precisely three-eighths of an inch below the rim of its cup. And, of course, you *knew* you would end your meal with a favorite ice cream flavor—buttercrunch, coffee, and maple walnut have been some of the time-honored specialties—made using a specially developed scientific formula known only to Howard Johnson's.

Ice cream was what first put Howard Johnson's on the map. Howard "Buster" Johnson had such success selling a trio of extra-rich standard flavors (chocolate, vanilla, and strawberry) from his drugstore soda fountain in Wollaston, Massachusetts, starting in 1925, that within a few years he had opened ice cream stands all around the Boston area. In 1929 he started a full-service short-order restaurant serving hot dogs, hamburgers, and the local specialty, fried clams, in addition to a growing number of flavors of his high-butterfat ice cream. Franchising had proved tremendously successful for White Castle hamburgers, which had begun as a single diner in Wichita, Kansas, in 1916, and by 1930 had expanded to more than one hundred franchised outlets around the country. In 1935 Johnson decided to franchise his name to a former schoolmate, Reginald Sprague, who opened a Johnson's Restaurant that featured the now-proverbial twenty-eight flavors and an orange roof, alongside a busy tourist thoroughfare on Cape Cod. Five years later there were 130 franchised Howard Johnson's along the East Coast, including a huge one on Queens Boulevard in New York with a view of the 1939 World's Fair.

An exclusive deal struck with the Turnpike Authority made Howard Johnson's restaurants the *only* place to eat along the Pennsylvania Turnpike (America's first limited-access superhighway) when it opened in 1940, and thanks to their vivid orange-shingled roofs, you could see them a mile away. After World War II, the creation of the interstate highway system effected a subtle but certain change in the HoJo's image. In its earliest days, the orange roof had meant a breezy kind of place for vaca-

tioning families on their way to the beach, but when it was made into the only sanctioned food-service establishment along eight major American turnpikes, including the interstate highways of Connecticut, New Jersey, and Massachusetts, Howard Johnson's became better known as a symbol of inescapable sameness.

Phil Patton, in *Open Road*, called Howard Johnson's precise formula "just the note of the Modern Olde the traveling public was interested in. Everything was just like colonial times—and right up to the minute; completely new—and just like Grandma made." Howard Johnson's dramatically modernized many of its restaurants in the 1950s and 1960s, moving from the Olde New England look to a low-slung suburban ranch-house style, complete with starburst clocks on the walls and picture-window views of the parking lot. In 1954, following the inspirational success of Holiday Inn, HoJo's plunged into the motor lodge business, creating well over a hundred motels by 1960. Each one had a cupola on an orange roof and all were connected to a Howard Johnson's restaurant. In the early 1970s, when there were nearly a thousand orange-roofed HoJo's across the land, and when McDonald's proliferating golden arches hadn't quite yet eclipsed the ubiquitous orange roofs, the company motto was "Howard Johnson's—the Taste of America!" But by this time, the reliable standardization that had once made those bright orange roofs such a welcome relief along the highways was beginning to seem like yet another example of the blight of franchised commercial architecture.

HoJo's food lost some of its charisma, too. The well-known menu had come to seem a little dowdy, and the salutary, quasi-regional Yankee flair that had once made it such an infallible American institution was passé. A newly sophisticated America was no longer enamored with frankforts and baked beans, or, for that matter, with scientific assembly-line precision; and HoJo's ice cream, once the class of the field, had been outflanked first by Baskin-Robbins, then, by Häagen-Dazs (see p. 203). Restaurant critic Gael Greene, who had fond memories of eating Howard Johnson's sinfully rich chocolate fudge cake years earlier while on family vacations, called the modern progeny of the formula "both hideous and strangely comforting . . . predictably clean, predictably carpeted, predictably low-brow, predictably mediocre, predictably turquoise and orange." Greene's ambivalent reaction to the franchise's predictability, titled "Help! I'm a Prisoner on the Turnpike," lamented that even Howard Johnson's most celebrated specialties weren't nearly as good as they used to be, at least as she sampled them alongside the New Jersey Turnpike. Her frankfort was shriveled, her bun was unbuttered, and her chicken pot pie was filled with stringy meat.

Howard Johnson's had in fact long since taken extraordinary measures to bolster its reputation and to ensure its status as a source of good food that was a cut above self-service hamburger joints. In 1960 it hired Pierre Franey away from the most respected restaurant in America, New York's Le Pavillon, to become head chef and elevate the kitchen. Chef Franey added beef burgundy and curry to the menu, but rued the fact that truck drivers were too impatient to wait even five minutes for their frankfort to be grilled in butter. (Jacques Pépin has worked for HoJo's, too, as director of research and development.)

In 1969, in an effort to circumvent the eyesore reputation of the orange roof and the inevitable association of its plebeian cuisine with junk food, Howard Johnson's made a bid to recapture the family dining trade. In the tradition of its upscale Red Coach Grill restaurants (fancier HoJos), the company began to open dining rooms with comfortably nostalgic decor of old advertising memorabilia and historic photos of Americana, and with tasteful brown-shingled roofs instead of the loud orange ones. They weren't called Howard Johnson's; they were known as the Ground Round, signifying something better than franchised hamburgers. Ground Rounds weren't fancy or expensive, but neither would you go to one for a frankfort or a clam roll; and the trademark soda fountain with twenty-eight flavors of ice cream was gone. There was no portrait of a strict Howard Johnson hanging up inside, and no childish weathervane of Simple Simon and the Pieman twirling overhead.

Poor HoJo's almost died in the 1980s, a victim of corporate football. Howard B. Johnson, son of the founder, sold all 1,040 restaurants and 520 motor lodges to Imperial Group, Ltd., a British conglomerate. But the Britons didn't like HoJo's, so they sold it back to the Marriott Corporation, which replaced many of the old restaurants with its more profitable Big Boys. Then in 1988 Marriott announced its intention to give all Big Boys and all Howard Johnson's a totally new name—Allie's (after Alice Marriott). In 1988 Otto Friedrich reported in *Time* magazine that some of the old-time Howard Johnson's operators had fought back and managed to get control of at least 137 of the restaurants, where they intend to continue the tradition, even if they cannot manage to stock twenty-eight flavors of ice cream anymore. A spokesman for the new Howard Johnson's group promised a minimum of eighteen.

"HOWDY DOODY"

Howdy Doody was television's first nationally known celebrity. The freckle-cheeked, wood-bodied marionette from Doodyville scaled unprecedented heights of fame, and in his wake came such flesh-and-blood TV pioneers as Milton Berle, Gorgeous George, and Lucy and Ricky. But none of those mere humans had shows that lasted half as long as Howdy's, from the dawn of television in 1947 to September 1960.

Howdy was a marionette whose ancestry traces back to a 1945 children's radio show on NBC called "Triple B Ranch," named for its host, Big Brother Bob Smith, a living human being who co-starred with an imaginary hick-from-the-sticks named Elmer. Elmer was supposed to be a dim-witted ranch hand on the Triple B; and whenever he came on the air, he said, "Ho, ho, ho, Mr. Smith and boys and girls—well, howdy doody!" Children in the listening audience relished hearing the semitaboo word "doody" on the air; so when "Triple B Ranch" was transferred to NBC television as "Puppet Playhouse" on December 27, 1947, Elmer's name was changed to Howdy Doody. However, because no puppet had been designed yet, Howdy stayed in a drawer during the first televised show and said—still sounding like a hick—"Gorsh, Mr. Smith, Ah'm too dern bashful to come out!"

Soon, marionette maker Frank Paris unveiled the first Howdy Doody. He was a loathsome-looking being with jug ears, a messy mop of blond hair, and a moronic grin—all made to fit the coarse voice of the original Elmer. Doody wore work clothes and cloddish boots, and when he was pulled out of the desk drawer and introduced, he

Bob Smith (Buffalo Bob), Photo Doody, Marti Barris (Peppy Mint)

terrified kids in the Peanut Gallery (the bleachers where the studio audience sat). Still, "Puppet Playhouse" was a huge success, praised by *Variety* for its ability to "keep the small fry intently absorbed and out of possible mischief" during the late-afternoon hour when it was a broadcast.

The dilemma of what to do about Howdy's appearance resolved itself within weeks when Frank Paris walked off the show in a dispute over who owned the merchandising rights to Howdy's image. The audience was told that Howdy had left to campaign for the office of President of all the Boys and Girls (on a platform of bigger ice cream sodas and higher allowances). Until a better-looking marionette could be made, Bob Smith introduced a figurine with its head swathed in bandages, told the kids in the Peanut Gallery it was Howdy, and asked them, "Do you know what plastic surgery is?" He explained that Howdy Doody had gone under the knife to gain an edge on his handsome opponent in the presidential race, Mr. X (who was running on a platform of abolishing comic books). A month later, when the improved Howdy Doody marionette was ready, the gauze was removed, revealing the postoperative countenance that American children grew to love. With his new face, leaner body, and sportier wardrobe, Howdy Doody made history. (Meanwhile, Bob Smith assumed the name "Buffalo Bob," supposedly given to him by Indians who lived near the circus town of Doodyville, actually in honor of Smith's home, Buffalo, N.Y.)

The new Howdy Doody was created by Velma Dawson, a former employee of Walt Disney Studios, based on audio tapes that Bob Smith (who always did Doody's voice) had recorded for her, using the friendlier, more boyish tone he wanted to give the new model. Howdy was now a big-cheeked, freckle-faced lad with tousled hair, dressed in blue jeans and cowboy boots, plaid shirt, and bandanna. A second Howdy Doody that Ms. Dawson had made for safety's sake (in case the original got damaged) had its nose shaved and chin reshaped and became John J. Fadoozle, a private eye who appeared frequently on early shows. A third model (which turned out to be top-heavy) became known as Double Doody and sometimes appeared as Howdy's twin. Soon there were Phineas T. Bluster, the mean mayor of Doodyville; the Flub-a-Dub, a polymorphous doglike creature who loved eating spaghetti and meatballs; Heidi Doody, Howdy's sister; and Phineas Bluster's brothers, Hector Hamhock and Don José. (There was even one character known as Photo Doody, who never actually appeared on the show but was made without any strings for picture sessions.) In addition to the marionette cast and a clay figure named Gumby, who appeared on the show in an animated series, Doodyville's inhabitants included Clarabell, the clown (mute because nonspeaking actors didn't have to be paid as much), whose main activities were squirting Buffalo Bob Smith with a seltzer bottle and honking a bulb horn; Chief Thunderthud, the Indian (who first uttered the exclamation "Cowabunga!"); Pierre, the chef; Ugly Sam, the wrestler; and beautiful Princess Summerfall Winterspring.

Each show had a plot, frequently involving Howdy and Buffalo Bob getting together to outwit the ill-tempered Mr. Bluster, who was fiercely jealous of everything Howdy had, including his intimate relationship with Buffalo Bob. The story was always loose enough to allow for songs, including "duets" sung by Howdy and Bob (who prerecorded Howdy's voice), film shorts, and games, and always much pouting and seltzer-bottle mischief from Clarabell (originally played by Bob Keeshan, who became Captain Kangaroo [see p. 80]). In the 1980s, long after Howdy had retired, Jeff Greenfield analyzed the dynamics of the show for *TV Guide* and declared Howdy "the first hippie," noting that all the show's good characters were either kids, native Americans, or clowns and that all its middle-class adults (except for Buffalo Bob) were evil.

In fact, from the beginning "Howdy Doody" drove parents insane. It always started with forty kids in the Peanut Gallery answering Buffalo Bob's question "Say, kids, what time is it?" by screaming "HOWDY DOODY TIME!" at the top of their lungs, then basically continuing to scream for the entire hour. Critics said the show agitated children to the point of dementia— and just before dinner time! "After witnessing it once," New York *Herald Tribune* columnist John Crosby moaned in 1951, "the exasperated parent is likely to head for the cellar or the roof to escape the darned thing.... The program is conducted at a noise level roughly five times that of Berle, or about twenty times that of Lou Costello."

But kids loved it. Howdy was their hero (he got more votes for President of all the Boys and Girls than Progressive party candidate Henry Wallace got for President of the U.S. in 1948), and such a national institution that when Charles Schulz created his cartoon strip, his syndicate named it "Peanuts" (see p. 376) for the kids in the Peanut Gallery. Howdy Doody merchandise included clothes, school supplies, toys, furniture, and even eggs (edible ones) that he endorsed. On January 27, 1952, when "Howdy Doody" became the first network show ever to have a run of one thousand performances, its guests stars included Kukla, Fran, and Ollie in a live remote broadcast from Chicago, Milton Berle, Ed Wynn, Dave Garroway (pre-"Today"), and Happy Tooth and Mr. Tooth Decay (the latter two courtesy of Colgate, the program's sponsor).

Howdy Doody met his Waterloo in Mickey Mouse. When "The Mickey Mouse Club" went on the air in 1955, beginning a half-hour before "Howdy Doody" in the afternoon, the stringed marionettes and costumed vaudevillians of Doodyville suddenly looked awfully tired compared with the glamorous likes of such cute Mouseketeers as Annette Funicello and Cubby O'Brien. While old Clarabell was lumbering after Buffalo Bob with a seltzer bottle for the millionth time, handsome-as-a-movie-star host Jimmy Dodd was introducing "The Adventures of Spin and Marty" to enraptured viewers of "Mickey Mouse." Television had grown up since 1947; and children —of every age—had learned to expect more from kiddie shows. "The Mickey Mouse Club" was modern and pert; it made "Howdy Doody" look dowdy. In June 1956, Howdy was relegated to Saturday mornings —the kids' ghetto—where it limped along for four more years. At the end of the final show, September 24, 1960, all the residents of Doodyville packed their bags—on the air —and left town. The Peanut Gallery was empty as the show began; and instead of screaming, the peanuts filed in quietly. Howdy fluttered his wooden eyeballs and bounced with that peculiar walking-on-air gait shared by all inhabitants of Doodyville as he reminisced over a 1948 "Howdy for President" poster. Mr. Bluster announced he had fallen into a deep, irreversible depression. At the very end, after Buffalo Bob's final "Goodbye Song," Clarabell turned to the camera, began to cry, and *spoke:* "Goodbye, kids," he whispered, and the Peanut Gallery was silent.

Buffalo Bob and Howdy Doody performed in live nostalgia shows through the seventies and eighties; and in 1976, there was an attempt to syndicate a new, modern version of "Howdy Doody," for which Howdy grew his hair out in a sort of disco pouf, but the new program was a flop. In 1983, the Associated Press reported that Howdy Doody had been decapitated, and sent out a grisly picture that showed Howdy's headless remains. In fact, the corpse in the picture was Photo Doody, attacked in his NBC storage room by an unknown assailant; and Photo has since been fixed. (That same year, when Bob Keeshan's successor as Clarabell had heart surgery, the New York *Post* headlined, CLARABELL FIGHTING FOR LIFE!) Buffalo Bob and the original Howdy Doody are now retired and live in Florida; Photo Doody is safe in a private collection in New York; and Double Doody is institutionalized at the Smithsonian in Washington, D.C.

WALTER HUDSON

*J*et magazine reported Walter Hudson's weight at six or seven hundred pounds in October 1987. The following month, *Jet* reconsidered and listed him at a thousand and said that he was being investigated by the *Guinness Book of World Records*, which was considering his inclusion as the heaviest person in the history of mankind. *People* said he tipped the scales at twelve hundred, and *Forbes* listed his gross weight at a full fourteen hundred—seven tenths of a ton. It was all speculation, as there was no known method for actually measuring Walter Hudson's mass, considering the fact that he was too fat to get out of bed, and the one time he was lifted onto a farm-animal scale, he broke it. So we cannot say for sure that Walter Hudson was the fattest human ever (*Guinness* did determine he was then the fattest man alive), but he was certainly the world's most famous fattest man, having made headlines and television news shows all over the country when he was discovered in the fall of 1987.

His story was revealed after his sister Barbara had to call the rescue squad to help upright him when he fell on the way from his queen-size bed to the bathroom in his little red brick suburban house in Hempstead, Long Island. Some reports erroneously said Hudson had been stuck in a doorway; in fact, he was not stuck, but the door frame had to be removed so that eight rescue workers could roll him over from his stomach, on which he had landed, to some wooden planks, which were used to hoist him back into his bed, belly up.

Walter Hudson, age forty-two, had spent nearly all of his life in bed, since he was thirteen years old and three hundred pounds, when doctors ordered him to rest

up after a bad fall. Hudson decided he preferred staying in bed and eating better than going out. "The things that go on, I just don't like," he said. "I just hate to see it." And so, starting in 1970, he never once left his house. He read the Bible, he watched television, and he ate; and his sister, a practical nurse, brought him food. On an average day, Walter Hudson ingested approximately five pounds of bacon and sausage, a dozen eggs, and a loaf of bread for breakfast; eight to twelve double-decker cheeseburgers with the works, a few pounds of French fries, and six quarts of soda for lunch; and a brace of chickens, four heads of broccoli, a half a dozen potatoes, and a cake for dinner. Plus snacks, which consisted of a thousand pounds of potato chips every year, as well as untold numbers of Twinkies, Yodels, and Ring Dings. "Walter is such a happy person," said his brother George. "He enjoys food so much."

But Hudson was sad, too, because he had really wanted to attend his mother's funeral, but was unable to get up that day, and so after the rescue in 1987 he resolved to trim down to 195 pounds, with his first major goal being a visit to her gravesite (after conquering his fears of leaving the house). Nearly every exercise and diet guru around offered to help: Walter Hudson had become the weight-loss business's supreme challenge. He chose Dick Gregory as his guide, and he was soon eating raw fruits and vegetables and Dick Gregory Health Enterprise candy bars and milk shakes made with sugar cane. The new high-fiber diet helped him lose hundreds of pounds almost overnight, if for no reason other than the fact that it stimulated more frequent bowel movements: Prior to going on the Gregory regime, Hudson took a dump only six times each year. He was also helped by a regular exercise program which, because he couldn't get off his back, consisted of waving his arms in the air for several minutes every day, like an orchestra conductor. Walter Hudson and Dick Gregory eventually had a falling out, but by 1990 the formerly immobile man had trimmed down to 520 pounds and was photographed as he walked out the front door of his house.

One of the things that had bothered Walter Hudson when he was lying in bed at maximum weight, with his hair in twin braids intertwined with orange ribbon, was that even if he had wanted to go out, he couldn't, because there were no clothes that would have fit him. In fact, he had been naked for about ten years. So the first thing he did once he was able to move was to create the Walter Hudson Collection of clothes for women who weigh up to a thousand pounds, in sizes that top out at 9X and 9X plus, meaning measurements of 94–86–96 or more. Included in his catalog were all manner of high-fashion shawls, stirrup pants, pullovers with bat-wing sleeves, and jumbo jumpsuits, also sexy teddies and lace caftans, as well as a special 108-inch tape measure ("Just imagine the joy of actually knowing exactly what your waist is").

In addition to clothes, Walter Hudson also marketed a selection of handy appurtenances such as a water pouch for wearing on one's back (to sip from and prevent dehydration), elongated shoehorns and extra-wide clothes hangers ("How many times have you practically broken out in a sweat trying to put on a pair of shoes with a shoe horn that's much too short, or had a good outfit wrinkled because it fell on the floor due to the fact that your hanger was too small?"), and a selection of long-handled bathing devices ("There won't be a part of your body you can't reach") as well as a book titled *Personal Hygiene for the Ample Person.* "I believe the time for fat acceptance has arrived," Mr. Hudson wrote in his introduction to the catalog, reassuring fat shoppers, "You are me and I am you, and I will never forget that."

He was forty-six years old and back up to 1125 pounds when he died in 1991 after suffering the flu. The New York *Daily News* described Hudson's family as "overwhelmed by the task of removing his body for burial." The emergency rescue squad cut a passageway in the wall of his home to extricate the remains, which were borne away on a fork lift.

HULA HOOPS

Every now and then America goes bonkers over something idiotic, such as goldfish swallowing in the 1920s, pet rocks (see p. 379), or Ronald Reagan's multicolored jelly beans. Few fads were as phenomenally popular or as quick to die as the Hula Hoop of 1958.

The men who created it were Richard Knerr and Spud Melin, who had built a nice business, called Wham-O, in the fifties selling slingshots, paddle balls, and boomerangs. One day at the toy fair in New York in 1957 they were discussing boomerang techniques with a visitor from Australia, who happened to mention that back in his native land, people put bamboo hoops around their waist and set them spinning by twirling their hips. It was a form of exercise that according to Charles Panati, author of *Extraordinary Origins of Everyday Things*, descended from a game that used to be played in Edwardian England: Children and adults twirled wood or metal hoops around their waists . . . and doctors treated them for twisted backs. Panati says that the origins of this peculiar activity actually go back to 1000 B.C., when Middle Eastern children devised similar diversions using hoops made of grapevines.

The men at Wham-O had a unique talent for fabricating fads, and they had already had good luck in their home state of California selling a new gizmo known as "Flying Saucers" (soon to become the Frisbee; see p. 184), so they invented the Hula Hoop. The first test models were wood, which were too expensive and looked less like a toy than a piece of gym equipment. They began working with plastic and created a three-foot hoop out of brightly colored, lightweight, injection-molded polyethylene. The hoop had no purpose other than to encourage people to put it around their waists, slightly above the hips, and start whirling around and around so as to keep it suspended in the air like a lopsided ring of Saturn.

When it was introduced in the summer of 1958, Wham-O had no advertising budget, so they gave hoops to kids in Pasadena parks. The hip-swinging youngsters were picked up by local television news broadcasts, and soon all America, and then the world, went wild for the Hula Hoop—so much so that nearly a hundred million $1.98 hoops were sold in a year. A dozen more companies came out with their own versions, including Hoop Zings, Hooper Doopers, one called Spin-A-Hoop produced by Art Linkletter, and giant-size six-foot hoops for two. "All Labor Day weekend," *Newsweek* reported, "on the beach and at home, children were using them as boomerangs or jump ropes, but most people were doing a hula inside them. . . . It takes a child five minutes to master the thing, but adults take longer; it all depends on the waistline." In December, *Time* noted that Hula Hoops were now being seen along the Champs-

Elysées, in "the stodgiest of London shops," in Tokyo geisha houses, in Jordan, Belgium, South Africa, Finland, and Holland. "Not since the Yo-yo has a U.S. craze spread so far so fast," *Time*'s article exclaimed. "The Hula Hoop has circled the globe." Françoise Sagan in Paris became the first intellectual to Hula Hoop; ex-world-champion boxer Max Schmeling was seen Hula Hooping in Germany; and in Switzerland, the latest phrase for expressing bewildered surprise became "Hula-la!"

Like the twist, which would follow in 1960, the Hula Hoop was a wild, swinging frolic that was youthful but seemed to appeal to nearly every age, and there wasn't a popular magazine that didn't have funny pictures of oldsters, toddlers, nuns, law officers, couples, and bubble-blowing teens rotating one, two, sometimes dozens of hoops around their waists, and also around their arms, legs, and necks.

Doctors reported a rise in reports of neck pains, wrenched backs, and torn abdominal muscles. *Pravda* condemned the Hula hoop as proof of "the emptiness of American culture." A newspaper in Amsterdam seriously worried that so much plastic tubing was going into make Hula Hoops that countries around the world were running short of tubing needed for house construction. One New Jersey school banned the Hula Hoop from playgrounds on the ground that it made kids who used it too wound up. Dr. Gerald T. Miles, head of the child guidance unit at the Karen Horney psychiatric unit in Manhattan, offered a geometric explanation for the craze: "When a child first begins to draw a human body, it starts with a circle. A favorite game—ring around the rosy—is played in a circle. The child feels secure in the family circle."

As with the twist, there was something vaguely naughty about the below-the-waist gyrations Hula Hooping required (it was banned in Indonesia for its powers to "stimulate passion"), and also like the twist, it demanded a willingness to let yourself go and look mighty silly in front of other people. By the end of the fifties, a decade that had begun to worry so much about being bland and conformist, swiveling with a Hula Hoop around your waist seemed a perfectly wonderful way to let the world know you had a touch of mischief in your soul.

The Hula Hoop sank as quickly as it had blasted off. "Hoops Have Had It," said the *Wall Street Journal* in November 1958, and for the next few years Hula Hoops lingered in many people's memories as an embarrassing reminder of this country's unconscionable frivolity. While the Russians were sending Sputniks into space and training their children to be rocket scientists, our rockets were crashing because our kids, instead of studying higher mathematics, were drooling over Elvis or jiggling with Hula Hoops on their hips.

By the late sixties, when nostalgia for the carefree days of the fifties started growing, scenes of happy-go-lucky Americans Hula Hooping were resuscitated as reminders of how lighthearted life used to be before drugs, the Beatles, and the war in Vietnam. In fact, in 1968 Wham-O reformulated the Hula Hoop with ball bearings that rolled around inside its plastic tube as it twirled. At the time, their Frisbee was going great guns, and their high-resiliency Super Ball had been a big success in 1965, so they figured it might be an opportune moment to fabricate a Hula Hoop revival. But they were wrong. Whereas Frisbees delighted people with their aerodynamic magic, the new "Shoop Shoop Hula Hoop" was a dud, without the Frisbee's hypnotic powers of flight. Like automobile tail fins, the Hula Hoop was destined to be remembered as an artifact unique to the speed-crazed pop culture of the 1950s.

"I LOVE LUCY"

"I Love Lucy" established the rules of television comedy. It was the first show to use a three-camera setup (created by the great Hollywood cinematographer Karl Freund) to film episodes before a live audience and thus include real laughter, and it perfected an archetypal pattern of husband-wife antagonism and domestic double-dealing that infused vast numbers of sitcoms that followed. The premiere episode, broadcast on October 15, 1951, was titled "The Girls Want to Go to a Nightclub," and told how Lucy Ricardo (Lucille Ball) and her neighbor Ethel Mertz (Vivian Vance) connive to get their husbands, Ricky (Desi Arnaz) and Fred (William Frawley), to take them to the Copacabana for the Mertzes' eighteenth wedding anniversary (the men want to go to the fights). This plot line was typical of what *TV Guide* described as a program "revolving around problems arising in a household where the wife is stage-struck and the orchestra leader husband thinks she should stay home." For six seasons, Lucy, abetted by Ethel, schemed so that Ricky would (a) appreciate her more, (b) introduce her to a celebrity he knew, (c) give her more money, or (d) put her into his stage show.

Lucy was an immensely frustrated individual, and nearly all the show's humor comes at her expense as she bungles attempts to somehow get Ricky to allow her the freedom and opportunity she wants. Her perpetual yearning for more out of life has been seen by some social-minded critics as symbolic of the repression of housewives by a chauvinistic culture that discouraged female independence; the show has even been called "the first feminist sitcom." In fact, in the early 1960s it was banned in Saudi Arabia because censors there decided that it showed a wife with too much power over a husband. Lucy indeed exercised extraordinary power in the Ricardo household, but Ricky was always the boss, and she was frequently reduced to her famous gape-mouthed "Whaaaaa!" when her schemes went awry and she needed Ricky to forgive her.

Lucille Ball had already perfected her character as a scatterbrained housewife in a late-1940s radio comedy called "My Favorite Husband," in which she played Liz Cooper—a madcap, giddy banker's wife who was known for loud crying fits when she didn't get her way; and she and her real-life husband, Desi Arnaz, had developed a traveling slapstick vaudeville act called "Desi Arnaz and Band with Lucille Ball," built around the premise of a movie star (Lucy, who indeed had a minor career going in the movies) who tries desperately to join her husband's band. CBS wanted to bring Lucille Ball to television but was worried that Desi's thick Cuban accent would hurt a show's appeal to middle America, so they suggested hiring Richard Denning, her radio husband, as a TV mate. But Lucy and Desi, who believed they needed to work together to save their troubled marriage, insisted on doing the show as a couple and chose the title "I Love Lucy" because it put Desi first. Lucy's stage-show character was changed from a movie star to a starstruck housewife so ordinary viewers could identify with her ("Everybody *wants* to be in show business," she said), and much of Lucille Balls's own biography was incorporated into the character, including her childhood in Jamestown, New York. To play the Ricardos' neighbors and friends, Fred and Ethel Mertz, William Frawley and Vivian Vance were hired, the former on the condition he never miss a day of work because of his notorious drinking habits, the latter with a clause in her contract insisting she remain twenty pounds heavier than Lucille Ball so as to always be the frumpier one.

By its second season, "I Love Lucy" was number one in the ratings, where it stayed until 1955–56, when "The $64,000 Question" beat it out. It returned to the top spot for the 1956–57 season, after which production of the half-hour show ceased.

Bart Andrews, author of the definitive *The Story of "I Love Lucy,"* enumerated these signs of early Lucymania:

- The telephone company reported a "substantial reduction" in calls between 9:00 and 9:30 P.M. on Monday night, when "I Love Lucy" was on the air.
- Marshall Field department store in Chicago switched evening shopping hours from Monday to Thursday so customers and employees could watch the show.
- Members of the Lynn, Massachusetts PTA picketed the local CBS station demanding the show be broadcast at an earlier hour so children could see it and get to bed.
- The water commissioner of Toledo, Ohio, reported that pressure plummeted during "I Love Lucy" commercial breaks.
- "Lucy Goes to the Hospital," the episode in which she delivered a baby (Little Ricky),

aired January 19, 1953, and attracted a record forty million viewers; the next day, history's first televised presidential inauguration drew only half as many. Lucille Ball, who delivered her own actual child, Desi, Jr., the same day Lucy Ricardo did on the show, was the first pregnant person ever on TV, although that word was still taboo, and so she had been described with euphemistic politeness as "expectant" or, in the famous episode title, "Lucy Is Enceinte." Desi, Jr., was the cover boy of the first issue of *TV Guide*, dated April 3–9, 1953.

- When the "I Love Lucy" bedroom suite was introduced in 1953, a million sold in ninety days.
- At the height of the House Un-American Activity Committee witch-hunting in 1953, when Walter Winchell broke the news that Miss Ball had once declared her intention to vote Communist, she was so popular that the revelation had no effect on her career, and she was swiftly and efficiently exonerated by the patriots in the U.S. Congress. "The only red thing about Lucy," Desi said, "is her hair. And even that's not real."

Although they were hardly typical, the fictional Ricardo family found themselves, like so many Americans in the 1950s, moving up the ladder of success as material prosperity washed over the land. They moved from their lower-middle-class urban apartment at 623 East 68th Street (which, on a real map, would have put it in the East River) to a ranch home in Westport, Connecticut; they spent time in California as Ricky tried to break into the movies (in the role of Don Juan); they toured Europe, visited Florida and Cuba. And Ricky went from a $100-per-week employee at the Tropicana Club to proprietor of his own Ricky Ricardo Babaloo Club.

After "I Love Lucy" went off the air (because Lucille Ball and Desi Arnaz were exhausted), thirteen hour-long shows with the original characters and cast were made between 1957 and 1960, and after Lucy and Desi got divorced in 1960, she went on to star as Lucy Carmichael in "The Lucy Show" (1962–68), Lucy Carter in "Here's Lucy" (1968–74), and Lucy Barker in "Life with Lucy" (six weeks in 1986). All these subsequent roles reprised the scatter-brained vivacity that had made Lucy Ricardo so funny, but with diminishing success. All but one of the 180 original "I Love Lucy" shows were rebroadcast by CBS in the late 1950s, again in 1961, and on daytime on CBS through 1967. (The one missing show, from December 2, 1956, was kept out of the package because it had a Christmas theme—Lucy trims a tree—and featured flashbacks from other episodes.) In syndication, "I Love Lucy" was as much a television pioneer as it had been in its original run, establishing the fabulously lucrative market for syndicating old shows long after their first life. No other television program in history has been shown as many times and for such an extended term. Even today, thirty-five years after it ceased production, at every minute of the day "I Love Lucy" is being broadcast somewhere in the world.

INFOMERCIALS

Some of the most heart-rending moments on television are when Richard Simmons, wearing exercise shorts and a strap T-shirt, pays a surprise visit to someone who has lost lots of weight and he and the newly thin person begin to cry long and intimately as they share the joys and sorrows of yo-yo dieting. The happiest thing on television is when Mike Levey, host of "Amazing Discoveries," watches stupid high-school dropouts develop self-esteem and self-confidence by using a system called Memory Power to transform themselves into human calculators as Mr. Levey's studio audience claps and cheers.

Richard Simmons, who is selling the Deal-A-Meal diet plan and *Sweatin' to the Oldies* exercise videos, and Mike Levey, who is selling instructional audio tapes, are two of the brightest stars of infomercials—a form of television that gets its name because it looks like information but is actually a commercial. Their target market,

according to Greg Renker, who produces infomercials from a studio in Palm Desert, California, is "the *National Enquirer* audience." Hopeful culture boosters who believe that TV has the potential to be educational, uplifting, or enlightening tend to loathe infomercials because they are inane, confusing, and sometimes fraudulent. But such critics' wishful thoughts aside, the fact is that they are an example of television doing what television does best: numbing viewers into a trance that is equal parts passivity and greed.

When they work, infomercials give you the craving to buy something but take away your will to get it any other way other than by dialing the 800 number that flashes on the screen. Within minutes, and without ever having to go out shopping, you have put yourself on the receiving end of such marvels as a Snack Master (the one that turns two pieces of white bread and a glob of jelly into an individually sized lump of Mom's fruit pie); a jet-powered oven (cooks a twenty-pound turkey in one hour); skin cream that makes wrinkles disappear (for up to eight hours); the Brain Supercharger, which promises purchasers "a brain transplant from a self-made millionaire" and suggests that people who use it will feel like Mozart did when he wrote a symphony—*at the age of nine!*; or a tooth-whitening chemical that will make your mouth the envy of every dentist. Among the "Amazing Discoveries" success stories are:

- Europainter: "the cleanest painting system ever invented."
- Purr-fect Punch: "Anyone can design their own unique, embroidered garments."
- Vertical Roaster: "Cook chicken, turkey, and game hens in half the time."
- Picture This: "custom portrait designs to beautify every garment."
- Power Steamer: "makes old-fashioned ironing obsolete."

Never mind that every on-the-level consumer report reveals that the same (or much better) products are available in stores at lower prices. Where is the joy of going shopping in a store, where merchandise just sits, gathering dust, and surly clerks ignore customers? Infomercials are successful because they have restored the lost thrills of salesmanship to shopping. Sit back and relax and watch Richard Simmons blubber his little heart out; see Mike Levey gasp in awe at the incredible car wax that protects a bright red Rolls-Royce even when it is *set on fire* (and a hamburger is fried on it); listen to Meredith Baxter and Ali MacGraw be earnest and frank about their makeup techniques (and the brand of makeup you, too, can own). These people are turning somersaults for you: They bake cream-puff pastries while you watch; they make pretty stained glass windows (like medieval artisans used to, but in one one-hundredth the amount of time); they demonstrate how their IQs got raised thirty points by listening to a set of audio tapes; they turn a junk-shop chest of drawers into a valuable antique by applying instant furniture restorer; they exercise with the fabulous bag-o'-water (the same one Olympic athletes prefer) until they are ready to drop. In real life (outside television), you never meet people who work so darn hard for your money; and that is why it is almost impossible not to be at least a little bit impressed by their pitch (and also why Mike Levey receives up to a thousand fan letters every week).

Infomercials are a relatively new phenomenon that started in 1984 after the Federal Trade Commission lifted all restrictions on how much commercial time local TV stations could sell. Most of them run late at night, when entire hours can be bought cheap (and when bleary-eyed, lonely viewers are most susceptible to suggestions)—a slot known in the television trade as "remnant air time"—and although they cost little to produce, they can make fortunes. *Time* magazine reported that the thirty-minute Kitchenmate Mixer infomercial, which shows a lady turning skimmed milk into luxurious whipped cream, bread into bread crumbs, and oil into mayonnaise, was produced for $125,000 and generated $55 million in sales. Over twenty thousand different infomercials are broadcast on stations around the country; four out of five stations run them; and their total take is estimated at about a billion dollars a year. In 1991 the Home Shopping Network started a twenty-four-hour-a-day infomercial-only channel.

"A sixty-second spot goes by so fast," said Nancy Langston of infomercial producer Media Arts International. "In a half-hour, we allow time to demonstrate and repeat and demonstrate and repeat. It's really an incredible way to sell a product." Some products, however, have defied successful infomercialization. According to Bernice Kanner, writing in *New York* magazine, these include back-pain cures, improve-your-garden products, and a videotape starring Walter Cronkite, Nancy Reagan, and Morgan Fairchild titled *How to Raise Drug-Free Kids*. Greg Renker explained, "Our audience wants instant, effortless success, fame, or beauty.... God forbid you offer a product that requires a little effort or more than thirty days to see results."

One way to look at the big-time success of infomercials (even General Motors has produced one) is that they are a sign that television is returning to its true nature. Crass, tacky, loud, unabashed program-length commercials for marvelous products were a staple of the airwaves in the early years, and even many of the best-remembered shows incorporated blatant advertising in the days when sponsors bought whole programs. ("The Milton Berle Show" began as "The Texaco Star Theater"; Howdy Doody and Buffalo Bob frequently sang about Happy Tooth and Mr. Tooth Decay on behalf of their sponsor, Colgate.) As television time grew more expensive and was sold by the minute rather than by the show, long commercials disappeared, and

most respectable programs put a seemly distance between themselves and their advertisers.

In the sixties, Ronco marketed the Veg-O-Matic with the kind of hard sell reminiscent of television's early days, but Ronco commercials were short, and they didn't pretend to be anything other than a sales pitch. The gauntlet of shameless advertising vulgarity was carried into the seventies and eighties by Dial Media ads for kitchen knives (see "But Wait, There's More," p. 74) and special record offers (see "Slim Whitman," p. 560). But it is safe to say that the golden age of trash TV advertising is now.

After deregulation, the pioneers of long-form salesmanship were not hucksters selling mere household products or record albums; they were successful people selling the secrets of their health, wealth, and happiness. Self-improvement schemes abounded, including calisthenics videos; Y-Bron (the cure for impotence); the stick-on EuroTrym Diet Patch (hosted by Ronald Reagan's son Michael); and one set of tapes called *Where There's a Will, There's an A*, which held out the promise of photographic memory to students, salespeople, and anyone who wants to get ahead in the world.

Riding high aboard the real estate boom of the eighties came hordes of television pitchmen with surefire plans for getting rich, which they sold via half-hour infomercials that took the form of talk-show testimonials with such intoxicating titles as "The Millionaire Maker," Credit Card Millionaire," "Get Rich With Real Estate," and "Fortune Formulas." One of the best-known and longest-lived of these programs is Dave Del Dotto's, which sells the "Cash Flow System," contained in a book he wrote titled *How to Make Nothing But Money*. Dave's show is hosted by John Davidson, who stands in the midst of an audience and interviews people lined up in chairs on a stage about how they have been rolling in clover ever since they sent away for Dave's tapes and book. (Typical Del Dotto suggestions: Underwrite a trip to Spain by bringing home cheap leather purses and selling them to your friends for fifty dollars apiece; rent VCRs to tourists stuck in local motel rooms on rainy days; hang out at Little League games and Girl Scout meetings to meet children of wealthy people, then ingratiate yourself with their parents.) The people in the infomercial who have profited from Dave's techniques—which mostly have to do with buying or building low-budget housing, then collecting government subsidies—are ordinary schleps (or worse), suggesting that any moron can do it; and the show is taped outdoors, in a tropical location, with sunshine and pleasant breezes, suggesting to us moles at home sitting in a darkened room with a glowing TV set just how great life could be if we only get our hands on the secrets that Dave is selling. A similar infomercial, called "Second Paycheck, Hawaiian Style," features wheelbarrows full of money lined up on the stage.

Among true connoisseurs of infomercials, the cream of the crop are considered to be those produced by Tom Vu. Vu's are unique in that they aren't directly selling anything. Designed to entice viewers to come to a local motel where Tom Vu will be conducting a seminar in getting rich, they are broadcast in saturation campaigns that promise viewers that the secret to great wealth can be found in just three little words, which Mr. Vu will reveal at the seminar. The commercials consist of videotapes in which you can see (but not hear) other people receiving The Words, and many scenes of Mr. Vu enjoying his fortune: driving a Rolls-Royce, riding in a yacht surrounded by beautiful gold-diggers in bathing suits, being waited on and toadied to by servants. Although Vu doesn't even hint at what the three words might be in his infomercials, he does tell viewers what to say when their friends or family argue that they are insane to spend good money to attend a Tom Vu seminar. He advises that you push all cynics aside and yell at them, "Get out of my way, you loser!"

MICHAEL JACKSON

M ichael Jackson is more charismatic than anyone else who ever lived, except maybe Jesus; and there are some Jehovah's Witnesses who are certain he *is* Jesus, in the returned-to-earth form of Michael the archangel (who, Witnesses believe, manifested himself 1992 years ago as the Messiah who got written about in the Bible as Jesus). Michael was reborn on September 1, 1958, two days after Jehovah's Witnesses held their biggest gathering in history, filling Yankee Stadium and the Polo Grounds in New York with 253,000 believers—one of whom was Michael Jackson's

mother, nine months pregnant with the Prince of Peace who has since gone on to rule the world.

"Star of records, radio, rock video. A one-man rescue team for the music business. A songwriter who sets the beat for a decade. A dancer with the fanciest feet on the street. A singer who cuts across all boundaries of taste and style, and color too." That's how *Time* described Michael in a 1984 cover story that enumerated the many ways he was a savior—of some sort—not only for the music business but for all of popular culture. Later that same year promoter Don King summarized his status: "Michael Jackson has transcended all earthly bounds."

Fanatic displays of Michaelmania have ebbed since the mid-1980s, when he won an unprecedented eight Grammy awards in a single year (1984), his *Thriller* became the best-selling album of all time, and his "Victory" concert tour with the other Jackson brothers (a show with 750,000 pounds of equipment carried in twenty-four tractor-trailers and requiring three times more elec-

trical power than had ever been used for a rock-and-roll performance) grossed over a hundred million dollars. Jackson and his promoters were roundly criticized for the "Victory" tour's high ticket prices (thirty dollars) and short sets (ninety minutes)—especially compared with Bruce Springsteen, who was on tour at the same time but charged half that amount and performed for more than twice as long. Also, by the time "Victory" was over, critics began to complain that Michael was "overexposed." In 1987 *Newsweek* observed that "up-to-the-minute American kids may have become bored with Jackson" (but did note that he was more popular than ever among the "hip youth" of Addis Ababa and that in Ethiopia his "androgynous image is everywhere").

Even when he keeps to himself, and even if he isn't at the cutting edge of popular music anymore, Michael Jackson continues to be the most famous man in the world (according to *People*), and every move he makes is gobbled up by the press and public, who delight in how unusual his life is. When, for example, he sought to buy the bones of John Merrick, the nineteenth-century English freak known as the Elephant Man, it set off waves of wonder: *WHY?* (He did not succeed in getting the remains out of England . . . but he did purchase the song copyrights to the entire Beatles catalog.) When he began to pal around with young Macaulay Culkin (of *Home Alone*), who was then featured in Michael's "Black or White" video, tabloid tongues wagged. And who can forget the time his hair caught on fire while filming a commercial for Pepsi-Cola —and Pepsi sales went through the roof? When Elizabeth Taylor got married for the eighth time in 1991, Michael was in the news again because the wedding took place at his home, and he gave her away in a ceremony to end all ceremonies. "I want Elizabeth to think she's in paradise," said

Michael, who at one point planned to decorate the grounds of his estate for the occasion with statues depicting great moments in Miss Taylor's life. For ring bearer at the ceremony, Michael selected his beloved chimpanzee, Bubbles II, successor to the original Bubbles, who was fired by Michael after an altercation. (When it turned out that Bubbles II could not perform, the job was done by hairdresser-to-the-stars Jose Eber.)

The highest-paid entertainer on earth was born poor and normal, one of nine children, in Gary, Indiana. He was five years old when he and his brothers, calling themselves the Jackson 5, performed in public for the first time, in a local nightclub in 1963. Some time later, Gladys Knight (or, according to other stories, Diana Ross or Bobby Taylor of the Vancouvers) happened to hear them sing. Whoever their discoverer was, he or she was so enthusiastic that he or she told Motown president Berry Gordy about them. By the late 1960s, they had become the opening act for Diana Ross and the Supremes. In October 1969 they debuted nationally on television's "Hollywood Palace," and three months later a song called "I Want You Back," from their first album, *Diana Ross Presents the Jackson Five*, hit number one on the *Billboard* pop chart. Within the next couple of years the Jackson 5 became the fastest-selling act in Motown history and the only group ever to have its first three singles all hit number one (after "I Want You Back" came "ABC" and "The Love You Save").

Despite the overwhelming, overnight success, Michael didn't seem at all weird in the beginning, except for his prodigious talent. In a 1971 story about "Rock Stars at Home with Their Parents," *Life* magazine quoted Michael's father, Joseph, as saying about the Jackson boys, "They go to school, do their chores, play ball. They have to

maintain their personal lives, because if an entertainer doesn't, that's when he can get the big head." It was obvious that none of the Jackson 5—Michael, Tito, Jackie, Marlon, and Randy—had the big head. They were pictured at home, sitting on motorcycles, dirt bikes, and all-terrain vehicles, smiling like happy, prosperous, all-American teenagers.

Michael's first solo chart-topper was the theme song from *Ben*, a 1972 movie about a sad, sick boy and a misunderstood rat. "I loved the song and I loved the story," Michael wrote, comparing *Ben* with *E.T.*, which came later: "People didn't understand the boy's love for this little creature. He was dying of some disease and his only true friend was Ben, the leader of the rats in the city where they lived. A lot of people thought the movie was a bit odd, but I was not one of them. . . . I have always loved animals." Don Black, lyricist for "Ben," said he knew as he wrote the words for the song that Michael was the one to do it, because only he was sensitive enough. Said Black, "He enjoys anything that crawls or flies."

From being a Motown sensation, Michael Jackson turned himself into a life force when he went to Epic Records and made two solo albums, *Off the Wall* (1979) and *Thriller* (1982). Coming at a time when pop music had declined into a monotonous throb of synthesized leftover disco chic ("Boogie Oogie Oogie," "Le Freak," "Funkytown"), Michael's newfound power electrified record buyers. Along with Bruce Springsteen (the working-class hero), Michael Jackson (the sequined pixie) rejuvenated pop, making 1984 the record industry's best year in a decade. At the same time he helped transform music videos from quirky art films into slick sales vehicles and desirable products unto themselves. In fact, the video *The Making of "Thriller,"* which showed the working-out of some of the elaborate choreography (by Michael Peters) and meticulous direction (by John Landis), became a million-seller and established a pattern for innumerable "Making of" programs with behind-the-scenes chatter and candid shots giving hungry fans even more of their idol. The videos from *Thriller*, including "Beat It" and "Billie Jean," were themselves landmarks because they broke the color line on MTV (see p. 344), and their inescapable success signaled the return of black artists to the Top 40. "Black music had to play second fiddle for a long time," said Jackson's producer, Quincy Jones, in 1984. "Michael has connected with every soul in the world."

It isn't accurate to say Michael Jackson represents the mainstreaming of black music; in fact, his audience has always been conspicuously white, and his music, while drawing on his Motown background and soul stylists such as Little Richard and Chuck Berry, is by no stretch of the term rhythm and blues. His songs defy all the categories into which pop music is usually pigeonholed: punk, new wave, disco, hard rock, soul. He has taken something from each but has been bounded by none, and has added his own taste for cornball show tunes to the strange mix. Among his personal music inspirations, Michael Jackson lists soul singers Jackie Wilson and Stevie Wonder but also Prokofiev's *Peter and the Wolf*, "My Favorite Things" from *The Sound of Music*, and Gordon MacRae belting out "Oh, What a Beautiful Mornin'" in *Oklahoma!*

It wasn't only Michael Jackson's music that gave the world a lift when everybody discovered him. It was the unbelievable way he moved when he performed—an utterly original blast of maneuvers that combined the frenzy of James Brown, the grace of Fred Astaire, and the determination of an attacking mountain lion. "The sexual dyna-

mism irradiating from the arch of his dancing body challenges Government standards for a nuclear meltdown," observed the generally clearheaded *Time* magazine. *TV Guide* proclaimed his nine-minute performance at the 1988 Grammy Awards possibly "the most passionate appearance ever televised."

His signature "moonwalk," in which he seemed to defy the laws of physics by striding forward but moving back, became the single best-known bit of celebrity body language since the four Beatles shook their shaggy mop tops. "It was born as a breakdance step," Jackson explained. "Black kids had created [it] dancing on street corners in the ghetto. Black people are truly innovative dancers. They create many of the new dances." Three street kids taught it to him; then he polished it up and unleashed it while singing "Billie Jean" on May 16, 1983, on the television special "Motown 25: Yesterday, Today, and Forever." That performance helped send *Thriller* into the stratosphere, and the moonwalk was subsequently imitated by millions of kids in his thrall. When Fred Astaire watched him do it on TV, he called Michael and said, "You're a hell of a mover."

Every detail of Michael Jackson's act was doted on by a fascinated public. A single, sequined glove, for instance, which he wore during his "Off the Wall" tour, became *the* Michael Jackson totem, worn by all impersonators, and by thousands of fans at his live performances. His brocaded coat, dark glasses, white socks, and spit curl all became emblems that signified him, in a way that only the most iconic superstars can be broken up into pieces. Elvis was a sneer, swivel hips, and gold lamé suit; the Beatles were long hair and lapel-less jackets. Jill Klein, the stylist who helped pick out the auspicious wardrobe for Michael's "Billie Jean" video, said no one had more natural style than he, something she realized as soon as she saw that his house was full of mannequins. In fact, she paid Michael her highest compliment: "He's like a mannequin."

But even more than his looks, his music, his dancing, and more than his much-publicized estrangement from sisters Janet and LaToya (themselves superstars), the most mesmerizing thing about Michael Jackson has always been Michael Jackson the human being (if he is a human being): the boy in the bubble, fragile as a leaf, painfully lonely, eternally young, the sensitive sprite whose dream is to someday play Peter Pan. "I feel strange around everyday people," he once said, and he looks strange, too. First introduced to the public back in 1969 as a sweet-looking, cherub-faced, African-American boy, he has since changed, dramatically and magically—an accomplishment he personally credits to growing up and a strict vegetarian diet. His nose is narrower, his chin has developed a cleft, his eyes look almond-shaped, his cheeks appear to have been hollowed, and his skin has assumed a strange pallor, resulting in an alien physiognomy that looks neither white nor black, male nor female, child nor adult, but is uncomfortably similar to the face of his mentor Diana Ross. "I didn't invent plastic surgery," he protested in his autobiography, *Moonwalk*. "A lot of very fine, very nice peo-ple have had plastic surgery." Just to set the record straight, he declared: "I have never had my cheeks altered or my eyes altered. I have not had my lips thinned, nor have I had dermabrasion or a skin peel. . . . I have had my nose altered twice and I recently added a cleft to my chin, but that is it. Period. I don't care what anyone else says—it's my face and I know." Furthermore, his mother has insisted that despite rumors to the contrary, Michael is not gay. Jehovah's Witnesses don't allow that sort of thing.

Among the curious facets of his private life dug up (or manufactured) by a relentlessly inquiring press are: He keeps an Elizabeth Taylor shrine in a room at home to which only he and Miss Taylor are allowed entrance; he bathes in Evian water; he sleeps in a hyperbaric oxygen chamber to forestall aging; he keeps a private zoo of exotic animals, including llamas, peacocks, three parrots, two swans, and a boa constrictor; his home, named Neverland Valley, is a personalized theme park (including video arcades, carnival rides, snack bars, and soda shops) where Michael, who is painfully shy everywhere except on stage, can play with his friends, many of whom are children. "It's a nice place Michael comes from," said director Steven Spielberg, who likened him to a faun in a burning forest. "I wish we could all spend some time in his world."

JEEP

"The Jeep of my dreams . . . a grand passion . . . a monument to American ingenuity," Art Carey rhapsodized in an "Elements of Style" column in *GQ* magazine in 1989 devoted to the open-air, hard-sprung, noisy, and uncomfortable cross between a car and a truck originally designed over a half-century ago but still "a perfect

These Soldiers Go Up in the Air to Prove They Can Take It, Camp Hood, Texas

gadget" (according to the Museum of Modern Art) and "the ultimate boy toy" (according to *GQ*). Carey called the Jeep "a rugged, Spartan, macho vehicle that stands for freedom and independence and a can-do, take-no-prisoners, four-wheel-drive approach to life." Like pickup trucks (see p. 385) and cowboy boots, the Jeep is a form of transportation originally known for its ability to fulfill strictly practical needs; and also just like them, it has assumed bristling prestige as a psychosexual fetish.

The rough-and-tumble image of a Jeep is based on many things, including its lack of creature comforts and its venerable history as a military vehicle, but the underlying reason for its appeal is that it doesn't get stuck. It is a set of wheels that will take you where ordinary cars cannot go. In a blizzard or a sandstorm, in the backwoods or a muddy swamp, people in sedans are helpless. The man or woman in a Jeep equipped with all-terrain tires and a stump-pulling low-range transmission is about as close to being master of the earth as a driver can be, unless you include caterpillar half-tracks and M-1 tanks. But that's just the point: A Jeep is a passenger car with the muscle power of a weapon and the added bonus of wind-in-your face, convertible fun.

Long before their acclaimed service in World War II, Jeeps had a short life as playthings among Hollywood stars. They weren't yet called Jeeps (which was a wartime construction from "GP," for General Purpose Vehicle); they were known by their brand name, American Austin. Austins were first developed in 1929 when Sir Herbert Austin of England decided to build a sporty little vehicle for the American market. His go-anywhere dune bug became a popular photo prop for outdoorsy actors, but few ordinary Americans in the 1930s could afford a play-toy car: American Austin went bankrupt in 1934 and was reorganized as the Bantam Automobile Company. The Bantam roadster was hardly more successful than the Austin had been, but it was used for its sporty connotations by Coca-Cola and Firestone in advertisements, and it led the opening-day parade at the New York World's Fair in 1939. The following year, with war imminent, when the U.S. Army asked all auto manufacturers for bids on an all-purpose four-wheel-drive vehicle, Bantam had the inside track. The original Jeep was designed by a committee of military and civilian engineers, and although it was based on the Bantam, most of the wartime Jeeps were built by Willys and Ford—bigger car companies able to met the Army's seventy-five-Jeeps-per-day quota. Most of Bantam's minuscule wartime production of three thousand Jeeps was sent to Russia.

"By the end of the war, half of America wanted to buy a Jeep," Arthur Pulos wrote in *The American Design Adventure*. This was not just because Jeeps were the only vehicles readily available (ordinary car production had stopped in 1942) but also because of their well-earned reputation for ruggedness and reliability: "America's greatest contribution to modern warfare," according to General George C. Marshall; "the most revolutionary thing to come along in military transportation since the horse," according to *Popular Mechanics*. Not since the Model T had any vehicle so captivated the imagination of the American public. It was the mechanical mule that wouldn't quit, and when the war was over, many soldiers in Europe and the South Pacific wangled ways to strip down their old four-wheeled hinny and ship it home.

Car companies that had supplied Jeeps to the armed forces went back to passenger car production, and Bantam went out of business, but Willys decided to abandon the traditional passenger car market (temporarily, until 1952) and make nothing but Jeepsters—two-wheel-drive convertibles that looked like a cross between a military Jeep and a European sports car (complete with whitewall tires and luxury upholstery) as well as station wagons with all-steel (rather than the traditional wood) bodies.

Willys Jeepsters never found a market niche, but in 1964 the Kaiser-Jeep corporation introduced a two-and-a-half-ton station wagon known as the Wagoneer, which was almost as revolutionary as the original Jeep. The Wagoneer was the first of America's "sport utility" vehicles, combining four-wheel drive with passenger comfort and a high sticker price; it pioneered the way for a whole world of Ford Broncos, Chevy Blazers, and Dodge Ramchargers, as well as more recent Japanese four-wheeling imports such as the Isuzu Trooper and Mitsubishi Montero. While all these vehicles have metamorphosed and modernized over the years, the Wagoneer, amazingly, remained essentially the same car for over a quarter-century until its demise in 1991—the last of the automotive dinosaurs.

The unchanging Wagoneer became a favorite means of transportation among the horsey set, not only because it was suitable for towing a trailer but also because it was so dowdy and tenaciously unstylish. Powered by a big, inefficient V-8, equipped with a panoply of appurtenances for passenger comfort but utterly invulnerable to decades' worth of safety, ergonomic, and engineering advances, the Wagoneer was for many years the only choice for new-car buyers who were not enamored of aerodynamic, Euro-look styling and jet-age technology. Its hallmark was its exterior decoration: one of the last examples of sculpted, wood-look plastic sides, reminiscent of estate wagons from the 1940s. In fact, antistyle has always been the Jeep's style. In the 1940s, when America fell in love with it as the faithful ugly duckling (like the Model T before it and the VW Beetle in later years), it stood in marked contrast to the efforts at longer-lower-wider streamlining that had swept through Detroit in the late 1930s, then returned with a vengeance after the war. A Jeep has always seemed obstinately oldfangled; and no matter how chic it has become, there is still something clunky and musclebound about it, suggesting machinery rather than fashion.

As for the classic Jeep, it has hardly changed in fifty years. The CJ-5, introduced in 1954 as an only slightly softened version of the military Jeep, was made until 1983, when it was discontinued in favor of the similar-looking but somewhat modernized (with roll-down windows!) CJ-7, which is still manufactured today as the Wrangler. Like pickup trucks, Wranglers are frequently tricked out in chrome, racing stripes, styled wheels with decorator all-terrain tires, and Day-Glo accessories, but none of that foppery ever seems to diminish the formidable cachet of the army styling, removable doors, and collapsible windshield. An open Jeep announces an adventurer at the wheel. As Art Carey put it in his *GQ* paean, "When I drive one of my Jeeps, I always wear my grandfather's old leather bomber jacket and suddenly I'm no longer in a suburban world of Volvos and Saabs."

JET SET

Rich people used to go places at a processional pace: in well-appointed railroad coaches or the staterooms of ocean liners. The pleasures of the upper crust tended to be thought of as slow and ceremonious, whereas only people with too little time of their own felt compelled to rush. But in 1960 a new notion of swank life was born. The jet set didn't dawdle in trains or on big, clumsy boats like their profligate forebears. When they wanted to have fun, they had fun without delay, they seized their pleasure NOW! They zoomed where they wanted to go at more than five hundred miles an hour—"faster than a bullet," according to one thunderstruck spokesman for American Airlines' jet passenger service. Then, as soon as they gulped their fun, they zoomed somewhere else. Speed became a status symbol and the pop-culture banner of wealth and power.

Not just travel but everything the jet set did was speeded up. They danced furiously in hyperkinetic discothèques; they skied down the highest mountains of the world and careened from casino to casino in fast, open cars while the wind tousled their hair; and they even made the leisurely activity of getting a tan seem frantic, as they greedily soaked up the most sun in the least time to cultivate the darkest skin. They sometimes seemed so busy having fun that *everything* about them was brisk and abbreviated, even their names, which—although they might be duchesses or counts—tended to be silly quickie nickies such as Kiki, Nikki, Sukie, Shugsie, and Soupsy.

It was the dawn of the go-go age, and they supplied an image of frenzied pleasure-seeking whose time had surely come. The jet set were like the flappers of the 1920s, but richer and more famous . . . and faster. The world had become their playground, which made them the "innest" in-crowd ever, and although no one ever figured out how many of them there were (if, indeed, there were any), and none of them would ever dare call him- or herself a jet-setter (how gauche!), the *image* of these live-to-the-max, globetrotting hedonists mesmerized the early 1960s and has never quite gone away. Even as the idea of going somewhere in a jet plane has sunk from future-chic (as it was in 1960) to feeling more like being herded in a winged cattle car, the notion of a jet set, and the mastery of time and space it implies, is still a viable (if less charismatic) cultural ideal.

The ascent of the jet set to a pop paragon signaled many of the lifestyle changes that defined the dreams and fantasies of restless Americans, including the sexual revolution, the gourmet revolution, the rise of the miniskirt, and the formulation of discothèque society. Jet-setters were modern pathfinders who were up on all the latest ways and places to have a really good time; and ever greater numbers of Americans believed they could follow in their footsteps, at least a little bit: by reading *Playboy* (which wrote breathlessly about their comings and goings); by buying a ticket for a two-week package tour of fourteen swinging European cities or spending a vacation at Club Med; by serving Swiss fondue or rock-lobster-tail kabobs with flaming coffee for dessert. Few admirers of the good life actually sought to join the exclusive ranks of the jet set, but nonetheless the perks and prerogatives of the modern world that were the basis of the jet set's fantastic life were increasingly available to most upwardly mobile citizens. The jet-setters were seen as supreme hedonists by an era that felt it was discovering pleasures for the very first time.

As a concept, the jet set popped into being in 1960, a year after the first scheduled passenger flight of a jet-powered Boeing 707—American Flight #2, Los Angeles to New York in four hours and three minutes. It was named by Igor Cassini, who used the pen name Cholly Knickerbocker to write a column for the New York *Journal-American* called "The Smart Set." The Knickerbocker name had long been a gossip institution in New York, and Cassini's predecessor, Maury Paul, had coined the term "café society" back in the 1930s to describe the bluebloods and bons vivants who spent their evenings in top hats or evening gowns gallivanting from one festive nightclub to another, sipping champagne and exchanging worldly witticisms.

The term "café society" had become démodé by the 1960s because cafés were so earthbound, and too associated with remnants of earlier decades' nightlife, such as café society doyenne Elsa Maxwell, who, despite her attempt to join the twisters at the Peppermint Lounge in 1961, was simply too dowdy and too . . . yes, too *old* to be a leader in the youth-worshipping 1960s. Besides, all the avant-garde society people had long ago given up on such places as the Cub Room at the Stork, El Morocco, and the Harwyn Club; those old haunts were for stick-in-the-muds, or worse: suburbanites, visiting firemen, prom kids on dates. The real haut monde no longer merely told their driver to take them downtown to find their merriment. They got on a jet plane! And in 1960, strange as it may seem to anyone who has flown anywhere on an old scow jet in the last ten years, jet planes were the razor edge of chic. In his wide-eyed panegyric *Boeing 707* (1960), Martin Caidin took a ride in the new jet and exulted, "Up, up, soaring into the deepening blue, scorning the cloud mountains, gaining mastery of them all." Those doomed to never experience this wonder, Caidin said, were "people who have never lived . . . trapped in a two-dimensional world, blind to the beauty which soars about their heads."

Who, exactly, were the jet set? Hard to say. A *New York Times* article about the phenomenon in 1962 estimated there were a few thousand of them "in various western capitals," but noted that the really snobby jet-setters said there were only a few hundred true high fliers who deserved the name. Here's how the *Times* described their ranks:

> Post-debutantes, scions of bigwigs in business and government or sons of just plain millionaires, Greek ship owners' sons, people with titles (many of these spuriously used), a few who have done well in the arts (mostly in the commercial arts and are touted as geniuses), models, successful businessmen trying pathetically hard to be casual hangers-on, social climbers and foreigners of all the above varieties. Everybody has a nickname.

They were people that gossip columnists like to write about, pretty much like old café society but generally younger and much more impatient. Specifically, their numbers included such fun-lovers as Britain's Marquess and Marchioness of Tavistock; semiprofessional escort Porfirio Rubirosa; Lady Jeanne Campbell (granddaughter of British press mogul Lord Beaverbrook); Mrs. Robert Sarnoff (wife of the NBC chief, who was generally too busy working to really have fun); Princes Ira von und zu Fürstenberg; Loulou de la Falaise and her date Giorgio Sant'Angelo; top models from Chanel and the Ford agency; Veruschka (the first supermodel); Valentino (the jet set couturier); such well-cultured actresses as Virna Lisi and Sophia Loren; ultra-rich Paul and Talitha Getty; Princess Luciana Pignatelli (author of *The Beautiful People's Beauty Book*); and (arguably) Richard Burton and Elizabeth Taylor. Fictional jet-setters made appearances in James Bond books (Bond himself shared much with the jet set, but he was just too serious about his job and didn't have the necessary joie de vivre) and *Once Is Not Enough* by Jacqueline Susann, and one jet-setter manqué actually appeared as a character in a TV sitcom in 1966—"the Pruitts of Southampton," starring Phyllis Diller as a former bonne vivante who is suddenly poor and has to open a boardinghouse. (In 1974, two of the surviving Three Stooges were cast in an R-rated comedy called *The Jet Set*, but Moe fell ill and died, and the movie was retitled *Blazing Stewardesses*.)

Jet-setters were, if you'll pardon the Euro-multilingual farrago (itself very jet-setty) the *crème des cognoscenti*. They decided what was "in," and once they chose a hot spot (the Mid-Ocean Club in Southampton or L'Eléphant Blanc in Paris), it became *le dernier cri*, and the place all social climbers craved to get in and be seen. They ratified such dances as the twist, the hully gully, and the Madison, and transformed the Peppermint Lounge from a sleazy midtown dive into the center of the trendy universe for a short while in the early 1960s, then lent their imprimatur to the raging disco club scene of the 1970s at such hot spots as Studio 54 and Xenon. In the beginning, they brought the bouffant hairdo from Paris. They made Pucci dresses the epitome of chic. They created the (still extant) fashion for women's outrageously oversized eyeglass frames (originally worn because they suggested ski goggles). They helped make anorexic thinness all the rage: "If you want to have a good figure and look divine, you have to diet," said C. Z. Guest as she came out of her lunch at La Grenouille on the arm of Baron Alexis de Rede. "Anyone who tells me he doesn't diet is a liar."

The most important thing about the jet set was not any one trend they established but the very fact that they existed, at least as an ideal. Like the hippies, who came after them (see p. 212), they embodied a lifestyle that expressed a fantasy existence that a lot of people dreamed of living. Strangely, though, the idea has persisted. Whereas the hippie era now seems almost quaint, and the few who remain true to its principles appear stuck in time, the jet set never really went away. If you doubt that, tune in to "Lifestyles of the Rich and Famous" (see p. 286). The difference between now and thirty years ago, however, is that in 1962 the jet set signified a glorious, leisure-filled future. Today, the notion of traveling all the time, even if it is to go skiing or get a tan, seems like an awful lot of work.

CHRISTINE JORGENSEN

December 1, 1952, was a big news day: An H-bomb had just been exploded on Eniwetok in the Pacific, Elizabeth had become the new Queen of England, and the Korean War was raging. The New York *Daily News* pushed aside all those lesser stories to fill its front page with a real blockbuster of a headline: EX-GI BECOMES BLONDE BEAUTY: OPERATIONS TRANSFORM BRONX YOUTH. George Jorgensen, a ninety-eight-pound photographer, had gone to Denmark in his suit and tie and was coming back a showgirl in a full-length mink coat. Christian Jorgensen was the world's first celebrity sex change.

Nowadays, transsexuals are a dime a dozen, and they periodically make the rounds of television talk shows to tell their tales of triumph and woe, but in 1952 this story was so astonishing that Christine Jorgensen became the most written-about person in the history of newspapers (according to trade magazine *Editor & Publisher*). Her transformation reverberated through the tabloids (WEDDING FOR CHRISTINE!... CHRISTINE BANNED IN LATIN QUARTER... "I HAVE FALLEN IN LOVE—WITH CHRISTINE"... DISILLUSIONED CHRISTINE TO BECOME MAN AGAIN), and it instantly inspired the publication of a semifictional account of what had been the world's first, but little-known, sex change (when Danish artist Ernar Wegener became Lili Elbem in Berlin in the 1920s) as a book called *Man into Woman:* "Here, in all its startling truth, is the fearlessly told, factually complete drama of a man who surrenders to his destiny and becomes a woman—a beautiful woman who falls hopelessly in love!" Also in 1953, Edward G. Wood directed a "docu-fantasy" motion picture called *Glen or Glenda?* (also

Christine *(top)* and her parents

known as *I Led Two Lives* and *I Changed My Sex*), narrated by Bela Lugosi and considered by many to be the worst movie ever made, in which Glen spends most of his time worrying about how to tell his fiancée that he would like to borrow her panties and brassiere.

George Jorgensen had not been happy as a boy growing up in New York. He felt different and was painfully shy and hated the fact that little boys weren't allowed to cry. Once, his teacher in grade school scolded him in front of all the class because she found the piece of needlepoint he used to like to keep in his desk to fondle. Although honorably discharged from the U.S. Army (in 1946), service had been hell for him: He couldn't even bring himself to pull the trigger of a gun. "I was underdeveloped physically and sexually," Christine recalled in her autobiography. "My thoughts and responses were more often womanly than manly."

After the Army, while studying photography in New Haven in 1948, George came across a book called *The Male Hormone* by Paul de Kruif, about the effects of testosterone and estrogen on the human body: "At that moment it seemed possible to me that I was holding salvation in my hands." George got hold of some female hormone pills and started taking them. On the eighth day of his self-prescribed treatment, he felt "refreshed and alive" and thought he noticed new sensations in his breasts, which seemed to be growing. He began to wonder if surgery could complete the process by removing his penis, or as he called it, his "malformation." When he learned that such experiments had already taken place in Sweden and Denmark, he was on his way.

Under the supervision of endocrinologist Christian Hamburger, George took two thousand hormone injections, and went under the knife for the first of five operations on September 24, 1951. In May 1952 he went to the American embassy in Copenhagen, still dressed in suit and tie, and applied for a new passport, as a woman. Calling herself Christine, the feminine of "Christian" (to honor Dr. Hamburger), the new woman got dressed properly for the first time one morning in June—green skirt, pale brown jacket, and brown suede shoes ("I liked what I saw," she wrote)—then went to a beauty salon for the works: manicure, facial, and permanent. That afternoon, walking through Tivoli Park, she got her first wolf whistle. Several weeks later, on the eve of her return to the United States, Christine wrote her parents, who had thought their son had gone to Denmark to pursue a career in photography. "Nature made a mistake," she explained to them. "I am now your daughter."

The *Daily News* was not impressed: "The lad who became a lady arrived home from Denmark yesterday, lit a cigarette like a girl, husked 'Hello,' and tossed off a Bloody Mary like a guy, then opened her fur coat.

Jane Russell has nothing to worry about." But a lot of women who believed they were trapped in men's bodies found Christine an inspiration. In fact, by February 1953 so many Americans had appealed to Dr. Hamburger to help them realize their true sexual identity that the Danish minister of justice decided to restrict the sex-change operation to native Danes. (It was only in 1966 that sex-change operations became readily available in America, at the Gender Identity Clinic of Johns Hopkins Hospital.)

Christine overcame her shyness as soon as she was back in the States. She had never wanted any publicity, she said, and in fact, the original story had been leaked to the *Daily News* by a medical technician in Copenhagen. But once it was out, she and her family made the most of it. Her life story was sold to *American Weekly* for $30,000, which her parents said would be used to help others "suffering in the no-man's-land of sex." And Christine became what *Time* called "Manhattan's No. 1 glamour girl": "A blonde with a fair leg and a fetching smile, she seemed to be everywhere that was anywhere, with everybody who was anybody. Columnist Leonard Lyons introduced her to a gaggle of celebrities, Broadway Star Yul Brynner and she grinned at each other over a couple of highballs at El Morocco . . . and she was photographed in a soft *tailleur* for the Easter Parade."

She developed a nightclub act that included her singing "Getting to Know You" and "I Enjoy Being a Girl," doing an impression of Marlene Dietrich, and talking about her operation. She was banned in Boston (the mayor called her "a travesty") and ordered not to use ladies' rooms in Washington, D.C., but Las Vegas and New York couldn't get enough of her. Walter Winchell wrote, "She's a star who was a stare a year ago. The audience loved her and called for more, more, more!"

After touring America and Europe for six years, making a record (with Nipsey Russell, called *Christine Reveals*), and appearing on television's "The Arthur Murray Party" to speak on behalf of the Damon Runyon Cancer Fund, Christine believed her career in show business was finally on its way to the heavens in 1959 when she signed a contract to star in *She*, a new motion picture version of the H. Rider Haggard fantasy about an eternally young, love-starved sex goddess. However, both Hedda Hopper and Louella Parsons sternly and publicly disapproved of her as immoral (strictly because of the sex change; she was not promiscuous), and so the project was shelved . . . until 1965, when the movie was made with all-woman Ursula Andress taking the role of She.

The biggest tragedy of Christine's life was that she could not get married. Because her birth certificate listed her as a man, she was denied a marriage license in 1959, after which her fiancé dumped her. For the rest of her life, she dated often but simply could not find her Mr. Right. Still, she had her career, and as she stated in her autobiography, "I had come to love and enjoy show business." Until her death in 1989 of bladder cancer, she made a nice living starring in local theater productions and giving lectures on "How to Deal With Being Different."

KENNEDYS

W hatever the accomplishments of its members as elected officials, the Kennedy family of Massachusetts has been a breathtaking source of entertainment since Jack ran for President in 1960. The most remarkable thing about them as pop-culture characters is how dramatically their public image has changed since the early 1960s, going from America's young knights in shining armor to America's naughtiest partiers. In fact, *they* haven't changed much at all: Most of the prominent Kennedys in the last three decades have expressed high ideals, which they sometimes betray. What has changed is the way their behavior has been interpreted by the popular press and the public. Once a widely accepted standard of culture and virtue, the Kennedy name has become a titillating emblem of wanton misconduct.

Back in 1960 it was considered quite cool that JFK was known as a "ladies' man"; his star gleamed all the brighter for his connections to Frank Sinatra's vaguely nefarious Rat Pack (see p. 450), and even for the (then-) rumored liaisons he had with such beauties as Marilyn Monroe and Angie Dickinson. Jerry Lewis, who helped JFK add jokes to his speeches, called him "one of the great cunt men of all time—except for me." Today, however, as stories are told about Jack getting regular amphetamine shots and smoking pot in the White House and joking about being high with his finger on the nuke button, and about his going after anyone and everyone in a skirt (includ-

ing a Soviet spy and a mobster's girlfriend), and maintaining a party suite in the Mayflower Hotel known to the FBI as "JFK's playpen," and even carousing with a prostitute just minutes before his television debate against Richard Nixon in 1960, most concerned citizens gasp with horror. And when we hear about JFK and RFK *both* carrying on with Marilyn Monroe, and consider the possibility that Bobby might have been in her room, up to no good, the day she died, the Kennedy saga begins to assume a morbid fascination—like an accident you cannot help staring at, even while it sickens you.

Most of this behavior is stuff the public didn't know about when it happened (although there were rumors, and the Kennedy boys' romp with Monroe was used by Jacqueline Susann in her roman à clef *Valley of the Dolls*), but as it has become general knowledge in recent years, the Kennedys have become all the more mesmerizing: not mere two-dimensional heroes but *hugely* flawed heroes. There can be no question that morality in America has become a slippery subject in the last thirty years, but at the same time, we as a nation have become downright puritanical in our attitude towards politicians. Today, fewer people are

willing to wink and look the other way at the escapades of dead Kennedys. Public figures are no longer allowed to have private lives, and therefore we are privy to all their lapses, in every awful detail. And while the prominent living members of the family, scrutinized by a gossip-hungry press, find few admirers for their moral, sexual, and substance-abuse indiscretions, they are ever more the stuff of pop mythology, not to mention moralizing.

The one thing that has not changed is America's thorough fascination with this big, rollicking clan of relentlessly procreative guys and all the pretty gals who serve as their handmaidens. (With the current exceptions of Jackie O, Maria Shriver, and Jack's daughter, Caroline, Kennedy women have always seemed like second-stringers.) At the dawn of the 1960s, they emerged as fair-haired symbols of youth, energy, self-made success, and unimpeachable idealism. No one cared to remember patriarch Joseph Kennedy's bootlegging past and his Nazi leanings prior to World War II (and few knew about *his* sexual recklessness with, among others, Gloria Swanson), and America fell in love with his gallant sons, who were depicted in thousands of articles and books as well educated, witty, eloquent, handsome war heroes. After the homespun Ike-and-Mamie 1950s, Jack and Jackie Kennedy (and brother Bobby and even chubby little brother Teddy and certainly Hollywood-connected in-law Peter Lawford) all signified a fresh new beginning for a country eager to frolic and to feel more worldly.

The Kennedys sailed and jogged and played tennis; they enjoyed high-spirited games of touch football on the lawn at their family compound. And although certainly not to the manor born, they were ever so sophisticated (and they married so well!). When they arrived at their new home on Pennsylvania Avenue, Jack and Jackie booted out the meat loaf chefs and served nothing but fancy French food. When the First Couple went to France, Jackie wowed the locals by speaking French fluently; and in Berlin, even Jack tried to show he was not an ugly American by saying *"Ich bin ein Berliner,"* which he took to mean "I am a Berliner" but in fact informed his German-speaking listeners that he was a jelly-filled donut. No matter, it was the thought that counted.

America was so in love with the promise of the Kennedys that Jack's assassination in November 1963 is remembered by a lot of people like a hard punch to the solar plexus. Never mind that he had sent Green Berets to Vietnam, had played heretofore inconceivable nuclear brinksmanship with Russia over Soviet missiles in Cuba, had embarrassed the country with a halfhearted invasion at the Bay of Pigs, and had delivered nice talk but little in the way of action to the emerging struggle for civil rights in the South. Despite the ambiguity of his actual accomplishments, John F. Kennedy had become a symbol of national idealism. He had given America the concept of a "New Frontier" where, individually and collectively, we could all be heroes. His death was popularly understood as nothing less than a moment when Evil overcame Good in this land, and when all the visionary promise of a short administration known as Camelot was overtaken, if not by pure wickedness, then certainly by a kind of unpleasant pragmatism. (This feeling was confirmed when JFK's place at the head of the country was appropriated by the ultimate pragmatist politician, Lyndon Johnson.)

In a bustle of folklore formerly reserved for the likes of such matinee idols as Rudolph Valentino and James Dean, Jack Kennedy's death inspired a still-burgeoning body of elaborate and imaginative conspiracy theories, and Kennedy himself was kept alive in the popular mind by all manner of pop apocrypha, including:

- He did not die in Dallas, but his brain was destroyed and he is now living in a vegetative condition in a secret suite in Dallas's Parkland Memorial Hospital.
- He was suffering from a disfiguring disease so hideous that the family decided to fake his assassination and spirit him away to an asylum in New Hampshire.
- He was killed by the Mafia, the CIA, Fidel Castro, big business, Jimmy Hoffa, Texas oilmen, J. Edgar Hoover, etc.: Take your pick.

Paul Krassner, editor of *The Realist*, added to Kennedy lore in a fabulous story, written as straight reportage, about the plane ride back from Dallas after JFK's assassination, during which Lyndon Johnson is described as being so excited by his assumption to the presidency that he opens up the coffin and has intercourse with the bullet wound in the former President's neck. Incredible as it seems, this anecdote swept through the youth culture in the 1960s and many people accepted it as gospel truth.

When Bobby Kennedy was assassinated in June 1968, the two dead brothers became even more exalted symbols of virtue, hope, and martyrdom; along with Martin Luther King, who was also killed in April 1968. The three slain leaders became a popular motif on wall rugs, souvenir plates, and reverential calendars as reminders of the ideals that used to be. They also came to be handy symbols of America's violent streak, which by the end of the 1960s seemed to be eradicating so much of the optimism and self-assurance that the Kennedys originally represented. "I hate this country," Jackie said after Bobby's funeral. "I despise America."

And so the worm began to turn. Throughout the 1960s, Jackie the bereaved widow had been transformed from a First Lady who signified elegance and class into a gossip-magazine cover girl bigger than Elizabeth Taylor, inspiration for endless rumors about whom she would marry (Alan Jay Lerner or Mike Nichols, according to *Movie TV Secrets* in October 1966; Lord Harlech of England, according to *TV Radio Talk* in April 1968). Four months after Bobby's death, when she married Aristotle Onassis, one of the richest old men in the world, Jackie's place in tabloid history was ensured by the three-million-dollar cash dowry and over six million dollars' worth of gems Mr. Onassis gave her for a wedding present. When her husband died in 1975, it was estimated she came away with a cool $45 million settlement.

In 1969, just months after Jackie became Mrs. Onassis, the only remaining Kennedy brother, Teddy, ran a car off a bridge at Chappaquiddick and his companion, Mary Jo Kopechne, drowned. Some theorists contend that Ted was too hysterical or too self-interested to get help in time. No one, except probably Ted himself, knows exactly what happened that night, and for more than twenty years the unexplained death has set the tone of pop culture's scandalmongering interpretation of the Kennedy clan, despite such happy tidings as Maria Shriver's television success and her marriage to Arnold Schwarzenegger and JFK, Jr., being named the world's sexiest man by *People.*

It is embarrassing and unpleasant to enumerate all the Kennedy drug and alcohol problems and sex scandals that have made headlines in the last few decades, up to the most notorious one of all—the William Kennedy Smith Palm Beach rape case, which finally ended in Mr. Smith's acquittal and a big Kennedy bash to celebrate the event. So we have selected a handful of quotations from contemporary books and magazines to describe the changing image of the family America most loves to gape at:

1960

At Hyannis Port they threw themselves eagerly and loudly into the family touch football games on the front lawn, paired off in slam-bang mixed doubles tennis matches on the court behind the house, sailed in inter-club races against boats from Wianno and Osterville, organized trips to Turners on Route 28 for ice cream, and, every evening after dinner, they still gathered with neighbors downstairs in the family's private projection room to watch a new first-run movie.... [A friend said,] "There was something doing every minute. The conversation at the dinner table was wonderful, lively, and entertaining. I don't think America has ever had another family like the Kennedys—independent, wealthy, and yet so realistic, unaffected and down to earth and so deeply and seriously concerned with what's going on in the world and so anxious to work hard in public service."

—The Remarkable Kennedys
by Joe McCarthy

1961

Jacqueline Kennedy, the dark-haired, dark-eyed, young beauty who, at thirty-one, has become the nation's new First Lady, has captured the imagination of the American public in a way that no other hostess to preside over the White House has done in many, many years.... The beautiful young woman "has everything," including more glamour than many a movie star [and] a great many traditionalists are frankly shocked by the idea that the First Lady of the land should be so young, so chic, so stylishly dressed, and should wear bouffant hair styling.

—Jacqueline Kennedy
by Deane and David Heller

1962

They are men adept at such sports as skiing, tennis, and ski diving, and yet equally at home in contemplation of intellectual matters.... [They include] his father, who built his fortune with his own ingenuity; his mother, who reared a family of rare talents with love and common sense; R. Sargent Shriver and his wife, Eunice, the President's sister, he the head of the Peace Corps, she a former social worker; Peter Lawford, the movie actor, and his Kennedy wife, Patricia, full-fledged members of the legendary Hollywood "Rat Pack"; and the youngest brother of the President, Edward (Ted) Kennedy, married to a glamorous blonde who was once a model and a debutante.

—*JFK: An Informal Biography*
by William H. A. Carr

1965

From his very first days in public office, as a young Congressman from Boston, John F. Kennedy showed that he had the rare gift of bringing laughter to others. As his career developed and flourished... his wit became a Kennedy trademark. Here is John F. Kennedy in his own words, as family man, Senator, and President... with that famous warm smile and unforgettable wit that were an integral part of this great American.

—from the introduction to *More Kennedy Wit*
edited by Bill Adler

1968

Robert Francis Kennedy had a marvelous sense of humor. He was able, through his warm and gently teasing humor, to draw a shy child out of its shell or relax a tension-ridden meeting. His wit blossomed even at formal occasions.

—from the introduction to
The Robert F. Kennedy Wit
edited by Bill Adler

1968

They booed Jackie Kennedy in Montreal. A few months later she was bitterly criticized by the press corps who called her haughty, aloof, and cold. All of this added up to a spectacular reversal of public sentiment. Only a short time before, Jackie had been the most respected and beloved woman on earth. To say a word against her was to demean all that was noblest and best in womankind—almost a sacrilege. But suddenly Jackie has become fair game for every kind of criticism—personal, political, religious.

—*TV Radio Talk*

1968

Last week, to the shock and dismay of most of her admirers, the Queen [Jacqueline Kennedy] abandoned her reign and, many felt, her reputation [when] she chose as her consort shipping magnate Aristotle Socrates Onassis.... "The Lady," it seemed, had surrendered to the lotus-eaters. Candles burned brightly in café society, but the lights were going out all over Camelot.

—*Newsweek*

1970

A girl was dead and a dream died. The picked-up torch was dropped and doused in an eight-foot pond of water.

—*Jackie, Ted, Ethel: The Kennedys' Year of Crisis*
(Dell Publishing Co.)

1979

"I need a woman every day!" JFK boasted, and she usually wasn't Jackie!

—*Kennedy's Women*
(Lexington Library, Inc.)

1979

"I'm David Kennedy. This can't get into the press. I'm David Kennedy, one of the sons of Robert Kennedy."

—from a story in the *New York Post* in September, titled "I Was Buying Drugs, Says RFK's Son" (David Kennedy later died of a drug overdose)

1991

Jack had his brother-in-law Peter Lawford and pal Frank Sinatra fix him up with oodles of women including sex symbol Jayne Mansfield. She told Peter later there was "a coldness to him, a hard flat coldness which must make his personal life with Jackie less than satisfactory."

—*The Kennedy Scandals*
edited by Michael J. Irish

1991

From Camelot to Dante's Inferno: Eighty Years of Sin and Scandal by the Kennedy Family Men: Startling new facts on the Palm Beach rape, Jack, Bobby, Teddy, Chappaquiddick, the booze, the drugs, and the broads!

—reading lines for *The Sins and Scandals of the Kennedy*'s [sic] by George Carpozi, Jr.

1991

Will accusations of rape on a debauched Good Friday be the scandal that finally buries Camelot? Dominick Dunne reports on three generations of tragedy and trespass, and the twilight of America's First Family.

—introduction to a story called "Damage" in *Vanity Fair*

STEPHEN KING

When *Carrie* was published in paperback in 1975, the name of the author wasn't on the cover. He was a nobody, so it didn't matter. In fact, the *title* of the book wasn't even on the cover, just some words written by the publisher's promotion department, which hoped they would attract readers: "A novel of a girl possessed of a terrifying power." Now, when the once-unknown writer from Maine writes a book, it could easily be published without any such tantalizing come-on. It could be published without a title. All it needs is two words on the cover—"Stephen King." If he wrote it, it's golden.

There is no way to talk about Stephen King without savoring some numbers: A hundred million copies of his books have been sold; in 1988 *Forbes* listed him as twenty-third among the forty top-grossing entertainers in America (he had earned $25 million in two years); and a recently reported deal with a publisher will net him $35 million for four books—an all-time record. In the winter of 1989–90 he had five different books on the hardcover and paperback *New York Times* bestseller lists. Readers love what he writes (and so do millions of people who aren't normally readers, but who always make an exception for him), and they are constantly hungry for more; lucky for them, he is almost as prolific as he is successful, having produced nearly thirty books in the last fifteen years. In the world of publishing, Stephen King is in a class by himself. The *Economist* declared him "as much of a star as Michael Jackson or Eddie Murphy."

The point may seem obvious, but King has done so well because he is a good storyteller. He does what storytellers have done since prehistoric humans gathered around a fire for warmth, and one of them started spinning out a tale that drew them all close together, and bestowed not only excitement and wonderment but a sense of community for having shared the experience, and made them crave to hear what happened next. Because he often writes in the horror genre and tells stories of fantastic goings-on, and because he is the only person with such a commanding power over our collective attention, the comparison of King to some kind of tribal shaman seems especially apropos. His work has the quality of legend and parable; he taps into the hiding places of the mind and scares out demons; and even when he is not writing occult stuff as in *Salem's Lot*, *Pet Sematary*, or *The Shining*, there is something primal about the intoxicating sense of awe he imparts (as in "The Body," the short story he wrote that became the movie *Stand by Me*).

One of the reasons Stephen King's fables are so effective is that they take place in the real world, frequently in the fictional but familiar town of Castle Rock, Maine. He is no sci-fi space cadet or H. P. Lovecraft type writing about some totally exotic gothic universe populated with hyperborean demons. Even when there are supernatural spirits in his stories (there are plenty), they are spirits that seem to rise up out of a world of human dimensions; and all his human characters (even the ones who possess supernatural powers) are endowed with commonplace human traits. Like the best Alfred Hitchcock movies, Stephen King novels are set in the kinds of places that most average, middle-class citizens know very well—a landscape of 7-Elevens and strip malls, workaday Coke machines and Walkman radios, typical high schools and knickknack shops and small towns where ordinary people live. By mining such prosaic details for their disturbing resonances, King transforms a numbingly familiar Coke machine into a presence so malev-olent you can never again buy a Coke with indifference, and reconceives the ubiquitous Walkman as a technological incubus capable of literally blowing your mind. There is more to this strategy than simply scaring the pants off readers (which King does brilliantly). By investing real life with magic and creating ordinary characters who face down monsters, Stephen King has—singlehandedly—invented a modern mythology that serves its readers just as Zeus and Company served the Greeks: as inspiration, escape, shared adventure, and a reminder that the divine and the devil exit in the here-and-now.

King's style, like the things he writes about, seems mundane. There are few belletristic flourishes and none of the kind of self-indulgence that infuses pretentious novels as a way of reminding the reader that they are holding an Important Work by a Talented Author. King seems to just plow ahead and tell the story, piling on mountains of details with no evidence whatsoever of an intervening intelligence (*It* was 1,338 pages and weighed three and a half pounds). But such apparent simplicity conceals what is truly a remarkable art—the art of eradicating all the esoteric folderol that separates the teller from the tale, and the tale from the listener. Ralph Vincinanza, the literary agent who sells foreign rights to King novels (they are bestsellers overseas, too), described the feeling to *Publishers Weekly:*

> You're not reading his books, you're living them. It's a good writer who can make you feel he's sharing his experiences with you, but it's a genius who can make you feel that you are sharing your life with him. You feel so comfortable in Steve's world that you feel as if the author has become the person who is listening. Somewhere along the line you begin to feel you're telling the tale.

All the things that make Stephen King such a commanding writer with an audience of millions are the same things that have earned him eternal damnation in the eyes of some people who consider themselves guardians of important literature. In the last few years, even many literary prigs have come to appreciate his talents, but it is still not unusual for critics to damn him with faint praise by lauding his talents as a *mere* storyteller. "Like eating Cheese Doodles" is how the *New York Times'* Christopher Lehmann-Haupt described King's 1991 novel *Needful Things* in a generally very positive review that admired his "prodigious capacity to milk every situation for its dramatic possibilities [and] to activate one's every anxiety" and yet qualified the commendation by saying that only momentum kept him reading to the end.

"I regard King as the chief cancer on our republic of letters," announced one juror on the 1986 Pulitzer Prize fiction committee when a colleague suggested (only half in jest) that they give at least an honorable mention to Stephen King's *It* and acknowledge that "he was an American writer immersed in American culture and one hell of a good storyteller." Frank McConnell, who made the suggestion, then wrote about the incident for *Commonweal* magazine, where he lauded the "immense current of tenderness and nostalgia that underlies [King's]

gothicism," and said that the literary establishment simply could not accept Stephen King *because* he was such a good storyteller —like Shakespeare and Mark Twain— which made him too accessible to nonacademics and rendered critics irrelevant. Furthermore, the narrative drive of his stories makes nearly all of them ripe for translation into TV and movies, a fact that has ensured his high status in the pop-culture pantheon but has also ensured low status in the eyes of those dogmatists who see TV and movies as colloquial forms of expression inferior to abstract, untranslatable literature.

King's crimes of being too successful an entertainer and working in an unworthy genre are compounded by the facts that he is much too prolific and too nice a guy (he is famous for giving quotes of praise to other authors); worst of all, he seems to have lots of fun writing. The literary stereotype demands that serious authors be more like Harold Brodkey—tortured geniuses who spend years grunting out a book, all the while wearing the burden of the awful process like a crown of thorns. Not Stephen King. He merrily goes about his business, making it look easy, directing scary movies in his spare time, posing for pictures in graveyards with eerie lights under his chin, and being the most prosperous writer in the history of the planet.

EVEL KNIEVEL

No one in recorded history has broken his bones more times than Evel Knievel, who is listed in the *Guinness Book of World Records* for having fractured, cracked, snapped, and crushed various

parts of his skeleton 433 times in his career as a daredevil specializing in long-range cycle jumps.

Evel Knievel invented cycle jumping. In a 1973 book called *The Cycle Jumpers*, Mar-

shall Spiegel called him "as courageous a pioneer as any in history," explaining: "When we speak of courage, we refer to those pioneers who have done what others have not, pioneers like the first man to walk on the Moon or the first man ever to eat a clam."

Knievel came upon his own personal New Frontier after a childhood of petty thievery and juvenile delinquency in Butte, Montana. It was in Butte in 1952, when he was arrested at age fourteen for stealing hubcaps, that he got his name. Christened Robert Craig Knievel, he was thrown in jail with another crook, named Knauffel. The next day, the local newspaper complained that taxpayers would have to pay for an extra guard to watch over the two of them. The headline called them "Awful Knauffel and Evil Knievel." Knievel liked the wicked moniker, which he altered to Evel, to match the spelling of Knievel.

He was in his mid-twenties when he began to wonder just how far it was possible for a man to jump while riding a motorcycle; and starting in 1966 he dedicated his life to finding the answer via his own newly invented occupation, "professional risk taker." Before that, he had sold insurance ("I sold 110 policies one day in an insane asylum," he once boasted) and had competed in ordinary motorcycle racing,

which soon grew dull because, by his accounts, he always won. "I was a terror on wheels!" he recalled, and said that he invented jumping to alleviate boredom.

As he devised it, cycle jumping was similar to broad jumping: He started way back, built up as much speed as possible on a straight track that led to a ramp, rode up the ramp, then sailed over a bunch of cars and landed on a downhill ramp, preferably without crashing. He began with a dozen cars between the ramps, then stretched the distance up to nineteen. He jumped over vans and trucks, over water tanks full of man-eating sharks, over hissing rattlesnakes, and over the fountain in front of Caesars Palace in Las Vegas (where he crashed and put himself in a coma for a month).

Knievel may have invented the sport, but by 1974 there were enough professional jumpers to fill a book: *Evel Knievel and Other Daredevils* by Joe Scalzo, which profiles:

- *Speedy Babs:* A seventy-one-year-old motordrome rider (they pilot a motorcycle around in a tight circle along the walls of a vertical cylinder) with fifty-six broken bones to his credit, Speedy claimed to be the only daredevil to have gone into a bullring to fight a wild bull on a motorcycle.
- *Lee "Iron Man" Irons:* The safety-minded motorcycle daredevil whose specialty was being dragged behind a speeding motorcycle while sitting on a coal shovel blade.
- *Super Joe Einhorn:* "Other car jumpers zoom off their take-off ramps low, then allow their flying motorcycles to nearly skim the car tops. But Super Joe deliberately shoots his bike up high, then lets it plunge straight down, and not infrequently he comes crashing down on his skull." After three years of cycle jumping, Super Joe boasted of having broken his back twice, flattened his nose three times, mashed his

ribs, shattered his collarbone, been on the hospital critical list on two separate occasions, and in a coma "more times than he can count."

- *Captain Joe Monfort:* The man responsible for what the author of *Evel Knievel and Other Daredevils* says is "the most revered accomplishment in the entire history of lunacy aboard a speeding motorcycle." He sped off the rim of the Grand Canyon, then parachuted from midair a mile to the canyon's floor carrying a six-pack, which he drank when he landed.
- *Bobby Gill:* The first man to jump a cycle over cars in a foreign country (Venezuela).
- *Debbie Lawler:* "The Flying Angel," who fought to open the sport of cycle jumping to women, was known for not wearing a brassiere, except for her "lucky" bra, worn only for jumping, under her hot-pink leathers. Her goal was to jump two naval destroyers at once, but she cracked her back in an ordinary car jump and at last report was confined to a wheelchair.

Of all the jumpers, Evel Knievel was definitely the best—at getting publicity. There seemed to be no end to him in the media in the early 1970s. At one time he actually convinced the United States Department of the Interior to grant him permission to jump the Grand Canyon, and when that permission was rescinded after environmentalists protested against the ugly ramps he was planning to build and the damage spectators would cause, he sought in vain to lease the canyon from Navajo Indians for $100,000. (Instead, he jumped Snake River Canyon in Idaho.) "I know someday someone may outjump me," he once said. "But no one will ever out-promote me." For sure, no one ever out-injured him: A miscalculation on March 23, 1972, when he tried to leap over thirty-six cars in the Houston Astrodome, resulted in a crash after which astounded doctors declared that he had broken every

bone in his body. They were exaggerating; actually, he broke only ninety-three.

Two films were made of his exploits, the first, in 1972, a biography called *Evel Knievel*, starring George Hamilton in the title role (but featuring actual gory crash footage from the Caesars Palace fiasco), followed by *Viva Knievel!* in 1977, in which Evel plays himself in a fictional melodrama about kidnappers and drug runners, featuring a "stratocycle" that can fly and a daring jump in which Evel lands on a moving truck. *Viva Knievel!* has since become a kind of cult favorite as one of the worst motion pictures ever made. Leonard Maltin, who rated it "BOMB" in his *TV Movies and Video Guide*, said, "Don't miss the opening scene, in which Our Hero sneaks into an orphanage at midnight to distribute Evel Knievel plastic model kits—whereupon one little boy miraculously throws away his crutches!"

About the time Evel turned fifty, too old to jump anymore, his oldest son, Robbie, took up the gauntlet. After having broken his father's car-jumping record by flying over twenty-two vehicles in one jump, Robbie went on to successfully execute the Caesars Palace fountain jump that had nearly killed his dad in 1967. As five paramedics and a brain surgeon stood by on emergency alert, he sailed 150 feet into the air on a Honda (Dad had ridden a Harley-Davidson) and landed without incident. Before the jump, Evel boasted that "Robbie is the true heir to the Knievel name. He can not only jump better than me, but he does it with no hands on the bars." Robbie returned the compliment by telling the crowd, "There will never be another Evel Knievel." Pay-per-view spectators at home paid $14.95 to watch the jump (during which Robbie *did* hold on to the bars), which lasted four seconds. Evel declared it to be "one of the greatest sporting events of the century."

KOHOUTEK

Named for Lubos Kohoutek, the astronomer who discovered it on March 7, 1973, Kohoutek was the great celebrity comet of our time. But like so many celebrities of our time, it didn't have a lot of staying power. It was the New Kids on the Block of outer space: It generated an astonishing amount of press for a while; then it disappointed people because it wasn't as grand as it was supposed to be; then interest in it evaporated. People shrugged and wondered what the fuss was all about, and Kohoutek returned to the existential obscurity of the cosmic void.

- *November 5, 1973:* "May become the most spectacular comet of this century. . . . By early January, its tail may stretch across one-sixth of the evening sky." (*Time*)
- *December 17, 1973:* "Kohoutek is a reminder of great events—and even greater mysteries—far beyond the earth. [It may be] a messenger—of light and knowledge for all mankind." (*Time*)
- *January 14, 1974:* "Kohoutek has faded almost to a fizzle, and red-faced astronomers were predicting that most earth-bound comet watchers would be lucky if they could get so much as a glimpse of it. It will be fully visible only with the aid of scientific instruments available in advanced astronomical laboratories." (*Newsweek*)
- *January 21, 1974:* "Dud" (*The New Yorker*)

Dr. Kohoutek's detection of what he called Comet 1973F, a hazy blob between the orbits of Jupiter and Mars, about 480 million miles from the earth, might never have been known to the public were it not for the fact that news of his scientific discovery (which was at the time invisible to all but the earth's most powerful tele-

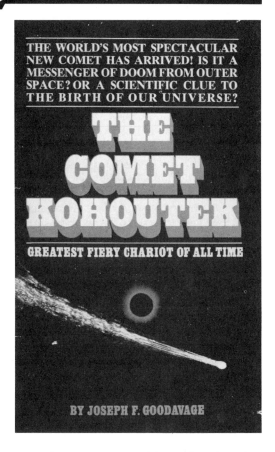

THE WORLD'S MOST SPECTACULAR NEW COMET HAS ARRIVED! IS IT A MESSENGER OF DOOM FROM OUTER SPACE? OR A SCIENTIFIC CLUE TO THE BIRTH OF OUR UNIVERSE?

THE COMET KOHOUTEK

GREATEST FIERY CHARIOT OF ALL TIME

BY JOSEPH F. GOODAVAGE

scopes) was announced just when America was enraptured by disaster movies. *The Poseidon Adventure*, in which an undersea earthquake flips a crowded cruise ship upside down, had been a huge success in 1972, and *The Towering Inferno* and *Earthquake* were in production, scheduled for release in 1974, which is when scientists were predicting that Kohoutek would streak within a mere thirteen million miles of our own sun.

If this trillion-ton heap veered off course, it could slam the puny little earth into a jumble of unrecognizable space flakes—

and even if the dirty iceberg (comets are mostly frozen vapors) happened just to pass by, it was almost certain to wreak havoc. Halley's Comet was recalled by disaster aficionados to have caused hideous calamities when the earth passed through its tail in 1910 (it rained really hard in Paris). And Halley's Comet was a pipsqueak compared to Kohoutek—a mere one-twenty-fifth the size of what overenthusiastic sky-watchers were beginning to call the Killer Comet, the Fiery Chariot of the Apocalypse, or the Cosmic Messenger of Doom. Astrologer M. K. Gandhi of London predicted "subterranean upheavals and disastrous inundations of the Pacific Coast by tidal waves," plus "an epidemic of strikes and sabotage" in Europe. Om Tat Sat, writing in *The Astrological Magazine*, predicted an "epidemic of permissiveness in sex relations." Brigadier Firebrace of England (also an astrologer) foresaw "anarchists, saboteurs, and purveyors of interracial violence," not to mention "increased volcanism in the Ring of Fire." The parting of the Red Sea, the Plagues of Egypt, the assassination of Julius Caesar: All have been linked to the arrival of comets. It was also remembered that the Black Death of 1347 *and* the Black Plague of 1665 both occurred immediately after a spectacular comet sailed through the skies: Could this possibly be a coincidence, or was there a chance that Kohoutek might also be carrying a big lode of evil spores from outer space?

Joseph F. Goodavage, author of *The Comet Kohoutek* (1973—"The world's most spectacular comet has arrived!"), wasn't quite as hysterical as the astrologers, but he did remind readers that history tells of no comets that have brought good news to earth: "Comets have always been associated with revolutionary (usually violent) changes—wars, epidemics, volcanic erup-

tions, drought, and famine, horrendous earthquakes, tidal waves, bloody uprisings, the overthrow of governments and downfall of leaders—every catastrophe the human mind can recall." And if such garden-variety cataclysms weren't impressive enough, Mr. Goodavage included a chapter called "Rendezvous with . . . ?" in which he pointed out that an awful lot of strange things can rain down from the heavens when a comet pulls into town. He enumerated well-documented reports of falling coffins, transistor radios, carburetors, and bikinis, as well as frogs, eels, snails, worms, goldfish, periwinkles, even—on rare occasions in the desert—manna ("It's consumable, too—can be ground into flour that makes delicious bread. Some of the large kernels are like corn and taste like honey").

Tabloid reporters went digging and reminded readers that in 1890 a Kansas farmer had been killed in his field by a falling meteorite. In 1953 a housewife in Alabama had been beaned on the head by a meteor chunk as she slept on her living room couch. Even conservative astronomers began predicting that Kohoutek might very well provide a heavenly light show brighter than anything since the Jefferson Airplane played the Fillmore.

Alas, Kohoutek was a flop. Instead of blazing across the heavens, wreaking havoc, or heralding a millennium, it was an inconsequential dot in the sky that you had to look very hard to find. Its tail, flaring backwards due to solar winds, was practically invisible, with none of the dirty gases that reflect the sun and make a comet really vivid. No toads fell to earth, and no one had an opportunity to bake manna bread. Some wiseacres tried to make a feeble attempt to connect the shame and shock of the ongoing Watergate hearings with Kohoutek's arrival, but such an argument did nothing to assuage those who had paid good money for a stateroom aboard the *Queen Elizabeth II* on its scheduled Kohoutek-watching cruise off the Carolinas.

Even if Kohoutek did not live up to its billing as the most brilliant heavenly vision of modern times, it did help establish a new genre of pop hysteria: fear of falling space junk. Next came Skylab, America's space station (from which astronauts had tried to get spectacular pictures of Kohoutek), which wobbled out of orbit in 1979 and threatened to plunge to earth and land who-knows-where. In Times Square, street vendors sold cone-shaped hats with little magnets on top designed to repel pieces of the falling space station; but some people were not so flippant. Among those who really panicked was singer Liza Minnelli, who at the time was under the influence of severe addictions to drugs and liquor. In Lawrence O'Toole's profile of Miss Minnelli for *New York Woman*, she recalled that she honestly believed Skylab was looking for her and planned to flatten her, personally, when it fell. To get away from it, she fled to the Long Island home of Halston, the clothing designer. Halston reassured her that yes, Skylab would fall, but in the middle of his lawn rather than on Ms. Minnelli's head; so he set up lawn chairs at the edge of his property and the two of them sat down with a view of the impending crash site, waiting for the great event. (Most of Skylab fell in Australia.)

It has been some time now since such hair-raising skyborne disasters have weighed on people's minds. The epidemic of fear seemed to come to an end with the last of the 1970s' big-budget disaster movies, *Meteor* (1979), which had originally been inspired by Kohoutek fever and turned out to be just as big a disappointment as the real thing. But just in case you think Kohoutek-style Chicken Little delirium was strictly a 1970s phenomenon, consider this headline from the *New York Times* in the summer of 1991: THERE'S A "DOOMSDAY ROCK," BUT WHEN WILL IT STRIKE? The *Times* informed its readers that the National Aeronautics and Space Administration was busy researching ways to detect and prevent what it called "killer asteroids." One had come perilously close to earth in 1989, nearly causing "a disaster unprecedented in human history" the *Times* gulped, noting that some scientists had suggested setting up a nuclear-armed missile defense system against future threats. The scary article was accompanied by a chart warning that for an average American, risk of death by asteroid impact was considerably higher than risk of death by tornado, airplane crash, fireworks, or food poisoning.

At least one thing we can tell you, by way of reassurance, is that the Killer Rock predicted in the *Times* will definitely not be Kohoutek. That briefly famous Messenger of Doom isn't expected back to terrorize us earthlings for another thirty million years.

LAMBADA

Fads happen so fast nowadays that sometimes they come and are gone before anybody is really aware of them. The best example of this peculiar time-warp effect is the lambada. For three or four months early in 1990, it was widely believed to be the hottest dance craze since the twist. There were stories heralding its arrival in all the newsweeklies, in the *New York Times*, the *Wall Street Journal*, and *USA Today;* it was demonstrated on television talk shows, and it inspired Hollywood to quickly produce two movies to cash in on the craze: *Lambada! The Forbidden Dance* and just plain *Lambada*. In New York, the Palladium dance club marquee announced THE RAGE OF THE '90s, and inside there were free lambada lessons every Friday night. But by the end of the summer of 1990, the lambada was gone and forgotten.

The problem was that, despite all its heralded appeal, few Americans could do it, and those who could do it didn't want to do it because it was so embarrassing. Supposedly discovered in 1988 on the coast of Brazil, where publicity releases said it had once been banned as too sensual, the lambada (whose name comes from a Portuguese verb meaning "to whip") is a dance in which the man jams his right leg up between the thighs of his partner, who is supposed to wear a short skirt and bikini underwear. The woman rides the man's leg, rubbing up and down in tune to a salsa beat. In the summer of 1989, it actually did become a club craze in France, especially on the Côte d'Azur, where visiting dancers from South America showed adventurous continental vacationers how to do it. After "Lambada," a song credited to Chico de Oliveira and Lamotte d'Incamps and re-

corded by a vaguely third-world-looking band called Kaoma, sold five million copies and two million albums worldwide, CBS's Epic Records began marketing the idea in America, proclaiming the feverish new dance "an alternative to sex in the age of AIDS."

In January 1990, when *Newsweek* attended lambada night at a New York nightclub, the magazine reported that the dance floor was packed with curious trend-seekers, but that nobody danced when the music played. The conclusion: "Lambada may be the perfect fad for this pre–Super Bowl season, when hype traditionally outstrips reality." By April, *Time* wrote about the "hurricane of hype," chronicling the appearance of skimpy lambada skirts and tops in clothing stores, as well as of lambada videos, books, towels, bandannas, T-shirts, and cocktails, but wondering about the fad's staying power.

In July the lambada scandal broke. The French Society of Musical Authors, Composers, and Editors canceled the copyright held by Lamotte d'Incamps when it was discovered that his co-author, Chico de Oliveira, did not exist; and that in fact Mr. d'Incamps had stolen the melody to "Lambada" from a song called "Llorando Se Fue" by Gonzalo and Ulises Hermosa . . . who were not even Brazilian! They, and the dance they invented, actually came from Bolivia.

By the time the real origins of the lambada were revealed, no one cared. The fad was dead, as were five of the movies that had been rushed into production in the spring, as well as the band Kaoma. Despite the extraordinary promotional efforts and record-company predictions that the beat of

the 1990s had arrived, no one in America was interested, and except for a few oddball lambada clubs that still exist in city neighborhoods, the dance is as passé as a pet rock.

You would hardly know lambada had come and gone were it not for evidence on the shelves of video stores, in the form of the two astonishingly execrable movies, *Lambada! The Forbidden Dance* and *Lambada*, both of which were produced so quickly that they were completed before lambada's death, but were released, alas, as it was expiring. It's hard to say which is more deliciously awful. *Lambada! The Forbidden Dance* is the more exotic of the two —about a Brazilian Indian princess who saves the rain forest by winning a television dance contest. But *Lambada*, set in Beverly Hills, has a neo-realistic social consciousness going for it. It's about a mild-mannered high school teacher who leads a secret life: Every night he sneaks out of his house, dresses in leather, and rides a hot chopper into East Los Angeles, where he lambadas all night long with juvenile delinquents as a way to encourage them to do their math homework.

LASSIE

Lassie is not, and never has been, a bitch. The character of Lassie is indeed a female dog, but ever since the first Lassie movie, *Lassie Come Home* (1943), co-starring eleven-year-old Elizabeth Taylor and Roddy McDowall, the actual animal actor has always been a male.

It wasn't planned that way. A bitch had been cast to play the part, which was a plum

role for a dog if there ever was one. Lassie, created in 1938 in Eric Knight's short story "Lassie Come Home" (later expanded into an international bestselling children's book), is a collie belonging to a Yorkshire family so poor that they sell her to the mean Duke of Rudling, four hundred miles away in the Scottish Highlands. But Lassie pines for her family, especially their lad, Joe. So she

comes home: "Ah, a thousand miles of tor and brae, of shire and moor, of path and road and plowland, of river and stream and burn and brook and beck, of snow and rain and fog and sun, is a long way, even for a human being. But it would seem too far—much, much too far—for any dog to travel blindly and win through." Nothing stops Lassie in her quest. Joe finds her waiting for him at the school gate, lying weakly and blotched with dirt and burrs from the journey, able only to whine when she sees the boy she loves.

The animal chosen to play this poignant role was a beautiful champion of noble lineage, with a panoply of trophies and blue ribbons to her name. However, *Lassie Come Home* was to be filmed in the summer, and the dainty superstar began to shed terribly—as female collies tend to do in warm weather. "The leading lady looked like a jackrabbit," said Rudd Weatherwax, an animal trainer who happened to have his own collie, a male named Pal. Pal was anything but a champion. His ancestry was unknown, and he had been acquired by Mr. Weatherwax as settlement of a ten-dollar debt. He had suffered from mange and distemper, chased cars, and didn't even know how to walk at the end of a leash or sit on command. But Weatherwax nursed Pal back to health, taught him the ABCs of canine conduct, and, in a show-business moment straight out of a Busby Berkeley backstage musical, sent Pal in to play Lassie.

What followed was, according to the *Saturday Evening Post*, "the most spectacular canine career in film history." Seven Lassie movies later (including *Courage of Lassie*, co-starring Elizabeth Taylor in her last juvenile role, in 1946), Pal had a five-year contract with MGM, a radio show on 163 NBC stations every Saturday afternoon (in which he barked, whined, and panted), was reported to be earning well over a thousand dollars a week—not only from the movies but from endorsements for Red Heart dog food and personal-appearance fees—and was getting thirty thousand fan letters every year. Plus, he got to keep his testicles (clever mise-en-scène kept them hidden from view in nearly every shot), and he sired a whole line of Lassies (all men) to follow in his pawsteps. Meanwhile, collies, which had once ranked twelfth in popularity among all breeds registered with the American Kennel Club, rose to number three. Lassie was America's sweetheart. Rin Tin Tin, once the best known dog in show business, had become practically a nobody.

Writing in the *New York Times Magazine* in 1949 (just after the Christmastime release of *The Hills of Home*, the fourth Lassie picture), Helen Colton said:

> By beauty standards, Lassie's too fat (80 pounds), too tall (26 inches), her face is too wide and her upper jaw sticks out

too far over her lower one, and yet she is loved for her looks. The parent of fifty children, she still retains her youthful allure. Despite having had six mates, she has no moral clause in her contract. She takes a bath only once every three months. In fact, she is really a he. What other star can make these claims?

By 1956, Pal was fifteen years old. He was blind and had retired to Rudd Weatherwax's ranch along with dozens of other canine motion picture veterans too old to work anymore. But his son, also a collie with a white blaze down his forehead, was earning enough to support them all—a hundred thou a year starring in the television series "Lassie," which was a staple on CBS from 1954 to 1971, then until 1974 in syndication, and until today in reruns. Rudd Weatherwax died in 1986, but his son Robert trained yet another descendant for the syndicated "The New Lassie," and was reported in 1992 to be readying the latest Lassie for a remake of the original film. Lassie's most memorable TV moment was during the last network season, which cast him as a loner with no human family whatsoever. In a special seven-part story, he gave birth, practically on camera, to a litter of puppies. Seven generations of Pal's progeny have played the role of Lassie, and in 1978 one

was featured in the Radio City Music Hall stage show in conjunction with the release of *The Magic of Lassie*.

Why has Lassie been so popular? In 1949, at the peak of Lassie's film career, when his character was featured in sermons, pep talks, and inspirational addresses throughout the land, and the book *Lassie Come Home* had become official reading matter in thousands of schools, Dr. Lucien Warner, an authority on animal psychology at Claremont College, explained that Lassie exhibited courage, loyalty, and dependability —qualities too often lacking in human beings. "Uncertain of the responses of our fellow man, we make of Lassie a substitute who represents a constant in a changing, insecure world."

Everyone has always loved Lassie except the actors who have had to co-star with him in movies. Like a few other powerful screen legends, Lassie's scripts have always been written to show him in the very best light, and to minimize the other players' importance, so Lassie's expendable human family has regularly changed personnel in the movies and on television. Cloris Leachman, who played the mother in the 1957–58 TV family, said about the scripts: "They had to find reasons for us to be morons so the dog could outsmart us."

"LAUGH-IN"

Thanks to "Laugh-In" (technically titled "Rowan and Martin's Laugh-In"), these expressions became an unavoidable part of vernacular American English in the late 1960s:

- "Sock it to me."
- "You bet your bippy."
- "Ring my chimes."
- "Verrrrry interesting!"
- "Look that up in your Funk and Wagnall's."

- "Welcome to beautiful downtown Burbank."
- "Here come de judge" (previously the trademark of vaudevillian Pigmeat Markham, who became a "Laugh-In" regular).

And these once-unknown performers became famous:

- Lily Tomlin (the sarcastic, nasal-voiced telephone operator)
- Arte Johnson (A German soldier peering out from behind a potted plant and puffing a cigarette)
- Ruth Buzzi (a little old lady named Gladys Ormphby who whacks men on the head with her umbrella)
- Henry Gibson (a befuddled poet or priest)
- Gary Owens (the pompous announcer)
- Judy Carne (the "sock it to me" girl)
- Jo Anne Worley (the big mouth)
- Goldie Hawn (a dumb blonde, frequently dressed in a bikini, dancing the boogaloo, with funny sayings written on her bare skin).

When it first appeared on television as a one-hour NBC special on September 9, 1967, "Laugh-In" was such a hit among viewers that it was a regular weekly series by January, the number-one-rated show for the next two years, a *Time* cover story in December (in which it was proclaimed "the smartest, freshest show on television"), and Emmy winner as outstanding variety series of 1968–69. Conceived by George Schlatter, who had earlier produced "The Judy Garland Show" in 1963 and then later went on to produce "Cher" (1975) and "Real People" (1979–84), it was indeed a variety series, but there had never been anything that looked quite like it on television. It was filled with references to current events and social issues (a rarity in American television outside the news), and, like an "Ed Sullivan Show" on an LSD trip, the comic spectacle spun in and out of control at a demented pace. "The first-time viewer can hardly believe the proceedings," *Time* raved. "Silly punch lines fly like birdshot." Some examples given were:

- If Shirley Temple Black had married Tyrone Power, she'd be Shirley Black Power.
- A myth is an effeminate moth.

A touch of normalcy was provided in the form of the program's hosts, Dick Martin (the suave, handsome one) and Dan Rowan (the goofy one), who stood up on stage like a pair of old-fashioned nightclub comics about to do some tired and familiar routine. Rowan and Martin had knocked around television for well over a decade, with limited success; their vague familiarity and somewhat square show-biz image made them perfect as the vortex of a bizarre barrage of cockeyed sight gags, irreverent one-liners, off-color blackout sketches, and surprise cameo appearances by celebrities, from Tiny Tim premiering "Tiptoe Through the Tulips" to presidential candidate Richard Nixon saying "Sock it to *me?*" in 1968. Never fully part of the action, Rowan and Martin stood there looking amused and befuddled by the whirlwind of hip badinage that encircled them.

Critics lauded "Laugh-In" as the first show to exploit the nature of TV as a primarily visual medium. Instead of relying on hoary, plotted skits, it flooded the screen with faces, phrases, and fragments of conversation that worked less like a stage-bound variety show and more like television commercials, grabbing your attention every fifteen seconds or less. It was—in the parlance of the time—a happening. Its apparent defiance of the traditional TV variety show format made it seem practically avant-garde, although in fact its relentless fusillade of wisecracks harkened back to classic vaudeville (*Hellzapoppin*) and Borscht Belt comedy. It was a program filled with pies in the face, people falling through trap doors, a running gag in which Judy Carne got a bucket of water dumped on her head whenever she said "Sock it to me," and plenty of smirking persiflage about women with large breasts.

Just like "All in the Family" a few years later, "Laugh-In" traded on its image as a brave demolisher of taboos, not afraid to challenge television's priggish standards and have some fun with such issues as war, protest marches, sex, and procreation ("I should have danced all night," sang a pregnant woman). "We broke the marijuana ban," Dick Martin boasted to interviewer Gordon Javna, referring to such witticisms that flashed on the screen as "Lawnmowers are on grass" and "BULLETIN: U.N. Agrees on Everything! Police seeking culprit who put the grass in the air conditioner" and "Acapulco Gold is a Mexican tailor." Martin was also known for occasionally wearing an ankh medallion on his turtleneck—symbol of the Legalize Marijuana movement.

A major category of vulgar humor using double entendres was perfected (if not actually invented) on "Laugh-In," and it continues to be one of the primary aesthetic principles of automobile bumper-sticker writing to this day. MINERS GET THE SHAFT, PAPER GETS REAMED, STETSON IS OLD HAT, PRUNES MOVE ME, and CON EDISON TURNS ME ON are all signs and slogans that appeared on the show. Frequently, the verbal wit was sexual, arising from the premise that you couldn't be direct about sex on television. So "Laugh-In" writers concocted all kinds of amusing ways to insinuate sex into jokes but avoid censorship ("Laugh-In" was the only show on television that had its own on-premises censor, Herminio Traviesas). On one occasion cited in the book *Inside Laugh-In*, Dick Martin was given a line in which he said he made so many long-distance phone calls he was known as "Direct Dial Dick." Traviesas wanted to cut it because "dick" means penis; but after some discussion he was talked into allowing the phrase because Dick also happened to be Martin's real name. Other examples of the kind of naughty sexual allusions for which "Laugh-In" was known include:

Q: "Why are jockeys so short?"
A: "I don't know. When you wear them, it's just hard to stand up straight."

and

Goldie Hawn to Terry-Thomas: "Do you still use the metric system over there [in England]?"
Terry-Thomas: "Not since my wife took the pill."

and

Ruth Buzzi as Gladys Ormphby: "Harry said I ought to be a cover girl. Then he covered me."

and

Arte Johnson as a guru: "The snake that striketh at the feet of a hunter is naught but a pain in the grass."

Frequently, the puns and double entrendres took the form of signs placed around the set or written on the body of Goldie Hawn. For example:

- This is national broad jump week. Make a broad jump.
- The KKK is full of sheet.

"Laugh-In" developed not only a huge repertoire of familiar characters who reappeared show after show but also recurrent skits that provided a forum for gags: the Cocktail Party (at which everyone who was doing the frug and watusi suddenly froze so someone could deliver a quick gag); "'Laugh-In' Looks at the News" (fractured headlines from the past, present, and future); "Hollywood News" with Ruth Buzzi; and the Flying Fickle Finger of Fate Award, which gave such prizes as "a winged weenie," "a rigid digit," "a nifty knuckle," and "a wonderful wiggler" to such dubious achievers as William F. Buckley, Jr. ("for his philosophy—never clarify tomorrow what you can obscure today") and Eldridge Cleaver ("for putting the hood back in

brotherhood"). The show always ended with the Joke Wall, where the cast regulars, guest stars, and occasional surprise visitors would pop their heads out of doors and deliver bons mots such as "Incest is a relative term" or "Is Ben gay?"

Within a year of its going on the air, "Laugh-In" had become a mini-industry of official as well as unauthorized souvenirs, especially because its use of one-line quips lent itself so well to T-shirts, coffee mugs, cocktail napkins, even punching bags with some of the regular characters' faces on them. There were "Laugh-In" record albums, jogging outfits, comic strips, fortune cookies, and even graffiti wallpaper. However, after reigning at number one in the Nielsens for two years, "Laugh-In" lost viewers almost as quickly as it had found them. It dropped to number thirteen in the 1970–71 season, then ended its run in 1973, by which time its fractured format, drug jokes, and leering sexual innuendo had become very unhip legacies of the once-swinging 1960s.

RALPH LAUREN

Ralph Lauren is nothing less than a fashion Messiah, the best known clothing designer ever. You won't have to feel anxious if you buy something with his label on it. It will be well made, it will be handsome, it will let the world know (subtly, of course) that you are a person of breeding. This annoys the hell out of some people, particularly snobs, because fashion used to be one of the most convenient ways to distinguish between people who have fine old money (with fine old-style clothes to match) and those who are nouveau riche

(and tend to buy the vulgar apparel of the moment). Ralph threw a monkey wrench into that time-honored system of instant ID; he created, popularized, and mass marketed the kinds of clothes that used to signify social pedigree. And the strangest thing about it is that people with social pedigrees buy his clothes, too! Prince Charles and Princess Diana wear Ralph Lauren apparel because he now makes some things that are more traditionally English than anything made in England!

It would be hard to say whether the conspicuous success of Ralph Lauren or of Martha Stewart (see p. 482) has been more confounding to social critics and commentators over the years. Both of them have been immensely successful selling the accoutrements of good taste; but the difference between them is that Martha's fans want to *be* her. Although Ralph is famous for starring in his magazine ads, dressed in well-worn jeans, weathered Stetson, and chambray shirt and leaning on a vintage pickup truck, it seems fair to say that most Ralph fans aren't really interested in *being* him. They want to buy the wherewithal to make themselves into a fantasy character suggested by his various lines of products, which are given such names as "Log Cabin," "Thoroughbred," "Chintz," "Knightsbridge," "Regatta" and the ever-popular rubric for nearly everything he makes, "American classics."

More than any other designer, he has opened up the romance of fashion to every shopper who yearns for it. He can help you feel like a rugged trail rider or a mountain man, like a witty bon vivant in a 1930s Ernst Lubitsch movie, like a studious graduate of an Ivy League university, or like a sheltered member of the landed gentry. Or he can simply make you feel—if, indeed, you crave such feelings—that you have some roots and venerable values, you are partaking of

a heritage that's yours, sort of. After all, his clothes are "American classics," aren't they? And what's America if not a land of opportunity? There is indeed something disarmingly New World about the anyone-can-do-it attitude implicit in Ralph Lauren's marketing; and if he has done nothing else, he has helped make American sportswear into a worldwide symbol of prestige the likes of which were once available only from a place like Savile Row, and only to a chosen few. Rugged, confident, understated: These adjectives, applied to him by fashion critics, were always connected to praise for his having brought something uniquely, refreshingly American to the formerly snobby fashion world. He called it "an attitude, a sense of freedom."

Amazing as it now seems, considering that *timelessness* is one of the bedrock ideas of Ralph Lauren fashions, he began his career by designing big, wide polka dot neckties. In 1967 he was wholesaling ties from drawer space he rented in a closet of someone's office in the Empire State Building. The ties were three inches wide, but Ralph knew the mod look was on its way to even more outrageous extremes. So he designed some really wide ties and began selling them using the label Polo Fashions. The ties were so big that when they were knotted they totally eclipsed the collar of an ordinary shirt; so in 1968 Ralph Lauren designed shirts with extra-wide collars, soon followed by sports jackets with really wide lapels. In 1970 he introduced his first full menswear collection, which was judged by the press to be "elegant and relaxed"; that year he won the Coty Fashion Award and opened the first Polo boutique to showcase his clothes at Bloomingdale's. "Nostalgia with subtle updating" is how the Los Angeles *Times* described his line in 1972 (by which time he had introduced women's wear too), calling his work "the most complete and handsome of the new breed of traditional taste."

He has been called the outfitter of New Traditionalism, which is the term for middle-age baby boomers who long for old-fashioned values but don't want to appear stuffy or unhip. Polo Fashions have always embodied those values: tradition with panache and the nostalgic reassurance of the not-too-distant past that some people remember, but many know only from movies.

He always had a taste for clothes that embodied a certain heritage. As Ralph Lifshitz growing up in the Bronx (his father changed the family name to Lauren when Ralph was fifteen), he saved for weeks while working as a stock boy at Alexander's so he could buy himself a Brooks Brothers suit, even though most of his neighborhood friends were hoods who preferred black leather jackets. His high school yearbook listed only one aspiration for him: millionaire. Even while working as a tie salesman, Ralph became famous in the fashion industry for stylish (but never shocking) clothes he had custom-made from fabrics he selected, and his impeccable taste was the subject of a 1967 profile in the *Daily News Record*, an industry newspaper.

An idealist and a romantic, Lauren has said that his inspiration for remaking so many cowboy classics, from jeans to traditional flap-fronted shirts, was a trip out west during which the clothing he saw on real American westerners appalled him: "Every collar was big, and the shirts were flowers and they were polyester," he lamented to *Manhattan, Inc.* "I said, *Where are the shirts that Randolph Scott wore?*" When he went to New England, he saw a lot of discount stores and shoppers in big down coats; so again, he wondered, *"Where are the country stores, the flannel shirts, the colorful little woven baskets, the plaid hunting caps?"* Finding none of these

things he wanted to see, he realized that it was up to him to reinvent America. "I'm sort of bringing back a world that doesn't exist," he said.

Everything he brought to market was made of pure, natural fibers—suede, tweed, leather, and silk. No polyester was allowed. Probably more than anything else since the leisure suit in the mid-1970s, Ralph Lauren fashions were responsible for consumers' obsession with fiber snobbery, and the radical downgrading of anything artificial to a status of low-class ignominy. He sold clothes guaranteed to wrinkle, to fade, and to quickly develop a patina of age and nobility.

Along with this new concept of marketing a whole lifestyle rather than merely articles of clothing, Ralph Lauren began creating some astonishing advertisements, every bit as tasteful as his clothes and his furnishings: pictures of incredibly handsome people in stunning environments (indoors and out) wearing (but never seeming to model) his fabulous clothes. The ads had no copy to read whatsoever, except the words "Ralph Lauren."

In 1985 he opened a flagship store in the former Rhinelander home at Seventy-second and Madison Avenue, one of New York's most famous old mansions. Writing in *Manhattan, Inc.* in 1989, James Kaplan called it "the citadel of dreams . . . a fantasyland of an advanced order." The Ralph Lauren store is to ordinary stores what Ralph Lauren ads are to other ads: too tasteful to have such impolite things as signs and cash registers and uniformed help. It is rather more like the imaginary mansion of some fantastic Anglo-American nobleman whose family has spent generations amassing the most incredible mahogany furniture, classic-looking (but never worn) clothes, finely cobbled shoes, stylish hats, and ever-so-elegant accessories, awesome oil portraits of hundreds of ancestors and bucolic paintings of contented animals grazing on the family fiefdom. And the great thing is that when you visit this impeccable, noble home, you can take away anything you want! Ralph Lauren said: "I can't tell you how many people walk into my store and say, 'I want the whole room.' They buy everything out of the room at once. The walls—they take everything. They'll take the salesman."

TIMOTHY LEARY

"Tune in, turn on, drop out," Timothy Leary told America in the mid-1960s, and an amazing number of people listened to him. Leary's antidote to all the problems of the world, personal as well as societal, was LSD. If everybody took it, he believed, good and groovy things would happen inside and outside their heads, and he predicted that by 1990 America would be "an LSD country." There were plenty of other messiahs delivering this message at the same time, including Allen Ginsberg and Ken Kesey, but Ginsberg and Kesey and their proto-hippie ilk were clearly outsiders, sacrilegious anarchists intent on upsetting the status quo. Leary, so it appeared at least on superficial examination, was the voice of reason, or at least he had passed as something like normal within the respectable establishment. And that is why he, more than anyone else, became the symbol of psychedelic mind-voyaging in those heady days when drugs were honestly believed by reasonable men and women to be capable of helping save the human race.

He first got noticed in 1962, when as a Harvard psychologist he and fellow professor Richard Alpert wrote an article for the *Bulletin of Atomic Scientists* warning that in the event of war, the Russians might lace the American water supply with LSD, wait for the entire population to get stoned, then seize control. In order to be prepared, the professors suggested, everyone ought to voluntarily take a dose of LSD and thereby get comfortable with their karma.

Leary and Alpert did their bit for American civil defense by organizing the International Foundation for Internal Freedom at Harvard, where they conducted a notorious series of unconventional experiments with various hallucinatory drugs, including psilocybin and LSD. Their laboratory at the Center of Personality Research consisted of a "psychodrama room" with mattresses on the floor, Hindu ragas on the stereo, flickering candles, and posters of Buddha. The Harvard *Crimson* reported plans for a graduate "Mushroom Seminar" in which students would get stoned once a month. In the fall of 1962, Leary gave doses of psilocybin to each pupil in his introductory clinical psychology course. Only one refused to do the assignment.

Leary's circle of LSD acolytes was inventoried by fellow faculty member Charles Slack, who attended one of his early "experiments in nonvisual perception" in 1961:

Aldous Huxley and Johara, a dancer—very exotic...jazz musicians, writers, artists, at least one big-name actor, a young lady reputed to be the richest girl in the world. The other half were just the opposite—as in "how the *other half* lives": a couple of ex-inhabitants of a well-known Massachusetts prison for young men, one person just out of a public mental hospital, several garden-variety beatniks, and a smattering of student types.

The men at the experiment, Professor Slack noted, wore "the kind of bathrobes worn by judo contestants." The lady of the house passed around a jar full of LSD that looked "not unlike a child's soap bubble kit." The next morning, when the experiment had ended, Slack, still reeling, told Leary, "That was really *something.*"

"Just a teenage fad," Leary joked back.

By 1963, LSD was enough of a curiosity that planners of the 1964 New York World's Fair considered (but rejected) including a mind-expansion pavilion. Some clinical psychologists had begun to laud its wondrous ability to short-cut analysis and lead patients to quick cures of complex mental disorders. In secret, the CIA was testing its powers for mind control and psychological warfare, but to most people who read about it in the popular press, LSD was little more than a chemical novelty. The more of it Timothy Leary took, however, the more he was convinced it was the true road to Truth and Joy.

He started a church, known as the League for Spiritual Discovery (note the initials), with branches in a basement ashram on Hudson Street in New York and a grand Victorian mansion in Millbrook, New York. The maxim of the church was "You have to be out of your mind to pray." Leary advocated one LSD trip per week and marijuana every day, the goal of which was heavenly revelation. "The sacraments marijuana and LSD should only be used by initiates and priests of our religion and used only in shrines," he declared. "We consider our re-

ligion to be highly orthodox. Our temple is the human body." He told *Look*, "I am convinced that the present generation of young, under 25, Americans is the . . . holiest generation since mankind began."

Few Bible-thumping evangelists were ever as convinced of their mission as was Leary when he began campaigning on behalf of LSD. In the summer of '66, the League for Spiritual Discovery placed advertisements in the *East Village Other:*

ANNOUNCING PSYCHEDELIC RELIGIOUS CELEBRATIONS . . . Mythic voyages through seven levels of consciousness, guided by the great world religious dramas, employing sermon, lecture, prayer, mediamix, symbol-overload, sensory meditation, gesture, pantomime, light sculpture, sound, noise and music. (Death and rebirth of Jesus Christ, illumination of the Buddha, the last trip of Lao Tse, Bhagavad-gita, Eleusinian Mysteries, et al.)

Aspirants were invited to write to Timothy Leary's place in Millbrook for a full catalogue description of the divine experience that awaited them. And in order to make sure more people got holy, Leary hit the road with his message, lecturing at colleges, on a stage surrounded by flickering candles, wearing white pajamas and chanting "om."

Hippies on the West Coast were proclaiming the joys of LSD, too, but there was a fundamental difference about the way they went about it. The trippers of Haight-Ashbury, as personified by Ken Kesey and his Merry Pranksters, called LSD "acid" and weren't into the old-fashioned religioso embellishments with which Leary draped the LSD experience. *Ramparts* magazine (published in San Francisco) described the contrast this way: "The leaders of the booming psychedelic bohemia in the seminal city of San Francisco are their own men. . . . [Allen] Ginsberg and Leary may be Pied Pipers, but they are largely playing old tunes. The young men who make the new scene accept Ginsberg as a revered observer from the elder generation; Leary they abide as an Elmer Gantry on their side, to be used for proselytizing purposes only."

For many disaffected citizens who craved to tune in, turn on, and drop out, but weren't quite ready to leave *everything* behind, Dr. Leary (Ph.D., University of California) had the proper credentials: affiliation with Harvard (so much the better that he had been dismissed in April 1963, for dilating student brains with psilocybin) and a Brooks Brothers suit (worn with J. Press tie and Egyptian mandala). This Hippie Pope, as he was labeled in *The Hippy's Handbook* "Who's Who," was no spaced-out loony freak with war paint on his face and bells on his toes like the blown-mind be-in trippers of the West. Leary granted intelligent interviews to all the magazines, pleading the

seriousness of his quest for inner knowledge and its venerable precedents in all the finest religions. The Boston-based *Avatar* showed him on its cover wearing a crown of thorns. Nonetheless, despite the underlying seriousness of his intent, Leary did manage to punctuate nearly all of his pontification with a sense of play and irony. "I have never felt any rancor against Harvard," he once said about his firing. "It is the mainline of American transcendental thinking."

After the Age of Aquarius came to an end, Timothy Leary had a lot of trouble with the law (mostly for breaking out of jail, where he was incarcerated on drug charges) and campaigned (unsuccessfully) for President of the United States. Recently he wrote an autobiography (*Flashback*) and has toured college campuses performing a point-counterpoint show with Watergate felon G. Gordon Liddy.

LEVITTOWN

B etween 1947 and 1951, over seventeen thousand identical houses were built in rows on Long Island land that used to be potato farms. They were constructed using assembly-line techniques, with teams of mostly unskilled laborers moving from house to house putting up prefabricated parts. As many as 150 were finished in a day, and within hours of the last workmen moving on to their next house a family took up residence in the just-completed one. On weekends, mile-long lines of cars crept along the newly paved roads and through muddy fields to gape at this wondrous new place, which was named Levittown, after its

builder, William J. Levitt, who liked to call his company the "General Motors of the housing industry."

William Levitt, described in a 1950 *Time* profile titled "For Sale: A New Way of Life" as a "cocky, rambunctious hustler" with a voice hoarse from three packs of cigarettes a day, began planning his community while serving with the Seabees in World War II. He had been in the construction business with his father and brother since the thirties, and they had already created one planned community of two hundred houses, called Strathmore-at-Manhasset, in 1934, and another one, which failed, in Virginia in

1943. During the war Levitt started buying up Long Island potato farms for as little as $225 per acre, anticipating the huge housing needs of GIs when they began returning home ready to start families. "Any fool can build homes," he told the *Christian Science Monitor*. "What counts is how many you can sell for how little." He sold plenty, cheap; and Levittown became an example that changed the landscape from coast to coast. It was not the first suburb, but it was the first mass-produced one, and its name has become a symbol—for better and for worse—of the way most middle-class Americans like to live.

Levittown's Cape Cod–style, single-family houses sold for $6,990—no money down and $65 per month—and they provided their occupants with a taste of luxury heretofore reserved for rich people. For returning veterans, many of whom had been forced to live in "garages, coal sheds, chicken coops, barns, tool sheds, granaries,

and smoke houses" (according to a Senate committee report at the time), these homes were the American dream come true. Each one was equipped with a washer and a dryer, the latest kitchen appliances, and a television set. There were newly planted trees in the yard, and public swimming pools and shopping centers for neighbors to share. The *New York Times* called the new householders "suburbia's V.I.P.'s," and said that among the things they enjoyed about their new life were "the baronial splendor of going upstairs to bed and coming downstairs to breakfast," "going out and clipping the grass, listening to the birds," and "being able to throw the kids out in the back yard and not having to worry about them." Many Americans moved to suburbia because it was supposed to be a good place to raise children, and at Levittown there were parks and baseball diamonds, and so many newborn baby boomers that for years in the fifties, pregnancy was commonly known as the "Levittown look."

For its occupants, Levittown may have been—in one ex-GI's words—"like being emancipated," but pained social critics demurred. They slapped the people who lived there with just about the meanest label anyone could apply in the fifties: They were conformists. They spent their energy keeping up appearances (Levittown rules demanded the lawn be mowed once each week; wash could not be hung out to dry on weekends or holidays), and there were no community cultural activities whatsoever. Long Island's "horsy set," according to *Time*, "watched aghast as the Levitt houses have marched towards their sacrosanct land of polo, privet, and croquet." John Keats's book *The Crack in the Picture Window*, written in 1957, told about a couple named John and Mary Drone, citizens of a Levittown-like development, who are driven insane by the tedium of their tasteless lives.

"Even while you read this," Keats warned readers, "miles of identical boxes are spreading like gangrene." Six years later folksinger Malvina Reynolds wrote a song called "Little Boxes" about houses that all look the same and are all "made out of ticky tacky."

After visiting Levitt's second Levittown, in Pennsylvania, in 1952, architecture critic Lewis Mumford complained about the "multitude of uniform, unidentifiable houses, lined up inflexibly at uniform distances, on uniform roads, in a treeless communal waste, inhabited by people of the same class, the same income, the same age group, witnessing the same television performances, eating the same tasteless pre-fabricated foods from the same freezers, conforming in every outward and inward respect to a common mold." It was Mumford who made the famous prediction that Levittown, and all developments like it, would be the "slums of the future." Two years later Levitt said that he had made efforts to keep Levittown from turning into a slum by not selling any of his houses to people of color. "If we sell one house to a Negro family," he was quoted in the *Saturday Evening Post*, "then ninety to ninety-five percent of our white customers will not buy into the com-munity." He was abetted in this policy by the Federal Housing Administration, which declared integrated areas poor financial risks and therefore ineligible for government-guaranteed mortgages.

Far from turning into an instant slum, Levittown has become valuable real estate, with homes that originally went for under seven thousand dollars now worth a quarter-million. When Ron Rosenbaum visited in 1983 for an issue of *Esquire* about fifty people who made a difference in the way Americans live (his subject was William J. Levitt), he noted that virtually every family had individualized its home by adding a garage, a terrace, extra rooms, a new facade, dormers, a roof, a breezeway. He wrote that a "nonstop remodeling craze has been a peculiarly Levittown phenomenon from the beginning," and concluded that the planned development was "an almost perfect laboratory demonstration of the inexorable workings of the American individualist impulse." In 1987, to celebrate the beginning of their town's fifth decade, nearly all of them—some sixty thousand strong—turned out to honor William J. Levitt with a parade along streets now lined with lush, forty-year-old shade trees.

JERRY LEWIS

What do people love about American pop culture? It is fun, bright, irreverent, irrepressible, unabashedly sentimental, sometimes brilliant, and almost always surprising. What do people dislike about American pop culture? It is loud, lowbrow, blasphemous, mawkish, sancti-monious, sometimes obscene, at times predictable, and almost always impolite. Jerry Lewis is all of the above.

Fans around the world consider him one of this country's greatest talents. There are millions of Americans who adore him, too, but the chances are that if you are reading

this book without moving your lips, you are not one of them. Jerry is a people's hero, an everyman (or every*boy*) in his movies, and a champion of the downtrodden on his annual Labor Day Telethon. He has railed against the highbrow critics who have condemned him as tasteless, maudlin, and insincere: "They like to denounce things, because if they didn't they'd be part of the masses that like it." But it is impossible not to believe that Jerry Lewis has drawn strength from his enemies. From the snobs who turned up their noses at his vaudeville act in 1950 to film critics who damned him in the 1960s to the hecklers with muscular dystrophy who have recently griped that they don't want his patronizing charity, Jerry's adversaries always seem to be the exceptions who prove the rule that there are millions more who venerate him. When you see him now in public, Jerry Lewis is a man who visibly basks in the love of his people, just as he did forty years ago.

Some of Jerry Lewis's accomplishments and honors are indisputable. As a filmmaker he helped design and pioneered the use of the portable Nagra tape recorder, facilitating location sound recording (now an indispensable tool of the trade); he was the first director to use video instant replay to immediately check a scene (now standard procedure), a technique he developed when he was directing himself and needed to critique his own acting; and he shares credit with French filmmaker Jacques Tati as a pioneer in creating comic bits around the syncopation of sound and image (he moves his mouth and musical notes come out; he devised noises to convey the sense of being waterlogged). Furthermore (and this is the kind of thing that used to gall his American critics to distraction), he and Alfred Hitchcock are the only Hollywood filmmakers ever to receive the French Legion of Merit —an award he shares with Louis Pasteur, Albert Schweitzer, and Emile Zola.

About this French thing: They especially love Jerry Lewis, not only because he is so American (loud, brash, ridiculous, rude, and inventive) but also because he is—or, actually, *was*, now that he hasn't directed a feature film in a while—one of the rare heirs to the tradition of the cinema's great silent clowns. When Jean-Luc Godard, writing in *Cahiers du Cinema* in the 1960s, proclaimed him even better than Chaplin and Keaton, it wasn't only for literary effect. He really believed that Jerry had improved upon their tradition of sight gags and had continued their antielitist democratic social perspective (particularly Chaplin's).

From the French point of view, Jerry Lewis's unruly and self-pitying screen image is every bit as universal and evocative of the human condition as the Tramp and the Great Stone Face, but with the addition not only of sound and color (both used to remarkable effect in his movies) but of the self-awareness Jerry has as a second-generation Hollywood artist. Writing in his book *The Total Film-Maker* (1971), Lewis made these observations about his strategy and its inspiration:

> Chaplin was both the *shlemiel* and the *shlimazel.* He was the guy who spilled the drinks—the shlemiel—and the guy who had the drinks spilled on him—the

shlimazel. He also played a combination of shlemiel-shlimazel [who] does it to himself. My Idiot character plays both the shlemiel and the shlimazel, and at times the inter-mix. I'm always conscious of the three factors—done to, doing to self, and doing to someone else by accident or design—while playing him.

It should be no big surprise, considering the hypersensitivity with which Jerry Lewis has endowed his screen persona, or as he calls him, the Idiot, that the one property he always wanted to buy, so he could direct it and star in it, was J. D. Salinger's *The Catcher in the Rye.*

Jerry may have seen himself as—in his words—"the Jewish Holden Caulfield," but his circumstances were considerably less prosaic when he burst into the American consciousness as the funny half of Martin and Lewis, an act he formed with singer Dean Martin in Atlantic City in 1946. They were polar opposites who mostly seemed to hate each other: Dean was cool, mellow, and romantic; Jerry bubbled over with ambition and impudence, described by Michael Angeli in *Esquire* as "a kid with an air-raid siren for a voice and a head like a porcupine stuck on a baton." The chemistry was dynamite, and within a few years they were far and away the most popular act in American show business—Dean crooning and making time with ladies, Jerry mugging and yelling and acting like an imbecile. They made sixteen movies together, including Frank Tashlin's masterful *Hollywood or Bust* (1956), which captured the seething tension between the two stars in aching detail. Jerry's yearning to break out of his role as the funny half of the duo (and Dean's exasperation at being Jerry's straight man) led to a much-publicized and bitter separation in 1956, after which Jerry starred as a bathetic misfit antihero in some very funny

Tashlin movies, including *It's Only Money* (1962), *Who's Minding the Store?* (1963) and *The Disorderly Orderly* (1964).

The case for Jerry as a genius is based mostly on the comedies he directed as well as starred in during the early 1960s. Robert Benayoun, a French film critic, described the elements of his art as "the magisterial playfulness of the visual element in his films; the emotional manner of handling actors (worthy of Renoir, Kazan, or Visconti); and the *technical* sensuality that one scarcely finds in mainstream American cinema, but which he has adopted with freshness and incomparable purity."

This is not the place to analyze the "technical sensuality" of Jerry Lewis movies. If you want evidence of it, look at the Jekyll-Hyde transformation scenes in *The Nutty Professor* (1963) or the sumptuous use of the spectacular boardinghouse set in *The Ladies' Man* (1961). Such undeniably impressive technical tours de force have never been the issue that made Jerry Lewis movies controversial. The sticky point is their common theme—the fundamental and endlessly fascinating (to Jerry Lewis) question: Who really is Jerry Lewis? In the autobiographical show-business parable *The Patsy* (1964), he is a sweet, innocent, and immensely talented guy victimized by Hollywood jackals; in *The Family Jewels* (1965), he is half a dozen enigmatic characters, including an emotionally spongy schlep and a malevolent clown; and in his most audacious movie, *The Nutty Professor*, he has a personality that bounces unpredictably from meek, mousy chemistry professor to unctuous lounge lizard.

What is fascinating about *The Nutty Professor* is that its comic (and dramatic) punch comes from the fact that the personality changes from nebbish to swinger are induced by a potion to which the tormented hero becomes addicted and over which he loses control, allowing the embarrassing "Professor Kelp" to intrude on the suave "Buddy Love" at the most awkward moments. And what is especially provocative about this battle between the two personalities is that, grotesque as they both are, each is clearly a projection of the Jerry Lewis that all of us have come to know and love and/or loathe in his role outside the cinema as host of the yearly telethon, as Las Vegas casino entertainer, and as an unavoidable, all-around show-business Prometheus.

Jerry Lewis is not really controversial anymore, although the *National Enquirer* has beat its drums about episodes in which he allegedly assaulted a crippled midget (he grabbed the guy's lapels) and in which he was going to be kicked off the telethon (he was not); and the *Star* has exposed his "sexcapades" with various starlets. Such prattle notwithstanding, in recent years more and more tastemakers, even in America, have begun to think about Jerry Lewis as—if not a genius—then certainly an important person. (We recently saw a show devoted to his *art* on educational television.) This may be due to the fact that in the last several years he hasn't been nearly as offensive or outrageous as he was in the 1950s, and 1960s, and 1970s. No doubt, he has mellowed. He received universally glowing notices for his low-key dramatic performance in Martin Scorsese's sublime *The King of Comedy* (1983) as well as his role in a five-episode series of the TV show "Wiseguy"; and even the annual Labor Day Telethon on behalf of the Muscular Dystrophy Association has become a practically dignified affair.

In older days (before Jerry's open-heart surgery in 1983, and until he kicked a life-threatening Percodan habit in 1979), the telethon was always one of television's most agonizing events, because it was unscripted, long, and frightfully unpredictable.

It could be at once painful and inspiring to watch—so sincere, so truly sad, so overwrought, and such a strange combination of money lust, charity, and tragedy that it was hypnotic. On live TV, you shared the gut-wrenching moments as real cripples paraded forth and begged, and Wayne Newton and Lola Falana sang, and all of Jerry's friends from show business gave testimony to his devotion to the cause. It was awful, and it was righteous, as in 1973 when Jerry, holding a suffering child in his arms, explained to his audience, "God goofed, and it's up to us to correct His mistakes." In recent years, however, more and more of the telethon has been devoted to film clips expertly produced to tug at heartstrings with all the strength of a good television commercial, but with little of the raw power of live people struggling to express themselves. Instead of Jerry mugging and screaming and sweating and pouting and smoking, the typical telethon image is now of polite men in suits from big corporations handing Jerry multimillion-dollar checks. Jerry hardly ever loses his composure. He doesn't have any tantrums or berate the audience for not giving enough money, and he never walks and talks like a spastic the way he used to. Also, he allows himself enough rest so he doesn't seem ready to collapse at any moment—always one of the old telethons' greatest sources of suspense.

Like the telethon, Jerry Lewis has changed. You cannot help feeling happy for him as a man, because he seems to have found peace and is no longer so ravenously hungry for attention. But, to be honest, we miss the insanity. Once known as "the Kid," with all the inspired, obnoxious, unconstrained joie de vivre of a divine idiot who knew no limits of taste or talent in his pursuit of an audience's love, Jerry Lewis has become a dignitary: the grand old man of American show business.

"LIFESTYLES OF THE RICH AND FAMOUS"

Test your knowledge of rich and famous people with this quiz, which consists of questions that television personality Robin Leach said he was most frequently asked during the mid-1980s:

1. Whose is the most lavish, most gadget-filled yacht of them all?
2. How does the world's richest man make his money?
3. What's the price tag on the poshest cruise of them all?
4. What's the ultimate shopping spree of the rich and famous?

The answers to these questions, and thousands more like them, can be found on television's "Lifestyles of the Rich and Famous," a show that first went on the air in 1983, into syndication the next year, onto the ABC network in 1986, and, amazingly, is still being broadcast, sometimes more than once a day, in many cities across America. There isn't another television program or cultural artifact of any kind (with the possible exception of one of Nancy Reagan's borrowed designer gowns) that so totally expresses the infatuation with money and celebrity that has become the signature of a voluptuary decade when living high on the hog was in style.

Every episode of "Lifestyles of the Rich and Famous" takes the form of a travelogue, usually with plenty of scenic vistas and aerial photography to introduce the mansion, castle, or villa of each of that show's three or four celebrities and megamillionaires. As dreamy go-go music provides a background serenade, the camera swoops among a famous person's formal

Robin Leach

gardens or garage full of exotic cars, or around the person sipping from a glass of champagne while relaxing in a hot tub, while narrator Robin Leach (or one of his lesser-known comrades-in-awe) fills in viewers about the extent of the famous person's wealth and renown. Sometimes there are humble people who were born poor and got rich (Tom Jones, Loretta Lynn, Rick James); occasionally there are famous people who don't live very exorbitantly (Pam Dawber, Dorothy Hamill, Linda Blair); but "Lifestyles" has always excelled at profiling high-living types who have cultivated their spending habits over a lifetime, or possibly even for generations. Malcolm Forbes, King Hussein of Jordan, and the Maharajah of Jaipur (known to his friends as "Bubbles") have been special favorites because of their unstinting profligacy.

It's with the super-rich that Robin Leach does what he does best, which is to effervesce with wonder. A former celebrity columnist for the *Star*, he served as roving show-biz and society reporter for "Entertainment Tonight," and began "Lifestyles of the Rich and Famous" as a two-hour special in August 1983. The time was right—big spending was in fashion—and when "Lifestyles" debuted as a series, it was a hit overnight...and Robin Leach became an instant icon of conspicuous consumption, as well as an inspiration for parody by countless comedians. Always sounding slightly out of breath and a little bit too close to the microphone, Leach ejaculates superlatives with a shrill twang, falling into dizzying paroxysms of admiration as he itemizes excess, luxury, and the astonishing price tags of things jet-setters own. His booming voice and relentless enthusiasm, which are reminiscent of those of a carnival barker luring customers with the amazing things they are about to see, are the soul of the show, every bit as much as its filthy-rich subjects. In fact, Leach's ardor is frequently so ridiculously intense that it is possible to feel the throb of irony as he goes gaga over such wonders as Liberace's $200,000 tea set (once owned by Napoleon), Zsa Zsa's closets full of Giorgio gowns, or Donald Trump's impeccably waxed personal underground bowling alley.

The basic formula of "Lifestyles" was to visit celebrities at home, a concept pioneered by "Person to Person," which Edward R. Murrow hosted on CBS-TV from 1953 to 1960. Murrow generally liked to have interesting discussions with his guests, who although always famous were sometimes not rich, and the show-and-tell portion of the program, during which they allowed Mr. Murrow to see some of the unusual things in their homes, was hampered by then-cumbersome television lighting and camera equipment. Many "Lifestyles" episodes have no intelligent discussions whatsoever: They are nothing *but* show-and-tell, and Leach's lithe modern cameras have allowed viewers to see everything, including Englebert Humperdinck's heart-shaped swimming pool (in the Beverly Hills home once owned by Jayne Mansfield), Bob Guccione's bathtub (over which hangs an original painting by Picasso), Hugh Hefner's bedroom, and the state-of-the-art home gym where Cher keeps in shape.

Sometimes "Lifestyles" goes places with people, in a segment known as "Getaways," which spun off into a whole other show, titled "Runaway with the Rich and Famous," in 1987. For these on-the-road adventures, the cameras follow a famous person on vacation, accompanied by Robin Leach, or at least by Leach's voice, so viewers can marvel at luxuries to be found in the playgrounds of the world. Morgan Fairchild took the Orient Express to Venice and exclaimed, "The really beautiful thing about a city like this is that you realize the insignificance of any one life in terms of world history!" Lana Turner went to Egypt, where she said "I believe in reincarnation" from the top of her camel. Brooke Shields "watched in horror and fascination as hungry lions...devoured hunks of freshly slaughtered meat" in Kenya. Valerie Perrine went hot-air ballooning in champagne country, and although she didn't talk much, she looked just great eating Moët & Chandon grapes. And when the cameras went to the beaches of Rio de Janeiro (without a celebrity, just to look around), Robin Leach nearly busted a gut extolling what he called "the tantalizing *tonga*, a string bikini so tiny it's called 'El Band-Aid'!"

One of the most memorable rich and famous people that Robin Leach visited was the Pope. John Paul II did not personally escort the "Lifestyles" cameras around the Vatican, but Robin Leach did get a picture of His Holiness greeting "Dynasty" star Linda Evans, and also had a chance to admire the papal art collection, especially the nude classical statues in the Belvedere Pavilion. After surveying the treasures, Leach finally had to conclude that the Pope's things were so fantastically rare and valuable that he couldn't even put a price tag on them. Another unforgettable episode showed Donna Mills of "Knots Landing" covered with mud at the Stresa spa, which Robin Leach clued viewers was the Italian fountain of youth and "the secret of the rich and famous."

Whatever the particulars of any week's journey through "the twenty-four-karat corridors of success" or its quest to explore "fortune, the final frontier," the show always ends with scenes of utmost beauty (sunsets) and/or sybaritism (swank yachts, casinos) and Robin Leach's signature farewell, the long form of which goes as follows: "Remember, you too can be rich and famous and live life to the hilt, fulfilling your champagne wishes and caviar dreams." (The usual abbreviation was merely "Champagne wishes and caviar dreams.")

Today, "Lifestyles" seems nostalgic, not to mention politically incorrect and perhaps even worn-out—a reminder of the glittering materialistic delirium of the haute 1980s, which are now commonly condemned as an elitist era. But Robin Leach didn't see himself and his show as the least bit elitist. In fact, he considered the success of "Lifestyles of the Rich and Famous" to be a truly democratic event, and a demonstration of his own trickle-down theory of television programming. In the introduction to the *Lifestyles of the Rich and Famous* book (1986), which featured gold-embossed type across a royal red front, he wrote: "We like to think we've pioneered a new form in television. Before we came along, the rewards of hard work and good fortune were seen and appreciated by only a precious few. Now we've brought them out—gloriously— into the open and everyone can share a

taste of what this richly endowed planet has to offer and what dreams money can buy."

The answers to Robin Leach's "Lifestyles" quiz, by the way, are:

1. Movie producer Robert Stigwood's 280-foot yacht, the *Jezebel*, with wall-to-wall silk carpeting, held top honors as the most lavish yacht until Adnan Khashoggi, the Saudi arms dealer, built one two feet longer in 1980. Khashoggi announced plans to build one with accommodations for his own seven-passenger submarine, his-and-her helicopter pads, four Rolls-Royces, and a battery of surface-to-air missiles, but he didn't; and his big boat eventually went to Donald Trump (see p. 529) in 1987—for $29 million, plus about $8.5 million for incidental repairs and remodeling.

2. The Sultan of Brunei became the world's richest man by appropriating the bulk of his country's oil and gas income.

3. $325,000 buys the ultra-luxury suite on a ninety-five-day around-the-world cruise on the *QE II*.

4. Rodeo Drive in Beverly Hills is where "the world's most expensive boutiques line the exclusive blocks of a billionaire's bazaar where stars and moguls, movie producers and princes come to be seen and pay the premium prices for prestige designer labels."

"LOUIE LOUIE"

"Louie Louie" has been recorded by nearly one thousand performers and has sold an estimated quarter-billion copies in the last thirty years. Since it was waxed by an obscure Portland, Oregon band called the Kingsmen in 1963, it has set the beat for untold numbers of wild parties and has become the definitive "frat rock" tune—suitable for dancing all night, drinking beer and puking, and jumping up and down in conga lines or lacing trees with rolls of toilet paper. No other song in rock history has become so famous for its power to loosen inhibitions.

Aside from its eminently danceable 1-2-3, 1-2, 1-2-3, 1-2 three-chord progression, "Louie Louie" was a landmark when it first got popular because people thought it was dirty. So many listeners were convinced that the raggedy, indistinct lyrics included the line "I'll tell her I'll never lay her again," or possibly "Every night at ten I lay her again," and another line that could be heard as "I got my boner high in her hair," that late in 1963 the FCC instituted an official investigation, playing the song at various speeds and interrogating its writer as well as the lead singer of the Kingsmen, finally announcing that no matter how hard it was listened to, "we found the record to be unintelligible." Nonetheless, the investigation sparked even greater curiosity about "Louie Louie," and millions of people bought it because they were convinced they did hear dirty words when they played it.

Silly as all the uproar was, the notoriety of "Louie Louie" was a significant moment in cultural history. Since its start in the 1950s, rock and roll had been seen by friend and foe alike as a new way of sharing feelings among the burgeoning ranks of baby boomers now growing into their teens. But music's power to actually contain forbidden messages—secret messages, no less!—took that premise one step further. Kids positively relished the idea that if they listened hard enough, they could share in the taboo meaning of "Louie Louie": hearing those dirty words evoked a feeling of solidarity with other kids who were listening. And similarly, many of rock and roll's enemies were eager to hear evidence of the devil's voice lurking in this disruptive music. The wicked reputation of "Louie Louie" ensured its standing as the first clear sign that rock and roll was on its way to becoming counterculture code, a nearly instantaneous means of tribal communication among those who were in the groove and outside the adult mainstream. Later in the decade, recordings by the Beatles, the Stones, and Country Joe and the Fish consciously loaded songs with esoteric messages, usually about sex and drugs, and as recently as 1991 Van Halen produced a number-one album titled *For Unlawful Carnal Knowledge* (wow, note the naughty acronym!). But the elevation of "Louie Louie" to cult status as a trove of off-color mischief was strictly accidental.

The original recording of the song, by its author, Richard Berry, as the B side of "You Are My Sunshine" in 1956, was smooth, slow moving, and totally audible, similar to Chuck (no relation to Richard) Berry's "Havana Moon," which was currently popular. Richard Berry's inspiration happened one night in 1955 when he was in his dressing room at the Harmony Club Ballroom in Anaheim, California, waiting to go on stage to sing with the Rhythm Rockers. The Rockers were doing an instrumental with conga drums and a Latin beat, and Berry was moved to write a song with a Caribbean feeling. The lyrics just came to him, and because he had nothing to write on, he inscribed them on a length of toilet paper. Louie was a guy the singer was talking to, telling about the girl he longs to see. These are the actual, original words, as told to Bob Greene, who interviewed Richard Berry for a 1988 article in *Esquire* magazine:

> Louie Louie, me gotta go
> Louie Louie, me gotta go
>
> Fine little girl she waits for me
> Me catch the ship for cross the sea
> Me sail the ship all alone
> Me never think me make it home
>
> Louie Louie, me gotta go
> Louie Louie, me gotta go
>
> Three nights and days me sail the sea
> Me think of girl constantly
> On the ship I dream she there
> I smell the rose in her hair
>
> Louie Louie, me gotta go
> Louie Louie, me gotta go
>
> Me see Jamaica moon above
> It won't be long, me see my love
> I take her in my arms and then
> Me tell her I never leave again
>
> Louie Louie, me gotta go
> Louie Louie, me gotta go

Berry sold the rights to "Louie Louie," along with four other songs he wrote, in 1957 for $750.

As it is painstakingly detailed in the liner notes of Rhino Records' *Best of Louie Louie* (an album consisting of nothing but ten versions of the song, performed by groups ranging from the Rice University Marching Owl Band to punk rockers Black Flag), the important steps in the transition of the song from a laid-back calypso love chant to the all-American beer-bash standard were these:

- In 1961 in Seattle, a singer named Rockin' Robin Roberts discovered Richard Berry's "You Are My Sunshine" in the bargain bin of a record store. With a group called the Wailers, he recorded "Louie Louie," but with an urgent wail to the words that made them sound more like rock and roll than Caribbean blues.
- In 1962, the Wailers' "Louie Louie" became a hit in the Pacific Northwest, but failed to break into the national Hot 100.
- Late in 1962 in Portland, the Kingsmen were playing a gig with another local dance band, Paul Revere and the Raiders. During a break, both groups watched in awe as Portland kids gathered around a jukebox and danced to the Wailers' "Louie Louie"; and both groups vowed to add it to their repertoire. When the Kingsmen's lead singer, Jack Ely, taught the song to the group, he forgot the original 1-2-3-4, 1-2 progression and accidentally sped things up.
- In May 1963 the Kingsmen played their version of "Louie Louie" for forty-five minutes straight at a dance: The audience went wild and begged for more.
- The day after the astounding forty-five-minute case of mass hypnosis, the Kingsmen paid fifty dollars for two hours of studio time to record "Louie Louie." The recording facility was primitive, and Jack Ely had to yell the words up towards a microphone dangling from a high ceiling, which made the song almost unintelligible. (The next day, Paul Revere and the Raiders went into the same studio and recorded their own "Louie Louie.")
- Arnie "Woo-Woo" Ginsberg of Boston's WBZ got a copy of the song and began playing it frequently. Listeners wanted to know who the Kingsmen were. Other deejays in the Northeast, thinking they were a New York rhythm group, began playing it, too.
- In September 1963 the Kingsmen's "Louie Louie" broke onto *Billboard*'s Hot 100 chart, at ninety-four. By this time, however, Jack Ely had left the band. Ely went on to

record his own "Love That Louie," which went nowhere.

- Goosed up the charts by the FCC investigation, the Kingsmen's "Louie Louie" rose into the top twenty, where it stayed four months, then continued for years as a party standard, selling well over ten million copies. "Does anyone have recollection of a school dance in the 1960s that *didn't* feature a version of 'Louie Louie'?" asked Doc Pelzell, who wrote the liner notes to Rhino's album.
- In 1978 "Louie Louie" was introduced to a whole new generation of party animals when it was used as the theme song of the toga party scene in the movie *Animal House.*
- In 1980, KPFK in Los Angeles began weekly "Battle of the 'Louie Louie'" contests, for which deejays would play several versions and listeners would phone in to vote for their favorite.
- In 1981 KFJC of Los Altos Hills, California, broadcast thirty-three versions of "Louie Louie" in a row, lasting about ninety minutes. Two years later, on August 19, 1983, they aired a marathon program called "Maximum 'Louie Louie'": three hundred different recorded versions of the song, plus several live bands' performances and a guest appearance by Richard Berry, who sang the song the original, slow and mellow way.

Although it is probably the most popular rock-and-roll song in history, "Louie Louie" tends to annoy serious critics of rock and roll, who like to think of rock as important. The reason is simple: "Louie Louie" doesn't sound important. It sounds cheap and tinny, and if you do manage to make sense of the indistinctly shouted words, they aren't very profound. As a recording it is generally dismissed, in the words of *Rock of Ages: The Rolling Stone History of Rock and Roll,* as "heavy-footed." Traditional rock history gives 1963 to the early Beatles, prime Motown, surf music, and Phil Spector, and in this noble company "Louie Louie" is only an anomaly. Despite such lack of musicological significance, it was, and continues to be, a pop-culture phenomenon unlike any other song.

LUNCH BOXES

E very hero and demigod of preteens in the fifties and sixties was emblazoned on a lunch box. From Howdy Doody through the Beatles and James Bond to the Brady Bunch, from cowpokes to astronauts, they all got carried to school with their faces and their glory lithographed on metal or heat-embossed into vinyl. Well over a hundred million lunch boxes were sold between 1950 and 1970—one and a half for every baby boom child; and according to Scott Bruce, editor of the *Hot Boxing* newsletter and author of the definitive book *Lunch Box,* they were "as essential as a rifle had been to early pioneers—a shield against an uncertain future, a badge of membership, a friend."

The image of Mickey Mouse had been on lunch boxes since 1935, and Mr. Bruce's book describes some other early theme

lunch boxes as "resembling pressed ham cans [or] glorified tobacco tins"; but most kids who carried their lunch to school before 1950 did so either in a rumpled paper bag or a plain tin box indistinguishable from the kind used by their dads. Hopalong Cassidy changed all that. In 1950, Aladdin Industries of Nashville put a decal of Hoppy crouching among cactuses in the desert, with both six guns raised and ready for action, onto the side of an ordinary red lunch box, and a picture of him with his horse onto a vacuum bottle to be carried inside. The Hoppy kit sold six hundred thousand copies in a year. Roy Rogers was jealous, and when Aladdin refused to put him on a lunch box ("One cowboy is enough," they said), he went to American Thermos in Connecticut; in 1953 the Roy Rogers and Dale Evans lunch box was introduced. It was new and improved—no mere box with a decal on the side. Roy, riding Trigger, and Dale, waving to him from beneath the gate of the Double R Bar Ranch, and Bullet the dog, running merrily along, had all been lithographed onto the steel in an edge-to-edge scene with a wood-grain, consolelike border that foreshadowed Swanson's TV dinner box, introduced in 1954. Two and a half million of these kits sold the first year, and Aladdin and American Thermos (later known as KST) found themselves waging a lunch box war (also involving some lesser

manufacturers, all of whom are known in the trade as "boxmen") to get licensing rights to every popular movie and TV character.

The rivalry among boxmen was fierce. "They hated our guts and we hated theirs," said a KST spokesman about Aladdin, which was offered—but didn't buy—the rights to Barbie and Peanuts in the sixties, because they thought both of them too adult. On the other hand, KST passed on Batman—a big mistake. As for the smaller manufacturers, they didn't have a chance against the free promotion kits and store displays offered by the big boys. In the aisles of supermarkets, where most lunch boxes were sold, the Aladdin or KST display came to be known among store managers as "the whine sign" because it was where children would mewl until their mothers bought them the box they wanted.

Improvements in lunch box design included 3-D characters stamped into the metal; box sides (known as the waist) decorated with images of tooled leather, bandoliers, etc.; dome-topped boxes (perfect for depicting barns, covered wagons, and treasure chests); vinyl boxes ("a piece of shower curtain plastic heat-sealed over cardboard," according to KST); and long-handled Brunch Bags in 1962, which were sold with such "sophisticated" characters on them as the Beatles and the Flying Nun. In the late sixties, due to complaints from teachers that metal boxes were too noisy and, worse, heavy enough to be used as a dangerous weapon, many boxmen began phasing out metal in favor of (cheaper) injection-molded plastic. Florida, and then several other states, actually banned the sale of metal boxes. "Lunch box manufacturers," Scott Bruce writes, "wept into their hands."

Today, lunch boxes are coveted by collectors, with the most valued being those made of metal and vinyl. Highest on the list of desirables are the ones without a known surviving example. They include a 1961 vinyl "Ballet" box by Universal and two 1959 vinyl "Lunch 'n Munch" boxes by American Thermos, one with a river raft theme, the other showing outer space.

Among the less valuable lunch boxes is a metal one designed by Andy Warhol. It is shaped like a loaf of bread with a Campbell's soup can vacuum bottle inside, and it was a flop when it was introduced in 1968. According to Scott Bruce, "Kids thought the whole idea dumb."

MAD

What rock and roll did for the bodies of the baby boom, *Mad* magazine did for our minds. It was cultural liberation in the form of parody, and for many who grew up reading it, *Mad* was every bit as titillating and taboo as *Playboy* or Elvis Presley's pelvis. It was a monthly dose of blasphemy and disrespect that was the polar opposite of the Walt Disney pieties well-behaved children were supposed to be ingurgitating. And make no mistake, it was kids who composed most of the *Mad* readership: kids who were beginning to feel rebellious; not yet empowered, but on their way to creating a serious generation gap. "If you were growing up lonely and isolated in a small town, *Mad* was a revelation," recalled "Head Comix" artist R. Crumb. "Nothing I read anywhere else suggested there was any absurdity in the culture. *Mad* was like a shock, breaking you out."

It began publication in 1952, looking like a horror comic book, with a cover that advertised "Tales Calculated to Drive You MAD" and the subtitle "Humor in a Jugular Vein." It contained four features, each a parody of a comic book. The cover showed a couple cowering in the dungeon.

"That thing, that slithering blob coming towards us!" screams the man.

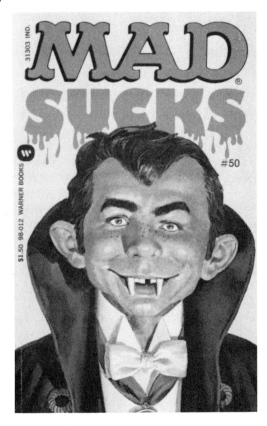

"What is it?" screams the woman.

And piping up from the ground, a finger digging deep into one nostril, their gnome-like child delivers the answer: "It's Melvin!"

Of such wisenheimer non sequiturs and deflated expectations was *Mad* made. Eventually, each issue contained well over a dozen different features: essays, comic-book and TV and movie parodies, sheet-music spoofs, fold-ins (as opposed to *Playboy*'s expanding centerfold), articles pretending to advise readers how to improve their lives. Nothing was ever serious, and nothing was sacred. *Mad* ripped into almost every respected institution and accepted wisdom, into fringe groups and conformists, into trendy lifestyles (from 1950s suburban to 1980s yuppie), into politics (the John Birch Society, the Ku Klux Klan, black militants, the New Left, the Kennedys, Nixon, Bush), into psychoanalysis and the New Age human potential movement, into Shakespeare as well as the lowest-brow pop culture, into Barbie dolls and bikers. Like its post-1960s progeny the *National Lampoon* and *Spy*, it has always been a wild, anything-goes mess on the pages; it looks like utter chaos, and you can be sure there will be something, somewhere in the magazine, that insults or offends beliefs you hold dear.

Early issues of *Mad* made fun of Christmas, Superman and Wonder Woman, Mickey Mouse, Howdy Doody, Picasso paintings, the Gettysburg Address, comic books and—most deliciously—advertisements for all the products that billed themselves as essential to a happy life in these United States. Cigarettes, cars, barbecue grills, and fashionable clothing were all rendered stupid-looking by *Mad*'s ad parodies; and even the most juvenile readers couldn't help looking at such ridicule and begin to cultivate their own countercultural point of view. *Mad* presented itself as an antidote to sanctimony with only one consistent principle: to give the raspberry to all the overly anointed aspects of American life. (Its best-

known cover, from 1974, shows a larger-than-lifesize painting of a human hand, flipping the bird out towards readers.) Nowadays, *Mad* has plenty of company in its impolite crusade, but in the 1950s and early 1960s it was alone. By wrapping its derision in juvenile buffoonery, it helped ensconce subversion as a fundamental attitude of postwar adolescence.

Mad came into full flower after the institution of the moralistic Comics Code in 1954, which effectively eliminated gore, sadism, and offbeat sexuality from comic books (until the late 1960s, when they all resurfaced). Among those who had been responsible for the most effective of the pre-Code horror comics were William Gaines and Harvey Kurtzman, publisher and editor of *Mad*. In 1955, as their comic-book business went down the tubes, they transformed *Mad* from its original comic-book format and cheap newsprint stock into a slick-papered magazine, which would be unaffected by the Code, and where they could give free rein to their smart-aleck sensibility. Among the writers for the new *Mad* were Ernie Kovacs, Carl Reiner, Jean Shepherd, and Roger Price; founding artists Will Elder, Wally Wood, and Jack Davis were joined by Don Martin, and in 1955 Al Feldstein took over as editor. Those who created *Mad* were always referred to on the masthead as "the usual gang of idiots."

Like *Playboy* and *The New Yorker*, *Mad* stands for values, traditions, and a distinct perspective that its readers expect and depend on as a cultural beacon. For those who have treasured it, *Mad* has always been much more than just a magazine; it has provided a viewpoint applicable to all of life, and a reassuring consistency. It is peopled by a well-known cast of regular characters, including the Joke and Dagger Department's "Spy vs. Spy" duo, Don Martin's

("*Mad*'s maddest artist") lantern-jawed, pot-bellied goons, and the ever-present grinning-idiot mascot, Alfred E. Neuman (a pop-culture symbol of stupidity going back to postcards and advertisements of the late nineteenth century), whose motto is "What, me worry?" It also has a huge constellation of expected features, ranging from arcane marginalia, the "Mad Mumblings" page, and Dave Berg's "The Lighter Side" to a language of its own, including not only real Yiddish words ("ganef," "farshimmelt") and pidgin-Yiddish such as "furshlugginer" (an all-purpose adjective to express contempt) but also such totally absurd comic cues as "frammistan" (no known meaning), "axolotl" (actually, a salamander), "hoohah!" (originally an EC comics horror parody, but generally used as a resigned "hurrah"), "zilch" (zero), "blecch" (an expression of disgust), and "potrzebie" (a complete nonsense word). Among *Mad*'s best-remembered contributions to the English language were the words cartoonist Don Martin invented to show sounds. For example, a slap on the face was "FRAP"; a scene of people eating ravenously was festooned with "CHOMP . . . BLOOF . . . FARP . . . BLUK . . . SHPLIK . . . BLICH . . . BORP . . . FLUBBLE"; a gang of cockroaches moving through the Acme Ritz Central Arms Waldorf Plaza Hotel went "AGH . . . UGH . . . IG" and the sound of them being squished underfoot was "GOOSH."

If you need to be convinced of *Mad*'s depth and scope, we recommend you have a look at Maria Reidelbach's astonishing volume *Completely Mad*, which profiles every artist and writer, reproduces every cover, and gives practically a month-by-month history of the magazine as well as a thematic analysis of its satire. Ms. Reidelbach includes chapters devoted to *Mad*'s most famous forms of parody: of advertise-ments, of popular television shows and movies, and of the all-American family. She noted: "In *Mad*, as in real life, fathers sometimes came home drunk, mothers were lousy cooks, and sullen teenagers hung out on corners looking for trouble. By not only mentioning these unspeakable events, but chortling, guffawing, and belly-laughing at them, *Mad* helped alleviate the stresses of modern living." At a time when Americans began to worry about conformity, and when kids coming of age were feeling estranged and impatient with the old social order, *Mad* was a breath of fresh—very fresh—air.

In the process of ridiculing culture, *Mad* has itself become a pop-culture institution, owned by Time-Warner and with a circulation of 800,000. It has been given credit for creating the generation of skeptics, rebels, and war protesters who began to feel their oats in the 1960s, and despite the editors' protests that it is not political, there has always been something alluringly rebellious about it for those who crave a beacon of dissent. Candice Bergen once said, "Without *Mad*, it would have been harder to survive a Republican upbringing" (and in her TV series, "Murphy Brown," framed covers of the magazine appear in a place of honor on her office wall). It should, then, come as no surprise that *Mad* has been accused (by the Ku Klux Klan, in 1979) of undermining the American way of life and condemned as "sexual and satanic." Even intellectually respectable cartoonist Jules Feiffer has condemned it as a poisonous screed in which "everything stinks, everything is a gag, a joke, a put-on . . . so there are no changes to be made and no reason to be involved." It has also been celebrated as a prime example of modernism, along with Picasso and the Marx Brothers (this by Marshall Mc-Luhan). Although its editors are hesitant to call it anything but unredeeming trash,

Completely Mad did quote publisher William Gaines on how he believed Mad educates its readers: "Editorially, we're trying to teach them 'Don't believe in ads. Don't believe in government. Watch yourself—everybody is trying to screw you!'" When Gaines died in June 1992 the New York Daily News headlined his obituary, "What, Me Dead?"

MADONNA

In 1985, the year Madonna Louise Veronica Ciccone became a superstar faster than anyone else in history, an instant paperback book was published to satisfy fans who wanted to know all about her. It was called *Holiday with Madonna*, and it included this childhood reminiscence: "I played with my Barbie dolls all the time. I lived out my fantasies with them. They were sexy. Barbie was mean. Barbie would say to Ken, 'I'm not going to stay home and do the dishes. You stay home! I'm going out tonight. I'm going bowling, okay, so forget it!' You know? She was going to be sexy, but she was going to be tough."

There you have Madonna: sexy but tough . . . you know?

Since Elvis, it has been traditional for pop music idols to be—or at least to seem—somewhat innocent and rather bemused about their devastating effect. Not Madonna. She wallows in her power to arouse adulation, outrage, curiosity, and pseudo-sexual desire. It is that particular talent as a provocateuse that is the secret of her success, far more than her singing voice, which is seldom the issue when critics or fans debate her talents. Even her work to date as a film actress seems peripheral to her true career, although many critics were impressed by the offbeat and vaguely unpleasant screen persona she debuted in *Desperately Seeking Susan* (1985), and she

had a big role (but earned little praise for her performance) as Breathless Mahoney in *Dick Tracy* (1991). (We'll be considerate and not discuss her other films, *Shangai Surprise* [1986] and *Who's That Girl?* [1987].) It seems safe to say that there are millions of people around the planet who couldn't name a single Madonna song or movie role, who couldn't tell you anything she has accomplished in the world of art or culture, but could easily describe the way she looks and acts and offer an opinion about whether it is proper or scandalous. Irrespective of her amazing accomplishments in the worlds of music and uncouth fashion and her not-so-amazing film career, Madonna has surely outstripped all stars and starlets who came before her in the fine old art of attracting attention. Her life is a publicity stunt. "She doesn't want to *live* off camera," Warren Beatty said of her. "Why would you want to say something if it's off camera?"

She was born in Bay City, Michigan ("a smelly little town," she once recalled); when she came to New York she got a job at Dunkin' Donuts and a scholarship at the Alvin Ailey dance school until she got bored with what she called "all those little, horrible ballerinas." She starred as a dominatrix with three slaves in an "art film" called *A Certain Sacrifice* in 1979 and posed for some dirty pictures, then became a drummer for a band called the Breakfast Club. Nothing much happened until the early eighties, when New York's club scene began to heat up with the rumble of a new countercultural energy known as hip-hop, which included rap, break dancing, boom-box radios, and a resurgence of graffiti and rag-tag street fashion. It was a milieu made for Madonna's talents. She gave herself a graffiti name—"Boy Toy"—and began Magic-Markering it all around the city. She wrote songs, made demo tapes, and went to clubs every night in hopes of being noticed by the right people.

Her first single, for the Warner Bros. subsidiary Sire Records, was called "Everybody," and it made critics talk about her as the next Debbie Harry (the original New Wave bad girl); it was a big success in disco clubs and on black radio stations. Not long after she recorded her first album in July 1983 (*Madonna*), Warner Bros. decided to promote her using big-budget music videos. *Madonna* went triple platinum and her "Borderline" and "Material Girl" videos got prodigious play on MTV in 1984 and 1985, by which time it was clear that Madonna was going to be a phenomenon of a whole new order of magnitude. That was obvious at the first MTV Music Awards in 1984, when she staged a dance number for her soon-to-be-released single, "Like a Virgin." Playing Icarus in a parable she had choreographed, Madonna seemed to sail up off stage; but then when her wings melted and she fell, her dress flew up and she exposed her ass (in close-up) to the camera. "I was upset because everyone took it the wrong way," she said. As soon as "Like a Virgin" was released, it flew like Icarus to the top of the charts . . . but stayed there, at number one, for five straight weeks.

Madonna is the grand master of merchandising songs via music videos. They have been condemned by the Catholic Church and by moralists upset about their forthright sexuality, and one—"Justify My Love"—was so risqué that even MTV refused to broadcast it. But such complaints are no obstacles to Madonna's momentum. On the contrary: her success thrives on her talent for going too far. When *High Society* published topless pictures from her art film and when Bob Guccione's *Penthouse* ran a spread of the low-rent nudie shots she had done in her early New York days—exposure that might have ruined or at least embarrassed a star with a decent image—the impropriety only added to her charisma. And when her "Justify My Love" video was banned by MTV but aired uncut by ABC's "Nightline"—"in the public interest," according to producers—"Nightline" got its highest ratings of the year. "America's Smartest Business Woman?" asked *Forbes*. WHAT A TRAMP! headlined the New York *Post*.

It is a curious attraction she generates, this "superstar sex goddess of the video generation" (according to rock impresario David Geffen), because for all her ritualized sexuality, Madonna is one of the most sexless idols in pop music history. Whatever obscene things she does on stage and however shocking her costume, her carnal gestures are always calculated rather than lustful. Unlike sex goddesses and gods who preceded her, such as Elvis, Marilyn Monroe, James Brown, and Tina Turner, Madonna never, ever appears carried away by the passion she simulates on stage, and she manages to affect an ironic attitude even about the tabloid melodrama that is her real life. Control is the key: She plays with herself with more detachment than children use when they enact scenes with a Barbie doll (which perhaps explains her appeal to little girls more than to boys).

Madonna's ascension happened about the same time as the Valley Girl fad (see p. 546), and her wardrobe, in the beginning, pretty much defined the Valley Girl look: torn leotards, net tops over black T-shirts, clumsy shoes and pounds of clunky bracelets and necklaces, and, always, an exposed stomach. "I have the most perfect belly button," Madonna observed. Her rude street-urchin look and attitude became a paradigm for teenage and preteen girls all over America. For nearly a decade now, Madonna has been the most important arbiter of street fashion for adolescent girls, as well as for many mature women whose taste is inspired by the clothing of the young. If she had done nothing else, Madonna would have earned her place in the pop-culture pantheon for popularizing underwear as outerwear: brassieres, bustiers, corsets, garters, and all manner of lacy dainties that used to be known as ladies' "intimate apparel" are now—thanks to Madonna, on stage and off—suitable attire in public or at least for going shopping at the mall.

Whatever Madonna does has the quality of a public event. Her marriage and breakup with Sean Penn, and all the fistfights and screaming matches it entailed, were doted over rapturously by gossip columnists and supermarket tabloids. When her lips seemed to inflate into a bee-stung pucker in early 1991, suddenly hordes of other aspiring rock singers and movie actresses started pouting and getting facial collagen injections. Physically, everything about her changes constantly, and when it does, it's news: Nancy Kruh of the Dallas *Morning News* offered these "Idle Musings on the Subject of Madonna" in 1990: "Flat or full-figured? Gay or straight? Blonde or brunette? Artist or opportunist?" These are questions that fans, or at least reporters, never seems to tire of asking, and even when there is nothing new about her, no raunchy video or steamy outfit to discuss, everybody loves to think about Madonna the publicity hound. In fact, at the Cannes Film Festival in 1991, when Madonna didn't really have much to offer in the way of shock (other than a newly brunette hairdo, an evening ensemble composed entirely of underclothes, and an excruciatingly intimate documentary about her recent tour, *Truth or Dare*), much of the press coverage about Madonna was about . . . press coverage of Madonna. "Good Lord, the ink never stops flowing," *Entertainment Weekly* commented when it named her one of the top entertainers of 1991.

She is big business, so much so that she has become the president and sole owner of a multimedia corporation devoted to marketing her acting, video, music, and merchandising ventures and in 1992 struck a deal with Time-Warner, which agreed to advance her approximately $60 million. "Madonna, Inc.?" asked the *New York Times*, and *Forbes* declared her "America's No. 1 Business Woman," with an estimated gross sales of $1.2 billion since her climb to stardom. In light of that development, we thought it might be nice to remember back to 1985, when Madonna was a person rather than a capitalist institution. *Holiday with Madonna* offered these insights into her character:

- Madonna's favorite movies usually come from France or Germany. She does not like

- *Star Wars*–type movies that rely on special effects.
- Madonna tries to reread *Catcher in the Rye*, *Tender Is the Night* and *The Sun Also Rises* at least once a year.
- She once made a movie of an egg being fried on her stomach.
- She was a baton twirler and cheerleader in high school.

- Madonna has a burning desire to succeed.
- She is a girl on the go who at age twenty-five has lived an amazingly full life.
- Her wildest ambition: "To be a memorable figure in the history of entertainment in some sexual comic-tragic way."

CHARLES MANSON

During the "Summer of Love," hippies were widely known as flower children: merry imbeciles who wanted only to drop acid, walk barefoot through the grass, make love, and be mellow. Two years later, in August 1969, a gang of them brutally slaughtered seven people, and suddenly a deeply disturbing side of the love generation surfaced. *Life* magazine called it "the dark edge of hippie life" and a crime that "struck innumerable Americans as an inexplicable controversion of everything they wanted to believe about the society and their children." On its cover *Life* ran a terrifying picture of the man who planned and instigated, but did not personally commit, the murders: Charles Manson, his eyes wide and pupils dilated, looking like a totally stoned hippie . . . or like the devil himself.

After he was caught, Manson became one of the most famous criminals in modern history because he was so terrifying in so many ways. He relished the publicity of his capture and the trial that followed, making funny faces for photographers, and during the legal proceedings it was alarmingly evident that the members of his cult who had done the killings (and several dozen others who may have been involved in murders

that remain unsolved today) were still his subjects. When jailed, they demanded peanut butter and honey so they could perform a Mansonesque purification ceremony, and they insisted on being naked all the time. They yipped like coyotes, and in his cell Charles Manson yipped, too. The women shaved their heads as part of some incomprehensible ritual on his behalf; they chanted and prayed for him; when he carved an X into his forehead, they did, too; and when he changed the X to a swastika, they followed his example. As recently as 1991, Sandra Good, a Manson follower for over twenty years, eagerly told *Esquire* writer Ivan Solotaroff that she remained in his thrall. Ms. Good said that it had been a good deed to murder Sharon Tate's unborn child, because the fetus was "a baby that would grow up to be a fat fucking hamburger-eating, Earth-destroying . . . soul-destroying piece of shit."

Throughout the trial, as members of his "family" who had not been arrested held a vigil outside the Hall of Justice, "waiting for our father to be set free," he stared at his followers in the courtroom with Svengali eyes; he and they giggled and smirked when grisly details of their crimes were enumerated; and he showed no remorse, and certainly no fear of punishment. (He was sentenced to die in the gas chamber, but because the death penalty was abolished in California, he got life.) From prison, Manson later offered this explanation of why incarceration doesn't bother him: "My eyes are cameras. My mind is tuned to more television channels than exist in your world. And it suffers no censorship. Through it, I have a world and the universe as my own. At my will, I walk through your streets and am right out there among you."

Perhaps even scarier than the psychopathy of Manson and his small band of followers were the reactions of some of the counterculture to his crimes. *Tuesday's Child*, a Los Angeles underground paper, selected him its Man of the Year in 1970 and featured him on the cover, crucified like Jesus. Jerry Rubin, the leader of the yippies, said that when he saw Manson on TV he fell in love with his "cherub face and sparkling eyes," and later wrote, "His words and courage inspire us." During the trial, according to District Attorney Vincent Bugliosi, it be-

came evident that the Manson family was growing—Charlie's notoriety held a special attraction for a certain kind of demented thrill seeker. In a speech before the radical Weather Underground in Flint, Michigan, Bernadine Dohrn extolled Manson and his followers as model revolutionaries. "Dig it," she said, "first they killed those pigs, then they ate dinner in the same room with them, then they even shoved a fork into the victim's stomach! Wild!"

For many, the terror of Charles Manson wasn't the gruesome crimes of which he and four of his followers were convicted; it was the sudden, awful realization that the Aquarian shibboleths that so many well-intentioned people had come to believe about the innocence of hippie life had been so readily perverted into a reason to commit deranged atrocities. Free love, spiritual liberation through drugs, the joy of communal living, and half-baked religiosity were all tenets of many sixties people's lives, believed even by some who weren't card-carrying hippies. It all seemed so beautiful, so childlike and natural. Then, along came Charles Manson and his band, living what seemed to be a typical hippie life out on a ranch near Los Angeles: They practiced free love, took drugs, lived as a communal family, and espoused their own cockamamie religion—a lot like hippie communes everywhere. About the three women in the Manson family finally convicted of murder, Jerry Adler wrote in *Newsweek*, "They could have been any family's daughters, caught up in the wave of drugs, sex, and revolutionary blather that had swept up a generation of young people." Except in this case, their guru, Charlie, was a dangerous criminal, and his childlike love-and-peace followers became Silly Putty in his hands.

In fact, Charles Manson was no hippie. He was a con man for whom the trappings of hippie life were a perfect scam. He had been a criminal all his life—a pimp, a car thief, a forger—and was described by one of his parole officers as "the most hostile parolee I've ever come across." But as *Life* put it in its story about "The Love and Terror Cult," Charlie was clever enough to realize that the innocence flaunted by the hippie culture was ripe for exploitation, and hippies, who veritably cultivated simple-mindedness, were pushovers. "Criminals and ex-cons have discovered a new sort of refuge in the last couple of years: They grow hair, assume beads and sandals, and sink—carnivores moving in with the vegetarians —into the life of hippie colonies from the East Village to Big Sur."

When Manson arrived in Haight-Ashbury in San Francisco in the summer of 1967, he described himself as "a roving minstrel," let his hair grow long, and started picking up girls and offering to "break down their inhibitions." Many lost souls who came to the Haight that summer were eager to have their inhibitions broken down, so they took drugs and did whatever self-confident, all-knowing, twinkle-eyed Charlie told them to do; some even became Charlie's girls. There is no good logic that explains why any of them willingly acted as his slave (there really never is a satisfying reason for why any cult attracts followers)—they panhandled for him, they had sex with straight guys from whom he wanted something, and eventually they butchered innocent people for him. One psychiatrist described them as "hysterics, wishful thinkers, seekers after some absolute." Charlie was their man.

David Smith, founder of the Haight-Ashbury Free Clinic, said "Charlie Manson as a spiritual leader is probably more typical than we care to believe. He would probably be diagnosed as a schizophrenic, but ambulatory schizophrenics were very much looked up to in Haight-Ashbury because they could hallucinate without drugs."

Charlie, whom his followers called either Death or Devil or God (when he was booked by police it was as "Manson, Charles M., a.k.a. Jesus Christ, God"), had a very religious point of view. He believed that all people were part of one great, mystical whole; so there was really no such thing as death, and killing wasn't really all that bad. He also believed that if you listened very carefully to the Beatles' song "Helter Skelter," you could hear exactly what was going to happen in the not-too-distant future: an apocalypse, which would start when all black people rose up and killed all white people, except for righteous white people like the Manson family, who would emerge at the end of the battle to rule the world. When Charlie and his bunch moved out to the Spahn Movie Ranch, a scruffy riding stable used occasionally in the past as a setting for westerns, it was to prepare for that day. (They got the ranch by paying owner George Spahn, who was blind, five thousand dollars, which Manson had conned from one of his rich followers. Subsequently, Manson retrieved most of the money from Spahn when he held him hostage and brutalized him.)

People drifted in and out of Manson's family; sometimes there were as many as six or seven men and a couple of dozen women. Charlie's word was law. He dictated who should sleep with whom, and frequently rearranged partners and choreographed evening group sexual encounters to suit his mood. He taught his followers that everything in the world belonged to everyone, so there was no such thing as theft. They stole cars that they would need in the coming conflagration. He sent follower Patricia Krenwinkel on the garbage run most days —to get the family's food by foraging in other people's dumpsters and garbage cans.

He and his bunch on the ranch spent a lot of time gathering ammunition and fixing up their stolen cars as desert-worthy dune buggies with gun mounts. Charlie believed that it was his job to trigger the apocalypse by killing as many people as he could. He was mad at Doris Day's son, record producer Terry Melcher, because Terry wouldn't help him become a rock-and-roll star (later, when he was in prison, an album of his songs was actually released), so on August 8, 1969, he announced, "Now is the time for Helter Skelter" and dispatched four members of his group, led by Charles "Tex" Watson, to Terry's house to kill him. It would be the beginning of the end. Terry wasn't there, so they killed the people who were: Sharon Tate, Abigail Folger, Voytek Frykowski, Jay Sebring, and Steven Parent. Although some were strangled, hanged, or cut and disemboweled with dinnerware, Tex shot everyone, too, yelling, "I am the devil and I have come to do the devil's work." After everyone was dead, the killers tasted the blood they had spilled (Susan Atkins later said she enjoyed it because "it's warm and sticky and nice"), then scrawled the word "PIG" on the wall in accord with Charlie's order to "leave a sign . . . something witchy"; but they felt there wasn't enough time to extract all of their victims' eyes and cut off their fingers, as they had hoped to

do. The next night they broke into another house, selected because it was owned by middle-class white people, and murdered its occupants, Leno and Rosemary LaBianca, leaving forks and knives protruding from their corpses and the word "WAR" carved in Mr. LaBianca's stomach.

The murders were supposed to be a catalyst for the great war to begin, and there were plans to encourage it by sending phony letters to local newspapers, but the Manson family forgot to write them. They went back to the ranch and spent the next few days taking pep pills and getting ready for the revolution, then retreated to an encampment of abandoned shacks on the edge of Death Valley, where they set up defenses and waited. When the police finally raided the hideout in October (with warrants on charges including car theft and arson, but not yet murder), they rounded up nearly everyone except for Manson himself, who had vanished. They then noticed a hank of hair dangling from a twelve-by-sixteen-inch cupboard underneath a bathroom sink. Charles Manson, scarcely five feet tall, had wedged himself into the tiny cubicle to hide; but his hippie-length hair, sticking out the door, gave him away.

MICKEY MANTLE

There is no sport that inspires nostalgia more than baseball, and there is no modern baseball player people enjoy remembering more than Mickey Mantle. The fair-haired, crew-cut, broad-shouldered Oklahoma boy who led the New York Yankees when the Yankees were great was a natural athlete, a combination of power and

speed such as the game had never seen. He might have been invincible, but he was hobbled by his own body's weaknesses, and his career—magnificent through it was—always seemed a little less than it might have been were it not for all his injuries. The pain he endured and played through—sometimes collapsing on the field in agony from

shinsplints, bone fractures, and bad knees; frequently limping around the bases after hitting a home run—made him all the more admired. When he was booed, as he so often was when he struck out swinging for the bleachers, it was because so much was expected of him; and when he was cheered, he was cheered wildly, for what he represented as much as what he did. Writing in *Holiday* magazine, John O'Hare remembered the August day in 1963 when Mantle stepped to the plate to pinch-hit after being sidelined with knee problems for eight weeks and slugged a home run into the left-field stands. "I jumped to my feet, let out a yell that was heard in my kitchen, and then sat down and cried. I was happy for Mantle, happy for the Yankees, and happy for the human race."

When he played, Mickey Mantle was reason enough for baseball to be America's favorite sport. Now football has replaced it, and his reign as Yankee number 7 (his jersey was retired when he quit) has come to signify a time when it was easy to think of the major leagues as a privileged world

apart, and of its players as quintessential American heroes. The very texture of the game was different then: Stadiums had grass fields, not Astroturf, and uniforms weren't yet made of rubber-waisted polyester. No one had heard of free agents, drug tests, or George Steinbrenner, and if you were lucky you could catch the Mick in a good mood before or after the game, or during the seventh-inning stretch, and get him to sign a baseball for you . . . *for free.*

All that has changed now. Mickey Mantle seems as much a part of another era as "Leave It to Beaver." Hardly anyone thinks of professional baseball as a game anymore. It is entertainment; it is big-time show business, and its participants are businessmen, and it is unlikely you will get any of them to sign a ball for free. They have deals, you see, with promoters; and they sign balls for a price, so you can buy them at a sanctioned baseball-card show after paying admission to get in. Not only is baseball itself big business; even its memories have become expensive. Just last year, a number 7 jersey Mickey Mantle once wore sold at auction for $71,500. A signed bat he used in a game is worth $10,000. An autographed Mickey Mantle ball goes for $50.

It is easy to sugarcoat the past—especially easy when remembering the 1961 season, when Mantle and teammate Roger Maris both stalked Babe Ruth's home run record, or if you begin daydreaming wistfully of the summer of '56, when Mick won the triple crown (a feat not accomplished since 1937) and the Yankees licked the Brooklyn—yes, Brooklyn—Dodgers in a seven-game World Series during which Mick saved pitcher Don Larsen's perfect game by nabbing Gil Hodges's left-field drive. It's awfully tempting to idealize such glories when, in fact, as Jim Bouton revealed in *Ball Four*, even Mickey Mantle could be a pretty sleazy guy after hours: He caroused, he drank too much, he swore, and he was sometimes grouchy and thoughtless towards fans. We're not saying that what has happened to baseball is all wrong: Astroturf and stupid-looking uniforms notwithstanding, there are arguments to be made in favor of the principle of free agentry and for players getting salaries commensurate with their drawing power. But still, the fact is that baseball was a whole lot more fun thirty years ago, which helps explain the recent boom in nostalgia for it (baseball cards and memorabilia from the era have never been more valuable), and also helps explain why Mickey Mantle has returned to being what he was in his heyday as a player: a national god.

He joined the Yankees from a farm club in Missouri in 1951, the year Joe DiMaggio retired. DiMaggio was cool, elegant, unflappable. Mickey Mantle was hot—hugely talented and hugely flawed, more famous in his first few years for his ability to strike out than for his ability to hit. But, as Ross Wetzsteon recalled in an elegy written on the occasion of Mick's sixtieth birthday in 1991: "In 1956, the first of Mantle's three MVP [Most Valuable Player] seasons, his talent suddenly erupted, and by 1961 . . . he'd

become an object of adoration not only in New York but across the country. . . . Though always the shyly grinning kid who never seemed to age, Mantle added a decade and a half to the Yankee dynasty and a never-to-be-forgotten radiance to our recollections."

By the mid-1960s, his injuries were getting the better of him, and after his retirement (1969) and his election to the Baseball Hall of Fame (1974), there were some bad business deals, including an ill-starred restaurant chain called Mickey Mantle's Country Cookin' Kitchen, the slogan for which, Mantle joked, was "to get a better piece of chicken you'd have to be a rooster." In 1983, after he took a job as a spokesman for an Atlantic City casino, he was banned from any official association with baseball by a righteous commissioner who felt the connection with gambling was unseemly, but the ban was lifted in 1985, and today Mickey Mantle is the most popular of all of baseball's living legends. You can see him table hopping at Mickey Mantle's Restaurant and Sports Bar in New York, selling memorabilia at baseball-card conventions, or letting fans pay to play with him at fantasy baseball camp in Fort Lauderdale, Florida.

"THE MARY TYLER MOORE SHOW"

M ary Richards, the main character in "The Mary Tyler Moore Show," was a television sitcom first: a single woman who wasn't ravening for a man. She was in her thirties and unattached because she wanted to be. The original concept was

to make her a divorcée, but CBS executives decided that American television viewers didn't like divorced women; widowhood was also considered, but rejected because it was determined that a widow couldn't be perky enough; and even when it was finally

Gavin MacLeod (Murray Slaughter),
Ed Asner (Lou Grant), Ted Knight (Ted Baxter);
bottom: Betty White (Sue Ann Nivens),
Mary Tyler Moore (Mary Richards),
Georgia Engel (Georgette Franklin)

agreed that she could be a single woman with no past, CBS pleaded with Grant Tinker (then Mary Tyler Moore's husband, and head of *MTM* Productions, which produced the show) to give her a steady boyfriend. Mary Richards didn't even get that. But she did get birth control pills, along with a fulfilling life as an associate producer at WJM-TV in Minneapolis.

When the show premiered in 1970 it signaled not only the arrival of the sexual revolution but also the disintegration of the nuclear family—at least on prime-time television. "I thought about something last night," Mary said at the end of the final episode of "The Mary Tyler Moore Show" in 1977. "What is a family? And I think I know. A family is people who make you feel less alone and really loved." By the time the show went off the air, Mary's definition of family had become the basis of a new kind of situation comedy about an ensemble of characters who, although they are not kin, spend a weekly half-hour together as a tight-knit group that can be as supportive —and occasionally as maddening—as blood relations. From "Barney Miller" and "M*A*S*H" through "Cheers" and "Murphy Brown," this formula has been at the heart of some of the best TV sitcoms.

The customary assumption of situation comedy history is that Norman Lear's "All in the Family" (see p. 11) marked the beginning of a sitcom revolution and a decade that would become its golden age. No question, it was revolutionary in the way it tackled serious issues head-on; but formally it was old hat: a living-room comedy about a bickering family. "The Mary Tyler Moore Show," which premiered four months before "All in the Family," was actually the more innovative form, even though it didn't provide a forum for debate about current events, and was considerably more circumspect than Norman Lear when it handled such once-taboo subjects as sex, illness, death, and aging (and it *did* handle them). Its setting in the workplace (an extension of Mary Tyler Moore's previous series, "The Dick Van Dyke Show," which was set half at home, half at work), and its focus on an independent single woman really were different than what had come before; and its positing of friends as family was in some important way a more accurate reflection of genuine social trends than the traditional "All in the Family" couplings of the Bunkers and the Stivics.

In its uniquely gentle nature, "The Mary Tyler Moore Show" was the polar opposite of "All in the Family," which consummated a style of humor based on the mockery of caricatures. Almost no one ever yelled at other people in "Mary," and although they frequently made fun of one another, they never went out of their way to humiliate another character, as so often happened when the Bunkers and the Stivics argued. In "The Mary Tyler Moore Show," the fun came not from seeing someone put down but from empathy.

Not that the people in "Mary" were *realistic.* Such regular characters as Rhoda

Morgenstern (Valerie Harper), the neighbor, and Sue Ann Nivens (Betty White), the "Happy Homemaker," were as overpronounced in their prevailing traits (Jewishness and lust, respectively) as any characters in the most polemical Norman Lear sitcom. Even the most annoying individuals in the show, such as Phyllis Lindstrom (Cloris Leachman), the pretentious landlady, and Ted Baxter (Ted Knight), the egomaniacal anchorman, were inevitably *lovably* annoying, or at least vulnerable in ways that made them sympathetic. The likable people on the show were exaggerations, too: Lou Grant (Ed Asner), the bearish but kindhearted boss, and Murray Slaughter (Gavin MacLeod), the well-intentioned schlep, but even though each was a type with a dominant aspect that was played for laughs, the laughs were almost never mean. Mary herself was a parody of normalcy, and a lot of the show's humor came out of her relentless niceness—a screen personality she had developed not only as Laura Petrie in "The Dick Van Dyke Show," but as a nun in the Elvis Presley movie, *Change of Habit* (1970), and even in her first television appearance in the 1950s as the miniaturized Hotpoint Pixie who danced around the kitchen stove in commercials during "The Adventures of Ozzie and Harriet."

"The Mary Tyler Moore Show" was about adults, and there was very little physical humor in it. Neither cute nor slapstick, it was built upon brilliant repartee, of which its writers supplied an abundance unknown (before or since) in television situation comedies. In 1971 the *New York Times* observed that many young adults, who had given up watching the tube in the 1960s (when rock music and movies seemed so much more relevant), were coming back to watch "Mary." Its attraction was a truly modern point of view combined with so-

phisticated writing, both of which had been conspicuously missing from prime time, not only in such obviously lowbrow fare as "The Beverly Hillbillies" and "Hee Haw" but also in such allegedly hip (but actually quite square) nitwit variety shows as "Laugh-In" (see p. 272) and "The Flip Wilson Show." The *Times* observed, "Mary is so IN, actually, that it has become fashionable to drift into the den at a party or even to go home at nine on Saturday because you simply must not miss this program."

It seems safe to say that "The Mary Tyler Moore Show" was, and to this day remains, the best-liked show on television. It won more Emmy awards than any other (twenty-seven) and generated three successful spin-offs: "Rhoda," "Phyllis," and "Lou Grant" (not a comedy). It became so popular, Rick Mitz reported in *The Great TV Sitcom Book*, that the Victorian house in which Mary Richards was supposed to have had her apartment became a tourist attraction in Minneapolis, and the owner, a woman who had originally allowed the crew to film it for exteriors (interiors were shot in Hollywood), became fed up with people driving by and taking pictures. A few years into the series, when the crew returned to film more exteriors, she hung a banner out the window that was supposed to be Mary's saying IMPEACH NIXON. The next season, Mary Richards lived in a high-rise apartment building.

"The Mary Tyler Moore Show" was still rated in the top twenty in 1975–76 when the decision was made to end it the following season, and the concluding episode, in 1977, in which all the characters bunch together in a love huddle (despite rumors that the series would end with Mary finally having sex with her boss, Lou Grant), rates with the final "Howdy Doody" (see p. 232) as one of television's most bittersweet farewells. Andrew J. Edelstein and Kevin McDonough recalled Saturday nights with "Mary" in their book *The Seventies*, describing how deeply viewers really cared about the characters on the show: "For seven years, even if Watergate, gas lines, or WIN ["Whip Inflation Now"] buttons got you down, there were always friends you could turn to.... Thanks, guys, for making the decade that much easier to get through."

MAYBERRY

Folks who live in the imaginary small town of Mayberry, North Carolina, are almost never in a hurry. They sit on the front porch in rocking chairs, they go fishing, they sip sodas at the drugstore, they take time to chat as life passes slowly and sweetly. They almost never tell a joke, never zing each other with clever one-line rejoinders, never *ever* get sexually suggestive. By current standards, this hardly seems like the material of a great television situation comedy, but once, thirty years ago, it was. "The Andy Griffith Show," set in Mayberry, was among the top-ten-rated programs on

Don Knotts (Barney Fife), Jim Nabors (Gomer Pyle), Andy Griffith (Andy Taylor)

the air every season it was broadcast, from 1960 to 1968, and since then its reruns have garnered a following of extraordinary size and loyalty. There are plenty of things people love about the show, but what makes it unique in the pop-culture pantheon is the world in which it's set: Mayberry, the Platonic small town, the home you *can* go back to, a setting of hypnotic peacefulness.

The appeal of Mayberry is timeless, but it was especially embraced in the 1960s, a time when everything in the real world seemed to be so uncertain and changing so fast. There were no hippies in Mayberry, and certainly no drugs; no protest marches; no mention of the war in Vietnam. Racial strife was not an issue, because everyone who lived there was the same color; and besides, you honestly got the feeling that if a black person (or a Jew, or any kind of alien) ever did come to town, he'd be treated with the same dignity and respect that all the people in Mayberry tendered towards one another. Mayberry was a town without a single mean person in it, except maybe for Ernest T. Bass, the mischievous hillbilly, who sometimes threw rocks at neighbors' homes.

There was a slew of eccentrics in Mayberry, most notably Deputy Sheriff Barney Fife, who was played by Don Knotts, winner of five Emmys for his performance. To this day, Barney is one of television's greatest characters—a sublime nincompoop who yearned to be a martinet but inevitably made himself look silly. Knotts, who at that point in his career was a dead ringer for the Rolling Stones' Mick Jagger, played his beanpole body, livery lips, and buggy eyes like too-tight strings on a Stradivarius, turning every posturing move Barney made into an excruciating comic rendering of a man desperate for someone to take him seriously. Barney had a melodramatic view of life and constantly yearned for something big to happen, although if it ever did, he was bamboozled and helpless. He was overeager (frequently practicing quick draw, although he was allotted only one bullet, which he tried to keep in his shirt pocket but sometimes lost), hilariously incompetent and self-important, but such a basically sweet-natured character that everyone in town pretended not to notice his conspicuous failings (he often accidentally locked himself in jail).

The other Mayberry regulars included kindly Aunt Bee (Francis Bavier), who had a tendency to be oversensitive to any slight; Gomer Pyle (Jim Nabors), the village idiot, who worked at the gas station; equally half-witted Goober Pyle (George Lindsey), known for his little beanie—Gomer's replacement when Gomer got his own spin-off sitcom; Otis, the town drunk (Hal Smith), who voluntarily locked himself in jail whenever he tied one on; Floyd (Howard McNear), the anxious barber; Elly Walker (Elinor Donahue), the pretty drugstore clerk; Helen Crump (Aneta Corsaut), the schoolteacher; and Thelma Lou (Betty Lynn), waitress at the Bluebird Diner and Barney Fife's main squeeze.

The central character was Sheriff Andy Taylor (Andy Griffith), a widower (and Barney Fife's cousin), who didn't carry a gun and tended to exercise his authority by getting wrongdoers (the really bad ones were always from out of town) to see the error of their ways. Once, he cornered a crook by leaving one of Aunt Bee's warm pies to cool at an open window—a snare no human who came to Mayberry could resist. Although the original conception of the show was to make Andy a bumbling hick, all the goofy qualities went to Barney and the other characters. Andy was the cool, steady straight man, gently orchestrating law and order in a town full of nice citizens whose wacky ways sometimes got them into trouble.

Andy's young un', Opie (Ronny—now Ron—Howard), grew up as audiences watched over the course of eight seasons, and while the other characters' idiosyncrasies were mostly a source of laughs, the rapport between curious, impressionable Opie and his soft-spoken father provided some real ethical weight nearly every week as Opie learned about life. Connoisseurs of Mayberry affairs consider the epitome of this aspect of the show (and the best of all the 249 shows) to be the 101st episode, first broadcast September 30, 1963, titled "Opie the Birdman." Being a typical young lad, Opie has a slingshot. Thoughtlessly, he kills a mother bird in a backyard tree. He expects to get whipped, but instead Andy opens the window of Opie's room and asks the boy to listen to three baby birds calling for their mother. Opie (who has no mother) takes the nestlings for his own and raises them (helped by Barney, who claims to have a special understanding of the chicks' language) until they outgrow their cage and Andy convinces his son that they ought to fly free. When he reluctantly releases them, Opie tells his father how sad he feels to see them go. "Cage sure looks awful empty, don't it, Paw?" he pines. Andy looks up to where the birds are perched and singing and says to him, "But don't the trees sound nice and full?" At that point the camera soars overhead and looks down from a bird's-eye point of view at the father and son standing close and sharing their enjoyment of the freed birds' song.

The most remarkable thing about life in Mayberry was that despite such ineffable moments of resounding sentiment, it was rare to hear a lecture about right and wrong. Moral as it may have been, "The Andy Griffith Show" was never preachy and rarely maudlin. Some of this has to do with Andy Griffith's acting; although Don Knotts won all the Emmys for his tour-de-force portrayal of excitable Barney Fife, Griffith (who had virtual creative control over the show) fashioned the drawling voice, easy manner, fatherly posture, and compassionate facial cast of Andy Taylor with such tender aplomb that he could bring a lump to your throat if he sat in his rocking chair by the fire and read the telephone book to his son. He *was* Andy Taylor. Mayberry *was* his hometown; in fact, it was modeled after Mount Airy, North Carolina, where Griffith was born and raised (although the show was filmed entirely in California). "Andy never left," one Mount Airy resident told *TV Guide* in 1966. "He plain took it to Hollywood with him." The show felt so natural that its humane lessons, as well as its humor, seem to flow artlessly out of the characters who peopled it; even those who were exaggerated burlesques tended to be sympathetic sorts. Mayberry was a fantasy world that was mighty easy to like. It was also featured in the sequel to "The Andy Griffith Show," called "Mayberry, RFD," which proved just how much the unique appeal of the original show had to do with the interplay of its main characters. Without Andy, Barney, and Opie (but with Aunt Bee, Goober, and some other leftover supporting cast) the new show felt like a strange impostor; and although it was among the top ten rated programs in its three seasons on the air, starting in 1968, few TV aficionados

consider it in the same lofty league as the original.

Although it provided a blissful escape from the pressing social issues of the time, Mayberry was a town where personal dilemmas were dealt with directly and sensitively (as well as humorously), even if many of them—such as Aunt Bee's yearning to be someone important and Barney's underlying loneliness—didn't have neat and tidy answers. In the pilot show for the series, which ran as an episode of "The Danny Thomas Show" (both were produced by Sheldon Leonard), Opie comes crying to his father because a lady has stepped on his pet turtle and killed it. Opie wants Andy to bring the turtle back to life, but Andy explains to him it cannot be done: "When your Ma died, I didn't get another Ma." Opie stops crying and pauses to think about what his father just said, then asks, "Who stepped on Ma?"

Like no other television series except maybe "Star Trek" (p. 479), "The Andy Griffith Show" has inspired legions of followers to chronicle, analyze, and systematically adore its every nuance and detail. There are at least two clubs devoted to it (the "Andy Griffith Show" Rerun Watchers Club of Nashville and the "Andy Griffith Show" Appreciation Society of North Carolina), and when most of the cast got back together for a reunion, their *Return to Mayberry* became the top-rated TV movie of the 1985–86 season. The most wondrous example of continuing affection for the world of the show is Stephen Spignesi's book *Mayberry —My Hometown* (1987), which is to the town of Mayberry what the Bible is to the known universe. Here is *everything* anyone could ever want to know, including floor plans of the back room of the town courthouse and of Floyd's barbershop, as well as a detailed rendering of the exact location of every piece of furniture in Andy Taylor's bedroom. Here are the first few lines of the theme song, which is whistled at the beginning of every show but was never sung. Here is an extensive interview with Jim Nabors (Gomer Pyle), in which he tells about the time Andy Griffith discovered him in a Santa Monica nightclub, doing an act in which he talked like a hayseed but sang as prettily as Robert Goulet: "I really don't know what you do," Griffith told him, "but you do it very well." Here is a list of every animal and pet ever mentioned in every episode, including Queenie, Fluffy, Spot, and a thirteen-inch, one-blue-eyed, part-of-his-tailfin-missing fish. And most astonishing, here is an A-to-Z encyclopedia exploring every possible subject related to Mayberry, its history and inhabitants. Entries include:

- *Nectarine Crush:* Soda from the cooler at Wally's Service Station. Floyd had already opened one when he realized that there was a new flavor in there he had been wanting to try, Huckleberry Smash.
- *Golllly!:* Another of Gomer Pyle's all-purpose expletives and expressions of amazement. Surprisingly—for such a notable trademark—we can only find one instance of Gomer using "Golllly!" in the entire run of the original "Andy Griffith Show" series.
- *Punch Supreme:* Andy's specialty. It consisted of orange sherbet, tomato juice, root beer, and molasses.

- *Web-Footed Red-Crested Lake Loon:* The bird Andy invented and imitated in order to lead Barney back to camp without Barney knowing he was being helped.

Mayberry—My Home Town also includes a guest essay by Richard Kelly of the University of Tennessee, who has written his own evocative book, *The Andy Griffith Show* (1981). Titled "Staying Alive in Mayberry," Professor Kelly's comments provide a good summary of what makes the setting of "The Andy Griffith Show" such a fetching landmark of modern TV folklore:

> The focus of Mayberry is always upon life in its simplest and most affable form. The town sparkles with energy, love, and eternal youth. Perhaps it is best to allow it to remain what it was in our first mind, in that far away world where all the complex shades of reality were reduced to black and white, a world built around a father, his son and aunt, his friends and neighbors, a world where getting a haircut or going on a picnic was a notable event . . . where Aunt Bee is still making her pickles, Floyd is evening up someone's sideburns, and Andy and Barney are still drowsing on the Taylors' front porch. Those characters will never age; they are immortal, and whenever we join in their company we share, for a brief moment, their extraordinary longevity.

McDONALD'S

Combine car culture with junk food, apply assembly-line techniques and rigid standardization, season it with a fetish for cleanliness and absolute control, and serve it to the baby boom. The result is an empire that, right up there with Coca-Cola, Walt Disney World, and devotion to handguns, has come to symbolize America all around the world: vulgar, expedient, cheap for anyone to buy a little piece of on a plastic tray, but a cash-bearing bonanza for the men in charge.

real good

look for the golden arches... **McDonald's**®

In 1954, when Ray Kroc made a deal with the McDonald brothers to franchise their restaurant idea nationwide, they had a clever, profitable little hamburger stand in San Bernardino, with a dozen branches scattered in California and Arizona. Twenty years later the McDonald brothers had been put out to pasture; McDonald's, with four thousand stores coast to coast (and beyond), had become the largest minimum-wage employer in the country. Now, nearly twenty years after that, it has eight-and-a-half thousand stores, and it owns more real estate than any other company on earth.

There are two ways to think about McDonald's growth and phenomenal success. On one hand it is a rags-to-riches fable of a man who dared to dream in a land of unlimited opportunity, the story of pioneering business acumen and the thrill of taking risks, of hard work, wholesome idealism, selfless philanthropy, and Ronald McDonald, America's beloved ketchup-coiffed clown. On the other hand, cynics see McDonald's ascension as a horror story. Its villain is Ray Kroc, a shrewd megalomaniac who began by screwing the McDonald brothers, then built a billion-dollar business on the backs of low-paid teenage help and franchisees who got hoodwinked, all the while despoiling the environment in North America (by building ugly restaurants and littering the highway) and South America as well (by consuming so much beef that nations were encouraged to turn their rain for-

ests into cattle land), and hardening the arteries of millions of customers who have grown accustomed to baneful robotic food. "McDonald's," Tom Robbins wrote, "represents mediocrity at its zenith."

The facts are these: The McDonald's phenomenon started in 1948 when Mac and Dick McDonald, who had done well selling hamburgers at their little California drive-in since 1940, decided they didn't like how much of their income went to pay car hops, dishwashers, and fry cooks. So, in what would later look like godly prescience on the eve of the stupendous postwar boom in car sales, highway building, and the move to suburbia, the McDonald brothers changed strategies. Instead of a full menu with the usual choice of condiments for each sandwich, customers would henceforth pick from a small, standardized menu and receive exactly the condiments that the McDonald brothers ordained. In exchange for giving up freedom of choice, burger buyers were treated to unbelievably fast service (under a minute), low prices (15-cent hamburgers; ten-cent fries; 20-cent milk shakes), and freedom from tipping. By 1952 the new McDonald's was so successful that it was featured on the cover of *American Restaurant* magazine in a story that told how the formula had cut operating costs in half. A sign in front of the brothers' restaurant (where the mascot was a winking, burger-faced cartoon character named Speedee) boasted of six million hamburgers sold. So many entrepreneurs came to them wanting to copy their method that the McDonalds decided to franchise. In September 1952 they ran an ad in *American Restaurant* for "McDonald's Self-Service System Drive-Ins." "Imagine," it urged, "no car hops, no waitresses, no waiters, no dishwashers, no bus boys...no more glassware, no more dishes, no more silverware. The McDonald system eliminates all of this!"

Ray Kroc, who had become acquainted with the McDonald's business as a salesman for Multimixers (milk shake machines), liked everything about the formula. He liked the french fries, which always seemed fresh because the McDonalds had invented a shelf that kept them warm under a heat lamp; he liked the fact that everything was served in throwaway paper with no utensils whatsoever, because it eliminated not only dishwashing but the threat of pilferage; he liked the building's stark simplicity, without any landscaping or interior decor that needed tending; but most of all he liked the streamlined efficiency: There was no waste; customers were in and out in minutes; no one—especially no teenagers, the bane of drive-in operators—loitered in the parking lot. In 1954 Kroc, who was then fifty-two years old, made a deal with the brothers to sell franchises, and six years later he paid $2.7 million for the kit and kaboodle—all trademarks, copyrights, and secrets. At first Kroc held rigidly to their formula, although he did add benches for people to sit on alongside some stores' kitchen windows; the benches were tile, so they could be hosed down quickly. The McDonalds kept their original San Bernardino store, renaming it Mac's Place because Ray Kroc now owned their name. But a few years later another hamburger shop opened up directly across the road. Like Mac's Place, the competitor had red and white tiles and golden arches, as well as an identical menu. In fact, it was a McDonald's . . . franchised by Mr. Kroc. The McDonald brothers could not fight the national chain. "I ran 'em out of business," Kroc rejoiced after the brothers were forced to close.

McDonald's grew with the suburbs (a switch from previous chain restaurants' concentration in cities), building its early stores in places convenient for growing families with cars (and with kids) and trying to appeal to the kind of middle-class customers Ray Kroc liked best, which he described as "fussy . . . clean and proud." Kroc sometimes hired a plane so he could fly over towns and suburbs to spot churches and schools, taking them as signs of a community that would be right for McDonald's. He discovered a new way to make money by not merely franchising the name but by becoming landlord to the franchisees. He sold territorial licenses to men who made millions for themselves (and hundreds of millions for the company) filling towns, cities, and whole regions with McDonald's. Some who were with the company from the beginning grew fantastically wealthy; one— Jack Simplot of Idaho, who provided the potatoes—is now the richest man in Idaho, and rated by *Forbes* near the top of America's list of billionaires. June Martino, Ray Kroc's bookkeeper in the mid-sixties when the company went public, took stock instead of a salary. A dollar's worth of that stock is worth well over two thousand dollars today. (Once, after *Fortune* magazine criticized the golden arches as visual pollution, Ms. Martino wrote an angry letter defending the proliferation of McDonald's as a way of making highways less monotonous and "humanizing" the oppressive natural American landscape.)

In the early days, McDonald's worked hard to create an image Ray Kroc described as "a combination YMCA, Girl Scouts, and Sunday school." Early editions of the Operations Manual used at McDonald's Hamburger University in Illinois (where ambitious employees went to get degrees in "Hamburger Science") specified:

A man should shave every day, clean his fingernails every day, keep his teeth and breath fresh and clean all the time, bathe often to prevent underarm and other body odors and use a deodorant. . . . Personnel with bad teeth, severe skin blemishes or tattoos should not be stationed at service windows. Your windowmen and outside order takers must impress customers as being "All American boys." They must display such desirable traits as sincerity, enthusiasm, confidence, and a sense of humor.

For many years, McDonald's hired only male help. Female counter attendants, Ray Kroc felt, would "attract the wrong kind of boys."

The sixties was a boom decade for franchising schemes, and the number of McDonald's stores more than doubled, including not only hundreds of new franchises but also stores operated by McDonald's itself (McOpCo)—a strategy that freed Kroc from having to depend on others to uphold his standards and allowed Hamburger Central to keep more profits. By 1966 two billion burgers had been sold. It was in the sixties that McDonald's began positioning itself as not merely a restaurant but an expression of America and of American values. Franchising, which in theory gave the little guy a chance to make it big, was pitched as the essence of free enterprise. NEW CAPITALISTS ARE FOUND IN MOTEL, DRIVE-IN INDUSTRY, headlined the Hartford *Courant* in an article that quoted Ray Kroc as saying, "We're teaching people how to become successful small businessmen." Later, in the seventies, Kroc boasted, "We've been a leader in advancing black capitalism," and television ads began to feature black franchisees and black employees, with theme songs about how they were serving the "community," a code word for black neighborhoods. Every McDonald's franchise was required to have a flag and flagpole, and was offered a wall plaque of an eagle holding a banner in its beak that read, "McDonald's. The American Way."

Not just McDonald's business practices but the hamburgers themselves were touted as Americana in a bun. A children's book the company published in 1965 called *Let's Eat Out* told about an American family that decides to show a young German visitor named Hans the American way of eating. Directed by their son Tom, whose ten-year-old palate determines where the family goes out to eat, they drive to the edge of town and pull into a McDonald's:

> Hans was looking at a flat, steel table, the grill. His eyes popped open when twenty-four hamburgers were being prepared at one time. "That's pretty American," said Tom. "It's called mass-production." ... Hans had scarcely spoken on this whole trip. Suddenly he grinned, sat up straight, and said in his best English, "Say, I can be as American as a hamburger sandwich."

In the late sixties, the company image changed—subtly but certainly. Carefree, eat-in-the-car highway drive-ins had disreputable connotations (as hangouts for bad elements of society, as sources of traffic congestion and litter, and as junk architecture eyesores), so the design of the stores was altered to appear more authoritative and rigidly polite—a corporate-controlled environment that didn't tolerate deviation. The first McDonald's with indoor seating opened in Huntsville, Alabama, and in 1968 the original garish red-and-white-striped buildings began to give way to the new-look, more sedate McDonald's: brown brick walls, indoor dining, mansard roofs, and eventually even some hanging plants and imitation stained glass.

By the time Ronald McDonald, the squeaky-clean corporation clown (first played by Willard Scott), made his national television debut in the Macy's Thanksgiving Day Parade of 1966, the McDonald brothers' rather mischievous-looking mascot, Speedee, was ancient history. Surveys have since shown that Ronald is recognized by 96 percent of all American schoolchildren, second only to Santa Claus. In January 1967 McDonald's sponsored the first Super Bowl telecast, completing its growth from a fun hamburger business to a corporate giant; and in 1973 a *Time* cover story declared Big Mac "the Burger That Conquered the Country." The year before, in an interview with *Institutions* magazine, Ray Kroc explained the secret of his awesome success: "It is ridiculous to call this an industry. This is rat eat rat, dog eat dog. I'll kill 'em, and I'm going to kill 'em before they kill me. You're talking about the American way of survival of the fittest."

Throughout McDonald's history, the drive towards corporate hegemony has been balanced by powerful efforts to humanize the company, not only by crusading for kids' loyalty and by conspicuous community service (Ronald McDonald House serves families of children with cancer) but with advertising slogans, accompanied by misty-eyed television commercials, to make customers feel respected rather than like cash cogs in the burger assembly line. The most successful one was "You Deserve a Break Today," introduced in 1970 and phased out in 1974. (Its theme was used by Ray Kroc as the door chime for his Fort Lauderdale home.) Others have included "Your Kind of Place" (1966–70), "You, You're the One" (1975–78), "Nobody Can Do It Like McDonald's Can" (1978–82), "Together, McDonald's and You" (1983–84), and "It's a Good Time for the Great Taste of McDonald's" (1984–90), which was frequently abbreviated to "Good Time, Great Taste." When the anthem "Food, Folks, and Fun" debuted in 1990, a company executive said it "puts the humanity back. It establishes this friendly, homely turf as ours."

Typical "Food, Folks, and Fun" television spots showed cute kids surviving their first day at school (then eating at McDonald's), working moms sharing quality time with daughters (over hamburgers), and an attractive, nervous couple on a first date (guess where they go to eat). In the summer of 1991, however, "Food, Folks, and Fun" went on what company executives suggested would be a temporary hiatus, replaced by "McDonald's Today," in an effort to reprise the success of "You Deserve a Break Today" and to be—in the words of a McDonald's marketing executive—"more relevant." "Food, Folks, and Fun" never came back; in its place came "Whatever It Takes: That's McDonald's today"; and as of the Super Bowl of 1992, "Whatever it takes . . ." was eclipsed by "What You Want Is What You Get."

Ray Kroc had been proud of his hands-on leadership. In his autobiography, a photo of him with a garden hose reads, "That's me washing down the front of the store. I may have been the owner, but I wasn't too proud to clean up. That's still true." Everything about the McDonald's operation was under his rigid control, and he was fanatic about details, from the precise "ten patties to a pound of meat" rule (except for the HUGE Quarter-Pounder) to the "Thank you" and "Have a nice day" employees were required to say to customers. But the stunning growth of the corporation made it impossible for Kroc to exercise that level of control, and by the early seventies trouble was brewing. In 1973 disgruntled franchise owners formed the McDonald's Operators Association, claiming that Hamburger Central aimed to buy them out when their standard twenty-year license expired, and leave them in the cold; in fact company-owned stores went from 30 to 40 percent of the total in 1973 and 1974. McDonald's said they were moving in only to ensure that every branch measured up to Ray Kroc's high standards. Today, about a quarter of the eleven thousand McDonald's businesses around the world (including Moscow and Beijing) are company-owned, although Hamburger Central holds title to every site and every building.

One of the things Ray Kroc had liked best about the original McDonald's was the severely restricted menu. But as McDonald's faced competition, the menu expanded, and since Ray Kroc's death in 1984, the McDonald's menu has grown nearly as large as that of a normal restaurant. One of the earliest additions to the basic bill of fare was Filet-O-Fish, added after a franchisee in Cincinnati pleaded for something to help business in his battle against Big Boy fish sandwiches in Catholic parts of town; Big Mac was invented to compete against Burger King's Whopper. After a friend of Ray Kroc's said that he loved the french fries so much he sometimes bought two bags, Large Fries was invented. In 1972, a franchisee in Santa Barbara invented the Egg McMuffin, and suddenly McDonald's found a whole new source of revenue: breakfast. Chicken McNuggets appeared in 1983, and in a short time McDonald's had become the second-largest chicken merchant on earth (after Kentucky Fried).

Dessert was always a problem, because it is more difficult to mass produce and keep fresh. After failing with pound cake and strawberry shortcake, McDonald's introduced fried pies, which Ray Kroc said he liked because they had "that special quality, that classiness in a finger food, that made it perfect for McDonald's." Fried pies, the only dessert for years, have now been replaced by such "healthful" items as fat-free frozen yogurt and fruit sorbet.

In recent years, new additions have included salads (in 1987, because they are "nutritious"), the McDLT (which, by keeping hot and cold parts of the sandwich separate, eliminates the soggy lettuce problem), and the McLean burger (in which the use of seaweed extract helps reduce the fat content from the usual 19 percent to 9 percent). Many McDonald's menus now also include reduced-fat McNuggets, low-sodium breakfast sausage, burritos, fajitas, and pizza. In the summer of 1991, the company even tried test-marketing fettucine Alfredo and Chinese egg rolls; and there are now plans to create a whole separate dinner menu, including roast chicken and spaghetti with meatballs ... but not including alcoholic beverages (which *are* available in some European McDonald's) or table service. When the *Wall Street Journal* discussed the expanding menu with Dick McDonald (who is retired in New Hampshire), the forefather of fast food warned that it was the elimination of complicated menus that made him and Mac (who died in 1971) successful in the first place. "They should be very careful," Mr. McDonald said, "or fast food will be history."

MICROWAVE OVENS

Zap it, nuke it, atomize it: These are popular ways to describe the process of agitating water molecules inside food until they get hot—so hot that the food cooks itself from the inside out. What gets the fibers shuddering is electromagnetic energy radiated by a microwave oven, which, along with TV remote control devices (see p. 418), cellular telephones, and tubs of Cool Whip, has become one of America's most beloved (and burlesqued) icons of just how wondrously effortless modern life can be. While not quite as significant as the cave dwellers' discovery of fire, the popularization of microwave ovens has revolutionized the middle-class kitchen, providing home cooks a world of easy, shortcut recipes that formerly required time, care, and culinary expertise.

Popular as they are, microwave ovens are still so mysterious to most people that there is a thriving branch of cautionary folklore about people who misuse them. Little old ladies are alleged to have tried to dry a small pet (a chihuahua, a cat, a parakeet) after its bath by putting it in a microwave. The result: The pet explodes, and in some such stories, the door of the oven bursts

open and the hapless lady is hit in the face by flying pet parts. Hippie babysitters, high on drugs, used to be featured in variations of this tale, in which they put the baby in the microwave oven after its bath. The theme that energizes all versions of the story is indolence. By trying to use the quick and effortless microwave instead of an old-fashioned towel and elbow grease, the perpetrator invites disaster. The moral is a puritanical one: You will be punished for being lazy. The microwave oven is a featured player in these stories because it is a quintessential symbol of sloth.

In fact, microwave ovens are now considered perfectly safe (unless you wear a pacemaker, or try to use them for deep-fat frying, or cook whole eggs in them—the yolks might explode—or put metallic things in them, or are unaware that the *inside* of a piece of freshly zapped food can be lava hot even if the outside is cool enough to handle). However, before Federal standards for microwave ovens and their latches were established in 1971, they really could be dangerous. As late as 1977 food writers John and Karen Hess, authors of *The Taste of America*, wrote, "If you've already been conned into buying one, you might also consider buying a pocket Geiger counter." Documented cases of radiation leakage had led to a nationwide microwave oven scare in 1968, and some radiation-wary doomsayers warned that people who stood near a leaky one, staring bug-eyed at the oven door and panting eagerly for their instant dinner to get hot enough to eat, ran the risk of inadvertently cooking their corneas.

Although they were not popular enough to worry anybody until the late 1960s, the earliest ones actually predate TV dinners.

And the first food known to be "cooked" by microwaves was an accident. It happened in 1942 one day when Percy Spencer, an inventor employed by Raytheon in Waltham, Massachusetts, was testing a radar component called a magnetron tube. Dr. Spencer liked chocolate. He liked it so much he often kept a bar in the pocket of his pants. After testing the magnetron, he reached for a piece of his chocolate bar and found he had a pocket full of goo. The chocolate bar had melted. He put a bag of corn kernels near the magnetron and they popped inside the bag. Next, he blew up an egg. He knew he was onto something big.

As soon as the war was over, in 1946, Spencer created a prototype microwave oven. "Foods prepared with sealed-in flavor *quick as a flash!*" Raytheon boasted, sending out photographs of wieners in buns and hot apple pie à la mode emerging from the monstrously large, brushed-metal machine they patented as the Radarange. They were "duds for a decade," according to the *Wall Street Journal*, which blamed their failure on "bilious grey meat and limp french fries" —problems that have been addressed in recent years by the addition of conventional "browning units." Despite such workarounds, the miracle ovens continue to be notorious for their propensity to transform bread into limestone, steak into gelatin, and chocolate into glue if used incorrectly. But in the future-worshipping postwar years, such lapses were insignificant compared to the wonder of instant cookery. Waldemar Kaempffert, science editor of the *New York Times*, wrote an article in the early fifties about a hypothetical family named the Dobsons, living in America in the year 2000: "Cooking as an art is only a memory in the minds of old people. . . . Jane Dobson has an electronic stove. In eight seconds a half-grilled frozen steak is thawed; in two minutes more it is ready to serve." (The

Dobsons, by the way, eat mostly food made out of recycled sawdust, discarded paper tablecloths, and old rayon underwear.)

The earliest home-kitchen microwaves sold for more than a thousand dollars, but in the mid-1960s Keishi Ogura of New Japan Radio invented a compact electron tube that made cheaper, home-size ovens a reality, and in 1967 Amana Refrigeration (which was part of Raytheon) introduced a $495 Radarange. Norma Whaley, Amana's resident home economist, showed the press how to bake a cake from scratch in fifteen minutes and fry bacon in fifty seconds. She poached an egg, too, and she astonished reporters when she pricked the soft-cooked center with a fork and it burst into a torrent of hot yellow yolk. The era of nuked food was at hand.

Still, it took a while for the microwave oven to find its place in the kitchen. Much early advertising pitched it as yet another keep-up-with-the-Joneses, suburban-style small appliance—wonderful because it was so portable, in the tradition of tabletop rotisseries, toaster ovens, and corn poppers. "Cooking is no longer confined to the kitchen!" rejoiced the 1971 Montgomery Ward catalog about its new electronic oven. "Cook wherever the action is. Kids will love having a 'cookout' in the recreation room. You can even have a spur-of-the-moment 'barbecue' on the patio." The following year, Montgomery Ward de-emphasized portability in favor of the microwave oven's lasting appeal—immediate gratification. The catalog now boasted that the Signature brand oven, with "wood-look control panel," could cook a hot dog in one minute and a baked potato in five. A book called *The Microwave Way*, written later in the decade by Dorothy McNett, proprietor of the first microwave oven specialty store in San Francisco, began this way: "Welcome to the world of microwave cooking! You can cook foods in just minutes with this remarkable space-age appliance."

"Imagine, no after-meal clean up of pots and pans!" raved Amana's Radarange instruction booklet. "In just a short time you will be using the Radarange for most of your food preparation. It will help you prepare 75–80% of the foods that you serve your family." Included in the book were recipes for the likes of "Chunky Pizza Sticks," "Rice & Spice Hamburger Casserole," "Chewy Chocolate Log," and "Pretzel Peanut Butter Pie."

No appliance has better fit the restless disposition of a nation in love with fast food. In 1989, when United States sales of microwave ovens were running at over ten million per year, the *New York Times* re-ported that fast-food restaurants were scrambling to fulfill the expectations of high-strung customers who had grown to expect instant eats from their home microwave ovens. "There are never any lines at home," said one food marketing consultant to account for people's impatience with service in franchise restaurants that prepared their vittles the old way, using fire and heat. "With the microwave, you just reach into your freezer and pop it into the oven and zap! it's done." Culinary historian Harvey Levenstein explained the mania for instant eats as "Americans getting back to their roots" in the early nineteenth century, when food was generally so bad that "The idea was 'why not get it over with?' "

MITCH MILLER

Most people who remember Mitch Miller remember him for "Sing Along with Mitch," a prime-time television show that ran from 1961 to 1964, and as the inspiration for countless record albums that encouraged people to not just sit there in their La-Z-Boys but stand up, take a deep breath, and SING ALONG! At about the same time that hootenannies were becoming popular among campus and coffeehouse folk singers, Mitch reached out and touched the musical yearnings of folkies' parents and anybody else who wanted to enjoy the old-fashioned fun of a communal songfest but had little interest in protesting social injustice, singing sad old ballads, or trying to mimic the grunts and groans of teenage pop idols. Mitch has gone down in popular memory as the king of the

squares—not only because of his weekly join-the-fun sing-alongs on television but also because he despised rock and roll.

Back when rock and roll was young and provocative, it had important enemies, and Mitch Miller was the biggest of them. As

A&R (artists and repertoire) man at Columbia from 1950 to 1961, he had been what *Audio* magazine called "one of the most important figures in the history of the record industry." He invented the concept of the "greatest hits" album (for Johnny Mathis), and he produced more hit records than anyone else, with a chart-dominating list of artists that included Doris Day, Tony Bennett, Rosemary Clooney, Frankie Laine, the Four Lads, Jerry Vale, and Mahalia Jackson, too. He produced the "Colonel Bogey March" from *Bridge on the River Kwai*, an all-whistling song whose actual lyrics, sung by soldiers during World War II, were:

> Hitler, he has no balls at all.
> Goering has some, but very small.

It was he who had the words to the theme from *High Noon* rewritten as a love song—a song that became the best-known movie theme since *Gone With the Wind*. His own recording of "The Yellow Rose of Texas," a Civil War–era tune originally about "high yellow" (light-skinned) African-American women, was the second number-one single of the rock era (after "Rock Around the Clock") in 1955. And his "Sing Along with Mitch" albums sold over twenty-two million copies and made him the most famous record producer ever.

It all seems like ancient history, doesn't it? That's because history is written by its winners, and as successful and significant as he was in his time, Mitch Miller got clobbered when rock and roll came along. He is now inscribed in pop music chronicles as an evil schlockmeister and sworn enemy of all that was good, young, fresh, and creative. Even before he fought the battle against rock and roll, Miller was despised by many music cognoscenti. In his book *Jazz Singing* Will Friewald condemned him as "the worst in American pop [who] aroused the ire of intelligent listeners by trying to turn

—and darn near succeeding in turning—great artists like Sinatra, Clooney, and Tony Bennett into hacks. Miller chose the worst songs and put together the worst backings imaginable . . . with insight, forethought, and perverted brilliance." According to *Rock of Ages: The Rolling Stone History of Rock & Roll*, "Under the torpid leadership of Mitch Miller, Columbia [was] perhaps the stodgiest of major labels."

As an A&R man, Miller wanted to develop artists capable of sustaining careers and recording whole albums. When he heard it in the mid-1950s, rock and roll didn't sound like it could do that. Its hits were one-shot singles, not albums, and his only real response was to produce Perry Como's "Ko Ko Mo," a kind of nonsense tune with a lilting beat, but hardly rock and roll. Rock's artists—he hated to use the word "artist" to describe people who he said "couldn't ad lib a burp after a radish dinner"—had no serious musical ability that he could discern. (Miller himself had been considered America's finest oboist in the 1940s.) Unlike the sermonizers of the time who opposed rock and roll, with its throbbing beat, as the devil's music, Mitch Miller didn't like it simply because he thought it was monotonous. "You can't call any music immoral," he said.

It was the immaturity of the songs that Miller opposed. In a story he wrote for the *New York Times Magazine* in April 1955, at the dawn of the rock era, Miller asked, "Is popular music changing—from the sweet and sentimental to the nonsensical and neurotic?" His answer, curiously, was an emphatic no, because he explained that a little bit of nonsense had always been part of the popular song repertoire (going back to "Vo-Do-Do-De-O" and "Mairzy Doats"). In fact, as an A&R man, Miller was known for being an eccentric kind of prodigy who frequently made hits out of records that verged on being nonsensical novelties, such as "I Saw Mommy Kissing Santa Claus" and Frankie Laine's huge hit "Mule Train" (complete with the sound of a cracking whip). One contemporary said of him, "If an octopus could sing, he'd make a record called 'Drown Your Blues in My Lovin', Squeezin' Arms.'"

Before rock and roll's triumph, Miller was widely thought of as a genius, and a man of progressive beliefs. In his 1955 *Times* article, he said that he considered the current interest among young people in rhythm and blues to be a healthy indication of the breaking down of color barriers. However—and this is a mighty big "however"—Miller insisted that "for all these occasional shifts in emphasis, the basic structure of popular music remains constant." He listed the three factors that characterized a good song:

- Self-identification. The song says to the listener what the listener has in his own mind but can't quite put into words for himself.
- Universality. In articulating his own emotions, the song makes the listener aware that he is not alone.
- Simplicity. The ability of the listener to hum the tune, and to pick up the lyric quickly, is essential.

Most rock-and-roll songs, Miller postulated, did not fit the three criteria. They were, in his words, "musically illiterate." Furthermore, he was convinced that rock and roll was bad business for radio stations. In a notorious speech he delivered to a convention of disc jockeys in 1958, Miller accused his audience of abdicating to the "preshave crowd that make up 12 percent of the country's population and zero percent of its buying power." He told them that the eight-to-fourteen-year-olds who listened to rock and roll would attract no advertisers other than for such products as soda, candy, and complexion cream. "God help them they should buy a bar of soap," he later said.

Radio knocked Mitch Miller off his pedestal. Todd Storz, owner of a chain of stations in the Midwest, began developing what he called a "Top 40" format: a list of records given to the disc jockeys that they were instructed to play over and over again, in rotation. Many deejays hated the idea, because it took away their prerogative to play what they liked and their power to make hits. For station owners, however, it was a brilliant idea, because it gave them control of what was played; it also lessened the possibility of payola (slipping cash, drugs, or sex to a deejay to get him to play a record). The Top 40 format was a success that went beyond Storz's stations, and it began to standardize the national play list. Mitch Miller, who pleaded for "a balanced diet of music," said it was turning radio stations into "automated jukeboxes."

After Mitch Miller made his anti-rock-and-roll speech in 1958, all Columbia records were banned from airplay on Storz's Top 40 stations. Then, about the time John Hammond, Sr., returned to Columbia and signed Bob Dylan, Mitch Miller went from being an A&R man to a new level of fame. The first "Sing Along with Mitch" album had come out in 1958, originally conceived as "barracks ballads"—army songs for listeners to join in singing. Miller finessed the idea into an album of sing-along party songs that sold terrifically well; then, in January of 1961, "Sing Along with Mitch" went on NBC and became a surprise hit, regularly topping its competition, "Route 66," in the ratings.

"Sing Along with Mitch" featured a chorus of twenty-eight hearty, ordinary-looking, middle-aged American men and Mitch Miller standing up front conducting them as his famous beatnik goatee merrily wig-wagged to the beat. There were preteen Sing-Along Kids, and featured vocalists (including Leslie Uggams) who performed some solos, and even some choreographed acts for visual variety. But the heart of the show was Mitch and the Gang belting out such feel-good tunes as "Toot, Toot, Tootsie," "I've Been Working on the Railroad," and "Beautiful Ohio" as the lyrics were flashed on the screen so viewers at home could join the merriment and sing along as a ball bounced from word to word. With the possible exception of "The Lawrence Welk Show," nothing else in all of popular culture had a spirit that ran so absolutely contrary to the steamrolling ascent of rock and roll.

A lot of people frustrated by what was happening in popular music loved "Sing Along with Mitch," and it was a ratings success for four years. "We're filling a psychological need," Miller said. "In times of stress, people look for the tested values. They find them in reminiscing enjoyably about the past. . . . People say over and over again that this is the first real family experience they've had with music. Children are discovering fresh, new songs, while parents remember the old days." In September 1964, however, "Sing Along with Mitch" went off

the air at the peak of its popularity. The reason for its demise: Although the numbers were big, demographics were bad. Mitch Miller's appeal was to older viewers, and the coveted twelve-to-twenty-year-olds —who, it had been discovered, bought a whole lot more than pimple cream and candy bars—were ignoring him and paying attention to such hitmakers as the Animals, Manfred Mann, the Shangri-Las, the Supremes, and, of course, the Beatles—who began to dominate the pop charts during Mitch Miller's last few months on the air.

In 1970, at the height of protest over the war in Vietnam, the sing-along concept was revived for another album: *Mitch Miller and the Gang: Peace Sing-Along.* Always a liberal, Miller wanted to do something to express his opposition to the war. So he led his gang of enthusiastic basses and lilting tenors in such songs as "Where Have All the Flowers Gone?," "We Shall Overcome," and John Lennon and Paul McCartney's "Give Peace a Chance." Since then, Mitch has done many conducting tours around the world, specializing in Gershwin symphonies and frequently staging benefits with local orchestras that need money.

MINISKIRTS

A slender, tight little tube of material ending six, eight, possibly even ten inches above the knee, the miniskirt was, in its heyday, less an article of clothing than a flag of revolution. To wear one in 1965 was to stake your allegiance to the go-go generation—to mod London instead of formal Paris as your fashion beacon, to youthful audacity instead of matronly cor-

rectness, to the promise of a footloose future where anything would go rather than a dour past of rules and constraints. In 1989, looking back on its debut, even *Ms.* magazine's Susan Anthony found reason to hail it (although many feminists like to point out that it pandered to pubescent male fantasies): "Sexist or sexy, the mini was certainly a symbol of real social change."

No question: A new era of fashion (and more!) was dawning. Women had had birth control pills since 1960; the proliferation of pantyhose (see p. 374) made cumbersome garter belts and stockings virtually obsolete and allowed for unheard-of heights in hemlines; disco dances like the twist (see p. 542), the frug, and the watusi demanded total leg freedom. For women who wore them high enough to expose more thigh than had ever been considered seemly in polite society, miniskirts were a way to tell the world you intended to HAVE FUN!

Mary Quant, known among fashion historians as "the Mother of the Miniskirt," described the new attitude as "Wow—look at me!—isn't it lovely? At last, at last!" Quant began her career as fashion pioneer at Bazaar, the boutique on the King's Road in Chelsea that she and her husband, Alexander Plunket Greene, had opened in 1955. Once a neighborhood of small family shops, Chelsea became known in the late 1950s and early 1960s for its cellar clubs and beatnik joints and for a new kind of street-fashion pioneer called the Chelsea girl, outfitted in leather boots and black stockings, with feather boas and dramatic eye makeup,

looking, in Quant's words, "like some contemporary counterpart of a gay musketeer."

The Chelsea girl, whom Quant helped outfit with amusing handbags, poor-boy sweaters, fishnet gloves, outrageous horizontal stripes, patterned stockings, and short-shorter-shortest skirts (and whom Vidal Sassoon coiffed in drastic, short, asymmetrical hairdos), reversed the traditional dynamic flow of fashion trends. Whereas most young girls had once longed to "dress old" to appear more sophisticated, the new look took the exact opposite approach. In *Popism* Andy Warhol recalled that "everything went young in 1964... everything was reversed—the mothers and fathers were trying to look like their kids." Sophistication of the customary sort (pearls and pumps; bouclé suits; bouffant hair) was passé. A girlish appearance and fresh-as-a-daisy attitude became the marks of a new kind of irreverent sophistication.

Chelsea was its home, but soon the new look captivated London, the Left Bank, Greenwich Village, Haight-Ashbury, and eventually the whole world. By the mid-1960s, no groovy person wanted to look mature anymore. Clothes had ceased to serve their traditional purpose, to distinguish between rich and poor; they had become symbols of the gap between the young-at-heart and fuddie-duddies. "Many items shouldn't be worn by people over twenty-eight," announced Mr. Plunket Greene, whom the *New York Times* called "an elder statesman of the Mod movement" (he was over thirty).

Although hemlines had been going up for quite some time, the debut of the miniskirt in the windows of Bazaar in 1965 was—like Rudi Gernreich's topless bathing suit the year before—a challenge and a dare to propriety, and a defiant thumb in the eye of haute couture. Within months, miniskirts were everywhere in swinging London, and on the streets of hip neighborhoods in

American cities as well. When asked by a reporter to explain the social significance of the miniskirt, Mary Quant answered without equivocation: "sex." By the following year, when the Beatles had conquered the world and the myth of swinging England peaked, Quant's miniskirt had become as much a symbol of the new moral order as men's long hair and marijuana. Some American schools, in an effort to hold back the tide of cultural insurrection, instituted the kneel test, requiring the hems of girl students' skirts to touch the floor when they knelt. Old-guard couturiers hated the miniskirt because it was so unflattering to their staid clientele; in January 1967 *Women's Wear Daily* observed, "Everybody keeps saying it's going to go away like it's some kind of a disease."

It was, at first, an outlaw fashion, and strange as it may seem today, when such blatant sexual display is generally considered reactionary, miniskirts were originally adopted by many who considered themselves at the forefront of the women's movement. For them, the short-short skirt wasn't merely groovy. It became, for a while, an emblem of female liberation—an announcement by its wearer that she was indeed a sexual being, and not afraid to show it. Along with go-go boots, extremist makeup (including Body Paint), patterned tights, mod-colored body stockings, and the peace symbol, the miniskirt was a way for a woman to signify she was bold, sexually free, and unfettered by male-chauvinist notions of modesty and Victorian propriety. She could do as she pleased, and that included the freedom to be sexy. Even Bernadine Dohrn of the ultra-radical Weather Underground was known for her miniskirts, as were women's movement pioneers Gloria Steinem and Marlo Thomas.

However, the semiology of short skirts changed dramatically in the 1970s when many in the movement became more militant and adopted a sober, earth-tone, unisex look. The miniskirt soon took on the stigma of clothing worn to titillate a man, and as it grew shorter and evolved into the crotch-high micro-miniskirt, it became, along with hot pants, the well-established uniform of hookers all over the world.

The respectably long miniskirt (four inches above the knee) is now everyday fashion for many women—still a wee bit daring but nonetheless fully acceptable clothing in polite society. In his enlightening analysis of 1960s fashions, *Radical Rags*, Joel Lobenthal pinpointed the moment when miniskirts became okay as occurring in December 1966, when Jackie Kennedy wore a fairly modest one to lunch at a restaurant in New York. (Jackie hedged her bet, Lobenthal pointed out, by wearing her short skirt with long, formal gloves and other such "genteel accoutrements of yore.") Miniskirts were heading for the mainstream, and by the early 1970s Mary Tyler Moore—television's quintessential nice girl (see p. 304)—was wearing them just as casually as she wore pantsuits, ponchos, and bell-bottom slacks.

THE MOB

The criminal underworld has been called all sorts of things through the years, including the Mafia and the Cosa Nostra, the syndicate, the brotherhood, Murder Inc., and organized crime, but nearly everybody knows it simply as the mob. There is no other subculture so storied for its denizens' irredeemable villainy. They kill, steal, extort, pander, deal drugs, gamble, drive too fast, dress too loud, and talk like either stupid oafs or sly flim-flam men . . . all of which has made them not only archetypal twentieth-century bad guys but also an underlying source of popular entertainment. In books and on stage, especially in the movies, but also on newspaper front pages, professional gangsters have charisma unlike any other type of criminal.

In real life their ranks have included such colorfully named (and badly behaved) characters as "Scarface" Al Capone; "Legs" Diamond; Earle "Hymie" Weiss, the first known crook to give a victim a "one-way ride," in 1921, thus making cars a fundamental gangster tool; "Lucky" Luciano, who with Meyer Lansky and Louis "Lepke" Buchalter first established a national crime syndicate in the 1930s; Vince "the Chin" Gigante; Joe "Bananas" Bonanno; "Three-Finger" Brown; "Blue Jaw" Magoon; and Tony "Big Tuna" Accardo. These characters have in turn inspired over a half a century of bewitching fictional mobsters, ranging from the underprivileged dead-end kid gone wrong played by Jimmy Cagney in *Angels with Dirty Faces* (1938), to the roster of sadistic psychopaths headed by Richard Widmark in *Kiss of Death* (1947), the movie in which he laughingly pushes a crippled old lady down a flight of stairs, to the merry musical chums of *Guys and Dolls* (which

Edward G. Robinson *(far left)* in *Little Caesar*

opened on Broadway in 1950, based on Damon Runyon characters and was revived in 1992), to wise and avuncular Marlon Brando of *The Godfather* (1972), to the cretinous con men of Martin Scorsese's *Goodfellas* (1990).

Along with the trigger-happy gunslingers of the Old West, these racketeers in fedoras and double-breasted suits are America's most symptomatic leading men—as red-white-and-blue as a blazing tommy gun or a snub-nose .38. In fact, when Euro Disney world was being planned, the French wanted Main Street to be a 1920s recreation, populated by gangsters and their molls shooting at each other and running illegal booze, but an abashed Disney organization disallowed the idea as unbecoming. Be that as it may, there can be no denying that mobsters have just what it takes to succeed in the land of the free and the home of the brave: blazing ambition. The traditional underworld character (in fiction and in real life) starts with nothing, customarily as an immigrant, then rises to glory by his wits and by treachery, creating his own success with passion and self-confidence and a kind of perverse bravery like the star of some haywire Horatio Alger story. Gangsters live the American dream, but turned inside out. They are, in a philosophical sense, quintessentially free men—unbounded by law or even by ordinary moral scruples. They are compulsively violent but often sympathetic, immensely powerful, foolhardy to the point of insanity (and frequently beyond)—qualities that have made them anathema to civic-minded taxpayers and law-enforcement officers but have endeared them to generations of moviemakers in need of exceptional protagonists. From Hollywood studios in the 1930s to the French New Wave directors of the 1950s and 1960s and even for action filmmakers of today, gangsters always provide a tantalizing opportunity to tell a life-and-death story with not only jeopardy and thrills but also social consciousness and sermonizing.

This book is not the place to examine the preposterous debate about whether or not there is, or ever was, a Cosa Nostra operating in the United States: The inner workings of the mob were revealed in excruciating detail when former hit man Joe Valachi testified to the U.S. Senate in 1962 all about ritualistic blood oaths with gun and dagger, being "made" (becoming a sworn member of the crime family), and the kiss of death (marking an imminent victim). However, it is important to note that there is a big difference between the everyday cruelty of most real-life criminals and their rousing pop-culture image. Just as actual cowboying was a whole lot less fun than the thrilling lives of the heroes and desperadoes who populate most western movies, so the generally scurvy doings of genuine gangsters are only dimly related to the grandiose mythology that has made gangsterism a mainstay of entertainment and American folklore. Nearly all mobsters in movies, no matter how evil and repugnant they may be,

are larger-than-life figures who, if seldom actually heroic, frequently enact dramas loaded with moral significance.

Semiorganized criminals have been movie characters since D. W. Griffith's *The Musketeers of Pig Alley* (1912), but it was in Josef von Sternberg's *Underworld* (1927) that the now-familiar image of a well-organized gangster society first began to take shape as an inversion of corporate society on the other side of the law. Bull Weed, boss of Sternberg's underworld, behaves a lot like any take-charge boss and meets his end, as has become requisite in nearly all fictional accounts of the mob, in a cathartic shoot-out and violent death. Bull Weed, however, was merely a diamond thief taking things that didn't belong to him; when bootlegging became the central activity of gangster movies in the early 1930s, the underworld assumed a whole new social dimension, populated with importers, distributors, enforcers, and petty criminals eager to work their way to the top of the gangland hierarchy. There were over sixty such movies made between 1930 and 1935, some of which, including the classic *The Public Enemy* (1931, starring Jimmy Cagney) and *Scarface* (1932, starring Paul Muni), made their eager-to-succeed outlaw heroes so sympathetic that they were amended with preachy prologues reminding audiences that the illegal activities they were about to see were wrong.

What has made so many movie mobsters attractive (aside from their pluck and prosperity) is their peculiar code of honor. Strange as it may seem for people defined by moral turpitude, the mob (the movie mob, we repeat) lives by a set of old-fashioned rules that includes loyalty to kin and comrades, respect for elders, eye-for-an-eye retribution, and reward for hard work. As depicted in all three *Godfather* movies, the mob isn't just an accidental extended family; it is nothing less than a scrupulously structured alternative society, headed by its all-powerful Godfather, who, more like some wondrous fairy godmother, can grant any wish to a loyal follower who kisses his hand and shows proper respect. In contrast to the square, gray, implacable and often dishonorable bureaucratic government (personified for decades by J. Edgar Hoover of the FBI), this unpredictable, hot-blooded, all-too-human bunch of gunsels is an enthralling group, even when they are up to no good. Indeed, most gangster movies focus so much on the machinations of the underworld that the law and its drab enforcers seem practically extraneous.

The appeal of the mob as an alternative to priggish straight society crystallized in the early 1960s when Frank Sinatra (see p. 450) and his Rat Pack expressed a hip, flip, and mischievous infatuation with organized crime in the films *Ocean's Eleven* (1960) and *Robin and the Seven Hoods* (1964). In both movies, gangsters are cool, handsome, lighthearted, and sexy, and the crimes they commit are mostly for kicks, never hurting anybody (unless he deserves it). That's one of the strangest aspects of the mob in pop culture: Notwithstanding its well-known and well-deserved reputation in real life as a bunch of vicious thugs, the mob so often appears in entertainment as an almost harmless source of wry delight. In May 1992, in an article about career opportunities for young adults, *Details* magazine offered readers a merry parody board game titled "The Mob Game: How to Whack Friends and Influence People." Players moved from a square that said "Your uncle the capo sets you up as a coffee distributor. Restaurants are told to buy from you—or else" through "The Feds bug your social club" to the penultimate achievement: "Martin Scorsese options your life story." In April 1992 the Toronto *Star* noted, "Real life

mobsters and molls are already standard fare afternoons on 'Oprah' and 'Geraldo.' . . . One suspects if a movie about Abe Lincoln was released this year, we'd see at least one underboss."

Another reason people have tended to dote on the mob despite its essentially atrocious nature is that the mob is (in folklore) so damned efficient—much more so than the government or legal businesses. These boys get things done, usually without a hitch, and they don't leave a trace. In the late 1960s, about the same time it grew generally apparent that the United States government was bungling the war in Vietnam, the mob started getting credit in many conspiracy theories as the unseen (and implicitly omnipotent) force behind the assassination of JFK; it has since been revealed that Chicago crime boss Sam "Momo" Giancana was actually employed by the CIA to purvey dirty tricks (including an attempt to give Fidel Castro an exploding cigar). On a less fantastical level, it has become a familiar conviction in many American cities that the only really safe neighborhoods are those in which mobsters live. Park your car on their street, walk along their sidewalks after midnight: No petty-ante crook or mugger would dare disturb the peace where mobsters live because mobsters, unlike cops and DAs and all timid minions of the law, always get their man . . . and get him good. This belief was best rendered in Don Siegel's masterful *Charley Varrick* (1973), about a small-time thief who robs a bank that happens to be used by the mob as a depository. Varrick, played by Walter Matthau, has no fear whatever of the police or the feds getting him for bank robbery; but when he realizes he has taken Mafia money, he knows he is in deep, deep trouble. The mob enforcer, played by Joe Don Baker, is inexorable, inescapable, and absolutely self-confident. This is an image of the mob very much alive today in real life, as evident in the federal prosecutor's summary statement in the 1992 trial of New York Mafia don John Gotti, in which the government openly acknowledged that, of course, jurors had reason to fear for their own safety if they delivered a guilty verdict.

Mr. Gotti, who went from being the Dapper Don (because of his high fashion wardrobe) and the Teflon Don (because the feds could never make any charges stick) to winding up as the Velcro Don (when he was stuck with a murder rap because a fellow killer named Sammy "the Bull" Gravano ratted on him for rubbing out another mob boss), was the last (or perhaps we should say the most recent) in a long line of mobsters who have relished pop celebrity. Gangland's best-known glory hogs have included Arnold "Mr. Big" Rothstein, who strolled the streets of New York in the 1920s placing thousand-dollar bets with sidewalk bookies; Harry "Pittsburgh Phil" Strauss of Murder Inc., known for his taste in gaudy jewelry and for gleefully popping (his word) over five hundred victims in the 1930s; and Benjamin "Bugsy" Siegel, who befriended George Raft and tried to insinuate himself into the movie business, then dreamt up Las Vegas in 1945. However, most real-life mobsters have preferred—for obvious reasons—to stay out of the spotlight. Only when they are caught, or when one of them decides to sing, as described in the book *The Valachi Papers* or in Nicholas Pileggi's *Wiseguy*, is the real mob exposed.

Ten recommended mob movies:

- *Little Caesar* (1930; director: Mervyn LeRoy). This tale of Enrico Caesar Bandello —the role that made Edward G. Robinson a star—established the classic formula: from small-time grifter to king of the rackets to corpse lying face-down in the street.
- *The Public Enemy* (1931; director: William A. Wellman). The first movie in which bootlegging was the central gangster activity. Jimmy Cagney's performance as Tom Powers has made it a classic. His volatile, brutish behavior (as when he squashes a grapefruit into Mae Clarke's face) added a psychopathological dimension to the genre, and his demise—trussed up like a mummy, delivered to his mother's front door—gave the film's violence an especially macabre twist.
- *Scarface* (1932; director: Howard Hawks). As Tony Camonte, Paul Muni created a haunting image of a man who is at once savage and sympathetic, terrifying and funny. "Do it first, do it yourself, and keep on doing it," he advises his friend Gino (George Raft). Tony's abnormal love of his sister and intimations of a taboo relationship between him and Gino make *Scarface* a rich character study and shade its violence with inevitable sexual undertones. Remade by Brian DePalma in 1983 with Al Pacino in the lead (as a cocaine dealer from Cuba rather than a bootlegger from Italy).
- *The Roaring Twenties* (1939; director: Raoul Walsh). The first cycle of gangster movies at the beginning of the 1930s focused on rise-and-fall stories of extraordinary individuals. The law entered the picture mid-decade, in *G-Men* (1935) and *Bullets or Ballots* (1936), and soon gangster movies began to offer a social context for their characters' aberrant behavior. In *The Roaring Twenties*, one of the quickest and most tightly plotted of the genre, the misdeeds of its criminals (Cagney and Bogart) are seen to have risen out of the violence of World War I and the hopelessness of social conditions that followed. Crime—bootlegging in particular—was the only chance these guys ever had.
- *Kiss of Death* (1947; director: Henry Hathaway). Although there is a quasi-documentary quality to *Kiss of Death*, typical of many postwar crime movies (*Boomerang* [1948] and *Force of Evil* [1949]), it is best remembered for its moral gravity: Can Vic-

tor Mature stay honest and out of the mob? The shadowy visual web in which the characters are trapped, as well as Richard Widmark's seething dementia, make this a definitive gangster film noir.

- *White Heat* (1949; director: Raoul Walsh). Deliciously unhinged James Cagney plays Cody Jarrett, a man who loves his mother so much that he doesn't mind killing everybody else. One guy is disfigured by scalding steam; another is thrown in a car trunk then blasted full of holes; and in the most explosive movie ending ever, Cody stands atop a giant gas tank, salutes his dead mom, then blows himself to kingdom come. The mob as an organization scarcely matters in this movie, but as a professional mobster, Cody Jarrett provides the ultimate definition of antisocial depravity.

- *The Big Heat* (1953; director: Fritz Lang). One honest man (Glenn Ford) against the syndicate: a formula popular in such other fine 1950s gangster pictures as *The Phoenix City Story* (1955) and *The Brothers Rico* (1957). *The Big Heat* is almost unbearably violent, beginning with a close-up of a revolver and a gunshot, then hurtling through scene after scene of cruelty and treachery, many featuring Lee Marvin in one of his favorite roles, as sadist Vince Stone. Gloria Grahame gets her face burned by scalding coffee; another woman is tortured and strangled; the hero's wife is blown up in a car. The mob is so all-powerful and so well insinuated into officialdom, as well as so vicious, that the happy ending attached to this movie only underscores its essential cynicism.

- *Underworld USA* (1961; director: Sam Fuller). War between the feds and the syndicate is told in very personal terms: One man (Cliff Robertson) sets out to get revenge on the mobsters who killed his father many years earlier. Boss Connors runs the underworld just like a respectable corporation and even masquerades as a charitable guy, letting underprivileged kids swim in his pool (but ordering his henchman, who acts as lifeguard, to murder the little girl of one of his enemies, which he does by running over her with his car), and with characteristic Sam Fuller irony Connors dies in his pool, too: gasping for air under his avenger's feet. His lifeless body bobs up and floats alongside a day-old newspaper with a headline that reads, CONNORS DEFIES UNCLE SAM.

- *The Godfather* (1972; sequels in 1974 and 1990; director: Francis Ford Coppola). Based on Mario Puzo's colossally successful novel (67 weeks on the best-seller list after it was published in 1969); this is essentially a roman à clef about the life and times of Vito "Don Vitone" Genovese, who rose up through the ranks of the New York Mafia by killing off his rivals, eventually becoming the *capo di tutti capi*—boss of all bosses. The most successful gangster movie ever (the biggest-grossing movie of all time until *Star Wars* and *E.T.*, and winner of ten Academy Awards), *The Godfather* has become a cultural institution; its multigenerational sweep has assumed the aura of a great national fable. Its theme song is played at countless weddings (and is available as a car horn and a musical toilet-paper dispenser); its ominous line "Make him an offer he can't refuse" has become one of the best-known clichés in the language; the rotund, stuffed-cheek don created by Marlon Brando is modern cinema's most recognizable character, parodied and spoofed ad nauseam, even by Brando himself (in *The Freshman*, 1990). Since this movie's release, the word "godfather" has been adopted as a sign of power and authority in nearly every aspect of American life, from soul music (where James Brown [see p. 70] declared himself the Godfather of Soul) to franchised food (Godfather's Pizza). More than any other single movie or real-life event, *The Godfather* has ensured the lasting status of the mob as a pop-culture obsession.

- *Goodfellas* (1990; director: Martin Scorsese). An exhilarating deconstruction of genre mythology in which the mobsters (Robert De Niro, Ray Liotta, and Joe Pesci) are shown to be trite, petty, and sordid; gang activities that may seem glamorous to the outside (and to the lead character, in the beginning) are rendered as dismally banal. Real-life mob turncoat Henry Hill, upon whose life *Goodfellas* was based (from the book *Wiseguy*), became a widely known talk-show guest following the success of the movie in 1990, regaling media hosts from ABC's Ted Koppel to morning shock-jock Howard Stern with his hair-raising adventures as a member of the mob.

THE MONKEES

In the first few months of 1967 the Monkees were the most popular band on earth, outselling the Beatles, the Beach Boys, and the Rolling Stones combined. Two years later, they were rock laughingstocks. Whatever their charms and talent, however distinguished their achievements in music, television, and movies, the four lads who were put together as a singing and performing group in 1965 and began breaking up in 1968 became a long-lasting symbol of fraud in rock music. Long before the righteous wrath of fans and critics made Milli Vanilli into a living sacrifice for the crime of lip-synching songs that other people actually sang, the Monkees were crucified for not being real enough. In the late 1960s, being real—or at least appearing to be real —was essential to gaining audience respect in rock and roll, which was hard at work positioning itself as the youth culture's honest alternative to the slick stylings of the old pop establishment (see "Mitch Miller," p. 318). They never lost all their fans, especially among very young kids, who always liked them because they were so cute, and in recent years, like so many odd 1960s things, they have inspired campy Monkees cults, as well as a big market in Monkees

Peter Tork, Micky Dolenz, Mike Nesmith, Davy Jones

collectibles. But by the time Woodstock Nation gathered to the beat of Jimi and Janis in 1969, it was hard to find any hip person over the age of sixteen who would admit to liking them.

Critically approved rock-and-roll acts were supposed to rise up out of their circumstances, as the Beatles had done from Liverpool or Ike and Tina Turner out of East St. Louis, and sing about the real life they had encountered along the way. Being honest meant being yourself and thumbing your nose at the establishment. The Monkees, however, were nobody and came from nowhere, and didn't sing about anything real. They were, in fact, invented out of whole cloth, the idea being to create another musical phenomenon and sell millions of records, like the Beatles, but instantly and more efficiently, via a television show. Conceived by Bob Rafelson and Burt Schneider as a fast way to make heaps of money, their television show was commissioned by Screen Gems well before they existed. Rafelson and Schneider had discarded such names as the Creeps ("too negative," Schneider explained), the Turtles, and the Inevitables, deciding on "the Monkees" because, like "the Beatles" and "the Byrds"— both big successes—it was a misspelled animal name. On September 9 and 10, 1965, they placed this advertisement in *Daily Variety:*

(Ben Frank's was a popular cafe on Sunset Strip where the mod crowd hung out. "Must come down" was supposed to be a clever reference to being high.) Four hundred and thirty-seven applicants came down to attend the audition, including Charles Manson (see p. 299), who was rejected because he wasn't cute enough, and Stephen Stills, who got cut because of his receding hairline and a bad tooth and because he wasn't uninhibited enough (and, he now claims, because he insisted on writing his own music).

Micky Dolenz, already under contract to Screen Gems from his days as a child star in the TV show "Circus Boy" (1956–58), was a shoo-in; Davy Jones, a Brit who had played the Artful Dodger in *Oliver!* on Broadway two years earlier, was a cinch. Mike Nesmith (whose mother invented the secretary's friend White Out) was pulled into audition when a studio guard spotted him on the street carrying his laundry to the laundromat. Peter Tork, chosen in open auditions, had been a folksinger in Greenwich Village before coming to California. Each of the four designated Monkees had qualities that were supposed to parallel those of the four Beatles. Eric Lefcowitz, author of *The Monkees Tale*, described them this way: "David Jones had the cuddly cuteness of McCartney, Michael Nesmith had the mercurial arrogance of Lennon, Micky Dolenz mirrored the happy-go-lucky Ringo, and Peter Tork was similar to the inward, mystical Harrison." Lefcowitz went on to note that, like the Beatles, each Monkee had a target audience: "Jones was the teen heart-throb; Nesmith appealed to the intellectual nebbish crowd; Dolenz won fans with his free-wheeling, wise-cracking demeanor. Tork's appeal was [as an] empty-headed caricature on the television series . . . [and a] gentle 'peace, love, and flowers' image off screen."

Before the show started filming, the Monkees underwent five grueling weeks of rehearsal and improvisational sessions in which director James Frawley taught them to be funny all the time, especially when a camera was pointed in their direction. Some of Frawley's techniques included having them do everything in slow motion and to pretend they were different animals (a crab, a giraffe, an elephant), and even to behave as though they were inanimate objects (a teapot, a tree). Meanwhile, the Monkees' look was established: full-blown mod wardrobe, including bell-bottom pants, flowered shirts (later, Nehru jackets), and long hair. The hair was so important that the hair stylist on the set was reportedly paid more per week than all four Monkees put together. And although they drove a woody station wagon (like surfers) in the pilot episode, it was soon traded for a Monkeemobile—a bright red, souped-up Pontiac GTO designed by customizer George Barris.

Just as the boys replicated the Beatles, their TV show was made to remind viewers of the Beatles' movie *A Hard Day's Night*: a jumble of speeded-up action, upside-down frames, and visual non sequiturs; lots of madcap romping around; only the shreds of a plot; and many shots in which the boys made funny faces. In almost every episode of its two-year run, there were moments when the boys, as themselves, talked directly to the camera. And although they used their real Monkee names, the characters they played were not pop superstars; they were supposed to be ordinary fellows who find themselves in funny situations, as described by Edward Reilly, Maggie McManus, and William Chadwick in their incomparably exhaustive catalogue of Monkee facts, statistics, and day-by-day (!) chronology, *The Monkees: A Manufactured Image*:

- "Royal Flush" (the first episode): Uncle Otto plans the untimely demise of his niece, Princess Bettina, but the Monkees have a plan all their own.
- "The Spy Who Came In from the Cool": Look out, James Bond, here come the Monkees. It's high intrigue and high comedy as the boys are mistaken for spy contacts.
- "Don't Look a Gift Horse in the Mouth": The excitement begins when Davy receives a pony as a gift, but it will be a horse of a different color when their landlord finds out.

- "I Was a 99 Pound Weakling": To win the heart of a beautiful girl, Micky takes a course in body building.

"The Monkees" won Emmy awards (best comedy show and best director, for the first episode) and nice notices from the *New York Times*, which called its stars "the Marx Brothers in adolescence," *Newsweek* ("fresh stuff for TV"), and *Time* ("bright, unaffected, and zany"), but it never even made it into the Nielsen top twenty-five, a fact that Monkees fans continue to blame on the number of local NBC affiliates that refused to run the show because they believed it was subversive. "Our show gives you the idea of being an individual," Micky Dolenz told *Seventeen* magazine, asserting that "The Monkees," unlike ordinary television programming, encouraged viewers to question authority. Timothy Leary, the LSD guru, agreed with him, writing in *The Politics of Ecstasy* that the show was "a classic Sufi put-on. An early-Christian electronic satire. A mystic-magic show. A jolly Buddha laugh at hypocrisy ... burlesquing the very shows that glue Mom and Dad to the set during prime time." Producer Burt Schneider put it this way: "It wasn't 'Father Knows Best.' It was the kids know best. The heroes were young people and the heavies were older people."

Whether or not the message of "The Monkees" meant anything, the show did establish an avenue for exploiting talent by combining television and the music business in a new way. For one thing, its appeal to preteens, who viewed it as a kind of live-action cartoon, corralled heretofore untapped enthusiasm into the marketplace for records and souvenirs. Prior to its debut, television had helped boost record sales on some notable occasions (Chubby Checker on "American Bandstand," Elvis and the Beatles on "Ed Sullivan"), but "The Monkees" was the first time TV created and sustained a musical phenomenon, establishing a lucrative merchandising pattern that is now the soul of MTV (see p. 344). Every episode featured segments in which the Monkees sang (or pretended to sing) their hits, and unlike Ricky Nelson's staid performance before an audience on "The Adventures of Ozzie and Harriet," these showcases for their records gleefully broke all the rules of how to present a rock-and-roll performance. Instead of standing up in front of a docile crowd to sing and play (neither of which they did particularly well), the Monkees were shown doing what they were really good at: cavorting. As one of their songs played in the background they rode merry-go-rounds, ran up and down sandy beaches, crossed their eyes, and jumped in the air while a jerky camera peered at them through a fish-eye lens. This marriage of pop music with dissonant imagery was the beginning of rock videos. It sold millions of records by making the Monkees into inescapable visual icons—today virtually a prerequisite for success in the music business. "Just as man evolved from apes, rock video evolved from the Monkees," Bob Shannon and John Javna wrote in their book *Behind the Hits*, pointing to the fact that the Monkees' "Valleri" became a top ten hit for no reason other than the fact that it had aired on TV once, and only once.

"Hang on to your granny glasses," said a 1966 *Teen* magazine advertisement for Colgems, the new label established by RCA to market Monkees records. "The Monkees have made the scene!" Their first release, "Last Train to Clarksville," sailed to number one on the pop chart after the debut of their TV show; and their next single, "I'm a Believer" (backed by ["I'm Not Your] Stepping Stone"), sold ten million copies. By early 1967 Monkeemania had arrived, and it wasn't only the records that were selling.

Their manufactured image had become the best-selling logo in the world; their likeness was on lunch boxes, wool hats (like Mike wore), and underwear; there were paint-by-numbers Monkees kits and a chain of Monkees Soft Drink Night Clubs for underage fans. They were huge hits in England when they arrived in June (it was reported that more journalists covered their press conference at the Royal Garden Hotel in Kensington than attended Winston Churchill's at the end of World War II), and there were soon imitation Monkee bands in America, including Monkey Business and the Banana Splits.

Serious rock fans hated them from the beginning, because serious rock fans were already into heavyweight stuff like Barry McGuire ("Eve of Destruction"), Simon and Garfunkle, and the new, intellectual, no-longer-cuddly Beatles. But all the squealy teens who had made the Beatles such a hit in the first place needed someone to love now that John Lennon and his pals were getting so pretentious, and the Monkees were nothing if not lovable.

Then the Monkees did something weird —entirely in character for the guys they portrayed on TV, but shocking to their handlers. They rebelled. Rocketed to overnight success like no other humans in history, the four boys suddenly found that they were very unhappy. They didn't like being puppets, or as Davy Jones put it, "mechanical toys told to go here, do that, don't talk about the war in Vietnam or whatever." So they blew the whistle on themselves. At the beginning of 1967, when their song "I'm a Believer" (written by Neil Diamond—and by some accounts sung by him as well) rode the top of the pop charts for ten straight weeks, they told the press they were phonies. "We're advertisers," Davy Jones told the *New York Times*. "We're selling a product. We're selling Monkees." And Mike Nesmith, explaining that "there comes a time when you have to draw the line as a man," informed the *Saturday Evening Post*, "the music has nothing to do with us. It was totally dishonest. Do you know how debilitating it is to have to duplicate somebody else's records? That's really what we were doing."

Music publisher Don Kirshner had completely controlled their sound, allowing them to merely dub their voices onto prerecorded tracks, then used editing and electronic wiles to create the final record (sometimes adding the voices of Neil Diamond and Carole King to flesh out the Monkees' sound), on one occasion actually releasing a record without even bothering to notify the Monkees he was doing so. From their first "concert," in September 1966, when (because they had just been put together) they merely stood up and introduced themselves, there had been rumors that they didn't really do their own music; and once they did figure out how to perform live together, stories circulated that there was a real band somewhere offstage that was actually playing and singing while they only went through the motions. All this remained rumor until early 1967, when at the height of their fame they came clean.

TV Guide's cover story about their revelations was titled "The Great Revolt of '67" and described their craving to be—like Dylan, the Beatles, the Stones, et al.—their own men. Don Kirshner was fired. The Monkees began to make their own music, and some of it was pretty good, even successful (Nesmith's hard-rocking "Circle Sky"; Jones's "You and I"). But it was too late for the Monkees to redeem their image. In the words of Eric Lefcowitz, "The Monkees became the counterculture's favorite whipping boy." They were clear and present symbols that the establishment was venal, phony, and unscrupulous. Producer Bob Rafelson, who had realized his goal of making

enough money to get into movies (he directed *Five Easy Pieces*), said: "Now that the word had gotten out that the Monkees were not responsible for their own music, the older kids said, 'Fuck the Monkees, let my kid sister watch them. I want to listen to Jim Morrison and Jimi Hendrix, not ersatz Beatle records.'" In fact, before he became popular Jimi Hendrix went on tour to open for the Monkees, and when he grew frustrated because the teenybopper crowds were unmoved by his psychedelic hot licks on "Purple Haze," booing him and chanting "We want the Monkees!" throughout his set, he quit the tour. The Monkees issued a phony press release saying that he had quit because the Daughters of the American Revolution had protested his act as too erotic.

In 1967 the Monkees sold thirty-five million records, but they were doomed, and not only by their reputation as frauds. The Beatles' *Sgt. Pepper's Lonely Hearts Club Band* rewrote the rules of pop, and the Monkees' 1968 movie, *Head* (co-scripted by Jack Nicholson), was a terrible flop (except in France, where it was proclaimed a masterpiece). Pauline Kael said that its "doubling up of greed and pretensions to depth is enough to make a pinhead walk out." *Head*, which in some ways is a culmination of their hyperkinetic style, is today one of the finest time capsules of soft-centered Aquarian iconoclasm, but in 1968 no one wanted to see it. After their last number-one song, "Daydream Believer," in December 1967, they placed a handful of hits on the *Billboard* chart, including "Valleri" and the psychedelic "Porpoise Song," before Peter Tork quit the group in December 1968. They appeared as a trio on Paul Revere and the Raiders' TV show, "Happening," and on "Laugh-In," made a flop television special called "33-⅓ Revolutions Per Monkee," and played to half-empty houses on a 1969 summer tour. Their old TV show, with new songs, was rerun at noon on Saturdays in the fall of that year, accompanied by commercials they had made for Kool-Aid and breakfast cereals. In conjunction with the reruns, specially marked boxes of Frosted Rice Krinkles, Honeycomb, and Alpha Bits were sold in grocery stores with actual Monkees records, pressed on card-board, as part of the packaging.

On February 23, 1986, MTV broadcast twenty-two and a half consecutive hours of original Monkees episodes in a marathon titled "Pleasant Valley Sunday" after the Monkees song of the same name, written by Gerry Goffin and Carole King, that attacked the superficiality of suburban life.

MARILYN MONROE

Blond, buxom, outrageously sexy, and profoundly sad, Marilyn Monroe is the supreme symbol of Hollywood. When she was alive, she was the world's most famous pinup girl, but she got only intermittent respect as an actress, and her career wasn't all that impressive. However, in the thirty years since she died, she has risen to become a cultural life force, an alluring embodiment of the movies' ambivalent ethos of glamour and exploitation. The tragedy of her life has combined with the triumph of her image to make her, in death, into just about every ambitious writer's favorite opportunity to expound about the relationship between personal psychopathology and popular culture. No other dead human being in this century has inspired such far-flung expository delirium, some of it so curiously sensual it verges on necrophilia:

- To Jane O'Reilly, who as a feminist said she felt uncomfortable watching "a grown woman act like a baby," Marilyn Monroe was nonetheless "astonishing, a riddle, a joy, phosphorescence in the midnight water."
- To Norman Mailer, who devoted a ninety-thousand-word "novel-biography" (*Mari-*

lyn, 1973) to her charisma, she was "a lover of life and a cowardly hyena of death who drenched herself in chemical stupors; a sexual oven whose fire may rarely have been lit . . . more and less than the silver witch of us all . . . the magnified mirror of ourselves."
- Writing in his book *Cult Heroes,* Deyan Sudjic observed, "Our idea of Marilyn Monroe is not that of a walking, talking human

being, but of a static figure forever poised over a Manhattan pavement grating, her skirts whirling around her neck, her candy-floss hair molded into baroque contours, her smile an unfocused glint."

- In a 1982 *Film Comment* David Thomson wrote, "Possibility slips in and out of her open-mouth smile, like fellatio in a daydream. Time and photography's staying power have gently lifted the smile into simile." Thomson then goes on to compare her death, at age thirty-six, with that of Jesus Christ, at thirty-three: "Think how blurred Christ might have been if he'd been photographed as often as she was."

- Pop-culture professor Michael Marsden of Bowling Green State University told the Los Angeles *Times* that Monroe had become a "super icon" like Abraham Lincoln, "an incredibly magnetic personality" who transcended her particulars to become a symbol of generational values far beyond her time.

Once cast as America's pre-eminent sexpot—every guy's wet dream and every woman's nightmare image of femininity reduced to breathy squeals and jiggling breasts—she is now one of pop history's favorite victims, embraced especially by feminists (including Gloria Steinem), who have come to see her as a woman who was never allowed to fulfill her potential in a male-dominated business (and society) that demanded she be nothing but pretty and hot. As film critic Molly Haskell put it, Marilyn Monroe has in recent years been canonized "as a martyr to male chauvinism."

Any way you choose to look at it, Marilyn Monroe had a pretty miserable life. Born Norma Jeane Baker in 1926, the illegitimate child of an absent father and a demented mother named Gladys Pearl Monroe who abandoned her with an aunt when she was three, she was alternately abused and neglected, raped at age nine by a "family friend," and shuffled from an orphanage to twelve different foster homes until age sixteen, when she got married (to a sailor named James Dougherty) to escape. As a worker in an aircraft factory during the war, known for wowing fellow employees by wearing tight sweaters, she posed for cheesecake pictures (for which she was paid a total of fifty dollars), including nude calendar shots that became some of the best-selling soft-core pornography of the early 1950s—one of them recirculated in the first issue of *Playboy* (see p. 388).

She was on the cover of five different magazines in 1946, which got the attention of Howard Hughes, who gave her a screen test. "Sign her up," said Darryl Zanuck, admiring what he called her "flesh impact." Zanuck said, "Some girls have flesh that photographs like flesh. You feel you can reach out and touch it." She was given platinum blond hair and a new name, as well as a surgically improved chin, and began her movie career with a one-word role ("Hi!"—cut out of the picture) in *Scudda Hoo! Scudda Hay!* (1948). She got her first serious role in John Huston's crime drama *The Asphalt Jungle* (1950), and a comic one in Joseph Mankiewicz's *All About Eve* (1950), in which she plays "Miss Caswell, a graduate of the Copacabana School of Dramatic Art." She posed for countless pinup pictures and publicity shots (dressed in nothing but a burlap potato sack, inside a jumbo Christmas stocking) and gradually slept her way to stardom, simultaneously projecting the image of a farcical bimbo and that of an earnest actress who yearned to be taken seriously. In April 1952 she made the cover of *Life*, for an article that called her "the talk of Hollywood."

Joe DiMaggio, America's favorite retired New York Yankee, had seen a publicity picture she had done posed as a baseball player, and found a way to meet her. Sparks flew, and in January 1954 she and Joe exchanged vows in the fairy-tale marriage of the decade. Joe, however, grew upset over her relentless publicity-seeking and her outrageously sexy image. "I shall never forget the look of death on Joe's face," recalled director Billy Wilder about the time in 1954 when Marilyn's new husband grimly observed the filming of the skirt-blowing scene in *The Seven Year Itch*. Joe pleaded with Marilyn to give up her career to stay home and be his loving wife. They were divorced in October.

Next, as part of her program to gain respectability and intellectual cachet, she married playwright Arthur Miller (dubbed "the wedding of the egghead and the hourglass"), who had become one of the movie industry's least favorite writers because of his refusal to buckle under to anticommunist witch hunters. Marilyn had two miscarriages during her marriage to Miller, one of which she blamed on overwork during the filming of *Some Like It Hot* in 1958. Eventually, Marilyn and Arthur Miller divorced, too, mostly because of Marilyn's escalating drug and alcohol abuse.

Marilyn had temporarily left Hollywood in the 1950s to study acting in New York because she was so frustrated by her movie roles as a dumb blonde. (She wanted, she said, to play Grushenka in *The Brothers Karamazov*.) Her teacher, Lee Strasberg, said she was one of his finest pupils, but the die had been cast, and even when she finally got her serious and important role—in *The Misfits* (1961), written especially for her by Miller—she received little respect from a Hollywood establishment that had come to resent her because she seemed to take special pleasure in setting herself apart from them. "This is supposed to be an art form, not just a manufacturing establishment," she scolded in her last published interview in *Life* magazine in August 1962. Her knack for positioning herself as a sensitive artist

who had been chewed up and spit out by an insensitive, exploitive industry has endeared her to generations of admirers who see her as the quintessential casualty of the entertainment business's voracious appetite for wayward souls. "It is the lost possibilities of Marilyn Monroe that capture our imaginations," Gloria Steinem wrote. "It is the lost Norma Jeane, looking out of Marilyn's eyes, who captures our heart."

In the legend of Marilyn Monroe as a sacrificial lamb on the altar of celebrity, it wasn't only Hollywood that eviscerated her. She had an affair with President John F. Kennedy (and in one of the more grotesque pop epiphanies of the 1960s, sang "Happy Birthday" to him at Madison Square Garden); but then JFK treated her like dirt. And when brother Robert Kennedy took his turn, she began to realize, as Jane O'Reilly put it, "that to Jack and Bobby Kennedy [she] was like so many other women, just another beach ball." She was a wreck by the early sixties: Her career was floundering; neither Kennedy brother would return her phone calls; and candid movies from the last few months of her life are nearly as hideous as pictures of Elvis in the final years. Addicted to sleeping pills and booze, Marilyn Monroe seemed barely able to stay conscious or utter a coherent sentence.

Her death on August 5, 1962, supposedly from an overdose of Nembutal (deemed suicide, but there have been a host of conspiracy theories over the years, including some indicting the Kennedys), was a kind of deliverance—not only from the pain of her life but from the impossible prospect of Marilyn Monroe growing old. Along with those of Elvis, JFK, James Dean, and Hank Williams, Monroe's death at a young age has become one of pop culture's favorite tragedies, doted over with grotesque fascination by fans, idolators, curiosity seekers, and skeptics. In personal terms, it was very sad that she died, victim of her own internal demons as much as of the star system; but it is now hard to imagine the alternative of her turning forty and beginning to look like a woman with sound judgment and the wisdom of experience. Her image was forever young and innocent and amazed by the world; and it was an image by which she felt trapped. In his autobiography, *Timebends*, Arthur Miller wrote, "She was 'Marilyn Monroe,' and that was what was killing her." And yet, struggle as she did, she was unable to convince anyone, including herself, that she really was something more than the wide-eyed, child-voiced Daisy Mae caricature of overripe sexuality on which her film career was built.

It is strange today to look at the movies made by Marilyn Monroe and consider that she was so rarely cast opposite an appealing, handsome man her own age—they were usually squares, or too old, or in some way defective, and she was thus rarely given the chance to play anything like a normal woman. It was more typical to find her on the arm of an old goat (Charles Coburn in *Gentlemen Prefer Blondes*), leered at by the likes of Tom Ewell *(The Seven Year Itch)*, disdained by one who was her cultural superior (Laurence Olivier in *The Prince and the Showgirl*), or—most tellingly—as the object of desire by a horny male who finds himself forced to impersonate a woman (Tony Curtis in *Some Like It Hot*). And just as most of her leading men are unable to function as her sexual equal, the roles Monroe played almost invariably turned femininity into a surreal burlesque of whispery squeals, pursed lips, swelling bust, and ricocheting hips. Certainly by today's lean standards of beauty—and even by those of her own time—Marilyn Monroe was literally larger than life: busty, verging on fat, with a fleshiness that caused Jack Lemmon (in *Some Like It Hot*) to describe

her walk as "like Jell-O on springs." The prevailing images of her—skirt blowing up, mouth open with inviting lips, breasts heaving, butt swaying—became some of the fundamental icons of femme-crazed camp culture in the 1960s and beyond, and continue to make her a favorite among outrageous comic impressionists.

Her fame has always been as an image and a symbol more than as an actress, and it has been noted by many students of her charm that her one enduring love affair was with the still camera, in front of which she always looked great, whereas she always seemed to be squirming and ill at ease in her movie roles. She had a bad reputation among nearly all the directors and actors with whom she worked as unreliable, unprofessional, nervous, and narcissistic; she forgot her lines, locked herself in her dressing room, and was ultimately so difficult she was fired from her last movie, *Something's Got to Give.* "What the hell is that girl's problem?" *Misfits* co-star Clark Gable asked, describing the trouble she put the cast and crew through, and how director John Huston actually had to shut down production so Marilyn could detox long enough to arrive on the set before noon and to remember her lines. "She damn near gave me a heart attack," Gable said; and the day after filming of *The Misfits*, he *did* have a heart attack, and he died ten days later. Some of Marilyn's detractors blamed his death on her.

No movie she ever made was a blockbuster hit, and she seldom got good reviews. In all her roles, even the best of them, such as in *Some Like It Hot* and *Gentlemen Prefer Blondes*, she is curiously out of sync with the proceedings around her. Unlike such screen goddesses as Marlene Dietrich and Bette Davis, who seemed to totally *become* their best characters and *live in* their best movies, Marilyn Monroe always appeared to be at least a little bit outside the character she played. "There is a strain, in the editing and among the other actors, as well as in her woefully distracted face," David Thomson wrote in *Film Comment*, "that tells us about the communal worry as to whether she would remember her lines and know when or where to move." It was almost as if she were too busy figuring out who she was to bother with the particulars of a mere part in a movie. This quest of hers—which actress Lee Remick called "a long search for the most elusive role of all, herself"—is what has helped make Marilyn Monroe into a legend.

It also made her persona non grata in the film community, where her famous fragility and sensitivity drove hard-boiled types into a frenzy. In the book *Close-Ups* Alvah Bessie quotes a 1961 article in *Frontier* magazine, written by one of her Hollywood admirers, describing why she was ostracized by most of the Hollywood old guard:

> The bitch-goddesses hate her cordially and spare no pains to run her down, rip her up, castigate her for being late or "uncooperative" or not properly "grateful" to the industry.... But more important are other facts: She has not in years lent herself to the whole-cloth publicity which provides these parasites with their filet mignon and champagne; she does not call up Dear Hedda or Louella Dear to let them "be the first to know...."

Posthumously, all the resentment, envy, and jealousy aimed towards Marilyn Monroe when she was alive has been transformed into thirty years of ghoulish infatuation. Even in death, her image has been milked eagerly just as it was in life, and not only by Norman Mailer (in *Marilyn* as well as in *Of Women and Their Elegance*, which Mailer described as being told in

MM's "sweet little rinky dink of a voice"). Madonna (see p. 296) boosted her career as a kind of Monroe mimic in her "Material Girl" video, as well as in her neo-Monroe singing in the movie *Dick Tracy*, and in a half-naked photo session for *Vanity Fair* in which she reprised poses Monroe made famous. Elton John scored a top ten hit singing about her ("Candle in the Wind"); all photographers who took pictures of her have made fortunes packaging them in books; and Andy Warhol's *Red Marilyn* painting was sold at auction in 1989 for four million dollars, more than any other Warhol painting ever. On what would have been her sixty-fifth birthday in 1991, six blond bombshells, four women and two men, vamped on stage of Mann's Chinese Theater in a look-alike contest, while a ceremony was held in New York at Lexington Avenue and Fifty-second Street (where, to promote *The Seven Year Itch*, she had posed above a subway grate for the picture of her skirt being blown up to reveal her panties), and dozens of admirers filed past her grave at Westwood Memorial Park.

The image of Marilyn Monroe, as marketed by her estate for use on commemorative plates, dolls, cards, shirts, towels, socks, and salt and pepper shakers, is second only to that of Elvis Presley in all-time dead-celebrity popularity. Even her outlandish fizz of a singing voice earns big bucks as every note she ever breathed, in movies and elsewhere, gets packaged and repackaged in CDs for fans who cannot get enough. Her footprints outside the Chinese Theater in Hollywood, according to the Los Angeles *Times*, share top honors with John Wayne's as the most-photographed on the sidewalk. There has even been a wine named for her: a Napa Valley 1985 vintage called Marilyn Merlot. Anything she touched or even came near is now a valuable piece of Hollywood memorabilia: a polka-dot swimsuit she once wore sold for $22,400; her junior-high-school diploma went for $90; and the burial plot adjoining her crypt was long ago snapped up for $25,000 by one of her great-est admirers, an anonymous fan who is still alive but intends one day to join his cherished Marilyn Monroe and spend all eternity as close to her as a corpse can be.

MOTOWN

The Supremes

Named for Detroit, the Motor City, where it began as a record label, Motown is now a multimedia entertainment corporation headquartered in Hollywood and owned jointly by MCA and Boston Ventures. But it is in Detroit that you can still see the brick house at 2648 West Grand Boulevard, with a small backroom studio where Stevie Wonder, the Supremes, Smokey Robinson and the Miracles, the Marvelettes, the Temptations, the Four Tops, and the Jackson 5 recorded their first hit records. The house, once emblazoned with a sign across the front that read HITSVILLE, U.S.A., is now the Motown Museum, dedicated to the pop sound that mesmerized both black and white Americans at a time when rock music was young and vital and seemed to express all the stirring passions of a new age.

Modern Motown continues to turn out important records, including those of Stevie Wonder, Diana Ross, and Lionel Richie, as well as some by fresh voices such as Another Bad Creation, Boyz II Men, and M.C. Brainz, but its legendary name will be forever linked to America in the 1960s, and a wondrous era when the throbbing rhythms, enthusiastic finger snaps and hand claps, lush orchestration, and echoing gospel call-and-response of Motown's Martha and the Vandellas ("Heat Wave," "Dancing in the Streets," "Nowhere to Run") were truly the heartbeat and soul of popular culture. Motown brought a joyful (essentially blues-less) gospel fervor to the pop charts. It was called "the sound of integration" at a time when pop music was becoming a guiding light and the secular anthem of students, soldiers, protest marchers, factory workers, and just about everyone who shared the ideals of liberation through harmony, brotherhood, and love.

"This organization is built on love," Berry Gordy told *Newsweek* in 1965. "We're dealing with feeling and truth." Mr. Gordy was too modest. It wasn't only love, feeling, and truth that made Motown so special, and it wasn't only raw talent, either. It was a system—an elaborate hit-making apparatus that included not only the exalted songwriting team of Eddie Holland, Lamont Dozier, and Brian Holland ("I Can't Help Myself," "Baby Love," etc.) but also a complete course in deportment, wardrobe, and charm

—onstage and off—for every Motown artist. Berry Gordy believed in nurturing artists' careers over the long run, his goal being to see African-American acts break out of the rhythm-and-blues ghetto and onto the pop charts as well as onto swank stages in Las Vegas and even (in the case of the Supremes) at New York's Copacabana. An ability to sing well was only the beginning for recruits, many of whom were high school students from the slums of Detroit. Gordy believed that for them to gain acceptance, they had to learn how to behave properly; and by the early 1960s he had established a highly disciplined training program in the house on West Grand Boulevard (where he also lived). Peter Benjaminson in *The Story of Motown* describes the setup: "One floor was for choreography, another for musical arrangements, and a third for wardrobe design. The training began with grooming, etiquette, diction, elocution, table manners, and personal hygiene. The would-be stars learned how to put on makeup, how to handle a fork, how to climb up on a piano."

Motown became famous not only for its satin-slick sound but for its performers' dazzling visual showmanship, which was fastidiously crafted by the Motown machine. The Contours did choreographed flips and splits; the Four Tops were outfitted in impeccable tuxedos, the Supremes in glamorous matching evening gowns and a trio of baroque wigs; and the Jackson 5 were introduced with matching Afro hairdos, glittering costumes, and a dance routine worthy of Busby Berkeley.

Berry Gordy, a former employee at the Lincoln-Mercury plant, truly made Motown into a hit-making factory, starting with eight hundred dollars he borrowed in 1959. In the beginning, all artists punched in on a time clock and were assigned specific tasks on specific days. At one point he took out ad-vertisements in trade papers describing his company as "Detroit's other world-famous assembly line." Songs were produced according to a master plan: Writers wrote, arrangers arranged, singers sang; and frequently artists had to suppress their own protean talents to fit the Motown sound (the Jackson 5 were not allowed to write their own music or play their own instruments in recording sessions). Singers and musicians sometimes laid down background tracks with no idea what they were the background for. In fact, in 1975, at the height of discomania, Berry Gordy released an album called *The Magic Disco Machine* consisting of *nothing but* leftover background tracks recorded by various artists but never matched to lead parts.

A few performers were allowed to write and produce as well as sing (Smokey Robinson the greatest among them), but most were expected to do specialized tasks and maintain clear-cut musical identities from which they weren't allowed to deviate. Gladys Knight, for instance, yearned to do a blues or a gospel album, but did so only after she split with Motown; and by the late 1960s a number of artists wanted to do songs with overt social consciousness, which Berry Gordy nixed until Diana Ross and the Supremes recorded "Love Child" in 1968.

Frustrating as the system may have been to some multitalented performers, it worked stupendously well for several years. Its success had a lot to do with the fact that Berry Gordy had a clear vision of what a hit song should be: It had to tell a story, preferably in the present tense (not "You broke my heart" but rather "Stop before you break my heart"). Furthermore, it had to sound good on a car radio (which in the 1960s produced low-quality sound) as well as on an expensive home stereo, so he insisted technicians listen to master recordings on low-quality, nineteen-dollar turntables, and he encouraged writers to create what one critic called "continuous loop melodies" that didn't require a listener to follow along but allowed for instant and total immersion in an all-embracing sound. In the beginning, when Studio A was simply a converted downstairs room on Grand Avenue, all Motown songs shared a booming echo that first worried Gordy but soon became the label's trademark, and an effect technicians worked hard to copy in later years.

Motown's most successful product was the Supremes, who sent twelve songs to the number-one spot on the *Billboard* pop chart, a feat topped only by the Beatles, Elvis, and Michael Jackson. At first they were a quartet called the Primettes, named as an echo of the Primes, whom they knew in high school and who later became the Temptations. With Florence Ballard and Diana Ross alternating as their lead singer, they won first prize at a local talent contest in 1960 and went on (as a trio) to get the full beauty-and-charm course at Motown, but their first eight songs went nowhere. Berry Gordy decided he didn't like their name, so he presented Ballard with a list of alternatives. She later recalled she chose the only one that didn't end in "ette," but her partners, Diana Ross and Mary Wilson, were displeased by her choice of "Supremes," which they considered too masculine. ("Supremes" had been the original name of the Romantics, a quartet of men who, with Ruby Nash, had made a big hit of "Our Day Will Come.") For a while, they were known around Motown as "the No-Hit Supremes," and they earned their keep doing handclaps and background harmonies for other artists' songs. But in 1964, when they got a good Holland-Dozier-Holland number called "Where Did Our Love Go," which had been rejected by the Marvelettes as "junk," they soared to number

one. Two months later, their "Baby Love" hit the top of the charts, and two months after that "Come See About Me" repeated the achievement. Three months later, they became the first group in history to send four songs in a row to number one, with "Stop! In the Name of Love."

By the time of their fifth chart topper, "Back in My Arms Again," in June 1965, the Supremes were America's most popular singing group, but they weren't talking to one another anymore. Florence Ballard resented becoming a background singer for Diana Ross (a move engineered by Berry Gordy, who believed Ross had more charisma), and after Ballard was told to resign in 1967, her life spiraled out of control until she wound up broke and broken down and died at age thirty-two in 1976. "Diana Ross and the Supremes" went on to more success; then Diana Ross left the group and became a multimedia superstar, beginning with lead roles in the Motown-produced movies *Lady Sings the Blues*, *Mahogany*, and *The Wiz*, and transforming herself from a glittery soul singer to a jazzy pop chanteuse. "What's this?" *Time* magazine wondered. "Diana Ross, ex-Supreme, making like Barbra Streisand?" The Supremes continued, too, but without Ross and Holland-Dozier-Holland (who split with Motown in 1967) and with numerous personnel changes. In 1988, when the (original) Supremes were inducted into the Rock and Roll Hall of Fame, Little Richard said, "I love them so much because they remind me of myself: They dress like me."

Motown's stunning power to churn out hits in the mid-1960s began to wane as successful artists broke away to have the freedom that Berry Gordy's paternalistic system would not allow (Marvin Gaye's ambitious Motown-produced "What's Goin' On" notwithstanding), and as Stax and Atlantic became powerful and more relevant-seeming alternative labels for soul performers. Mary Wells, David Ruffin of the Temptations, Gladys Knight and the Pips, the Four Tops, Edwin Starr, and (for eight years starting in 1981) Diana Ross all lit out on their own, sometimes under a cloud of vitriol. The Jackson 5, for instance, were enjoined by Motown from using their name and so had to begin performing as "the Jacksons." (One Motown executive proclaimed, "We can put together another Jackson 5 any time we want.") Lawsuits flew back and forth about withheld royalties and breached contracts, and in 1970 Motown shut down its assembly-line training school for new artists and Berry Gordy moved operations out of Detroit. Motown's most recent really big hit was not a record at all but the television miniseries *Lonesome Dove*.

The Motown sound of frenzied handclaps and tambourines, sweet polished harmony and revival-meeting shouts was a rallying cry for many people who came of age in the 1960s. But it was a sound that began to seem out of date in the following decade, when music fragmented into acid rock and disco pop, and the trademark lockstep choreography of Motown groups was starting to look as anachronistic as Chubby

Checker's twist. In his 1971 book *Motown* David Morse observed that "the idea of Black Power and the new role of pop music as an outlet for white American dissent have made Motown and its tuxedo-clad artists seem both square and Uncle Tom." Morse called Motown a "prisoner of its own image" and worried about its ascent from a label in touch with youth and street culture to "showbiz nobility." Of course, what Morse could not see from his perspective in 1971 was that Motown's transformation from a vibrant voice of countercultural audacity into the cultural establishment was what was happening to most of rock and roll in the aftermath of the 1960s.

As a record label, Motown weathered a quarter-century of rock history and survived its best artists' defections, ultimately moving—in the words of *Rock of Ages: The Rolling Stone History of Rock and Roll*— "ever closer to the conventions of the pop/ supper club mainstream." Berry Gordy sold the company in 1988, and now Motown is as anonymous as any other major record label. But to those who remember its glory days, it still smacks of "Hitsville, U.S.A." and a unique brand of haute pop that helped define a generation.

MOUSSE (STYLING)

In the postwar struggle to make hair into a precise sign of its wearer's class and attitudes, mousse just may be the ultimate solution. No can of spray or tube of Brylcreem, no gummy setting gel or oily lotion has ever allowed so many women and men to create such exquisitely expressive yet invulnerable and perfectly behaved

heaps of hair. Those girls cruising through the mall with their grand facades of piled waves and billows soaring up and out (but, strangely, seldom backwards)? Mousse did it. That TV anchorman with the perfect corona of greaseless groomitude all around his intelligent face? Mousse did it. The punk on the park bench with spikes sticking up?

Maybe mousse did that, too. There is almost nothing you can't do with your hair if you use mousse.

Mousse is less than ten years old and was named to evoke images of classy French pudding (although *mousse* can also mean moss). When it was introduced by L'Oréal early in 1984, as Free Hold, it promised hair that was shiny, smooth, soft, manageable, never stiff or sticky, and, most delightful of all, "bodiful." Some consumers didn't know what to do with the aerosol can that fizzed out foam when its nozzle was nudged. "When I first tried it," wrote Bernice Kanner of *New York* magazine, "globs of the stuff sailed across the bathroom." That was exactly the fun of it, explained one stylist at New York's La Coupe salon (where, according to *People* magazine in September 1984, Lauren Hutton and Raquel Welch and even Dustin Hoffman had already had their hair moussed): "Having seen foam used all these years as shaving cream, now women have a cosmetic foam of their own."

The appeal of mousse was more than novelty or the fun of spraying foam from a can. Mousse allowed ordinary people—men as well as women—to do something that only sticky arduous lacquer spraying techniques could heretofore even approach, and that is actually *sculpt* their hair with minimal effort and skill. Sculpting hadn't seemed so important in the 1970s, when the first, prototypical mousse—Breck Salon Hair Finishing Formula—had flopped. People with long, free hair or giant frizzy perms (both still fashionable in the 1970s) didn't need mousse. But in the designer decade that followed, the long-hair extremism that had started in the 1960s was finally superseded by cropped, shaped, relatively tidy layered styles that needed to be kept in control. The trick was to manage them without having the greasy, tamped-down, or oversprayed look of 1950s hair, and the only way to do so was to use plenty of mousse. It was a miracle whose time had come. "Everyone had an alias, an ambition, and an aerodynamic haircut to match," Dylan Jones wrote in *Haircults*. "In the controlled chaos of the decade, the haircult reigned." And mousse was the haircult's holy foam.

Prior to L'Oréal's invention, cosmetological textbooks lamented that it was impossible to combine the qualities of manageability and body in one hair-grooming product. But as *Time* reported in a story titled "Mousse Is on the Loose" in autumn 1984, "chemistry is the key" to the combination of negatively charged polymers (which create fullness) and positively charged polymers (which create shine and manageability). Old-fashioned hair sprays had polymers, too, but not electrically charged ones, so instead of clinging to hair as mousse did, they got combed away. Mousse clung, and although all evidence of it disappeared once it dried and got combed, it allowed the wearer to precisely shape waves, curls, prows, or smooth planes of hair wherever they were needed.

By the end of 1984 there were more than two dozen different brands of styling mousse on the market, including flavored ones (chocolate for brunettes, lemon for blondes, strawberry for redheads) that were reportedly eaten by some consumers who mistook them for dessert. First popularized among the high-fashion salon set, mousse's magical powers rendered it practically essential for anyone who cared to make a clear and powerful statement with his or her hair. In September, when it was still something of a novelty, one dazzled executive from a company selling flavored mousses predicted, "If young people get hold of it, it's going to go through the roof." They did, and it has.

MTV

MUSIC TELEVISION®

"The Biggest Advertising Merger in History" is how MTV introduced itself to the trade with a full-page announcement in *Billboard* magazine on August 1, 1981. The merger—of stereo sound and television—had been conceived by John Lack, a vice-president of Warner-Amex Satellite Entertainment, who surmised that the record-buying public might be an untapped market for cable TV, which was itself still a relatively undeveloped system of programming. The *Billboard* advertisement predicted "a whole new dimension to the way people watch TV," an all-music channel composed of "video records [that] are more than just a tape of a band playing and singing. They are highly stylized visual interpretations of the music, using the most advanced video techniques." The most promising thing about MTV, according to the notice in *Billboard*, was that companies who advertised on the new music channel would be able to reach a very desirable demographic group because MTV gave them "the best of both worlds—the 'low taste' audience selectivity of radio and magazines, and the broader reach of television."

There is no doubt that MTV has fulfilled its promises, and it continues to be a stupendously good place to sell products to brand-hungry consumers, although its ratings today are scarcely half of what they were in the salad days of the mid-1980s. Even if the MTV audience has thinned, advertising revenues are healthy because those who do watch it are known to spend lots of money, not only on records by video phenomena ranging from Sinead O'Connor to Poison but on sports shoes, hair mousse, breath freshener, jeans, and all the must-have appurtenances of a street-smart lifestyle. Furthermore, MTV is considered by a lot of people, even television critics, to be pop's cutting edge—daring, irreverent, and more seriously multicultural than any other network or, for that matter, any important radio station. But the most amazing thing about MTV, beyond its own actual achievements, is how broad its influence has been.

The unmistakable MTV style has saturated television. Quick cuts and extravagant imagery, combined with an aggressive music beat, are now a language that is used to sell not only pop recordings and lifestyle paraphernalia but also cake mix and dog food and Pontiacs and deodorant. And starting with the razzle-dazzle imagery of "Miami Vice" in 1984, through the formerly exalted "Pee-wee's Playhouse" and the now-familiar, emotion-charged advertisements that are made to sell political candidates, MTV's hyperactive sensibility has infiltrated nearly every other form of television programming as well.

Ever since the New York World's Fair of 1939 (which promised a wondrous future that included TV), audio-visual buffs had been predicting that the tube would someday evolve its own language, a unique vocabulary that would short-circuit the hoary conventions of theater and cinema. MTV was it. Borrowing free-wheeling, nonnarrative constructions that had been typical of twenty-minute art films of the 1950s and 1960s (including animation and surreal special effects) and infusing them with the impudence that had been the original soul of rock and roll, MTV gave birth to a language brilliantly suited for communicating not complicated ideas but cool attitudes (Madonna's "Vogue") and compelling urges ("I want my MTV!": the company slogan, introduced in 1982). That is why the MTV look has become practically ubiquitous in advertising, particularly in commercials pitching products that are supposed to help consumers perfect a pose (sports clothes, cosmetics, cars, beer). Its high-energy, quick-burst vernacular has been an ideal way to grab the attention of a generation of viewers with downsized attention spans and quickly clue them in to what is hip.

MTV went on the air with five "video jocks" (Martha Quinn, J.J. Jackson, Alan Hunter, Mark Goodman, and Nina Blackwood), in a format that seemed to echo radio; but its first broadcast video was the Buggles' two-year-old song "Video Killed the Radio Star." Within a few years that tape, which showed televisions erupting up through the ground and knocking over radios, would seem prophetic. Although it went on the air with a mere thirteen advertisers, access to a meager 2.1 million households and a total library of 125 videos, and wasn't even carried by cable companies in New York and Los Angeles, MTV had become *the* hot venue for pop music by 1983, when Michael Jackson's *Thriller* album went through the roof with forty million

sales (the most ever) featuring seven top-ten songs and stunning videos to match (see p. 244). Radio hadn't exactly been killed, but now suddenly it seemed more like the poor relation of MTV—parochial, old-fashioned, and predictable.

The rules of pop music had been changed. In the post *Thriller* era, music required some interesting visuals to go with it if it was to become really popular; and even many good live performers had to develop stage acts that approximated the glossy wonderment that was typical of music videos. It became vital for a pop star to be videogenic—which usually meant outlandish, bizarre, heavily tattooed, bald, bearded, or otherwise odd rather than pretty or handsome. Within the high-strung world of music videos, mere pretty or handsome were qualities that all too easily got overwhelmed by the sturm und drang of ambitious and often very pretentious video makers who quickly learned that the rule of this new medium was that nothing succeeds like excess.

Nearly every significant early music video used baroque technique to fragment, shred, crystallize, heighten, and polish its star's performance in ways that the mere playing of a track on the radio could never do. "Image"—a vital component of pop music since Elvis—had become almighty, a fact borne out when fabulously successful MTV stars Milli Vanilli were exposed in 1990 as nothing but poseurs who pretended to sing in their videos because "we just wanted to live the life—the American way."

Thriller was a video breakthrough in more ways than one. In MTV's first couple of years, every video in regular rotation was by a white musician. The logic of this strategy was the belief that rock fans with cable TV were essentially middle-class Caucasians and would therefore be more interested in seeing such acts as Duran Duran and Men Without Hats—white guys whose music may have been slight, but whose videos seemed visually audacious. In early 1983, when *Thriller* was already number one on the pop charts *without benefit of MTV*, CBS (it is rumored) threatened to pull all its artists from MTV unless they broke their whites-only policy. MTV complied, and Jackson's "Billie Jean" and "Beat It" videos became monster hits. The color line had been broken, and more recently *TV Guide* has credited MTV with turning rap music—once ghettoized as strictly black—into a mainstream form with the program "Yo! MTV Raps," which debuted in 1989.

Of all the careers made by MTV, no one better expresses its true character than Madonna (see p. 296), who has released more videos than any other artist (thirty-six), and whose fame was originally built upon her mastery of the mini-movie formula, as in "Borderline," "Like a Virgin," and "Material Girl." Whatever her talents as a performer, Madonna knows how to project attitude, and has therefore found her perfect medium in music videos, which provide a carte-blanche opportunity to pose and posture and attitudinize without the cumbersome, old-fashioned demands of a plot or character or intelligent ideas.

Madonna went so far in her video "Justify My Love," which featured nearly naked people and same-sex kissing, that MTV refused to air the tape. Acting as a minister of propriety was an unusual role for MTV, which has more often found itself the object of criticism by detractors who denounce it for its lack of standards. In the continuing tradition that began when rock and roll was first accused of being the devil's music, MTV has been seen as a forum for occult and degenerate perverts whose leering, sweat-drenched, snake-kissing, tongue-wagging, microphone-stand-humping performances encourage viewers to think evil thoughts and presumably to become immoral people. The National Coalition on Television Violence found that 40 percent of the videos they studied contained acts of aggression, and 39 percent of the aggressive acts were sexual. Many feminists have complained that women in most male musicians' videos are nothing but brainless, scantily dressed, sexualized trollops, although it can also be argued that most men in those videos—certainly all men in heavy metal videos—are brainless, scantily dressed trollops, too.

One reason parents in particular have gotten exercised over MTV is that it is usually offered in conjunction with basic cable services, so if they want any cable at all, they have to take the music videos as part of the package. Furthermore, the nature of MTV is that you rarely know what you're going to encounter when you flip it on. There are some programs that are shown on a regular schedule, but they are not listed in *TV Guide*, so most of the time tuning in means diving headlong into whatever video happens to be on at any moment: Anthrax or Public Enemy are as likely to appear as Whitney Houston. MTV boosters assert that this is its greatest quality. Rather than absolutely segregating different kinds of music, as happens on the radio (on stations that are all-country, all-soul, all-golden-oldies), MTV shows and plays nearly everything; it is closer to universal than any other pop music forum. Some people bemoan this strategy as a lack of standards, and in 1991 the TCA Cable company of Tyler, Texas, which operates systems in six southern states, responded to viewers' objections to what they considered too much lewd, suggestive programming by announcing it was no longer going to offer MTV as part of its basic package. Great uproar ensued. TCA was accused of censorship, and many subscribers said that getting MTV was their *right*. It was not taken away from TCA subscribers.

Occasional irate reactions notwithstanding, there is a sense among many viewers that MTV fell into a rut in the late 1980s and has lost its ability to provoke and its cutting-edge aura. Part of the problem is that so many other media have copied it, it is no longer unique. The once-brazen style that made it seem avant garde and refreshing is now all too familiar. Describing what for many years was the typical outrageous video on MTV—a heavy metal band of sweaty guys without shirts on smoky sets surrounded by sultry bimbos—MTV chairman Tom Freston said in the late 1980s, "Our audience wasn't shocked. It was bored." Some believe the basic reason behind MTV's stagnation is the music on which the all-music channel depends. Innovative pop music seems to have evaporated into a long, dry spell of repetitious, copycat, lip-synced stagnation. In 1991 David Benjamin, producer of "Friday Night Videos," told *TV Guide*, "When the music is cool, MTV is cool. We're in a cool, if not cold, period. Music is boring now."

ARTHUR MURRAY

The year Arthur Murray started teaching Americans how to dance, the *Ladies' Home Journal* summarily fired twelve of its employees because they were discovered dirty dancing—doing the turkey trot—during lunch hour. In 1912 to wrap an arm around a partner's neck, to press close, to swivel your hips or shoulders were all outrageous things to do on the dance floor. Arthur Murray helped make the new steps respectable, and from the jazz age into the television age (and even today, via the studios he began) his name has been America's best-known symbol of the kind of dancing in which two partners touch, hold, and handle each other in ways that are absolutely polite but unmistakably erotic.

Born Murray Teichman in East Harlem, New York, in 1895, he came of age at a time when dancing—jazz dancing in particular—was considered a tantalizing sin. The controversy heated up in 1913 when a Broadway performer named Harry Fox invented

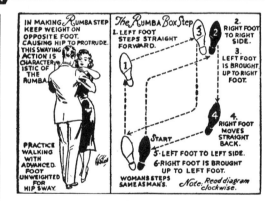

a fast variation of the two-step that quickly became a dance hall sensation known as the fox-trot. It was one of several provocative new dances, including the crab step, the kangaroo dip, the chicken scratch, the bunny hug, the toddle, and the grizzly bear, that swept across a nation where, previously, adults seldom danced at all. Those Americans who did dance customarily did it in a festive group to the sound of a fiddle, or possibly in the stately European manner of quadrilles and waltzes, for which partners were required to keep a seemly arm's-length distance between themselves. The modern, hopped-up beat was something altogether fresh, and it soon set the pace of nightlife in clubs, swank hotel ballrooms, and new dance halls called Roseland in Philadelphia and New York where staff hostesses (known as taxi dancers) were available at a dime a dance for single men.

Murray Teichman was a shy teenager who convinced a neighbor to teach him how to dance because he thought it would help him meet girls. He was light on his feet, and after winning some waltz contests at a local settlement house, then at Manhattan's Grand Central Palace ballroom on Forty-second Street, he enrolled in a program for dance instructors at Irene and Vernon Castle's Castle House. The Castles were the most famous dancers of their time, at the vanguard of dance mania, but they were no bunny hoppers or chicken scratchers; they didn't even approve of the fox-trot. They taught high society how to waltz and how to do the Castle walk, which was an elegant, gliding step they hoped would help "turn the tide against the orgy of the turkey trot." Kathryn Murray, whom Arthur married in 1925, recalled that at the time ballroom dancing was mostly an activity for the idle rich, and "to the average person, it seemed a frivolous, self-indulgent, and even shocking pastime." In fact, when Murray Teichman changed his name to Arthur Murray and started to give private lessons, his mother worried that he had become a dance bum. But to be a dance bum in the dance-crazed teens and twenties was to have irresistible social charm.

That's how Arthur Murray convinced customers to take lessons: If they could dance, they would be popular. He began the business in 1919 during a great mail-order boom, when all sorts of self-improvement programs were available just by sending away some money: exercises in poise and charm, piano lessons, muscle-building courses, art instruction, even long-distance psychoanalysis. So when you signed up for Arthur Murray, it wasn't just to cut a rug: It was a way to become a happier, more appealing person. Murray's plan was to sell dance lessons along with kinetoscope projectors—primitive devices that flipped still cards with pictures on them and created an illusion of motion, thus showing how a step was done. He announced his program with this advertisement in the *New York Times:*

"HOW I BECAME POPULAR OVERNIGHT": Girls used to avoid me when I asked for a dance. Even the poorest dancers preferred to sit against the wall rather then dance with me. But I didn't wake up until a partner left me standing alone in the middle of the floor. That night I went home feeling pretty lonesome and mighty blue. As a social success I was a first-class failure.

Not only was learning how to dance a fine way to make new friends and gain self-confidence; Murray even convinced many people in the calisthenics-crazed 1920s that ballroom dancing was as good as the popular Daily Dozen (see "Aerobics," p. 1) as a way to limber up and get one's circulation going.

However, there was a major problem to his plan: The kinetoscopes broke down all the time. So Murray, who had originally trained to be a draftsman, literally went back to the drawing board and came up with what is still the world's best-known device for teaching people how to dance: numbered silhouettes of shoeprints resembling the chalk outlines cops draw on the floor of a murder scene, each print corresponding to a single step of a dance. Lay them on the floor in the proper pattern, then follow the numbers . . . and you are dancing before you know it!

One of the reasons Arthur Murray became a success was that he was such a stiff. Smooth as silk on the dance floor, with impeccable manners and a well-learned air of upper-crust hauteur, his demeanor resembled that of an undertaker. He insisted that all his instructors deport themselves with the same excruciating formality. Any girl suspected of being "fast" or guy with gigolo potential was rejected as an instructor, no matter how well they danced; and doors to rooms for private lessons were designed with built-in portholes so Arthur or another supervisor could cruise past and make sure instruction was proceeding on the up-and-up. He knew that most people who sign up for dance lessons are a little embarrassed about it, so rather than reminding students of their social failings, as he had done in the earliest advertisements, he learned to treat them as potential swells who had come not to learn to dance but to learn a new step. "Does your dancing say 'New York' or 'small town'?" one ad from the 1930s asked, boasting of the Arthur Murray Studios as a place "where chic meets chic."

Murray was a tireless entrepreneur. By the mid-1930s he had convinced several New York department stores to give their employees dance lessons during lunch hour; eighty teams of Arthur Murray instructors were stationed on cruise ships and at resort hotels; at one point he had six different press agents on retainer to plant items about him in the papers; and by the 1950s his slogan "Arthur Murray taught me dancing in a hurry" had become nearly as famous as "Ding-dong, Avon calling." Arthur Murray jokes, usually about his homely face, bald head, or dour personality, were in

the repertoire of nearly every stand-up comedian:

- "I used to take dancing lessons from Arthur Murray until I found it was more fun dancing with a girl."
- "I took lessons from Charles Atlas and Arthur Murray. The trouble is, now I dance like Charles Atlas and look like Arthur Murray."
- "My girl won the Arthur Murray Award." "For dancing?" "No, for looking the most like Arthur Murray."

One of Murray's biggest successes in pre-television days was his popularization of the Big Apple in 1937. It was originally an African-American step, discovered in the South. In her book, *My Husband, Arthur Murray*, Kathryn Murray described how the dance was done when an Arthur Murray emissary first saw it at the Big Apple Club in North Carolina: "The couples formed a circle and stomped around in jazz tempo, following calls shouted by a leader. Every so often a couple would be called to 'shine' in the center of the ring and, now and then, the leader would call 'Praise Allah' and everyone would rush forward, hands waving high, howling and yelling." The Big Apple was publicized via a line of Big Apple jackets in department stores, as well as by teams of teachers sent forth to hotels all around the country with stacks of records and portable phonographs. Murray's troupes gave demonstrations to hotel guests, and when he saw how successful this was, he created the Arthur Murray Studio system of franchised dance schools.

Television was a venue he couldn't resist, and in 1950 he started buying fifteen minutes each week on CBS so he could give lessons on the air—and attract paying pupils to his schools. "The Arthur Murray Party," which starred Kathryn Murray as host, was a thundering critical flop ("The amateur spirit should be resisted in television," the *New York Times* critic complained), and ratings were low; but production costs were low, too, and the program's unpolished enthusiasm won it a certain so-bad-it's-good fame. Kathryn Murray recalled an encounter with a taxi driver who offered his critique: "You know, Mrs. Murray, when you first went on TV, I didn't think you'd last.... You ain't got talent; you don't sing; you're not exactly a glamour girl—and, if you'll excuse my saying so, you ain't a spring chicken either. But you got one thing. You got courage." Between dance demonstrations, the "Party" featured performers ranging from Yma Sumac (descendant of Inca kings) singing six-octave exotica to Helen Hayes doing dramatic readings from Shakespeare. There were comedians, jugglers, and movie stars; in addition to doing whatever it was that made them famous, they all danced the tango, the jitterbug, or the waltz with Kathryn or Arthur. Starting in 1956 the show featured an amateur dance contest during which different theme categories of people competed for prizes: all fat partners, all baseball players, all boxers. Television made Arthur Murray a household word, and his dance party lasted on the air intermittently until 1960, usually as a summer replacement.

The year he left TV for good was also the year of the twist (see p. 542), which ignited as big a dance fad as the turkey trot nearly a half-century before. However, the twist was a big blow to the kind of dancing Arthur Murray taught. It involved learning NO steps at all, just wiggling; it didn't demand that a man know how to lead, because twisting partners never touched; and it certainly called for no lessons—its appeal was that anyone could do it without having to learn a darn thing. For a while in the liberation-happy 1960s, the permissive freedom of the twist made Arthur Murray's kind of dancing look uptight, formal, and square, although he did begin to teach the twist and hully gully.

The do-your-own-thing style inaugurated by the twist can still be seen on many a public dance floor, but touch dancing, complete with real steps and choreographed moves, has come back. Its biggest boost was disco mania in the 1970s, as inspired by the movie *Saturday Night Fever* (1977), which, according to Arthur Murray Studios, "brought to the public the message that it was fun to be a good dancer." It was a message conveyed once again in the 1987 movie *Dirty Dancing*, which featured especially sexy variations of the kind of hot dips, flicks, and sways that Arthur Murray had started teaching over sixty years before. Murray himself, who retired from the business in 1964, enjoyed *Dirty Dancing* so much that he saw it twice when it came out. "I'm always interested in the way young people dance," he said in 1990. He died the following year at age ninety-five. He estimated that he had taught more than twenty million people how to dance.

There are currently over two hundred fifty Arthur Murray Studios around the world. Company literature enumerates these advantages to taking the course:

- Dancing will burn six hundred calories per hour.
- Dancing can iron out the stiffness of carriage and walking—the foremost signs of aging.
- Dancing leads to meeting new people and romance, getting to know them very closely, in a socially proper way, yet intimate in a non-threatening way. In today's society, getting to *"know your partner"* has many aspects of meaning and impact.
- Through dancing many people experience personal improvements in other areas, too—hair styles and general appearance.

- A positive personality can be developed through exposure to a dance environment such as that found at the Arthur Murray Franchised Dance Studios.

- Leading physicians and psychiatrists refer their patients to dance schools as a form of emotional and physical improvement.

MUSTANG

The Mustang wasn't just a new car when it was introduced in the spring of 1964. It was a new *kind* of car. It had bucket seats and a stick shift on the floor; it was low and had a body sculpted like a zestful Italian roadster; the very name suggested wild kicks. And yet for all its pizazz, it wasn't idiosyncratic the way real European sports cars tended to be. "The American public doesn't like a sports car," said Lee Iacocca, the shrewd Ford executive who brought it to the marketplace. "It wants one that *looks* like a sports car." That was Mustang's appeal. It was comfortably familiar, but it seemed completely fresh. It was the first "personal car" that was affordable and exciting, and it sold faster than any new car ever had—a million in less than two years.

Mechanically it wasn't all that different from Ford's sedate Falcon, the compact car from which its chassis, instrument panel, and other components had been borrowed. But it sure was sporty looking! A dramatically elongated hood gave the impression (to the person behind the wheel as well as to onlookers) of a big engine with plenty of power. The passenger compartment had only a token backseat, and there was a perfunctory trunk. This was a car designed to indulge a driver and a special friend—not for Mom, Dad, 2.7 kids, luggage, and the family dog. At a time when big four-door

sedans still dominated highways, the Mustang had the look of youth. And in 1964 youth was adored. Family cars—like the family itself—were beginning to seem old-fashioned.

Wilson Pickett recorded one of his wickedest, hardest-driving soul songs, "Mustang Sally," in 1966—about a girl behind the wheel who just cannot slow down. The new sporty car had that effect on people. "Life was just one diaper after another," advised an early advertisement, "...until Sarah got her new Mustang." To those who fell in love with it during a decade that craved to break free, the original Mustang really looked like a vehicle of liberation.

In addition to its spiritual charisma, the Mustang is important as a landmark in the march of postwar materialism because it was a car that gave people the opportunity to indulge themselves and feel pampered, but at bargain prices. "Class for the mass" is how Lee Iacocca described the strategy of pricing the car low ($2,368) but offering an irresistible array of fifty different extra-cost options. The Mustang was available with four different engines, three clutches, seven transmissions, two drive shafts, three kinds of wheels and tires, three suspensions, four types of steering, four brake options, a vinyl roof, a special handling package, and deluxe dashboard gauges. Even decked out in full regalia, it cost less than a top-of-the-line (but terminally dowdy) Ford or Chevrolet sedan. A *Time* cover story told about piloting one along a suburban street: Heads turned, drivers of other cars gaped, and a busload of schoolchildren began chanting, "Mustang! Mustang! Mustang!"

The Mustang was so successful that nearly every company tried to copy it with their own "pony car," but none had the magic combination of youthfulness, affordability, and novelty that made car buyers fall in love in the spring of '64. By the time Chevrolet introduced its Camaro in 1967 (with a "building block" system of options even more extensive than the Mustang's), the appeal of personal-size cars had shifted dramatically. Camaro was sold not for its ability to set drivers free and inspire lighthearted rambling but as a brute car with "a mean streak so ominous it goes by its code name [Z-28]." By the end of the sixties, in cars as in other areas of popular culture, the allure of power had superseded the charm of being carefree. Even the Mustang forsook its original jaunty personality and pumped up; by 1972 the Mustang had developed the macho muscle car personality that continues to distinguish the marque today: It was eight inches longer, six inches wider, six hundred pounds heavier, nearly twice its original price, and available with a huge Cobra Jet Ram-Air V-8 or a 375-horsepower engine that Ford called "the Boss." A Boss might rule the road, but how much fun could it be?

RALPH NADER

In January 1968 *Newsweek* put Ralph Nader on its cover and called him "Consumer Crusader." He was outfitted in a suit of armor and looked ready to slay dragons. By this time, crusader Nader had already dealt a mortal blow to General Motors' Corvair, had licked the American Dental Association, and was working on the fishing industry, the meat industry, the coal industry, the natural gas industry, and poultry producers. The prime mover of the consumer rights movement went on to establish over two dozen public interest groups, helped pass the Freedom of Information Act and the Occupational Safety and Health Act, and was declared by *The New Republic* in 1985 to be "responsible for more concrete improvements in the society we actually do inhabit" than any other living American. *Life*, listing him among the hundred greatest Americans, called Nader "the champion we never knew we needed against an enemy we never suspected was there."

The most explosive and influential best seller of the decade!

UNSAFE AT ANY SPEED

The Designed-In Dangers of the American Automobile

RALPH NADER

Aside from his specific achievements in the marketplace and politics, Ralph Nader spearheaded a major reformation in many citizens' belief systems, and it is his role in that reformation that has made him as much a cultural icon as a social activist, and as natural-seeming when he hosts "Saturday Night Live" as when he testifies before Congress. Before Ralph Nader, most Americans liked big business. We were proud of it. We even trusted it and considered its success an expression of this country's unique strength. It made sense that what was good for General Motors was good for the country. Ralph Nader changed that perspective. He taught Americans to be cynical, not only about big business itself but about its cozy relationship with the federal government. As he saw it, and as he convinced millions of heretofore unwary citizens to see it, cor-

porate America was all about corruption, greed, and deception. In a *New Yorker* profile in 1973, he said he refused to accept a situation in which "the manufacturer is the lord and the marketplace the manor," and he has spent his life trying to make big business do what he—speaking on behalf of the public interest—wants it to do.

He was born in 1934 in Winsted, Connecticut, and even as a boy, he had a mission—to become "a people's lawyer," once boasting that he had read "all the muckraker books" before he was fourteen years old. At home, his parents conducted regular family seminars on citizenship and ways to combat injustice; and when little Ralph wanted a snack he got no frivolous candy bars: Mrs. Nader set out bowls of healthful chick-peas for him and his three older siblings. At Princeton, he refused to wear white bucks like all the other boys and he tried (unsuccessfully) to get the university to stop spraying campus trees with DDT. He went to Harvard Law School, where in 1958 he published an article in the *Harvard Law Record* titled "American Cars: Designed for Death"; and although he opened a small, private law practice in Hartford in 1959, he soon realized that highway safety could be the issue to get his life's work under way. He described that work as nothing less than "the qualitative reform of the Industrial Revolution."

His first book, *Unsafe at Any Speed*, was published in 1965, the most successful year in history for the American automobile business, which was selling power, speed, and fun, with the new Mustang (see p. 351) at the head of the pack. Nader began, "For over half a century the automobile has brought death, injury, and the most inestimable sorrow and deprivation to millions of people," then alleged that General Motors had covered up safety defects in early models of the compact Chevrolet Corvair.

Today these types of accusations against corporations are commonplace, and Nader's goal—to shift the blame for accidents and injuries from consumers to manufacturers—is an everyday strategy among trial lawyers who handle product liability lawsuits. But a quarter-century ago, Nader's indictment was dynamite—so much so that General Motors hired private detective Vince Gillen and told him to "get something, somewhere on this guy to get him out of our hair and shut him up."

Nader found out about the gumshoe and told what he knew to a United States Senate committee on auto safety to whom he was testifying. After the story broke, GM president James M. Roche publicly apologized before a righteously indignant Congress, and the Traffic and Motor Vehicle Safety Act of 1966 was passed. "One man could still made a difference," declared the *Washington Monthly*. "To millions of Americans chronically addicted to rooting for the underdog, there was something irresistibly appealing in the sight of a slender, boyish, vulnerable figure standing up to a giant industry," *Newsweek* said, describing him as "a latter-day incarnation of a Jimmy Stewart hero in a Frank Capra movie."

The really delectable thing about the GM story was that the private dick couldn't find anything at all to make Nader look bad. He proved himself immune to anonymous phone threats, and even to the charms of prostitutes who had been hired to try to trap him into having sex. The more people learned about his private life, the more he assumed the status of a superhuman saint. He lived like a monk in an eighty-five-dollar-a-month rooming house, didn't own a television set or automobile, and was far too busy doing good deeds to socialize, vacation, or date. Some of his high-minded qualities made him seem alarmingly austere: An

Esquire "dossier" on him reported that he refused dinner invitations from anyone with a pet, apparently because pets are such frivolous things; he once told teenagers to ignore their adolescence and concentrate on "the future of civilization"; he frequently lectured cafe waitresses about the evils of Coca-Cola; and he was once described by the *New York Times* as "speaking in a colorless cant that has earned him a reputation as tedious." No slave of fashion or vanity, Nader was long known for sports jackets with skinny lapels and narrow ties left over from the early 1960s; and in a profile written in 1983, Ken Auletta revealed that in 1959, when Nader worked as an army cook, he had bought twelve pairs of low-cut, army-issue black dress shoes for six dollars apiece, along with four dozen pairs of socks at thirty-five cents a pair. He hadn't had to buy any shoes or socks since then, and he said that his only regret was that he hadn't bought several dozen more pairs of socks to last him for decades hence.

Hailed as a shining example of individualism, Nader appeared incorruptible; this, along with his proven ability to stand up and make a difference, were inspirational to citizens who, by the end of the 1960s, felt alienated from the government and helpless in the face of its evil policies and corrupt officials. By 1971 he was the sixth most popular public figure in the United States (between Spiro Agnew and Pope Paul VI), and the following year Democratic presidential nominee George McGovern seriously considered selecting him as a running mate (when Senator Tom Eagleton got bumped off the ticket after he admitted having had electroshock therapy).

Nader's ascetic lifestyle made him perfect for the role of professional scold and public conscience during the seventies, when it seemed that so many people were drifting away from social responsibility into discos, cocaine, and self-indulgent Me Decade faddism. One former FTC chairman called him "the voice and persona of a contemporary Old Testament prophet . . . calling society to account for its drift from its own professed morality." Nader's Raiders, as his muckraking group of idealistic, underpaid lawyers came to be called, exposed fraud, waste, mismanagement, and other bad things in the Federal Trade Commission, the Food and Drug Administration, the nuclear power industry, the Educational Testing Service, the U.S. Postal Service, public utilities, and the home heating oil business, and they were the force behind dozens of new regulations about products from baby food to spackling compound.

Nader was, in the words of the *New York Times*, "eclipsed in the Reagan decade," and perceived by many to be the reason nothing seemed to work right anymore. Thanks to him, everything was overregulated, and we had become a nation of worrywarts and lawsuit-crazed troublemakers. His confrontational style seemed like a hoary legacy from the sixties and lost much credibility at a time when we were supposed to be learning from the Japanese how to cooperate in search of excellence rather than join in battle—worker vs. employee and class vs. class—as Nader always seemed to see it. "In this sense," Ken Auletta wrote, "Ralph Nader is preaching a discredited and perhaps dangerous gospel." However, in 1989 *Business Week* announced "Ralph Nader is back"—campaigning against fluorocarbons, congressional pay raises, and rising auto insurance rates; and the next summer *Life* named him one of the century's one hundred most influential Americans. In response to articles that noted he was "coming back," Nader liked to remind reporters that he never went away: "It's the press's own creation. We've been doing what we've been doing."

In 1990 *Forbes* magazine did a cover story called "Ralph Nader, Inc." that tried to chip away the old monastic, goody-twelve-shoes image and present him as a power-hungry, paranoid hypocrite who traveled in limousines and lived in a $1.5 million townhouse and was funded by trial lawyers who made fortunes doing what Naderism has enabled them to do—sue like crazy. In response, Nader threatened to sue *Forbes* and noted that the townhouse belonged to his sister, and that money from rich lawyers was a mere one percent of his fund raising.

In another apparent attempt to discredit him, *Vanity Fair* reported that Mr. Nader had been seen sucking on a piece of hard candy containing a dye he had described as unhealthy and eating an ice cream bar despite his diatribes against foods containing sugar. To these charges, Nader responded that he took the candy when his throat was dry and it was the only salve he could find; and he blamed the ice cream bar on the *Vanity Fair* reporter, who insisted on buying it for him.

JOE NAMATH

His Nickname is "Broadway Joe"

His trade is football

His hobbies are good times, girls, and winning Superbowl championships

These were the boasts on the cover of *SuperJOE*, a paperback book published in 1969 after Joe Namath's spectacular performance as quarterback led the American Football League's New York Jets to a 16–7 victory against the invincible Baltimore Colts in Super Bowl III—a contest so soul-stirring that sports writer Mike Lupica once described it as "the only pro football game worth talking about." The win served to confirm a belief that had been growing since he came to New York from the University of Alabama (where he had set Orange Bowl records for passing and yardage) and signed with the Jets for an unheard-of annual salary of $427,000: Joe Namath was the best quarterback who ever lived. Born in 1943, the son of a Pennsylvania steel worker, he became the first pro football player ever to pass for more than 4,000 yards in a season; he threw the ball like a bullet; his accuracy was second to none; he was an inevitable winner. The image of Broadway Joe raising one finger high announcing "We're number one" as he ran off the playing field is an emblem of a decade in which football became a national passion like no other sport (see "Super Bowl," p. 485), as glamorous as show business.

He was more than football—much, much more. In 1969 Joe Namath became lord of the free world. In October of that year *Esquire* devoted a cover story to him, titled "The Higher Truth of Joe Namath," featur-

ing cartoons of him dressed as Superman to illustrate page after page of effusive words of praise, lust, and admiration from four pretty girls in short skirts and analyses and considerations of the meaning of his magic by Rex Reed, William F. Buckley, Jr., and Jack Richardson. To introduce this extraordinary coverage of a single subject, *Esquire*'s editors explained: "Once in a generation, more or less, a chosen figure detaches himself from the social matrix and swims into mythology, hovering somewhere near the center of the universe, organizing in himself our attention, monopolizing our hopes and fears, intruding on our dreams, compelling our hearts to beat as his. Such a figure is Joe."

Joe Namath had charisma. In addition to elevating football to a cultural status it had never had before, he made himself one of pro sports' first modern media superstars. He was handsome, outspoken, and outrageous. Like Muhammad Ali (see p. 8)—with whom, it must be said, he shared the kind of mythological symbolism described by *Esquire*—he was egotistical in a way no sports figure (and few celebrities of any kind) had ever allowed themselves to be. His autobiography, published in the glory year of 1969, was titled *I Can't Wait Until Tomorrow . . . 'Cause I Get Better Looking Every Day.* "I like my girls blonde and my Johnny Walker Red," he joked. "I don't want to go a day without seeing a woman." He didn't. Joe Namath was the original swinger, one of the great pubcrawlers in history—out and about every night, in all of New York's then-ebullient singles bars. "I don't date," he said, "so much as I just, you know, run into something."

Skirt chasing was not invented by Joe Namath, but in earlier eras a more discreet press tended to overlook professional athletes' after-hours carousing, because they were supposed to be role models who upheld traditional values. But with the sexual revolution well under way and Aquarian morality on the ascent, Joe Namath, armed with his much-publicized sex drive, was a hero whose time had come. "He has taken great pleasure," William F. Buckley, Jr., wrote in his *Esquire* paean, "out of humiliating the mores and the folkways of the republic." (In fact, the FBI's J. Edgar Hoover considered him dangerous and had his phone tapped.) Here was a new kind of role model for a generation of rebels, men who were feeling eager to have some naughty fun, let their egos on the loose, and give free rein to their drives and emotions.

It wasn't only braggadocio and sexual adventurism that made him a new kind of star. Broadway Joe Namath cried, *in public*, demonstrating he was sensitive. Machismo and sensitivity, all in one: Is it any wonder Kaye Stevens (one of his frequent dates) declared, "I think Joe Namath is good for the country"? The famous crying episode happened not long after the Super Bowl, when football commissioner Pete Rozelle found out that known gamblers were frequenting a bar called Bachelors III, which Namath co-owned. Rozelle ordered Namath to sell his share. "I was pretty damn angry. I knew

I hadn't done anything wrong," Namath recalled. "I wasn't going to take that. I wasn't going to sell my half of the club." Wearing his brown-and-white-striped bell-bottom slacks with a jumbo belt and a blue tuxedo shirt, he held a press conference at the bar and announced his retirement from football. "It's principle," he said, his voice quivering with emotion. "I'm not selling." That night, after he ate dinner at Trader Vic's, a fan came up to him on the street and shook his hand: "Man, you got a lot of balls," he said.

Joe's balls were already the subject of an embarrassing amount of press coverage. On one infamous occasion, when being interviewed by a female writer at a cocktail party (where he supposedly had consumed seven or eight martinis), he took the writer's hand and placed it on his crotch, telling her, "That's all America wants from me." But it wasn't really just Joe's hyperactive testicles that America admired and wanted more of. It was his ballsy attitude. He was his own man and delighted in telling the rest of the world where to go—and because he was Mr. Cool himself, he got away with it. "Beards and sideburns and long hair," he wrote, were a "symbol of the way I feel about things. . . . I'm up-to-date, I'm mod, and I don't really care too much what anybody else thinks."

He was known for conspicuous self-indulgence, which many fans admired because it was a sign that he was honest (no false humility) but critics condemned as spoiled and immature. It was rare indeed for any athlete, let alone a big football player, to be a pretty boy and a dandy (pro wrestling's Gorgeous George was the closest thing anyone had seen) at a time when many American men were still stuck in a 1950s plain-macho wardrobe. Not Broadway Joe, who was known for his snappy white shoes, his buckskin-fringe jacket, his long, curly hair and Fu Manchu mustache, and his color-coordinated warm-up clothes. Thousands of pictures were taken of him at his bachelor-pad apartment on First Avenue in the singles district of New York, with the camera peering up through the elongated fluff of his white llama rug, or into the bedroom, where a mirror was strategically mounted on the ceiling above his oval, satin-sheeted bed. He flaunted his sexual appetites and party-hearty attitude in a way that only movie stars had previously done. He was so sure of his machismo, he even posed for a pantyhose commercial and was photographed in a five-thousand-dollar mink coat.

When he cried and quit the game, there were rumors that the Bachelors III problem was just a cover story to camouflage his real reason for bowing out of pro football—his dramatically bad right knee, which was the one flaw that signaled his mortality (and kept him out of the army). In June, after his resignation, he left New York for Hollywood to take his first leading role in a motion picture, a motorcycle drama called *C.C. and Company* (in which *Life* described him as

looking "more like a hippie Tarzan than another Wild One"). But in July he and pro football had a reconciliation: He sold his interest in Bachelors III and reported to the Jets' training camp.

Joe Namath was back, and he stayed in professional football until 1978, although he never regained the devastating charisma of his post–Super Bowl apotheosis. He cultivated his talents as a television personality, hosting his own talk show (with Dick Schaap) starting in 1969, then branching out to theater, in *The Caine Mutiny Court Martial*, *Li'l Abner* (as Abner), and *Picnic*. He even starred in a short-lived 1978 sitcom called "The Waverly Wonders" as a history teacher and basketball coach. Namath, who is now the television spokesman for Nobody Beats the Wiz appliance stores in the New York area and does commentary for football games on NBC, says he especially enjoyed his recent stints acting in summer stock because they offered some of the same thrills football once provided. "I love that rush of adrenaline every night," he told Mike Lupica, revealing that his favorite role was Sky Masterson in *Guys and Dolls*.

NATIONAL ENQUIRER

"Anyone reading it should call up a psychiatrist," said a Columbia University professor of journalism about the *National Enquirer* in 1965, before it became the respectable publication it is today. America's second-largest-circulation journal (topped only by *TV Guide*)—which, its editor recently announced, "doesn't make up stories"—has shown its readers a pho-

tograph of Elvis in his coffin, Rock Hudson in his body bag, Liz Taylor at the detox clinic, the world's biggest horse, and an overweight Delta Burke alongside a psychic's prediction that Ms. Burke would soon shed fifty pounds. It has told all about the voodoo curse Roseanne Arnold put on her ex-husband, revealed that Cabbage Patch dolls can be possessed by the devil, re-

358   *NATIONAL ENQUIRER*

counted Liberace's lover's exclusive story, and exposed Jackie Kennedy for wearing an outfit she had worn four years earlier.

Before it realized these journalistic achievements, the *National Enquirer* used to be sleazy:

- MADMAN CUT UP HIS DATE AND PUT HER BODY IN HIS FREEZER
- I WAS TRAPPED IN A WELL—WITH MY WIFE'S CORPSE
- HE BUTCHERS WIFE AND THREE KIDS TO KEEP HIS ATTACK ON DAUGHTER A SECRET
- MOM USES SON'S FACE FOR AN ASHTRAY
- I CUT OUT HER HEART AND STOMPED ON IT
- I'M SORRY I KILLED MY MOTHER, BUT I'M GLAD I KILLED MY FATHER.

These are a few headlines from the *Enquirer* of the early 1960s—its sociopathic days of unalloyed shock, gore, and horrific perversion. In ugly black-and-white it regularly featured photos of mangled corpses, deformed children's faces, and grisly crime scenes alongside articles that told foul and horrid melodramas about the dregs of soci-

ety. "If a story is good," said the paper's editor in 1965, "no matter how vile, we'll run it." There was nothing in its pages about politics or current events as ordinary publications reported them; there were no sports or culture features. The *Enquirer* was a fifteen-cent-per-copy weekly weirdo's delight filled with what one critic called "all the news that's *un*fit to print." As of 1965 it had a circulation of 1.1 million, with virtually all copies sold at city newsstands alongside nudie magazines. (The fifty-thousand-odd subscribers received their issues through the mail in plain brown wrappers.)

It hadn't always been so scummy. Founded as a Hearst publication in 1926 as the *New York Enquirer*, it took a relatively high road among tabloids, in contrast to the city's *Daily Mirror*, *Daily News*, and *Graphic*, all of which fought with one another for the most scandalous stories and shocking pictures (including the *Daily News*'s notorious, illicitly snapped page-one photo of Mrs. Ruth Snyder, who had been convicted of murdering her husband, frying in Sing-Sing's electric chair in 1928). It was their no-holds-barred circulation war in the twenties that gave tabloids (named from the French word *tabloide*, meaning something capsulized or condensed) the reputation for sensationalism; but the *Enquirer* soon became known as much for its thorough sports coverage (including horse racing) as for its cheesecake pictures of pinup girls. Still, by 1952 its prurience seemed a remnant of another era, and circulation had dropped to 17,000 when it was sold by the Hearst Corporation to Generoso Pope for the bargain price of $75,000.

Mr. Pope, whom *Forbes* once described as "a combative man who looks and acts like the late Vince Lombardi," was well prepared to take the *Enquirer* to a new level of success. He already had experience in the newspaper business, having boosted circulation of *Il Progresso*, an Italian-language daily founded by his father, by livening it with maudlin editorials, goggle-eyed features about fashion extremes and zany personalities, and stunts staged in conjunction with press-hungry celebrities. Before that, after graduating from MIT at age nineteen, Pope had worked as an employee of the Central Intelligence Agency in the psychological warfare division.

Mr. Pope, who said he was inspired by auto accidents' uncanny ability to draw crowds, sought "something jazzy" for the *New York Enquirer*. His publishing vision was described by the *New York Times* in his 1988 obituary (he died at age sixty-one, of a heart attack) as "a showcase of the bizarre, with tales of mutilation, sadism, murder, and gory accidents." This formula made circulation skyrocket. The *New York Enquirer*, soon renamed the *National Enquirer* to reflect its growing readership, hired some of the cleverest writers away from legitimate papers by offering them double their usual salary, and had them use their talents to transform humdrum wire-service copy and free-lance writers' perfunctory stories into salacious melodrama. Word went out to newspapers in cities throughout the world that whenever they had an item or photo too gross and disgusting to print themselves, a hefty fee could be earned by selling it to the *Enquirer*.

By the late 1960s, the porno-violence magazine business was getting very competitive. Censorship had all but vanished, and so the marketplace was crowded with periodicals every bit as repulsive as the *Enquirer*, and some (like the *National Tattler*) even more so. To make matters worse, city newsstands were dying off; magazine sales were shifting into supermarkets, where the brutal old *Enquirer* would never fit. In 1968

Generoso Pope performed a miracle: He regenerated the soul of his newspaper and made it fit for supermarket shoppers. He hired an all-new staff and completely cut out gore and crime in favor of lighter-weight features about aliens from outer space, test-tube babies, dogs with ESP, children's essay contests, marvelous hemorrhoid cures, evangelistic columns by no less than Billy Graham, predictions by psychics, appeals to help the handicapped, and spy photos of Jackie Onassis—what one critic called "soft core sensationalism," or what was known during the tabloid wars of the 1920s as "gee-whiz journalism." Pope explained the source of his new publishing philosophy: "I went back and read some old *Reader's Digest*s of the 1930s, when the *Digest* was having its greatest growth. Most of the stories were about triumphs over adversity, breakthroughs in medicine, UFOs, and nutrition. The most important element was that most of it was *uplifting*."

The *Enquirer* was still no competition for the *New York Times*, but its publisher didn't want it to be: "What you see on page one of the *New York Times* does not really interest most people," he said. "And interest is our only real rule." In particular, the *Enquirer* began to specialize in what is known as *human* interest—stories about weird, lucky, heroic, and pitiful people, and always stories about celebrities. The formula was so successful that Rupert Murdoch copied it in 1974 when he began publishing the *Star*, which trumped Pope when it became the first of the tabloids to use color pictures on the cover.

About the time of its editorial about-face, *Enquirer* offices were moved to New Jersey; then, in 1971, they were relocated in the small town of Lantana, Florida, where the born-again newspaper sponsored a Little League team. In 1972, circulation was up to 2.6 million copies every week.

More and more since the move to Florida, the *National Enquirer* has focused its cover and its articles on stars of TV, movies, and popular music. Dismissing *People* magazine as "too highbrow," Generoso Pope sharpened a style of journalism that had been pioneered by Hedda Hopper and Louella Parsons in Hollywood, then by *Confidential* magazine: the journalism of embarrassment. Sometimes it features nice, laudatory stories about celebrities, but mostly the *Enquirer* is known for its ruthless dish, and like the famous gossip columnists of an earlier Hollywood, it is rumored to use its power to humiliate people to get them to talk (or to coerce stars' agents into feeding them stories about one client in order to protect another). "Prod, push, and probe the main characters in the story," Generoso Pope wrote in a 1973 memo to his staff. "Help them frame their answers. Ask leading questions like, 'Do you ever go in the corner and cry?'"

The *Enquirer*'s voracious hunger to dig, really dig, into people's private lives has sparked its reporters to rummage through garbage, fly over weddings and funerals in camera-equipped helicopters, and pay huge sums of money with what was described by *Rolling Stone* as "the fattest checkbook in journalism") to anonymous sources for spy photos, medical records, and other confidential information. Such relentless tactics have been abetted in the last fifteen years by an influx of veteran reporters from London's Fleet Street tabloids, who perfected the arts of stunt journalism (dress up like a bum and see how people treat you) and of turning little shreds of fact into blockbuster revelations. Attracted by the big salaries paid by the *Enquirer* as well by other tabloids that have set up offices near Lantana (the *National Examiner*, the *Globe*, the

Sun), these experienced masters of stake-out reportage (who, according to *Time*, "are able to weasel their way into anything") have helped elevate the *Enquirer*'s circulation to over four million copies and an estimated weekly readership of twenty million people. "The *National Enquirer* is like a pack of wild dogs," one such reporter boasted. "Let us loose and we'll savage you."

For better or for worse, by the 1980s the *Enquirer* had clearly made itself a publication whose time had come. In earlier eras, there was news and there was gossip, and the two were treated differently by readers and by the press. News was considered important, whereas gossip was thought of as trivial and generally unworthy of intelligent people's attention. Some newspapers had gossip columnists, or possibly even a gossip page, but they were segregated from the rest of the paper; as for the *Enquirer*, which according to one critic "preyed on that which is most reprehensible in human nature," no one took it seriously. Now, although it has plenty of enemies and people who loathe it and on at least one celebrated occasion in 1981 (a libel suit brought by Carol Burnett) has been forced not only to eat its words but pay $1.6 million in damages, the *Enquirer* has pretty well managed to shed its reputation as a freaky and essentially irrelevant sideshow; it is a pop culture force to be reckoned with.

By the end of the celebrity-crazed 1980s, even such apparently consequential periodicals as *Esquire* and *Vanity Fair* might just as easily be expected to run pictures and articles about Donald Trump or Nancy Reagan as about Henry Kissinger or Teddy Kennedy. Which was news and which was gossip? It has become increasingly difficult to know the difference, and so the *Enquirer*, which is nearly all unabashed gossip (verified and 100 percent factual, its editors guarantee), has been transformed into a deliverer of what is now considered news. If you doubt that fact, remember that it was the *Enquirer* that, in 1988, ran the career-destroying photo of Senator Gary Hart cavorting with girlfriend Donna Rice; and it was *The Enquirer*'s competitor, the *Globe*, that led the media in savaging presidential contender Bill Clinton in 1992. Although it is still unapologetically scandalous and often utterly preposterous, it has become as mainstream-seeming (and as trivializing) as nearly any other popular periodical.

In a 1990 *New York Times* story about the increasing respectability of the *Enquirer* among the advertising community, one executive with J. Walter Thompson said that forward-looking advertisers simply had to overcome their negative feelings about the tabloid. Staid old Procter & Gamble had already bought ad space in the *Enquirer* and the *Star* (now owned by the same company) because P&G was eager to tap the buying power of the paper's readers, half of whom, according to demographic surveys, are women eighteen to thirty-four years old —a group of consumers with prodigious buying power. "The people who plunk down their money and read these publications," said the ad exec, "they don't think they're schlocky people."

NAUTILUS

"I had the arms and legs of a gorilla and the body of a spider monkey," Arthur Jones said about himself, reminiscing back to 1948 when he was living at the Tulsa, Oklahoma YMCA and working out every day with dumbbells. Mr. Jones, a high school dropout, yearned to be strong and have a good physique. Lifting weights just didn't do it for him. So he set off on a twenty-year quest to invent a better way to build muscles. The result was Nautilus, a brand name for a set of exercise machines based on a cam similar in shape to a nautilus mollusk's shell. The machines are designed to isolate each muscle group, and the cam varies resistance as the weight stack is lifted and lowered, allowing the user to thoroughly exhaust each set of muscles.

Since they were introduced at a weightlifters' convention in Los Angeles in 1970,

Glenn Chippindale works out.

Nautilus machines have become what Kleenex is to tissue and Xerox is to copying machines: a brand so big and familiar that it defines the field and dominates all competition. "Nautilus is in a class by itself," *Forbes* magazine quoted the manager of one

New York health club in an early-1980s article that described Nautilus machines as "the ultimate gear for honing the body beautiful."

Unlike barbells and dumbbells which, as dead weight, have never really shaken their reputation as the workout tools of grunting Neanderthals, Nautilus is a modernistic apparatus that seems to express a designer's scientific intelligence and has therefore appealed to the more upscale gym-goers of the last twenty years. The cam principle on which these thinking man's weight machines' movements are based is a Bauhaus-like example of less-is-more engineering, and the fact that it is derived from one of nature's forms makes it all the more appealing to a generation of fitness buffs for whom natural is always good. Nautilus equipment brought class to the gym; along with running shoes (see p. 430) and aerobics (see p. 1) it has become one of the fashionable appurtenances of physical fitness.

Given the status achieved by Nautilus machines among the upwardly mobile, health-conscious middle class, you might expect their inventor, Arthur Jones, to be a politically chic sort of fellow, perhaps like an athletic Steven Jobs, inventor of Apple computers, or like Ben and Jerry, of hippie ice cream fame, or like Jim Fixx, who helped popularize running. Not on your life! Mr. Jones, who earned millions selling Nautilus machines at up to five thousand dollars per unit, is a right-wing vigilante survivalist who once made a living capturing and transporting exotic animals and selling them to carnivals, and has boasted that he killed dozens of people while employed as a soldier of fortune in third world countries. When his machines became the rage in the early 1980s and annual sales reached an estimated $400 million, it was reported by an aghast press that he chain-smoked Pall Malls, drank pots of coffee all day long, gob-

bled Hershey's kisses and Cheese Doodles by the bowlful, and packed a pistol in his waistband at all times. He liked to say that the only three things that mattered in his life were "younger women, faster planes, and bigger crocodiles." In fact, he was married five times, each time to a teenager; he owned (and piloted) three 707 passenger jets; and he boasted a collection of forty pet crocodiles, dozens of snakes, tarantulas, and the largest privately owned herd of elephants on earth.

Despite his own dim view of what he frequently called *homo lunaticus*, humankind —at least that high-profile portion of it that lived in America in the 1970s and 1980s and became obsessed with developing beautiful bodies—adored his invention. The *Wall Street Journal* called Nautilus "the biggest name in muscles" and said that Arthur Jones was considered "a genius among fitness gurus." Tennis pro Billie Jean King said she used Nautilus machines; so did Bo Derek (whose supposedly perfect body starred in the movie *10*), Victoria Principal, and whole pro baseball and football teams —all of whom found Nautilus far more efficient at building strength than old-fashioned workouts. Some advocates of aerobic conditioning denigrated Nautilus principles because the machines only increased muscle mass but did nothing for the cardiovascular system, but Arthur Jones never doubted his own genius. "Every single innovation in the field of exercise since the barbell has come from Nautilus," he told *Newsweek*. "Anybody who says otherwise is either a liar or a fool."

As far as Jones was concerned, Nautilus exercise equipment was just the beginning. The next step was to be the Nautilus Television Network, NTN, in direct competition with ABC, CBS, and NBC. He spent twenty million dollars building the Florida broadcasting facilities, which included a set for a talk show hosted by his personal friend G. Gordon Liddy that included a huge saltwater tank in the background full of live sharks. "TV viewers, whom [Jones] calls morons, would be more likely to tune in with the sharks there to captivate their attention," one story reported. He also planned a show starring himself and his newest, youngest wife, Terri ("The more you undress her, the better she looks," he said), titled "Younger Women, Faster Airplanes, and Bigger Crocodiles." A few of these shows were taped, but none aired: NTN never came to be, and in 1986 Jones sold the Nautilus company, including his jets and his elephants.

Despite Nautilus's unique reputation, sales had peaked and had begun to slip by the mid-1980s. Mr. Jones, who refused to hire professional managers and had once had himself photographed wearing a name tag inscribed "God," blamed his problems on the failings and corruption of lesser beings. Worst among them were design-stealing competitors, although some of his financial pickle was due to the fact that he insisted on running the company so that it never showed a profit, thus never had to pay taxes. (He does not believe the government has a right to tax citizens.) Although some rivals clearly infringed on Nautilus's patented designs, Jones would not sue them —to the dismay of his distributors, who lost millions. The reason: He hated lawyers and refused to get involved with them. "The one good thing about Communists," he once observed, "is that when they take over a country the first thing they do is kill the lawyers."

Jones also blamed his company's woes on enemies within his own ranks; he spent millions of dollars developing high-tech surveillance systems so he could observe Nautilus personnel as they worked. According to G. Gordon Liddy, on one occasion, while lecturing a recently hired man on the importance of loyalty, Jones took the newcomer to a big freezer and said, "Let me show you what happened to the last employee who double-crossed me." Jones opened the freezer. It was crowded with piles of frozen, severed human limbs, kept on hand for muscle research. "The guy freaked," Liddy recalled. "Arthur thought things like that were funny."

WAYNE NEWTON

When Wayne Newton, "the Midnight Idol," plays Vegas, which he does more than any other superstar, he grosses over a million dollars a month— exceeding the takes of Elvis and Sinatra. His records don't sell all that well; he has never had a number-one pop hit; most of the songs in his repertoire are cover versions of other artists' work. But live and in person, in Las Vegas (and also in Reno, Tahoe, and Atlantic City), he has no peers. Wayne Newton is the highest-paid nightclub entertainer ever, and since the late 1970s he has reigned undisputed as the King of the Strip. "Las Vegas without Wayne Newton is like Disneyland without Mickey Mouse," Merv Griffin once said.

There is only one way to understand his charisma: Be in an audience when the curtain rises and the drums begin to beat, the fog machine starts puffing, and a spaceship descends onto the stage, depositing an imposing figure with terrific posture in a wide-open shirt and great gold eagle-buckle belt. Glittering in the mist, the Newt steps forward to the edge of the stage. The throb of the tom-toms escalates; the crowd shrieks and gasps with anticipation of what is about to happen. Then, wielding the microphone like a quick-draw cowboy with a Colt .45, he belts out Neil Diamond's "[Coming to] America" like you've never heard it belted out before. Only if your flesh is made of wood can you resist tingling with the thrill.

Described by reporter Jefferson Graham as "Al Jolson, Elvis Presley, and Sammy Davis, Jr. all rolled into one," by *People* as "a showbiz glitz blitz [who] looks like Liberace's nephew," and by himself (on stage) as "the Indian all dressed up like a wedding cake," Wayne Newton, a.k.a. Mr. Excitement and Mr. Las Vegas, originated the concept of giving an audience 110 percent. When he puts on a show, it's twice as long

as anybody else's. He sweats, he cries, he laughs, he plays the fiddle, cornet, and piano, he sings hard rock, soft ballads, misty love songs, the best of Elvis and Sinatra and Barbra Streisand, he kisses ladies in the front row, and he convincingly reassures the cheering fans that they are very, very special. And they return the compliment by giving him roses, or if they are really carried away, by taking off their underpants and throwing them at him.

The ultimate casino crooner came to Las Vegas as a chubby fifteen-year-old boy with a strange, high-pitched voice and a repertoire of country-western songs he performed with his older brother Jerry. Born in Virginia to parents who were both half-Cherokee, Wayne was a musical prodigy who at the age of six had his own radio show, on which he sang hymns and pop tunes every morning for an hour before school. When he was eight, he auditioned for "Ted Mack's Original Amateur Hour," but flunked. For young Wayne, however, rejection was the best motivator he ever had, and in his autobiography, *Once Before I Go*, he recalled telling himself, "Damn it! I'm going to do it!" He also noted, "There are two people I know who flunked 'Ted Mack's Original Amateur Hour' audition: Elvis Presley and me."

Wayne was sickly, so stricken with asthma that his family moved to Arizona so he could breathe. In Phoenix he and his brother sang on local radio and television shows; in 1959, two weeks before the end of Wayne's junior year in high school (and just after he was elected student body president), the Newton Brothers opened at the Carnival Room Lounge at the Fremont Hotel in Glitter Gulch, downtown Vegas. Wayne's trademark song was a gushing version of the Irish ballad "Danny Boy," and although the act was so successful that they stayed on for five years, Wayne was lonely and sad. Too young to wander around the casino (where he required a special adult escort to the stage), he spent all his spare time caring for a pet skunk, or at a soda fountain across the street eating strawberry shortcake and pie. He got fat and became known as a cherubic clown; his brother Jerry was the sexy one.

Wayne began to believe he was doomed to be typecast as a downtown lounge singer, which meant he would never have a shot at the bigger and far more lucrative venues out on the Las Vegas strip. Then one day in 1963 Bobby Darin called him and asked him to listen to an acetate demo record done by a German baritone. The song had been recorded at 33-1/3 rpm, but Darin played it at 78 rpm, and that is how Wayne Newton recorded it, sounding less like a boy or a man than like a transsexual fräulein in the throes of desire. "Danke Schoen" was a major hit, and Wayne went national, singing it on the Jackie Gleason and Ed Sullivan shows, where television audiences loved him for his politeness and puerile smile. Soon he was out of Glitter Gulch and packing the Flamingo on the strip. The Newton Brothers became Wayne Newton with Jerry Newton, then just Wayne Newton (with Jerry playing guitar and exchanging jokes on stage until his retirement in 1970). "Danke Schoen" was followed by "Red Roses for a Blue Lady," which was also a hit; but finally Wayne's voice changed, and when he stopped being a soprano, the records stopped selling.

Still, they loved him all the more in Las Vegas. The huskier-voiced lounge singer made fortunes belting out such audience pleasers as "When the Saints Go Marching In" and "Bill Bailey, Won't You Please Come Home," and developing an act that featured laser light effects, rousing musical virtuosity, and some of the tightest tuxedo pants in history. Still, big as he was on the Strip,

Wayne Newton was getting very angry: While he was wowing capacity crowds at the casinos, he had turned into a national joke. Because of his tendency to show excess weight as baby fat, there were stories that he wore a frogman suit underneath his clothes to keep the blubber compressed (which helped explain why he sweated so much on stage), and there were nasty jokes, too: "Wouldn't it be interesting to be a straw in Wayne Newton's ear," McLean Stevenson used to say, "and blow up his head to match the size of his body?" And because of Wayne's early high-voiced recordings, there were sissy jokes, too, in the days when homosexuality was a giggle. "I saw Wayne Newton and Liberace together in a pink bathtub," Johnny Carson quipped one night in a 1973 "Tonight Show" monologue. "What do you think that meant?" The next day, Wayne—who had become a black belt in karate and was now six-foot-three with muscles of iron and a burly voice to match —stormed into Carson's office and demanded that Johnny cease implying he was gay. "I'm telling you right now it had better stop or I'll knock you on your ass," Wayne remembers saying. Carson turned white, apologized, and never told another Wayne Newton joke.

By 1980 Wayne Newton had a mustache and had completely transformed himself into a symbol of hairy-chested machismo on stage, as well as a shrewd and implacable businessman in private life, known as much for his stupendous wealth as for his talents. Today he lives in two homes: an Arabian horse ranch complete with a specially designed swimming pool just for the horses, and Casa Shenandoah, a fifty-acre oasis ten minutes from the Strip, complete with private lakes and streams, eight separate guest houses, a fleet of twenty cars, a private, five-passenger helicopter to take him to his private jet, flocks of exotic birds (including the world's largest collection of albino peacocks), a raptor rehabilitation center, and a vast library of Civil War literature. In his own words, it is "the American dream come true."

Believed to be one of the wealthiest people in show business, Wayne Newton has devoted a lot of time in recent years not to earning money but to a task beyond cash value: upholding his pride and honor. When he bought the Aladdin Casino in 1980, he blew the whistle on the mob, saying they tried to extort money from him; and when an NBC News broadcast implied that he was in fact cozy with the mob, he sued the network for defamation, claiming they had been put up to it by Johnny Carson. After years of legal wrangling and millions of dollars in legal bills, he won. "They hit me where I live, my dignity and my honor," he said to explain why he could not give up until he prevailed. Still, ferocious as he is about protecting his pride, Wayne also has a sense of humor about himself, and has taken movie roles in *Licence to Kill* (1989), as a sleazy TV evangelist, and *Ford Fairlane* (1990), as a deaf record-company executive, that are inspired parodies of his superslick Vegas image.

Whatever course Wayne Newton's career takes, he now seems to have established himself as an inviolable symbol of proud, moral wholesomeness. Ever since he demonstrated impeccable manners as a boy when he talked to Arthur Godfrey on television, he has been especially cherished by manners-minded Americans because of his admirable social skills. Sure, he's sexy, but his crotch thrusts on stage are not lewd, and the kisses he bestows on lady fans are chaste. Wayne Newton is clean and good, and his fans love him for that.

Ronald Reagan's secretary of the interior James Watt loved him for being clean, too, and because of that Wayne Newton became embroiled in one of the silliest cultural confrontations of the 1980s. Watt asked him to perform on the Mall in Washington, D.C., for a Fourth of July concert in 1983 after Watt had determined that the originally scheduled musicians, the Beach Boys (see p. 38), would attract "the wrong element." Watt's decision caused an uproar, known in the press as "the Great Beach Boy Brouhaha." Beach Boy fans (and Watt enemies) threatened to riot or simply boycott the event, and it was predicted that Wayne Newton's concert, the failure of which had now become a cause célèbre among anti-Reaganites, would be a cataclysmic bomb. When interviewed by TV news beforehand, Wayne threw down the gauntlet: "If the American public is truly sick of drugs and truly sick of overdoses and truly sick of fights and truly sick of not being able to go out of their houses on the Fourth of July and celebrate the nation's birthday, they have to do one thing—they have to show up for that concert." They did. Despite a heavy rainstorm, 350,000 Wayne Newton fans came to show which side they were on, joining their idol in singing his "American trilogy" concert climax: "Dixie," "Battle Hymn of the Republic," and "America." When he wrote his autobiography he described his feelings after that event: "The two things that I have never done in my life is lose faith in God or the American public."

900 NUMBERS

Money & Success

1-900-370-4401
Only $3.50 per minute

onely? Horny? Broke? Want a valuable free gift? Want to talk to the Easter Bunny, the Ninja Turtles, or a law firm eager to sue on your behalf? Would you like to win a Hawaiian vacation for two or a mink coat or a round-trip, all-expenses-paid ticket to Mir, the Soviet space station? Do you crave to hear the voice of Arnold Schwarzenegger, giving you a "personalized" message about why you should go see his newest movie?

You name it, you can have it by dialing 1-900, then seven digits that connect you to the wonderful world of voice information services. The cost? Don't worry: You will discover the cost later, much later, on your phone bill at the end of the month. Americans spend about a half a billion dollars every year calling 900 numbers to fulfill their needs and fantasies, and unless the government does something to stop it (a threat Congress has made since 1990, when 900-number fraud and abuse became a national issue), it is expected to be a $1.2 billion business by 1995.

The first use of 900 numbers was a noble expression of democracy in action, but for a price. During the 1980 Carter-Reagan televised debate, home viewers were invited to call in and say who they thought had won. Seven hundred thousand people picked up the phone and paid fifty cents for the privilege of expressing their opinion (67 percent picked Reagan). The next notable use of 900 numbers wasn't quite so high-principled, although it was certainly well meaning: Nearly half a million viewers called a 900 number in April 1982 to plead that "Saturday Night Live" not boil a live lobster (named Larry) on the air. Later that summer, NASA gave callers an opportunity to

pay money and listen in on space-shuttle conversations. By 1990, 900-number use had matured to the point that George Burditt of Santa Barbara, California, won a million dollars by making a $2.99 900-number call to a telephone contest called "The Game" and correctly answering this question: "How many eggs are in three dozen?"

There are many virtuous and charitable kinds of calls you can pay for: The March of Dimes and Red Cross and even Nelson Mandela have collected money by taking advantage of 900 lines. There is useful information to be bought, such as sports scores, stock quotes, and earthquake forecasts (dial 1-900-USA-JOLT). And there is plenty of lowbrow (if high-priced) fun: horoscope readings by Micki Dahne (including, at no extra charge, her seance with Elvis), dial-an-insult, previews of soap opera plots, and the Adventures of Gastroman ("No sound effect is spared to drive home the message that the body's noisiest expulsions are choice grist for America's comedy mill").

Despite such apparently harmless hijinks, 900 numbers have a lot of people worried. They "have turned your phone into a time bomb," said Congressman Bart Gordon of Tennessee, who has lobbied to curb their abuse. *Reader's Digest* called 900 numbers "the Pandora's box of the 1990s" in an article that told about an eleven-year-old boy who ran up a $120.72 phone bill trying to win a trip to Hawaii for his parents. A mentally handicapped boy in North Carolina accrued over nine thousand dollars in charges by dialing "talk line" services. The girls he talked to coerced him into giving out his home number, and now, according to his mother, they regularly call him at home and ask him for money to bail them out of jail. The *Digest* warned its readers that if you dial a 900 number, "you'll likely find yourself ripped off, knee-deep in sleaze, or hounded by bill collectors." In a report on parents' "phone bill shock," *Nation's Business* said, "Teenagers and 900 numbers go together like matches and gasoline."

Many of the tackiest pay-call schemes are advertised on television, which is obviously the best way to reach people whose communication with the outside world tends to be restricted to what they can reach via their remote control or telephone. Prurient talk shows use 900 numbers so viewers can pay to call in their opinions about the issue du jour (Should transvestites be allowed to use opposite-sex bathrooms? Should we ban bare buns on the beach?); sweepstakes sponsors invite homebodies to pay a mere $9.90 per call to phone in and check to see if they have won a new car; jobless people with bad credit ratings are enticed with credit cards if they call a number that, for a charge of $50, does nothing more than mail them a list of banks around the country that might be willing to consider their credit application.

In 1990 children were promised free gifts and fun stories if they called a "secret" Easter Bunny number. The call cost two dollars for the first minute, then forty-five cents for each additional minute. Many of them never got their presents because they were unable to follow complicated instructions, and their parents wound up paying for the call, because the kiddies didn't do as the Easter Bunny directed them to do: Send a photocopy of their end-of-the-month phone bill, with a stamped self-addressed envelope, for the gift and reimbursement. Another scheme, aimed at tots too young to know how to dial, told them they could talk to Santa Claus if they held their phone up to the TV, at which point the television played the tones that dialed the 900 number: charges accrued by the minute until the child hung up on Santa or until a responsible grown-up discovered what was going on. The Federal Trade Commission now requires 900-number ads to warn children about the cost and tells them to hang up if they don't have their parents' permission to call.

Idiotic though most 900-number schemes seem to any adult with a full-functioning brain, it must be said that there is something fascinating about some of the come-on ads for dating lines that are broadcast on television during the wee hours when, presumably, people are home alone and unable to sleep because they feel so forlorn. At least one has offered a famous sexy person with whom callers can talk (Jessica Hahn's "Love Line"), but most feature nobodies. With such names as "Live Model Line," "Dream Dates," "True Confessions," "Party Time," and "One on One," they promise hot, intimate conversations with other sensual lonelies (or sometimes even with whole orgies), but the real fun part, at least for voyeurs, is that they actually *show* such people talking on the phone: handsome hunks and lovely lasses lounge on couches looking passionate and disease-free as they begin to reveal their innermost fantasies and desires. You never hear the calls get really steamy

—just the opening lines ("Hi, I'm Kandi, I'm an aerobics instructor, and I'm tired of the dating game").

Actually calling love lines can be embarrassing, not to mention ultimately unsatisfying, but as television programming, the ads for the numbers are fun indeed. Watching sex objects pretend to talk dirty on the telephone isn't the least bit embarrassing for the simple reason that television's greatest gift is its power to transform intimacy into an entertaining public spectacle.

NINTENDO

In 1981 Shigeru Miyamoto designed an electric hominid to run around the screen in the video arcade game of Donkey Kong. It was a short, nondescript character with a red cap and a mustache that gave him the look of a stubborn guy who just wouldn't quit. He was named Mario by the American staff of the Nintendo company (after their building's landlord), and he and his brother Luigi, the Super Mario Brothers, can now be found in well over thirty million American homes. They are the most popular—but by no means the only—characters who populate the several hundred Nintendo game cartridges that feature heroes chasing through booby-trapped landscapes, slaughtering enemies, rescuing maidens, and usually dying with a sorry transistorized whimper some time before the goal is reached.

Nintendo wasn't expected to be the biggest phenomenon in electronic games since Pac-Man (see p. 373). When the system was introduced in 1986—it is an eighty-dollar box that hooks up to the television set and is controlled by a joystick, Power Pad, Power Glove, or wireless U-Force—most American toy companies believed that video games were passé and that kids were bored with little beeping characters who chased around a screen. But Nintendo, a

Japanese company that had begun as a playing-card manufacturer in 1888, initiated what the *Wall Street Journal* called "one of the great consumer-product success stories of the 1980s." They sold three hundred million dollars' worth of Entertainment Systems and cartridges in the first year, getting consumers hooked on the Legend of Zelda, an action-adventure game in which an indomitable swordsman named Link must find the Golden Triforce of Wisdom in the labyrinths of the Underworld in order to rescue Zelda. Sales tripled the next year: Nintendo begat Game Boy, a portable version so you never have to be without your boinging blips; and soon Nintendo had competition in the marketplace, with the likes of Atari, NEC, and Sega offering their own entertainment systems and games (some with liquid crystal 3-D glasses!). The home video game market is now a $5-billion-per-year industry.

The real thrill of such classics as the Legend of Zelda, Super Mario 2 (a quest to defeat the evil Wart), and Punch-Out!! (fight Mike Tyson) is that the course of the games is always unpredictable. Using computing power equivalent to that of an Apple II, a Nintendo console with a good cartridge plugged in is an adventure, even if you've played the game a hundred times before. You never know, and the instruction books do not tell you, where all the trapdoors and secret passageways are going to be, or ex-

actly what defense strategy to use when you are playing Renegade, which presents you with a gang of muggers about to attack in a subway. The only way to learn is to play and play again, or possibly to read *Nintendo Power* magazine (two million readers), which is filled with clues and tips that help you survive.

But even labyrinthine Nintendo grew boring to the eight-to-fifteen-year-old boys who are its prime market, and so in 1991 Nintendo introduced Super Nintendo, based on a sixteen-bit computer chip rather than the old eight-bit chip. Super Nintendo, designed to stop erosion of Nintendo's market share to other game companies and to counteract consumer ennui, promises sharper graphics, clearer sound, and brighter colors. "Kids all over America are going to go 'Wow!'" predicted Nintendo's vice-president of marketing, who envisioned a happy future selling the $190 system (plus about $60 per game) to millions of families who are bound to realize that their old Nintendo player and all its games have now become yesterday's fun.

OAT BRAN

Approximately once every decade Americans become fixated on the importance of healthy bowel movements; inevitably bran is touted as the best way to produce them. Beginning with Sylvester Graham's prescription of "whole wheat" flour in the 1830s (and its contemporary fad of drinking gallons of water as a way to purge), the history of American food flummery is mostly a chronicle of good-health evangelists telling people to eat bran

so they can go to the bathroom more often. Oat bran is the basis of the latest such regime.

It began with *The 8-Week Cholesterol Cure*, a 1987 book by Robert E. Kowalski that was more about healthy circulation than about expediting alimentary activity. But the bran-heavy diet prescribed by the book, which was a two-million-copy bestseller, didn't only reduce serum cholesterol; it also encouraged cataclysmic bowel

movements. Six months after its publication, the federal government issued guidelines that supported Mr. Kowalski's theories, and since then the best part of the oat has found its way into bagels, brownies, potato chips, spaghetti noodles, and dozens of cereals. America's oat crop, most of which had previously been used to feed livestock, was suddenly so scarce that oat imports skyrocketed and the price tripled.

The best-known forefather of modern bran mania was John Harvey Kellogg, who in 1895 invented the cereal flake (first called Granola, then Granose, then Toasted Wheat Flakes) at his Battle Creek Sanitarium because he believed it would help people chew more vigorously, thus stimulate healthy digestion; he even wrote a "chewing song" for sanitarium patients to sing as they ate. Kellogg believed that all illness was the result of a lazy colon, which he cured by submitting sufferers to fifteen-gallon enemas and breakfasts of pure bran and paraffin oil. One of Kellogg's patients, C. W. Post, was so inspired by his stay that he went on to write a book called *The Road to Wellville*,

which prescribed a physic cure using the system-cleansing products he invented, including cereal-based Postum and Grape Nuts cereal, which was alleged to be "more soluble than any other food."

In 1975 psychiatrist David Reuben, who had previously written *Everything You Always Wanted to Know About Sex (But Were Afraid to Ask)*, came out with the "Save-Your-Life Diet," based on studies done in Africa by an English doctor, Denis Burkitt, who became known in the United Kingdom as "the bran man." These theories, an update of Kellogg's and Post's, held that overprocessed foods and refined sugar caused colon cancer and high serum cholesterol; conversely, a diet based on mostly raw fruits and vegetables, and especially unprocessed bran, was the secret of long, disease-free life as well as bowel movements that Reuben promised would be "large in amount, well-formed, low in odor, and passed without straining."

Of all brans, oat bran is still the one loved best by today's bowel boosters, although some recent studies have shown that barley, carrots, onions, and cabbage are just as effective in lowering cholesterol levels, and probably better-tasting. A 1989 article by Marian Burros in the *New York Times* groaned about the "idiotic lengths to which some people have gone in an effort to ingest enough oat bran to lower their cholesterol," and concluded that "a steady diet of oat bran seems more like medicine than like a satisfying meal." David Liederman, a New York cookie merchant who lost more than a hundred pounds and lowered his cholesterol count from 324 to 180 on an oat bran diet (and was selling one hundred thousand oat bran muffins per week in his shops at the height of the craze), said, "It's bizarre when you walk along Central Park South, a horse may be eating the hottest food around."

PAC-MAN

In Japanese folklore there is a character who is always hungry. He lives to eat, the word for which is *paku*. Never satisfied, the Paku Man gobbles everything in sight. When he came to America late in 1980, he feasted. Pac-Man became a national obsession: in video arcades, at home on televisions equipped with Pac-Man cartridges, as a top-ten record ("Pac-Man Fever" by Jerry Buckner and Gary Garcia), as two bestselling books (*How to Win at Pac-Man* and *Mastering Pac-Man*), as a Saturday-morning cartoon show, as a decorative motif on jeans, lunch boxes, pajamas, and toys, and as *Time*'s Man of the Year in 1982. "I think we have the Mickey Mouse of the 1980s," said one Pac-Man executive when it was noted that Americans were spending about $6 billion per year on the game and its spinoffs—more than the gross of all the Las Vegas casinos and the motion picture business. "Pinball is obsolescent, and the jukebox is nearly extinct," *The New Yorker* announced in the fall of 1982 in an article devoted to the doings in the game room of Mike the Greek's, a cafe in Ocean Beach on Fire Island.

In case you were out of town in the early 1980s, we should explain that Pac-Man is a little yellow character shaped like a pie with a single slice missing—his mouth. He scores points by speeding through a video maze gobbling up dots and fruits or an especially valuable (2,000 points) Galaxian, while trying to avoid being gobbled by the four ghosts who inhabit the maze. In the glory days of 1982, good arcade players could pilot Pac-Man through his twisted environment for hours on a single quarter, scoring 20,000 or 200,000 or even a million points . . . unless they succumbed (as many

impassioned Pac-Man fanatics did) to inflamed tendons, blistered index fingers, joint pain, and tennis elbow.

Pac-Man's sway over American kids (and even over some adults) was a cause for great concern among guardians of public morals. Surgeon General C. Everett Koop worried that kids were becoming addicted, "body and soul." What were children learning when they succumbed to this eat-or-be-eaten fixation? A *Natural History* article about the phenomenon quoted one Pac-Man ace, described as a "political refugee from South Africa," as saying that video games' aggressive themes seemed very American to him because they encouraged "aggression against anything alien. If it's not an American, you try to shoot at it. Anything alien must be insulated against. Any foreign thing must go down." Although Pac-Man was about devouring enemies rather than shooting them, a social psychologist at Stanford expressed concern that it was sexist and violent because it "fed into masculine fantasies of control, power, destruction."

In fact, Pac-Man was one of the first games that attracted girls into video arcades, which throughout the late 1970s had been all-boy places where the popular games were such military confrontations as Space Invaders, Missile Command, and Defenders. Danielle Brisebois, the child star of TV's "Archie Bunker's Place," told *People* magazine that she especially liked Ms. Pac-Man because it was "cuter." In those days when personal computers were still a novelty, there were plenty of experts who eagerly defended Pac-Man as an avenue that led kids from passive TV viewing towards computer literacy. "Drugs are used to avoid problems," explained Dr. Stephen Leff, a psychologist at Harvard. "Video games get people fascinated with problem-*solving*." Another psychologist pointed out to *TV Guide* that the more money kids spent on Pac-Man, the less they would have for undesirable activities such as expensive rock concerts and large drug purchases.

Although a hundred thousand Pac-Man games were sold to arcades and tens of millions of cartridges were bought to attach to home televisions, the fad evaporated like all toy fads, replaced by more sophisticated, or at least different, video games such as Galaga, Centipede, Donkey Kong, and eventually Nintendo (see p. 370). Still, Pac-Man holds a unique position as a turning point in pop play. Before it, arcades were a dying form of fun, filled with remnants of earlier styles of amusement such as old pinball machines with mechanical paddles and real metal bouncing balls, Skee-Ball, and primitive tests of marksmanship. Throughout the 1970s there were glimmers of a new style of game, including PONG in 1972, the first to have a video screen, and Space Invaders in 1979, which used computer microchips to vastly complicate the challenge. Pac-Man ushered in a new era. After it, video arcades blossomed everywhere, and the sound of kids having fun became the beeps, boings, and sirens that technology can synthesize so well.

PANTYHOSE

No other product debut in history ever caused the pandemonium of nylon stockings when Du Pont first put them up for sale on May 15, 1940—"Nylon Day"—and riots broke out among women eager to get a pair of the wear-forever, miracle-yarn legwear that had been announced at the previous year's world's fair in New York.

Hardly anybody blinked in 1959 when Glen Raven Mills of North Carolina introduced Panti-Legs, the first pantyhose, simply because no one knew what to do with them. Glen Raven's president, Allen Gant, had listened to his wife, Ethel, complain about her nylon stockings and garter belts —what trouble they were, especially when she was pregnant—which is why he en-

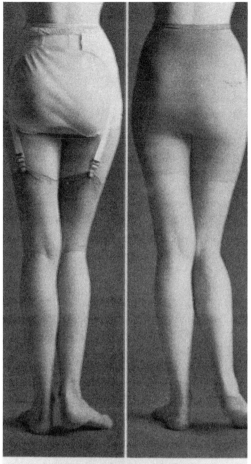

now you have a choice

to a woman's chin in order to get the feet to fit and the legs smooth. Panti-Legs originally came in ten sizes, which weren't nearly enough to fit all women, but one person who did find a perfect fit was stripper Sally Rand, who sent a photo of herself wearing a pair (and not much else) to Glen Raven, pleading with them to make Panti-Legs without seams in order to help her achieve a more totally nude look.

Improved seamless Panti-Legs were much more elastic than the original model, which made them easier to put on and take off (although instructions were included with all the early pairs), and they soon became available in many more sizes, including queen. And it's a good thing, because by 1965, when Mary Quant introduced the miniskirt, women needed them. Suddenly garters with clip-on stockings and girdles, which hung below the miniskirt's hemline, were obsolete. Unless a woman was willing to go bare-legged, a pair of pantyhose was the only possible thing to wear with a mini or, even more revealing, a micro-mini. (There was one eccentric alternative: Body Paint. Introduced by Coty in the late sixties for women who loved "mini, kicky, bare-as-you-dare fashions," Body Paint came in green, blue, mauve, and four shades of flesh. Advertisements showed a woman with a roller and pan, which were supplied with each can of paint, making her legs appear to gleam flawlessly.)

For a garment that at first had a rather sensuous appeal because it seemed so revealing, pantyhose have gone through a strange evolution. As Ellen Melinkoff wrote in *What We Wore*, "Pantyhose edited legs. They hid the hair, the blotches, the cellulite." *That* was their real value: They freed women not only from garter belts but from the arduous task of leg grooming. Strangely, this made them more like cosmetics than like intimate apparel, and in 1970 the Hanes

couraged the company to develop a new kind of leg covering that would be more convenient. Nylon sales were slow in the late fifties, while stretch tights in opaque colors (pioneered as beatnik wear) had been gaining in popularity. Gant believed a new product combining tights' convenience and nylons' cachet might renew consumer interest.

The first Panti-Legs, which were full-fashion form (with seams), were created by stitching a pair of stockings to a big nylon crotch. The result was a billowy garment with a waist that had to be pulled up nearly

company started selling pantyhose called L'eggs just like soap or toothpaste—packaged in plastic containers in supermarkets and convenience stores.

Now pantyhose seem more prosthetic than provocative. For working women with aching legs, they are a godsend, and even many varieties not specifically designated as "support hose" boast that they are made of durable, iron-tough spandex designed to compress fat stomachs (control-top), disguise panty lines, and support tired muscles. They may have lost the sex appeal once commanded by all the secret folderol of stockings and garter belts, but American women buy over a hundred billion pairs every year, and pantyhose today are an axiomatic American product: cheap, convenient, practical, comfortable, and disposable.

"PEANUTS"

When it comes to clout in the world of entertainment, musclebound masters like Arnold Schwarzenegger and Sylvester Stallone are pipsqueaks compared with the balloon-headed, stoop-shouldered, worrywart kid named Charlie Brown. A few years ago when *Forbes* surveyed the biggest moneymakers in show business, Charles Schulz, Charlie Brown's creator, not only scored above Arnold and Sly but also beat out heavyweight champ Mike Tyson, talk-show mogul Oprah Winfrey, and frightmeister Stephen King. "Peanuts," the comic strip in which Charlie Brown stars along with a round-bellied beagle named Snoopy, a bird named Woodstock, and a gallery of sympathetic and sagacious tots including Lucy and Linus and Schroeder, is the most popular comic strip in history, a pioneer of spin-off merchandising (about $1 billion gross each year) and of network television special programming (starting with "A Charlie Brown Christmas" in 1965). Its popularity is global. You can read "Peanuts" in Chinese and Serbo-Croatian and twenty-four other languages, and American astronauts brought it with them when they went to the moon. "He has taken over our collective consciousness and become a part of our everyday lives," declared French Minister of Culture Jack Lang about Snoopy, on the occasion of the opening of a "Peanuts" show (for which 150 top designers made clothes for the beagle) at the Louvre in 1990.

Another museum show featuring the "Peanuts" gang opened in America in 1990, at the National Museum of American History in Washington. It was titled "This Is Your Childhood, Charlie Brown: Children and American Culture 1945–1968," and its

Snoopy, Lucy, Charlie Brown, and Linus

theme was the distress induced by a contradictory world that presented its children both a vision of perfect happiness ("The Adventures of Ozzie and Harriet") and the threat of nuclear Armageddon. Curator Charles McGovern used strips from "Peanuts" throughout the exhibition to illustrate this ambivalence because he said that Charles Schulz was "tapped into the greater currents." In one strip the ever-apprehensive Linus (he's the one who won't let go of his security blanket) becomes terrified about a snowstorm, crying, "It's happening, Charlie Brown, just like they said it would!" When Charlie Brown reminds him that it's winter, and it's snowing, and asks what else he could expect this time of year, Linus says with bruised relief, "Snowing! Good grief, I thought it was the fallout."

"Peanuts" takes place in an adult-free playland where children, in their innocence, give voice to all the primal feelings of fear and fatalism, as well as needs for comforting, that grown-ups may experience but seldom feel comfortable expressing—from the ingenuous "Happiness is a warm puppy" to Charlie Brown's favorite word for the slightly bemused state into which he is so often thrown by people and events around him: "*SIGH*." Before "Peanuts" (and even today) most comic-strip kids were hyperkinetic mischief makers, and most comic strips have always expressed a fairly aggressive or at least sarcastic point of view towards the flaws and foibles encountered by their characters. The charm of "Peanuts," and the reason people have fallen in love with its kids, is that it takes such a tender (but not sappy) point of view of characters who are far from perfect. Charlie Brown is weak, one of life's victims; even Lucy is vulnerable and insecure beneath her tough facade. They worry about everything from nuclear disaster to their own personality flaws. "Fears and anxieties" is how cre-

ator Charles Schulz once explained the theme of the strip. "It's getting down to the problems that people have." More than a few observers have compared "Peanuts" to a religious text, noting, as did Gary H. Koerselman in *The Lost Decade: A Story of America in the 1960s*, that Charlie Brown's dilemmas "relate exactly to such theological questions as original sin, neighborly concern, and the worship of graven images."

The world's favorite comic-strip artist received a grade of C+ for his only-average drawings of children when he signed up for a correspondence course in cartooning when he was seventeen years old. He had liked drawing from the time he was a little boy, and had a special affinity for comic strips ever since his father nicknamed him Sparky, after a racehorse named Spark Plug in the "Barney Google" comic. After serving in the Army as an infantry machine gunner in World War II, Schulz returned to his home in Minneapolis, applied for a job carving tombstones, and taught drawing in art school. In 1950 United Feature bought and began to syndicate (to seven newspapers) a comic strip he had devised called "Li'l Folks," featuring a (then-) smiling tyke called Good Ol' Charlie Brown. At the time, the hottest child star in the country was Howdy Doody (see p. 232), the TV marionette whose studio audience of children sat in a "peanut gallery" and were known as "Peanuts." Over Schulz's objections, United Feature renamed "Li'l Folks" after the tots in the TV show—"Peanuts."

"Peanuts" grew in popularity throughout the 1950s until Charles Schulz won the Reuben (like an Oscar, for cartoonists) in 1956, but it was in the intellectually restless 1960s, as Americans began to really worry about such issues as whether or not God is dead, that "Peanuts" time truly arrived. Old beliefs were crumbling, and thrilling as that may have been, it was also disorienting and scary. The kind of guileless aphorisms spun out by Charles Schulz's characters, not only in the comics but in *Happiness Is a Warm Puppy*, a best-selling compilation published in 1962 (and the start of over two hundred million "Peanuts" books sold so far), provided just the remedy of plain truth and whimsy that millions of people needed. Charlie Brown, founder of the Great Pumpkin Movement (which postulates a beneficent gourd but can offer no proof of its existence), became a beloved antihero for an age of anxiety that has never really ended. Wide-eyed and innocent, everybody's fool, frequently tormented and sad, but never totally without hope, he has become an eternal symbol for the possibility of postnuclear optimism (as well as spokesman, with his cartoon pals, for Metropolitan Life Insurance Company). His kite *will* fly, he *will* kick the football, the Little Red-haired Girl of his dreams *will* appear; and some day the Great Pumpkin *will* arrive with the toys he knows are his.

CLARA PELLER

In the ruthless hostilities among America's purveyors of fast-food hamburgers, McDonald's and Burger King have always been champion and challenger. Wendy's, since its founding in 1969, has the dubious honor of perpetual third place. This hierarchy was almost overthrown in 1984 by a four-foot-ten old lady named Clara Peller, who yelled "Where's the beef?" on behalf of Wendy's in a pair of television commercials.

In the first commercial, Ms. Peller and two elderly friends examine a hamburger doled out by a restaurant that calls itself "Home of the Big Bun." In a gruff, angry voice that sounds like gravel being crushed with a sledgehammer, she yells, "Where's the beef?" In the sequel, Ms. Peller telephones the restaurant's boss, who is sailing aboard his yacht, the S.S. *Big Bun;* when she asks the famous question, her bellow knocks him out of his captain's chair.

Not long after the first commercial's six-week network run, Wendy's sales had jumped 31 percent. Even more impressive, advertising-industry awareness surveys ("Name the first TV commercial that comes to mind") showed that Ms. Peller's spots were breaking all previous records of ad recognition. Three times more people named her than named Michael Jackson, who was then doing ads for Pepsi. In the burger business, where McDonald's traditionally got twice the recognition of Burger King and ten times the recognition of Wendy's, suddenly Wendy's was at the top of the heap.

Clara Peller became a star: She appeared on the "Today" show and was profiled in *People;* there were Clara Peller coffee mugs, beach towels, and T-shirts, a Clara Peller

doll, and much talk about the octogenarian's forthcoming MTV video (which never actually materialized). Saying "Where's the beef?" became a national fad. Walter Mondale used it frequently during his run for President in 1984 in an attempt to suggest that Democratic rival Gary Hart was all fluffy bun and no meaty substance. Joe Sedelmaier, who directed and produced the commercials (as well as the famous fast-talking TV ads for Federal Express), said, "If Walter Mondale could have said the line like Clara, he would have been our President." Radio stations around the country held sound-alike contests in which listeners tried to say "Where's the beef?" just as churlishly as she did. It was reported that when visiting teams entered the gym at Watterson High School in Columbus, Ohio (where Wendy's was founded), they were greeted by jeering hometown fans yelling, "Where's the beef?" *Advertising Age* said that Wendy's was "reveling in a wave of free publicity worth many times the $8 million spent on the campaign."

Not everybody was ecstatic. The Michigan Commission on Services to the Aging asked Wendy's to withdraw the ads, which they felt made old people seem cantankerous and overly fussy. Wendy's demurred, arguing that the ads showed no such thing: They demonstrated an old lady being "strong-minded enough to demand quality."

Also upset were some advertising executives who had commissioned Joe Sedelmaier to make a commercial two years earlier for Rhodes frozen bread dough. Sedelmaier, who had discovered Clara Peller in 1970 in Chicago, where she was working as a manicurist, and had used her in at least two dozen local ads since then, cast her in the bread dough spot as a cranky old lady who asks, "How's it taste?" The bread dough people were unhappy because they felt "Where's the beef?" was too much like "How's it taste?" but Sedelmaier pointed out that in the bread dough commercial, the advertising agency had actually *deleted* Ms. Peller's distinctive foghorn growl because they thought it was too awful, substituting the dulcet voice of someone else. It was her grating sound that made Wendy's ads distinctive, Sedelmaier argued.

The following year Wendy's fired Clara Peller. Her crime? She had appeared in a commercial for Prego spaghetti sauce saying, "I found it." A vice-president at Wendy's explained, "Clara can find the beef only in one place, and that is Wendy's."

"Wendy's made millions because of me," responded Ms. Peller, who was deaf and had to be pinched in the ankle as a cue to say her line when the famous commercial had been made. "I've made them millions, and they don't appreciate me." She died two years later, at age eighty-six.

PET ROCKS

Gary Dahl, a California advertising man, was having drinks with his buddies one night in April 1975 when the conversation turned to pets. As a lark, Mr. Dahl informed his friends that he considered dogs, cats, birds, and fish all a pain in the neck. They made a mess; they misbehaved; they cost too much money. He, on the other

hand, had a pet rock, and it was an ideal pet —easy and cheap, and it had a great personality. His buddies started to riff with the off-the-wall idea and pretty soon they were all tossing around the notion of a pet rock and all the things it was good for.

Dahl spent the next two weeks writing the *Pet Rock Training Manual*—a step-by-step guide to having a happy relationship with your geological pet, including instructions for how to make it roll over and play dead and how to house-train it: "Place it on some old newspapers. The rock will never know what the paper is for and will require no further instruction." To accompany the book, Dahl decided to actually create a Pet Rock. He went to a builder's supply store in San Jose and found the most expensive rock in the place—a Rosarita Beach Stone, which was a uniform-size, rounded gray pebble that sold for a penny. He packed the stone in excelsior in a gift box shaped like a pet carrying case, accompanied by the instruction book.

The Pet Rock was introduced at the August gift show in San Francisco (the gift market is much easier to break into than the cutthroat toy market), then in New York. Neiman-Marcus ordered five hundred. Gary Dahl sent out homemade news releases of himself, accompanied by a picture that showed him surrounded by boxes of his Pet Rocks. *Newsweek* did a half-page

story about the nutty notion, and by the end of October Gary Dahl was shipping ten thousand Pet Rocks every day. He appeared on "The Tonight Show," *twice*. By Christmas, when two and a half tons of rocks had been sold, three-fourths of all the daily newspapers in America had run Pet Rock stories, often including Gary Dahl's tongue-in-cheek revelations about how each rock was individually tested for obedience at Rosarita Beach in Baja, Mexico, before being selected and boxed. A million rocks sold for $3.95 apiece in just a few months, and Gary Dahl—who had decided from the beginning to make at least one dollar from every rock —had become an instant millionaire.

Copycat rocks flooded the market, including one cleverly marketed as "the Original Pet Rock," and dozens of quick-buck entrepreneurs joined the action selling such ancillary fun as Pet Rock Obedience Lessons and Pet Rock Burial-at-Sea Services. Immediately after Christmas 1975, Gary Dahl himself relabeled leftover Pet Rocks as Valentine's Day gifts for loved ones in need of a low-maintenance pet, but the Pet Rock quickly became last year's fad.

Dahl quit his job in advertising and formed Rock Bottom Productions, and two years later he was interviewed by Don Kracke, the inventor of Rickie Tickie Sticky bathroom appliqués, for Mr. Kracke's book *How to Turn Your Idea Into a Million Dollars.* Dahl confided to Kracke, "I've got four more ideas. Wait'll you see 'em!" We have been unable to determine if any of the four ideas have seen the light of day.

Whatever his fortunes after the Pet Rock, Gary Dahl has become one of the great motivational figures of recent times. To Don Kracke and to other inventors, like Ken Hakuta (author of *How to Create Your Own Fad and Make a Million Dollars*) and Robert L. Shook (author of *Why Didn't I Think of That!*), the story of the Pet Rock is a never-ending source of inspiration to create new crazes that sweep the nation and make millions for the genius who thought of them. To most noninventive people who remember it, the Pet Rock, like Deely Bobber head antennae and the Hula Hoop (see p. 237), has become one of the mind-boggling examples of inexplicable marketplace mania.

But Ken Hakuta does have an explanation for the periodic success of what he calls "useless dumb jokes" like the Pet Rock: It gave people a few moments of absolutely meaningless pleasure in a troubled world—no small accomplishment. "If there were more fads," Hakuta observed, "there probably would be a lot fewer psychiatrists. ...Instead of paying for $100-an-hour therapy sessions, you could just get yourself a couple of Wacky Wallwakers [a rubber toy that sticks and wriggles on a wall, which earned Hakuta $20 million] and a Slinky and lock yourself up in a room for a couple of hours. When you came out, you'd be fine."

PEYTON PLACE

There is no way to know exactly how many boys and girls growing up in the 1950s got their sex education by studying the good parts of *Peyton Place*, but one thing is certain: Grace Metalious's novel, published in September 1956, aroused the nation. It is believed that one in six Americans read at least parts of it. And there are certain parts—Rodney and Betty's nude moonlight swim, Helen's perfect heaving breasts and the hard nipple she flicks with her fingernail, the torrid sexual reawakening of Constance MacKenzie, and Bradley Holmes teaching Allison to "kiss like a woman"—that are remembered by a lot of once-young-and-curious readers more clearly and precisely than the details of their own personal sex lives. What a naughty thrill it was in 1956 to surge through the novel and dote on the passages about young Allison's swelling passions, about handsome (and intelligent) sex god Tomas Makris, about quiet Norman Page and his odd relationship with his mom (he liked it when she whipped him!), about the

Grace Metalious

shame of beautiful Selena Cross (raped by her stepfather!), and about rich Rodney Harrington and his forbidden love affair.

Peyton Place sold twenty million copies, inspired a sequel, a movie, a movie sequel, a long-running television series, and a sequel to the television series, and became a provocative symbol of sex for years to come. You may recall Jayne Mansfield in her signature movie role, as blonde bombshell Rita Marlow in *Will Success Spoil Rock Hunter?* (1957), reads *Peyton Place* while she and her clipped poodle enjoy a bubble bath together. But sex alone is not what made the book so controversial. There were some other equally explicit novels floating around in the 1950s (by Henry Miller and D. H. Lawrence), but the special titillation of *Peyton Place* was that it took sex out of its usual faraway romantic meadows or European castles or beatnik pads in San Francisco and put it into a respectable New England village. Its throbbing body parts did not belong to counts or duchesses or lusty pirates of yore; the people getting it on in *Peyton Place* were a schoolteacher, a seamstress, and pretty little teenage girls. Lust in the here-and-now not only made the book steamier and more fun to read; it also stirred up torrents of controversy.

It was banned in Canada, in Rhode Island, and in Fort Wayne, Indiana. Bookstore owners were fined for selling it to minors. Although the *New York Times* compared it with the works of Sherwood Anderson and *Time* praised it for capturing "a real sense of the temper, texture, and tensions of a small town," a lot of people who lived in small towns hated it. It was bad enough for city know-it-alls to moralize about country life, but Grace Metalious was herself a rural New Englander, and for her to wag her finger seemed a little bit like treason. One Vermont newspaper called it "a murky pool of drunkenness, sex outside of marriage, family violence, and uninhibited language." Some provincial libraries refused to buy it, and many that did wouldn't let it out on loan. *Yankee* magazine recently recalled that the Beverly, Massachusetts library posted a sign at the circulation desk advising customers, "This library does not carry *Peyton Place*. If you want it, go to Salem."

Peyton Place endured as a cultural symbol because it was an exposé. Beyond the then-lurid details in the sex scenes, it riled everybody up because it was an ugly portrait of a part of America that had formerly been held sacred. The idyllic New England setting was depicted as a hotbed not merely of sex (which was naughty enough in 1956) but of incest, brutality, suicide, abortion, and drunkenness; even its puritanical moralists were shown to have sinning on their minds. To this day, decades after the novel topped the bestseller list (it is now out of print), the words "Peyton Place" have become a familiar term to describe jerkwater hypocrisy and to suggest a world of sin and secret concupiscence behind a polite facade.

"To a tourist these towns look as peaceful as a postcard," Grace Metalious said in one infamous interview. "But if you go beneath that picture, it's like turning over a rock with your foot—all kinds of strange things crawl out." To say the least, the village of Gilmanton, New Hampshire, where Grace Metalious lived, was not happy with the publication of *Peyton Place*. In an article titled "An Unpopular Best Seller," *Life* magazine said that the citizens of Gilmanton, who hated the book, had completely ostracized Mrs. Metalious and fired her husband from his job as school principal. (Technically, he wasn't fired; his contract was simply not renewed.) *Life* said that the residents not only didn't like Mrs. Metalious's book; they thought she was sloppy because she wore blue jeans and a man-tailored shirt and put her hair into a ponytail and didn't use makeup.

Grace Metalious certainly did not fit into the finely mannered social scheme of small-town Belknap County, New Hampshire.

Raised poor in the nearby city of Manchester, she came to Gilmanton in 1953 when her husband got a job there as a grade-school teacher. She was a twenty-eight-year-old aspiring author with three children, a serious drinking problem, and a novel no one wanted to publish. Her house was a mess, she was overweight, and she swore all the time. She felt so resentful about the way she was treated by townspeople that she put aside the novel she had been trying to sell and started work on another one, called *The Tree and the Blossom*, in which she intended to expose and ridicule the people who were being mean to her.

Grace had only one friend, but this friend was a gold mine: Laurie Wilkens, Gilmanton correspondent for the Laconia *Evening Citizen*. According to *Yankee* magazine, Mrs. Wilkens's job clued her in to *everything* that happened in town as well as to every nasty little rumor, and although she didn't write about such stuff for the paper, she told it all to Grace Metalious. Grace ate it up. It took her four months to write *The Tree and the Blossom*. Her publisher renamed it *Peyton Place* for greater sex appeal, and insisted that it be toned down (Selena's rapist-father was rewritten as her *step*father) and heated up (a really juicy sex scene between Constance MacKenzie and Tom Makris was added at the last minute). "Publishing circles are gabbing," gossip columnist Dorothy Kilgallen announced in the summer of 1956, and six weeks before its official publication day, *Peyton Place* was on the bestseller list.

Grace Metalious was pictured on the jacket of the book poised at her typewriter in casual clothes, with a caption that described her as "Pandora in blue jeans." Originally, her publisher had thought they would promote the book by playing up the contrast between its shockingly frank contents and the prim schoolteacher's-wife who wrote it. But Metalious couldn't play prim, and soon she was cast in the media eye as a scandal monger. Although book buyers went mad for it, many members of the press earned their brownie points by scolding her for snooping. "What gives you the right to pry and hold your neighbors up to ridicule?" interrogated Mike Wallace, who then hosted a television show called "Night Beat." Poor Grace did not know how to respond, and when Wallace concluded, "I thought your book was basic and carnal," all she could answer was a weak "You did, huh?"

Gilmanton was overrun with media people looking for sizzling sex going on in every sheep pen, barn, and parlor, but all they found was an embarrassed and embittered populace who didn't appreciate reporters and photographers coming to show how sanctimonious and narrow-minded they all were. Despite some harassment from the locals, and despite her husband's leaving her, Grace Metalious stayed in town, married a local disc jockey, and wrote *Return to Peyton Place*, *The Tight White Collar*, and *No Adam in Eden*, each of which got pitiless reviews and sold significantly fewer copies than its predecessor. When she ran out of money, she pleaded with her agent to help her get work writing gossip about Gilmanton, but no one was interested. At forty years old, in 1964, Grace Metalious finally drank herself to death.

PEZ

No other candy is like Pez. It is eaten from a hidden orifice atop its own little altar, which is a pedestal with a head on top designed to remind the eater of his favorite character from folklore, movies, cartoons, or comic books. In almost every variation of the disgorging icon, the sweet brick of candy comes out of the icon's neck, like a food pellet from the beak of a mother bird, proffered to supplicants at a confectionery shrine.

The Pez experience, which elevates sugar eating to a nearly spiritual event, seems so American, but actually its origins were in Vienna, Austria. Eduard Haas III, now known in the candy trade as the Wilbur Wright of Peppermint, had already made a fortune in baking powder before 1927 when he conceived the idea of combining peppermint oil with sugar and using heat, humidity, and compression to create tiny black-shaped lozenges. He named his product Pez, from the German word *Phefferminz*, and marketed it to adults as a breath mint.

For over two decades Pez was sold wrapped in stacks that required the consumer to pick one, then rewrap the rest. In 1948 the Pez-Haas Company introduced the Pez dispenser, which could be loaded with a stack of candy like staples in a staple gun, and which ejected the little bricks one by one, from a flip top. The first Pez dispensers had no funny heads on top: They were strictly utilitarian, and resembled cigarette lighters.

In 1952 Pez came to America in a dispenser topped with Mickey Mouse's head. Plain peppermint candies weren't of much interest to American candy buyers, so fruit flavors (and fruit colors) were introduced, and dozens, then hundreds, of different

heads were molded to fit on top of the dispenser. Snowmen, skulls, clowns, jack-o-lanterns, and witches (but never the likeness of a living or dead human being) have all been mounted, each with a lever at the back of its noggin that causes the chin to tilt back and the neck to open wide and regurgitate a candy. Mickey Mouse and Santa Claus are the all-time bestsellers, and the cast of heads is always growing, with about forty in production at any given time; according to Mike Robertson, editor of *The Optimistic Pezzimist*, a newsletter for about 250 aficionados, some collectors boast nearly a thousand characters in their collections.

Pez continued to be made in Austria and imported to the United States until 1973, when the company built a plant in Connecticut, where American Pez candy now comes from. (Dispensers are made in Austria, Yugoslavia, Hungary, and China.) European

Pez, like the American variety, is now positioned more as children's candy than as an adult breath mint. Scott McWhinney, president of the Pez Candy Company, told us that on occasion Austrian Pez makers produce "Golden Memories" peppermint-flavored candy, like the original, but so far American Pez has stayed fruit-flavored, and is available today in lemon, orange, strawberry, and grape.

Pez has never advertised, but Americans like it enough to ingest over a billion tablets every year. Although exact sales figures are a secret, it is known that in the mid-eighties, at the height of the Reagan-era boom in jellybean sales, Pez business went up nearly 50 percent. Pez is explained to the alien in *E.T.* (see p. 177), and in Rob Reiner's sentimental 1986 movie *Stand by Me*, which gazed back on a 1960s childhood, Pez is the romanticized little lads' favorite snack. "If I could have only one food for the rest of my life?" one boy asks. "That's easy. Pez. Cherry-flavored Pez." (Ironically, just before the movie was released, cherry-flavored Pez had been discontinued in favor of grape, a flavor and color that Pez makers felt was more fun for kids.) An article about the company by Jeremy Schlosberg in *Connecticut* magazine attributed Pez's continuing success to its nostalgic connotations, calling it "a favorite of the generation that refuses to let go of its adolescence." Schlosberg reported (although we have not been able to confirm) that in 1989 a rock-and-roll band named the Pez People performed golden oldies while dressed in human-size dispensers.

PICKUP TRUCKS

Sissies do not drive pickup trucks; hale, hearty folk do. It's not that pickups require a lot of muscle to drive. Most of the models sold today are as tractable as a Sedan de Ville, but despite the available amenities, there isn't another four-wheeler vehicle on the road that exudes as much blunt muscle power. Like a Harley-Davidson (see p. 205), a stretch limousine, or a Volvo station wagon, a pickup truck is a moving proclamation of the lifestyle and values of the person it carries.

The man or woman behind the wheel of a pickup truck is not likely to be the suave continental type who wants the world to know of his or her sophistication (for that, a BMW is needed), or a sugar daddy in a plush Lincoln, or a hopped-up speedster in a muscle car, or a sex kitten in a purring Jaguar. A driver of a pickup truck is playing the role of a down-home pick-and-shovel man. A good ol' boy, or possibly a good ol' gal, leading a good, ol'-fashioned life: like a farmer, maybe, with bales of hay or rocks to haul; or like a construction worker with a load of

bricks and lumber; or like a cowboy on his way to town to buy such provisions as seed, feed, and barbed wire, and shells for the lever-action carbine mounted on the gun rack in the back window of the cab.

In fact, a lot of people driving pickup trucks, especially in the South, are on their way to white-collar jobs at the bank or an office building, or to the assembly lines in a factory. They might just as easily be wearing pinstripes or Ultrasuede or a Metallica heavy-metal T-shirt as tattered farmer's dungarees, and it is very likely that the gun rack will be holding an umbrella so their well-moussed hair won't get deflated by the rain. The truth is that only a small minority of pickup trucks ever actually see hard labor. One out of five of all the new vehicles bought in America are pickups, and most of them are used for such tasks as commuting, grocery shopping, and possibly hauling the week's household garbage to the town dump. Equipped with ornamental metallic paint jobs, fragile magnesium wheels, and cabins outfitted in leather, plush velour, and high-pile carpet, many are strictly showboats, unfit for any grimy kind of task. These facts do nothing to diminish the reputation of the pickup truck as a sturdy tool for working people with red necks and blue collars.

The first pickups were nothing but Ford Model Ts with the backseat replaced by a platform, so farmers could haul bales of things around their land, or to and from town. Chevrolet made its first closed-cab pickup in 1931, and until the beginning of World War II all its trucks were essentially cars with a cargo box in back and the previous year's styling at the front end. During the war, almost all light trucks went to the military, and to anyone who could prove he would put the vehicle to use in the war effort (drilling oil, for instance). When the war was over, car companies started designing trucks that had their own bigger bodies with rigid frames, double-walled boxes, and swing-down tailgates. Dodge called its line the "Practical Pick-Ups," offering a choice of colors for the cab but only basic black enamel for the box and rear fenders. Between 1947 and 1955, Chevrolet and GMC made what were known as Advance Design trucks, which are today recognizable as America's classic old, friendly pickup: big, bulbous hood atop a grinning grille flanked by buxom fenders, a split windshield, a mighty, eighteen-inch steering wheel, and no chrome.

There were few frills on these early halftons, but by the mid-1950s even trucks got caught up in Detroit's styling mania, and were available with two-tone paint, dual headlights, and high levels of trim and interior luxury, as well as racy V-8 engines. Ford, whose F-100 was far and away the sales leader of its time (riding on the reputation of Ford tractors), advertised its pickups with the slogan "Where men are men, trucks are Ford V-8s." Dodge trucks got push-button transmissions and color-coordinated fabric seats and, in 1957, tailfins on the sides of the box! Still, pickups continued to be sold less for their beauty or macho charisma than for strict utilitarian value. "If ever a pickup was built for farm work, it's the new GMC!" ballyhooed a 1960 advertisement that told of a suspension that "literally 'walks' over rough fields."

The reputation of pickup trucks as redneckmobiles reached its peak in the late 1960s, when each of the subcultures of the time had its own symbolic means of transportation. The silent majority drove family-size, gas-guzzling Chevrolets; hippies had winsome Volkswagens (buses, preferably, with psychedelic paint jobs); swingers bought sexy sports cars; surfers traveled in eccentric vans or woodies; and vast numbers of rural common folk were proud to announce their allegiance to the traditional work ethic by driving made-in-America pickup trucks. To many in the counterculture, a pickup truck became a symbol of the depravity and evil that lurked in rural America, as demonstrated in the last scene of *Easy Rider* (see p. 172), in which the heroes, on their motorcycles, are gunned down by a couple of tobacco-chewing, overall-clad morons in a rattletrap pickup.

When the 1960s went sour, some strange cultural realignments occurred. Rednecks started to grow their hair long (like hippies used to do), while a lot of former hippies tried to go back to the land and become self-sufficient homesteaders. For some of these back-to-earth secessionists who once feared and loathed what it represented, the pickup truck was redeemed, and not only because it was actually of use doing chores around the commune. Its sturdy masculinity was just what many individualists in the 1970s craved as an antidote to the decade's ditsy fashion extremes, which included not only glitter disco wear and leisure suits but also such vehicular extremes as luxury Lincolns designed by Bill Blass and Pucci as well as Chrysler Cordobas that swaddled their occupants in plush velour or soft "Corinthian leather."

By the mid-1970s, when America was infatuated with the rugged lives of long-haul truckers, pickup trucks became a way for ordinary drivers to express a similar machismo. Like blue jeans, which got duded up as designer jeans in the late 1970s, pickups were a totem of working-class life that was easily repackaged as chic and sporty. No matter how many dashboard doodads, spotlights, quadrophonic stereos, and simulated wood-grain door insets it has, a pickup always maintains its down-home soul. To signify the dual character of its Adventurer, a two-tone rig with air conditioning, padded dash, and flip-up glove compartment, Dodge

hired Don Knotts, still riding on his popularity as Deputy Barney Fife in "The Andy Griffith Show," to play a dual role in advertisements as a slick lothario going to town and his identical twin, a ranch hand going out to string fence: Both of them want the Adventurer. "Only a clod would treat a good-looking, fully carpeted, air-conditioned runner with power steering like an ordinary truck," says the dapper Don. His virile brother replies: "Anything that can walk away with up to fifteen hundred pounds ain't ordinary, friend." They conclude that their Adventurer is more than a pickup. It is a "Sportruck" that leads a double life.

The practical advantage of the backwoods pickup truck became the inspiration for one of the most improbable sports ever invented: monster truck racing, in which competing pairs of ten-thousand-pound vehicles with eight-foot tires and flame-thrower engines speed up ramps, then smash down onto the roofs of cars as their drivers try to keep them upright and aimed towards a finish line. Developed in the mid-1970s as a way to show off a truck's ability to ride over any obstacle, this surreal event is a crowd-pleaser in rural America, often coupled with such other power-happy vehicular dramas as tractor pulls, demolition derbies, and drag races.

Pickup trucks are truly country-western, and like the music that best expresses their personality, they display a strong streak of cowboy style. Ever since Chevrolet's introduction of the Apache pickup in the mid-1950s, a lot of trucks have been given names that evoke the rugged and romantic Southwest. Chevrolet has made El Caminos, Scottsdales, Silverados, and Bonanzas; GMC has offered trim packages called Sierras and High Sierras; and Ford is known for Broncos, Rancheros, and Explorers, available with Lariat trim packages. Always favored as ranch transportation in cowboy country, where they are actually useful, pickups fulfilled their destiny in pop culture as fashion accessories when cowboy style started getting chic in the 1980s.

Pickup trucks appeared prominently in ads for Ralph Lauren clothes, for Coke, for jeans, and for dozens of other products eager to appropriate their aura of honesty, vitality, and tradition.

PLAYBOY

It began as a magazine. It became a lifestyle, then a full-scale philosophy of life. For a while, it was a global empire; now it is pretty much back to being a magazine, with a cable television channel on the side. However else it has evolved, matured, and changed with the times, one thing about *Playboy* has remained constant—inviolable and untouchable—and that is its centerfold. A million jokes have been told about randy oglers who swear they buy the magazine because it contains interesting articles; in fact, many people do read the articles, which frequently are as literate and as hightoned as those in any other popular journal. Despite the intellectual ballast, the world knows *Playboy* for its monthly picture of a voluptuous, young woman who isn't wearing any clothes, and it seems safe to say that whatever editorial course it takes in the future, nothing will alter this one fundamental purpose that has been, literally, at the center of the magazine since its debut in the fall of 1953: to allow readers to look at naked women and feel good about it. In this sense *Playboy* is, and always has been, as all-American as apple pie.

"We are not interested in the mysterious, difficult woman, the *femme fatale*, who wears elegant underwear with lace," publisher Hugh Hefner told *Look* magazine in 1967. "She is sad, and somehow mentally filthy." Centerfolds, also known as Playmates, are never sad, and they certainly are not filthy. They are smiling, happy, wholesome, completely unintimidating, and they are available. Invariably, they look into the camera, directly at the viewer, with friendly eyes. And they have identities. Their names, hobbies, likes, and dislikes are all enumerated to make them even more familiar. And they also always tell what kind of man turns them on: None are too particular.

That wasn't quite the plan at first, when a cheesecake picture of Marilyn Monroe was used in the premier issue and labeled "Sweetheart of the Month," but in the next *Playboy*, the pinup became "Playmate for the Month," and in 1954 the feature grew into an article called "Photographing a Playmate," complete with behind-the-scenes pictures of the model's arrival, undressing, and makeup session, accompanied by a two-page center spread. The story's extended caption advised:

Each month *Playboy* devotes its center two pages to a lovely, full-color unpinned pin-up. This pulchritudinous Playmate of the Month is the most popular feature in the magazine. She is fast replacing wallpaper in the college fraternities of the nation, businessmen hide her in their desks, service men in their foot lockers. She is becoming the new American Love Goddess, and her admirable proportions have been credited with an assist in the early demise of Christian Dior's Flat Look.

Finally, in July 1955, the Playmate was no longer an anonymous model. She was Janet Pilgrim (real name: Charlaine Karalus), not just another lovely body but actually a cute little human being who happened to work in *Playboy*'s circulation department and was delighted to strip for the camera. Her caption reassured readers, "Potential Playmates are all around you: The new secretary at your office, the doe-eyed beauty who sat opposite you at lunch yesterday, the girl who sells you shirts and ties at your favorite store." Gosh—Playmates all around. What a wonderful world!

That was *Playboy*'s genius: to take sex out of the closet, to make it clean and available and ubiquitous. Pretty, naked girls were shown in a context of refined articles amidst a world of tasteful advertisements for luxurious appurtenances of the good life, with none of the traditional "male" magazine ads for such unpleasant, lowbrow stuff as hernia trusses, muscle-building courses, and shyness cures. It used to be that an awful lot of young men got acquainted with the female form via dirty pictures, French postcards, or sneaking peeks at airbrushed, smooth-crotched nudist magazines on newsstands. Now they could thumb through *Playboy* and read Norman Mailer, learn about Ibsen and Sartre, study such acceptable subjects as which sports car was best and how to grill lobster tails on the hibachi . . . and also look at busty undressed women.

Before *Playboy*, for most Americans, sex and sophistication were opposites. Sex was stag films, obscene jokes, pitiful prostitutes, the backseat of the Buick at a drive-in movie. Sophistication was literature, gourmet cuisine, fine art, international travel, and witty conversation. By putting the two together, and taking out any suggestion that sex was shameful, filthy, taboo, or vulgar, *Playboy* put itself at the vanguard of a new, swinging lifestyle. Advertisements selling space in the magazine were always headlined "What Sort of Man Reads *Playboy*?" The answer, as any reader could tell you, was a supremely modern man. A world traveler, an oenophile, a sharp dresser, a man (in the words of one such ad in 1966) "of action and acquisition [for whom] the name of the game is fun." If you had the desire, *Playboy* had the plan (and the products) to fulfill it, and it delivered them meticulously. In an article for *Canadian Photographer* in 1961, *Playboy*'s picture editor told aspirants what they had to do to sell a photograph to the magazine:

> *Playboy* describes "the good life" and dictates "the elegant taste." . . . Too often has a photograph had to be redone because, *hypothetically*, a chair in the picture was not the Scandinavian imported original desired but a cheap poorly designed imitation; or again, *hypothetically*, because the car key on a key chain suggested that the owner drove an economy car when he should be driving a fast, stylish sports car. . . . Photographs have to contain all of the *Playboy* elements of fun, romance, excitement and the immediacy of being alive now and enjoying every minute of it.

Even in the beginning, when it was only a magazine, it was so much more. It was a guidebook for a new kind of individual, hungry for pleasure and status but also for culture and cool (cf. James Bond). It wasn't only about acquiring stereos and sports cars and no-wrinkle slacks and learning how the jet set has fun on ski slopes and at Cannes (although there were plenty such nuggets in every issue); it was about developing an attitude, about liberating the body and the mind, learning to live life to the hilt. Coincident with the sexual revolution, but not bounded by it, *Playboy* guided its readers into a new era of libertinism, permissiveness, and loosened morals, all the while cultivating a supreme sense of savoir faire. In 1962, Unitarian minister John A. Crane delivered a sermon about *Playboy*, which Hugh Hefner liked to quote:

> *Playboy* comes close now to qualifying as a movement, as well as a magazine. It strikes me that *Playboy* is a religious magazine. It tells its readers how to get into heaven. It tells them what is important in life, delineates ethics for them, tells them how to relate to others, tells them what to lavish their attention and energy upon, gives them a model of the kind of person to be. It expresses a consistent world view, a system of values, a philosophical outlook.

In the 1960s writer Gay Talese called *Playboy* "probably the most influential publication of my lifetime."

Its influence wasn't only as a spearhead of the sexual revolution or as an arbiter of fashion and status. No more than ten years after it began publication, *Playboy* had assumed the titanic responsibility of keeping up with all important and enlightened things going on in the world, from the battle for civil rights in America (major interviews with Martin Luther King, Jr., and Malcolm X) to Albert Schweitzer and the Beatles. If something was au courant or trendy, you could learn about it in *Playboy*; if it wasn't yet hip, and *Playboy* wrote about it, it soon would be. Although anything square, bumpkinish, or narrow-minded was likely excluded from the *Playboy* mix (except as an

Hugh Hefner with unidentified companion

opportunity for ridicule), the range of ideas to be found around the pictures of naked women and paintings by Leroy Neiman was truly remarkable. Here were profiles of Federico Fellini and Terry Southern, criticism by Alfred Kazin, Jules Feiffer cartoons, fiction by Vladimir Nabokov, essays by Mortimer Adler, original James Bond stories by Ian Fleming, reviews by Nat Hentoff, and interviews with Bertrand Russell and Miles Davis. The magazine that began as fifty pages of "Entertainment for Men" in 1953 had become a three-hundred-page (in its holiday issues) intellectual concordance by the late 1960s, with a circulation of over six million and a readership with interests beyond looking at big bosoms.

It was almost called *Stag Party* when Hugh Hefner planned the first issue—with no date on the cover and no subscription form inside, because there was little confidence that a second issue would ever get printed, but when *Stag* magazine complained Hef rummaged in the past and found a term long out of use in the vernacular: "playboy." He had been a publisher since he was fifteen years old, when his *Shudder* magazine, devoted to horror movies, premiered (1941) for five cents a copy, available only to members of the Shudder Club, who were all kids who liked scary movies. *Shudder* had a print run of one, which was passed around among the members, who were Hughie Hefner's friends. The next year in high school he began a series of cartoon books about a character named Goo Hefner ("a lanky, Sinatra-like guy with a love for loud flannel shirts and cords in the way of garb, and jive for music"), and he and two friends invented a fifteen-hundred-word language called Muphbekian. Hef went on to the Army, college (the University of Illinois, where he started a humor magazine called *Shaft*), the circulation department of *Esquire*, and a year with the Publishers Development Corporation, whose several magazines included one called *Modern Man*, featuring pictures of half-dressed women and real articles of interest to guys—about guns and antique cars.

The idea of *Playboy* as Hef conceived it was to hybridize *Modern Man* and the old, cosmopolitan *Esquire* and create what he described as "an entertainment magazine for the city-bred guy—breezy, sophisticated! . . . a really class look." It would be a magazine that would "thumb its nose at all the phony puritan values of the world in which I had grown up." The naked girls were one way to give the raspberry to puritans, but so was *Playboy*'s devotion to an unabashed, sophisticated, pleasure-seeking way of life. Those two elements together— nude boobs and refined fun—became nothing less than a new declaration of independence for the modern male. *Playboy* proclaimed freedom from prudish taboos, stultifying traditions, and class snobbery.

Go for the gusto—work hard and play hard, it said—and it proselytized with religious zeal for what it liked to call "creative nonconformity." In 1963, Hefner wrote, "Blessed is the rebel. Without him there would be no progress." Here was a truly avant-garde approach to life, encouragement to go beyond the rules and experience all the pleasures of the mind as well as those of the senses. The only real crime in what Hef liked to call "the Upbeat Generation" was being conventional, as was made clear in a satiric "*Playboy*'s Ten Commandments" written by the Reverend Roy Larsen for *Motive*, the magazine of the Methodist Student Movement:

Thou shalt not wear double-breasted suits.

Thou shalt not swing and sway to Sammy Kaye.

Thou shalt not drive a Dodge.

Thou shalt not serve breakfast coffee after dinner.

Thou shalt not attend the P.T.A.

Thou shalt not eat Velveeta Cheese.

Thou shalt not be crude or cavemanish in love-making, and above all, thou shalt not be guilty of chastity.

Thou shalt not travel by bus.

Thou shalt not be stuffy and intellectual.

Thou shalt not read the *Reader's Digest*.

The fundamental beliefs of *Playboy* were only implicit in the kind of articles and pictures it ran until December 1962, when Hugh Hefner began writing "The Playboy Philosophy," which spelled it all out. Hefner originally planned it as a four-part statement of his principles, but once he got rolling the ruminations seemed to build momentum, and his "Philosophy" flowed out in thousands of words every month for well over a decade, becoming what must be considered the most painstaking manifesto of social, sexual, moral, and legal theory in human history. Joe Goldberg, writing in his book *Big Bunny*, called it "a strange, home-grown, sometimes contradictory combination of civil libertarianism and the collected works of Ayn Rand." Among the sacred cows slaughtered in various early installments: the House Un-American Activities Committee, the Organization Man, J. Edgar Hoover, America's "purityrannical" heritage, Sunday blue laws, the influence of the church over state affairs, and the U.S. Postal Service; singled out for acclaim were the American Civil Liberties Union, the F. Scott Fitzgerald era, the Supreme Court's decision against school prayer, and naked women. To write his essays, Hef holed up in his mansion, sometimes locked in his room on his round bed for sixty hours at a stretch, fueled by a diet of amphetamines and Pepsi.

Reading *Playboy* made you feel like you were part of a private and exclusive club. Articles regularly took readers behind the scenes: to a swinging party at Hef's mansion in Chicago; to a Playmate photo session; inside Hef's private DC-9 airplane (which was outfitted with a big, round bed covered with Tasmanian possum skins). Front-of-the-book sections "On the Scene" and "Playboy After Hours" clued readers in to cool people and events that the general public might not know about, and "The Playbill" served as an insider's guide to the magazine itself. Few magazines have ever told so much about how they were put together—the story behind the story, how the jazz poll was conducted, who the authors are, and who did what at the last party at Hef's house. To consolidate readers' closeness to the Big Bunny (Hef's name for the whole shebang), you could (and still can) buy lit-

erally hundreds of *Playboy* products (tie tacks, billfolds, etc.), all imprinted with the *Playboy* logo, a bunny. Hef described such items as "a mark of identity in common with the publication—the sort of honor a man usually reserves for his fraternity, or a special business or social association."

Starting in 1960, there really were Playboy Clubs, first in Chicago, then all over the world. One of the magazine's editors joked they were "as hard to get into as the Red Cross," but actually some effort was made to make the men-only niteries seem exclusive. Members received identification keys (they didn't open anything), and a registry of names was kept by the door—when someone entered, his name was posted on a board (any attending celebrities were posted in the top row) titled "At the Playboy Club Tonight." Clubs catered to adults—they served good liquor and red meat, and featured cool jazz rather than hot rock and roll. They were staffed by Bunnies—well-built girls in little satin outfits with rabbit ears on their heads and fluffy tails on their rumps. Bunnies were overseen by a Bunny Mother, and their foremost command was to refrain from having sex with customers. "The girls are there for their attractiveness and personality," Hugh Hefner said. "But it's a no-nonsense, no-hanky-panky sort of situation." The idea for patrons was "Look, but don't touch." The philosophy and rules of Bunnydom were described in a leaflet given to new recruits, titled "What Is a Bunny": "A Bunny—like the *Playboy* playmate—is the girl next door. She is the American romanticized myth—beautiful, desirable, and a nice, fun-loving person. A Bunny is not a broad or a 'hippy.' She may be sexy, but it's a fresh, healthy sex—not cheap or lewd." The Bunny manual also included this commandment: "Your proudest possession is your bunny tail. You must make sure it is always white and fluffy."

For a while there at the end of the 1960s, *Playboy* was IT for a lot of men who wanted to be fashionable but could not buy into the sloppy youth culture. Although its battle cry was liberation, its vision of a liberated world was eminently civilized and, even if morally unfastened, always mature and polite. *Playboy* provided its readers an adult vision and an adult world of fun, including the clubs and the magazine, resort hotels, *Playboy*-produced movies and plays, a book-publishing business, and a limousine service. Its unswerving liberalism and devotion to good taste supplied an ironclad answer to a world where morality was getting ever more slippery and the sexual revolution appeared to be crossing over the line from the healthy frolics of *Playboy*'s "Party Jokes" and "Ribald Classics" to kinkier realms.

As the world changed, however, *Playboy*'s place in it shrunk. The revolution in morals it had cheered and inspired had been so successful that in some ways the magazine had made itself obsolete. By the time the 1960s ended, there was no longer such a crying need for people to speak out against stultifying traditions and sacred cows: Most of them had been pretty well demolished. Also, for the first time since its founding, *Playboy* faced serious competition: *Penthouse*, which was introduced in the United States in 1969 (after debuting in England in 1965), was a lot like *Playboy*... but it didn't just show nice, friendly boobs on girls wrapped in clean sheets and bath towels; it showed girls with their legs spread and nothing hidden! And its models were definitely not cheerleaders and girls-next-door. They were hot and horny, accompanied by text that was frankly designed to turn readers on and ads for dirty movies and sex aids. This ran completely contrary to the formula of uplifting philosophy, high-status materialism, and sanitary sex that had made *Playboy* such a

success. Despite Hefner's introduction of *Oui* magazine in 1972 (described as "more continental," which meant more emphasis on genitals and less on bosoms), *Penthouse* suddenly looked for a while like the daring, courageous, and truly nonconformist magazine—and by the mid-1970s, it actually topped *Playboy*'s circulation for a while.

In 1975 Christie Hefner, Hef's daughter (born in 1952), joined Playboy Enterprises as her father's assistant, and in 1988, with the magazine's circulation at 3.4 million, half its peak in the 1970s, she became CEO. "If she had not been born to it," Hef said, "the promotion department would have had to invent her!" Christie swept away a lot of dead wood: The clubs, hotels, and most of the various enterprises begun when *Playboy* could do no wrong were sold, as was the original Chicago mansion. She declared a new era, which included not only corporate streamlining but certain editorial changes in the *Playboy* product: the appearance of more naked famous people in the magazine, cheesecake pictures with captions in which models reveal that they are intelligent, and such special single-subject publications as *Playboy's 1988 Book of Lingerie*. In 1990, after years of losing so much money that Hef had to sell off some of his valuable art collection, *Playboy* showed a profit once again; and management estimated that one in nine American men still read it. "*Playboy*'s Philosophy Still Pays Off," headlined the *New York Times* in an April 1992 article that described it as "a mix of consumer pieces, pop culture, humor, and, of course, unclad women."

The first issue of *Playboy* had warned readers, "If you're somebody's sister, wife, or mother-in-law and picked us up by mistake, please pass us along to the man in your life and get back to your *Ladies Home Companion*." That kind of macho attitude had come to seem antediluvian and sexist by the 1980s, as had the whole original concept of *Playboy* and the very name itself. "Can Christie Hefner remake an empire built for men only?" *Business Week* asked. Gloria Steinem didn't think so, advising any females who worked for the magazine, which she thought was still degrading to women (despite its outspoken support of feminist causes), to quit. Christie, on the other hand, said, "If I thought our products were degrading to women, I'd be working someplace else."

As for Hef, a bachelor since his first marriage ended in divorce in 1959, he married former Playmate of the Year (1988) Kimberly Conrad, age twenty-six, in 1989, explaining to his ninety-three-year-old mother, "I'm too old to marry someone my own age." When Hef and the missus had a baby in 1990 (the first of two, so far), he raised some eyebrows because, unlike so many modern dads, he refused to go into the delivery room to experience the wonder of birth up close in all its obstetric detail. He explained, "I'm a very romantic guy."

POP ROCKS

"**K**ids are like junkies," *Time* magazine observed in 1978 when it investigated American children's craving for a bizarre candy that provided them a new kind of kicks. Called Pop Rocks, it was brightly colored shards of sugar-sweet, fruit-flavored gravel that crackled and fizzed furiously when they were sprinkled onto a moist tongue. Never before had a candy been so spectacularly, instantly popular. Marketed only in select locations, Pop Rocks were being sold on the black market in Louisiana (where they were not available in stores) for up to a dollar a packet—over six times their fifteen-cent retail price. Five hundred million packages were sold between 1975 and 1980.

Then production ceased. The hottest-selling candy ever became history, done in by a rumor: Pop Rocks had killed Little Mikey, the adorable three-year-old who had starred in TV commercials for Life cereal in the early 1970s. In the Life ads, Little Mikey had gobbled up a whole bowl of cereal—wordlessly but with gusto—as his two slightly older brothers exclaimed, "He likes it!" His tragic mistake, according to the rumor—which coursed through kid society as fast as the candy had gotten popular—was that he went at his Pop Rocks just like he had eaten that bowl of cereal. Instead of putting just a few little fragments on his tongue like good, mannerly kids were supposed to do, hungry Little Mikey swallowed

three packets of Rocks, then washed them down with a can of Coke. The supercarbonated combination was TNT. Moments later, Little Mikey exploded.

The Little Mikey of this cautionary tale was not all that different from most juveniles, for whom maximum backfire was a goal devoutly to be wished. After years of disappointment with such loud-named but essentially inert confections as Atomic Fireballs and Gob Stoppers, at last here was a candy that really delivered what it promised. When Pop Rocks first came to California in 1977, *Newsweek* interviewed ten-year-old David Oliver of Menlo Park, who said, "If you swallow them fast, they crackle all the way down." *Newsweek* also reported that in Seattle the Food and Drug Administration had set up a Pop Rocks hot line to allay parents' fears that their children would choke or erupt.

Early in 1979 General Foods ran a full-page advertisement for Pop Rocks in the *New York Times* and newspapers around the country. The ad was addressed to parents and spoke about how much fun Pop Rocks were, and it happened to mention, by the way, that the "wild rumors" about them were completely untrue. The ad didn't specify what the rumors were; in fact, the demise of Little Mikey was only one of the stories going around about the fulminating candy. According to the *Wall Street Journal* in a 1979 article about "Rumor-Plagued Firms," the stories began to circulate within a week of the product's introduction in a market. Jan Harold Brunvand, author of *The Choking Doberman and Other "New" Urban Legends*, catalogued not only Mikey's detonation but also accounts of Pop Rocks' containing illegal drugs or spider eggs (the latter a rumor that also plagued Bubble Yum), as well as stories that they had been declared illegal by the U.S. Government, and that self-combustion awaited anyone who swallowed an undiluted Alka-Seltzer tablet.

General Foods tried additional damage control by sending letters to fifty thousand school principals and sending Pop Rocks' inventor, William A. Mitchell, on tour to show everyone that he was a sweet, kind, grandfatherly guy and not some evil warlock with a plan to make all of America's children burst. Mitchell had stumbled upon the Pop Rocks concept back in 1956 when he was experimenting with methods for trapping carbon dioxide inside a hard tablet, the point of which was to create a way to make instant carbonated soda pop—like Alka-Seltzer, but sweet and without the medicine. (An instant-soda tablet called Fizzies actually was marketed between 1962 and 1969.) Mitchell found that little nuggets of the carbon-dioxide-infused candy popped and bubbled when exposed to moisture, as on a tongue; but no one in the mid-1950s believed that kids would be much interested in candy that seemed to jitterbug in their mouth. It was nearly twenty years before General Foods began marketing Pop Rocks in selected areas.

After their premature extinction in 1980, Pop Rocks seemed doomed to lie in candy limbo, along with Fizzies, Flav-R-Straws (as you suck, the straw secretes chocolate or strawberry into the milk coursing through it), and cherry-flavored Pez. But in 1985 they returned. Now sold by Carbonated Candy Ventures of Buffalo, New York (again in limited locations, for limited amounts of time), modern Pop Rocks are marketed as an "action candy" that "provides entertainment for the entire mouth." They pop as ferociously as ever, but they come in strawberry, grape, and orange flavors that have been intensified from the original. According to a press release issued by the company, they were tested and found safe by the FDA, which was unable to confirm any stories of Pop Rocks–related injury or spontaneous combustion. As for the supposedly exploded Little Mikey (played by John Gilchrist), he continues to appear, as an adult, in television advertisements for Life cereal.

POP-TARTS

Test your knowledge of convenience food: Of course, you know that Kellogg's Pop-Tarts come two to a packet, but su ppose you choose to eat only one. Admittedly, this is an unlikely scenario, because, as comedian Paula Poundstone is fond of pointing out in her stand-up routine, after the packet is open it seems illogical to leave half of it uneaten. But for the sake of argument let us hypothesize that you are on a diet and you are forced to limit your intake to only one 200-calorie toaster pastry —which, according to the "Nutrition Information" area on the side of the box is in fact a single serving. What do you call it?

If you said "a Pop-Tart," you are wrong. According to Kellogg's, which conceptualized toaster pastries and introduced them to the world in 1964, even a single slab of the world's most famous heat-and-eat table tile is properly referred to as a Pop-Tart*s*. The *s* on the end not only confirms Paula Poundstone's craving to eat them in multi-

ples; it also suggests the profusion of Pop-Tarts among America's daily rations.

Pop-Tarts aren't merely very popular; they have become a paramount symbol of corporate creativity—an ingenious method for harried eaters to ingest warm, complex foodstuff almost instantly and utterly without exertion. Plucked from a foil packet in a cardboard box on an unrefrigerated pantry shelf, they need only a few minutes in a toaster to become something that resembles freshly baked food! Although the name was originally conceived because they "pop" out of the toaster when they are ready, we don't think it's at all far-fetched to suggest that their appeal—in addition to their flavor—is that they embody a whole constellation of philosophical values that are the essence of the kind of "pop" that is the focus of this book: They are modern, quick, easy, sweet, sturdy, and oh-so-pretty (especially the frosted and spangled ones). Pop-Tarts are edible pop culture.

We asked Kellogg's to tell us who, exactly, eats them, and their creator responded (and we quote): "Everyone in the country." A representative in the department of corporate communications advised us that the age range of Pop-Tarts eaters was between two and thirty-five, but that most people who eat them are between six and seventeen. The bigger the family (3-plus kids), the more likely it is that Pop-Tarts will be a regular staple. At one point the

"My Three Sons" television family were Pop-Tarts spokespeople.

Eighty percent of all Pop-Tarts are eaten warm; in fact, "warmth" is one of the top three reasons people like them ("taste" and "convenience" are the other two). The cold ones are generally eaten out of lunch boxes or as snacks for people who don't want to bother (or are unable) to prepare anything more complicated for themselves. Actress Colleen Zenk Pinter (see "Soap Opera") recalls performing in the first national Pop-Tarts television advertisements in the mid-1960s: She played a gabby teenager who couldn't get off the telephone . . . but could very easily manage to feed herself a fruit-filled Pop-Tarts as she talked.

Although nobody mentioned it in the Kellogg's surveys to which we were privy, one of the truly remarkable qualities of Pop-Tarts is the way they feel: They are substantial pieces of food, denser and heftier than any pastry you would find in a bakery, and whether they are cold or toasted, fresh from the foil packet or abandoned on the kitchen counter days before, they are relentlessly crisp. A Pop-Tarts' shelf life (in the box) is six to nine months, depending on whether or not it is a fruited variety. No matter how you treat it, it always feels ready to eat—so wieldy that most people don't even bother putting it on a plate. The one terrible exception to this rule is microwave cooking, which seems to be the only thing that can really kill a Pop-Tarts. Once, when we were too impatient to wait the two full minutes required in our toaster oven, we nuked a Frosted Strawberry one for forty-five seconds in the microwave oven. The result was disastrous. The distressed pastry had transformed into a hideous clump of sodden, fissured dough engulfed by sticky globules of the corn syrup, partially hydrogenated oils, dextrose, gelatin, and xantham gum it had once encased.

Aficionados rue the loss of Cherry Chip, Chocolate Chip, and Peanut Butter & Jelly —all discontinued flavors—but 1991 provided reason to rejoice in the form of unfrosted Apple Cinnamon Pop-Tarts, which joined a repertoire that now includes Strawberry, Blueberry, Cherry, and Brown Sugar Cinnamon (all available with or without frosting), as well as unfrosted Milk Chocolate, frosted Chocolate Fudge, Vanilla Creme, Raspberry, and Grape.

POTATO CHIPS

Potato chips are to raw potatoes what "Jeopardy" is to serious scholarship: an addictive, ready-to-digest pop-culture variant of something that traditionally requires time and effort. There are many junk foods a person can snack on, but chips are the supreme emblem of this country's love affair with things that are convenient, greasy, bad for us, and ever so much fun to eat. They imply leisure time, soda pop or beer, and all-American voracity. Is there anyone out there who actually sits down and limits himself or herself to the six to ten chips that are considered a single serving? Don't be ridiculous. Potato chips are for gorging.

One great thing about them is that they are better than ever, which is not true of a

lot of foods. (Consider wooden tomatoes, low-fat beefsteaks, and wan baseball stadium franks.) Potato chips' new age of excellence began in 1980 when Cape Cod began nationally marketing what it called kettle-style chips: sliced thicker than ordinary chips, crunchier, and with a real potato flavor. Kettle chips, which cost more than ordinary ones, are made in small batches in fry kettles rather than by the ton on conveyor belts. In the last ten years, other brands—from New York's strictly local Bronx Chompers to Frito-Lay's nationwide Crunch Tators—have joined the kettle-cooked revolution. Potato chips are not exactly in style—they are too fatty and too salty to be N.C. ("nutritionally correct," as determined by health-food killjoys)—but they are in the midst of a renaissance. They are being gobbled down in record numbers (six pounds per person per year); regional varieties of chips are burgeoning; and some companies have even introduced oxymoronic low-salt and low-fat chips.

The first known potato chips were cooked by chef George Crumb at the Moon Lake Lodge in 1853 when, so the oft-told tale goes, Cornelius Vanderbilt returned an order of french fries to the kitchen because he thought they were cut too thick. To spite Vanderbilt, Crumb sliced a potato wafer-thin—too thin to be spearable by a fork—and fried the discs. When he sent them into the dining room, instead of getting angry at the sight of see-through slender, brittle spuds, Vanderbilt was delighted. He threw down his fork and ate the fried chips of potato with his hands. America's most popular snack food was born.

At first, "Saratoga chips" were known only among people in the Northeast, served at the home dinner table to accompany meat or fish and by seafood restaurants as a companion for raw clams and oysters. It wasn't until the 1920s that they began getting popular in other regions, and by the end of the next decade, as James Beard later recalled, "the ghastly potato-chip-dip invention had . . . begun to spread across the country." After World War II, potato chips' popularity soared because they were so handy for suburban-style casual entertaining in rec rooms or on patios, at teen parties, and—most important of all—as the munchable best suited for television watching. Furthermore, the very shape of potato chips seemed to match the era's adoration of things with swoopy curves. *Populuxe*, Thomas Hines's imaginative exegesis of the Golden Age of American materialism, observed, "The potato chip, with its free-form shape and double curving plane, recalled some of the high-design objects of the day —Danish coffee tables and American molded fiberglass and bent plywood chairs. Formally, it is a very short jump from the standard potato chip to the great double-curving furniture of Charles Eames and Eero Saarinen."

The great date in the ascent of the potato chip to supremacy among snack foods is 1954, when California dip was invented (see

p. 78). A simple amalgam of Lipton's dehydrated onion soup powder and sour cream, California dip was designed to eliminate any need for utensils, plates, or napkins. All it required was potato chips, which were used like a shovel to scoop out a mouthful from the serving bowl. The resultant instant canapé was an inspired confluence of creamy soft stuff and crunchy chip, and a dazzling saline harmony from the two of them. However, California dip and the hundreds of other hot and cold dunks popularized as party food in the fifties tended to be weighty compounds, and ordinary chips frequently broke when plowed into them or, worse, on the way from serving dish to mouth. The solution was the corrugated chip, known by such brand names as Ridgies, Ruffles, and Dipsy Doodles, which was strong enough to dig through even hardened, day-old dip without cracking.

Potato chips were a familiar staple in the American pantry by the 1960s, and home cooks were smitten with the kind of creative cookery that uses already-made groceries from bags, boxes, and cans (casseroles made with soup, cookies made with chow mein noodles, etc.), so manufacturers seriously developed recipes to encourage using potato chips as something other than a snack, including "Chip-Coated Oven Fried Chicken" (from Lay's), "Chip Stuffing for Turkeys" (from Wise), and "Eggs 'N' Chips Casserole" (from the National Potato Chip Institute of Cleveland). To inspire cooks, the Potato Chip Institute made an instructional film called *Thank You, Mr. Chips*, in which the kindly potato man comes to the aid of poor Mrs. Whipple, whose husband's boss is coming to dinner and who doesn't know what to serve. The solution? A meal in which nearly every course is improved by the addition of pulverized potato chips, followed by this recipe for "Rich, Chewy Brownies":

4 squares unsweetened chocolate
1/2 cup vegetable shortening
4 eggs
2 cups sugar
1/2 teaspoon salt
1 teaspoon vanilla
1 cup flour
1/2 cup crumbled potato chips
1/2 cup coarsely chopped black walnuts

Preheat oven to 350 degrees.

Melt chocolate and shortening in top of double boiler. Remove from heat.

Beat eggs and add sugar. Beat until smooth. Add salt, vanilla, and cooled chocolate mixture. Mix well. Add flour, potato chips, and nut meats. Mix lightly.

Line an 8 x 8 x 2–inch pan with waxed paper. Grease paper with butter or margarine. Pour brownie batter into pan. Bake 30 minutes. Cool in pan 5 minutes after removing pan from oven. Turn onto cake rack and remove waxed paper. Cut brownies into squares.

As Americans settled down at their televisions to watch Super Bowls and mini-series in the seventies, many grew accustomed to bleached-white chips with only a shred of potato flavor, enjoying them for their high salt and fat content and because they are such convenient ways to ferry dips and dunks up from the bowl without having to divert any attention from the screen. Following the lead of Pringles, a mass-produced chip of uniform size and shape that is sold stacked in a can, many modern chip purveyors now market "potato snack chips" reconstituted from dried potatoes and potato starch, a process that eliminates the inconveniences of actually slicing and frying potatoes (real spuds stick together and vary wildly in color depending on the sugar content, which changes from season to season).

Sales of bland-tasting, blemish-free chips have never faltered, but at the same time, serious potato chip connoisseurship has thrived, too. America's myriad regional brands continue to have devotees who treasure their real potato look (mottled, irregularly shaped), their distinctive feel (thicker, brittle, and more fragile), and their actual potato taste. Since the beginning of chip history, local companies have remained an important part of the landscape if for no other reason than the fact that it is not practical to ship potato chips long distances.

Today there are hundreds of kinds of soulful chips across the land—made the old-fashioned way, some of them with shockingly idiosyncratic flavors, including dill pickle chips from Poore Brothers in Arizona, ketchup-flavored chips from Humpty Dumpty in Maine, and alder-smoked salmon-flavored chips from Tim's Cascade of Washington. Allison and Margaret Engel's cross-country treasury of regional mail-order specialties, *Food Finds*, lists an abundance of local potato chip makers (a disproportionate number of them in Pennsylvania, where it is not unusual to see a grocery store's shelves stocked with several dozen different brands). The best potato chips, which probably taste something like the original Saratogas, are always made in small batches, and most of them—the unbearably addictive ones—are still fried in lard and are still salty as hell.

PREPPIES

Preppies are scions of the WASP upper crust who got their name because they went to prep school. They have been around for at least a hundred years, and a fictional one of them became a favorite 1970s hero in Erich Segal's bestselling *Love Story*, a novel about the affair between Oliver Barrett IV and a working-class girl who insists on calling him "Preppie." But it was not until the publication of *The Official Preppy Handbook* in 1980 that the subculture of people nicknamed Buffy, Muffy, Biff, and Skip became a mainstream obsession. Once refused to all but those who were born to its manners and rituals, the preppy life was transformed into a life*style* any willing player could affect. If you had the money to buy a pair of go-to-hell country club pants and Top-Sider shoes, plus $3.95 for *The Official Preppy Handbook*, the status and privileges of America's pseudo-aristocracy could be yours. "Stop thinking you're a lost cause simply because you've never been to either the Harvard-Yale game or Martha's Vineyard," the book's introduction reassured readers. "It is the inalienable right of every man, woman, and child to wear khaki. Looking, acting, and ultimately being Prep is not restricted to an elite minority."

With its madras plaid cover and how-to-do-it line drawings, this little paperback helped provoke an astonishing cultural phenomenon. Bored and sickened by the rampant extremism of the 1970s (huge hair, wide bell-bottoms, the glittery disco scene, and a general sense of overwhelming vulgarity in dress and behavior), fashion pioneers were out cruising for a set of values to help define a more tasteful time, something refreshing, clean-cut, and new. In this case, the new thing was old: old money, old

traditions, and things so timelessly unhip that they became chic again.

The weird thing is that *The Official Preppy Handbook* was a joke, a merry all-in-good-fun parody of haute-WASP style that began by promising readers, "In a true democracy everyone can be upper class and live in Connecticut. It's only fair." But it did such a good job of describing its subject that people bought it not only as a put-on or an amusing field guide to the very rich but as a learner's manual that described exactly how to emulate them. It told readers where to shop (L. L. Bean), what to do on vacation (ski), what to drive (a Jeep with a horse hood ornament), and even which breed of dog to own (an ill-behaved retriever). It didn't ask to be taken seriously, of course; but remember that at the same time, Ralph

Lauren (see p. 275) was beginning to very seriously revolutionize pop fashion by rein-troducing classic—yes, preppy—clothing: loose-fitting, natural-fiber, traditionally tai-lored garments that seemed to smell of horses (thoroughbreds) and salty spray from a weekend cruise on a wood-decked boat rather than of poppers and rubber spandex halter tops at Studio 54. As Ralph began to sell mass quantities of class to all who wanted it, *The Official Preppy Hand-book* rocketed to the top of the bestseller list (where it stayed and sold about a mil-lion and a half copies). Tongue-in-cheek or not, America went crazy for the preppy style.

The old hippie notion that everyone was beautiful in his or her own way was getting superseded in the early 1980s by a sense of how much more beautiful rich people were (see also "Lifestyles of the Rich and Fa-mous," p. 286). And even if you couldn't ac-tually be rich or privileged, you could act that way, or dress that way, at least a little bit. "Remember, Preppies don't have to be rich, Caucasian, frequenters of Bermuda, or ace tennis players," the book said. This no doubt came as quite a surprise to graduates of St. Paul's and members of such patrician clubs as the Myopia. The book's promise to the great unwashed that they, too, could pass for bluebloods brought its editor, Lisa Birnbach, plenty of angry mail from appar-ently insecure old-line preppies who had no intention of sharing their yacht slip and em-broidered whale pants with parvenus. But most readers—prep and nonprep alike—took the whole thing as a hoot, and merrily dressed themselves in layered-look clothes and acquired monogrammed cases for their tortoiseshell specs, drank "G and Ts" (gin and tonics), and practiced speaking with the preppy accent known as Locust Valley Lockjaw ("draw out all accented vowels as long as possible. Reeeeally.").

The preppy style remains popular not only among real preppies but among preppy wannabes, too, and such accoutrements as Lacoste shirts, boxer shorts, and khaki A-line skirts are readily available at Sears and J. C. Penney as well as from the approved stores like Cable Car Clothiers, Paul Stuart, and the Country Store of Concord. What's most curious is how much preppy vocabulary, once the telltale mark only of highbred sorts, has saturated vernacular slang at every level of society. The lexicon of *The Official Preppy Handbook* included:

- *awesome:* "terrific, great."
- *dorky:* "that which is characterized by clumsiness or ignorance of, for instance, how to mix a Bloody [Mary]."
- *Eat my shorts:* "Drop dead, go jump in the lake." Now a favorite expression of that most unprep of characters, Bart Simpson (see p. 447)!
- *Go for it:* "Let's get carried away."
- *intense:* "anything really fun."
- *outstanding:* "synonymous with *excellent* but delivers bigger wallop (pronounce with drawn out second syllable)."

- *really:* "universal term of agreement and emphasis. Can be used as a complete sentence."
- *to the max:* "all the way." This entered common language via Valley Girls (see p. 546), who inherited many preppy affectations but no class.

The preppy fad was a strange mixture of adulation and ridicule, demystifying behavior formerly thought of as exclusive and at the same time exalting class consciousness. The *Handbook* made it into a fun game because it took such an ironic attitude, but an unfortunate legacy of America's suddenly heightened infatuation with the semiology of status is that the trappings of the preppy look became the stuff of yuppie dreams (see p. 571). Yuppies were similar to preppies, but totally materialistic, with no interest in deportment or breeding—they just wanted to have all the adornments of the good life. Their avarice tended to blot out the memory of what fun it was, for a while in the early 1980s, for people to affect the embellished mannerisms, and the joie de vivre, of America's imaginary upper class.

ELVIS PRESLEY

Those in the business of marketing Elvis Presley's name, likeness, and image get upset when you compare the Elvis phenomenon to a religion. Religions, after all, can have a life of their own —beyond the control of their prelates—and religious zealots tend to be loose cannons. True believers sometimes even resent the church because it gets between them and their idol. That is the way many who love Elvis have felt ever since Colonel Tom Parker started managing him in 1956. They consider themselves so personally close to him that they don't like anybody who dares get in the way—that includes the Colonel; Elvis's wife, Priscilla; and the estate of Elvis Presley, which works hard to sustain belief in Elvis as a great rock-and-roll performer —maybe the best ever—and a really neat guy, but certainly no deity.

The estate of Elvis Presley doesn't want anyone to worship Elvis; they much prefer to think of him as a latter-day Mickey Mouse—a source of wholesome family entertainment, and a manageable image whose powers can be respectfully packaged and tastefully exploited in licensing agreements, royalties, and the tourist trade. However, religions, once they start, cannot be controlled so easily, and there ought not be any doubt about it: Elvisism has begun. For an awful lot of people around the world, Elvis Presley is about as close to a spiritual icon as any American since Father Divine, the preacher who told his followers, "I am God." Fifteen years after the death of Elvis, Elvisism has believers around the world; it has pilgrims, holy sites, Good Books (and evil ones), acolytes and infidels, passion plays performed by professional impersonators, a calendar of epiphanies, and a rich literature of apocrypha.

There are many nonbelievers who do acknowledge the beauty of his unique voice and his truly remarkable achievements (over a billion records sold) as the first rock-and-roll superstar. Nearly all music critics pay their respects to him as the catalyst, if not the creator, of modern pop music and of a new youth culture, and it is common to bemoan the tragedy of his squandered talent. Even these points, however, are not universally accepted. Throughout his life, and especially since his death, skeptics have worked hard to discredit Elvis, even as a man. They have said his voice was nothing but a gimmick, his mammoth success was simply the result of mammoth exploitation, and furthermore, he stole rock and roll from black people. The vehemence of those who curse Elvis—from the ministers who labeled him obscene, insane, and evil in 1956 to ghoulish biographer Albert Goldman, who was as obsessed by his bowel habits as by his moral turpitude—is the kind of sanctimonious passion rarely stirred up by anyone other than a messiah . . . or a false messiah. As is true about all religions when they are new, there are more cynics than there are believers.

The story of Elvis has become at least folklore, if not theology. From the day he was born to the present, every epoch of the Elvis phenomenon has a canonical version as well as a heretical interpretation. And so, to help clarify the creed of the Elvis cult, we hereby set forth **The Eight Ages of Elvis:**

I. GENESIS
(1935–1948)

Born dirt-poor in a shotgun shack, Elvis was the second-born of a pair of twins. The first-born, Jesse Garon Presley, was born dead or died soon after birth. Some (rare) apostate accounts hold that the first twin did not actually die; he lived a secret life, and when

Elvis supposedly went into the army in 1958, he actually vanished, and his place was taken by Jesse Garon. This explains the apparent change of character during the Fourth Age of Elvis (Exile). Elvis's mother, Gladys Presley, smothered him with love, and the disbelievers' account of this era finds the beginning of a profound agoraphobia in their unnatural closeness. The earliest known testament of Elvis's boundless charity was during the First Age: Although destitute himself, Elvis gave his bicycle to a needy playmate. At the age of ten, Elvis sang "Old Shep" in a contest at the local fairgrounds and won second prize for the performance. Genesis ends when the Presley family moves north to Memphis, hoping for a better life.

II. BOYHOOD
(1949–1953)

"Velvet Lips" Presley became known to other kids in his Memphis housing project, Lauderdale Courts, for his elaborate hairdos (frequently changed, and on at least one occasion created by using his mother's curlers) and his fancy clothes, which he bought on Beale Street, home of the blues. Sometimes calling himself Valentino, he finally decided to fashion his hair after that of Tony Curtis—dyed dark and well-greased—and he began to formulate his life's ambition: to be a handsome movie star. He also loved gospel music, which he learned to sing in church, and as a young teen he began to jam with Bill Black, whom he met at Lauderdale Courts (and who later backed him on his first recordings). He sang in a high school talent contest and was happily flabbergasted when the other kids liked his performance. In his yearbook, there is a reference to his being a teacher's pet; in the class prophecy his future is described as a "singing hillbilly of the road." In 1953, his picture appeared in the newspaper for the first time: as "Mr. Safety," for his flawless demonstration of automobile parallel parking techniques.

III. ASCENSION
(1954–1958)

The true coming of Elvis began on July 5, 1954, when he and two friends went to the Sun Records studio and tried to come up with a nice, slow ballad that Sam Phillips, who owned the studio, would be willing to put on a record. During a break, Elvis—just for fun—belted out a speeded-up, high-key version of "That's All Right," a rhythm-and-blues number he might have heard on Beale Street. Sam Phillips, who figured he could make a million dollars if he could ever find a "white boy who sounded black," was delighted and recorded the song. "That's All Right" was the rage of Memphis that summer; and the high-energy chorus of "dee, dee-dee, dee-dee" that Elvis sang became a signature that teens whistled and hummed to each other throughout the city.

What followed was a fast-rolling delirium that spread from Memphis through the mid-South, then coast to coast, and had all America in a dither by the summer of 1956. Elvis mesmerized teenagers and horrified adults. To kids, he was liberation; he was sex; he was *theirs*. To many parents and moralizers he—and the fans' behavior he inspired—signified juvenile delinquency, unleashed profanity, and bad taste. It was the great moment of emancipation for teen culture, and the beginning of what would later be known as the generation gap.

There is no question that Elvis popularized a kind of music that had previously been ghettoized as black. That was one of the reasons many of his early white critics feared his effect. His libidinal style of performance (swiveling hips, flying hair, and lots of sweat) had precedents only in church revival music (white as well as black). Admirers consider him the Zeus of rock and roll, because he infused the sensuality of black rhythm and blues with country insouciance and a gospel resplendence. The result was a new musical form . . . and a new superstar status and superindulgent pop lifestyle to go with it. To heretics, the Ascension of Elvis represents the exploitation of a genuine folk culture by commercial interests.

IV. ELVIS IN EXILE
(1958–1960)

In every myth of triumph there is a moment of humiliation, and just as Samson was shorn, Elvis got his hair cut off, too—by none other than the government of the United States. At the peak of his career, when he was King of Rock and Roll in a ten-thousand-dollar gold lamé suit, he was taken by the U.S. Army. His beloved mother died the same year. Within months, Elvis lost everything that mattered to him. This great sense of loss is one of the most poignant moments in the Elvis legend. Not only was Elvis deprived of his happiness, but the fans were deprived of him, too.

But lo! The dangerous rebel with his sneer and gyrating hips proved to be a good, obedient soldier. Veteran El-fans, who were devastated by his exile, now love talking about the Army years because they are incontrovertible evidence of his goodness. Cynics have suggested that it was while Elvis was on guard duty that he first started taking drugs—pep pills to stay awake, and also, perhaps, to help alleviate the pain of his mother's death—which was an ominous development that would lead ultimately to his demise.

V. THE BLAND YEARS
(1960–1969)

The Elvis who returned from the Army was different from the wild child who had once alarmed the culture's guardians of propriety. There were no more live concerts—those Dionysian revels at which young girls melted into puddles of desire before him. And with a very few exceptions, the torrid rock-and-roll songs vanished, too. His movie career took a new direction. No longer playing the rebel, as he had in such pre-1960 pictures as *Jailhouse Rock* and *King Creole*, Elvis turned into a pussycat. In nearly each of the more than two dozen films he made in the 1960s, he is polite, pleasant, happy-go-lucky, with a nonsensical song for every occasion (including "There's No Room to Rhumba in a Sports Car" in *Fun in Acapulco* and "Yoga is as Yoga Does" in *Easy Come, Easy Go*). Rock critics tear out their hair over the Bland Years, but many of the most unswerving Elvis fans treasure these movies, and even their music, because they show how nice and polite and virtuous he was.

VI. REBIRTH
(1968–1973)

One of the famous apocryphal stories in the saga of Elvis is the day in 1968 when he walked along Sunset Boulevard and nobody recognized him. The rock culture he had once inspired had become so big and loud and important-seeming, and he himself had gotten so bland, that nobody cared about Elvis anymore. Of course, this is not true. The faithful ones always believed in him; and his movies, however drab, made money. But it is important for the myth of Rebirth to think of Elvis as a has-been, a washed up nobody on the skids. His blazing return to superstardom is marked by four events:

- "The Singer Special," 1968 (named for the sewing machine company that sponsored it): Elvis performs on television for the first time since 1960, wearing black leather and singing hot rock and roll.

- The American Sound Studio Sessions, 1969: Elvis returned to a Memphis recording studio (rather than Hollywood), to his rhythm-and-blues and country roots, and produced such songs as "Long Black Limousine" and "In the Ghetto," both featured on the *From Elvis in Memphis* album.
- Triumph in Las Vegas, 1969: Elvis returned to Las Vegas (where he had flopped in 1956) with a big orchestra and an elaborately choreographed performance, including dazzling karate moves incorporated into his stage rites. He played to sell-out crowds at the International Hotel (now the Hilton), the biggest venue in town, and he was able to use the success as a launching pad for eight years of on-the-road concerts. Until his death, he was the unrivaled king of Vegas show biz.
- "Elvis—Aloha from Hawaii," 1973: A satellite television broadcast that idolators like to say was seen by half the population of the planet. Elvis looked terrific—tan, thin, alert—and even if the music wasn't his very best, the hyperbolic reach of this manufactured event helped create a cosmic aura that stuck with him to the end, and beyond. Elvis had become omnipresent.

VII. BLOAT
(1974–1977)

Elvis had seemed bigger than life from the time he burst into the public eye in the mid-1950s; but in the last few years of his life, he became gigantic. He literally ballooned to about 250 pounds, but far more important than his actual weight gain was the way everything about him seemed to inflate. His grandiose stage shows came to resemble a coronation ceremony, and his on- and off-stage costumes grew ever more embellished. His retinue swelled to dozens of friends, helpers, relatives and steprelatives, and hangers-on. For touring, he bought his own four-engine jet plane (formerly owned by Hugh Hefner) and outfitted it with bright shag rugs, velour, and teak. His urge to give presents (which he called "happies") became stupendous, and it was in the mid-1970s that some of the most renowned incidents of his charity were recorded: new Cadillacs to perfect strangers, a house to one of his maids, a yacht to Danny Thomas (for St. Jude Hospital), his own diamond wedding ring to a stepbrother (for good luck), thousands of dollars to Jerry Lewis for the muscular dystrophy telethon. Elvis museums around the country display many five-figure checks he signed as "loans" to friends and relatives during this time.

Elvis was always an extremist, and in the last few years of his life everything he did grew to maximum size. He ate like a pig (a dozen cheeseburgers and two pounds of bacon at a time); he watched three televisions at once; he bought the largest limousine Mercedes-Benz ever manufactured; and he took more drugs than any other human in recorded history. Acolytes will tell you that he was in tremendous pain (worse than anybody else's, ever) from gastrointestinal problems, and that all the drugs he took were by prescription—doctor's orders. Debunkers relish listing all the various unorthodox prescriptions (most of which were issued by a doctor who was his close friend and a regular member of his entourage), which chief blasphemer Albert Goldman, author of *Elvis*, says were "enough to stun an elephant." Although drugs were not the official cause of his death (it was cardiac arrhythmia), only the most pious votaries deny that they are what did him in.

When Elvis died on August 16, 1977, there was pandemonium on the street outside his home. Devastated fans wept and fainted on the lawn of Graceland (it was 100 degrees that day). From all around the country people came to be in Memphis—just because they needed to be there, to stand witness, and, if they were lucky, to file past his body, which lay in state in his mansion on the hill. The lawn of Graceland was crowded with floral bouquets (as it now is each year before August 16); every florist for a hundred miles around Memphis ran out of stock.

VIII. AFTERLIFE
(1977–)

There might not be an Elvis religion today if he hadn't been martyred. He suffered much abuse throughout his professional life —from angry parents and moralizers in the 1950s, from movie critics in the 1960s, from disappointed rock-and-roll purists who condemned his kitschy flamboyance in the 1970s. But it was not until he was gone— actually, just before he died—that his enemies began to crucify him. *Elvis: What Happened?*, written by three former bodyguards and published just weeks before his death, exposed Elvis to the world as a bad-tempered, drug-crazed megalomaniac. Fans were outraged—not by what they learned about Elvis, but that anyone dared desecrate his image—and to this day there are many who blame the book for his death: He was so embarrassed by its revelations.

Next came Albert Goldman's book, *Elvis* (1981), a screed that attempted to discredit not only Elvis (as a hillbilly drug fiend) but his family, his fans, and his music. Since then, all loyal proselytes have made it a duty to—in their words—"take care of Elvis." They believe the attacks on their boy, and on them, are simply the work of elitist snobs afraid of the popular energy Elvis signified. As for the snobs, they see Elvis and his defenders as crass, commercial, and vulgar—democracy at its very worst. It is a fundamental rift that has energized Elvisism since 1956, when defenders of proper culture closed ranks against the onslaught of rock and roll's impudence.

As much as Elvis himself was worshiped when he was alive, it has been in the Afterlife that Elvisism has taken on the true ardor of a religious faith. If you doubt it, consider some of the holiest souvenirs, such as the biblically bound, self-published books of pictures taken by amateur photographers at his concerts in the 1970s, or votive candles with his face imprinted in the wax, or the poster that shows him ascending to the gates of heaven, where his mother waits and Hank Williams comes to greet him. One of the popular icons is a breathtaking painting (on black velvet) that shows him bathed in saintly light, microphone in hand, with a single tear running down his cheek. It is a picture of a man crying not only for his own sorrows but for the sorrows of all the world. Many devout Elvis fans keep little shrines in their home—a corner of a recreation room where they display photos, favorite records, relics from concerts, and perhaps some of the more personal souvenirs available, such as a vial of his sweat ($9.95), or a teaspoon of dirt from near his grave ($4.95), or a scrap of carpet that once was on the Graceland floor and underneath his feet.

Fans love to talk about his beautiful voice and his good looks, but ask the real devotees what it was that made Elvis so magnificent, and it is just as likely they will talk about his charity, his compassion, his love. Elvisism only starts with his talents and achievements; it's the spirit behind those facts that inspires serious adherents. They like to recall how much he loved his mother—more than any other good boy ever has—and some will tell you that he loved Priscilla, too, too much for his own good, so much that when she left him for another man, some of those who ached for him swore they would put a bullet in her adulterous head, and haven't yet forgiven her. Listen to them sing his praises, repeating stories over and over again—as they feel they must do, because they are the first Elvis generation, the generation who knew him and saw him and agonized with him until the day he died, and they are now duty-bound apostles who are privileged to keep the flame alive. And so they talk about how he loved his daughter; he loved his step-brothers; he loved his maid; he loved his friends; he loved his hairdresser (and nearly all of the people he loved have written books that tell how much he loved them).

Most of all, the witnesses remember that Elvis loved his fans. He loved them so much that he gave himself to them. Even when he was sick and fat and woozy, he put on the jumpsuit and went on stage, and he threw out the souvenir scarves for them to catch, and sweated for them while he sang to his Heavenly Father, "How Great Thou Art" and "Glory, Glory, Hallelujah." To witness Elvis perform in the final years, to see him falter and die as the faithful watched in awe and wonder, was to see him give everything so his fans could be happy: That's the way they interpret those last, stumbling concerts. They have not forgotten how hard Elvis struggled to give them what they wanted, and they don't want anyone else to forget. And so, to honor him today, many Elvis clubs around the country regularly raise money for poor and sick people and donate it in his name, as a form of remembrance; they buy wheelchairs for the needy and do the kind of good deeds they know their Elvis would have liked.

There is a Christian calendar year and an accountant's fiscal year, and there is also an Elvis year. Those who live by the Elvis year mark such days as his birthday (January 8), the birthday of Lisa Marie (February 1), his Army induction (March 24), the "Aloha from Hawaii" TV special (April 4), his wedding anniversary (May 1), and the holiest of holy days, the day he died: August 16.

August 16 is the climax of Elvis Week in Memphis, and the ultimate testament to his Afterlife. Disciples come from around the world to share their love for him. They visit all the important sites, including Sun Studios, the Lansky Brothers' clothing store (where he shopped for zoot suits as a teenager), Lauderdale Court housing project, Super Cycle (where he bought his Harleys), Humes High (where he went to school), Poplar Tunes (where young Elvis bought records), and the Memphis Funeral Home (where his body was prepared for burial). They travel down to Tupelo, Mississippi, to see his boyhood home. And of course they tour Graceland, where he lived and died and is buried. On the eve of his death day, around sunset, fans gather at the Graceland gates, and throughout the night, sometimes until dawn on the sixteenth, they walk reverently up the long driveway, each carrying a candle, to file past his grave, in the Meditation Garden to the side of the house.

There aren't a lot of fans who honestly, in their heart of hearts, believe Elvis is really still alive. That's mostly a tabloid gimmick. But just as Jesus sometimes manifests Himself on a tortilla (in Lake Arthur, New Mexico) or an oil tank (in Fostoria, Ohio), or as a nine-hundred-foot-tall giant (in Tulsa, for Oral Roberts), Elvis makes appearances, too: at the Burger King and the J. C. Penney store in Kalamazoo, Michigan, or—every year, without fail—among the thousands of people gathered at the Graceland gate on the evening of August 15. The strange thing about his yearly appearance in Memphis is that there are so many Elvis impersonators among the crowd—some merely wearing Elvis hairdos, some in full regalia and singing with a boom box, some so quiet and withdrawn that they seem to want to hide their Elvisness—that spotting the real one is well-nigh impossible. But you can count on it happening: As the sun gives way to the humid summer night on Elvis Presley Boulevard, fans waiting to go up to the grave start to murmur that they have seen him; and a bolt of chain lightning will shoot through the crowd; and a hundred or more impersonators among them will begin to sneer like he did, and pose with their capes spread, and gyrate their hips and sing "Heartbreak Hotel." Suddenly, for a moment, it is easy to believe that whether or not he is dead, Elvis is, like God, everywhere.

NATHAN PRITIKIN

After Nathan Pritikin committed suicide by slitting his wrists in 1985, a spokesman for the Pritikin Longevity Center he had founded revealed the autopsy results: His heart was in superb condition; Pritikin's corpse "had the arteries of a preadolescent boy."

A college dropout, a free-lance inventor who held almost fifty patents in chemistry, electronics, and physics, Nathan Pritikin likely would not have been offended or sur-

prised to hear a postmortem panegyric about his circulatory system. He had nurtured his heart and arteries for over a quarter-century (after an acute angina attack) and built a phenomenally successful career telling other people how to rehabilitate and care for theirs. Although he had no medical degree, he was probably the most influential health guru since Horace Fletcher (who at the turn of the century advocated "thorough mastication"—chewing each mouthful of food a hundred times—as a means of producing odorless stools and attaining prime health). To this day, among some doctors and many lay people for whom proper nutrition has become a personal obsession, Pritikin's theories are more than a method for losing weight or lowering cholesterol levels: They are a new way to live.

"There are only two basic diets," Pritikin announced when his bestselling *The Pritikin Program for Diet and Exercise* was published in 1979, "the Western World and the Third World." He based his plan on the latter, which had one-fifth the fat and one-tenth the cholesterol, and he developed a regimen of eight small meals a day based almost entirely on vegetables, fruit, grains, and plainly cooked fish, with no oil, sugar, dairy products, or red meat. No coffee, no tea, and no tobacco were allowed, and alcohol was limited to a single glass of wine per day. After doctors told him he was about to drop dead in 1957, Pritikin had eaten his way back to health using exactly this self-invented diet, which lowered his cholesterol count by more than half. Starting in 1976, at Pritikin Longevity Centers in Santa Barbara (and then in Santa Monica, Miami, and Maui), he gave the public a chance to enroll as "patients" (at fees that ranged from three thousand to six thousand dollars, plus medical expenses) for a twenty-six-day course in his version of how to live right. Despite his lack of medical or scientific credentials, Pritikin had a true inventor's faith in his theories. "For forty years, studying the human body has been my avocation," he explained.

Many graduates of his program—some of whom arrived at the centers in wheelchairs or on stretchers but left with spring in their step—became tireless proselytizers for the Pritikin way of life. Mrs. Eula Weaver, a ninety-one-year-old woman admitted with congestive heart failure, left the Pritikin center and went on to win a gold medal in the Senior Olympics' mile run. The *New York Times* called her a "miracle." By 1980, with the jogging fad in full swing, Pritikin's ideas began to seem not only healthy but socially fashionable and even politically correct. (Eating Third World food apparently eases people's guilt about being an overfed American.) California governor Jerry Brown lost thirty-five pounds thanks to Pritikin. Senator George McGovern took the cure and became a believer. Not since Audrey Hepburn's debut in the fifties had there been a more convincing argument in favor of extreme, nearly anorexic thinness. Big men and women who discovered Pritikin and became crusaders for his puritanical way of life frequently reduced themselves to cadaverous shadows (but with clean-as-a-whistle arteries). Doctors worried about

amino acid deficiency as a result of Pritikin's stringent regime; they questioned Pritikin's unscientific (and nonmedical) research; and they worried that the diet was so unpalatable that no one but a fanatic could stick to it. For many people who tried the severe Pritikin regime and failed, its privations were proof of what Mark Twain had said: "The only way to keep your health is to eat what you don't want, drink what you don't like, and do what you'd rather not."

Pritikin's severest criticism came from rival diet pitchman Robert Atkins (an actual cardiologist), whose theories were nearly the complete opposite: Lose weight and get healthy by eating massive amounts of fat— all the steak, bacon, and eggs you like— sending your metabolism into a condition called ketosis (similar to kidney failure) in which the body burns fat for energy. "My patients can eat meat or any other main course in whatever quantity they wish," Atkins boasted. "They never go hungry." Said Pritikin: "His diet is a monstrosity. It's really a malignancy of nutrition." Atkins counterattacked, hitting at the cost of Pritikin indoctrination: "His primary interest in longevity is in the longevity of the Longevity Center. After they go to Pritikin, they haven't got any money left for food."

Time has been kinder to Pritikin's theories than to Atkins's. In 1979 Pritikin predicted, "In the next five years, half of the country will be on my diet." Perhaps half the country isn't actually eating Pritikin-approved meals, but his condemnation of meat, fat, and sugar and his celebration of grains, vegetables, fruits, and plain fish have become the unquestioned nutritional dogma of late-twentieth-century America. When he killed himself at age sixty-nine (because he was suffering leukemia, anemia, diabetes, kidney failure, and intense pain), Pritikin was still hoping to prove unequivocally that heart disease could be reversed by diet. "It's unheard of for a layman to receive a Nobel Prize in medicine," said Dr. Monroe Rosenthal, an endocrinologist employed by the Pritikin Centers, "but I think he could have done it."

RAP

Rap started as part of a subculture called hip-hop in New York's South Bronx in the 1970s. Young, urban, black, and mostly male, hip-hop (named by the early rap master DJ Hollywood, who used to chant "Hippity hip hop, don't stop") started as music, but soon developed into a charismatic set of signals that included spray-painted graffiti nicknames and murals on subway cars and building walls, breakdancing on the sidewalk to the sound of jumbo boom-box radios played at maximum volume, hooded sweatshirts, baggy workout pants and clean white sneakers, and outrageous gold jewelry such as heavy necklaces and rings. The soul of this subculture was rap itself, a synthesis of disco's throb with old-fashioned African-American toasts and boasts. It combined up-to-the-minute audio technology, the passion of rhythm and blues, and the sardonic braggadocio of spaghetti western soundtracks. It was *fresh*, and for the first time since the invention of the electric guitar, popular music regained the strength to scare the daylights out of those who find comfort and security in the social order that rap music assaults.

Rap's martial beat was created in basement clubs by deejays such as Kool Herc who could play a pair of record turntables like a musical instrument, cutting back and forth between songs, pushing tracks backwards to create a bizarre musical texture,

cuing and recuing snippets of everything from old Monkees tunes to bits of disco hits. Over the resulting collage, Kool Herc and other early rap masters (including the Treacherous Three and Grandmaster Flash) belted out rhyming pairs of street-jive exhortations as a way of getting dancers to move and also to boast of their own magnificence. Ringing with echoes of inspiration that ranged from the African-American insult game, "the Dozens," to Cab Calloway's "hi-de-hi-de-hi-de-ho" and James Brown's "Get Up, Get Into It, Get Involved," rap was something altogether new, a ferociously innovative musical form so impertinent that it simmered as a cult sound for years before it finally propelled its way out of the ghetto into the pop idiom.

Even more than most early rock and roll, rap and its practitioners were contemptuous of commonly accepted standards of taste and decorum. Rap musicians presented themselves as theatrical versions of street gangsters. Their lyrics were about violence, sex, and drugs and openly defiant of authority. And although the common rapper image as a badass street tough was frequently colored by irony, and the songs often contained cautionary messages, the point of the music—at least to its critics—seemed to be to drive listeners into an antisocial frenzy. In a 1986 article about Run-DMC, whose inflammatory concerts became famous as flashpoints for audience hell-raising (even though their lyrics encouraged people to stay in school and keep off drugs), *New York* magazine reported that "critics say the rap group, with its exaggerated street-kid image, is playing with fire." Playing with fire is what made rap so exciting. "Rap is rock," B. Adler wrote in the book *Rap!*, "and rock has *always* been at least incidentally about pissing off the old folks."

Rock and roll's original strength had been as a battle cry of yearning for people who felt powerless—teenagers. This was an outlook borrowed from rhythm and blues, which expressed the outsider status of African-Americans. But by the 1970s, rock music seemed middle-aged and had been eaten up by big business, retaining the attitudes of disenchantment and rebellion but little of the menace that had made it such a thrill for rebels and social outcasts in the 1950s. Rap music went back to brutal basics. It was the nasty voice of the street, uncompromising in its complex, sometimes grating musical form, and relentless in lyrics that *Newsweek* called "a series of bulletins from the front in a battle for survival"

—including N.W.A. (Niggas with Attitude) shouting "Fuck Tha Police" and threatening to "smoke [shoot] any motherfucker that sweats me." This kind of pose was nothing less than musical guerrilla warfare.

Rap emerged into a musical world that was dominated by such homogenized, hyper-produced sounds as those of the Village People, the Bee Gees, Donna Summer, and Abba. At just about the same time "Rapper's Delight" by the Sugar Hill Gang became the first rap song to climb the *Billboard* pop chart (to number thirty-six) the first week of January 1980, the number-one hit on the chart was the lighthearted "Escape (The Piña Colada Song)," in which Rupert Holmes croons melodiously about a girlfriend who's nice because she likes piña coladas and doesn't mind getting caught in the rain. It was very pleasant to hear Mr. Holmes's romantic words, but they meant nothing to black teens at the Disco Fever club in the South Bronx. "The Bronx wasn't into radio music no more," announced Afrika Bambaataa, a community organizer and one of the original rap supporters. "Hip-hop was against the disco that was being played on the radio."

The appearance of "Rapper's Delight" on the pop charts was a remarkable achievement considering it got virtually no play on any white rock station. The next year, Kurtis Blow's "The Breaks," a seven-minute harangue about all of life's bad breaks, chanted in couplets at once bellicose and hilarious, also edged its way out of the ghetto, but most record business executives still considered rap a minor and ephemeral genre with little or no audience beyond the black urban community. That perception began to change in 1983 with the arrival of Run-DMC, whose lead rapper, Joey Simmons, began as Kurtis Blow's onstage deejay, known as "Run Love, Son of Kurtis Blow." Although he was a middle-class boy from Queens, Joey (Run) perfected his street attitude, and Run-DMC established a belligerent style that jabbed rap into the public eye. Outfitted in black Kangol hats, black leather suits, heavy gold jewelry, and white Adidas, Run-DMC (Run and his partners, Darryl McDaniels and "Jam Master Jay" Mizell) were proud of their gangster image. "A lot of the kids who like us are impressionable," Run told *New York* magazine. "I got a lot of juice with them. It's like I'm cooler than their teacher, I'm cooler than their mother, I'm cooler than their father. So when we say don't take drugs and stay in school, they listen." Tipper Gore of the Parents' Music Resource Group was not amused, contending that Run-DMC music "says it's okay to beat people"; even Kurtis Blow was worried that the feigned violence in their act was giving kids the wrong impression. Whatever the moral implications, Run-DMC were selling millions of records by 1985 and selected collectively as one of the "25 Most Intriguing People" of 1986 by *People*, which declared them "kings of Queens."

Rap's big breakthrough came in January 1989, with the debut of "Yo! MTV Raps" on cable television. Suddenly everyone in America with a remote control device could tune in to the Fat Boys, L.L. Cool J, Stetsasonic, Salt 'n' Pepa, and Fab 5 Freddy, and a pop mythology that had been pumping up its muscles for more than ten years exploded into the mainstream. M. C. Hammer's *Please Hammer Don't Hurt 'Em* album sold ten million copies; rapper Will Smith of DJ Jazzy Jeff and the Fresh Prince got his own prime-time sitcom, "Fresh Prince of Bel-Air"; the rapping duo Kid 'N' Play starred in the movie *House Party* and sequels, including *Class Act;* even cartoon character Bart Simpson had a hit rap song, "Do the Bartman"; and advertisers selling everything from family sedans to refriger-

ated crescent-roll dough started using rap music in their TV spots. Begun as a powerful vocal weapon of the urban underclass, rap suddenly became a fad, and a pretty silly one at that. In the summer of 1990 the *Wall Street Journal* reported that Congressman Major Owens had decided to "use the language and the attitude of a street constituent" to express his opinions about the federal budget in such rap verses as:

> At the big white D.C. mansion
> There's a meeting of the mob
> And the question on the table
> Is which beggars will they rob.

It was also reported that Japan had fallen in love with "rappu," and their home-grown rap artists were laying down tracks about such subjects as the perils of monosodium glutamate and the pleasures of watching "Sesame Street" on television. Born-again rap songs, performed by such groups as P.I.D. (Preachers in Disguise), S.F.C. (Soldiers for Christ), and DC (Decent Christian), encouraged the Reverend Jerry Falwell to call himself a convert to rap, and there was at least one Jewish rap group, called Shlock Rock, whose leader, Lenny Solomon, explained, "It's a way of getting a point across . . . to tell people to be proud they're Jewish." Shlock Rock's raps included "Rockin' Rabbi," "Minyan Man," and "Yo Yo Yo Yarmulke."

There have been some very successful white rappers, including the Beastie Boys ("Fight for your Right to Party") and Marky Mark, who brought rap to white teeny boppers, but the most notorious, and successful, deviation from the traditional rap ethnology was Vanilla Ice. Vanilla is a Caucasian boy who was named best new artist of 1990 by the American Music Awards, and whose single "Ice Ice Baby" was the first rap song ever to hit number one on the *Billboard* pop chart—much to the dismay of rap supporters, who had always boosted the music as a natural-born expression of the African-American community. "Rap is from the streets and I'm from the streets," Ice protested, but critics said he had phonied up his life story ("I was the king master rapper from the neighborhood," he wrote in *Ice by Ice*, his autobiography) and that he was really more an expression of the middle-class Dallas suburb where he went to high school than of the mean streets of Miami where he was a preteen. Writing in *Billboard*, Janine McAdams complained that "what ultimately galls us is the guy's *attitude*. While rap thrives on macho braggadocio, it is also grounded in a street reality and an earned respect. Ice fudged by fabricating his background and then showing us his posterior in thanks [he mooned the audience at the American Music Awards]." McAdams complained that there were "dozens of artists more innovative, less derivative, better skilled, and certainly more grounded in the black urban tradition" than this white guy, whose high school classmates remembered him driving a nice white Camaro Z-28 (very unsoulful) around town after school. ("It's true, I did have a Camaro," Ice later admitted, explaining that a white car is easy to keep clean, and that he used it to create a challenge to other drivers.) McAdams also noted that some people were even expressing reservations about the success of Hammer, who *is* an African-American but had been accepted by the establishment too easily to please purists, who like rap because of its power to kick ass and to offend white people. Hammer, who has starred in Pepsi-Cola commercials on TV, was called "the Michael Jackson of rap" by *TV Guide*, which praised him for having "made an inner-city style safe for the suburbs [and giving] the mass audience a style of rap that's no more controversial than a good time."

Although rap, like rock, showed that it could easily be commercialized and defanged, many rap groups have steadfastly maintained an image as combative street fighters unwilling to compromise with propriety and the "Positive Image Mentality" that says that it behooves successful black people to be polite and take their place in the conventional social order. "P.I.M. hates rap because it's nappy, pissed-off, loud, lewd, irreverent, confrontational," B. Adler wrote in praising such groups as Public Enemy (accused of Jew baiting) and Ice Cube, whose debut album, *Amerikkka's Most Wanted*, featured the song "The Nigga Ya Love to Hate." Some such rappers go beyond loud-lewd-irreverent to out-and-out political treatises set to music, as in Public Enemy's song "Shut 'Em Down," which laments the lack of minority-owned small businesses and blames this situation on the difficulty black entrepreneurs have getting start-up loans from banks. *Entertainment Weekly* described the "Shut 'Em Down" album *(Apocalypse '91: The Enemy Strikes Black)* as "theorizing about black discontent with a close-up, street-life focus, while insisting that rap be more than the whine of crybabies or thugs," and praised the group for "advancing political awareness."

The best-known offensive rap group is 2 Live Crew, whose album *As Nasty as They Want To Be*, featuring the preposterously misogynistic "Me So Horny," was declared obscene by a federal judge in Florida in 1991, when police actually arrested some record store proprietors who sold it. Court-ordered martyrdom made 2 Live Crew just about the hottest rap act in the country (other than Vanilla Ice). Their album sold millions of copies, and rap's status in pop mythology was assured: It had become the most dangerous sound in the air since Chuck Berry and Jerry Lee Lewis were smote down as threats to moral order.

REDNECKS

Of all the bad guys who have lurked through popular culture in the last forty years, none other has been so delectably awful as the southern redneck. He has been the villain that northerners love to hate: a mean, slitty-eyed, overweight, tobacco-spitting bigot with a shotgun, eager to murder interlopers, or (as in *Deliverance*) to bugger them in lieu of his usual barnyard liaison. It has long been a tradition to make fun of rural people as hicks, and the term "redneck" has been popular since the 1930s, following H. L. Mencken's crusade to brand the South as a land of depraved nincompoops (e.g., "The Sahara of the Bozart"). But the image of the redneck as a truly wicked character didn't crystallize until the civil rights battles of the 1960s, when a righteous, mostly northern counterculture turned the depredations of some of the southern bigots they met into a stereotype that soon became applied to nearly every white southerner who wasn't an intellectual.

By the end of the 1960s, a southern accent almost automatically branded someone as stupid. Even President Lyndon Johnson's Texas mannerisms became a source of ridicule—his vulgar barbecues were contrasted with the Kennedys' elegant French soirées. Newspapers showed him mistreating his hound dog by yanking the pup off the ground by its ears; he was reported to career around his ranch in a Lincoln convertible, tossing empty beer cans by the roadside. Whereas JFK's Boston accent had been a source of lighthearted fun, the Johnson family's down-home ways were perceived as the loutish behavior of bumpkins.

To be a country person in the Age of Aquarius was to be a dunce. Look at the southern characters on television in the 1960s: the Beverly Hillbillies, Gomer Pyle, the Real McCoys, and all the slow-witted clowns who populated the town of Hooterville in "Petticoat Junction" and "Green Acres"—morons one and all (with the conspicuous exception of those on "The Andy Griffith Show" [see p. 307]), many of them sporting such yokel names as Bubba, Slick, Mavis, or Billie Joe Bob. Redneck men had dirty fingernails (from working on their car engines), drank bad whiskey, chewed tobacco, and ate greasy food; redneck women snapped their gum, sprayed their hair into jumbo bouffants, and worked as waitresses in diners.

Most of all, to be a redneck was to sweat. Throughout the 1960s and 1970s, you could not show the "real South" in movies without buckets of glandular excretions. Beads of perspiration—signs of heat and humidity, sure, but also of tension, claustrophobia, and pent-up perversity—define virtually all villains in southern-themed movies. Look at the two most famous—and sweatiest—southern movies of the 1960s, *In the Heat of the Night* and *Cool Hand Luke*. Both show an outsider (symbolically, the northerner) under the jurisdiction of a narrow-minded, sadistic southern authority figure. Life in these pictures is so horrible that everybody sweats, even the good guys.

In *Cool Hand Luke* (about the evils of a southern chain gang), the redneck is a mean little sumbitch known only as "the Captain," who makes it his business to squelch individuality and irreverence as personified by Paul Newman. *In the Heat of the Night* created the definitive redneck sheriff (Rod Steiger) as an ignorant, plodding, hostile loudmouth, much stupider than Sidney Poitier, the black detective from the North with whom he matches wits.

It became a common assumption among many citizens of Woodstock Nation that the nation from which they seceded—the rest of America—was basically a bunch of would-be Rod Steiger sheriffs and chain-gang bosses, a land of thick-necked bigots wielding axe handles and shotguns. Michael Rossman, in his late 1960s book *The Wedding Within the War*, traveled cross-country and saw such people "charging up with rage, hate, despair, frustration, and pain . . . rooted in a deep fearing of the sexual-sensualness of all life."

Menacing though it might have been, a cross-country journey into the land of the redneck became a fundamental rite of passage for many antiestablishment types who enlisted in the battle against the system. One hippie author described his trip into the belly of the beast as "a car full of wandering freaks in search of a home in our land." They are thrilled about the "New Age" people they find in California and the dope-smoking longhairs who help them change a tire in Nebraska, but the scenario for this type of trip demands that once among the rednecks, you find yourself staring into the heart of darkness. And so they did: "Restaurants won't serve us. Hostility surrounds us. Paranoia . . . bad vibrations . . . Does this same madness possess the citizens of every town we pass in the night?"

Yes, it was common knowledge among hippies that every southern town was populated by people who wanted to kill you if you had long hair or smoked grass or were against the war in Vietnam. The movie *Easy Rider*, made in 1969, demonstrated that (see p. 172). The rednecks in the town cafe hassle Peter Fonda and Dennis Hopper be-

cause their hair is long and they look like girls; they club Jack Nicholson to death because he is different; in the end, they gun down the hippie-biker heroes just for the hell of it.

The ugly and evil stereotype of small town southerners was undone at least a little bit in the mid- to late-1970s, when, for a while, country ways were in style. Truckers became knights of the road via CB radios (see p. 86); Burt Reynolds starred as a shrewd and likable good old boy in the first *Smokey and the Bandit* (1977); and on TV, "The Dukes of Hazzard" (starting in 1979) showed rednecks as playful sorts. When Jimmy Carter, a peanut farmer from Plains, Georgia, was elected President in 1976, his unvarnished, downhome manners seemed a welcome relief from the covert Nixon years. But Jimmy's charm as a rustic hero didn't last: along came his brother Billy, with a six-pack of beer under his arm (there was even a brand called Billy Beer) and an Alfred E. Neuman grin on his face, and a propensity for saying something stupid to reporters who soon made a mischievous sport of Billy-baiting. By the time the socially adept Reagans of California got to the White House four years later, Jimmy's Georgia charm, and more importantly, his brother's unredeemed redneck behavior, seemed something close to a national embarrassment.

Rednecks weren't much of an issue through the 1980s, and the big-time popularity of country music began to make the simpleton image seem almost obsolete. But redneck infamy was revived once again in 1991 as, simultaneously in the autumn, David Duke, former Ku Klux Klansman, almost got elected governor of Louisiana, and Martin Scorsese's remake of *Cape Fear* was released. *Cape Fear* featured Robert De Niro as a white trash mental case with a full repertoire of devilish redneck traits including sexual perversion, multiple jailhouse tattoos, an obsession with biblical vengeance, and—in his remarkable death scene—the power to talk in tongues. Red-necks may yet come back in style as an effigy of everything repulsive that virtuous and normal people want to shun.

REFRIGERATOR MAGNETS

I t is hard to imagine life before there were refrigerator magnets. How in heaven's name did anyone exhibit recent family snapshots, toddlers' crayon sketches, shopping lists, phone messages, interesting newspaper clippings, and coupons about to expire? All other ways of displaying such ephemera (photo albums, bulletin boards, note pads) seem so formal compared to the willy-nilly fun of affixing them to the refrigerator door with cute little magnets shaped like pudgy trolls and "Li'l Stinker" skunks or magnets with such amusing messages as FAT IS A FOUR-LETTER WORD and KISS MY GRITS.

Sticking things onto the refrigerator in order to bring them to the family's (or to friends') attention may be a practice as old as refrigerators themselves, but we believe it is possible to pinpoint the precise Moment of Creation of the first mass-produced decorative refrigerator magnet. It happened in 1964 when John Anasto (whose father had invented the Eskimo Pie) and his wife, Arlene (whose grandfather had invented one of the first water-heater coils used in New York City), had the idea to create and market decorative hooks for walls in people's homes. Arlene thought it would be fun to have a hook on a refrigerator, and realized that the best way to hold it there would be a magnet. Working in their New Jersey living room, as Arjon Manufacturing Com-

pany, the Anastos made a little magnetic tea kettle with a hook and bell. It sold well, and they followed it with daisies, roses, pots, pans, mugs, and mini-trivets, then with magnets for which they licensed brand names (Coke, Hershey's) because they figured housewives would be especially comfortable with familiar logos stuck to the refrigerator door. Arjon is still in business, specializing in magnets that, according to Arlene, reflect the American home and family.

Amazingly, refrigerator magnets have become collectibles. "Kitchen kitsch is gaining stature," *Newsweek* declared in 1989, reporting that "collectors are getting stuck on them" and noting that some especially rare issues, such as a Hallmark pixie stretched out on a green leaf, originally marketed in 1978 for $1.25, had recently been sold by Meredith DeGood, a collector with a three-hundred-piece magnet museum, for $150 to another collector. A set of 1978 "Frigidots," shaped like tennis balls and rackets, were going for $125, a hundred times their original selling price. And in 1991 the Loren & Pere art gallery in New York mounted a show (on old refrigerator doors) called "Marlou's Magnets," including several hundred of the choice magnets acquired by Marlou Freeman, a diner waitress from Maryland whom the gallery owner described as "an extension of Andy Warhol." Like pop art, however, the refrigerator magnet market is volatile. Marlou Freeman had no luck when she tried to sell her twenty-three-hundred specimens in order to earn the down payment on a new mobile home. And *Newsweek* observed that only *unused*, in-the-box magnets were worth anything to serious collectors. "If the magnet is sitting on your refrigerator," warned antiques columnist Harry Rinker, it is "noncollectible crap."

REMOTE CONTROL

I n 1956, a movie was released called *Forbidden Planet*—a thinking man's science fiction fantasy (starring Leslie Nielsen, Walter Pidgeon, Anne Francis, and Robbie the Robot) about Altair 4, a distant world of the year 2200 where mankind has figured out how to eliminate all manual labor. The geniuses of the future have managed to harness their brain power so effectively that all they have to do to make something happen is to think it. It seems like a crazy, far-out premise until you consider that the very same year, 1956, an inventor named Robert Adler actually made the effortless world of *Forbidden Planet* a reality, almost.

Robert Adler invented TV remote control. It isn't quite as good as life on Altair 4: There is still a small, intermediary step required between the thought ("What's on?") and the action (switching channels). But the mere touching of a button, compared to hoisting oneself out of a chair, walking to the set, turning a knob, then returning to the

chair and sitting down again, is scarcely more than a technicality. The remote control has, for all practical purposes, eliminated the need—among TV viewers—for muscles.

It is no coincidence that *Forbidden Planet* and remote control appeared at the same time. Since the end of World War II, America had been enamored of anything that promised to eliminate drudgery, and by the mid-1950s, as Thomas Hines points out in *Populuxe*, the most symbolic work-saver was the push button, which required even less effort than dial twisting or switch flicking. Chrysler came out with push-button PowerFlite transmission for its cars, as did Edsel in 1957. Soon there were stoves and washing machines and electric blenders bristling with rows of buttons to push; and there was even "push-button warfare," so that no one had to exert himself too much when launching weapons of mass destruction. In 1958 *Cosmopolitan* magazine featured an article titled "Push-Button Future," which predicted not only video recorders and ultraviolet guest cleaners that would rid visitors of all germs before they set foot in your house, but a series of buttons to press so you would be surrounded by the appetizing aroma of whatever food you were cooking in your push-button microwave oven.

Some televisions got push-button controls as early as 1954, but having the buttons on the set did nothing to eliminate the hardship endured by viewers who wanted to change channels and could not muster the energy to move. Zenith had a gizmo they marketed as "Lazy Bones" in 1955, which was attached to the set via a cord that, Robert Adler told the Chicago *Tribune*, "people stumbled over" and that "would get tangled up in the furniture." Zenith also sold a "Flash-Matic" control, which was nothing but a pinpoint flashlight that viewers could aim at any one of four photoelectric cells at the corners of the screen to change channels up or down, or turn the set on and off. However, Flash-Matic receptors could also be affected by sunlight and bright lamps, and most people forgot which corner's cell controlled what function. And so Adler, a physicist in Zenith's employ, was directed to create an improved control device that was simple to use, small enough to fit in the palm of the hand, and free of any wires or batteries.

His invention—the Space Command TV with a Sunshine Picture Tube—featured a remote control "Space Commander 400" a little bigger than a pack of filter king cigarettes. It had four buttons lined up in a row: one to turn the receiver on and off, one for channel up, one for channel down, and one to—in the words of an early advertisement —"shut off the sound of long, annoying commercials while the picture remains on the screen." It worked by sending high-frequency sound waves (inaudible to humans) to an electronic ear in the Space Command receiver. "NOTHING BETWEEN YOU AND THE SET BUT SPACE!" ads boasted, noting that the ultramodern device was available in Traditional, Modern, or Provincial-style cabinets. Its audio-wave technology, which could be tricked only by some pet parrots who learned to mimic the "inaudible sounds," thus adjusting the TV at their whim, was the way virtually all remote control operated until the early 1980s, when coded-light infrared beamers were developed, allowing for much more complex signals suited to elaborate VCRs and 100-station cable systems. Four out of five color sets sold in the United States now come with remote control; and you can buy stereo systems and even automobile locks and alarms with remote devices that require minimal physical manipulation to have machines do what you want them to do.

One unexpected result of the proliferation of television remote control is what the *New York Times* called "The Battle (Zap! Click!) of the Sexes"—the fact that men tend to click from channel to channel quickly, whereas women take twenty seconds or more to evaluate each show before clicking on. Comedian Jerry Seinfeld explained the gender gap: "because women nest and men hunt." But the *Times*, in a 1991 editorial about the problem, said that Seinfeld's explanation didn't solve the basic question: "Who, nester or hunter, controls the remote control?"

In a definitive Chicago *Tribune* article (titled "ZAP! Man Who Put Choice Into the Hands of Viewers") about the inventor of remote control, reporter Steve Johnson cited opposing views on the benefits and liabilities of the electronic-age technology —regardless of which sex wields it. One self-proclaimed couch potato called it "a milestone along with the TV tray and the VCR . . . one of the great boons to mankind." On the other hand, a concerned citizen from San Francisco's Public Media Center vilified it as "the next step in the evolution of television turning people into not only mindless beings, but into beings that are totally physically incapacitated as well."

MISTER ROGERS

Most civilized Americans used to formally shake hands when they took their leave of anyone other than close friends and loved ones. Now, a lot of us hug people we hardly know. If there is one individual responsible for this change in behavior, it is Fred McFeely Rogers, the nicest man on television. Using songs, puppets, and quiet chat, he has shown millions of tots how to cope with childhood crises ranging from a death in the family to the irrational fear of getting sucked up into a vacuum cleaner. But most of all, he has taught the viewers of "Mister Rogers' Neighborhood" to share their feelings openly. "Everyone longs to be loved and longs to know they are lovable," he said.

As Mister Rogers tells it, he had no intention of going into television when he went to Dartmouth, then Rollins College, and studied music composition. He wanted to be a songwriter, or possibly fulfill his childhood goal of becoming a Presbyterian minister. In 1951, when he was twenty-three, his love of music led him to New York and a job as an assistant producer of the "NBC Television Opera," then as floor director of "Your Hit Parade" and "The Kate Smith Hour." It was during this time that he happened to look at a kiddie show on television . . . and was appalled by its stupidity and violence: "people throwing pies at each other," he later recalled. He became a man with a mission.

Opportunity beckoned when WQED-TV, America's first noncommercial station, went on the air in Pittsburgh in 1953. With a production budget of $150 per week, he produced a daily hour-long show called "The Children's Corner," during which he sang songs and spoke directly to his audience about what he called "the bewilderments, the sadnesses, the joys, the lonely times, the angers." The show lasted seven years, and in 1955 and 1956 over two dozen episodes were aired on NBC. Meanwhile, Mister Rogers attended the Pittsburgh Theological Seminary, where he received a bachelor of divinity degree in 1962. The following year he was ordained as a minister, charged with the special mission of working with children through the mass media.

"MisteRogers" went on the air at KQED in 1963, and when production money ran out in 1967, its cancellation was announced. The hue and cry among parents and children, who had learned to love the gentle man in the baggy raincoat (before his cardigan sweater days), encouraged new funding, and the show went back on the air as "MisteRogers' Neighborhood." Production stopped in 1975, then resumed in 1979; today "Mister Rogers' Neighborhood" (as its title now appears) airs on three hundred stations and is consistently among PBS's top-rated shows.

The formula is simple: Mister Rogers walks onto the set like a dad coming home from work and puts on his sneakers and a sweater (actually knit by his real-life mother). He sings and carries on a private, one-way conversation with viewers about emotions, then sometimes talks to puppets and interesting human visitors to the "Neighborhood of Make-Believe," where his audience learns about life's ups and downs. "Before we got so mobile in this country,"

Mister Rogers once said (off camera), "there was always a grandparent or an uncle who could give a child undivided attention. I think that I'm this adult male who stops in." Unlike most other children's television, even high-minded "Sesame Street," "Mister Rogers' Neighborhood" is always leisurely paced, and instead of focusing on educational goals, Mr. Rogers talks about feelings—with few gimmicks and with lots of hugs. Psychologists have noted that whereas children tend to sit in a vegetative trance during ordinary television shows, they talk back to the screen and respond actively whenever Mister Rogers is on.

The homey format and cheerful tone of "Mister Rogers' Neighborhood" became so much a part of folk culture that "Saturday Night Live" developed two parodies—"Dr. Jekyll and Mr. Rogers" and the famous Eddie Murphy routine about a smiling, soft-spoken black man named Mr. Robinson, who sings a fractured version of Mister Rogers' theme song, "Won't You Be My Neighbor," that goes:

> It's one hell of a day in the neighborhood,
> A hell of a day in the neighborhood.
> I hope I get to move into your
>   neighborhood.
> But the problem is
> When I move in,
> You all move away!

Off screen, Mister Rogers is every bit as admirable as he is on the show. He doesn't smoke or drink (except for sacramental wine, which he likes because it is sweet as soda pop), and his favorite dessert is apple pie à la mode. He has been married to the same woman (Joanne Byrd) since 1952; the single great scandal that the press has been able to unearth about him is that the older of his two sons neglected to write or call home for a while when he went off to college in 1978.

ROLLING STONES

When the Beatles were nice, singing their jovial "Eight Days a Week," the Rolling Stones were naughty and sang "(I Can't Get No) Satisfaction." As the Beatles transformed their appearance from lovable, fresh-faced mop tops into bearded, brooding Bohemians, the Stones grew wicked-looking, until lead singer Mick Jagger was described in one 1969 review as the "clown prince of darkness; an angelic devil" as he sang such unrepentantly sadistic Stones hits as "Under My Thumb" and "Stupid Girl." It's a good thing the Beatles broke up when they did, or the Rolling Stones—who always made a point of being much meaner than their more popular British rivals—would now likely be singing nothing but songs about death, destruction, and the devil. Of course, they did sing such songs for a while in the early 1970s: "Sympathy for the Devil," "Sister Morphine," and "Dancing With Mr. D." In 1971 *Time* magazine said about them, "Rarely has rock music invoked such an invitation to hell."

That's been the image of the Rolling Stones for more than a quarter-century: mean, brutal, satanic, incorrigibly rebellious, and the embodiment of violent, rude rock and roll. They got so good at projecting this image of themselves that it seems almost impossible to believe that in the beginning it was simply a marketing plan to get them noticed. "We wanted you Americans to think that we were dirty and raunchy," Mick Jagger said in 1965. "If those dumb American birds dig that kind of shit, why shouldn't we do it?"

The nasty image was created for the Stones by manager Andrew Loog Oldham, who realized that the sextet—Jagger, Keith Richards, Brian Jones, Bill Wyman, Charlie Watts, and Ian Stewart on piano—would get nowhere performing as yet another jolly, Beatles-like band from England. Dressing in matching mod houndstooth suits with ruffled collars, they tried to bob their heads and smile as they sang like the Beatles did in 1963, but such merriment did not come naturally. The Stones had gotten together as blues aficionados, enamored of the rough-tempered, sexually suggestive songs of Muddy Waters and Willie Dixon. While the Beatles got wildly popular with their rollicking love ditties in the States in 1964, the Stones made a name for themselves in England singing such raunchy

Top: **Keith Richards, Charlie Watts, Mick Jagger;** *bottom:* **Bill Wyman, Brian Jones**

songs as "Little Red Rooster" and "Play with Fire." But when they came to America, they performed in half-empty concert halls and got no respect. "They're off to England to have a hair-pulling contest with the Beatles," Dean Martin quipped when they appeared on a TV show he hosted. The Stones needed a makeover.

Ian Stewart had been demoted out of the group by the time their first single was released (in public only; he stayed part of their recording talent until his death in 1985) because it was decided that six people were too many for fans to remember. Although they were all in their twenties, a few years were shaved for press releases so they could be talked about as teens. They were refashioned as symbols of rampaging rebellion, with articles planted about them pissing on walls in public and spitting at reporters; one story in 1964 described them as "wallowing in a swill-tub of their own repulsiveness." They cultivated sullen demeanors and sneers, and their stage act became so lewd that Ed Sullivan felt it necessary to apologize after they appeared on his show in October 1964, during their second American tour: "I promise you they'll never be back," Ed said. (They did come back.) An advertisement placed in *Billboard* by London Records, the Stones' label, boasted: "They're outrageous! They're rebels! They sell!"

It was a winning strategy, particularly at a time when so many teens and preteens were hungering for pied pipers to lead them in rebellion. The Beatles, who had been fashioned by their manager to be insubordinate but not indecent, served this role for many, but their well-packaged brand of upbeat defiance was too easily co-opted by the establishment, and after a while even responsible adults started to say they liked them. The Stones, on the other hand, by making themselves thoroughly repulsive

and beyond redemption, had a taboo charm that was irresistible to many. (John Lennon, who as a youth had actually been more of a badass then any of the Stones, especially college-educated Mick, hated his role as the socially acceptable rock-and-roll star.) English critic Geoffrey Cannon wrote in the Los Angeles *Times*, "The Stones are perverted, outrageous, violent, repulsive, ugly, tasteless, incoherent. A travesty. That's what's good about them."

A blasphemous attitude may have been responsible for getting them noticed, but it was not all that was good about the Rolling Stones. They were ingenious musicians who, more than anyone else, bridged the gap from old American blues to modern rock and roll. Keith Richards's restless, ripping guitar (an elaboration of Chuck Berry techniques) combined with the rhythm funk of Bill Wyman on bass and Charlie Watts on drums to create a unique sound, orchestrated (in the beginning) by a blues-savvy Brian Jones and fronted by the eager vocal stylings of Mick Jagger, who made up for his lack of musical savoir faire (in the beginning) with enthusiasm, an infectiously agitated stage manner, and big, blubbery lips that caressed every note he sang. All these talents came together when, one sleepless night while on tour in Florida, Keith Richards dreamt up a bloodthirsty chord progression inspired by the hard-pounding rhythm of Martha and the Vandellas' "Dancing in the Street." Although he thought it would work best if played by a horn section as background music, he tape-recorded the chords using his guitar and a Gibson fuzz box. When Mick Jagger heard them, he came up with the words "I can't get no satisfaction." They recorded "(I Can't Get No) Satisfaction" with Richards's scabrous riff echoing in the beginning like some kind of demented anthem of sexual detonation. It became their first American number-one hit, in July 1965, and it suddenly elevated the Stones from yet another English group to a force unto themselves. By any critical measure it stands at the pinnacle of rock-and-roll music—all power and menace at a full-tilt fever pitch.

The Stones' next number-one hit, "Get Off My Cloud," in November, began each chorus with the words "Hey, you!"; its arrogant narcissism firmly established them as authoritative bad boys as well as superstars in their own right. On tour in America in October 1965, they were nearly killed when desperate New York fans crowded onto the tops of their limousines, causing the roofs to cave in. From then on, they just seemed to get badder and badder. They dressed in drag for the sleeve of "Have You Seen Your Mother, Baby, Standing in the Shadow?" and *Newsweek* called them a "leering quintet" obsessed with pornographic lyrics. Their own private lives were exorbitantly scandalous, including numerous arrests on drug-related charges, a rapacious hunger for groupies (their song "Ruby Tuesday" was named after a famous one), and an undisguised contempt for law and order. "I'm not concerned with your petty morals," Keith Richards told the court during his 1967 drug trial. Brian Jones announced, "There is a young revolution in thought and manner about to take place"; the Stones, who released "Street Fighting Man" in 1968, aimed to put themselves on the front lines of that revolution.

Bad news helped solidify their status as the devil's minions: Brian Jones's 1969 death in a swimming pool was officially deemed "death by misadventure," but everyone—certainly all serious Stones fans —knew that he had been fired from the band the month before because he was so dissolute, or as rock critic Robert Christgau put it, he had "fucked and doped himself beyond usefulness." Later that year, in the

great bummer of all rock concerts, at Altamont Raceway in California, the Stones presided over what the Los Angeles *Times* called a "ragged, drug-ridden day" that included a killing in the audience, committed by the Stones' own chosen security guards, the Hell's Angels. The killing, captured on film, became the highlight of the brutal documentary film *Gimme Shelter* and has been interpreted as the symbolic end of the love generation. But the specter of real violence and death only made the Stones more attractive at a time when violence and street fighting was considered rather chic. The lyrics of their songs seemed to caress evil, and eventually, in the *Exile on Main Street* album, they grew ominously unintelligible, like speaking in tongues. On stage in live performances, they were menace incarnate: Keith Richards carried his guitar like it was a tommy gun, and Mick Jagger strutted, grimaced, and preened like an incubus in heat.

The Stones made a seamless transition from rock and roll's postadolescent bad boys to disreputable (but tantalizing) denizens of fashionable gossip columns in the early 1970s. Having stropped their insolence into a posture of willful, decadent evil, they sang such recalcitrantly wicked songs as "Bitch" and the racist-sexist-druggie "Brown Sugar." They had already added a measure of intellectual cachet to their image by appearing in Jean-Luc Godard's *One Plus One* (1969) and (Jagger only) in Nicholas Roeg's ode to degeneracy, *Performance* (1970). About the latter, Danny Peary wrote that it "makes you feel from frame one that someone is resting his dirtiest finger in the back of your throat." They enlisted celebrity-hungry pop artist Andy Warhol (see p. 547) to design the cover of their 1971 album, *Sticky Fingers* (blue jeans packed with an abundance of male crotch and a real zipper to pull) as well as their new logo—a big, slavering open mouth.

Also in 1971, Mick Jagger married Bianca Perez Mora Macias, a Nicaraguan socialite, at a Saint-Tropez wedding photographed by Queen Elizabeth's cousin Lord Litchfield. Meanwhile, Keith Richards was busy making himself into the world's best-known corpse-faced junkie.

The Rolling Stones became at least as celebrated for their fiendish night-life misadventures as for their music. They were banned in Japan and Australia; Keith was arrested in 1978 in Toronto on a cocaine and heroin possession rap and was marooned there, pending trial, for weeks; about the same time, Mick and Bianca got divorced in a tabloid-told battle of the sexes. When the Stones were the musical guests on "Saturday Night Live" in the fall of 1979, "they lived up to their legendary rowdiness," according to Doug Hill and Jeff Weingrad, authors of *Saturday Night*, "drinking scotch and vodka and snorting coke openly in the studio." At dress rehearsal on Friday night, Mick Jagger was so ripped he could not stand upright; Keith Richards's part in two comedy sketches had to be cut because he was unable to remember his lines or cues. Censors tore out their hair looking at the outline of Mick Jagger's penis in his pants; and you could hear the gasp in the audience when Mick stuck out his quivering tongue and licked the lips of guitarist Ron Wood (who had replaced Mick Taylor, who had replaced Brian Jones).

As they hit fifty years of age, the fact that (most of) the Stones are still alive has earned them a certain standing even among nonfans. "Not quite at the threshold of Geritol, pensions, and Social Security," *People* characterized them on the occasion of their induction into the Rock and Roll Hall of Fame in 1989. And later that year, Jay Cocks described them behaving "as if they were the oldest guys at the gym and trying to look good on the Nautilus." Still, even if the self-assurance of their youth has gone with the ages, the Stones' unswerving devotion to rock and roll has bestowed upon their music an inviolable aura of classicism . . . as well as the kind of respect earned only with age. It may be true that rock and roll originally posited itself as forever young, but the rhythm and blues that first drew the Rolling Stones into popular music was never just the voice of youth. It was also age-burnished songs of experience and hard-earned wisdom, which is exactly what the Stones produced in their masterful elegiac hit of 1989, "Slipping Away."

Personally, they are no longer Satanic Majesties, although they have had some ugly-sounding semipublic feuds with each other (Keith vs. Mick in particular). The Stones are quite respectable and decent-seeming, not to mention rich and powerful; they are now very much part of the establishment at which they used to wag their wicked tongues. Their 1981 hit, "Start Me Up," was sold to Budweiser to be used as promotion for a tour, and Mick, whom *Time* called "rock's foremost mandarin," cut a deal to market Rolling Stones–brand tank tops and leather jackets at J. C. Penney and Macy's, plus a line of collectible silver coins with all the Stones' portraits on them. Charlie Watts, who has assumed the mien of a fine old English lord, has done tasteful jazz recordings and was selected by *Arena* magazine as one of Britain's fifty best-dressed men ("once a rebel, always a gent"); Bill Wyman wrote an insightful book *(Stone Alone);* Ron Wood sells his artwork; and at one point Keith Richards was reported to have had all his old blood drained out and replaced with fresh drug-free plasma—a claim he denies.

Flashpoint, their 1991 album, was labeled "nursing home rock" by *Entertainment Weekly*, and when they toured five continents in 1990 as "the world's greatest rock-and-roll band," it became fashionable for critics to call them pop music's living dinosaurs. It is an ambivalent label, and doesn't really mean a whole lot, but it assumed some real poetic signification with the release in 1991 of *At the Max*, a documentary film that captured their stage act in the awesome five-story-tall IMAX format. IMAX films can be seen in those few select theaters equipped with IMAX technology— many of them located among the dinosaurs in museums of natural history.

ROSIE RUIZ

I t is not unusual for a long-distance runner to start a race but not finish it; Rosie Ruiz finished a race she didn't start. The first woman to cross the finish line in the 1980 Boston Marathon, initially credited with the third-fastest time in history (2:31:56), cheated, and in doing so became one of the (temporarily) best-known cheaters of modern times.

Ms. Ruiz slipped into the field of runners less than two miles before the end of the race and zoomed to apparent victory, receiving a crown of mountain laurel and a sapphire-and-gold medal for around her neck, both of which she wore at the post-race press conference. She was hardly sweating or panting as she sat alongside Bill Rodgers, first among the men, who turned to her and said, *"Who* are you?" (Later, to reporters, Rodgers confided, "I don't believe it. I don't believe that woman ran a marathon. She isn't tired enough.") When a chiropodist on duty examined Ms. Ruiz, he was perplexed, too, noting that her thighs were too flabby for an accomplished runner. When asked how a novice could top a field of expert marathoners, the triumphant Ms. Ruiz explained that her mother had prayed for her. Also, she told race officials, "I just got up this morning with a lot of energy." A week later she was stripped of her title, and

Jacqueline Gareau, who had been stunned to find herself in second place after leading for most of the race, was declared the winner.

Inept cheating in a sports event hardly deserves a footnote in the annals of popular culture except for some mitigating circumstances that *do* make Rosie Ruiz a proper footnote. First, her misdemeanor provides a symbolic end to the honorable era of modern running (see p. 427), when the charm of even the major marathons was that they were pretty much wide open to amateurs as well as to professionals, who ran alongside each other and competed in a spirit of Olympian trust. After Rosie Ruiz, the honor system was void; running had lost its innocence. Second, she enjoyed her bogus win in the spring of the first year of the 1980s, and thus stands as a conspicuous beginning of a decade in which winning was admired so much that bending rules to reach the top almost seemed acceptable and, even when exposed, often earned perpetrators celebrity as winners rather than ignominy as cheaters.

For Ms. Ruiz, however, fame as a trickster was short-lived. She explained that she had committed her scam because she aspired to be an actress and needed to get attention. She had endured nothing but bad luck since arriving in the United States from Cuba in 1962, during which time she had had a "tangerine-sized" tumor removed from her brain and a plastic plate installed in her head, and had been accused of robbing a boyfriend of all his credit cards. She reminded a skeptical press that she had finished twenty-third among all women in the previous year's New York Marathon (which had qualified her for the Boston debacle); however, investigating reporters revealed that she had dropped out of the New York field with a sprained ankle early in the race, taken a subway to the finish line, and limped across looking for medical help. Confused officials accidentally credited her with finishing, which apparently gave her the idea to cheat the next year in Boston.

Rosie Ruiz's hoped-for career as an actress has not yet blossomed, but her name did appear in the press one more time—in 1983, when she was arrested as part of an all-woman drug ring running cocaine in Miami.

RUNNING

U ntil the 1960s, running for extended lengths of time was, for most people, a special kind of torture they knew only from gym class or boot camp. Long-distance running was considered especially

odd as a sport, with none of the team spirit and camaraderie of normal ones like baseball and football, and no beer-and-peanut spectator appeal at all. Those who did it professionally or even semiprofessionally were frighteningly skinny, certainly no kind of ideal for a nation that tended to admire such hunky men as Mickey Mantle, Muhammad Ali, and Joe Namath: It was always fun to watch big guys like them win because they beamed happily and jumped up and down and looked hearty and victorious. On the other hand, there was something downright scary about watching the end of a long-distance race. Even the greatest milers of the time—such pioneers as Arne Andersson, Roger Bannister (the first to break four minutes), Jim Ryun, and Sebastian Coe—looked ready to die of exhaustion when they staggered over the finish line at their moment of triumph.

In the years following the first Super Bowl in 1966 (see p. 485), many sports seemed to turn into show business. Starting in 1970, Howard Cosell (see p. 109) began pontificating on "Monday Night Football." In baseball, free agents were demanding million-dollar salaries. Jim Bouton's best-selling *Ball Four* (1970) made the Yankees seem like boozy, pilled-up philanderers, and George Steinbrenner, who bought the Yanks in 1973, began a decade-and-a-half of public fighting with his team. In this context, it was not only refreshing but positively inspirational to start hearing about a new breed of athlete, the marathon runner. Bill Rodgers, who first came to the public's attention when he won the Boston Marathon in 1975, taught school for a living, drove an old Volkswagen, and splurged only occasionally . . . on chocolate chip cookies with ginger ale.

By the time Bill Rodgers got famous, there were a lot of Americans who knew about jogging, thanks in large part to Arthur Lydiard, who toured the States after the 1968 Olympic Games. Lydiard had trained a group of New Zealanders who went on to set marathon records, and encouraged large numbers of American athletes (professionals and advanced amateurs) to engage in what he called long, slow distance running (or as it became known in the slap-happy 1960s, LSD running), which was customarily done with a small pack of fellow LSDers, slowly and steadily, as a means of building up endurance.

For most people who took it up in the beginning, jogging was like playing Frisbee —a humanitarian sport, noncompetitive, and essentially very simple. It required no fancy equipment and no organization. You could jog whenever you were in the mood, for as long as it felt good, over hill and dale, through parks and on sidewalks. It was easy-going; all early proponents emphasized that jogging should be done at a relaxed pace— nothing like the intense self-torture of serious long-distance marathoning. There was something very natural-seeming about it, a

notion well expressed by distance runner Bill Emmerton in his book *Running for Your Life* (1970): "If you put a chipmunk in a cage and include one of those round things for him to run in, watch him go! Some primitive instinct tells him his body needs exercise, regardless of the circumstances, and he has sense enough to comply."

The original reason most people started running was good health. "Insurance against heart attacks," is how *U.S. News & World Report* described the fad that was making joggers part of the daily scene in cities across the country. "You see them everywhere—in the parks, on the streets, in offices, even in hotel corridors," the magazine observed in December 1967, just prior to the founding of the National Jogging Association, which was inaugurated when Secretary of the Interior Stewart L. Udall led an assembled crowd on a jog around Washington, D.C.'s reflecting pool. In May 1968, the cinder path around the Central Park Reservoir was officially declared a track for joggers. *U.S. News* declared, "Jogging—a kind of steady trot interspersed with periods of walking—is close to becoming a national health craze." It *did* become a national health craze within ten years.

Like so many totems of Aquarian culture that got big and more intense in the 1970s (sideburns, bell-bottoms, shag rugs, the disco scene), jogging sped up, and most people began to think of it as running. It was the same basic idea as jogging but more important-seeming, not nearly as relaxed, and there was much more emphasis among runners on goals, which could range from winning a race to better arteries or self-awareness. Of all the ways people in the Me Decade found to take their pulse (literally and spiritually), look inward, and obsess about bodily corns and souls' coronas, nothing was as popular as running. What was most revolutionary about running was that so many people who did it *loved* it. Instead of complaining about the discomfort of exercise, runners tended to dote on their agonies with masochistic pleasure, especially if they could get to "the wall" (the moment in a long run where you are certain you are about to die of fatigue), then run through it. Mike Spino, director of the Esalen Sports Center, wrote a book in 1976 called *Beyond Jogging: The Inner Spaces of Running*, in which he said that he had discovered his "larger self" while on the run. His advice to others searching for Nirvana: "Maybe you can find one moment where the sun is beginning to set, where the fog rolls in, and maybe you are running with just that person who gives you the right feeling, and the ground is smooth and fast. You have known the tension and now the freedom. There is only you and your companion and it is almost absurd how important you make it all. But why not important? What else?"

People ran for fun, for sport, to get fit, and to find peace of mind. Everybody did it, from President Jimmy Carter (who collapsed mid-run in 1979) to Senator William Proxmire (who said that it was "like being immortal") to Benigno Aquino (who became a devotee while in a Philippine prison). Ninety-year-olds did it; heart transplant recipients did it; even people without legs did it, in their wheelchairs. Jim Fixx, author of *The Complete Book of Running* (which sold more copies than any other nonfiction book in the history of Random House), was proclaimed by *People* magazine to be one of the most intriguing people of 1978, along with Brooke Shields, Meat Loaf, Jimmy Carter, and Miss Piggy.

Those who didn't run began to dress as though they did (see "Running Shoes," p. 430), and it soon became the height of fashion to be seen in a baggy warm-up suit with stripes down the legs and a headband, looking all sweaty as if you had just reached the end of a good run. Along with aerobic dancing (see p. 1), which got popular about the same time, running made athletic wear into fashion.

Other than Jim Fixx (who died while running in 1984), the best-known proponent of pounding pavement was Dr. George Sheehan, a "philosopher of sport" (according to *Sports Illustrated*) and author of *Running and Being: The Total Experience*. Sheehan, who was fifty-eight years old and ran more than thirty miles every week, described how running could not only give everyone the circulatory system of a twenty-eight-year-old but also provide "answers to the Big Questions about your soul." He wrote:

> Running made me free. It rid me of concern for the opinions of others. Dispensed me from rules and regulations imposed from outside. Running let me start from scratch. It stripped off those layers of programmed activity and thinking. Developed new priorities about eating and sleeping and what to do with leisure time. Running changed my attitude about work and play. About whom I really liked and who really liked me. Running let me see my twenty-four-hour day in a new light and my life style from a different point of view, from the inside instead of out.

Dr. Sheehan, a cardiologist, concluded *Running and Being* by reminding readers that ancient Egyptians believed that judgment after death began with weighing the heart of the deceased. The heart, he wrote, is "the measure of our days, of what we have done, of who we are." And nothing swelled the heart better than running. He then revealed that his own pulse, only one day after completing a marathon, was a steady, remarkably slow (and therefore reassuringly healthy) forty-eight beats per second. "My heart is capable of anything," he rejoiced.

RUNNING SHOES

In the beginning there was the athletic shoe. It was made for athletes engaged in athletic activities. It was a plain leather upper, with laces, sewn onto a flat rubber sole. At the turn of the century, Spalding produced three kinds: for running, for jumping, and for cross-country. To wear a pair of these athletic shoes anywhere other than on track or field would have been as weird as an athlete of today wearing his jock strap for a hat.

Then the U.S. Rubber Company, using a process invented in the 1860s called vulcanization, which bonded cloth to rubber, created the sneaker, so nicknamed because it didn't squeak like a leather oxford and therefore allowed its wearer to slink along in silence. The first sneakers were named Peds, in honor of feet. Because of trademark problems the name was changed to Veds, but someone at the company felt a snappier sound was needed, so on July 14, 1916, they were reintroduced as Keds, a contraction of "peds" and "kids" (who were supposed to especially enjoy wearing

them). Keds were marketed not as shoes for athletes but as the "shoes for every summer need." The next year Marquis M. Converse, who had been manufacturing low-cut athletic sneakers in Malden, Massachusetts, since 1909, created high-top sneakers (formally named "Chuck Taylor All-Stars" in 1936), of which well over three hundred million pairs have been sold.

Keds' high-top sneakers were proclaimed "temples of the feet" in 1983 by Betty Cornfield and Owen Edwards in their book *Quintessence: The Quality of Having It.* They were originally brown, then only black or white, and their stark appearance encouraged many of the kids who have worn them to customize them—with ballpoint pen, stick-on decals, spray paint, or weird-colored laces. Today high tops are available in suede as well as canvas, in neon-bright colors, and with air-cushion soles. But we are getting ahead of the story.

Until the sixties, there were high tops (basketball shoes) and low tops (tennis shoes) for playground wear and yard work and for amateur sportspeople, and there were serious athletic shoes for athletes. Then came Adidas: earnest shoes, from Germany, made by the same company that made Jesse Owens's shoes in 1936. Adidas were not for children or backyard badminton players. They cost twice as much as sneakers and they had a look that was more purposeful than playful. By 1968, when the *New York Times* declared jogging "the in sport," Adidas had become the in *shoe;* just as people began wearing jogging suits around town to let the world know they were in the good-health groove, Adidas gradually became fashionable and quite acceptable footwear in places other than the gym or the track. Only a few years later, clothing designer Ralph Lauren advised Woody Allen that it was acceptable to wear sneakers with dinner clothes.

Not all people who wore running shoes were fashion plates. For years, sneakers had been popular as children's footwear, and in 1974 the New York City Department of Recreation and the Police Athletic League began sponsoring a yearly "Jive to My Sneakers" poetry contest for people under eighteen. The object was to write and recite a poem about their shoes. One entry, in 1975, went:

In French it's called le sneakaire
In Russian it's sneakotsch.
In Japanese it's snikorru.
I'm not sure how it's in Dutch?

One entry, titled "The Sneaker and World Peace," included the lines:

When everyone will be wearing
    sneakers
It will be impossible to hate.

About the same time Adidas began to make their mark, two Oregonians named Bill Bowerman (a track coach) and Phil Knight (a 4:05 miler) teamed up to form Nike (first known as Blue Ribbon Sports), and in 1966 they created the Cortez, a long-distance running shoe designed with a pronounced wedge in the heel to help reduce Achilles tendon strain and absorb shock. The following year they put nylon in the upper to reduce their shoe's weight; and in 1972, according to official Nike company history, "Bill Bowerman turned his breakfast waffle into a radical new athletic shoe component" by creating what was then known as a "Moon Shoe," with high-traction, lightweight principles still in use today. Air cushioning, devised by Frank Rudy in 1979 and first sold as "Nike-Air," was the next big technical advance, and by the mid-

1980s running shoes had become the prosthetic-soled, bulging, high-tech clodhoppers they are today.

Big and clumsy-looking though they were, they swiftly became very stylish, and not just as casual wear. At the peak of a high-flying decade that for a short while venerated young, urban professionals on the go, running shoes became an emblem of executives (female executives in particular) speeding on their way towards higher rungs on the corporate ladder. Sober business suits and panty hose, attaché cases and microcassette recorders were complemented by big sneakers on the feet of bustling commuters (who generally changed into normal shoes once they arrived at their cubicle or office). Although the catalyst for this look was a 1980 New York transit strike that necessitated walking, the fashion endured. Dr. Michael Solomon of New York University, a specialist in the psychology of fashion, explained, "People who first wore sneakers to work did it for comfort. But now, for the yuppies, it is part of their product constellation—the uniform that's worn offstage. It makes them look like they are seriously running to get ahead." Although still occasionally seen on city streets, the sneakered look quickly became an emblem of *junior* executives and lower-level yuppies who had to walk between the subway station and their office building, as seen in the 1988 movie *Working Girl.* Upper-level management took taxicabs or limos and didn't want to affect a scurrying appearance.

Although now out of fashion among young executives (who are themselves out of fashion), sneakers remain immensely popular. Except for Keds, which has staked out the classic segment of the market with its ever-popular high tops ("no bells or whistles here," say the ads), running-shoe companies now sell millions of pairs of absolutely baroque footwear with dizzying doses of technical mumbo-jumbo reminiscent of Detroit in the glory days of 1950s moonstruck marketing. You can buy running shoes with "multi-port Hytrel elastomer lacing systems," a "visible energy wave," "recessed low-profile heel stabilizers," blown rubber outsoles, Kevlar torsion systems, ZO^2 sockliners, and untold varieties of air pockets, gels, and urethane skins for "cross training" (a term originally popularized by running-shoe companies as a label for doing two different kinds of activity in one kind of shoe). L.A. Gear advertises its "Catapult" with the tag line "It's not a shoe, it's a machine." You can even buy "sports sandals," which have high-tech soles like running shoes but open tops and a panoply of tethers to keep them secure while their adventurous wearer goes mountain climbing, kayaking, or sky diving.

No question: Running shoes have become show business, a multibillion-dollar industry known less for its connection to athletic activities than for its sports-star endorsements, its hundred-million-dollar television advertising campaigns, its role at the vanguard of commercialized street fashion, and its pithy slogans, including "Life Is Short—Play Hard" (Reebok) and "Just Do It" (Nike). The official policy at Nike, which holds nearly one-third of the running shoe market, states, "Make the best authentic athletic products for the authentic athlete, and the rest will follow," but a company spokesperson recently described its newest shoes as "performance costume design... for someone who is constantly playing on center stage." In 1990 Nike began opening Nike Town stores, which are huge sports-themed shoe-sales environments that the *New York Times* called "part Disneyland, part MTV." An official at Reebok International, second only to Nike in sales, said, "We don't consider ourselves an athletic footwear company. We are a marketing company. We build brands." In 1990 Reebok upped the ante in technological razzle-dazzle by introducing the "Pump," a shoe with an inflatable air bladder that surrounds the wearer's foot.

"Jogging shoes," *Esquire* declared in 1988, are "worn by all manner of trendy people nowadays, whether they jog or not." And among those discriminating young consumers who have made themselves connoisseurs of brand-name products and who respond eagerly to ad campaigns (for jeans, fast-food burgers, etc.), a fine pair of the newest bulky, air-bloated models has become one of the definitive totems of success—nearly as vaunted a status symbol as a car, and a sure sign of someone who knows how to live the Good Life. In fact, in a 1990 *Village Voice* article about new trends in designer running shoes, Phil Patton observed that "Nike's reputation has been scuffed by critics who say high-price sneakers encourage kids to deal drugs." Patton explained: How else could an ordinary teen get the money to buy a pair of hundred-dollar shoes?

SERGEANT BARRY SADLER

On March 5, 1966, Barry Sadler did something that parents, college deans, school principals, police officers, Bob Hope, John Wayne, J. Edgar Hoover, and other champions of law, order, and short hair had been trying to do since the Beatles stormed America in early 1964: He stopped the sixties. For the five weeks that Sadler's song "The Ballad of the Green Berets" held at number one on the *Billboard* pop chart (until toppled in April by the Righteous Brothers), it seemed almost possible to believe that life in these United States might go back to normal again. The dissent, fashion anarchy and hairdo mayhem, and even drugs and sex symbolized by such rock-and-roll chart toppers as the Rolling Stones and Sonny and Cher were all momentarily held at bay as Barry Sadler's song about heroic soldiers in Vietnam made America feel good about itself. It was the fastest-selling record in RCA history (faster than Elvis!). Sadler, an Army Sergeant who had come home with a Purple Heart after serving as a medic with the Special Forces in Vietnam, became the country's first (and arguably only) well-known 1960s war hero.

Ed Sullivan welcomed him on television. *Life* magazine showed pictures of him in his combat uniform with his wife, Lavona (in a giant-size bouffant), and son, Thor (in an outsize green beret). *Teen* magazine put a model wearing Special Forces gear on its July cover and named Sadler a "superdate" of 1966 (despite his being married), along with David McCallum (of "The Man from U.N.C.L.E."), Peter Noone (of Herman's Hermits), Luke Halpin (of "Flipper"), and Bob Dylan. Toymakers issued Barry Sadler

pop guns and field ration kits, and his face appeared on the cover of the paperback edition of Robin Moore's million-and-a-half seller *The Green Berets*.

Barry Sadler wasn't at all comfortable being the nation's pre-eminent symbol of patriotic righteousness. He didn't like being introduced as Vietnam's most decorated soldier (he was not, but many people believed he was), and when he actually had to get up and sing his number-one song—which was more a chant, recited to a tune he had borrowed from a German march—he looked pained. Sadler had wanted a musical career, not blind adulation; nothing had prepared him to be the love object of a two-hundred-thousand-member fan club. Before Vietnam he had played in a honky-tonk band in New Mexico, and fellow soldiers remember that during the war he

would often sit alone strumming a guitar and singing songs he wrote. He recorded "The Ballad of the Green Berets" originally only for military sales; when RCA picked it up and it suddenly became the biggest song of 1966, he couldn't handle the role of culture hero. He began to come unhinged: He drank too much; he womanized; it didn't take long for him to spend the half a million dollars he had earned.

Sadler took tremendous heat for what he represented: *Time* blasted "The Ballad of the Green Berets," calling it "banal and ridden with sentimentality"; some Special Forces troops were heard to complain that he had gotten rich being a celebrity while they were still slogging through jungles; there were even charges (false ones) that he had come back from Vietnam not because of wounds suffered in combat but to have hemorrhoid surgery. His follow-up song, "The A-Team," in late 1966 (well before the TV show of this name), was a dud, and by the time he was honorably discharged in 1967, the Doors' dionysian "Light My Fire" was number one on the charts. Barry Sadler's career as a songwriter stopped as quickly as it had started.

He then wrote a series of adventure novels about a character named Casca Longinius, who—cursed by Christ to wander until the end of time as history's "eternal mercenary"—shoots, strangles, decapitates, and disembowels his way through all the ghastly wars and revolutions ever fought. In 1978 he killed a man whose girlfriend he was dating (for which he served a couple of years in a halfway house), and in 1981 he shot and wounded a former business partner. The following year Sadler moved to Guatemala City, where he continued to drink and chase women, dispensed medicine and medical advice to locals, wrote more of what he called his "slaughter books," and encouraged his friends and publisher back home to think (wrongly) that he was fighting alongside the contras in Nicaragua.

In 1988 Barry Sadler was shot while sitting in the backseat of a taxicab. He lingered for fourteen months, paralyzed and incoherent, and died in November 1989. His death was listed as an accident, but some people who knew he was despondent thought it might have been suicide. One of his former buddies insists Sadler did not kill himself, that in fact he rallied in the hospital before he died and named his killer. The friend further points out that the former number-one performing artist—who had come to refer to "The Ballad of the Green Berets" as "a curse upon my soul"—always promised that he would kill himself with a hollow-point bullet from a handgun aimed into his mouth; his fatal wound, in fact, came from a full-metal-jacket round that entered the top of his head.

"SATURDAY NIGHT LIVE"

"Saturday Night Live" brought a new generation to television. Prior to its debut at 11:30 P.M. on October 11, 1975, most hip young people disdained the boob tube as hopelessly square. Even a supposedly groovy show such as "Laugh-In" (see p. 272), although stylistically daring, drew its sensibility from old-fashioned

Top: **Bill Murray, Garrett Morris, Dan Aykroyd;**
center: **Jane Curtin, Laraine Newman, Gilda Radner;**
bottom: **Chevy Chase, John Belushi**

show-biz shtick that only feigned irrever-ence. When something even a little bit naughty or sacrilegious got on the air, like "The Smothers Brothers Comedy Hour" (first broadcast in February 1967), it be-came more famous for what was censored out of it than what was left in, and even-tually it was canceled for its political and moral transgressions. Many members of a generation that had been raised on televi-sion in the 1950s grew alienated from it in the 1960s. They found their favorite means of expression in music, in movies (like *Easy Rider*), in underground comics, and—for some of the more adventurous ones—in the kind of street-theater life popularized by hippies. "TV sucks!" John Belushi ranted during his preinterview to become a regular member of the "Saturday Night Live" cast.

TV may have seemed irrelevant to most of the counterculture, but one venerable form of show business had been revitalized in the aftermath of the 1960s: stand-up com-edy. Comedy had always had a certain hip-ster appeal (e.g., Lenny Bruce), and the pro-liferation of rock concerts (needing opening acts) presented a whole new audience for comedians, especially comedians with an offbeat, psychedelic appeal. At the same time, improvisational comedy, given a shot in the arm by the street-theater tactics of such 1960 groups as the San Francisco Mime Troupe and the Yippies, was thriving, and portable video equipment (see p. 218) was beginning to allow for the development of what was known at the time as guerrilla television—shown on closed-circuit sets in city lofts, or transferred to film. *Saturday Night*, the comprehensive history of "Sat-urday Night Live" by Doug Hill and Jeff Weingrad, quotes Ken Shapiro, producer of a 1966 underground TV show called "Chan-nel One" (featuring Chevy Chase), then the hugely successful film *The Groove Tube* (1972), describing the new audience for comedy: "A gorgeous subculture, with their own language, their own jokes—and since so little of it can be broadcast over regular media, drugs and sex and such, it gives us a whole world of totally new material to work with. We like to think we're providing heads with their own CBS."

An antiestablishment sense of humor was in the air in the early 1970s: The *Na-tional Lampoon* spun away from the *Har-vard Lampoon* in 1970 and went on to produce *Lemmings*, a theater parody of the Woodstock festival, as well as the syndi-cated "National Lampoon Radio Hour." At Yale Garry Trudeau began drawing what would become "Doonesbury"; R. Crumb's "Head Comix" were ripping into the culture and counterculture equally; and Second City troupes in Chicago and Toronto were honing the satirical talents of such perform-ers as John Belushi, Bill Murray, Harold Ramis, Dan Aykroyd, Gilda Radner, and John Candy. The new sensibility came together in the cynical aftermath of the Watergate hearings and the end of the Vietnam War—as "NBC's Saturday Night," a variety show with a weekly shot of rock and roll, regular guest appearances by Jim Henson's Muppets (for the first season only), and an attitude of pissed-off impudence. It was a concept whose time had come, and it soon became a kind of cultural lightning rod for all the disillusioned creative energy that had nowhere else to go in the anxious mid-1970s.

The name of the program was changed in 1977 to "Saturday Night Live," and like the name said, it was not filmed or taped in advance, and it didn't have the safety net of retakes or a laugh track. The first show, in 1975, began without titles: John Belushi sat onstage opposite Michael O'Donoghue, and they did a bit of conceptual humor called "The Wolverines," in which Belushi, playing an earnest immigrant, learned such English phrases as "I would like to feed your fingertips to the wolverines," then dutifully imitated his instructor as his instructor had a heart attack and fell dead to the floor. "You knew you weren't watching George Gobel or Garry Moore, or whatever comedy had been," O'Donoghue said. The bit ended when Chevy Chase came on stage and hollered into the camera, "Live from New York, it's 'Saturday Night'!" This first show had many features that would become trademarks, including a "Weekend Update" satirizing the news, and comedy sketches by a repertory troupe called the Not Ready for Prime Time Players (a name chosen to mock the Prime Time Players on Howard Cosell's variety show). The show also presented Andy Kaufman nervously singing the theme from "Mighty Mouse" and a controversial monologue by guest host George Carlin, who speculated that God might be only a "semi-supreme being" because "everything he has ever made died."

Tom Shales of the Washington *Post* called it "the freshest satire on commercial TV" and praised it for being done "nakedly, brazenly, and perilously live"; although overall ratings were low, the *demographics* of the ratings were fantastic: Three out of four viewers were in the precious (to advertisers) eighteen-to-forty-nine age group. In her book *Saturday Night*, Susan Orlean recalled being at parties that would stop at 11:30 so everyone could gather around a TV set. "Watching 'Saturday Night Live' was like joining a better party that happened to be broadcast from NBC's Studio 8H," she wrote. "Getting together with friends to watch it became a social ceremony in itself." By the end of the first season, "Saturday Night" had established itself as the hippest show on television, a reputation on which it has ridden, sometimes deservedly, for the last decade and a half. Countless numbers of its regular characters, skits and bits have become popular folklore:

- John Belushi as the samurai warrior in a mundane job, starting with a "Samurai Hotel" sketch and including "Samurai Tailor" and "Samurai Psychiatrist"
- Gilda Radner as Emily Litella, who does an op-ed segment on "Weekend Update" based on her misunderstanding of a common term (such as "Soviet jewelry" rather than "Soviet Jewry"), then, when her mistake is pointed out, meekly says, "Never mind"
- Chevy Chase as a hopelessly clumsy President Gerald Ford
- Lisa Loopner and Todd DiLaMuca, the Nerds, played by Gilda Radner and Bill Murray, and Lisa's housecoated mother (Jane Curtin), known for her egg salad and Tang (The late Mr. Loopner, born without a spine, was said to have invented the Slinky.)
- The Coneheads, from the planet Remulac (Dan Aykroyd, Jane Curtin, Laraine Newman), masquerading as earthlings but never getting it exactly right

- Bill Murray as Nick, the unctuous lounge singer
- Steve Martin and Dan Aykroyd as Jorge and Yortuk Festrunk, the swinging Czech brothers, famous for their flowered shirts and geeky seduction techniques, which usually involved rhapsodizing about "large American breasts"
- Don Novello as Father Guido Sarducci, chain-smoking gossip columnist for the Vatican newspaper
- Mr. Bill, the animated clay character who winds up getting squished, usually because of his enemies Mr. Hands (human hands) and Mr. Sluggo
- Dan Aykroyd and John Belushi as the Blues Brothers (which started as a bit within a "Killer Bee" sketch, then became a preshow warm-up act)
- Dana Carvey and Mike Myers as the frizzle-brained denizens of "Wayne's World" in Aurora, Illinois.

Catch phrases viewers adopted from the show permeated pop culture, including frequent guest host Steve Martin's famous "Excuuuuse me!"; John Belushi's cry of "Cheeseburger-Pepsi" (from an ongoing sketch about the Olympia, a Greek diner); Belushi's "But nooooo!" as a zinger after reeling off a list of abuses; Dan Aykroyd's "You ignorant slut!" (to Jane Curtin on the point-counterpoint debate of "Weekend Update"); Gilda Radner's "It's always somethin'" (as huge-haired reporter Roseanne Roseannadanna). This direct line from "Saturday Night Live" into current phraseology has remained intact right up to the present: the Church Lady exclaiming "Isn't that special!"; the guy at the office copy machine festooning everybody's name ("Steve . . . the Stevemeister . . . Steveman . . ."); and the extremely popular negation of a declarative sentence by adding "not" at the end ("George Bush is doing a fine job in the White House . . . *not.*").

By the end of the 1970s, the performers of "Saturday Night Live"—no longer the Not Ready for Prime Time Players—were cover stories on national magazines, including *Newsweek, People,* and *Rolling Stone,* and they became known among an adoring press as "the Beatles of Comedy." Schoolchildren learned to give noogies to each other (a 1950s classroom torture of rubbing knuckles over someone else's head, revived by SNL nerds Todd and Lisa); the Blues Brothers were starred in a multimillion-dollar Hollywood movie (1980); commercial time on the show, which originally sold for $7,500 per minute, escalated to well over $50,000 per minute; and McDonald's was beseeching the producers to license the right to give away Roseanne Roseannadanna glasses with their hamburgers. At its peak, "Saturday Night Live" was being watched by an estimated twenty-five million viewers every week, and its guest host roster grew to include not only provocative comedians and hip young actors and musicians but also such totally straight men as Senator Daniel Patrick Moynihan of New York and consumer crusader Ralph Nader.

The program that had begun as the voice of the new video literati and the venue of a surly, defiant counterculture had become what Steve Martin called "a direct line into consumers of pop." Its popularity has varied in the last ten years, but it has continued, like Johnny Carson, to defy competition. Like so many cultural phenomena that are thrilling because they are young and brash, "Saturday Night Live" inevitably lost some of its electricity when it became so conspicuously successful. The exhilarating outlaw cachet of the first few seasons depended a lot on surprise; although it is still plenty naughty and impertinent, it is simply too familiar to be really shocking anymore. Instead, it has evolved into one of television's reliable institutions: a repertory theater for comedy writers and players who then go on to bigger and better things. Once a dangerous-seeming showcase for outsiders, "Saturday Night Live" has become the quickest and best way for an unknown performer to become a star, as has happened to, among many others, Chevy Chase, Steve Martin, Eddie Murphy, John and then Jim Belushi, Jane Curtin, Martin Short, and Billy Crystal.

ARNOLD SCHWARZENEGGER

Recently Arnold Schwarzenegger was asked why, after two decades in America, he hadn't worked harder to lose his heavy Austrian accent. He explained that he could be speaking the King's, or at least American, English by now if he had chosen to do so, but that he long ago realized he needed something "off" about him, a flaw to remind everyone that he is indeed a mortal human being. Other than the accent, and a perhaps slightly too large gap between his front teeth, Arnold is flawless. Nothing ever seems to have gone wrong in his life. He gets what he wants, and there is no apparent limit to his drawing power as a star. From the time he stepped down as the undefeated Mr. Olympia *and* Mr. Universe, he has gone on to become the highest-paid actor in the world; he has also married the woman of his dreams (Maria Shriver, in 1986), become an influential Republican and chairman of the President's Council on Physical Fitness, invested wisely in California real estate, and managed to do what so many people only dream of doing —maintain absolute control over his own perfect, fat-free body. He has enjoyed himself every step of the way, with just enough good humor and self-conscious irony about his dominion over the world of popular culture that hardly anyone resents him for his unchallenged supremacy.

With no exceptions, Arnold always portrays a character, human or not, who plays to win. Even in *Twins* and *Kindergarten Cop*, his two comedies, he gets to lick some

Arnold Schwarzenegger as Conan the Barbarian

bad guys; in his more typical action pictures, such as *Total Recall*, *Commando*, *Predator*, and the *Terminator*s, he wipes out thousands of enemies. He never gets tired, he never has self-doubts, he is never seduced by any distractions, and as he goes about his task of winning by intimidation and force, he almost always has a little grin or a wink for the camera—a bit of business that lets his audience know that he isn't really a mean son of a bitch and in fact he is having a very merry time play-acting in the role of a superhero. Because of the way he injects a soupçon of satire into every role, Arnold himself has become an idol bigger than any of the characters he has played. Like Elvis or Marilyn Monroe, it is Arnold the Star that moviegoers like to watch, not some screenwriter's invention. "In the last five years most people haven't really talked about the characters that I play," he told the *New York Times* in 1990. "I have parents coming up to me and saying you've been an example for our children and you've helped keep them off drugs, or somebody else off alcoholism, or my kids are training every day because of you," Arnold said, adding that the very hugeness of his success feeds upon itself: He is a living example of America being the land of opportunity; he is a man who came to this country as an unknown, worked hard, and made himself into a fabulous celebrity.

He wasn't exactly a nobody when, as "Arnold Strong," he acted in his first movie, *Hercules Goes to New York* (also called *Hercules Goes Bananas*), in 1970, in which the Greek superhero gets bored with life on Mount Olympus and comes to America to work as a professional wrestler. He had become Mr. Universe the previous year—the first of five such titles, as well as seven Mr. Olympias. You might have guessed back then, judging from the low standards of his

first film, that Arnold would have followed in the footsteps of Steve Reeves, the one bodybuilder before him who had managed to (barely) break out of the musclebound ghetto by playing oiled-up beefcakes in grade-B action movies.

Arnold was not like Reeves or any other bodybuilder. He made himself into the first real star of the sport—known even to people who weren't fans of bulging biceps. For him, though, it was more than a sport: It was an art. "I felt like Leonardo da Vinci," he said of his days as a teenage bodybuilder. "I was a sculptor shaping the body." From the beginning, he had a goal beyond creating a fantastic set of muscles. Arnold consciously chose bodybuilding because he believed that it would be the best way to get from the village of Thal (where he had grown up in a home without electricity or indoor plumbing) to America, where he could fulfill what he described as his boyhood "urge that I was meant for something big."

He was a winner. No one had ever dominated the sport of bodybuilding so totally, and it wasn't just because he had amassed a bigger, handsomer physique than his rivals. Arnold had charisma, and he was notorious among competitors for his scene-stealing antics during the climactic posedown, where his aggressive confidence combined with a penchant for ribbing the other contestants to always clinch the blue ribbon. In 1972, while at a Mr. America contest in New York, Arnold was recruited to be the focus of the documentary film *Pumping Iron* (released in 1977), which showed him (and other) specimens preparing for a Mr. Olympia contest. The movie was a cult hit, and its hip attitude towards huge muscles helped give bodybuilding an enlightened cachet it had never previously had. At a time when so many people were becoming obsessed with fitness and self-image, outlandishly pumped-up muscle tissue seemed especially fascinating. Arnold was certifiably the man with the best build on earth; his quick wit and the twinkle in his eye helped dispel old-fashioned ideas that guys like him had to be lunkheads; and furthermore, he bristled with ambition. There could be little doubt that this man was destined for some kind of show-business greatness.

But he was so abnormal-looking, no one would possibly accept him as an ordinary male lead in a movie: What could he do other than flex and look intimidating and add the occasional ironic zinger in the form of a cute, gap-toothed grin? Actually, that was all he had to do to become a star. Along with Clint Eastwood as Dirty Harry and Sylvester Stallone as Rambo, Arnold helped develop a new kind of film known to critics as the "Don't Mess with Me" genre and a new kind of Hollywood hero: a brutally efficient purveyor of violence whose human qualities are repressed or concealed, or in the case of Arnold's best roles, nonexistent. After *Star Wars* (1977) propelled Hollywood into the business of making high-tech, big-budget movies in which human characters are frequently less important than robots and special effects, he found his avenue to stardom by playing robots (with a sense of humor) and becoming what *Time* magazine called "a star whose body was its own stunning special effect." He played himself in *Stay Hungry* (1976) and a comic-book hunk of beefcake in the big hit *Conan the Barbarian* (1983), but his major breakthrough came as a cyborg in *The Terminator* (1984), in which the body count was significantly higher than the number of words he spoke. The role's combination of ferocity and fun fit Arnold like a tight black leather suit, and it provided the template for a career that made him, in the words of Richard Corliss, "the torch bearer, the sword wielder, the giant of American movies...the inevitable star of Hollywood's global era."

Arnold's unique mix of superheroics and comic detachment are box-office dynamite and have been the object of much analysis by social critics who get upset about the wanton violence in his movies and want to know what it means that filmgoers are so eager to root for the nonhuman brutes he plays. According to the *New York Times* in a 1990 article about his dominance of the movie business, the success of his movies "reflects something about the needs and spirit of the time," in particular the cravings for control in an insecure world and for the satisfying resolution of problems in an era of ambiguity. In all his movies, he plays characters who are virtually omnipotent and who solve problems with finality, but what is interesting about the *Times*'s analysis is that it is less about movie characters than it is about Arnold himself. He, as a cultural icon, is proving to be as invincible and indomitable as any terminator, or maybe more so. Terminators, after all, have a built-in vulnerability and are limited by the power of their microchips. Arnold, who began his career most auspiciously by literally creating himself as a physical image of perfection, has evidenced no such weakness.

SECRET AGENTS

The cold war wasn't all bad: If it weren't for the rivalry between communism and the West, popular culture might never have had its coolest 1960s role model, the secret agent. Formerly the stuff of specialized genre fiction and elaborate suspense movies by the likes of Alfred Hitchcock or Fritz Lang, spies had become very scary types of villains by the 1950s, when they were mostly presented as evil characters—slitty-eyed, sweaty, heavy-breathing Reds who intended to undermine the American Way of Life, as in Sam Fuller's *Pickup on South Street* (1952). But then a strange thing happened in the early 1960s: A new breed of spy breezed onto the scene in movies, on TV, and even in pop music. He was a good, groovy spy, a very attractive kind of spy who worked for our side. He was suave, deadly, and ever so much fun.

The new, heroic spies of the go-go years were classy individuals—not brutal hit men, perverts, or droning ideologues. They spied less for old-fashioned love of country than for a rather modish love of adventure. And they never took what they did too seriously, which made them ideal heroes for a time of disillusion and cynicism about politics. In fact, nearly every well-known pop-culture spy of the 1960s is a bit of a put-on, a parody, or a burlesque; in almost every case, the talents they have and the dangers they face are exaggerated almost to (and sometimes beyond) the point of parody. Their escapades are frequently so extremely heroic that they seem a little silly (on purpose), which makes them fun to watch without ever having to worry about the confusing business of real geopolitics. The operative word when looking at all the secret agents that shot, kissed, careened, and karate-kicked their way through pop culture during the cold war is "irony." Every one of them went about their deadly business with a wicked smirk.

The most famous smirk of all was Sean Connery's, as the movies' first James Bond, whose badge, 007, meant that he was licensed by the Crown to kill anybody he felt he ought to. Bond had been created in a series of books written by British writer Ian Fleming, starting in 1953 with *Casino Royale*. Fleming, who had once actually served in Her Majesty's Secret Service, created him as an intelligent, violent hero with a thrilling sex life and a propensity for getting into serious trouble, but it wasn't until he was elevated to the status of superhero, in the first James Bond movie, *Dr. No* (1962), that

Bill Cosby (Alexander [Scotty] Scott) and Robert Culp (Kelly Robinson)

spies started to become an obsession in America and around the world. His legitimacy as a hero was abetted by a 1963 *Life* magazine interview in which President John F. Kennedy revealed that Fleming's *From Russia with Love*, also a Bond book, was one of his favorite reads; then many other Bond novels and stories were serialized in *Playboy* (their ideal audience), for years after Fleming's death in 1964; and James Bond rose to become one of the dominant symbols of a swinging, sexually adventurous, and violence-prone decade.

Bond served as the point man for a worldwide love affair with England. He wore elegant clothes from Savile Row; he drove a Bentley and an Aston-Martin; he was well bred in a man-of-the-world way that more and more Americans yearned to be: sexually experienced, well traveled, with a finely honed taste for vintage wine and gourmet food. He was utterly unflappable, even in the direst circumstances, and he always had a witty rejoinder in every situation. He made espionage look like the most exciting job in the world; other than Hugh Hefner, he was probably the most admired man of his time.

Spying's ascent to everybody's favorite naughty amusement was facilitated not only by fictional James Bond but by the real-life British minister for war, John Profumo. As Bond's fortunes soared in 1963, Profumo's sank, but the results of their polar luck were the same: a fusion in the popular mind of espionage and hot sex with a British accent. Profumo became famous via a protracted unraveling of his life on the front pages of Fleet Street tabloids and the newspapers of the world. His problems began when he had an affair with call girl Christine Keeler, who happened to include among her clients one Captain Yevgeny Ivanov (i.e., spy). The liaison itself was racy enough, but the scandal was considerably juicier than the mere passing of tactical secrets during an illicit rendezvous (in fact, it was ultimately concluded that security had not been breached). Each time a tidbit of truth was revealed—Profumo's lies about his affair to the House of Commons, for example—torrents of crazy rumors accompanied it: Nine High Court judges regularly engaged in orgies with whores; an unidentified member of the cabinet had served dinner to a private party completely naked except for a mask and a card around his neck reading, "If my services don't please you, whip me"; another member of the cabinet had been caught with a prostitute beneath a bush in Richmond Park. No such slurs were ever proven, but all of England's leadership was suddenly fair game for the gossip mill. There was even a story going around about an unnamed member of the royal family getting it on with prostitutes.

By October 1963, as the James Bond craze was spreading worldwide, the Profumo spy-sex affair brought down the British government. It was a national shame, with the kind of moral onus Watergate later carried in America. But the important thing to know is how pop culture feasted on its forbidden mingling of secret agents, beautiful women, vital government secrets, and kinky sex. In a book called *Scandal '63*, authors Clive Irving, Ron Hall, and Jeremy Wallington suggest that the whole disgraceful episode was in fact "regarded as just one long glorious summer of vicarious excitement, novelettish intrigue, and sexual titillation...." That's pretty much what James Bond movies and a sudden worldwide glut of secret-agent heroes were supplying, too, by the middle of the decade.

Spies infested television programming in 1964 and '65, and by 1966 there were ten different shows about them on American TV. In England, "The Saint" had been popular since its radio days in the forties, and although not technically a secret agent, Simon Templar was an adventurer with exactly the qualities secret agents had to have —described by author Leslie Charteris, his creator, as "a dashing daredevil, imperturbable, debonair, preposterously handsome, who lives for the pursuit of excitement." The 1960s television Saint, syndicated in the States starting in 1963, was played by Roger Moore (later 007 in the movies). *TV Star Book* noted with amazement how much Mr. Moore had in common with the dapper detective: "quick wits, a bantering sense of humor, good looks, a fine physique, the ability to pack a punch, an appreciative eye for a pretty girl, a big following among the opposite sex, and a gay outlook on life."

Mr. Moore's qualities pretty much sum up the job requirements for all well-known secret agents during their heyday. Some of the more interesting television variations on the theme included:

- "The Man from U.N.C.L.E.," 1964–68: TV's most popular spy show, originally conceived with the help of Ian Fleming, who saw it as a tongue-in-cheek spoof of his original Bond books. Each week, Napoleon Solo (Robert Vaughn) and Ilya Kuryakin (David McCallum), agents from U.N.C.L.E. (United Network Command for Law Enforcement), enlisted the aid of an ordinary citizen to help them defeat the bad guys of T.H.R.U.S.H. (meaning unknown).
- "I Spy," 1965–68: A lighthearted drama about a Rhodes scholar (Bill Cosby) and a Princeton graduate (Robert Culp) who pretend to be a trainer and a tennis pro but are actually spies whose adventures take them around the world.
- "Get Smart," 1965–70: A spoof about inept Agent 86, Maxwell Smart (Don Adams), with a bright but long-suffering partner, Agent 99 (Barbara Feldon); also featuring an undercover dog named Fang. Agent Smart contributed many funny expressions

to 1960s vernacular, including "Sorry about that, Chief," "Would you believe . . . ?" and "Missed it by *that* much."
- "Mission: Impossible," 1966–73: This adventure differed from other secret-agent shows in that it had no single charismatic hero and little in the way of witty badinage, and there were seldom intimations of sex. But it had gadgets and gizmos galore, and more plot twists than a bag of pretzels as the Impossible Missions Force (IMF) executed a convoluted conspiracy that usually involved saving a third-world country in danger of being controlled by an evil dictator.
- "Honey West," 1965–66: Honey West (Anne Francis) was more a private eye than a secret agent, but she frequently got involved in undercover espionage. She had a pet ocelot and was billed as the gal who "packs a .38 automatic and a lethal command of karate [with] curves deadlier than a cobra."
- "The Girl from U.N.C.L.E.," 1966–67: Secret agent April Dancer (Stefanie Powers) was "108 pounds of dynamite with trained-to-kill reflexes and an IBM brain."

Bond-inspired spies populated movies as well as television. Big-screen agents ranged from merry spoofster Derek Flint (James Coburn) in *Our Man Flint* (1966) and its sequel, *In Like Flint* (1967), to stripper Chesty Morgan as herself in *Deadly Weapons* (1968), a motion picture in which Ms. Morgan used her capacious breasts to smother Russian agents. Dean Martin went spying as Matt Helm in four off-color, nudie-cutie send-ups, including *The Silencers* (1966) and *The Ambushers* (1967); and even Doris Day played the spy game in Frank Tashlin's jaw-dropping surrealistic caper flick, *Caprice* (1967), in which Miss Day, still wearing her taut girdle and ladylike silk suit from the glory days of *Pillow Talk*, outwitted a whole cast of international villains. There were hit songs about secret agents, too, including Johnny Rivers's "Secret

Agent Man" (from the TV series "Secret Agent") and Edwin Starr's "Agent Double-O Soul."

One of the characteristic aspects of virtually all the great spies of the James Bond era was their love of gadgets, which translated into big profits for anyone with espionage-related toys or fashions to sell: suave trench coats, hats like Oddjob wore in *Goldfinger*, toy spymobiles, all manner of leisure wear, including 007 ladies' panties (but not brassieres—rejected as "not sophisticated"), bubble gum, and a men's aftershave lotion called 007, that advertised it gave "any man the license to kill women." Spies became famous for having a marvelous tool for every occasion, which was a real inspiration to so many upwardly mobile members of the middle class, who were learning to modernize their lives, too, with appurtenances of all kinds, ranging from remote-control color televisions to push-button dishwashers. The basic idea, for spy as for ordinary homeowner, was that survival (or at least happiness) depended on possessing the right stuff. Included among the necessary tools were:

- *James Bond's attaché case.* It held a break-apart Armalite rifle with a telescopic sight, as well as solid gold coins and throwing knives; and it was booby-trapped in such a way that it gassed anyone who opened it without punching in the secret code. (Attaché cases were a requisite spy accoutrement, not only for carrying weapons but also for hauling around hundreds of thousands of dollars in neat little stacks, when necessary. The use of attaché cases to carry huge bundles of money, originally popularized by secret agents in the sixties [as a sign of their cool VIP demeanor], has remained a fundamental icon of pop culture. In older days, satchels and doctors' bags were the more common way to carry ransoms, etc.)

- *Maxwell Smart's telephone.* Conceived by "Get Smart" writer Mel Brooks, Agent 86's secret phone was built into the sole of one of his shoes. The earpiece was in the heel, which also had room for pills and other small oddments. It rang just like a normal phone, frequently flummoxing Smart during moments when he was trying to sneak somewhere quietly.

- *The "Mission: Impossible" tape recorder:* At the beginning of every episode, agent Jim Phelps (Peter Graves) would go to an inconspicuous phone booth or men's room where he would rendezvous with a little reel-to-reel tape recorder that played a message describing his mission, should he choose to accept it. Once the message was played, the tape recorder self-destructed in a belch of smoke.

- *Derek Flint's cigarette lighter:* Flint's only weapon, capable of performing eighty-three separate functions. It could transmit and receive secret messages, function as a blowtorch, and when thrown on the ground, release toxic smoke to immobilize a foe. Flint also had shirt buttons that pulled out of their buttonholes to become a stethoscope used for safecracking and a watch that put him into suspended animation so his enemies would think he was dead. The watch then woke him up at a predetermined time by gently tickling his wrist.

- *James Bond's car:* The best-known of all secret-agent gadgets, Bond's Aston-Martin was equipped with bulletproof glass, a machine gun, the power to lay down an oil slick and a smoke screen, and a high-powered ejector to shoot the driver out and up through the roof if a quick exit became necessary.

Secret-agent mania waned in the 1970s, and although Bond movies continued to be made (most starring Roger Moore), the gadget-filled, globe-trotting life of secret agents now seems a relic of another era. Back in the 1960s, one marketer of James

Bond souvenirs called 007 "Mr. Kiss-Kiss Bang-Bang," because there was sex for grown-ups and thrills for kids, but the tongue-in-cheek attitude that was the soul of secret-agent films has lost most of its appeal for young and old alike. One of the problems in appreciating the charisma of spies in recent years has been the unpleasant demeanor of real-life operatives who have surfaced in some of the well-publicized treason trials: dumpy Washington functionaries shown on TV news being escorted to and from the courtroom wearing ill-fitting spongy slacks, K-Mart polo shirts, and big nerd shoes. James Bond and all the other spies who populated the shared mythology of prehippie years weren't like these losers at all. They were the essence of savoir faire, always on their way to some fabulously interesting location, like a Swiss ski resort, to save the world—and while they were at it, to plunge into round-the-clock adventure, to exchange bons mots with rich and powerful people, to drive fast sports cars, to drink dry martinis, and to indulge in gymnastic lovemaking with gorgeous partners at a time when casual sex seemed guiltless, consequence-free, and the last word in sophistication.

7-ELEVEN

A sick child starts coughing at three in the morning. A lonely trucker highballing through the night craves coffee and a heart-to-heart chat with some fellow drivers. An eager young executive snares her pantyhose just minutes before an important meeting. A boy who fails to get the game-winning hit in a Little League game yearns for consolation.

What do these people have in common? They all find what they need at a 7-Eleven store: cough syrup for the tot; hot coffee and a good bull session for the gearjammer; pantyhose for the lady on her way up the corporate ladder; and two Slurpees for the kid who couldn't get a piece of the baseball. Their stories are contained in a mesmerizing book called *Oh Thank Heaven!* written by Allen Liles in 1976 to celebrate the fiftieth anniversary of America's premier convenience store. (The title of the book, by the way, comes from an advertising slogan ini-

tiated in 1969—"Oh Thank Heaven for 7-Eleven"—that inspired Jerry Lewis to write a song by the same name, which he sang during his 1976 Muscular Dystrophy Telethon. That year 7-Eleven gave over three million dollars to Jerry's kids.) This is how *Oh Thank Heaven!* (the book) begins:

> All day and all night they come. Mostly working people moving to and from their labors. . . . They flow in and out. . . . Slurpee cups are filled, ice cream novelties or candy chosen, an errand for Mom handled. . . . Milk, bread, groceries, beer, cigarettes and thousands of other products or services are waiting, ready to be found. . . . Several million people will enter the little stores before this day ends. Their lives will be touched, their needs will be served.

7-Eleven stores are the butt of a lot of comedians' jokes—about their third-world employees and corn-dog cuisine, about trashy teens who cruise the parking lot, and about the crime rate because they are open through the night—but it's hard to imagine America without them. We are a nation that demands convenience, so it is only right that convenience stores are what we get. Like car salesmen and politicians, they are ridiculed with gusto, but gosh, it sure is nice to know that wherever you are in this great land, at any time of day or night, you are never far from a Big Gulp, a Big Grab, and a Big Bite, which are 7-Eleven's tantalizing names for some of their culinary specialties —soda pop, french fries, and a quarter-pound frankfurter, respectively.

The world's first convenience store grew out of an ice station run by the Southland Ice Company in the Oak Cliff section of Dallas. The idea was to supplement ice sales (slow in winter) with groceries. When an employee came back from Alaska with a souvenir totem pole, Southland adopted it for a logo, and the dozen ice docks they ran became known as Tote'm Serv-Ice stations. By the mid-thirties, Tote'm stores were the biggest dairy retailer in the Dallas–Fort Worth area, and in 1946, with some seventy stores in north Texas, the name was changed to 7-Eleven, signifying good luck as well as operating hours from early morning to late at night. Within a few years the company expanded throughout Texas, selling ice-cold watermelons with a money-back guarantee and boasting of its own "sharp-frozen" heat-and-eat corn dogs. 7-Elevens opened in Florida in 1954, then in Louisiana and up the East Coast. In 1959 Southland bought 7-Eleven's main competitor in Dallas, Cabell's, Inc. (where double-dip ice cream cones had been invented in 1932); in the sixties, it bought Minit Markets (Arizona and New Jersey), Scotty Stops and E-Z Ways (Colorado), Speedee Marts (California), Quick Marts (Boston), Open Pantry (Illinois), and Pak-A-Sak (Louisiana and the Deep South). By the end of the decade there were 3,537 7-Elevens, plus 121 Gristede's grocery stores and 145 Barricini candy stores (both of which were now owned by Southland).

7-Eleven's best-known product, the Slurpee, was introduced in 1965, based on a substance invented in 1959 by Dean Sperry and Omar Knedlik of Dallas. Sperry and Knedlik had figured out a way to freeze water with carbon dioxide and flavored syrup just enough so the resulting suds could be dumped out of a freezer into a cup and sucked up a straw as it melted. They called their sweet secretion Icee, and they sold Icee machines to drugstores and drive-ins. Only 7-Eleven, however, which had years of experience in the refrigeration business, knew how to keep temperamental Icee machines running at full efficiency. The name was soon changed to fit the sound the festively colored lather made when going up a straw, and Slurpees became 7-Eleven's signature draft.

When 7-Eleven first went to round-the-clock operation at its Las Vegas stores in the summer of 1963, profits went up and a fringe benefit was noted: There were no after-hours burglaries. By the end of the sixties, there were ever more twenty-four-hour stores around the country, but now instead of burglaries they began to face a problem that has since become endemic in the convenience-store business: armed robberies, as depicted in nearly every movie and television show about urban crime in the last twenty years. 7-Eleven's expansion program (to nearly six thousand stores by the mid-seventies) began to face strong opposition from some communities who felt their mere presence actually attracted crime, or at least noisy and annoying adolescents who loitered in the parking lot smoking cigarettes and drinking beer. Just two years ago, some of its stores in the Northwest successfully dealt with the loitering problem by blasting music into the parking lot: *easy listening* music, which the local thugs couldn't stand to hear. "They won't hang around and tap their feet to Mantovani," declared a 7-Eleven spokesperson after a mellow-string concert cleared a parking lot in Tillicum, Washington, of all undesirables.

In 1991, when the Southland Corporation found itself sinking in an extra Big Gulp of debt, it was rescued from bankruptcy by the Seven-Eleven [sic] Company of Japan. Originally licensed by Southland, the Japanese had improved on the Texas-born convenience-store formula and made it ultra-efficient by the use of P.O.S. (point of sale) computers, which it is anticipated they will bring to America to improve business. Seven-Eleven Japan stores also added sliced octopus and boiled tofu to the inventory (which they are not planning to put into stateside stores), and they created a catalog of such luxury imported goods as Cartier gifts and Tiffany watches. The catalog is called *Shop America.*

"THE SIMPSONS"

These are some of the famous things Bart Simpson, star of the animated TV show called "The Simpsons," says:

- "Outta my way, man"
- "Eat my shorts"
- "Don't have a cow"
- "No way, man"
- "Aye, caramba!"
- "Cowabunga."

Bart Simpson was not the first to say any of these phrases, but now they belong to him, and they are displayed in dialogue balloons above his head on millions and millions and millions of T-shirts, bumper stickers, beach towels, and approximately one hundred other licensed (and God knows how many unlicensed) products. Not since the ascent of the Teenage Mutant Ninja Turtles (see p. 512) has there been such a profitable marketing phenomenon.

People love Bart Simpson because he's an adorable mischief maker. Unlike television's diligent and well-meaning children,

MATT GROENING

from Ozzie and Harriet Nelson's boys and Opie Taylor to the Cosbys, he belongs to the Dennis the Menace school of impishness. He doesn't keep his room clean, his skateboarding terrorizes pedestrians, he makes phony phone calls, he is an incorrigible cheater on school tests as well as home video games, he watches violent cartoon shows on television, and his favorite riposte to all authority figures is "Eat my shorts." Of course, he has a good heart—he tries to defend his sister against the school bully—and his hijinks and rudeness are tempered by a streak of adult sarcasm, not to mention an extraordinary command of language for a ten-year-old. "I paid the inevitable price for helping out my kid sister," he says when the bully stuffs him into a garbage can.

Like Bart, the other members of the Simpson family are antiheroes with good souls. His father, Homer, is nothing like those wise and judicious TV dads Ward Cleaver ("Leave It to Beaver") and Jim Anderson ("Father Knows Best"). He's a downtrodden type of guy who works in a nuclear plant where he spends most of his time eating donuts and sucking up to the boss. At home he loses his temper, has all the wrong answers to family problems, and feels sorry for himself. His wife, Marge, who sports a blue beehive hairdo that has been compared with the coif of the bride of Frankenstein, struggles in vain to make him and Bart more couth. And there are Lisa, the three-year-old who is a goody-two-shoes always baiting Bart, and baby Maggie, who brainlessly sucks on a pacifier.

As a group, they are crude and obnoxious, "the worst family in town" according to Homer, and they all treat one another with a kind of thoughtless disrespect that has made them the darlings of viewers who delight in the inversion of TV's more typical glorification of family life. "The Simpsons" is not the first program to play the ugly underbelly of home life for laughs. "The Honeymooners" did it (although the Kramdens were childless); "All in the Family" did it; and "Married...With Children," which came on the air the same time as "The Simpsons," is still doing it. One of the reasons people enjoy the antics of Bart and his family so much is that they seem to be an antidote to most of television's tendency to sugar-coat the notion of blood relations, who, after all, are not necessarily always so comforting. "This show gets to the heart of the family as few sitcoms have," wrote USA Today's TV critic Matt Roush. "It's all a love/hate relationship." When "The Simpsons" was scheduled opposite "Cosby" on Thursday night, it wasn't the usual programming battle of lookalike shows: It was a rivalry based on principles. Just as the Cosby family is a caricature of warmth, ethics, respect, morality, success, and high ideals, the Simpsons are a burlesque of boorishness, impudence, ineptitude, vulgarity, failure, and cynicism.

People magazine praised the series when it first went on the air as an example of the Fox network "busting through TV's archaic sense of propriety," calling it "the most subversive beast in the Fox den." Harry Shearer, who does many of the show's voices, including radio psychologist Dr. Marvin Monroe and Homer's boss, Mr. Burns, attributed the show's unusual level of irreverence to the fact that it became successful so fast that none of the executives in charge had a chance to test-market it, screen it for focus groups of typical viewers, tinker with it, and soften its sharp edges. "The networks listen to everyone," he said. "They try so hard to make the characters likable to everyone. There was no time for that with 'The Simpsons' because it all happened so quickly."

The way it happened is this: When James L. Brooks produced "The Tracey Ullman Show" for the fledgling Fox network in 1987, he added a series of short animated segments as buffers between the live-action skits and commercials. The cartoons were about the Simpsons, a family of bug-eyed misfits drawn by Matt Groening, who wrote and directed the shows, and whose "Life in Hell" comic strip, about a family of maladjusted bucktoothed rabbits, had gone from an underground cult to big-time success in over two hundred newspapers by the mid-1980s. Critics adored "The Tracey Ullman Show" for its creativity, but audiences were much more enamored of the thirty- and sixty-second cartoons, which Brooks expanded into a half-hour TV Christmas special in 1989 called "The Simpsons Roasting on an Open Fire" (in which Bart yearns to get a tattoo and Homer loses all his money at the dog track). The following month, "The Simpsons" was on the regular schedule, and by spring it was among TV's fifteen top-rated shows. That fall, it was scheduled opposite the heretofore invincible "Cosby,"

and although it didn't top the "Cosby" ratings, it did very well, and it has continued to be a ratings success and a mind-boggling pop-culture phenomenon.

What is especially remarkable about Simpson mania is that grown-ups like it every bit as much as children. Unlike Saturday-morning cartoons, which are mostly jumbles of mindless motion and kinetic kicks, "The Simpsons" has the same sarcastic bite that made the tortured and alienated rabbits of "Life in Hell" so popular. But there is a difference: Whereas "Life in Hell" and the thirty-second Simpson bits on "The Tracey Ullman Show" were relentlessly cynical, "The Simpsons" has been considerably easier to swallow since it became a half-hour TV program. Goofy and disrespectful as it continues to be, the show almost always offers a tidy lesson in life on a par with the most earnest live-action family situation comedies. "There's a real message for adults in this episode," critic Matt Roush noted about the one in which Bart is mistakenly put into a class for gifted children and feels uncomfortable about it. Among the messages delivered are skepticism about IQ tests, a critique of parents who base their love on a child's accomplishments, and an expression of the uneasiness children feel when joining a new class. Other "Simpsons" episodes tackled such issues as envy of other people's material goods (Homer wants a camper like the neighbors'), the undue emphasis put on popularity in school (Bart cuts off the head of a statue to win his classmates' admiration), male chauvinism (Homer treats a belly dancer as a sex object), and even child exploitation (Bart is taken advantage of by some wine makers).

"The Simpsons" is popular and also hip, as evidenced by the fact that many celebrities are eager to do the voices for its characters. Fans of the show delight in hearing guest roles played by such familiar old TV favorites as Marcia Wallace (Carol, the receptionist, on "The Bob Newhart Show"), Penny Marshall (Laverne on "Laverne and Shirley"), and Kelsey Grammer (Frazier on "Cheers"). Roseanne Arnold and Michael Jackson have supplied voices, too, and the recently published book *Simpson Mania: The History of TV's First Family* revealed that Whoopi Goldberg has volunteered to play Maggie if the baby of the family ever graduates from sucking sounds to words.

FRANK SINATRA

"The toughest minds in the entertainment world soften and melt into blobs of wonder when they contemplate the phenomenon of this man," wrote one enraptured journalist in 1961. For half a century now, fans and critics have contemplated Frank Sinatra, and most of them have melted into blobs trying to figure out how, exactly, to describe him.

In one way it's easy. He is a singer, or as he would put it, a "saloon singer," with a warm, husky voice that suggests not so much the craftsmanship of a trained vocalist as a guy simply singing what he feels. Sinatra has a way of making a song his, and crooning it with such convincing familiarity that members of the audience easily imagine he is singing only to them.

Whatever the dimensions of his artistry, he is without any question the most enduringly successful singer in the history of popular music. One of his earliest recordings, "I'll Never Smile Again," was the number-one song on *Billboard*'s first chart, the week of July 20, 1940; since then he has sold hundreds of millions of records, and established more pop standards than anyone else —from "Night and Day" and "Witchcraft" to "My Way" and the "Theme from *New York, New York.*"

Tremendous as his musicianship may be, Frank Sinatra is something more than his actual talent and achievements. From 1942, when young female admirers, known as "Sinatratics," packed New York's Paramount Theater to faint and cry and throw their brassieres and panties onto the stage as he sang, to 1991, when Nancy Reagan's unauthorized biographer, Kitty Kelley, hinted that he was the First Lady's steady

White House paramour (Secret Service code name: Napoleon), Frank Sinatra has always been a provocative symbol—a guy most people either love or love to hate.

Born in Hoboken, New Jersey, he decided to become a singer after being impressed by a Bing Crosby concert in Jersey City. It was 1936; he was twenty-one. After performing for a while with a group he assembled called the Hoboken Four, he went solo and by 1939 was a singing headwaiter at the Rustic Cabin nightclub in Teaneck. Harry James heard him and hired him to sing with his band; then he went with Tommy Dorsey, and in 1942 he set out on his own. When he stepped on stage at New York's Paramount Theater on December 30 that year, some members of the audience screamed with joy. Among the crowd was press agent George Evans, who, when he saw fans convulse in rapture at the sight of their Frankie, was inspired. Evans's subsequent work publicizing Sinatra is now a show-business legend. Building on an already fanatical core of followers, he paid bobby-soxers to yell "Oh, Frankie!" whenever Frank started to sing a slow song; he instructed them to yell "Oh, Daddy!" when he sang "Come to Papa"; he showed some how to faint; and he hired an ambulance to wait outside the theater to tend to those overcome inside. For every dozen girls hired to moan, hundreds more did so of their own volition. It is impossible to know how much of the early delirium was created by George Evans and to what extent Evans simply milked what was there anyway; whatever the case, Frank Sinatra became the first modern symbol of celebrity built by hype.

He symbolized more than that. In the early days he was called "the Voice" or—in honor of the bobby-soxers who fainted when he sang or caressed the microphone —"Swoonatra." As would happen with Elvis a dozen years later, his effect on fans scared the hell out of custodians of the moral order, who saw him as a bad influence and a sign that social decency and propriety were disintegrating. "We can't tolerate young people making a public display of losing control of their emotions," announced New York City's commissioner of education. On the floor of Congress, Sinatra was called "the prime instigator of juvenile delinquency in America." Elsa Maxwell described the fans at one concert as "emotionally unstable females who paraded naked and unashamed for the drooling, crooning, goonish syllables of a man who looked like a second-string basketball player." On Columbus Day, 1944, thirty thousand of them practically tore the Paramount Theater to the ground—"the worst mob scene in New York since nylons went on sale," according to the police chief. Earl Wilson reported that cries of "Frankie, Frankie!" could be heard blocks away: "a rumble like distant thunder."

Not everyone in attendance at the October riots was an idolater. One teenage boy threw raw eggs at Sinatra, and soon sailors outside were heaving tomatoes at his picture on the marquee. To young boys at home who lost their girls to the Doctor of Swoonology, but especially to those in the armed services, Frankie symbolized something else altogether: the insecurity they felt about girls acting so unabashedly sexual in his presence. This was especially annoying to soldiers overseas, starved for companionship, who were treated to Army newspaper photographs of Frankie surrounded by adoring girls. Writer William Manchester, who served with the Marines, called Frank Sinatra "the most hated man of World War II, much more than Hitler." Elsa Maxwell suggested that all the girls who loved him so uncontrollably be given "Sinatraceptives."

The next chapter in Sinatra mythology describes a painful descent into shame and ignominy after his initial blaze into the pop-culture pantheon. Record sales went downhill as bobby-soxers grew up, and Sinatra himself began having throat problems. He made many movies in the late 1940s and early 1950s, some of them fun *(Anchors Away, On the Town)*, but none earned him serious recognition as an actor. His TV series, "The Frank Sinatra Show," was unable to survive against competition from Sid Caesar and (in its second year) Milton Berle. Then, as with so many fabled careers with soaring comebacks (Elvis on TV in '68, Winston Churchill in England in '51), Sinatra reinvented himself. Considered box-office poison, especially in nonsinging roles, he begged Columbia's Harry Cohn for the role of the wry, pathetic Italian-American Private Maggio in the film version of James Jones's bestselling novel *From Here to Eternity* (1953). For a total paycheck of $8,000 (he had previously received $150,000 per picture), Sinatra got the part. He won an Oscar for his performance and suddenly had a booming new career—as a serious actor in such subsequent heavyweight pictures as *The Man with the Golden Arm, Some Came Running*, and *The Manchurian Candidate*. About the same time, he teamed up with music arranger Nelson Riddle at Capitol, who helped turn him, in the words of one biography, "from a down-and-out ex-crooner into the most magnetic musical communicator and the ace mood-pitcher of the era." On such albums as *Songs for Swingin' Lovers, Come Fly with Me*, and *Only the Lonely*, Sinatra established himself as a mature, masterful stylist, singing to what he called "the tempo of the heartbeat" in a deceptively unaffected manner that writer Daniel Okrent described this way:

He learned to lay back on the beat, to let the rhythm of his accompaniment tug him along, opening up the line of the song before him, making a lyric into a story. . . . In his ballad singing, the infinitesimal lagging accents his ache, his hurt. All but imperceptibly, the listener moves to the edge of his chair, soon to the edge of his emotions, longing for the rhythmic resolution that only comes at the end of a telling phrase.

No longer a fetish of teenage bobby-soxers, the new Frank Sinatra crystallized an image of masculinity supremely well suited to the new libertinism of the late fifties and early sixties (see "Playboy," p. 388). Nicknamed "the Chairman of the Board" by New York disc jockey Willie B. Williams, Sinatra became known for his practiced irreverence, his libidinous pleasure-seeking, and a treacherous emotional volatility with a placid veneer that simply defined the concept of "cool" at the time—and for many people, continues to do so today. *Ring-a-Ding-Ding*, the jaunty name of one of his first albums for his own label, Reprise, became an expression that epitomized his brand of macho appeal as much as "Go ahead, make my day" came to stand for Clint Eastwood's in a later time. "Ring-a-ding-ding": its jazzy, abstract joie de vivre perfectly communicated the devil-may-care swagger of the saloon singer who was nobody's man but his own.

As Chairman of the Board, Frank was the gang leader of a group of celebrities known as the Rat Pack. The original bunch by that name, a group of cynical Hollywood cutups that included Humphrey Bogart and Lauren Bacall, John Huston, Spencer Tracy, Judy Garland, agent Swifty Lazar, and Katharine Hepburn, had called themselves the Holmby Hills Rat Pack and actually had a stated purpose: "to spit in the eye of Hollywood custom and get away with it." Basically, what they did was drink, stay up late, make fun of people they considered square, and say outrageous things to the press. Sinatra's Rat Pack, also known as the Clan, was not quite so official; in fact, all its members denied that there even was such an entity. But the public loved the idea because it made so much sense to cast Frank Sinatra as the leader of a tight-knit group of high-rolling hipsters who had figured out the fine art of adult partying (in smoky rooms, with high-balls in their hands). They even had their own groovy language, which Sinatra explained to Art Buchwald for an article in the New York *Herald Tribune*:

> *Gas:* "A good situation. An evening can be a wonderful gas."
> *Gasser:* "A person. A big-leaguer, the best."
> *Harvey:* "A square, the typical tourist who goes into a French restaurant and says, 'What's ready?'"
> *Broad:* "An affectionate word for 'woman.' Calling a girl a 'broad' is far less coarse than calling her a 'dame.'"
> *Fink:* "A loser."
> *Clyde:* "If I want someone to pass the salt, I say, 'Pass the Clyde.' 'I don't like her Clyde' might mean 'I don't like her voice.' 'I have to go to the Clyde' could mean 'I have to go to the party.'"
> *All Locked Up:* Used when Sinatra has an engagement for the evening, usually with a broad.

In a 1961 book called *Sinatra and His Rat Pack*, Richard Gehman explained that the gang's name, as applied to Sinatra and his pals, first came into use during the presidential campaign of 1960, when all the guys did their best to get Kennedy elected. Republican reporters, resenting their efforts, started calling them the Rat Pack as a term of derision and contempt. But it conveyed just the right rude audacity to appeal to Sinatra's fans, who liked the way the pack seemed to relish sabotaging social order and convention. Gehman's analysis included a complete members' roster, with nicknames, titles, and positions—the obsessive details of which deliciously express people's fascination with the groovy little countercultural society in which Sinatra was the principal player.

> Frank Sinatra *(The Leader, The General, The Dago, The Pope;* also known to columnists as *Frankie-Boy)*: Boss.
> Dean Martin *(Dino, The Admiral)*: Sommelier.
> Sammy Davis, Jr. *(Sam)*: Tummler. (*"Tummler"* is a word used in Borscht Circuit resorts for someone who keeps the place in a tumult.)
> Peter Lawford *(Pete)*: Liaison Man With the Other Government of the Country.
> Joey Bishop *(Joe)*: Needler.
> Shirley MacLaine *(Shirl)*: Mascot.
> Tony Curtis *(Tony)*: Scout Leader.
> Jimmy Van Heusen *(Chester)*: Keeper of the Royal Exchequer.
> Sammy Cahn *(Sammy)*: Court Wholesaler. (According to Billy Wilder, Cahn has an ability to get almost anything wholesale for his friends, but this is not the only reason he is treasured by the clan. The members like his music, too.)
> Irving Paul Lazar *(Swifty)*: Director of Sanitation, Social Director, and Liaison Man With the Other "A" Group [important producers and studio heads]. (Lazar has entirely too much energy to hold down only one job; he therefore has three. He also is the only Rat Packer who moves into the "AA" group [the Hollywood establishment].)
> Harry Kurnitz *(Kurnitz)*: Roving Ambassador.

Mr. Gehman goes on to enumerate people who are "Rat Pack Affiliates," a list too long to reproduce here except to note that among its members is listed "John F. Kennedy: President."

It is also notable that Gehman says the full list of people who have been "in and out of the circle" includes "roughly five thousand girls, perhaps more." He has been married four times, to Nancy Barbato, Ava Gardner, Mia Farrow, and Barbara Marx; but beyond marital vows, he has always been a ladies' man. In the heyday of the Rat Pack in the early sixties, being smooth with the broads and bedding lots of them was considered by an awful lot of quite respectable people to be extremely suave. Consider such vintage culture heroes as James Bond, Hugh Hefner, and Warren Beatty, not to mention John F. Kennedy, whose secret appeal for many was his (then merely) rumored prowess with the ladies.

As leader of the Rat Pack, Frank Sinatra lived what was, by the standards of swingers' sophistication a quarter-century ago, a dream life: women by the dozen, booze and cigarettes aplenty, parties until dawn, close connections with the Kennedy clan (he staged the preinauguration gala in 1960) . . . and widely rumored friendships with Mafia figures. Despite a photograph of Frank apparently hobnobbing with the likes of Tommy "Fatso" Marson, Jimmy "the Weasel" Fratianno, Paul Castellano, and Richard "Nerves" Fusco, no one has ever legally proven anything bad about Frank and the mob, but facts are not the issue when it comes to his image as a culture hero. What matters is the prevalent impression that he has important friends on the wrong side of the law, and there are large numbers of Sinatra fans who relish that notion: It adds to what has increasingly been part of his peculiar glamour, which is the sense of danger he exudes, and his defiance of straight-laced propriety. Gay Talese said "He is [one of] what in traditional Sicily have long been called *uomini rispettati*—men of respect: men who are both majestic and humble, men who are loved by all and are very generous by nature, men whose hands are kissed as they walk from village to village, men who would *personally* go out of their way to redress a wrong."

Famous for spontaneous acts of charity to friends and strangers (he once sent money to Bela Lugosi when he heard that the former Dracula was now destitute and had checked into a hospital to shake an addiction to morphine), he is also known for equally spontaneous outbursts of violent temper. Just as friends can enumerate a lifetime of his charitable and humanitarian activities, critics like to trot out long lists of incidents that prove he is a mean bully: to people in the press he doesn't like, to coworkers, to a guy who didn't mix his martini the way he wanted it. Now that he is in his seventies, Sinatra's notorious willingness to speak his mind and—when he was younger —use his fists have made him seem rather like an elderly Godfather of pop music, still fearsome in his way, but with the roar muted to a snarl.

Sinatra's pre-eminence as an entertainer began to wane in the late sixties, when, like many adults, he had a hard time dealing with the cultural upheavals that transformed the United States from a nice place into a country that was, in his words, "so screwed up." Having once been the original teen dream, he found himself very much a member of the older generation in an era when almost all pop culture had been seized by youth, and when the kind of cool he once exuded began to look passé (although he still managed to send "Strangers in the Night" and "Something Stupid" to the top of the charts in 1966 and 1967 [the latter with his daughter, Nancy]). In fact, his glitzy, show-bizzy, annual one-hour TV specials from 1965 to 1970, during which he sang many of his classic hits, became a beacon for fans of old-fashioned pop music at a time when it seemed like rock and roll was everywhere.

The Rat Pack grew up and got old, and that was not a pretty thing to see. Instead of seeming like the insolent, fast-living Bohemians they used to be, their on-stage reunions—for the sake of TV specials and benefit concerts—have tended to have a pained air of sycophancy and self-congratulation. One newspaper described a two-hour TV show called "Sinatra: The First 40 Years" as "a display of public groveling that would have embarrassed anyone except the gentleman in question, Mr. Frank Sinatra." The article went on to say, "That such beautiful music should emerge from such vulgarity is one of the great mysteries of the age."

Although he retired from show business in 1971, he returned two years later for a TV special called "Ol' Blue Eyes Is Back" and has continued to record albums and make movies, including *Cannonball Run II* (1984), in which he played Frank Sinatra. In 1985 Ronald Reagan presented him with the nation's highest civilian award, the Presidential Medal of Freedom. It was an event much rued by anti-Sinatra people, who felt his associations with morally bad characters ought to disqualify him, and also by anti-Reagan people, who felt that an award to a mere saloon singer proved once and for all that the President wasn't a deep person. But in his presentation speech, Reagan explained why Sinatra deserved it: "His love of country, his generosity for those less fortunate, his distinctive art, and his winning and compassionate persona make him one of our most remarkable and distinguished Americans and one who truly did it his way."

SKATEBOARDING

Skateboarding has been a big fad three times, once in each decade since the 1960s, and in the interstices between the hype it has evolved into a subculture complete with its own lingo, fashion, and faintly peevish attitude.

It is hard not to think of it as the lesser version of surfing. That's how it got popular the first time, in the early 1960s—as a way for surfers to keep in shape and sharpen their balance when the surf wasn't up by riding on roller-skate wheels affixed to a flat board. But the fact is that, while surfing on an ocean wave has a more venerable history and far more prestige as a sport, it is

actually less dangerous than riding a skateboard over concrete and asphalt. Furthermore, many of today's most advanced surfing moves have been derived from skateboarding. That's what *Thrasher*, the skateboarders' magazine, said in August 1991:

> Surfing may have given skating its birth, plus a couple of moves like the bert and the layback, but skating is paying surfing back tenfold in the air/lip trick department with endless variations on lien airs, stalefish grabs, indy airs, ollies, rock and rolls, and cess slices.... Even the concept of wallrides translates into the vertical or over-vertical environment of gnarly shorebreak.

One reason skateboarding doesn't get the respect tendered surfing is that it appears by comparison mundane: Doing nose wheelies and belly whoppers or popping an ollie railslide into a bench at the K-Mart parking lot simply doesn't have the cosmic punch of conquering the storm waves at Waikiki. Also, while surfers tend to be athletic, sexy young men and women, nearly all skateboarders are pubescent boys. No one knows precisely how skateboarding came into being, but it seems logical to speculate that it may have been invented by a wannabe surfer too young to drive a car (necessary to transport board to beach), who simply attached roller skates to a slat of wood and made a modern variation of the old-fashioned soapbox scooter, but without a balance handle.

Like so many teenagers, skateboarders feel at odds with the rest of the world. In a letter to *Thrasher*, Shawn McCarty of New Jersey wrote: "I'd just like to give my definition of a skater: an outcast of society, a social misfit. One who rips and tears on concrete anytime, anywhere, and who defies the laws of gravity in an upward motion. A

human or such who grabs a simple piece of wood and flies down that surface like it was nothing."

The first time around, the boards were solid oak or ash with hard wheels, and they tended to be long and cumbersome, allowing only basic slalom maneuvers, storm drain 360s, limbo leaps, and high-speed downhill racing. Starting in southern California, spurred by Jan and Dean's 1964 hit "Sidewalk Surfin'" (which included actual sounds of skateboarding as a prelude to a tune borrowed from the Beach Boys' "Catch a Wave"), the new sidewalk sport became so popular that by the end of 1964 there were ninety-two skateboard manufacturers nationwide and boards selling for prices from $1.79 for shoddy el cheapos to $49.94 for a "Tiger Skate" with a little motor. The following year, ten thousand fans filled Anaheim's La Palma Stadium for the First Annual Skateboard Championships. Noel Black's artistic short film *Skater-Dater* won an Academy Award. Quarterly *Skateboarder* magazine started lobbying to get into the Olympic Games.

Then came the backlash. Doctors and hospitals began noting an upsurge in broken bones suffered by kids skateboarding on city streets and sidewalks and in drained swimming pools. Five children were reported to have died when their boards smashed into trees or hurtled into traffic. SKATEBOARDS: A NEW MEDICAL MENACE headlined a special bulletin of the California Medical Association. Aside from safety concerns, some adults complained that skateboarders, weaving among pedestrian traffic or darting among automobiles, were becoming pests. Signs went up in parks and at beaches announcing NO SKATEBOARDING ALLOWED; speed bumps were installed in parking lots and on banked walls of playgrounds. Cities in Utah and Florida actually confiscated skateboards as a public nuisance. Restrictive laws and doctors' warnings may have helped decelerate the fad; it is also possible that, like coonskin Davy Crockett caps, skateboarding had simply played itself out in a few years and the market for them had been saturated. In either case, 1967 was the end for fly-by-night surfboard manufacturing companies, and press coverage of the asphalt athletes dried up.

"But here's a secret," confides *Hot Skateboarding*, the complete guide to the subject, published in 1977 at the height of what looked like an all-new era of skateboarding. "Skateboarding didn't die like the hula hoop. The kids of Santa Monica Canyon never stopped skating." In skateboard history, the period between 1967 and 1973 is known as the prerenaissance, before the invention of urethane wheels. Originally designed for use on training roller skates, urethane wheels revolutionized boards and made riding them a national obsession all over again, one that has never totally gone away. The new wheels absorbed shock better than old hard skate wheels and provided fantastic grip that allowed much higher speeds and tighter maneuvers, and they were also safer because of their excellent traction.

Skateboarding's second coming was a lot less controversial than the first. No longer satisfied with outlaw antics, many of its practitioners set their sights on legitimacy. "This time around," *Newsweek* reported in 1976, "skateboarding is being taken seriously as a sport." At the first World Masters Invitational competition in New York, skaters rode slalom courses, raced at speeds up to 50 mph, and created freestyle routines as elaborate as figure skaters'—all for prizes worth $50,000. The revival was also marked by a 1977 movie called *Skateboard*, which sought to find excitement in the resuscitated fad. But movie viewers weren't impressed, and no film producers

were eager to exploit its theme of heroic riders into a sequel, as had been done with the surf-centered beach-party movies a dozen years before.

Newsweek's story, called "Rebirth of the Boards," noted that along with the skateboard revival was coming a new escalation of accidents: over twenty-seven thousand skateboard injuries in the previous year. But *Newsweek* also reported that serious proponents of it as a sport were armed with safety equipment (helmets, knee pads, elbow pads, gloves, and heavy shoes) that was color-coordinated with their fancy-painted fiberglass boards. *Hot Skateboarding* is filled with advice about safe riding and good public relations, including how to fall, how to convince park directors to provide places to skate, and how to avoid developing "hamburger feet"— the skateboarders' name for bruised, abraded, bloody toes caused by improper shoes or no shoes at all.

Skate parks started to open up in many towns and cities, providing riders with sanctioned banked tracks and concrete bowls so that no one had to worry about getting run over by a car or totaling a little old lady and her bag of groceries—and once again skateboarding faded from the public eye. "All the skate parks took the skaters off the streets," said Kevin Thatcher, editor of *Thrasher*. "Skating lost its visibility and things began to dry up."

But lo, it came back, *again*, at the beginning of the 1980s. Thatcher believes the latest renaissance began when a punk rock group started a skateboarders' club called Jaks. Unlike the sun-loving surfer types of the early days, the Jaks skate at night, when the streets are theirs and most cars are parked. They have inspired other similar clubs to form, including the YAA (Young Alluring Alcoholic) Girlz, the Deadly Sparks, and Nerdz. "Mostly these are punks," *People* reported, "mohawked, skinheaded, tattooed types, proud of their bravado and oblivious to the dangers of hard surfaces." Some of them skate wearing jackboots and Nazi regalia and carrying clubs—for self-defense, they say.

It isn't only antisocial punks who have rediscovered skateboarding. It has now become a thriving profession with traveling teams (such as the Bones Brigade, whose logo is a grinning skull) that travel around the country to compete and stage exhibitions. Tony Hawk, one of the best-known of the pros, inventor of such moves as the Madonna and the Frigidaire, was reported to be earning over $100,000 a year from prize money, stunt work, commercial endorsements, and his own lines of skateboards, shirts, and shorts. Recently, Tom Petty made skateboarding the leitmotif of his video for the song "Free Fallin'." Skateboarding has become part of the landscape; and the biggest worry today among most skaters, judging from what one reads in *Thrasher*, is parents, as revealed in a recent article called "Coping with Unstoked Parents," which included these thoughts:

> Lack of parental support is a far worse crime than any restrictive bounds placed on skaters by cops, neighbors, etc.
>
> Mothers are usually the main "stick in the mud" in a skater's household.
>
> Dads tend to have this scary notion that the *only* sports are football, basketball, and baseball. Therefore he will usually come up with statements like "You won't get a scholarship riding a skateboard."
>
> They don't know why it thrills you, day after day, to learn new moves and feel your board under your feet. You have to tell them.
>
> Skating is more than just a sport, it's a way of life. Stick with it. Your parents will get the idea sooner or later, so keep your chin up and skate with pride.

Another interesting thing we noticed in *Thrasher:* People who ride skateboards have found some joy in California's drought, because so many concrete viaducts and irrigation ditches are dry, providing them with vast networks of places to skate. "Actually, when it comes down to it," Vaj Potenza wrote, "skaters are promoting water conservation by encouraging the draining of all unnecessarily filled bowls, fountains, and pools."

SOAP OPERA

Five days every week, fifty-two weeks every year, for a significant part of the afternoon on all three major television networks, fantastic things happen to really interesting people. They keep happening, without end, sometimes for decades, and although events on the afternoon soap operas are sometimes predictable, they are never commonplace. The soaps tell stories with Homeric drive, peopled by a pantheon of heroes and villains snarled in dramas that reflect, dissect, and magnify—but never resolve—nearly all the important issues and concerns of life on earth as we know it.

Mark Pinter (Grant Harrison in "Another World")
and Colleen Zenk Pinter
(Barbara Ryan in "As the World Turns")

They are America's most prolific and popular art, and many viewers readily incorporate watching them into daily routine, like taking a shower or going for a morning walk. Whereas seeing a movie or reading a book, or even tuning in to a prime-time TV show, usually requires a certain degree of planning and can often feel like a break from routine, watching a soap opera ("my soap," so many people like to say) feels like a fixed part of daily life—natural, personal, dependable, and as reassuring in its own way as it must have been in prehistoric days to hear the tribal storyteller spin tales of gods and goddesses engaged in great moral battles. The soaps are late-twentieth-century folklore.

A measure of how different soap operas are from other forms of entertainment is the fact that many people who watch them feel so close to the drama that they believe it is real, and the actors are frequently treated by members of the audience as though they were the characters they play. Villains are spit on when they walk down city streets; mourning family members are sent sympathy cards when a character dies; and vulnerable characters are offered counsel by loyal viewers who really want to help them out. Amazingly, this sometimes happens even when an old role is taken by a new actor: Within weeks, the new person is totally accepted by loyal fans and treated like the character he plays. (Conversely, many actors have graduated from soaps and left their daytime drama personae well behind; their ranks include Warren Beatty ["Love of Life"], Jill Clayburgh ["Search for Tomorrow"], Dustin Hoffman ["The Edge of Night" and "Search for Tomorrow"], and Kathleen Turner ["The Doctors"]). Occasionally it happens that big screen movie actors or stars of prime-time TV shows are confused with the parts they play; but for actors in soap operas—the most intimate of all dramatic forms—it is a well-known occupational hazard.

Soaps got their name because they were originally sponsored by Procter & Gamble detergents (three still are) and were known for their operatic tales of woe and joy, as well as for the soul-stirring organ glissandos that italicized the histrionics. Also known as "washboard weepers" in the early days, they began in Chicago in 1930, with a radio program called "Painted Dreams," written by Irna Phillips (who later went on to create "The Guiding Light," "Another World," "Days of Our Lives," and others for radio and television). The unique idea of "Painted Dreams" was to keep its plot unresolved at the end of each episode, to create an ongoing drama that would keep listeners curious enough to tune in next time. "Oxydol's Own Ma Perkins," the first soap-sponsored soap opera, began on Cincinnati radio in 1933 and then moved to Chicago and the NBC radio network the following year. It starred Virginia Payne as a dispenser of folk wisdom to her extended and somewhat wayward family, who couldn't begin to solve one problem without finding themselves embroiled in two others. "Ma Perkins" spawned Ivory's "The Road of Life," Joy's "Young Doctor Malone," Duz's "The Guiding Light," Cheer's "Backstage Wife," and Tide's "Life Can Be Beautiful." A Procter & Gamble spokesman called the arrangement "a gold mine," because housewives, who could so easily listen to the shows while they did their chores, wept into their washloads as they listened, then went to market and bought tons of P&G soap.

Television was seen by soap manufacturers (and by many other upholders of the domestic status quo) as a threat to household management when it appeared in the late 1940s. If women replaced radio with TV as their companion through the day, they would have to knock off work to watch it (this was in the days before small, portable televisions, when the TV was a regal piece of furniture, usually in the place of honor in the living room), and if they were busy watching television, how could they find the time to keep house? Nonetheless, TV would prove a fantastic place to sell soap products (you could *show* how clean they make things), and the move to the tube seemed inevitable, even if it didn't happen immediately. One problem was that while radio performers had been able to stand around the microphone and read their scripts, TV required actors who could memorize dozens of pages of script every day . . . and who could really act, not just read well. Furthermore, the cumbersome production methods of early (live) television allowed little in the way of action or between-the-scenes filler: Everything had to happen via dialogue.

The first TV soap opera, "Faraway Hill," featuring an offstage voice as the lead character's inner conscience, lasted less than a year on the DuMont Network in 1946; a pilot of "Ma Perkins," produced in 1948, was never broadcast (although the show remained a radio staple until 1960); and "A Woman to Remember," about the backstage tribulations of the cast of a radio soap opera, went on the DuMont Network for six months in 1949 without a sponsor. Procter & Gamble sponsored "The First Hundred Years" on CBS for a little over a year, starting in 1950, but the big breakthrough came with Roy Winsor's "Search for Tomorrow," starting in 1951. "Search" stayed on the air until 1986; its main character, Joanne Gardner Barron Tate Vincente Tourneur, was played by Mary Stuart for the entire run, and she lived to see her mythical midwestern town of Henderson grow from a village to a thriving metropolis. (Roy Winsor also created "The Secret Storm," which provided Joan Crawford her conspicuous surprise visit to daytime television, when she temporarily took a role because her daughter, Christina, who normally played the part, had fallen ill.)

After Irna Phillips, whose "Guiding Light" went from radio to TV within months of the debut of "Search for Tomorrow" (and is still on the air), the most prolific force in soap opera writing has been Agnes Nixon. Nixon apprenticed with Phillips and helped create the august "As the World Turns" (1956–), featuring one of the great daytime miscreants, Lisa Miller (Eileen Fulton), who over the course of thirty years went through a total of six husbands and thirty-six lovers and even inspired a short-lived prime-time soap, "Our Private World," in 1965. Mrs. Nixon also created and produced "One Life to Live" (1968–); "All My Children" (1970–), which stars reigning soap opera diva Susan Lucci as scheming Erica

Kane; and "Loving" (1983–). Mrs. Nixon, who once explained that she came to television because she didn't want to go into the family business (manufacturing burial garments), has been more responsible than anyone else for transforming the fundamental sensibility of the soaps' intricate melodramas from Victorian to modern. Her characters might pine for lost love (hey, who doesn't?), but they also worry about race relations, adultery, drug addiction, venereal disease, pap smears, and POWs—all subjects once pretty much ignored by television, and not seen in prime time until long after they were dealt with in the afternoons. Nixon's defiance of old taboos helped pave the way for ever spicier material on Frank and Doris Hursley's "General Hospital" (1963–), on which Liz Taylor did a guest shot in 1981, and William Bell's "The Young and the Restless" (1973–), which recently featured a story line about babies born to crack-addicted mothers. The same week in 1991 that "The Young and the Restless" wrestled with teen pregnancy, telephone sex, and artificial insemination, the characters in "Loving" were coping with impotence, cough syrup addiction, and suicide.

In some ways the soaps have always been more daring, relevant, and realistic than prime time. In his book *Television: The First Fifty Years*, Jeff Greenfield suggests that because the soaps were aimed at women, they did what prime-time television didn't dare do—see problems from a female point of view. That meant they defined their subjects in terms of ambiguous feelings and complicated emotions and ignored the typical prime-time reliance on clear-cut solutions to problems. Unlike prime-time drama, which is customarily built around strong, confident, infallible heroes, daytime TV is peopled by men and women who are vulnerable, anxious, and flawed. They may be extravagantly good or evil, but it is rare for a soap opera character not to have some mitigating quality that makes him or her seem truly human—more human than the average prime-time TV character, whose predicament, you know full well, will be resolved at the end of the hour. They struggle, they win or lose, and they learn to live in a very imperfect world. And—unlike all prime-time characters (but like real-life men and women)—they *keep on struggling* for years on end; they change, they age, they sometimes even die. When "General Hospital" and "The Doctors" premiered in 1963, the soaps broke yet another TV convention by featuring women who were competent professionals—doctors as well as nurses—with serious nondomestic problems to worry about. This was a long leap not only from Irna Phillips's well-known dictum that "marriage is a woman's finest career" but also from the simpleminded image of women (not to mention men) seen in the number-one-rated prime-time show of that year, "The Beverly Hillbillies."

Outlandish as their plots may be, most soap operas take place in a familiar world peopled by characters who differ from real human beings only in that their emotional lives are tremendously magnified. One notable exception to this rule was "Dark Shadows" (1966–71), a strange Gothic tale set in Collinsport, Maine, about the tormented but sympathetic Barnabas Collins (Jonathan Frid), a two-hundred-year-old vampire. "Dark Shadows" characters frequently used seances and magic powers to travel back in time and interact with ancestors, including a pre-vampire Barnabas. It was a hit that developed an audience of young viewers and students far beyond the usual housewife crowd (and it was reincarnated as an especially lascivious prime-time soap in 1991), but in some ways it signaled a strange, anomalous point in soap opera history. Soaps have always reflected the values of the culture around them, and in the late 1960s and early 1970s, as so many traditional values seemed to be blurring or eroding, several long-running daytime serials, including Roy Winsor's "Secret Storm" and Irna Phillips's "Love Is a Many Splendored Thing," bit the dust. Robert LaGuardia, author of *Soap World*, attributed an early-1970s slump in soap opera popularity to "the absolute insensitivity on the part of many producers to what viewers really wanted to see." New life for soaps came in the form of stylish, savvy, streetwise programs—Bill Bell's "The Young and the Restless" and Claire Labine and Paul Avila Mayer's blue-collar drama, "Ryan's Hope" (1975–89), both featuring younger characters and candid, up-to-the-minute plots about such topics as obesity, rape, mastectomies, abortion, the right to die, and sexual harassment in the workplace. By the end of the 1970s, the look of soap operas was changing, too: Although they still relied on the tension of their dialogue and retained the classic videotaped intimacy of rhythmic close-ups and reaction shots, they now had the technical freedom to use exterior scenes and special effects, and on rare occasions, like Luke and Laura's wedding on "General Hospital" in 1981, to stage grand production numbers.

"Peyton Place," which started in 1964, is frequently credited with being the first soap opera to work as a prime-time show. Its pattern of turgid, never-ending triumph and tragedy did indeed bring the structure of daytime serials to prime time, but because this show was on film—and because it ran at night—it had a completely different feeling. "Peyton Place" had none of the pitiless closeness of the taped shows. It was less like eavesdropping—which is the common feeling induced by most soaps—and more like watching a movie, and so by comparison it seemed almost exotic. Fascinating though it was (it rated among the top twenty prime-time shows in its first year), "Peyton Place" went from three episodes per week to two, then out of production in 1969. Despite its high drama and continuing plot lines, it lacked the obstinate authority of the daytime shows, which somehow manage to signal, every moment they are on the air, that they will last as long as life itself. After five years it did what daytime soaps never seem to do: It simply ran out of steam. Similarly, Norman Lear's "Mary Hartman, Mary Hartman" (1976–77), which did have the raw, secular look of a taped show, assumed a far too fragile pose of quasi-parody to last longer than two fascinating seasons, during which audiences laughed at the ridiculous goings-on but also became involved in them. A syndicated show (because none of the networks would touch it), "Mary Hartman" was generally broadcast late at night and attracted an au courant audience that might previously have written off soap opera as simple-minded housewife fodder. It coincided with a huge rise in soap opera popularity on college campuses and signaled the fact that soaps didn't have to be for lonely ladies in housecoats anymore. "Mary Hartman" was proof, even to many anti-TV snobs, that serial drama could be cynical, hip, smart, and deliciously sacrilegious, and it helped pave the way for the phenomenal success of such cheeky and tongue-in-cheeky prime-time serials as "Dallas" (see p. 121), "Dynasty" (see p. 164), "Falcon Crest," "Knots Landing," and the briefly fashionable "Twin Peaks" (see p. 537).

People who don't know soap operas tend to think they all look alike, which is as big a mistake as thinking that all abstract-expressionist art is pretty much the same. So with the help of Mark Pinter (Grant Harrison on "Another World") and Colleen Zenk Pinter (Barbara Ryan on "As the

World Turns"), we have compiled this handy guide to some of the things that make each of the daytime soaps unique:

- "All My Children" (ABC): Set in Pine Valley, outside New York, "AMC" went on the air in 1970. It features larger-than-life characters, lavish sets and wardrobe, and highly charged situations. There was once an interracial romance, but the story, and the characters, were dropped quickly. At one time, twenty men in Erika Kane's past all came back to haunt her. According to *Soap Opera Digest*, plotting is the major strength of "AMC." However, *Soap Opera Digest* gave "AMC" a barely passing grade for character development. Its problem? It "has a habit of bringing on new characters who are not fully developed. [They] play out a story requiring one dimension and, when that is over, the character has nowhere to go." It is taped in New York, but "AMC" is known as a show with all the glamour of a California-made soap.

- "Another World" (NBC): Created by Irna Phillips in 1964, and set in Bay City, Illinois, "Another World" is a classic. The title refers to the difference between reality and what Ms. Phillips called "the world of feelings and dreams that we strive for." Psychological issues are emphasized as people sit down and have one-on-one, heart-to-heart talks, as in the earliest soaps. It was the first daytime serial to expand to an hour (in 1975). Taped in New York.

- "As the World Turns" (CBS): Written by the masterful Doug Marland, set in Oakdale, Illinois, "ATWT" is the most naturalistic of all soap operas. Less emphasis on glamour, costume, sets, and celebrity characters, and more on ensemble acting in group situations, make this the most respected soap among New York theater actors. Older characters are kept alive longer and some actors have been with the show for over thirty years, although many new characters were introduced in the 1980s to attract a younger audience. Taped in New York.

- "The Bold and the Beautiful" (CBS): The Los Angeles fashion business is the setting for this high-gloss show which went on the air in 1987, created by William Bell and his wife, Lee Phillip Bell. Taped in L.A., it features lots of beautiful and handsome actors who play what are known in the soap opera business as "super couples"—the high-profile pairings that tend to shift a program's emphasis from psychology to celebrity. This show features the most prominent cheekbones in daytime television, as well as a lot of sex; it is rare for an episode to go by without at least one beautiful or handsome character taking a shower.

- "Days of Our Lives" (NBC): This long-running (since 1965) show was created by Irna Phillips, Ted Corday, and Allan Chase. In the early 1970s it was the top-rated daytime show, and it continues to have a huge following, including well-organized fan clubs, even though ratings have slipped. The anchors of the show for twenty-six years have been Macdonald Carey as Dr. Tom Horton and Frances Reid as his wife. (It's Carey's voice that intones the famous preamble, "Like sands through the hourglass, so are the days of our lives.") Lots of trash romance here, and couples are always the focus. Recently, in an attempt to boost ratings, the story line echoed the exotic adventures of *Indiana Jones and the Temple of Doom*. Taped in California.

- "General Hospital" (ABC): Created by Doris and Frank Hursley in 1963, "GH" became the number-one soap in the early 1980s when producer Gloria Monty created the idea of the super couple—the charismatic Luke (Anthony Geary) and his rape victim Laura (Genie Francis), whose wedding in November 1981 was the most-watched soap opera episode ever. There were some strange science-fiction twists to the story after Genie Francis left, including one time when the entire town of Port Charles was about to be put into cryogenic suspended animation. Taped in California.

- "Guiding Light" (CBS): A genuine soap classic—still owned by Procter & Gamble. Set in Springfield, Illinois, and built (originally) around the Bauers, a close-knit (but eventually huge) family of German-Americans, it tends to develop stories that involve lots of interaction among the cast and less emphasis on celebrity super couples. In 1983 several members of the cast did a curious variation on their soap roles in the TV movie *The Cradle Will Fall*, based on the bestselling thriller by Mary Higgins Clark. Taped in New York.
- "Loving" (ABC): Created by Agnes Nixon and Doug Marland in 1983, "Loving" was the first daytime serial to be set on a college campus, the mythical Alden University—recognition of the immense popularity of soap operas among college students. In the mid-1980s, however, the focus tended to shift away from campus intrigue to the doings of the rich and famous. Recently, the college has begun to play a more important role again as part of a strategy to lift "Loving" from its status as the lowest-rated soap. Taped in New York.
- "One Life to Live" (ABC): Set in the East Coast town of Llanview, created by Agnes Nixon in 1968 with a surfeit of proper nouns beginning with double *l* (a mansion named Llanfair; Llantano Mountain) in homage to the Welsh-ancestored town in Pennsylvania where she lives, "OLTL" became known to soap buffs in the 1980s for its utterly fantastic story lines, such as an extended flashback to the Old West and scenes that took place in heaven. In 1991 Ivana Trump appeared on the show, as herself. Taped in New York.
- "Santa Barbara" (NBC): Of all the soaps, "Santa Barbara" takes itself the least seriously. Created by Bridget and Jerome Dobson in 1984, it has a campy point of view towards the tribulations of its super couples, who in the beginning were members of the rich upper crust but in recent years

have tended to slip down the socioeconomic ladder. Taped in California.
- "The Young and the Restless" (CBS): William Bell's masterpiece—number one in the ratings and winner of many awards, "Y&R" was created in 1973 and is known as the most glamorous of all daytime dramas. High production values (lighting, costume, sets) combine with good acting and a story line that slowly spins out with inexorable confidence to give this show a sense of grandeur, like a very long epic motion picture. The setting is Genoa City, Wisconsin; its characters tend to be young and good-looking (but not mere bimbos and hunks). The theme music from "Y&R" was used by Romanian gymnast Nadia Comaneci to set the mood when she won her perfect 10 doing the floor exercise in the 1976 Olympic Games. Taped in California.

"SOUL TRAIN"

Before 1983, when MTV decided to begin featuring music videos by black artists on the air, there was only one time slot on television that offered a regular dose of soul: "Soul Train," syndicated throughout the country since 1971 and—even after the ascendance of MTV—still the liveliest, as well as the onliest, venue for rhythm-and-blues performances not packaged as music videos. On "Soul Train" you watch real performers get up before a crowd and lip-synch their hits, and while they pretend to sing, the studio audience dances.

Regardless of the caliber of guests or how convincingly they move their lips, the dancing on "Soul Train" is always real, and always astonishing—a spectacle of innovative moves that take the best of vernacular soul dancing and broadcast it to the nation. The highlight of the dancing on "Soul Train" is the Line, when all the regulars part to form an aisle on the dance floor, and one by one (or two by two, in pairs) the show's best dancers start at the back and launch themselves up the aisle towards the camera, doing the most fantastic steps they can muster.

"Soul Train" has been called "the black counterpart of 'American Bandstand'" (see p. 15), and it does share the record-hop format originated in South Philadelphia back in the 1950s, but the level of dancing on the two shows is not comparable: Even at its best, "Bandstand" is like a nice gym dance in suburbia, while "Soul Train" is atomic-powered. Nor could you find two television characters more dramatically different than Dick Clark, host of "Bandstand," and Don Cornelius, who created and continues to host "Soul Train." Whereas Dick Clark has always been practically one of the kids—an eternally young, fun-loving manchild with a perpetual smile on his face—Don Cornelius is the epitome of groovy cool, with a honey-sweet baritone voice of absolute dominion. Like some great desert lizard in the sun, he stands inert at his podium and observes as all around him the "Soul Train" dancers wreak mayhem with their flailing bodies and the hottest acts in music kick out the jams. Then when the song is over, he moves and speaks with composure that verges on catatonia. His eyelids lift open and his mouth hardly seems to move as he invites his audience to climb aboard the Soul Train, "the hippest trip in America."

Don Cornelius was a radio disc jockey in Chicago when he got the idea for his show as an afternoon program for WVON, a UHF television station that was eager at the time to expand its appeal into the black community. "There are black television programs," Cornelius said in 1973, "but really no black entertainment programs." He financed his own pilot for "Soul Train," built a set, convinced Jerry Butler to be his guest star and some neighborhood kids to dance, and produced the first half-hour show in the spring. It was tough to get it on the air, because most advertisers weren't interested in the audience of a rhythm-and-blues music show aimed at teens, but with the backing of Ultra Sheen hair-care products, makers of Afro Sheen, "Soul Train" debuted October 2, 1971, and within six months it was on the air in half a dozen cities across the country —usually broadcast on Saturday mornings, but continuing in its original format five afternoons a week in Chicago.

"Soul Train" now appears in nearly a hundred TV markets, and there is a British version called "Soul Train 6:20" (because it airs at 6:20 P.M. on Fridays). It has moved from Chicago to Los Angeles, where, Cornelius said, he "discovered a totally new attitude towards dancing—it was wilder and more energetic, and made for extremely exciting television." As important as celebrity performers have been to the success of the show, it is the dancing, Cornelius believes, that has been the real engine pulling "Soul Train" since its beginning: "Twenty years ago every region of the country had its own style. But now dancing—at least street dancing—has become a universal language,

and I think that's due to television in general and 'Soul Train' in particular."

In addition to the dancing and two decades of showcasing the best black musical acts, from Chuck Berry, James Brown, and Aretha Franklin to the hot rappers of the moment, as well as a few white crossover artists such as Elton John and David Bowie, "Soul Train" is known for some of its extracurricular attractions. Among these are the avant-garde street fashions of the dancers: The "Soul Train" dance floor was the first place on TV to see the full range of oversize jewelry (including chandelier earrings), conspicuously labeled sportswear, and tapered "Philly cut" hair, and sculpted Afros that later permeated African-American culture. Another regular feature of the show has been the black history scramble board, on which letters spelling out the name of a famous soul brother are jumbled and a team of contestants has to rearrange them to spell the name correctly before the end of a song, during which everybody else dances around them.

SPANDEX

S pandex makes human bodies look naked, and usually a darn sight better. It cinches and compresses sagging flesh; it hoists and supports blubbery bosoms; it fixes flat fannies and muffles buttock bounce. It is everywhere: in nine out of ten swimsuits, in runners' and bikers' and pro wrestlers' suits, in jock straps and aerobics regalia, in unitards and halter tops and sexy casual wear that has nothing to do with sporting activity but nonetheless aims to project the sleek, skin-

tight look of an athlete stripped down to the essentials. It is hard to imagine that there once was a world in which the exact outlines of strangers' buns, breasts, stomachs, thighs, and pubes were not in our faces on the street as well as on the beach, but until 1957, when spandex was invented, most people actually believed in concealing their bodies.

Spandex was originally designed to *not* be seen, as material for ladies' dainties (girdles in particular) in the pre-Madonna days when underwear was considered a private matter. Based on research done during World War II, when natural rubber (made from tree sap) had become a frighteningly rare strategic material, American chemical companies developed a durable, elastic alternative during the fifties, in hopes of creating a girdle that was less bulky, easier to wash, and tougher than one made of rubber. A petroleum-based product that requires more complex chemical reactions than any other manmade fiber, the newly formulated synthetic was given the generic name spandex because of its unprecedented stretchability, but it was trademarked as Lycra (Du Pont's version) and Vyrene (U.S. Rubber's), as well as Glospan, Rheeflex, and Duraspun by other chemical manufacturers. Today, Du Pont's Lycra is by far the leading brand, found in nearly every fashionable swimsuit and bodysuit, support stockings, control-top pantyhose, and even "silken sheers" hosiery.

In 1962 *American Fabric* magazine enumerated the many virtues of spandex, which included *high stretch* (500 percent

"Vertical Dressing," demonstrated by
aerobicists from The Firm

without breaking) and *low set* (it springs back to its original shape) and also remarkable resistance to sunlight and water. The magazine went on to recount the fields in which the new material was already a huge success: bathing suits, support stockings, New York Giants football pants, and—its original purpose—girdles and bras, of which fully 50 percent already contained spandex. "Never before has there been such a dramatic and instant change in the look, the feel, the versatility of fashion fabrics," declared advertisements for U.S. Rubber's Vyrene, which showed not only a woman in a shoulder-to-knee all-in-one corset (made of "firm yet gentle material") but also a woman in a sexy swimsuit and another in a chic draped dress and high heels—both made of spandex! *American Fabric* proclaimed it "a radical new fiber concept," as important as nylon and polyester, with a bright future in garters, elastic waistbands, toreador pants, and golf jackets.

At the time, no one could possibly have predicted just how brilliant the future of spandex really was. Americans' growing concern with physical fitness, or at least with putting on the appearance of being concerned with fitness, was a boon. Back when spandex was invented, there were street clothes and there were exercise clothes, and the two were so different that it would have been embarrassing, not to mention impractical, to exercise in street clothes or walk along the street in gym clothes. Now that's all changed; it is fashionable to look like you are on your way to or from a workout, and it is also fashionable to flaunt a well-muscled body if you have one. There is no better fabric for flaunting than spandex, especially when its brilliant colors and skin-smooth sheen are compared to a fuddy-duddy old sweatsuit. The big breakthrough came in 1964 when designer Giorgio Sant'Angelo introduced his

"Lycra Collection" of stretch coordinates: bodysuits, bikinis, and tights, even wrap skirts and dresses. Clothes previously reserved to the gym were suddenly out on the street, and they were a sensation.

Nearly thirty years after the Sant'Angelo collection, body-hugging garments are not only high fashion but low fashion, too. Even relatively modest people, including plenty without well-muscled body parts to parade, don't think twice about appearing in public in spandex garments that show the cottage-cheese dimples, lines, and intimate contours of their flesh more clearly than if you looked them over in the buff with a magnifying glass.

The popularity of the sporting look probably did more for spandex than any other cultural phenomenon, but we cannot ignore the contributions of disco and other blasphemous musical trends to spandex's ascension. Although disco is customarily remembered for its enduring polyester gifts to the male livery, including the white three-piece suit and Qiana shirt (complemented by a batch of gold chains), club scene fashions were a major boost for spandex as well, in the form of ridiculously tight street clothes for women. Who can forget Disco Sally, the party-hearty grandmother of Studio 54, known for her nipple-hugging halter tops, skin-squeezing pedal pushers, and platform shoes? Disco stretch clothes—halter tops in particular—became a fundamental component of the cheap-trick-bimbo look so popular among teenage girls in the eighties. Then, thanks to the rise of heavy metal music, distended groins—as earlier pioneered by the likes of Mick Jagger and Jim Morrison—gained cachet among men of the fashionable white-trash-rebel set, and there is no better way to create the look of a whopper in the crotch than by filling up a pair of skintight spandex pants with a load of cotton sport socks and a foot-long weiner.

BRUCE SPRINGSTEEN

Let's be honest: A lot of guys who sing rock-and-roll music are pretty fruity. Even the ones who flaunt bare chests and padded crotches and two-day growths of grisly stubble on their faces seem so unnaturally concerned with projecting a well-crafted image of machismo, it makes you wonder what's really there. Rock and roll is so much about posing and primping and developing just the right attitude that an awful lot of its practitioners seem at least mighty narcissistic, if not downright dainty. Not Bruce. Bruce is a real guy in jeans and a T-shirt and a haircut you could get from the corner barbershop. He's from Jersey and he likes it there (Bruce fans don't like to talk about his mansion in Beverly Hills). He's clean and straight: no drugs, no kinky sex, and when he drinks, it's beer—by the slug, from a bottle. And for everyone who prefers real guyhood to the affectations of pretty boys and ambitious poseurs, Bruce is the Boss. Here are some of the wonderful things about him, as enumerated by *People* in a special issue devoted to the 1980s:

- He never sold a song to Madison Avenue. (The well-known story among Bruce fans is that he turned down $12 million to appear in a Chrysler ad and refused to let them use the music from his "Born in the U.S.A." for any price.)

- Tickets for his concerts cost half of those for one of Michael Jackson's.
- His shows are at least 50 percent longer than any other rock performer's.
- He had to be dragged into MTV because he's into music, not razzle-dazzle.
- He has never been androgynous, never had a face lift, and he has big biceps.
- When he did marry a model (Julianne Phillips), the marriage failed, and he took up with a girl in his band (Patti Scialfa)—a home girl, suitable for a guy from New Jersey. "Not a drop of Hollywood in him."
- He writes what he feels.

No one has chronicled Bruce Springsteen's excellent qualities and unaffected talents more thoroughly than his biographer Dave Marsh, who called him "the most brilliant American rock & roll performer to emerge in the last decade" (as of 1982) and "among the greatest, most ambitious artists rock has produced." Another music connoisseur, John Landau, wrote in 1974, "I saw rock 'n' roll's future and its name is Bruce Springsteen." Landau soon became Springsteen's manager, and Dave Marsh became what one journalist called his "media advisor."

Bruce Springsteen has been a performer loved at least as much by intellectuals who analyze pop culture as by fans. As a symbol, he inspires far more than blind adoration and has been the subject of massive critical analyses about such subjects as:

- what the lyrics he writes mean. As of the late 1980s, they signified the end of Reaganism, according to *The New Republic.*
- what his populistic persona signifies about American society. He is "the unassuming musical laureate of the working classes," according to *Rolling Stone.*

- the unique relationship that seems to exist between him and his audience. "Springsteen's followers are convinced he's just like them," *Rolling Stone* said, explaining that Bruce's gift was that he "glorifies the ordinariness of life."

One thing fans especially like about him is that he works so hard on their behalf. Ask any of them, and the first thing they'll tell you is how exhaustingly long and unbelievably loud his show is and how he sweats profusely and gets painfully hoarse every time, hunches over his guitar and struts and swaggers and slides and leaps across the stage with all the gusto of a serious aerobics instructor. He really cares about the followers who come to his concerts, and he's said so: "Before the show we go out and we check the sound in every section of the room. Because there's some guy sittin' back here, and he's got a girl with him, and you know, it's like, this is their seat." Who are the guys and girls who love him so (other than rock critics)? Nearly all of them are white, middle-class or lower middle, and a lot of them, like Bruce, are old enough to remember the 1960s.

That's what Bruce signified when he first got famous: a renewal of the promises and vitality of rock and roll, or as Earl Blackwell's *Celebrity Register* put it, "a pied piper to restless suburban youths who caught the tail-end of the 1960s rock-and-rebellion era and were hungry for more." By the mid-1970s pop charts were clogged with disco music and the soft rock of the Eagles and Olivia Newton-John and the fey stardust of David Bowie singing "Fame." Bruce, on the other hand, came from the planet Earth, from America, from Asbury Park and the highways and boardwalks and magic teenage nights that rock and roll seemed to have forgotten. "Not a golden California boy or glitter queen from Britain," *Time* exulted, revealing that he dressed in a leather jacket and a shredded undershirt and he walked with "an easy swagger that is part residual stage presence, part boardwalk braggadocio."

His third album, *Born to Run*, released in 1975, was an epiphany for music fans (and for the music business) hungry for the raw energy that had been missing from the pop charts. It conveyed big amounts of muscle and ambition in windblown tales about ordinary guys and girls coming of age and learning what life was all about . . . and you could dance to it. On October 27, 1975, when Neil Sedaka's "Bad Blood" (with Elton John singing backup) was number one on the *Billboard* pop chart for the third week in a row, *Time* and *Newsweek* both put Bruce Springsteen on their covers. The *Time* story was about "Rock's New Sensation," who was "directly in touch with all the impulses of wild humor and glancing melancholy, street tragedy and punk anarchy that have made rock the distinctive voice of a generation." *Newsweek*, slightly less bedazzled, titled its story "The Making of a Rock Star" and focused on Columbia Records' unprecedented marketing blitz on his behalf, concluding that "hypes are as American as Coca-Cola, so perhaps—in one way or another—Bruce Springsteen *is* the real thing."

He toured the country for twenty-three weeks and was hailed as the new Bob Dylan, with a personality similar to Dylan's in the beginning: the ramblin' street poet, a tousle-haired, road-weary hippie trying to make sense out of a crazy world. *Born to Run* eventually sold over five million copies. By 1980 *Harper's Bazaar* listed him as one of "The Ten Most Creative Bachelors" (along with Woody Allen and Burt Reynolds), saying:

> Passionate rock-'n'-roll paeans to urban life in New Jersey may not be your idea of poetry, but for pure energy, raw sex appeal and charismatic self-abandonment, there's no one quite like Bruce Springsteen. With his street dude good looks and his renowned ability to rivet an audience, he has often been a one-man movement for rock 'n' roll that galvanizes the heart in a way the sparer, harder sounds of New Wave music never can.

After *Born to Run* there were several important albums, including *Darkness on the Edge of Town* (1978), *The River* (1980), and *Nebraska* (1982), the last a gloomy, if not downright depressing, collection of introspective songs about loneliness, sorrow, and loss, including one that recalled mass murderer Charles Starkweather (see p. 475). According to Dave Marsh, *Nebraska* was "a cogent response to the deadening effect of the spirit of Reaganism."

Bruce (all his fans call him "Bruce"; like Cher and Madonna, he needs only one name) remained popular until 1984, when his *Born in the U.S.A.* album transformed him from a mere rock-and-roll star into a pop-culture phenomenon, or in the words of the *New York Times*, "something more than a rock icon, something more than an entertainer." Released in June, *Born in the U.S.A.* coincided with a stirring Annie Leibowitz photograph that showed Bruce in front of an American flag, leaping in the air and thrashing at his guitar, and sporting a brand-new body. No longer the grieving, battered waif, he had pumped up his muscles so much he seemed to be practically bursting out of his denim clothes (blue-jeaned buttocks were featured on the album cover), and although only five feet nine, he looked massive and strong. It wasn't a flamboyant, pretty-boy, bodybuilder physique like the one Sylvester Stallone had developed for himself; it was the honorable, beefy body of a man who works for a living. This was a body that stood in brilliant contrast to the elitist, prissy, power tie-and-suspenders values of the yuppie 1980s that were just starting to sour in a lot of people's minds. When Bruce went on his "Born in the U.S.A." tour—for *eighteen months* (grossing a hundred million dollars)—he donated money to food banks, homeless shelters, union funds, and Vietnam veteran groups in every American city he played. Here was an of-the-people hero with true populist charisma unknown since pre-Army Elvis.

Many people considered *Born in the U.S.A.* a sign that there was a revival of patriotism in America, also expressed in the Republican presidential campaign's dewey-eyed "Morning in America" video about the return of good, old-fashioned values. When *Rolling Stone* interviewed Bruce fans early in 1985, at the peak of Springsteen veneration, they said:

- "He's an American. He cares what we've done. He doesn't shun us. He's got spirit; he motivates us. I hear he's been givin' to charities."
- "Bruce is—he's America. He is exactly what America's about."
- "He's the most patriotic guy around. I feel patriotic—it's a real turnaround from the hippie days."

The title song, which begins with ringing chords like a martial reveille and features a rousing chorus that repeats the words "Born in the U.S.A.," is about a veteran of the war in Vietnam whose life was ruined and who now resents America for it. But the resentful, or at least ambiguous, words were overshadowed by the throbbing uplift of the music, which turned the song into a feel-good anthem for concertgoers, who waved American flags and joined Bruce in the chorus, shouting "Born in the U.S.A." with patriotic fervor. Nearly every candidate in that year's elections, including presidential rivals Ronald Reagan and Walter Mondale, claimed the words to Bruce's song as an endorsement of *their* kind of patriotism. Even left-wing skeptics found in the album a "theme of national rebirth," because the words encouraged people to come to grips with America's evil past—never mind the millions of fans who misunderstood the message and waved their jingoistic flags whenever Bruce ran out on stage to sing.

Bruce Springsteen had become a spokesman for all Americans who wanted to see themselves as regular folks—"rock and roll's Gary Cooper," according to *Newsweek.* "His songs," Mary-Ellen Banashek explained in 1985 in an article called "Bruce Springsteen: Why He Makes Us Feel So Good" in *McCall's,* "are peopled by Vietnam vets, the unemployed, factory workers, cops, convicts—each a microcosm of life in these United States." His career has since ebbed from that plateau, and his big 1992 releases, *Human Touch* and *Lucky Town,* sold a lot of copies but got only lukewarm critical response from rock critics who wondered if he was in a rut. Despite such slippage, Bruce continues to embody the blue collar virtues that defined him in the mid-1980s, as enumerated by Ms. Banashek for *McCall's* in yet another list of his terrific qualities, including:

> Bruce is a real man. No kid will ever come home wearing red lipstick and blue glitter eyeshadow because he's trying to emulate Bruce Springsteen. [On the other hand, Bruce must be given credit for pioneering the fashion of earrings among heterosexual men.]
>
> Bruce has nice buns.
>
> Bruce Springsteen is growing older, like the rest of us. And, by golly, you want him to be happy, with the house and the beautiful wife and the kids. Because he works hard for it.

SYLVESTER STALLONE

In a myth-making feat unequaled by any other movie star in history, Sylvester Stallone created two heroes who have not only become part of modern American folklore but are known to the rest of the world as quintessential Americans: Rocky and Rambo. For the last ten years, when-ever a foe of this country's foreign policy wants to wag a finger at American adventur-ism, you can bet he will invoke the name of Rambo, the Stallone character who is a symbol (for better or for worse) of a nation that is intuitively warlike. As for Rocky, Stallone once said of his best-known screen character that "you can't analyze Rocky's appeal. It's like trying to analyze the recipe of an apple pie." There have been four *Rocky* movies since the original in 1976, and although the most recent one wasn't the box-office champ its forebears were, the fable of Rocky Balboa—the incoherent neighborhood palooka with a sense of pride that just won't quit and a yearning to *be somebody*—has become every bit as American as apple pie.

Despite his indisputable accomplish-ments, Sylvester Stallone gets little respect from movie reviewers, who generally re-gard his work as melodramatic, or from so-cial critics, who tend to worry that he panders to the base instincts of the mass movie audience. "People think I rise out of the La Brea Tar Pits every year and do a film," he lamented. "People think I've got the IQ of a hockey score." In fact, he is quite an erudite and cultured gentleman—a novelist, a painter, an art collector, an avid polo player—and he once boasted of a vocabulary that he estimated "is larger than [those of] 90 percent of the writers I've met." He describes himself as more cerebral than physical ("I built my body to carry my brain around"), but no matter how intellectual or cultivated he is in private life, and regardless of how intelligently he has plotted (and directed and acted in) his stupendously successful movies, Sylvester Stallone the artist has been totally overwhelmed by the power of his screen creations. As far as American pop culture goes, he *is* Rocky and Rambo.

"He always fantasized about being the world's greatest," Stallone's stepfather once recalled. "He just wasn't sure at what." As a boy growing up in Philadelphia (after being born in 1946 in New York's Hell's Kitchen in a forceps delivery that severed a facial nerve and left him with a perpetual sneer), he was so inspired by watching Steve Reeves in *Hercules* that he fashioned barbells out of cinderblocks tied to broom handles. His teachers told him that his brain was "dormant," and so he focused more on physical development than on schoolwork. He fell so in love with Edgar Allan Poe's work that he bought a dictionary to help him understand it, and he vowed to learn a new word every day. When he got a standing ovation as Biff in a school production of *Death of a Salesman*, he remembers, he thought, "This is it! I've finally done something right! From here on, I'm going for it."

Stallone studied acting at the University of Miami and in 1969 moved to New York in search of work. While employed at the Central Park Zoo hosing out lion cages, he saw *Easy Rider* (see p. 172) and decided, "I couldn't write any worse." He sold a movie treatment called *Hell's Kitchen* about three brothers, one of whom is a wrestler, and when a producer, who liked the writing but not the story, asked him if he could do something else, he began to conceive a movie in which a Philadelphia cab driver becomes mayor of the city. Gradually it transformed into a boxing story, but a cynical one in which the hero throws the fight at the end. Then in 1975 he saw the boxing match between Muhammad Ali and Chuck Wepner, in which Wepner—an aging bleeder without a prayer—somehow managed to remain standing while getting beaten by the champ. Stallone was so inspired by Wepner's courage against all odds that he threw out the bitter story about a loser and made it into a heroic script about a loser who becomes a winner: a South Philly club boxer with no future who, miraculously, gets a shot at a heavyweight title match and, even more miraculously, goes the distance, and in the meantime develops self-respect and wins the love of a nice girl. The story was so unabashedly corny that Frank Capra once called it "a picture I wish I had made." It was a fairy tale, in Stallone's words, "about pride, reputation, and not being another bum from the neighborhood." He was so absolutely certain of his idea that he wrote the whole screenplay in eighty-six hours, fueled by caffeine pills, calling out "This is it, this is it!" as he shouted dialogue to his wife.

In fact, he was confident enough that *Rocky* would be a hit that he turned down $360,000 for the script when it was proposed that Ryan O'Neal play the role, and took a mere $20,000 plus 10 percent of the net profits to be Rocky himself. At the time he was a nobody. He had played only small parts in most of his movies, as well as a starring role in a skin flick called *A Party at Kitty and Stud's* and a critically well-received role as a 1950s greaser in *The Lords of Flatbush* (1974). *Rocky* was made quickly on a shoestring budget, but it became one of the great movie phenomena of the 1970s. It was nominated for ten Academy Awards (it won best picture), it grossed well over two hundred million dollars, and it created a hero that people wanted to stand up and cheer (many movie audiences actually did stand up and cheer during the movie's climactic fight). Stallone recalled walking out of the Goldwyn Theater after a screening for movie people and being applauded by the audience: "That moment was it. That's when it all fused together. It happened. John Wayne walked over and said, Hello, my name is John Wayne. I'd like to congratulate you. Like I didn't know who he was—John Wayne. It was like Mount Rushmore saying, 'How do you like the part?'"

Rocky was a people's champion—warm and earnest and full of heart, a common man who manages to beat the odds. Still smarting from the war in Vietnam and the bitter aftertaste of the Age of Aquarius, America was in desperate need of a winner like Rocky: a straight-shooting, plain-talking man who simply will not quit. Like Jimmy Carter, who got elected President that same year, he was an outsider who wasn't supposed to have a chance. But even long after the Carter era, Stallone kept making Rocky movies, each one's plot contrived to tell the story of the rough road from abject failure to triumph, and until *Rocky V* they were all big successes. The basic Rocky plot, and the hero who lives it, is timeless. As Franz Lidz wrote in *Sports Illustrated:* "Rocky Balboa has become more real than real people. Coaches losing at halftime quote him for inspiration. Politicians behind in the polls invoke him. Underdogs everywhere love him."

John Rambo started as one of life's losers, too (a rootless, traumatized Vietnam veteran), and in the three Rambo movies

(so far), he, like Rocky, has proven that heart and soul and determination are the stuff of victory. But Rambo is something very different from just Rocky with a machine gun. Rambo is a killer; Rocky is just a fighter. Rambo is merciless; Rocky is a soft touch. Rambo is always a well-honed fighting machine; Rocky must struggle to get in shape in every film. Rambo is a sociopathic loner; Rocky has a wife and family. And although Rambo is always, like Rocky, an underdog, he has no personal flaws—and little personality. The charm of Rocky, particularly in the first two, or even three, movies of the series, is that he is a very human character who—like most of us humans—screws up his own life, then—like a few of us—manages to set things right again. Rocky is an oaf who is loud, vain, sentimental, shy, even humorous—all of which tend to make him sympathetic, and make his victories a matter of spiritual redemption. Rambo, on the other hand, is a victim of evil forces outside himself: Communists, bureaucrats, an ill-conceived foreign policy, lily-livered politicians. He's a sort of militarized Dirty Harry (see p. 141). So when he whips his enemies, whether they are a corrupt sheriff or the Russian army, it tastes more like revenge than triumph. Stallone himself called Rambo "this frightening kind of thing. You step back and say, Whoa, Jesus Christ. But you wouldn't want his home phone number."

Rambo was created in the 1982 movie *First Blood* and helped establish what has been called the "payback" genre of movie, in which a lone Vietnam veteran is taunted or wronged and then spends the rest of the movie systematically eradicating dozens or hundreds of bad buys in a spectacle of gunfire, explosions, car and motorbike and helicopter chases, and an ever-accelerating *danse macabre* of cataclysmic special effects (see also "Arnold Schwarzenegger," p.

438). In *First Blood*, a survivalist fantasy that pits Rambo, armed only with his wits and his pectoral muscles, against local police and the National Guard, the pyrotechnics are relatively small, and the arena is a patch of wilderness in the Pacific Northwest, but in the 1985 sequel, *Rambo: First Blood, Part Two*, Rambo simultaneously takes on evil Communists and dishonorable officials in the U.S. government. It was this second film, as well as the not-so-successful *Rambo III* (1988), in which he fights the Russian army in Afghanistan, that defined a pop-culture hero who has since become a worldwide symbol of some disturbing contradictions in the American character. Writing about Rambo in *The New Republic*, Martha Bayles noted that "Stallone taps popular patriotism, but he also taps darker emotions, such as the resentment many veterans feel toward their government for not waging war against North Vietnam to the hilt, and toward their countrymen for ridiculing or ignoring their sacrifices." Rambo is brooding and in pain, also brave and patriotic—an avatar of American sensitivity as much as of global aggression.

Sylvester Stallone has tried hard to separate himself from the awesome aura of his screen creations, but so far none of his noncombat movies has softened his image as a macho warrior. "There was a fusing of my personality with Rocky's," he said. "We were genetically spliced. Spliced for life. And it became more compounded a problem when *Rambo* came up.... Again there is another gene splicing." Stallone's great unrealized dream is to someday make a movie from one of the first scripts he ever wrote, before *Rocky*, then *Rambo*, transformed his career and his life. It is a biography of Edgar Allan Poe, whom he yearns to play because he feels such empathy for the tortured poet. "No American artist was more misunderstood," he once explained. "He was scorned as a lunatic instead of hailed as a visionary.... He was like Rocky."

CHARLIE STARKWEATHER

One of pop culture's favorite themes in the 1950s was the specter of juvenile delinquency: wild teenagers on the loose. Most of the concern was overblown hysteria—confused reaction to an emerging youth culture that embraced the rebellious images of Elvis and James Dean and was eager to have its own kicks in its own way. Some anxiety was trumped up to market such movies as the high-minded *Blackboard Jungle* and kinky *Teen-Age Crime Wave* (both 1955), each of which in its own way was more a matter of exploitation than of insight. Rampaging teenagers sold tickets. *Cry Baby Killer*, Jack Nicholson's first picture, in 1958, was advertised with the line "Yesterday a teenage rebel ... today a mad-dog slayer!"

On one occasion, however, a couple of teenagers really did bring to life everybody's worst fears about the younger generation. TEEN-AGER BECOMES A MASS KILLER —WHY? read the headline in *Life* magazine after Charlie Starkweather, age nineteen, along with his girlfriend, Caril Ann Fugate, fourteen, went on a spree in the winter of

Caril Ann and Charlie

1958 and killed eleven people in Nebraska and Wyoming, just for kicks. The three-day hunt for the mad-dog slayer terrified the midlands and became front-page news all across the country. The story of Charlie and Caril, like that of Bonnie and Clyde before them, has since become compelling pop folklore with a weird romantic twist. Terrence Malick made it into an artistic movie, *Badlands* (1973), starring Sissy Spacek and Martin Sheen, and Bruce Springsteen sang about Charlie and Caril in "Nebraska" (1982), taking Charlie's voice and point of view, explaining his murder binge as a result of "a meanness in the world."

Charlie Starkweather, a native Nebraskan who was frequently described in the press as looking like a cross between Elvis Presley and James Dean, believed that his problems started the first day he went to school. "The kids picked on me, they made fun of my bowed legs and my speech." (He had a peculiar lisp that made him say "wowse" for house and "awong" for along.) As he grew older he became known to classmates as "Bantam Red Head," and he wore oversized cowboy boots to compensate for being five foot two. He grew sideburns and let his hair grow long enough so he could comb it like a greaser, and he affected all the mannerisms of a dangerous punk. Still, everyone laughed at him. "I built up a hatred as hard as iron," he later told a prison psychiatrist. Expelled from grade school for knife fighting, he quit high school in the ninth grade, then got a job as a garbageman's assistant in Lincoln, where he became known for yelling "Go to hell!" at perfect strangers from the window of the truck.

Only two things made Charlie happy. One was driving in demolition derby races, which his father explained by saying, "The idea was to smash into anyone that got in your way. He liked that best." The other thing Charlie liked was guns. He had bad eyesight and wore glasses, but he was a dead shot and would spend hours in front of a mirror, looking mean and tough like juvenile delinquents in the movies, and drawing his revolver against his own reflection, imagining how all the goddamned sons of bitches who made fun of him would feel if he ever pointed his .38 at them.

In 1956, Caril Ann Fugate came into Charlie's life. Legend says he first saw her in her front yard twirling a baton (at least that's what the movie *Badlands* shows and what Springsteen sings in "Nebraska"); in any case, she was even shorter than he was —under five feet tall, but with a pert figure —and she liked to go around in a big, floppy man-tailored shirt and tuck her tight jeans into the tops of tasseled majorette boots. Like Charlie, she was a rebel (she often told her stepfather to go to hell), and like him, she was bad in school (she had been held back a grade; he had been found to have an IQ in the "dull-normal" range). Caril thought

Charlie was cool. He said he had never met a girl who knew so much. When they met, she was thirteen years old.

Charlie gave Caril lots of presents: plush toys, a phonograph, and a gold heart to wear around her neck, with "Caril" engraved on one side and "Chuck" on the other. Charlie's sister, La Veta Jeanne, thought Caril was a bad influence—"a regular little snip, you know, a snot, and she treated him like dirt." Charlie's father didn't much like her, either, and one day when Charlie defied his father by letting Caril drive his car, Charlie's father kicked him out of the house—actually, pushed him out through a plate-glass window. He got a room at Mrs. Hawley's boardinghouse in Lincoln and planned for the day he and Caril would get married and run away together. And he decided to become an outlaw.

In December 1957 Charlie quit a job baling paper at the Western Newspaper Union. His reason: The long hours didn't allow him to pick up Caril at three in the afternoon when her school let out. Quitting was bad because it meant he had no more money to buy her presents. So early one winter morning when it was six below zero in Lincoln, Charlie took a twelve-gauge shotgun to a service station about a mile from Caril's house, stole $108, then shot off the attendant's head. The first thing he did was go to Caril's house and tell her. The two of them went out for a joyride together and spent the next two months going to every movie that had shooting in it, including *Escape from San Quentin* and *Last of the Badmen*.

For a while after his first killing, Charlie felt mighty good. He had evened the score for that first day in school when the other kids were mean to him. He had money, and he had his girl, with whom he spent every evening in his room, where they practiced knife throwing, listened to records, and ate candy bars. Sometimes Charlie drew pictures to amuse Caril. He was good at that. "Why, he could sit down and draw a pencil sketch of you, and you wouldn't know the difference!" his father told reporters after Charlie was in jail.

But there was a problem: Caril's mother and stepfather, the Bartletts. They didn't like Charlie one bit. On January 21 Charlie was at their house waiting for Caril to come home from school. They yelled at him, so he took his rifle and killed them just as Caril Ann was walking in the door. Caril Ann turned on the TV to watch her favorite afternoon show while Charlie killed her three-year-old half-sister, Betty Jean, whom he stunned with the butt of his rifle, then pinned to the floor by throwing his big knife into her throat. Charlie then made sandwiches and they watched TV together, after tacking a note to the front door that said, "Stay a Way. Every Body is Sick With the Flu. Miss Bartlett." The dead bodies were wrapped in paper and hidden in a chicken coop, and Charlie and Caril spent the next week living like teenage kings: bacon and eggs every morning, Pepsis and potato chips through the day, all the ice cream and chewing gum they wanted . . . and nobody telling them what to do and what not to do. After a week, when relatives got suspicious, Charlie and Caril took his revolver, the rifle, and Mr. Bartlett's .410 shotgun (Charlie had sawed the barrel down), got into his hot-rod 1949 Ford, and headed west.

It was a three-day, 525-mile ride into the badlands. They killed a seventy-year-old farmer, two teenagers, and two rich people and their maid. By the end of the second day, schools throughout Nebraska were posted with armed guards, and a posse of a hundred vigilantes carrying deer rifles and shotguns had gathered at the Lincoln courthouse, itching to go after the pair; police were given the order to shoot to kill; the National Guard was called up, and road-blocks were placed throughout the state. Somehow, Charlie and Caril avoided every-body, and twelve miles outside of Douglas, Wyoming, they spotted a nice new Buick by the side of the road. They were tired of the Packard they had stolen along the way, so they snuck up to the Buick, where the driver, a traveling shoe salesman, was sleeping. Charlie shot him nine times in the head, and Caril got into the backseat. But Charlie couldn't get the Buick's emergency brake to release. As he fussed, a passerby named Joseph Sprinkle stopped to help. Charlie pointed his rifle at Sprinkle and said, "Help me release this brake or I'll kill you." Sprinkle grabbed the gun and they started to fight. A sheriff happened by in his patrol car. Caril Ann Fugate leapt out of the Buick and ran towards him, screaming, "It's Starkweather! He's going to kill me."

Charlie leapt back into the Packard and sped off. He crashed through a roadblock but was finally halted when police bullets shattered his car's window. Glass nicked his ear, and it started to bleed. One of the offi-cers who captured him said, "He thought he was bleeding to death. That's why he stopped. That's the kind of yellow sonofa-bitch he is." As for Charlie, he told everyone who would listen that all the killings were in self-defense. "People kept coming at me, and I had to shoot. What else would you do? I wanted to be a criminal, but I didn't know it would be like this."

For a while, Charlie told authorities that Caril had been an unwilling accomplice. However, when he was being extradited back to Lincoln, he spent one night in a small jail in Gering, Nebraska, where he wrote these messages, faintly, in pencil, high on the cell wall:

Caril is the one who said to go to
    Washington State
by the time any body will read this i
    will be dead for all the killings then
    they cannot give caril the chair to
from Lincoln Nebraska they got us Jan.
    29, 1958.
kill 11 persons. (Charlie kill 9) all men
                  (Caril kill   2) all girls
                               ——
                               11
they have so many cops and people
    watching us leave I can't add all of
    them up

Below these words were a Valentine heart with an arrow through it and the words "Charles Starkweather and Caril Fugate."

When Caril Ann Fugate pleaded that she was an innocent hostage, Charlie changed his original story and said she had enjoyed their time together as much as he had, ex-plaining that they had simply devised the hostage hogwash during their happy week together after the first killings. "One time she said that some hamburgers were lousy and we ought to go back and shoot all them people in the restaurant," Charlie said, and one of his best-remembered remarks from the trial was "If I fry in the electric chair, Caril should be sitting in my lap." The jury didn't buy Caril's story; they were especially skeptical of her explanation that she didn't dare escape because Charlie had told her he would kill her family if she did. The pros-ecutor, who told the jury, "Even fourteen-year-old girls must recognize they cannot go on eight-day murder sprees," reminded Caril that her family had already been shot and that she had watched it happen. Caril never had been very bright. She was sen-tenced to life in prison.

To this day, Caril Ann Fugate asserts that she was a victim, not a criminal. Only re-cently, after nearly thirty years in prison with an unblemished record of good behavior, was she paroled. Charlie never said he was sorry about taking eleven innocent lives, but he certainly felt sorry for himself. In the days before his execution he told a psychiatrist, "I haven't eaten in a high-class restaurant; I never seen the New York Yankees play; I've never been to Los Angeles." And he placed the blame on everyone who made him do it by taunting him or getting in his way. They, not he, were the ones responsible for murder. "If you pull the chain on a toilet," Charlie asked, "you can't blame it for flushing, can you?"

Charlie Starkweather was electrocuted by the state on June 25, 1959. Robert J. Nash reports in *Bloodletters and Badmen* that the day before his execution, a local Lions Club asked him to donate his eyes to an eye bank after his death. His response: "Hell no! No one ever did anything for me." Thirty minutes before his scheduled execution, the prison physician dropped dead of a heart attack, but a new doctor was rushed to the scene to pronounce Charlie dead, and the execution proceeded on schedule. His last words, to the guards who took him to the chair, were "What's your hurry?"

When his passing was announced shortly after midnight, there were tears outside the gate of the Nebraska State Penitentiary. A cluster of bobby-soxers had gathered so they could be near Charlie at the end. Apparently, they had become smitten with the mass murderer, who was described in his cell by *U.S. News & World Report* as "the picture of a Hollywood-style 'tough' wearing blue jeans, leather jacket, cowboy boots, and sideburns." As the girls wept, gangs of hoods in cars cruised in circles outside the prison, blasting rock-and-roll music at full volume on their radios, drinking beer, and causing a commotion. Before Charlie Starkweather's body was removed from the prison, police were called to clear the area of all unruly teenagers.

"STAR TREK"

Science-fiction stories on film or television are customarily loaded with impressive special effects, especially since the overwhelming success of the high-tech movie *Star Wars* (1978), and more often than not their vision of the future is a scary one. "Star Trek," the television show that aired on NBC from 1966 to 1969 and has since become an unparalleled cultural obsession, is different. It is more about human and other beings, most of whom are pretty decent creatures, than it is about technological wonderment. (There are special effects in the series, based on tri-corders, transporters, phasers, and the like: "Star Trek" was nominated for, but did not win, an Emmy for them in 1967.) The future in which it takes place is a heartening one in which different life forms might co-exist in a relatively peaceful state if it weren't for the Klingons and Romulans.

In so many sci-fi movies of the last few decades, the common theme is that we humans become prisoners of our technology or are somehow diminished or jeopardized by it (*The Terminator* is a good example), and this has made "Star Trek" look all the sweeter in retrospect. Its heroes are en-

Leonard Nimoy (Mr. Spock) and Jane Wyatt (Mrs. Spock [his mother])

riched by their ability to warp themselves around the universe and beam themselves hither and yon; they use their powers on a noble quest to "seek out new life and new civilizations, to boldly go where no man has gone before"—their mission, as ordained by the United Federation of Planets—and they (usually) obey the Federation's Prime Directive, which insists on noninterference in the normal development of a civilization.

Furthermore, unlike a lot of the zap-'em-up rocket operas that went before it in the movies and on TV, "Star Trek" was a thinking person's series characterized by discussion and philosophizing among the crew of the starship *Enterprise*, especially between Captain Kirk (William Shatner) and the brainy but emotionless half-Vulcan Mr. Spock (Leonard Nimoy). Nearly all of its seventy-nine episodes had a message, usually about tolerance, that applied to twentieth-century life in America. "Star Trek" aired when this country was embroiled in the Vietnam War, and many of its fans have argued that it was replete with antiwar sen-

timent, not the least of which was the Vulcan salute—hand raised, palm facing forward, as if to say "How" (yet strangely similar to "Heil"), with the middle and index fingers separated, forming a V. According to Dawn G. Colt, writing in *USA Today*, the salute was "different from the counterculture peace sign, but the meaning was the same."

The most famous science-fiction series in history, created by Gene Roddenberry, who served as its executive producer, was a ratings flop in its three years of first-run broadcasts, never rising above fiftieth place, and especially unpopular among advertisers because of demographic studies that showed so many of its viewers were children and teenagers with low purchasing power. NBC started threatening to cancel it after barely a year on the air, but when they did, strange things happened: They got more protest letters than ever before in their history—over a million. "We are pleased to tell you that 'Star Trek' will continue," they announced one Friday night towards the end of the second season; but in February 1969 the axe finally fell. "Star Trek" was out of production for good, despite the letters and protests by fans (soon to be known as Trekkies, but now preferring the more dignified Trekkers), who believed they could revive it.

Even though no more episodes were to be made, NBC did air "Star Trek: The Animated Series," featuring the actual voices of William Shatner, Leonard Nimoy, et al. as well as stories from the prime-time show, on Saturday mornings in 1974 and 1975. But it is the original "Star Trek"—now all the more fun for its extremely dated-looking special effects and antiquated vision of the future (not to mention its quaint-seeming optimism about technology and racial harmony)—that has become a never-ending fountain of fascination to fans, who pore over the revered episodes as if they were the Dead Sea Scrolls. Serious Trekkers know all the dialogue from all the shows, as well as every tiny bit of business among the characters; at "Star Trek" conventions, known as cons, many of them enjoy dressing up like the crew of the *Enterprise*, in 1960s mod velveteen-polyester shirt-jacks.

For serious Trekkers, the original show has become, like the Old Testament, a text deserving not only detailed study but also further extrapolation. Many premises and situations were left unresolved when "Star Trek" was canceled, and since then, a vast universe of "zines" has opened up—homemade magazines that report on Trekker doings and also frequently feature fiction in which the "Star Trek" characters are brought back to life. "A good zine writer," Roberta Rogow, editor of the zine *Grip*, explained to *The New Yorker* for a "Talk of the Town" story in 1988, "might begin with 'Trek' characters the way a Greek bard might have begun with the same old crowd of gods and heroes. But then you go beyond." She said that 1976 marked the debut of "slash zines," named for their generic label, "K/S," which refers to the names of Captain Kirk and Mr. Spock, who always have sex in them. They usually feature Spock seducing Kirk, and they are invariably written by women, for women. "What the girls forget, though," Ms. Rogow fumed, "is that Spock is sexually active *only once every seven years.* . . . He may be a gay Vulcan. He might be a straight Vulcan. I'm open minded on that. But the one certain thing we know about all Vulcans' sex life is that *they are sexually active once every seven years.* When you ignore a rule like that, it seems to me you're not writing literature anymore." Ms. Rogow also said that one of the reasons she—and so many other women—originally became enamored of "Star Trek" was its Lieutenant Uhura (Nichelle Nichols), an African-American woman on the bridge alongside Captain Kirk. "In 1966 just to have a woman in contact with Star Fleet at all was a breakthrough," she said.

"After watching Kirk, Spock, and Bones [Leonard McCoy, the medical officer, played by DeForrest Kelley] recite the same corny lines year after year, I consider them almost like family," confessed Benjamin Svetkey, author of a 1991 *Entertainment Weekly* cover story titled "The *Enterprise* Turns 25." Svetkey concluded his paean to Trekkerhood by saying, "The thing I most love about 'Star Trek' is that it's just plain *fun.* Warp engines, phasers, Tribbles, transporters, tricorders, Klingons—life doesn't get much cooler than this." His story featured a picture of William Shatner and Leonard Nimoy, who had just completed the movie *Star Trek VI*, giving the Vulcan salute, and it offered the following evidence of the never-ending charisma of the show:

- Syndicated reruns of the original series are now broadcast over two hundred times a day in the United States. They have been translated into forty-seven languages.
- There have been six feature-length movies spun out of the concept, grossing over $400 million.
- An all-new TV show called "Star Trek: The Next Generation" is now in its sixth season on the air.
- There have been over one hundred "Star Trek" novels and nearly two dozen nonfiction books about the series.
- "Adults-only 'Star Trek' books, magazines, and videos are doing boffo business at 'Trek' conventions." They include a video called *Sex Trek: The Next Penetration* in which Mr. Spock's ears grow when he gets aroused.
- "Next to 'The Partridge Family,' the show has inspired more misguided crooning careers than any other TV series." Songs and

albums recorded by "Star Trek" alumni include William Shatner's "Lucy in the Sky with Diamonds," Leonard Nimoy's "Music to Watch Space Girls By," and Grace Lee Whitney's (Yeoman Janice Rand) "Disco Trekking."

- In 1976 the U.S. space shuttle *Constitution* was renamed the *Enterprise* after an intensive letter-writing campaign by Trekkies to President Gerald Ford.
- "Star Trek" merchandise, hawked at "Star Trek" conventions around the country, ranges from trading cards and glow-in-the-dark yo-yos to a $944 chess set populated by gold- and silver-plated "Star Trek" characters and a $200 gift set of videos (the first five feature films) accompanied by three cloisonné pins, a certificate from "Star Trek" producer Gene Roddenberry, and a piece of paper with William Shatner's signature on it.
- Vulcan, Canada (population 1,400), has made itself home of the world's first "Star Trek" theme park, "complete with parades, window displays, and a statue of the *Enterprise.*"

MARTHA STEWART

"Martha Stewart is no longer just a person," Martha Stewart announced in 1991. "Martha Stewart is an attitude. Martha Stewart is ideas." Martha Stewart, America's hostess with the mostest, was just too modest to come right out and say what nearly everybody knows Martha Stewart really is, and that is *perfect.* She is an ideal of success, poise, beauty, charm, domesticity, and good taste.

Over two million people have bought Martha Stewart books that tell them how to lead lovelier lives, but Martha is no mere instructor; she is the star of the show, a modern goddess of graciousness who is in the business of selling the secrets of her success. In books, videotapes, and *Martha Stewart Living* magazine, in thousand-dollar-a-head personal seminars and as million-dollar-a-year entertaining consultant to K-Mart stores, she has invented an aesthetic self-improvement program that *Newsweek* once compared to a religion: "The Cult of the Home, wherein the perfection of the place settings, the centerpiece,

and food is a reflection of the blissful serenity of the inhabitants." *Newsweek* didn't go so far as to suggest that Martha was herself the high priestess of this cult, but there was at least a little bitchiness in their analysis of the phenomenon. And let us say this before we go any further: A lot of people get infuriated by Martha Stewart and her relentless pursuit of loveliness. Diana White of the Boston *Globe* called her "the hostess from hell," but the fact is that millions of people want to be like her or at least relish what she has to say. And the Martha Stewart style has changed the look of pop culture.

Her first book, *Entertaining* (1982), created a new kind of cookbook: the plush, full-color, lifestyle bible meant to inspire its readers as well as instruct them. The recipes were criticized by many earnest food writers for being too derivative or too difficult, or for not working at all, but of course, such critiques missed the main point of the book, which was to present a blissful vision of entertaining. On every page of *Entertaining* is a picture of something wondrous to behold: poached pears with candied violets resting seductively in a cut crystal bowl filled with regal-colored wine; vodka bottles encased along with long-stemmed roses in frosty slabs of ice; deep-dish pies snuggled inside woven baskets; country kitchens and shoreline clambakes; Martha hoeing serenely in her garden, Martha surrounded by her gleaming copper pots, Martha creating her "signature basket": a huge wicker platter filled with about five hundred dollars' worth of the world's most beautiful strawberries ("plump, radiant, perfectly ripe," she advised).

Martha made this dreamy, soft-focus life seem accessible to anyone with the will to have it back in the early 1980s. Her beautiful world was not one of rare seventeenth-century antiques and priceless family silver; it was filled with cozy things: old handmade quilts, blue flowware platters, mason jars containing pretty homemade jellies (made from fruits from her hand-tended garden), well-worn gingham napkins, and adorably knobby baskets made of woven twigs. It cannot be said for certain which came first, Martha Stewart or the boom in country crafts, but it was clear by the middle of the decade that a new kind of rustic-themed romanticism was blooming in many American homes. Although Martha has been called the Barbara Cartland of food, her kind of enchantment was much more down to earth than pink chiffon and glittery tiaras: It was

a do-it-yourself kind of fantasy world, with less emphasis on spending money than on being creative. Why squander thousands of dollars on a chandelier, Martha asked, when you can snatch up an old, decrepit one at a tag sale and refinish it yourself? Why buy expensive French lace or Irish damask, when you can do as Martha did when she catered a party at the Whitney Museum in New York and use an airbrush to hand-decorate each of the secondhand rental tablecloths with modern art motifs borrowed from the paintings of the guest of honor?

The success of *Entertaining* was followed by more books, including the hugely popular *Weddings*, a fifty-dollar, high-gloss glorification of nuptial rituals that Martha had catered, and then came how-to videotapes and television holiday specials that showed Martha tramping through bogs of cranberries and smoking wild game in outdoor ovens. There were Martha Stewart compact discs with mood music for parties, Martha Stewart wedding organizers, and, starting in 1988, whole lines of Martha Stewart sheets, towels, kitchenware, lamp shades, and wallpaper specially designed for K-Mart, whose enthusiastic spokesman called the discount store's new line of products "everything from Martha's world."

Martha Stewart wasn't only a success. She became a cultural institution and a venerated idol to fans, whose devotion was of a magnitude heretofore unknown in the world of entertaining or recipe-writing. Explaining why she was happy to pay nearly a thousand dollars to attend a seminar at Martha Stewart's home in Westport, Connecticut, one pilgrim explained, "What we get is to see the real flesh-and-blood woman, the real Martha, the fabulous woman in those gorgeous books." At a K-Mart book signing in 1991, one devotee (not named Martha) boasted to Martha, "My friends call me Martha. My cousin and I call each other in Jersey and do Martha trivia." Martha also told one reporter that there are some fans who routinely set a place of honor for her at their dinner parties. Of course, they don't expect her to attend. Martha explained, "It's just their way of saying thank you."

For many people, Martha re-established housewifery as a venerable craft. The business of keeping house had suffered declining status for many years because such tasks as setting the table and making birthday party decorations seemed emblematic of women's second-class role. For a lot of women who had come of age and who had set up house in the years after the 1960s, it was simply considered socially incorrect to worry oneself with domestic trivia. But there were hordes of others who needed guidance, and for millions of successful baby boomers who were having kids and moving into the gracious middle class, Martha Stewart offered a plan and a role model and a pep talk. She showed that keeping house is not just a task; it is an art. *Yankee* magazine attended "A Day With Martha" in Hinsdale, Illinois, and eavesdropped on one of the eight hundred women (who had paid $38 each) in the audience: "There's never been anyone like her. Martha has done so much for women. She's so elegant, yet so down-to-earth. She's a successful businesswoman. She's beautiful. She has a perfect home and a perfect garden."

Like most phenomenally successful people, Martha Stewart has enemies. Some of them don't like her as a matter of principle. "Martha Stewart is possessed by her possessions and amorally oblivious of reality," the New York *Daily News* disparaged in a review that said her videotapes "will simply make a lot of women feel inadequate." "Artifice!" cried *Newsweek*. "No one can live like *Martha Stewart Living*, probably not even Martha Stewart." Some people don't like her because she is so tough in business

—a workaholic tyrant who, according to one former employee, "can be an incredible dragon." But most of her detractors don't like her because she is just too exemplary —the girl in school who is cheerleader, valedictorian, president of the student council, and head of the clothing-for-the-needy charity drive—and they are green with envy. "She is Martha Stewart," Kathie Lee Gifford joked on the TV show "Regis and Kathie Lee" one morning in 1990 after Martha demonstrated how to transform cast-off cardboard toilet paper tubes into festive Christmas gift containers. "*She* is Martha Stewart. And I'm not! And it makes me crazy!"

Martha has always been perfect, or close to it. If you need more things about her to admire (or to drive you nuts), here are a few achievements from her permanent record:

- When she was ten years old, she began staging children's parties, because she felt she could earn more than fifty cents per hour as a babysitter.
- She began modeling at twelve years old.
- She worked her way through college (Barnard, a dual degree in European history and architectural history) as a fashion model.
- She was selected by *Glamour* magazine as one of America's Ten Best-Dressed College Girls.
- She made hundreds of thousands of dollars as a stockbroker in the early 1970s.
- She paid $49,000 for her Westport home in 1971 and restored it herself; its current estimated value is several million.
- When she began her catering business in 1974, her earliest supporters and fans included Paul Newman, Robert Redford, Beverly Sills, and Ralph Lauren.
- She earns about two million dollars a year.
- She requires only four hours of sleep each night. She spends most of the night reading or working by flashlight in her garden.

It's hard to know now if Martha Stewart will be inscribed in cultural history as a

1980s person or if her magic will transcend the aspirations of that high-styled decade. One thing is certain, and that is that the 1990s have witnessed the advent of a new Martha. In 1991 her antique Victorian white aprons and flowing blond hair vanished in favor of gardening pants, a practical, short-cropped hairdo, and chic but sturdy shoes. (Not coincidentally, her 1991 Christmas gift book was *Martha Stewart's Gardening*.) On a "Today" show segment to promote her book, she appeared surrounded by piles of manure and mulch and showed Bryant Gumble how to make a compost heap. The impeccably attired Mr. Gumble looked as if he would rather be surrounded by Martha's cakes and cookies, but he did brighten up when he noticed that in order to lump together her rotting garbage, soil, and fecal matter on the NBC stage, Martha had put on a pair of lovely monogrammed gardening gloves.

SUPER BOWL

As an athletic contest, the annual January Super Bowl game between the two top teams in professional football is notoriously dull. It is seldom close; in fact, the margin of victory averages about two touchdowns. Known among sportswriters as the Stupor Bowl or the Super Bore, it is the single most watched, talked-about, and betted-on sporting event in North America (soccermania on other continents is at least its equal). It is billed as the Ultimate Game, but as Dallas Cowboys running back Duane Thomas once wondered, "If it's the Ultimate Game, why do they play it every year?"

They play it every year because it has become THE national pop-culture holiday. Super Bowl Sunday has a momentum all its own that has totally overshadowed the teams on the field and has less to do with sports than with a glorious celebration of leisure-time fun, American style. Unlike the World Series or the U.S. Open, which are mostly of interest to people who care about baseball and tennis, the Super Bowl—always the top-rated television show of the year—reaches far beyond the ranks of sports fans for its audience. You don't have to give a hoot about football (ten times as many people watch the Super Bowl on TV as watch an ordinary pro football game), but if you like to drink a lot of beer, eat junk food, bet your shirt, or lie in a reclining chair watching the best half-minutes that the best minds in television advertising can conceive, or if the great, commercial bigness of it all sends a shiver of awe up your spine, then why should that silly little game they're playing make any difference, any-

way? The Super Bowl has become what the Fourth of July used to be—this country's premier community jubilee, an event that general-interest polls have shown stirs more concern and attention than the outbreak of a shooting war in which the United States is directly involved.

The first Super Bowl, between the Kansas City Chiefs and the Green Bay Packers in 1967, was officially known simply as the "AFL-NFL World Championship Game," but when the five-year-old daughter of the Chiefs' Lamar Hunt was playing with her high-bouncing Super Ball that year, her drawling pronunciation of the ball's name gave Hunt an inspiration: Call the game a Super Bowl. The organizers were nervous that it wouldn't live up to that billing, but by the third game, the title had become official. For the fifth, when the Baltimore Colts played the Dallas Cowboys in a notorious flub-filled contest known among sportswriters as the Blooper Bowl, the name was appended with the Roman numeral "V," to help give the contest a classic aura—a tradition that has continued.

The great appeal of the Super Bowl when it began is easy to comprehend: 1966 was a year when many Americans felt overwhelmed by ambiguity; we were fighting a foreign war we didn't seem to want to win and arguing about issues like sex and drugs that had no easy answers. "We are in a time when society seems to have sympathy only for the misfit, the losers," said Vince Lombardi, the coach who led the Packers into the first Super Bowl. "Let us also cheer the doers, the winners!" In 1969 *Sports Illustrated* printed a letter from a Lombardi fan who wrote that America's "appetite for idealism and appreciation of romance has been starved on a diet of platitude, bombast, and forked-tongue aphorism as dished out by Washington's ruling-class population of politicians, bureaucrats, and the captains

of vested interests. A few *ararararararghs* can only be counted as a welcome sound." The Super Bowl provided *ararararararghs* galore. Unlike Vietnam, unlike the protest on the streets of this country, it allowed for an unambiguous celebration of winning, and of the old-fashioned principle that Might Makes Right.

From the point of view of professional football's promoters, it was a good way to extend the season; for television, it provided an opportunity to shake off the usual doldrums of January, when there were no exciting sports events to cover, and when advertising generally had to be sold cheap. Until the establishment of the third Monday in January as Martin Luther King Day, there were no holidays between New Year's Day and Lincoln's Birthday (now subsumed into "Presidents' Day"). Super Bowl Sunday was a wonderful way to fill that gap, and just as Mother's Day and Valentine's Day provided incentive for people to go out and purchase cards and gifts, the Super Bowl has helped activate consumers during an otherwise sluggish buying season.

Even if the game is an unpromising mismatch, the merriment that surrounds it in every city where it's played makes going to the Super Bowl a pilgrimage relished by anyone who wants to be where the action is, including fun lovers, party animals, pickup artists, prostitutes, business executives and their clients, and all gonzo journalists (starting with Hunter Thompson) who like seeing Americans let their hair, and sometimes their pants, down. The San Diego Convention and Visitors Bureau reported a thirty-six-million-dollar drop in spending by tourists in January 1989 compared with the previous year. The reason? Bureau president Dal Watkins said that in 1988, San Diego had hosted the Super Bowl, which had "poured money into the local economy." On the eve of Super Bowl XXIII in Miami, Carl Hiassen of the Miami *Herald* put it this way: "The prime mission of Super Bowl Week is to separate the tourist from as much of his money as can be pried from his pale little paws."

Hangers-on without tickets come for the fun, but to actually gain admittance to the stadium is one of the exalted accomplishments in sports fandom, like receiving an invitation to the coronation of a British monarch, and much rarer than attending a President's inaugural ball. Average people simply cannot get in. Unless you hold a season pass or know someone with pro football connections, you must buy your ticket from a "ticket broker," which is a nice name for a scalper, who might let you have a pair of good ones for three to four thousand dollars. The week before Super Bowl XXI, in Pasadena, California, one dentist advertised in the Los Angeles *Times* that he would trade a complete cap job for two seats anywhere in the stadium. A used car dealer said he would trade any car on the lot for "four good seats." A lawyer sought to exchange free legal advice—for life—with anyone who gave him two tickets. Conversely, an "art photographer" said he would give two tickets to a husband and wife willing to pose nude for him.

If you cannot go to the game, the place to be on Super Bowl Sunday is Las Vegas, where, it is estimated, somewhere near a hundred million dollars is wagered on the game (a fraction of the amount that is bet illegally around the country), and where—as at the game itself—you can't get in. All the big casinos book Super Bowl weekends at least a year in advance, and they are generally attended by high rollers and friends of the house. At Caesars Palace, the festivities usually include heaping buffets and champagne, real live pro football stars in attendance, jiggling cheerleaders at halftime, and the opportunity to lay down cash

on gaggles of "proposition bets" on such peripheral issues as who will score the first touchdown and which team will pass for the most yardage in the third quarter.

For most ordinary people the Super Bowl is a television event. For television advertisers, it is Judgment Day—despite apocryphal stories that cities' water pressure drops dramatically during Super Bowl commercials because so many people go to the bathroom and all flush at the same time. Every major corporate player in the American marketplace buys time during the game to reach the biggest audience it can ever hope to reach in one shot—well over a hundred million consumers. It was during Super Bowls that Michael Jackson debuted for Pepsi; the Macintosh computer was presented; Ronald McDonald introduced himself to America at large; Miller beer's bull terrier, Spuds MacKenzie, leaped to superstardom, as did all those garrulous guys on behalf of Lite beer; and starting in 1989, the commercial lineup included its own little "Bud Bowl," a kind of mini-parody of the game, for the purpose of selling beer. In fact, beer companies are the most conspicuous advertisers on the telecast—no surprise, considering that sales of such thirst-provokers as potato chips, pretzels, nuts, popcorn, and lunch meat reach their yearly peak as the Super Bowl approaches. Writing about the three-dimensional halftime show that Diet Coke sponsored in 1989 and that required special viewing glasses, Tom Shales of the Washington *Post* observed, "If you drank a beer for every beer commercial seen during the game, you probably saw the whole darn thing in three dimensions anyway. Maybe four or five, as a matter of fact."

SUPERMAN

"Super," which is now understood in virtually every language on earth, means a curious kind of excellence that does not necessarily have high rank, status, or dominion. It means only the greatest, without any sense of untoward arrogance or control—a really marvelous, outstanding, extravagant thing everybody can enjoy. In this country, we love just about anything that is super, or better yet, super-duper or super-colossal, and an awful lot of things that get that label (with the notable exception of countries that are superpowers) are in some way characteristically American: supermarkets, Super Bowls, superhighways, and supercriminals. Of all the super things this culture has produced, none is better known or more admired (here and around the world) than Superman.

Before Superman got famous as the blue-haired, red-caped muscleman who was a tireless champion of truth, justice, and the American way, the word was generally associated with German racism inferred from Friedrich Nietzsche, whose concept of an *Übermensch* (sometimes translated as "over-man" or "beyond man") was taken as a reference to a more highly evolved, superior kind of human who deserved to rule over lesser beings. It was no coincidence that seventeen-year-old Ohioans Jerry Siegel and Joe Shuster got their idea for Superman the same year Adolf Hitler was named Führer and became a world-famous villain by championing his own version of the superman myth, which asserted the whole Aryan race to be naturally better than all others. (In the 1950s, when the comic-book business was condemned as injurious to the mental health of children, some worried

guardians of morality pointed out that the lightninglike *S* on Superman's chest was uncomfortably similar to the Nazi police's *SS*.) Indeed, one of Siegel's first self-published, mimeographed comic books, done while he was in high school, was called *The Reign of the Superman*, about an evil scientist who wants to rule the earth. But as Siegel later conceived him (one night in 1934 when he couldn't sleep) and Shuster drew him, Superman was no megalomaniacal overlord. Based partly on the hero of the Philip Wylie sci-fi novel *Gladiator*, he was a friendly being from another planet who was a force greater than nature and truly superhuman—but he was duty bound to use his power to assist humanity. He had the strength of ten men and could jump over a tree; however, he could not fly, at least not at first.

Newspaper editors showed no interest in running "Superman" as a daily strip, but Detective Comics (DC) bought the idea to launch their new line, called Action Comics. Siegel and Shuster were paid $130 for their drawings and all rights to their characters and were hired, at ten dollars per page, to draw more Superman adventures. The first issue of Action Comics, in June 1938, with a cover showing Superman lifting up a car, sold out almost immediately (in 1991 one was sold by Sotheby's for $29,700), and the new pop hero became a hit within a year, inspiring countless copycat champions of virtue with extraordinary powers, including Batman, Captain Marvel, the Green Lantern, and Wonder Woman (not to mention Superboy, Supergirl, Superhorse, and a superdog named Krypto). In 1948 Siegel and Shuster left DC and sued to get some of the enormous profits the company was raking in (estimated at well over a billion dollars so far), but it wasn't until the late 1970s that they finally wrangled a small pension for themselves and had their names officially reinstated as Superman's creators.

Although he grew ever more powerful over the years (eventually able to move planets in and out of orbit), the basics of Superman's mystique were there in the first comic books: his disguise as Clark Kent, mild-mannered reporter (originally for the *Daily Star* before his paper was called the *Daily Planet*); his comely admirer Lois Lane, also a reporter, who thinks Clark Kent is a doofus but, defying logic, regularly suspects Clark is Superman until he disabuses her of the idea; and archvillain Lex Luthor, who wants to the rule the world.

Superman was turned into a radio series, first broadcast on February 12, 1940, with Bud Collyer (later host of TV's "Beat the Clock") as the Man of Steel, introduced with these words:

> Faster than a speeding bullet! More powerful than a locomotive! Able to leap tall buildings in a single bound! Look! Up in the sky! It's a bird! It's a plane! It's Superman!

It was Collyer who developed the trademark cue for a change from Clark Kent to the man of steel, announcing to no one in particular (but preparing the radio audience for the whistling sound of a man flying), "This is a job for Superman!" When Collyer wanted to go on vacation, the scriptwriters invented Kryptonite—a rock from Supe's home planet whose emanations are the only known thing in the universe that can diminish his powers—and used it in a plot that forced Superman into a closet, from which another actor groaned and grunted unintelligibly for two weeks until Collyer came back to resume the role.

After World War II (during which Superman kicked Nazi butt in the comics and starred in some high-budget feature-length Fleischer Brothers cartoons), dancer Kirk Alyn played him in two fifteen-chapter Saturday-matinee serials, shouting "Up, up, and away!" before each flying scene (the "special effects" for which were created by cutting to an animated character in an animated sky). When Alyn had had enough of the kiddie role, the part was taken (with some reluctance) by George Reeves for the first feature-length movie, *Superman and the Mole Men* (1951), a curious morality tale about a town full of frightened rednecks who try to destroy the tiny beings who climb up out of the world's deepest oil well until Superman (also a visitor to the earth's surface) saves the aliens. Reeves was chosen for his good profile and firm chin, but because of his stooped shoulders and indistinct physique, foam rubber was stuffed into the Superman suit to make him look stronger. There was no effort to make his disguise as Clark Kent believable—audiences were asked to accept the fact that a pair of glasses made his real identity unknowable to friend and foe alike.

The movie inspired a television series that lasted seven seasons and established Superman as TV's seminal action hero. The series was so cheaply made ($15,000 per episode, four of which were shot every ten days in the first few harried seasons) that it is filled with bloopers and flubs—on one occasion, a crook mispronounces Superman as if it were a German surname, like "Tupperman," barely enunciating the "man" at the end—and the flying scenes are all basically the same two pieces of footage, with Superman heading to the right or the left, repeated as necessary every time Reeves leaps off the ground by jumping on an invisible springboard. Also, because several episodes were always shot at the same time, all the principal players wore the same clothes, week after week. Nonetheless, "Superman" remains (in reruns) a bewitching program—fun to watch for its expository naiveté and the perpetual pseudo-tension of watching Lois Lane almost figure out who Superman really is. (She did actually learn the secret, once, in a 1957 episode called "The Big Forget," but then, thanks to eccentric scientist Dr. Pepperwinkle's antimemory vapor, she forgot what she knew.)

The main thing that makes "The Adventures of Superman" a high point in the evolution of America's superhero is George Reeves's performance. Reeves was a serious actor (he had been one of the Tarleton twins in *Gone With the Wind* [1939] and had starred in the Oscar-nominated *So Proudly We Hail* [1943]) and brought to the comic-book role a smidgen of embarrassment.

This infused his portrayal of supposedly ineffectual Clark Kent with a big helping of infectious irony; he knows perfectly well, as do we in the audience, that there is no jeopardy he cannot handle by stepping off camera and changing into his Superman getup. As for Reeves in costume, he seems to have a merry time boinging crooks' heads together, breaking through brick walls with a big smile on his face, and offering up his chest as an impermeable target for bad guys' bullets. In fact, he was so convincing in his role that it virtually ruined his career. No one wanted to see him as anything other than Superman, and his dramatic scenes in *From Here to Eternity* (1953) had to get cut because when he appeared on the screen preview audiences gleefully shouted "Superman!" and spoiled the picture's serious tone. Once, while on a promotional tour dressed in his unitard and cape, he was almost shot by a child with a loaded gun who really believed that bullets couldn't hurt him. (Reeves, not wanting to disillusion the child, explained that although the bullets would indeed bounce off him without doing any harm, they might ricochet and hit a mortal human.) He didn't work after the series went out of production in 1957, and when he was found shot in the head two years later, the medical examiner determined his death to be suicide. It was believed that he was despondent at having trapped himself in the mystique of the man of steel. However, there were skeptics, most notably Robert Shayne, who played Police Inspector Henderson on the TV series: "George wasn't the suicidal type," he said. "He had too much joie de vivre."

In the 1960s Superman was pretty much passé: too square to be taken seriously by anyone but the most juvenile comic-book buyers. But rock and roll was paving a curious new course of cultural transmission, from kiddie culture up into the adult mainstream, and as children who had watched "Superman" on TV grew up, they also grew nostalgic. So in 1978 Superman got a whole new life as a movie hero—the first of a new wave of cartoon characters, including Batman and Dick Tracy, to be mined for their big-screen potential. This time *Superman* wasn't just a quick, low-budget copy of the comics. It was a movie with state-of-the-art special effects (he really, really flies!), and with enough sexual tension to make it seem like a film for sophisticates ("How big are you?" Lois asks Superman). The new movie Superman, played by Christopher Reeve, was a campy kind of character, but he was played with utmost seriousness and respect. Reeve explained to *Time* that he couldn't allow himself to be silly: "I've seen firsthand how he actually transforms people's lives. I have seen children dying of brain tumors who wanted as their last request to talk to me, and have gone to their graves with a peace brought on by knowing that their belief in this kind of character is intact. I've seen that Superman really matters."

Four big-budget, all-star Superman movies earned hundreds of millions of dollars in box-office receipts between 1978 and 1987, but comic-book sales suffered a long decline. Market surveys have shown that the average age of a comic-book buyer today is about twenty (younger kids are too busy watching television to read comics), so in 1986 Superman got a makeover to appeal to a somewhat more mature audience of late teens and comic-collecting adults. In an article titled "Midlife Crisis for Superman," *Business Week* described the change as "yuppification." Superman's muscles grew to the point that his body resembled Arnold Schwarzenegger's, and he was frequently drawn with his traditional skintight pants and boots, but topless to show off his big, hairy chest. As Clark Kent, he slicked back his hair with mousse and wore power ties, worked out on Nautilus machines (to explain his pumped-up physique), and was a sensitive modern man who spent a significant amount of quality time sharing his feelings with Lois Lane. "He used to be *SUPER*man," explained an executive at DC comics. "Now he's a super*MAN.*"

SUPERMARKETS

Shopping in a supermarket is such a familiar and yet exhilarating part of life that it is the theme of one of television's giddiest game shows: "Supermarket Sweep" (originally on ABC for two years starting in 1965, now on cable). Three contestants are given empty shopping carts and a very short amount of time, then sent into the aisles. The player who fills his or her cart with the most expensive groceries, thus demonstrating prowess as a supermarket shopper, wins. Smart ones load up on meat, cheese, and concentrated detergent, while dopes fill their carts with fifty-pound bags of dog food, Circus Peanuts, and Cheese Doodles. It is a contest built on the basic principles of that irresistible supermarket sport: looking at what other people put in their carts and appraising their class and status accordingly.

King Kullen

Supermarkets are so much more than a convenient way to shop. They are a place to stroll through the aisles and say howdy to other people (like city streets used to be), to glance at (or buy) the weekly tabloids, and to admire the amazing abundance of the marketplace. We had an eye-opening supermarket moment early in 1992 when we happened to be standing near the Chicken Tonight display, chatting with neighbors we had met in the aisle. As we talked, half a dozen passing shoppers glanced at the jars of Chicken Tonight behind us and spontaneously began singing to themselves, or to their toddlers in the shopping carts, *"I feel like Chicken Tonight"*—the theme from a TV commercial for the product. We realized at that moment just how truly gratifying it can be to breeze through the supermarket's aisles and encounter not only friends and neighbors, but so many of the popular products that make being a consumer so entertaining.

Americans and many people around the world take supermarkets for granted, but as late as 1955 the *Silver Jubilee Super Market Cook Book* ("Dedicated to Mamie Doud Eisenhower, the housewife of America's №1 Household") gushed that "the supermarket is a symbol of America's attainment of a high standard of living through democracy, and is so looked upon as one of the great institutions in the world." According to this thesis, supermarkets were more democratic than old-fashioned grocery stores because self-service meat counters allowed customers to choose the cut they wanted, rather than submit themselves to the whims and favoritism of an autocratic butcher. That same year, a special issue of *Life* devoted to the country's "mass luxury," food, described shopping in supermarkets as "a major weekly ritual of American family life . . . filled with commerce, confusion, and lurking peril [that] swarms with preschool dynamos who crouch among the flour sacks, yip at elders in search of wheat germ, upset symmetrical towers of canned beans or seek to gash themselves on bargain knives."

The earliest known ancestor of the supermarket was Clarence Saunders's Piggly Wiggly grocery store in Memphis, which opened in 1916 and featured the novelty of aisles open to the public. Astonished customers were given baskets (shopping carts weren't yet invented) and sent through the store to pick what they needed—a job formerly reserved for clerks. Cheap and convenient, Piggly Wiggly was a huge success, and soon there were more than a thousand of them in forty states.

In August 1930, as the Great Depression descended on the country, the first truly *super* market was built. In an abandoned garage in Jamaica, Long Island, far from high-rent shopping districts, Michael "Mike" Cullen opened the King Kullen (with a K) Market, which he advertised as "the World's Greatest Price Wrecker." It was huge, it was cheap (many items were sold at cost), it was open at night (another innovation), there was plenty of parking, and it had everything a shopper needed: meat, vegetables, food in cans and boxes, even soap and pharmaceutical supplies.

The most important factor in the success of supermarkets was the invention of the shopping cart. By 1931, King Kullen offered crude wheeled baskets, but the big moment came in 1937 when an Oklahoma grocer named Sylvan M. Goldman introduced a wheeled, folding carrier (like a folding chair) that would hold two wire or wicker carry baskets and allow customers to buy much more than they could carry in their arms. Goldman's original fold-up carts were updated in 1947 to the "Nest Kart," which featured a child-carrier shelf near the push bar and the collapsible back still used on most carts today. (Goldman later invented luggage carts for airports.)

By 1940 there were six thousand supermarkets across the country. The old way of shopping was history. Piggly Wiggly's Clarence Saunders, after losing the business (which still exists) in a proxy fight known as the Piggly Crisis, tried to revolutionize the industry once again after World War II by creating automated grocery stores, called "Keedozzles," and "FoodElectric" stores in which customers not only shopped for themselves but checked themselves out and bagged their own groceries—innovations still being promised. Neither has yet been widely successful, and the logistics of shopping in a supermarket have stayed constant, with these new twists: prewrapped meat and produce to save shoppers time (introduced in the early 1950s); the service deli (an old-fashioned touch, complete with human contact, reminiscent of butcher shops); the do-it-yourself salad bar (1980s); bar-code scanners (first introduced in the 1970s); "talking aisles" that hawk products to passing customers (1990s), and carts with built-in video screens that alert consumers to good deals as they wheel near them (1990s).

Many modern supermarkets aim to counteract the image of overly sanitized, industrially wrapped food marketing built up in the 1950s and 1960s. They offer antiqued barrels of grains and seeds and nuts, bins of fruits and vegetables for people to pick through just as their presupermarket forebears did at village farm stands, and actual bakeries that perfume the air with tantalizing smells. At the cutting edge of such elevated shopping ambience, the Wild Oats supermarket chain based in Colorado disseminates gastronomic philosophy along with its groceries and wares, which include thousands of health-food products formerly the domain of wacky seed-and-sprout shops; in-store tastings of home-baked bread and vitaminized brownies; shelves devoted to helpful pamphlets about nutrition and organic farming; and public neck and back massages to help relax anxious shoppers. Cub Foods, a supermarket warehouse in Chicago, is such a people-pleasing kind of place that one couple who met there in 1991 chose to be married there—on an altar made from cases of Diet Coke. A portable organ was set up in aisle 15, and newlyweds Scott Wallace and Tami Weis strolled past cartons of diapers and rolls of toilet paper after exchanging their eternal vows.

SURFING

"Basking in the lush foliage and mild climate, the Westerner never knows constriction," Gael Greene wrote in her 1964 analysis of *Sex and the College Girl.* "The flowers (girls) on the beach wear polka-dot bikinis and mouse (neck) in the

SURFING ★ *493*

sun, inhaling hedonism with every breath."
A lot of people in the 1960s wanted what
those flowers in polka-dot bikinis had; and
surfing was the way they found it. It helped
crystallize the image of California as an
ideal place to drop out of the button-down
grind and find ecstasy in ocean waves and
the pulse of an electric guitar.

Of all the forms of pleasure seeking formulated in the go-go years, the surfer's life
is the only one that continues to be an attractive ideal. "More than just a sport, it's a
fever" is how the liner notes to the Ventures' *Surfing* album described the phenomenon. "Surfing has become a state of mind,
a wild, uninhibited existence that revolves
around the sun, the surf, and the sand." In
1963, surfing seemed to be the biggest national craze since the twist, and not just at
Huntington Beach and Waikiki. Surfing was

hot everywhere, even in landlocked places
like Des Moines and Tulsa. The *sport* of surfing was beside the point: Surfing as a state
of mind in no way required an ocean.

To zealous surfers—wavecrakers who
devote themselves to the search for a wind-
less day, an uncrowded beach, and the perfect wave—surfing was, and continues to
be, not only a strenuous sport but a religious experience and an opportunity to
challenge the very force of nature. But such
devotees are a tiny minority. Thanks to
Frankie and Annette (see p. 40) and the
Beach Boys (see p. 38), surfing was transformed from what it had been for years—a
demanding, loner's sport—into a fun fad
everybody could enjoy, a way to let the
world know you weren't a stodgy paper-
pusher or a square. Even Richard Nixon got
himself a surfboard—a gift from his daughter Tricia for Father's Day in 1969.

The apotheosis of the surfer's life in the
early 1960s was made possible by actual
technical developments in surfboards. In
the early days of California surfing, which
goes back at least to the 1920s, boards were
big and clumsy and weighed as much as a
hundred pounds, which made hotdogging
(trick riding) nearly impossible. Just after
World War II, Bob Simmons invented a
revolutionary lightweight "Malibu Board"
made of balsa wood encased in spun glass
and resin—terrific, until the skin around the
wood cracked and the board got waterlogged. The introduction of fiberglass-
coated polyurethane foam in the mid-1950s,
then Hobie Alter's foam plastic boards and
Dave and Roger Sweet's one-piece, high-
density molded boards gave the sport a
whole new appeal. Lighter and more ma-
neuverable because of their wider tails and
greater drag, these hotdog boards opened
the door for razzle-dazzle wave-riding techniques of power turns, dips, drops, spinners,
and leanbacks, which are the essence of

surfing today. Such techniques set hotdoggers far apart from the old-time purist surfers, whose focus was on the natural harmonics of nature's big waves.

A hotdogger knows how to take off with a drop turn (dropping straight down the slope of a wave, then suddenly making a power turn at the bottom); how to put his "toes on the nose" (also known as "hanging ten," which feels like skidding over the water on bare feet); how to climb-and-drop (stretch a mediocre wave into a long and exciting ride); how to execute "el spontaneo" (bending over and thrusting the head between the legs, thus riding upside down), the "Quasimodo" (dropping down on one knee, chin to chest, one fist thrust forward, the other back), the "coffin" (riding flat on the back, arms crossed like a corpse), and "el saluto" (riding at attention). He can do leanbacks and spinners and handstands, and he can ride tandem with his girl in a flying swan position on his shoulders.

As surfing techniques got more sexy, the surfing life attracted swarms of gremmies and hodads (uncomplimentary terms for show-off pseudo-surfers and hot-rodders). In *Surf and Sea*, an ode to classic surfing techniques written in 1965, John M. Kelly, Jr., worried that "feigned status is sometimes hard to distinguish from the real thing." Among the signs of phony surfers, he enumerated "the use of hair peroxide, wild skeg decor [a skeg is a surfboard's fin] and board pigmentation, doggers [multicolored canvas swim trunks], amulets, sacred beach rites and annual pilgrimages to the meccas of the devout, whether to the neighboring surfville, or to the sitting [i.e., nonsurfing] beaches of the Hawaiian north shore." All the things Mr. Kelly disdained are a familiar, essential part of the surfing life today.

By the mid-1960s surfer decals had become a fashion on boards and car windows;

Ed "Big Daddy" Roth began manufacturing a line of Weirdo T-Shirts (BORN TO LOSE, CATCH A WAVE) that identified the wearer as a member of the beach/car culture. Such songs as "Wipe Out," "Surfin' U.S.A.," "Surf City," and the "Surfers' Stomp" were throbbing in fraternity houses all across the land, and when the Beach Boys' "I Get Around" hit number one on the Billboard chart—on July 4, 1964—surfing had become a symbol of a new way to get the most out of life. This was a notion most vividly expressed in Bruce Brown's *The Endless Summer* (1966), a joyous documentary film about two likeable hunks who travel the globe in search of the perfect wave. Their sunny quest helped make surfing seem not only fun but also satisfying in a spiritual sense; and even today *The Endless Summer* is one of the most poignant reminders of just how optimistic life could seem before the social dislocations of the late 1960s. Although surfing was soon eclipsed in the public eye by hippie culture, it never lost its charisma for large numbers of physical, outdoorsy, party-hearty pleasure seekers.

The profound attraction of surfing is best seen in the way so many of its once-unique attitudes have permeated pop culture—not only in such beach fashions as bright-colored surf trunks (baggies) and floppy T-shirts, but in surfer jargon popularized by Valley Girls (see p. 546), whose vocabulary was taken almost entirely from surf-speak, and by Bart Simpson (see p. 447), whose "Aye Carumba!" (originally from Spanish) has long been a surfer exclamation to express awe at a great wave or a gorgeous person. There is no better documentation of the far-flung scope of surf culture than Trevor Cralle's astounding *Surfin'ary* (1991), a 200-page glossary of surfer terms from "aaaaahooo!" ("a yell of encouragement when watching another surfer get a hot ride") to "zup" ("What's up?"), including over a hundred surfboard construction terms ("dovetailed fin box"), surfing medical terms ("wax rash"), and two pages of words to describe waves, from the "A-frame barrel wave" to "wavelets" and "white elephant breaks." Mr. Cralle believes that surf lingo is especially spiritual because it is all about pleasure rather than work ... which is exactly why surfing itself remains such an enchanting myth.

JACQUELINE SUSANN

Writing fiction was once a profession plied by lonely litterateurs and souls too sensitive to spend much time in the hurly-burly world of cash and commerce. Now it is a lot like show business. The person most responsible for that development was Jacqueline Susann. "I don't think any novelist should be concerned with literature," she stated, and in the opinion of nearly every critic who deigned to review her novels, she practiced what she preached. Few highbrows said good things about her writing skills, but her *Valley of the Dolls* was until recently the best-selling novel ever, and helped make her into one of America's first brand-name authors. She was famous for her ability to publicize herself and her work, bypassing the once-omnipotent literary tastemakers to sell books by talking about them on television and radio, and to anybody who would listen. Professional celebrity-watcher Earl Blackwell marveled at how she had "parlayed a minor talent for storytelling into one of the most lucrative careers in contemporary letters."

She was an entertainer, and she herself was entertainment. More than simply a "good storyteller" (the reluctant praise most of her critics offered), she was a marketing genius. It can be argued that she helped democratize fiction by writing books

that attracted readers from beyond most novels' elite audience. In her biography, *Lovely Me* (named for an early, unproduced play Jacqueline Susann wrote), author Barbara Seaman quoted an executive from B. Dalton books as saying, "Starting with Jackie we began getting new customers in this door. People that had never been in this store before were coming in to buy Jackie Susann's books. They buy one book and they think, 'Hey, I haven't read a book in years, and I enjoyed this.' And then they'll read another book."

To be fair to the memory of Jacqueline Susann, it should be said that it wasn't only huge sales figures and her talent for promotion that made her a pop pioneer. She invented, or at least perfected, a major genre of literary trash—the glittering melodrama about the low-down miseries and fantastic sex lives of rich and famous big shots. Her books were populated by fictional characters who were always similar enough to real celebrities so that the stories read like gossip and provoked lascivious speculation about who was based on whom: Did Norman Mailer really have a tiny penis, like Tom Colt, the macho novelist in *Once Is Not Enough*, and was Marilyn Monroe really having an affair with Robert Kennedy, like Jennifer North in *Valley of the Dolls*? So this point was not lost on potential book buyers, Jackie began virtually every interview about *Valley of the Dolls* by announcing, "It's been said that *Valley* is a roman à clef, that Neely O'Hara is Judy Garland [originally cast to play the role of Helen Lawson in the film], Jennifer North is Marilyn Monroe, Anne Welles is Grace Kelly, Helen Lawson is Ethel Merman [upon whom Jackie had a crush]—all nonsense!" Before Jackie Collins and Judith Krantz (and about the same time as Rona Jaffe), Jacqueline Susann made herself into the original tell-all-but-keep-'em-guessing supernovelist, holding tens of millions of enquiring minds rapt with her tales about the private passions of Hollywood wives and starlets, high-powered industrialists, politicians, and show-business executives, fame-hungry nymphomaniacs, and handsome, jet-setting heirs and heiresses who yearn only for someone to love them.

Her first book, and her first bestseller, was about a poodle: her own beloved little toy, named Josephine, with whom she frequently wore matching mother-and-dog outfits. Subtitled "A Report from the Other End of the Leash," *Every Night, Josephine!* had no sex in it, but there were plenty of celebrities, including Josephine's friend from walking on Fifty-seventh Street, Greta Garbo, as well as Richard Burton, Laurence Harvey (who used to like to rub her belly), and Michael Rennie (who frequently scratched her ear as they both waited for the elevator). There were a few moments of high drama, especially the climactic knee surgery, for which Josephine is forced to stop licking the grease out of frying pans in order to lose five pounds before the operation, and there is an ambiguously happy ending: Josephine can leap and jump again, but is doomed to eat low-cal dog food for the rest of her life.

When asked to reveal her birth date, Jacqueline Susann sometimes told reporters "November 1963"—the month *Every Night, Josephine!* was published—because that was not only when she embarked on her career but the start of her first triumphant book-promotion tour. (Actually, she was born in 1918, in Philadelphia.) With Josephine dressed in a leopard-skin tunic and with a yellow bow in her hair and yellow polish on her toenails, the two of them appeared on New York television shows and were given a reception at the Waldorf Towers by the Duke and Duchess of Windsor. Then Jackie set off on dawn-to-dusk interviews in dozens of cities from coast to coast. In *Lovely Me*, Barbara Seaman says that Jackie frequently spent long nights visiting local bookstores and charming the personnel with what her publicist, Letty Cottin Pogrebin, recalled as "overblown Hollywood, glossy glamour." Pogrebin also remembered one of her own publicity stunts on behalf of the book that was just the kind of thing Jackie liked best: She managed to get a copy of *Every Night, Josephine!* into the hands of a character in a television soap opera. For Jackie, who once compared selling a book to selling detergent and insisted that her novels be advertised in newspapers on the movie pages rather than among the book reviews, there was no such thing as bad publicity.

Talk show hosts relished having her as a guest. Unlike so many authors, who are shy or abstract or unpleasant to look at, she was supremely telegenic—talkative, entertaining, theatrically glamorous, and to the point. "No matter what an interviewer may bring up, I can work the conversation back to the book," Jackie once boasted. Broadcasting the good tidings about her book came easy to her because she already had enjoyed careers in show business and promotion—first on stage as an almost-successful actress, starting in the late 1930s (having been chosen "the Most Beautiful Girl in Philadelphia" in 1935), then on television as a very successful spokesperson for Quest-Shon-Mark brassieres and for Schiffli lace, for which she wrote her own copy, including the memorable lines "Schiffli adds beauty to everything it touches: See how beautiful I am?" and "Lingerie without Schiffli is like Amos without Andy." For a short while she even hosted her own late-night television show, "Jacqueline Susann's Open Door," on which hard-luck guests (ordinary people who were out of work) would tell the studio audience what was wrong with their miserable lives, but instead of getting prizes, like on "Queen for a Day," they got advice and job-hunting tips from a guest celebrity.

Jackie was abetted in her talent for self-promotion by her husband, Irving Mansfield, a former press agent and creator of Arthur Godfrey's "Talent Scouts" and Dick Clark's "The World of Talent." On one occasion he suggested to Jackie's publicist that she concoct a story that a recently deceased starlet had died while reading *Every Night, Josephine!* The publicist refused, suggesting it might not be such a good idea to implicate the book in her death. Even Jackie balked at one of his publicity schemes: They were visiting Margaret Mitchell's home in Atlanta, and he thought it would be great press if Jackie could stand out in the street, on the same corner where the author of *Gone With the Wind* had been fatally injured when she was hit by a car, and get herself run down, too. "No," Jackie said. "Enough is enough." Mansfield is also credited with having invented the tactic of recruiting people in key cities to buy massive numbers of a book in order to get it onto the bestseller list.

Jackie's publisher wanted her to write sequels to *Every Night, Josephine!*, but she was not satisfied with being merely cute or having written a book that sold a mere one-point-seven million copies. "I had something to say about the pressure of life in the 1960s," she declared, and so she wrote *Valley of the Dolls*, about three Hollywood starlets fighting their way to the top, battling their dependence on pills, and enjoying plenty of throbbing—and for 1966, *graphic* —sex. Most of the editorial staff at her publishing company, Bernard Geis Associates, hated the manuscript, which they quickly abbreviated as *VD*. One in-house reader's report called it "painfully dull, inept, clumsy, undisciplined, rambling, and thoroughly amateurish." But when Bernard Geis took it home to his wife, Darlene, she said, "You've got to publish this book," telling him it made her feel "as if I'd picked up the telephone and was listening to two women telling about how their husbands are in bed. You can't hang up on a conversation like that." A lot of editing and rewriting were done, and then there was a major battle over Jackie's title, which everyone at the publishing house disliked. They worried that the word "dolls" would confuse booksellers, who might misstock it on the children's shelves. The book's flap copy was written to clear up any confusion:

Show business!—a world where sex is a success weapon, where love is a smiling mask for hate and envy, where the past is obscured and the future is oblivion. In this sick world where age and fading beauty are twin specters, the tickets to peace are "dolls"—the insider's word for pills—pep pills, sleeping pills, red pills, blue pills, "up" pills, "down" pills—pills to chase the truth away.

Published in February 1966 and promoted via a press release that looked like a doctor's prescription pad, *Valley of the Dolls* went to the top of the *New York Times* bestseller list, where it remained at number one for an unprecedented twenty-eight weeks. Today, its dirty parts seem tame indeed, but at the cusp of the sexual revolution it was dynamite. *Valley of the Dolls* became a lightning rod for controversy about sex, drugs, permissiveness, and pornography—all favorite issues of the time—and it was used by countless culture vigilantes as an example of the decline and fall of great literature. The few reviewers who bothered to critique it at all savaged both the writing and the subject matter. *Time* called it "the dirty book of the month," scolding its author for having "spent most of her time watching people swallow Seconal, slurp Scotch, and commit sodomy. Somebody does one or the other on almost every page." Jacqueline Susann defended herself by saying, "Way back, they didn't think Shakespeare was a good writer. He was the soap opera king of his day," and on a more contemporary note, "Nabokov and I are on the same level. But I'm better."

Valley of the Dolls made its author a household name whose fame was built outside the literary world: on talk shows, game shows, quiz shows, news shows, on the feature pages (not book pages) of newspapers. When she traveled in a city from interview to interview, a second car had to follow her limousine carrying her extensive wardrobe and makeup. *Saturday Review* called her the "Joan Crawford of popular novelists."

Barbara Seaman wrote: "By the summer of 1966 Jackie was one of the most recognizable women in the United States.... Omnipresent as Orwell's Big Brother was that tough, striking, showgirl's face: the false eyelashes fluttering beneath white eyeshadow; the bright-orange lips and nails; the wardrobe of dark, lacquered, shoulder-length falls; the vivid Emilio Pucci print dresses."

Her next book, *The Love Machine* (1969), was another blockbuster melodrama, this time built around a superhuman hero named Robin Stone: Harvard graduate, former fighter pilot, steak-and-martini man, eligible bachelor, and ruthless television executive. Nora Ephron described it as "a very long, absolutely delicious gossip column," and Liz Smith wrote that she "read it in one greedy gulp, enjoying every minute"; more "serious" reviewers, however, went for the kill. *Time* complained that "Miss Susann once again demonstrates her remarkable instinct for the varicose vein"; the *New York Times* found it to be evidence that literature was indeed dead. Jacqueline Susann's second novel remained at number one on the bestseller list for exactly half a year—twenty-six weeks.

One of Jackie's staunchest defenders was film critic Rex Reed, who, on a "David Frost Show" in 1969 devoted to her and her works, said he liked her books because they were in the *"Grand Hotel* style" and were "real storytelling." However, also on the show that day was critic John Simon, and when he went after Jackie and her work, the catfight that ensued became one of the most notorious television rows in history. Simon said he could bring himself to read only forty pages of *The Love Machine*, because "I couldn't stomach any more. I mean, how many swallows of a rotten stew do I have to swallow before I puke?" He said he would rather watch dogs fornicate than read her book, at which point a dog trainer in the audience stood up and shouted he would rather see dogs fornicate than listen to John Simon talk. Another member of the audience gallantly offered to punch Simon in the nose. Jackie defended herself, calling her accuser "Simple Simon" and making fun of his thinning hair and European accent, asking if his name wasn't really Goering or Goebbels.

Only a few weeks earlier, Jackie had done a little burlesque of author Truman Capote's lispy voice on "The Joey Bishop Show." Capote retaliated on "The Tonight Show" (the same evening the "David Frost" episode was taped) and ignited what became Jacqueline Susann's second juicy public feud of the summer of 1969. Capote said that she, not Raquel Welch, ought to be playing the part of Gore Vidal's Myra Breckinridge in the upcoming film because she was "a born transvestite in marvelous wigs and sleazy gowns" and reminded him of "a truck driver in drag." Irving Mansfield threatened to sue NBC and Truman Capote, asserting that "to refer to her gowns as sleazy is preposterous." When Johnny Carson invited her onto his show and asked what she thought of Truman, she answered, "Truman? . . . Truman? I think history will prove he was one of the best Presidents we've had." Capote then appeared on "Laugh-In," dressed, as he put it once again, "like a truck driver in drag," and he later apologized to truck drivers for his comparison. This battle royale lasted well beyond Jackie's death. In 1985 Capote gleefully took credit for killing her, saying in Lawrence Grobel's *Conversations with Capote* that his remark had caused her to fall out of bed onto the floor and start coughing up blood, precipitating her final bout with the cancer of which she ultimately died.

Jacqueline Susann's death in 1974 came as a shock to all but her close friends. In a melodramatic turn of events that seems like something she invented for one of her novels, she had first been diagnosed with cancer in 1962, before *Every Night, Josephine!* had been published, and at a moment when she considered herself washed up as an actress and a failure at life. In the twelve years after her radical mastectomy, she had become a superstar beyond her dreams, all the while fearing she didn't have much time left. In *Life with Jackie*, Irving Mansfield recalled that "after her first surgery, she had asked for a reprieve. She had asked God for only ten more years and she would prove she could make it as a writer, as the number-one writer." She got what she asked for.

She was in the hospital getting cobalt treatments when her third novel, *Once Is Not Enough*, was published in 1973, but she got out of bed to do an eighteen-city publicity campaign for it. This was her most grueling tour ever, because between encounters with the press she had to schedule time for secret visits to hospitals in every city for chemotherapy treatments. (She told some reporters she had a bronchial condition.) She lost her hair (no great loss—she had always loved wearing wigs), contracted pneumonia, and slipped below a hundred pounds, but on May 6 *Once Is Not Enough* hit number one on the *New York Times* bestseller list: the first time any author had sent three books in a row to the top spot.

When she finally succumbed the following year, she was cremated, and her ashes were put in an urn shaped like a thick book with this inscription on the spine:

JACQUELINE SUSANN
1921–1974

The birthdate was fictional, the way Jackie had always preferred. Her husband put the ashes on a shelf in their library, surrounded by her bestsellers, all of which are now out of print.

TABLOID TV

There was an empty spot in pop culture after the weekly tabloid newspapers gave up their coverage of gore, perversion, and mayhem in favor of soft-core sentiment and celebrities (see "*National Enquirer*," p. 358). The void has now been filled by television—syndicated daily programs that deliver lurid real-life (but frequently staged and always neatly fashioned) pulp tales about gruesome murders, sex scandals, Kennedy family shenanigans, and human depravity that staid network news establishments don't like to know about. "It's one big porno shop," deplored Don Hewitt, veteran producer of CBS-TV's esteemed "60 Minutes," which has often been accused of sensationalism but never of bad taste.

Television is not exactly renowned as a bastion of good taste in any case, but there used to be fairly clear lines between its news and its entertainment shows. And while hordes of entertainment programs have been allowed to tiptoe at the edge of vulgarity and beyond, network news was always a stronghold of sober, dignified, and frequently soporific propriety. It was never frivolous, never exaggerated, never blasphemous, and certainly never re-enacted.

Maureen O'Boyle, "A Current Affair"

Truth, not titillation, was the holy grail. When the big three networks ruled the air, it was rare indeed to see a news story that was in any way prurient, physically repulsive, or morally repellent; even if, on occasion, the subject was inherently odious, you could count on Walter, or Dan or Tom or Peter, to tell about it with taste and reassuring gravity, taking care not to seem emotionally upset or excessively obsessed with it themselves.

The modern era of tabloid TV began when Geraldo Rivera cried on the air in 1972. As a young reporter for WABC in New York (since 1970), he had snuck a camera into the Willowbrook State School for the mentally retarded and had come back with some gut-wrenching images of the horrendous way inmates were treated; when, in the venerable tradition of journalists unveiling society's ills, he showed his pictures on the air, he created a righteous scandal. But what was not traditional were the tears in his eyes. "This is what it looked like. This is what it sounded like," he said. "But how can I tell you about the way it smelled?" Geraldo just couldn't control himself, and what's more, it didn't seem as if he wanted to. He was proud to have the emotions of a human being, and to show them on the air. He became a specialist in exposés, and in 1986 he quit his post as muckraking reporter on ABC's "20/20" (where he had laid bare "The Elvis Cover-Up," about all the drugs Elvis's doctor had prescribed) in protest over the network's decision to kill a story (not his) that connected the Kennedy brothers to the death of Marilyn Monroe. It was only when freed from network supervision that Geraldo really found his calling, in a series of live specials that included:

- a you-are-there drug bust (the alleged perpetrator later sued Geraldo when charges against her were dismissed)
- "The Mystery of Al Capone's Vault" in April 1986 (the highest-rated syndicated special ever, even though the mystery turned out to be nothing more than two empty old bottles from the 1930s)
- an interview with Charles Manson, during which Geraldo turned to his subject and said, "You're a mass-murderin' dog, Charlie"
- a show about satanism (broadcast by a somewhat abashed NBC network) that doted on dismembered corpses and blood-drinking orgies . . . and became the highest-rated two-hour network special in history.

In 1986, as Geraldo Rivera was dazzling viewers with his investigative prowess, media mogul Rupert Murdoch came from Australia and started the Fox Network as a livelier alternative to the big three. One of the cornerstones of the new network was a show hosted by Maury Povich called "A Current Affair," designed to have a format similar to that of "60 Minutes"—an earnest person sitting at a desk introducing investigative stories—but focused almost exclusively on small-town violent crime, celebrity gossip, the drug trade, and any anecdote that provided the opportunity to show either corpses or women in bathing suits, or both. Producer Janice Kaplan provided *USA Today* with this list of the show's favorite promotional words: "shocking," "horrifying," "incredible," and "devastating." Its favorite subjects as of late 1991 were Liz Taylor, Michael Jackson, Marlon Brando, Ted Kennedy, and violent crime.

"A Current Affair" defined what now seems to be the golden age of tabloid TV, thanks in large part to the talents of its senior reporter, Steve Dunleavy. Brought to the show by Rupert Murdoch, who had already made his tabloid reputation in America as publisher of the *Star*, Dunleavy was himself an old hand at tabloid journalism. He had come to America (also from Australia) in 1966, when he began work as the New York correspondent for the Sydney *Daily Mirror*, a Murdoch publication. He wrote a book called *Those Wild, Wild Kennedy Boys;* he ghost-wrote *Elvis: What Happened?;* he got an exclusive interview with the parents of mass murderer David Berkowitz's (Son of Sam) last victim; and as metro editor of the New York *Post* (also owned by Murdoch) he was responsible for one of the most famous of all tabloid headlines: HEADLESS BODY IN TOPLESS BAR. At "A Current Affair," Dunleavy brought his experience as a no-holds-barred print journalist to the air and set the tabloid TV benchmark in stories such as these:

- an interview with a prostitute who had slept with the father of the Duchess of York, the former Sarah "Fergie" Ferguson
- a re-enactment of newswoman Jessica Savitch's accidental drowning, featuring the image of her dying face trapped behind the wheel of her car
- an exclusive showing of home videotapes featuring Robert Chambers, "the Preppy Murderer," partying with friends (and pretending to strangle a Barbie doll) while out on bail
- a convention for mercenaries featuring bikini-clad cutie-pies firing semiautomatic rifles
- the empanelment of a "shadow jury" during the William Kennedy Smith Palm Beach rape trial—a jury as demographically close to the real one as possible—charged with the job of listening to all the testimony so they could be interviewed as the trial proceeded
- a memorable tearjerker (Steve cried, too) about David Rothenberg, the thirteen-year-old boy who had been set on fire and nearly killed by his father.

Dunleavy, known alternately as "the Dog" (for his tenacity) and as "the Prince of Darkness" (because he covers so much death and misery), described his interests for *USA Today:* "sex, happiness, overcoming the odds, bravery, cowardice, elation, pride, humor, fear, distrust, and even disgust."

"What kind of people do we want to be?" the august *New York Times* cried in its hand-wringing review of "A Current Affair," calling it "nothing short of vile." Nearly all the critics agreed that this show, like Geraldo's specials, was inexcusably awful. "He really turns my stomach," said Pulitzer-prize-winning TV critic Tom Shales about Steve Dunleavy. "It helps to wear a gas mask," said the Los Angeles *Times* about "A Current Affair." The Washington *Post* declared Geraldo's satanism special "dirty-minded teleporn." But as Geraldo told *Newsweek* for an article called "Trash TV" that was itself highly critical of the new era of anything-goes (for ratings) television, "I have every ratings record there is on documentaries and nothing but scathing reviews. Are these handful of critics from a relatively narrow slice of American society right and all those fifty million viewers wrong?"

The tabloid TV show that simultaneously delighted the most viewers and irked the most critics was "The Morton Downey, Jr. Show," which started in 1987 on WOR in New Jersey, became a cult hit, went national the following year and mesmerized the viewing public, then just seemed to blow itself out of orbit and die in 1989. This was no "60 Minutes" manqué or crime recreation show. It was a talk show, but a talk show with a difference, and the difference was Mort. Once referred to as being possessed of "armpit eloquence," Mort did not speak to homemakers in a polite tone like most of the daytime talk show hosts. His show ran late at night, and his greatest fans

were young, rude louts, as could be seen at the beginning of the hour when Mort emerged to the roars, hoots, whistles, and screams of what was surely the rowdiest studio audience since the somersaulting kids who ran riot in the theater on Andy Devine's "Andy's Gang." What followed was a deafening cacophony of verbal (and occasionally physical) combat between a sneering Mort, a lynch-mob audience, and guests chosen to arouse righteous indignation.

Mort was not the first television personality to turn the talk show format into a battlefield of overwrought emotions. In the 1950s, Mike Wallace made his fame with a confrontational interview program known for mercilessly grilling guests, who were often ready and eager to fight back. Wallace, whom *Mad* magazine once parodied as "Mike Malice," mined truly sensational TV from such professional troublemakers as Ku Klux Klansmen, alleged gangsters, and driveling UFO experts. And Alan Burke had a show in 1966 on which he did battle with all manner of kook and crackpot, including psychics, strippers, sex changes, atheists, and pro- and antiabortionists. But Morton Downey, Jr.'s real spiritual forebear in his endeavor was a host named Joe Pyne, a chain-smoker who pioneered what he called "fist-in-the-mouth" television in the mid-1960s, which consisted of bullying and berating anyone with whom he disagreed. He delighted in giving a forum to Nazis, revolutionaries, and sex deviates and urging his audience to shout their views at the beginning of every show.

Mort, who smoked more conspicuously than any other television personality in history, frequently threatened to puke on people he didn't like. He once put an American flag on his ass and told an Iranian guest to kiss it. It was on this show that black activist Roy Innis knocked Reverend Al Sharpton off his chair as Mort smiled ear to ear and his massive white dental caps gleamed in the stage lights. Another time, Mort re-enacted the Preppy Murder on his stage: Playing accused killer Robert Chambers, he asked a woman to tie his hands with a pair of panties, then sit on his stomach while he tried to strangle her, as Chambers was supposed to have done. Within a month of going national in June 1988, "The Morton Downey, Jr. Show" had become the most popular syndicated late-night program of the 1980s, but fourteen months after that, its ratings had peaked and plummeted, and it was just as quickly out of syndication. Part of its decline may have been due to a weird occurrence that Mort claimed happened to him in the San Francisco airport: Skinheads had waylaid him and carved a swastika into his forehead. But no perpetrators were ever found, and some skeptical reporters noted that the swastika was backwards, as though it had been carved by someone looking in a mirror.

Mort's downfall notwithstanding, sensational tabloid television was a programming staple by the late 1980s, and "A Current Affair" (now in syndication far beyond the Fox Network) was joined by such similar shows as "Hard Copy," "Inside Edition," and Geraldo's own "Now It Can Be Told," as well as one called "The Reporters" that relied most heavily on crime re-enactments (including the wood-chipper wife-murder done in what had become standard form for the genre: slow-motion black-and-white with eerie music). One extremely popular variation of the formula was a program based *entirely* on crime re-enactments— "America's Most Wanted," which premiered in 1988, hosted by John Walsh, whose own young son had been kidnapped and murdered. "America's Most Wanted" augmented its dramatic exhibitions of heinous crimes with photographs of the actual crim-

inals and interviews with law-enforcement officials. In 1992 it boasted that its viewers, rallied to vigilance by watching the program, had helped nab more than 200 fugitives. Despite the re-enactments, this show is known as a pioneer of what is called "reality television"—because unlike traditional entertainment programs, which are fiction, and even unlike "Dragnet," which changed its characters' names to protect the innocent, it brought viewers right up close to genuine, real-life wickedness.

An even more real approach to tabloid television, also on the Fox Network, came in the form of "Cops" (1989–), which was conspicuous for the fact that it contained *no* re-enactments. Like some of Geraldo's early specials, it was done live as it happened—video verité, accompanying law-enforcement officials in various American cities while they arrested criminals, intervened in domestic disputes, sometimes aided law-abiding citizens in distress, and generally took viewers to all the bad parts of town. "Cops" was (and still is) a voyeur's delight, the only show on television that regularly lets you see the way real felons decorate the walls of their homes and trailers, and also lets you observe real cops eating jelly donuts as they go about their rounds.

In its "Trash TV" story in 1988, *Newsweek* lamented that "the tabloid virus, previously confined to the fringes of syndication, is gradually infecting prime-time network programming." The most conspicuous example of this phenomenon was "Saturday Night with Connie Chung," which ran on CBS one season, starting in the fall of 1989, and featured the highly respected newswoman hosting dramatizations of evil deeds, including the notorious Jonathan Pollard spy case. Connie Chung's show didn't make a niche for itself, and she went off the air for a while to try to have a baby with her husband, Maury Povich, but that didn't mean tabloid

TV was losing its ratings muscle, or that its emphasis on the—what shall we say?—less noble qualities of mankind has in any way diminished. It is now normal almost any day of the week to have one's choice from such interesting topics as these on the tabloid shows:

- Celebrity Murder
- Small Town Murder
- Murderer Who Tortured and Imprisoned His Victims
- Sex Abuse That Led to Murder

For all those champions of lofty journalistic ethics who found the ascent of trash TV repugnant, Van Gordon Sauter wrote an article for *TV Guide* called "In Defense of Tabloid TV" in which he told the critics to lighten up. "Do these shows sometimes exhibit excruciatingly bad taste?" he asked rhetorically, answering himself thus: "Do they ever!" But Mr. Sauter, who used to be president of CBS News, welcomed the new vulgarity as an enlightening alternative to the three straight-and-narrow networks' longstanding monopoly on TV journalism. He saluted the proliferation of sleaze and sensationalism as a reflection of "the spectrum of human experience . . . increasingly available to us on television, which is replicating in our living rooms the scope of the old-fashioned newsstand."

TANG

Tang is yesterday's drink of tomorrow. Introduced by General Foods in 1959 as a "breakfast beverage" made by mixing water with a spoonful of what the manufacturer called "aromatic, orangy-tasting powder," it was touted as convenient, nutritious (loaded with vitamins A and C, as well as tricalcium phosphate), pleasant-smelling ("like oranges, but with a flavor all its own"), long-lasting in its jar on the shelf, and, most wonderful of all, *modern*. To serve Tang for breakfast instead of orange juice was to say you were riding high on the wave of progress; history would not leave you behind with all the fuddy-duddies who still struggled to squeeze juice from oranges the way generations of unlucky home-makers had done before them.

To understand Tang's appeal some thirty years ago, it is necessary to remember that most Americans, especially in the 1950s and

1960s, put their faith in the march of progress. From the end of World War II until the 1970s, a lot of people honestly believed that the world was simply getting better and better, mostly because science and industry kept creating great new products and ever

more convenient ways of living. For many consumers who believed in progress, any foodstuffs that could be frozen, powdered, wrapped in cellophane or sealed in a jar, and stored indefinitely were automatically more appealing than old-fashioned ones that spoiled or required preparation. It was an age when convenience was king, and it included the popularization of TV dinners, the common acceptance of instant coffee, and a thriving industry devoted to can-opener cookery. Futurists were busy telling homemakers that they were anachronistic if they spent any time, for instance, baking bread or making gravy from scratch, or even selecting produce at a greengrocer, when all these things were available on supermarket shelves (see p. 491) already packaged, preweighed, and ready to serve. As early as 1942 in a "Report on Dehydrated Foods" for *American Cookery*, Eleanor Early predicted (with great enthusiasm) that as soon as the war was over, Mrs. Homemaker would be able to carry home an entire dehydrated, condensed dinner in her purse; milkmen would become obsolete, because all dairy products would be powdered; and when the ladies came for a bridge luncheon, this is what they would eat: "Cream of tomato soup, made from powdered milk, powdered tomatoes, powdered onions, and seasoning. Then, maybe, an entrée of dehydrated meat with powdered potatoes and powdered onions. After that, a dehydrated cabbage salad. And for dessert, cup custards made with powdered eggs and powdered milk."

Seventeen years later, when Tang was first marketed across the United States (and as "Sun Up" in Canada), General Foods was still predicting a dazzlingly modern future menu of scientifically reconstituted food-stuffs. "Picture an instant, king-sized steak —made of beef-flavored corn cereal—sizzling in the breakfast skillet," General Foods' *Monsanto Magazine* rhapsodized, going on to describe Tang as the logical next step after instant coffee in the march of progress from the laborious past to the effortless future.

It hadn't been easy to create a powdered breakfast beverage rich with the attributes of real fruit, the introductory article in May 1959 explained. Among the obstacles faced by scientists at the Post Division of General Foods were getting stable, water-soluble forms of vitamin A into the powder, finding just the right semiopaque orange additive (the precolored powder itself is white), and finding a way to keep the powder from caking in the jar. When it came time to package Tang, marketing people took an unusual step (for 1959) and created a label that actually told consumers what nutritional value they would get in every glassful of Tang. Soon after its introduction, General Foods was delighted to note that some consumers had added the new product to their repertoire of prepackaged mix-'n'-match cookery, and were using it—as they had cereal, soda pop, and canned soup—as an ingredient for creative recipes that combined several kinds of convenience food. Some were adding Tang to cake mix to create what was called an "orangy zest" (the word "orange," which might imply that there were actual fruits in Tang, was not used), and some were swapping recipes for Tangy cookies and Tangy coffeecake. One midwestern bank executive wrote to say he liked to mix his Tang with vodka for "a sort of pepped-up version of the popular 'screwdriver.'" General Foods responded, "If his preference becomes a fad, there's a good chance that a great many Americans will be getting their vitamins in liquid form—at the corner bar."

Tang made the leap from convenience food to pop culture in 1965 when it was taken on board the space capsules *Gemini*

IV (June 7) and *Gemini V* (August 21) as part of the astronauts' nutritionally balanced food supply. Tang was not the only brand-name food the spacemen consumed while circling the earth—they also ate Jell-O banana cream instant pudding and CVC freeze-dried apricots—but Tang hit the television airwaves within three days after splashdown in thirty-second advertisements that connected the astronauts' success to their enjoyment of the futuristic breakfast beverage. The ads recreated scenes inside the space capsule, showing the weightless men in their space suits using squirt guns to inject water into laminated plastic bladders containing powdered Tang, kneading the resultant mix, then gulping it down through a special mouthpiece. Shot on videotape instead of film, the commercials had an immediacy that suddenly made Tang something more significant than just another breakfast beverage. It went to the moon in 1969, and its space-age prestige as the ultimate symbol of futurefood was secured.

However, by the mid-1970s a major countercultural offensive against industrially created foodstuffs was under way. Many Americans were learning to distrust processed, chemicalized products, and soon the terms "fresh" and "natural" would displace "modern" and "convenient" as the highest commendation for what was on the table. Tang was the quintessentially modern symbol of scientific nutrition, and there was no way it could be called fresh or natural, and so although it has survived because it is indeed convenient (and because some people really do like its strange orangy zest), it has gone from being an emblem of the future to a quaint, even silly, reminder of what we used to think was groovy. On television's "Saturday Night Live" (p. 344), the totally nerdy Loopner ladies (Jane Curtin and Gilda Radner), you may recall, drank Tang by the pitcherful; and Beldar Conehead (Dan Aykroyd) consumed it dry, straight from the jar, with his average-American breakfast of "shredded swine flesh and fried chicken embryos."

ELIZABETH TAYLOR

The ultimate celebrity and the last great Hollywood-made star, Elizabeth Taylor is not famous because of her excellent performances as an actress, or because of her upstanding charitable efforts on behalf of AIDS research, or because she has big, hypnotic violet eyes, or because she was the movies' first million-dollar headliner. Nor can her unequaled grandeur be explained by the fact that she has been married eight times to seven different men. She did not become the world's most famous woman by eating such Homeric portions of fried chicken and mashed potatoes with gravy and buttered corn on the cob that for a while she was able to wear only caftans and muumuus. Her addictions were of mythological proportions—she was hooked on painkillers, sleeping pills, and bloody Marys for *thirty-five years*, she estimated— but even such notoriety isn't at the core of her celebrity. In fact, no personal attribute or accomplishment in her life is responsible for her status as the supreme star, although

all the extremes, good and bad, only add luster to the aura. Her charisma is greater than the sum of her parts. Elizabeth Taylor is famous because she is so famous; she is best known less for anything she's ever accomplished than simply for being well-known.

That's the way she longed for it to be when she was a twelve-year-old aspiring actress, doting on fan-magazine stories about the likes of Lana Turner and Ava Gardner and playing small parts in Universal pictures. Deciding her eyes looked "too old," Universal dropped her from the payroll, but then MGM cast her in *National Velvet* (1944), which instantly made her America's most beloved child actor—painfully sweet, shy, tender, girlish, and gorgeous beyond her years. Two years later Hedda Hopper declared her "the most beautiful woman in the world," a title that serious Liz fans believe she owns in perpetuity. At age sixteen, she was driving her own powder-blue Cadillac and going on studio-arranged publicity

dates with sports heroes and boys in uniform. Because of her physical elegance and faintly British accent (she had been born in London in 1932), her early roles were as a sophisticate or proper young lady (*A Date with Judy* [1948]; *Father of the Bride* [1950]), but with *A Place in the Sun* (1951), a torrid sensuality was added to the formula, and suddenly Elizabeth Taylor was no longer an ingenue. She was on her way to becoming a cinema sex goddess, infusing her tour-de-force performances in such films as *Cat on a Hot Tin Roof* (1958), *Suddenly, Last Summer* (1959), and *Butterfield 8* (1960) with a unique combination of voluptuousness and vulnerability.

She has always been the quintessence of glamour. At a time when many celebrated film performers, such as Marlon Brando and Shelley Winters, sought to be taken seriously as actors and shunned the trappings of the old-fashioned studio star system, and even Marilyn Monroe (see p. 334) went to New York to study "the Method" at the Actors Studio, Elizabeth Taylor mesmerized the press and public by testing the limits of high-priced self-indulgence beyond the profligacy of any movie star before her. She made her life into a melodrama bigger and more interesting than any mere movie role could ever be, the most glittery soap opera in Hollywood history. It started with her first marriage, at age eighteen, to hotel heir Nicky Hilton (Conrad's son), which lasted 205 days, during which he supposedly neglected her to gamble at the Cannes casino and she lost twenty pounds and started smoking. Her second marriage, to handsome British actor Michael Wilding, lasted four years, but was crumbling by the time she went to Texas to make the movie *Giant* (1956). *Confidential* magazine reported "When Liz Taylor's Away, Mike Will Play" in an article that told of her husband's cavorting with two strippers poolside at their

Beverly Hills home. Meanwhile, Elizabeth met movieland's most flamboyant showman, Mike Todd, Jr., who wooed her with gifts of original paintings by Monet, Renoir, and Pissarro as well as a Rolls-Royce. She ditched Wilding (calling him on the phone to announce the separation, so as to spare him the pain of reading it in the papers) and married Mike Todd as their friends (and America's favorite sweetheart couple) Eddie Fisher and Debbie Reynolds looked on. The marriage to Mike Todd was, in the words of fan magazine *Movie Life Yearbook*, nothing but "parties, trips, and love"; then Mike Todd died when his private plane, the *Liz*, crashed in 1958. Liz was alone, but not for long. "Who'll be number four?" *Movie Life* wondered in 1959, alongside a picture of Eddie Fisher, then a popular singer, grinning like a Cheshire cat and identified as her "forbidden lover."

In a love triangle that became a press agent's dream, Liz stole Eddie from Debbie. Gossip magazines went wild. Handsome Eddie Fisher was the prize in a contest that pitted sophisticated sexuality (Liz) against juvenile charm (Debbie). Debbie Reynolds was beloved by fans because she was cute as a button and had played a country-fresh teenager in *Tammy and the Bachelor* (1957), and she was the mother of Eddie Fisher's two young children, but she was no match for the worldly wiles of Elizabeth Taylor, who in 1958 was performing on-screen in her underwear and steamy décolletage as Maggie the Cat in *Cat on a Hot Tin Roof*. Analyzing the contrast between them, *Movie Mirror* noted that Debbie had grown up poor in El Paso, "surrounded by folksy family and friends," whereas Liz "was reared in London amid wealth and culture and was exposed from infancy to sophisticated society." It was no contest! Liz —the scarlet woman, the thief of husbands, the sex-hungry viper—won. Eddie got a di-

vorce and married her; Debbie, according to *Movie Mirror*, learned (too late) how important it was, if you wanted to keep a man, to have a sleek, upturned hairdo (like Liz), wear a chic chapeau (like Liz), dress in form-fitting dresses (like Liz), and broaden oneself by attending art exhibits and lectures (like Liz).

Stealing Debbie's man ensured Liz's status as a femme fatale with an image of insatiable lustfulness. She seemed even more treacherous as her rise to superstardom coincided with Eddie Fisher's decline, so that by 1961 some fan magazines were referring to him as a former singer and treating him as if he were Liz's male concubine and caretaker of her retinue of servants, pets, and medical personnel. Then Liz went off to make *Cleopatra* in 1962 and topped herself. Not satisfied with Eddie Fisher, who was now practically a nobody, she fell in love with Welshman Richard Burton, her hot-blooded, hard-living co-star. Their carousing (Burton was a world-class carouser) in their rented villa and the hot spots of Rome was a real-life reprise of *La Dolce Vita*— "the most public adultery in history" according to biographer Alexander Walker— and such a disturbing scandal that Ed Sullivan condemned it on his Sunday-night TV show: "I hope youngsters will not be persuaded that the sanctity of marriage has been invalidated by the appalling example of Mrs. Taylor-Fisher and married man Burton." 20th Century–Fox sued her, claiming that her conduct on and off the set made the budget of *Cleopatra* spiral out of control (to a then-unheard-of forty million dollars) and left the picture with a bad public image that ruined box office returns (it was a thundering flop). In fact, the Liz-Eddie-Richard triangle was probably the best publicity *Cleopatra* ever had, attracting audiences who hoped (in vain) to see onscreen evidence of the offscreen carryings-on. By the time Liz accompanied Dick when he went to Mexico to make *Night of the Iguana* the next year, poor Eddie Fisher was left in the dust (as was Richard's spouse, Sybil, who went on to open Arthur, a well-known New York discothèque).

In a 1971 interview in *Ladies' Home Journal*, Liz described why she felt Richard Burton was the man for her: "He is such a vast person. He has such a huge personality." Although some of Burton's friends worried that he would become Mr. Elizabeth Taylor, as had happened to Eddie Fisher, Dick and Liz were an even match. Their tempestuous relationship became one of pop culture's abiding symbols of excess— especially as measured by the diamonds he gave her. First came the 33.19-carat oblong Krupp diamond (which Helen Gurley Brown called "the most beautiful diamond in the world" and Princess Margaret called "the most vulgar thing I have ever seen"); then, to make up for an insult he hurled at her when he called her hands "ludicrously large and red as beetroots," Dick paid a little over a million dollars for a mammoth, 69.42-carat pear-shaped stone (henceforth known as the Cartier-Burton diamond). Liz hung the big rock on a hundred-thousand-dollar necklace designed so that the jewel would precisely cover her tracheotomy scar. The *New York Times* used Burton's purchase to editorialize: "It gets harder every day to scale the heights of vulgarity. But given some loose millions, it can be done—and worse, admired."

Liz and Dick fought, divorced in 1973, and married again in 1975, and their prodigal life helped make her into the world's best-known bonne vivante. For a while in the mid-1960s she was deemed by some fan magazines to be the West Coast leader of a clique of jet-setters who included Jackie Kennedy, Frank Sinatra, Mike Nichols, Princess Margaret, and Roddy McDowell. One

suggested that Liz might be considering running for Vice-President on a ticket headed by Bobby Kennedy! There seemed to be no bounds to the stories the gossip-mongers concocted:

LIZ TO HAVE TEST TUBE BABY!: Liz says another child is all she needs to make her completely happy with Richard. A test tube baby could be the answer to her prayers.
—*Inside Movie*, May 1966

LIZ WILL ADOPT A NEGRO BABY!: Friends of the Burtons believe the couple has already made arrangements to adopt an African child.
—*Movie Mirror*, April 1967

LIZ SAYS: "I LIKE MAKING RICHARD JEALOUS!": She finds a man to beam at, to hang onto his every word until Richard gets up and drags her away in the fashion of cave men of old. And Liz loves it!
—*Hollywood Screen Parade*, February 1966

At the same time that Liz was becoming the fan magazines' favorite cover girl (along with Jackie Kennedy and the Lennon Sisters), her career as an actress peaked with *Who's Afraid of Virginia Woolf?* (1966), directed by Mike Nichols from the Edward Albee play about an anguished college professor (Dick) and his sarcastic, sexually frustrated wife (Liz). The film was especially notable because for the first time, Elizabeth Taylor allowed herself to look less than magnificent on screen. To play the professor's middle-aged, falling-apart wife, she stayed fat (it had become customary for her to crash-diet before filming) and frowzy, and for her efforts she won her second Academy Award (the first was for *Butterfield 8*, which Liz had hated making because she thought the script was "a piece of shit").

By the 1970s, Elizabeth Taylor's private life had almost completely eclipsed her professional career as a source of interest; and although she made more movies (including the excruciating but strangely autobiographical *Ash Wednesday* [1973], about trying to stay young via plastic surgery), none of her performances was notable, and it was clear that her days as an important actress were behind her. After her first divorce from Burton, she declared she would never get married again, but she did, not only to Burton, whom she divorced again in 1976, but to Senator John Warner of Virginia (also in 1976)—a man arguably more important than she—and spent most of the marriage eating her way up to her maximum known weight of 182 pounds. "It's happy fat," Liz said, referring to her happy new role as a dutiful wife, content to tag along in her husband's shadow. "I eat because I'm so happy." But she was not happy as a politician's helpmate, and she was becoming the favorite butt of fat jokes by comedians, including John Belushi (who did a "Saturday Night Live" parody of her choking on a piece of fried chicken) and, most especially, Joan Rivers, who made Liz's corpulence a regular theme of her act with such rejoinders as: "Mosquitoes see her coming and scream 'Buffet!'"

After her divorce from John Warner in 1982, she went nearly ten years without another marriage, although she did have many steady pals during this time, including Malcolm Forbes and Michael Jackson. She even got back together with Richard Burton—but on stage only—for an ill-starred and short-lived revival of Noel Coward's *Private Lives* in 1983. Instead of concentrating on feature films in recent years, she has appeared in numerous television movies and miniseries and done a guest shot on the soap opera "General Hospital," and in 1987 she introduced "Elizabeth Taylor's Passion," a fragrance made by Chesebrough-Ponds, which was followed by "Elizabeth Taylor's Passion for Men" and, most recently, the super-expensive "White Diamonds." In 1988 she wrote *Elizabeth Takes Off: On Weight Gain, Weight Loss, Self Esteem & Self Image.* "Getting along in life is what Elizabeth Taylor has lately become most famous for," *People* magazine observed in a 1989 article that enumerated her husbands and chronicled the rise and fall of her weight and her various medical problems.

Frailness and vulnerability have always been a strange part of the Elizabeth Taylor allure, from the time she was a reedy-voiced child star through her many doomed romances. Illness has been the leitmotif of her adult life, too. She has undergone nineteen major operations; her Mike Todd honeymoon was cut short by severe back pain; she has had pneumonia several times, and was on the verge of death from it in 1961. In the 1980s she spent two well-publicized sessions at the Betty Ford Clinic in an attempt to shake her multiple addictions and to lose weight. She did kick her habits, and she did lose sixty pounds, but then put it on and lost it once again. At this writing, the muumuus are still in her closet and she is wearing her size 8 dresses, and Liz's turbulent life seems to be coming up roses. During her second Betty Ford stay, she met Larry Fortensky, a thirty-seven-year-old construction worker trying to overcome cocaine and alcohol problems, and in 1991 Liz and Larry were married in a ceremony at Michael Jackson's ranch (see p. 244). She and Larry celebrated her sixtieth birthday in a private party for one thousand friends at Disneyland. Barry Manilow sang love songs and fireworks exploded in the sky. "Happiness wasn't bestowed on me," she wrote. "I earned it."

TEENAGE MUTANT NINJA TURTLES

In the spring of 1984, news organizations around the country got a crudely made press release from Mirage Studios announcing the publication of "the first real comic book to be published in New Hampshire," to be premiered May 5 at the Howard Johnson's Motor Lodge, site of the Portsmouth (New Hampshire) Comic Book Convention:

> The comic follows the adventures of four teenage turtles who have been trained in the secret martial arts of the *ninja*—the shadow warriors of feudal Japan. They are also mutants, altered in form and intelligence by a mysterious radioactive ooze. The story unfolds as the four turtles—Leonardo, Michelangelo, Donatello, and Raphael—embark on a perilous mission to confront their sworn foe, the malevolent Shredder. Who will prevail?

In case you have been living on another planet in the last half-decade, we will tell you: The Turtles have prevailed. Kids everywhere love them; they have been turned into movies that gross hundreds of millions

of dollars, TV shows, toys, records, video games, underwear, singing toothbrushes, dinner entrees (turtle-shaped pasta), lollipops, and Rolets pork rinds ("See us munching Rolets in the awesome new movie!"). They have become a paradigm of marketing success and a new lesson in the boundless purchasing power of children. Some amazing Turtle statistics, from *Forbes* in October 1991:

> Ninety percent of American boys between three and eight own at least one Turtle toy.
> Teenage Mutant Ninja Turtles grossed $400 million, wholesale, in 1990: approximately 60 percent of the market of action-figure toys.
> There are some 100 different Turtles now on the market, including surfing Turtles, military Turtles, outer space Turtles, and talking Turtles.

Turtles were invented in November 1983 by Peter Laird and Kevin Eastman, two freelance artists who shared a house in Dover, New Hampshire. Laird occasionally sold illustrations to newspapers; Eastman had had some work published in underground comics but made a living bagging groceries and working as a busboy in seafood restaurants. One day Eastman drew a turtle wearing a mask, with numchuks strapped to its arms. They laughed at the idea, and so drew four and, just for fun, gave them art-history names that were, in the world of comic books, rather esoteric. They wrote, penciled, and inked a turtle book in black and white, with a red, black, and white cover, and spent fifteen hundred dollars printing three thousand copies. It was intended as a one-shot, but when UPI ran a story on these peculiar Turtles, the first printing sold out. They printed more and began a second issue. Teenage Mutant Ninja Turtles comic books now sell at the rate of a half a million copies every month.

The "retromutogenic" waste that turned four terrapin pets into hard-shelled teens with a taste for pizza and a vocabulary rich with urban African-American and Hispanic slang (as well as surfer lingo) gives the Turtle mythology a certain—what shall we say? —social relevance. From the beginning, the Turtles were designed with layers of meaning aimed at adults, or at least adolescents, beyond the kiddie market. Their big success among the very young is a good illustration of how energetically pop culture has overrun the lines that once separated children from adults. Just as many modern grownups enjoy rock music, goofy T-shirts, comic book collecting, and such major-motion-picture superheros as Batman, Superman, and Dick Tracy (all once considered strictly kid stuff), so millions of children have embraced a very savvy quartet of multi-cultural ethnic snappers with Renaissance names and a serious ecological agenda. No doubt about it: The Turtles are a children's thing; it's just that childhood isn't as childish as it used to be . . . as adulthood tends to be a whole lot less mature.

Today Peter Laird and Kevin Eastman wear Turtles clothing, sleep on Turtles sheets under Turtles comforters, and eat Turtles cereal, Turtles pizza crackers, Turtles macaroni and cheese, and Turtles chocolate cookies. "We're constantly amazed by what appears every day," Mr. Laird told the author of *The Official Teenage Mutant Ninja Turtles Treasury.* "It only varies by degrees of amazement." Just last Christmas, the image of the famous foursome appeared in supermarket dessert aisles on packets of powdered dessert mix. A press release announcing this event began, "What's green, slimy, jiggly—and tastes great?" The answer was Teenage Mutant Ninja Turtles Royal Gelatin Ooze Dessert. The press release suggested it was a food that "kids and parents alike can enjoy."

TELEVANGELISTS

Will wonders never cease?
As of late 1991, the most recent amazing tidings from the televangelists came when the Reverend Jimmy Swaggart got caught with a prostitute while the two of them were looking for a motel in Indio, California, that showed, in Mr. Swaggart's words, "fuck films." When asked how this incident would affect his television ministry, Swaggart revealed that it wouldn't: He had spoken with the Lord, who assured him that his doings with the hooker were

none of anybody else's business; God had instructed him to simply continue with his ministerial duties.

The incident happened only weeks after the resolution of a ninety-million-dollar slander and defamation suit that the Reverend Marvin Gorman had filed against Swaggart, charging that Swaggart had engaged in a smear campaign in 1986 to discredit him (they were airwave competitors) by spreading rumors that he was possessed by the devil and had engaged in gross sexual misconduct with members of his own flock. Gorman defended himself by contending that his sexual misconduct was actually not all that gross; he had in fact unzipped his pants in front of only one parishioner, then felt "very, very sorry" about it. Despite a trio of women on the witness stand who all said Gorman had "kissed and fondled" them, the jury decided that Gorman—now defrocked and bankrupt—had indeed been defamed, and awarded him ten million dollars (reduced to just under seven million in December 1991).

During the Gorman trial, the judge ruled that all evidence about Swaggart's own misconduct was irrelevant. Swaggart, you might remember, had admitted in 1988 that he had sinned by consorting with a prostitute, a fact that might never have been known were it not for the diligent detective work of none other than Mr. Gorman, who took spy pictures showing Swaggart entering a by-the-hour motel on the Airline Highway pickup strip in New Orleans. At the time, "The Jimmy Swaggart Telecast" was America's most popular religious TV show, raking in donations of $150 million a year. As soon as Gorman sent the pictures to the Assembly of God Church, Swaggart hopped into his personal Gulfstream jet, flew to a meeting of the elders, and said he was sorry. He then went on TV before his congregation and cried for all to see, proclaiming, "I have

sinned against You, my Lord, and I would ask that Your precious blood would wash and cleanse every stain until it is in the seas of God's forgetfulness." He got a standing ovation from the forgiving crowd, but even so, elders of the church (which was receiving a $14 million cut each year from the haul Reverend Swaggart was collecting from his viewers) banned him from broadcasting— for three whole months.

There were many in the church who felt that Swaggart's own fall from grace was only fair, because he had been the one who had blown the whistle on the Reverend Jim Bakker in 1987, when he informed the Assembly of God elders that Bakker—whom he called "a cancer on the body of Christ" —was carousing with church "secretary" Jessica Hahn. Their handling of church money was brought into question: Did they really need a Rolls-Royce, Vuitton luggage, and an air-conditioned doghouse? And worst of all, they were accused of bilking little old ladies out of their life savings by convincing them to invest in their theme-park community, Heritage USA. Jim was eventually defrocked and sent to prison for forty-five years. "The Gospel of Jesus Christ has never sunk to such a level as it has today," Jimmy Swaggart declared about Jim and Tammy Faye. "I'm ashamed, I'm embarrassed."

All in all, the late 1980s would seem to have been a lousy time for video vicars. "I'm afraid this will make Christians look like a bunch of fools," one courtroom observer worried during the Gorman-Swaggart defamation trial. But it was only televangelists, Swaggart in particular, who looked stupid, for he had gone to great measures earlier in his career to separate his kind of Christianity from any of the normal kinds. Roman Catholicism, he proclaimed, was "a false cult of liturgical religious monstrosities." He called St. Augustine a loser and Calvinism a lie; furthermore, he announced that Jews have brought all their sorrows on themselves (because they rejected Christ), that homosexual "limp-wristed preachers" don't belong in the pulpit, and that the United States Supreme Court and Congress are "institutions damned by God."

Swaggart was delivered his knowledge straight from God. He has been hearing from the Supreme Being, personally, ever since he heard Him speak when he was an eight-year-old boy waiting in line to go to the movies (God said the movies were evil). Since then, he has considered himself the Lord's chosen vessel. Shortly after he got married at the age of seventeen (to a fifteen-year-old girl), he started to preach wherever he could, especially to his evil, rock-and-rolling cousin Jerry Lee Lewis. "I will not be satisfied until I know Jerry Lee has entered the kingdom of God," he said. Swaggart considers Jerry Lee's repertoire to be the devil's music, but he has been a prolific recording artist himself, selling upwards of 150 million copies of his gospel records so far. In the 1960s, Swaggart received another message from the Creator, telling him to get into radio. "The ministry probably quadrupled with radio," he said. "With TV, it exploded."

The eruption of televangelists into American homes began way back in 1952, in Akron, Ohio, when Rex Humbard, a country preacher on the road with his Gospel Big Top revue, noticed a crowd of people outside a department store. They had gathered to look in the store window at a baseball game, and when Humbard saw their rapt attention, the light bulb went off above his head. Bishop Fulton J. Sheen was already on the air, hosting a thought-provoking, interdenominational show called "Life Is Worth Living" (for which he won an Emmy award, whereupon he thanked "my writers —Matthew, Mark, Luke, and John"), but

Humbard had other plans to take full advantage of television and its devoted audience. He had already had some success with a radio ministry, but he knew that if he could get his message out on the boob tube, he would have a huge audience in the palm of his—and his Lord's—hand. Starting with a single TV camera in a rented Akron movie theater, Humbard expanded his ministry until he built the Cathedral of Tomorrow in 1958 specifically for broadcasting—featuring a huge cross suspended from the ceiling with 4,700 red, white, and blue lights. In 1970 he supplemented his cathedral with the tallest building in Ohio, complete with a spinning gourmet restaurant and a 750-foot-tall transmitting tower. By 1980 he was being seen and heard on 207 stations around the world.

Even before the rise of Rex Humbard, and before the public humiliations of the Bakkers and Jimmy Swaggart, America's favorite multimedia evangelist was Billy Graham. Graham has never had a regularly scheduled television show, but his TV specials, which tell the viewing audience at home how they can be born again like those in the congregation of his live crusade, have been seen by hundreds of millions of television followers since the mid-1950s and have been heard on the radio since 1949, when William Randolph Hearst allegedly sent out a two-word memo to the editors of his newspaper chain: "Puff Graham." Graham became the world's best-known religious figure since Mohammed, a friend of presidents and kings, and—what's really amazing—a man untouched by even a wink of scandal. In the beginning, according to Graham's biographer William Martin, author of *A Prophet with Honor*, Graham established inviolable rules to avoid any seeming impropriety—for example, no man on his staff is ever allowed to be behind closed doors with an unrelated female. And

Graham himself, though financially comfortable and always impeccably dressed, is known for having plain taste, a modest home in North Carolina, and only a few pairs of shoes, their sturdy soles made of rubber.

One of TV's seminal pulpiteers was Oral Roberts, who started in the preaching business with "the World's Largest Gospel Tent" in the late 1940s. He went into TV in 1954, first from a studio, then directly from his tent. The first tent show (which, in pretape days, was put on motion picture film and distributed to stations around the country) begat a spectacular through-the-tube healing of a Wichita Falls woman named Anna Williams, who was confined to a wheelchair due to a train-car wreck as well as polio, phlebitis, and spondylitis, all of which doctors said were incurable and/or irreversible. Oral Roberts's autobiography, *The Call*, included this account of her revival from the Oral Roberts magazine:

> Oral Roberts appeared on the screen in a close-up. He urged everyone in the TV audience to place his hand on his heart and pray either for himself or for others who needed healing. Anna listened with both her mind and her heart as Brother Roberts prayed. At this precise moment, the Holy Spirit entered into Anna's frail body and there was a general tingling throughout her entire being. Her legs felt strange and alive. An overpowering compulsion told her to GET UP AND WALK.

Walk she did; in fact, she danced all around her living room. Roberts remembers that the story made the front page of newspapers in every major city, and the following week, Anna was interviewed by Paul Harvey on the radio. She told Harvey's audience, "If you believe and have faith, you will be healed."

Oral Roberts's tent show went off the air in 1967 and returned two years later in a less histrionic form, broadcast now from Oral Roberts University in Tulsa, which features a state-of-the-art television studio that has also served as video home of the Miss Teen-age America Pageant. Although Roberts has been roundly criticized for his princely lifestyle, he has never really taken a fall of *National Enquirer* proportions. But for many of his secular fans, the highlight of his televangelistic career was the time in 1986 when he blackmailed his viewers by telling them that unless they sent him eight million dollars right away, God was going to come down out of the heavens and snatch him. He then retreated to his two-hundred-foot-tall prayer tower for a ten-day vigil until he was saved from God's kidnapping scheme by a dog-track owner who contributed $1.3 million. (Apparently, God was willing to settle for $6.7 million less than His original demand.)

Robert Schuller was called "the only mainliner on the marquee of religious broadcasting" by Jeffrey K. Hadden and Charles E. Swann in their book *Prime-Time Preachers*. Hadden and Swann describe Schuller, whose "Hour of Power" show delivers a rational kind of Calvinist Christianity known as Possibility Thinking, as a kind of latter-day Norman Vincent Peale. Schuller began his ministry in 1955 preaching from the roof of a drive-in-movie snack bar to people in their cars, where he became famous as pastor of America's only drive-in church, and he has improved his congregation's lot all the way up to the spectacular Crystal Cathedral, a video-ready house of worship made from 10,611 panes of glass with a five-story-tall video screen outside for parishioners who choose not to leave their vehicles. As televangelist scandal-makers go, Schuller is a complete dud. Near as we can tell, there has never been a tabloid headline about him, and he's never done anything but try to help his audience and viewers lead more fulfilling lives.

The power of televangelism increased dramatically in the 1980s, thanks in part to the growth of cable television, but also because so many of the media's ministers started getting involved in public affairs, beginning with the presidential election of 1980. They helped make morality (the public kind) a big issue, using their pulpits to deliver a fundamentalist message not only to their own personal flock but to thousands of viewers at home. Among them was Moral Majority leader Jerry Falwell, whose "Old Time Gospel Hour" went on the air in 1956. Also in 1980 Pat Robertson—less an evangelist than a talk-show host—made his first move towards mainstream politics from his Christian Broadcasting Network's "700 Club." By the 1980s, TV preachers had become a regular part of the video landscape, and they are now the most-watched programming on basic cable service. Robertson's "700 Club," mild-mannered though it may be, was the breeding ground for Jim and Tammy Faye Bakker, who started as its puppeteers in the mid-1960s. In 1979, writing in *Christianity Today*, Bakker—who was already hosting his own fabulously remunerative "PTL Club"—declared, "It's not listed in the Bible, but my spiritual gift, my specific calling from God, is to be a television talk-show host. That's what I'm here on earth to do. I love TV. I eat it, I sleep it."

Well before Jim Bakker got himself into hot water, broadcast evangelism in America had had its share of spicy scandals, the biggest of them being Aimee Semple McPherson, whose Angelus Temple in Los Angeles featured not only an ultramodern radio studio that sent her "Foursquare Gospel" message around the world, but also a Miracle Room filled with crutches and wheelchairs left behind by cured believers. Sister Aimee found herself embarrassed in

1926 when she vanished for a month, then reappeared, saying she had been kidnapped. Reporters turned up evidence to show she had run off with the head of her radio station (a married man) for a month of hanky-panky in resort hotels throughout Mexico and southern California.

Probably the most (temporarily) famous sleaze artist among the media-mad evangelists was Marjoe Gortner. Given his name as a contraction of "Mary" and "Joseph," he was groomed by his parents, who were themselves revivalists, to become a Pentacostal Messiah. He began preaching fire and brimstone at age three, and performed his first marriage ceremony the following year. At age fourteen, he ran away, spent some time as a rock musician, then returned to the faith in the 1960s, combining religious ranting with the stage moves of Mick Jagger; Daniel Perry described him as "a hip Elmer Gantry, and the soul of hypocrisy." In 1972 he unmasked himself in a documentary called *Marjoe*, which made him a cultural celebrity while confirming skeptics' worst fears about the evil motives of those in the salvation business. He then went on to a semi-successful acting career.

Some modern media evangelists will never be exposed, because they hide nothing. They get right to the point: collecting bags full of cash. Robert Tilton of Texas advises his viewers to make a deal with God: Tell Him what you need—a new car, a high-paying job, a color television set, salvation—then give Him your best gift (God likes folding money, as does the Tilton ministry), and miracles are almost sure to happen. Another minister famous for keeping his eye on the dollar signs is Reverend Ike, who, although somewhat eclipsed now by the abuses and mortifications of the Assembly of God TV stars, deserves credit as the only modern evangelist to flat out tell his faithful followers that he was in it for the money. "Lack of money is the true root of all evil," Reverend Ike declared in 1965, offering his radio audience an opportunity to join God's Success and Prosperity Club, also known as the Blessing Plan, the entrance requirements for which are simple: Send Reverend Ike as much money as you can. He in turn guarantees that you will, somehow, get it all back (if you have faith), plus piles of interest. Then, when you get that money, you should spend it, as conspicuously as possible, the way he does—on Rolls-Royces, diamonds, and gold. "Don't wait for your pie in the sky by and by," he told an audience in Madison Square Garden. "Say 'I want my pie *right now*—and I want it with ice cream on top.'" Reverend Ike (whose real name is Frederick J. Eikerenkoetter II) made his original appeals on a quarter-million-watt border radio station, broadcasting from Mexico and immune to U.S. government interference, and has never made it big on TV: Maybe he's just too honest about his motives to control the me-

dium with the kind of pietism that worked so well for the likes of the Bakkers and Jimmy Swaggart.

As the latest round of scandals began to break in 1987, *Life* magazine said that video preachers' worldwide contributions amounted to nearly $2 billion per year from the "electronic faithful" who were eager to exchange their money for spiritual salvation, cures for incurable illnesses, and peace of mind. Since the infamies of the late 1980s, however, that figure has changed. And if you need proof that we do indeed live in a world of miracles, consider that the numbers have *gone up*. After the fall of Jim and Tammy Faye Bakker and after the multimillion-dollar, mud-slinging Swaggart-Gorman battle royale, the televangelism business is bigger and more lucrative than ever. There are now well over one thousand radio and TV ministries in America, and an estimated one-fifth of the population of this very religious nation continues to send them money.

"THIRTYSOMETHING"

"thirtysomething" was an hour-long dramatic television series broadcast Tuesday nights on ABC from 1987 to 1991. It never got strong ratings, but it did win Emmy and Peabody awards, and viewers who liked it didn't just like it—they *adored* it, were addicted to it, and celebrated it as an oasis of video reality and relevance. Calling it "exhilarating," the *New York Times* said it was "as close to the level of an art form as weekly television ever gets." Writing a "My Turn" column in *Newsweek*, Aric Press said it "offered models of behavior for the stymied and supplied a vocabulary for

the speechless." In the eulogy he wrote after the show was canceled, Mr. Press concluded that "the value of the Tuesday night meetings was that art, even on the small screen, reflected our lives back at us to be considered as new."

"thirtysomething," which referred to the age of all the main characters, was spelled as one word, suggesting their close-togetherness. And it always began with a lowercase *t*, which implied low regard for the authority of capital letters, and a desire to let every letter in the title stand without benefit of upper-case swagger. The affected humility and communal implications of the lowercase, all-in-one neologism perfectly express why "thirtysomething"—love it or loathe it—stands as the television show that best defined the baby boom in its middle years.

Allow us to explain:

One of the curious things about the social life of the postwar generation, so far, is how its members tend to always do things in groups. Even before the four-hundred-thousand-person love feast that was Woodstock in 1969 (see p. 567), the kids who came of age in the sixties had learned to clump together—in the Peanut Gallery of Howdy Doody (see p. 232) and on dozens of other kiddie TV shows with demonstrative mass audiences, then in teach-ins and pro-

Top left: Timothy Busfield (Elliot Weston), Patricia Wettig (Nancy Krieger Weston), Mel Harris (Hope Murdoch Steadman), Ken Olin (Michael Steadman), Polly Draper (Ellyn Warren); *below:* Melanie Mayron (Melissa Steadman), Luke Rossi (Ethan Weston), Peter Horton (Gary Shepherd)

test marches, and as emotionally incontinent fans sharing their joy at the sight and sound of favorite pop stars. Along came the commune movement of the late 1960s, as well as many noncommunalists who shared living quarters as overlarge "families." Even when boomers have lived apart, they have often done things en masse rather than as lone couples with kids: cook meals together, vacation together, discuss emotions together (in encounter groups, for instance, and also on soul-baring television talk shows) with intimacy that might have embarrassed most members of previous generations. This peculiar ultrasocial tendency was at the heart of John Sayles's first movie, *The Return of the Secaucus Seven* (1980), about a forgathering of communal-minded former sixties people, as well as of Lawrence Kasdan's *The Big Chill* (1983), about a bunch of people who have gone their separate ways but relish an opportunity to intimately share their lives the way they did when they were young.

"thirtysomething" luxuriated in this generation's yearning to SHARE EVERYTHING and to do it publicly. Prior generations tended to consider some things private—sex, how much money you made, the details of your illnesses, most feelings of jealousy, resentment, and hostility—but the characters in this show relished bringing such formerly personal subjects into the open. To bare the most intimate aspects of their lives, without modesty or embarrassment, served to create a valued bond with friends. When they proposed it to ABC, writers Marshall Herskovitz and Edward Zwick (themselves in their thirties) described "thirtysomething" as

a show about creating your own family. All these people live apart from where they grew up, and so they're trying to fashion a new sense of home—one made up of friends, where holidays, job triumphs, birthdays, illnesses, and gossip all take on a kind of bittersweet significance. Though each episode will be a complete story, it's the deeper currents among these friends that will be revealed over time.

They promised their series would consist of "small moments examined closely," and to create these moments they fashioned a cast of attractive but unexceptional people whose lives, presumably, mirrored those of typical baby boomers. Included among them (along with excerpts from the writers' descriptions) were:

- Michael Steadman (Ken Olin): "He always wanted to be a writer but somehow ended up in advertising."
- Hope Murdoch Steadman (Mel Harris): "Her fondest dream is a substantive conversation with anyone over seventeen inches high."
- Elliot Weston (Timothy Busfield): "The life of the party, but lately [he] finds fewer parties and less things funny."
- Nancy Krieger Weston (Patricia Wettig): "Recently . . . Nancy looked at her life, and her marriage, and asked, 'Where am I?' "
- Gary Shepherd (Peter Horton): "A passionate teacher [who is] very principled: never sleeps with undergraduates—more than three times a year, and really, never during finals."
- Melissa Steadman (Melanie Mayron): "Groping her way through singlehood . . . her life is a roller coaster of emotions, and she feels compelled to take all her friends along for the ride."
- Ellyn Warren (Polly Draper): "Her career keeps advancing, and so does her ambivalence."

Critics faulted "thirtysomething" for being self-absorbed and insular, relentlessly middlebrow, and oblivious to social and economic diversity. Everybody in it was white, well educated, relatively comfortable, and seemed to have little interest outside his or her own happiness and the doings of his or her cliquish little group of friends. *Psychology Today* quoted one critic of the "thirtysomething" characters who said, "Get real. They have everything and act like they are anguished. It's so yuppie, so trite." Even when Hope went to work at a shelter for abused women, her effort there seemed less about the problems of life's victims and more about her fulfilling her need to be a more satisfied and charitable-feeling human being. Ken Olin once countered the faultfinders by saying, "Nobody on this show is presuming that the problems of these characters are as serious as the problems of the homeless and the mentally ill and the tragedy of war. But that is not to say that this generation doesn't face a set of issues that are valid, too."

What issues did the "thirtysomething" gang face? Workplace tension, sibling rivalry, unfulfilled dreams of being a Creative Person, ovarian cancer, how difficult it is to lend a friend money, men's inability to express their feelings, a Jewish guy's discomfort over celebrating Christmas, idealism vs. selling out, the fine points of sexual etiquette (in one famous bedroom scene, in the first show of the second season, Hope pleads with Michael to let her get her diaphragm as he promises to withdraw before he ejaculates), homosexuality (two men were shown in bed together—a network first), even—in the very first episode—the problem of overanalyzing feelings: "God, I hate people who talk like this," Michael says after moaning and groaning about his perpetual depression.

"thirtysomething" was known for nonstop talking by its characters, who were fascinated by their own inner lives, and which fans found mesmerizing because it was so real. "I love playing those kinds of awkward moments where people at home have to get up and walk away from the TV, just flee from the room," Timothy Busfield told *Rolling Stone*, and it was not uncommon for producers to acknowledge that they were making the most annoying show on television. Annoying, yes, said devotees, even claustrophobic, but so, so *real.* "What is 'thirtysomething'?" Patricia Wettig asked rhetorically. "We eat, we talk, we make love, and we talk about eating and making love." Comedian Jay Leno once told this joke about turning on the tube to watch the show: "First I see the wife, and she's whining, 'What about my needs?' Then they cut to the husband, and he's whining, 'What about my needs?' And I'm sitting here saying, 'What about *my* needs? I want to be entertained. Can't you blow up a car or something?'" One of the regular writers of the show, Richard Kramer, explained, "We would never have a car chase. But we might be able to have a show about the characters' *feelings* about a car chase."

Instead of action, "thirtysomething" had fantasy sequences, daydreams, and scenes played back from different characters' perspective. In the best-known and most elaborate such episode, the show becomes a sitcom parody in which the characters find themselves playing scenes from "The Mike Van Dyke Show" (a homage to "The Dick Van Dyke Show," 1961–66) to demonstrate Michael's crisis of faith via a Christmas plot that concludes with him discovering that Santa Claus is a Jewish rabbi. "We wanted something silly to say something serious," the writers noted. In another well-remembered dream scene, Michael imagined himself on a carousel chasing a blond goddess as the speed increased and he begged to stop. Critics pointed out that this scene symbolized the frustration and dissatisfaction Michael felt in his (mostly successful) pursuit of the American dream.

The troubles and trepidations of the main characters made the show a favorite among some family therapists of the late 1980s, who used its episodes as object lessons for patients who were having trouble expressing their feelings. Marshall Herskovitz explained to *Psychology Today* that his show had been adopted by those in the mental health field "because we deal with ambivalence, we deal with inner conflicts." Some patients resisted being assigned to watch the show by their therapist, but one doctor explained that once they tuned in, many found that they related to the angst of the characters. He said, "The show gives them a language."

There was much woe and sorrow among loyal viewers when "thirtysomething" went off the air, due to poor ratings, in the spring of 1991. On the occasion of the final episode, in which Hope and Michael quarrel about his wanting to move to California (she prefers to stay where they are and continue working at the abused-women shelter), John J. O'Connor of the *New York Times* looked back on its four seasons, writing that "self-consciousness and anxiety never had it so good" and praising the show for its refusal to compromise. Network critics had wanted it changed; they had said it was too downbeat for prime time, and had objected that lead character Michael in particular had too much self-doubt to appeal to male viewers. The last show reveled in his agony over the move west, which would be great for his career. But after much discussion and argument, and a full hour of self-doubt, he decides to stay where he is because he comes to believe that his family is more important than the job. To its deeply ambivalent end, "thirtysomething" remained true to itself.

THE THREE STOOGES

The Three Stooges took slapstick comedy to its outer limits, creating a laugh-a-minute cinematic world of pain, sadism, and embarrassment. It has been over twenty years since they made their last movie, and although the moral and ethical standards of pop culture have slackened considerably since then, no one has matched their surreal brand of demented humor. In the days before MTV gave parents, teachers, and preachers of morality something serious to worry about, much right-minded concern was vented about the Stooges' wickedness and the evil effect they might have as role models for children. Back in the early 1960s, at the peak of their popularity (because seventy-eight of their short films had just been released to television for the first time), the National Association for Better Radio and TV labeled them "objectionable." The reason? Their films "degraded the dignity of man."

Even the biggest Stooges fan couldn't really disagree with that. Man's dignity, such as it is, never put a wrinkle in the style of Larry, Moe, and Curly as they poked each other's eyes with spiteful fingers or beaned noggins with hammers, or when Moe thrust Curly's bald pate into the spinning blade of a buzzsaw or put it into a vise and squeezed. Can you discover evidence of "the dignity of man" in such activities? As Curly used to say in his high-pitched squeal, "Why, *soitenly*" . . . not!

And therein lies the eternal appeal of the Three Stooges. They flouted the dignity of man. They embodied man as crude, stupid, annoying, and cruel. They thumbed their nose at man, knocked him on his ass, then squirted him with a seltzer bottle. And unlike such other anarchic comedy teams as

Top to bottom: **Larry Fine, Moe Howard, Curly Howard**

the Marx Brothers, Abbott and Costello, and even the antique Keystone Cops, the Three Stooges did their dirty work without a jot of sentiment or pity or even good intentions. The Marx Brothers, with whom they are frequently contrasted by critics (always unfavorably), sometimes acted just as naughty as the Stooges, but the Marxes were well aware they were being insubordinate, and there was a sense of plotted mischief about their misbehavior. They were unruly for a reason: to undermine pomp and pretense; they were artists of indignity. Not the Stooges. The Stooges never had any ulterior motive for acting bad. They behaved the way they did because they were cackling louts capable of nothing better. They were to comedy what heavy metal is to rock and roll: impossible to justify on any moral or intellectual grounds . . . and therefore tantalizing.

Most of us know better than to really behave like Stooges, and it's a darn good thing. Life would be pretty terrible if Stooge-like screwballs ran around all the time putting ants in your pants, wedging your face between the vane and the wall of a revolving door, and attacking your earlobes with scissors. But for any child (or adult) who feels a little bit constrained by all the right and moral injunctions to respect other human beings, such blatant imbecility can feel like glorious deliverance from moral and social correctness, in much the same way a lobotomy relieves a lot of stress. To immerse oneself in the world of the Stooges is to temporarily live life without a brain in a universe without moral scruples. Gary Lassin, president of the Three Stooges Fan Club, told *Entertainment Weekly* that he enjoyed the trio because they made him feel smart. "You do a lot of dumb stuff in this world," he said, "but when you see these guys, you feel like a genius."

The Stooges story began one night in 1922 when Moe Howard and his younger brother Shemp, who had already toured the country as singers, vaudevillians, and a minstrel act, went to see a show put on by their longtime neighborhood friend Ted Healy at the Brooklyn Prospect Theater. Healy was a comedian known for his dilapidated hat and a sweet, informal style, but when he called Shemp and Moe up from the audience (because his acrobats had walked out, leaving time to fill) and the three of them ad-libbed, there were comic fireworks. Healy realized his routine worked much better when he had some stooges to play off. He later explained: "A stooge always comes in handy when you feel like throwing something at somebody. Whenever I'm in doubt or feel mixed up, I always hit the nearest stooge. Makes me feel better. Noth-

ing like it. Hollywood's tired of yes-men. That's why the stooge is coming into his own. A stooge is a guess-man. You can never know what he's going to do next."

Healy convinced Larry Fine to give up his career as a violinist to become another stooge; and, as "Ted Healy, King of Stooges," the rowdy act toured the country. A few other stooges came and went during this time, and Shemp lit out on his own. Curly Howard, the youngest brother of Moe and Shemp, joined the act in 1932. At the time, Curly was known for his moustache and long, wavy hair. Healy made him cut it off (figuring a bald pate was funnier), which Curly hated because, according to Stooges experts Jeff Lenburg, Joan Howard Maurer, and Greg Lenburg, authors of *The Three Stooges Scrapbook*, he felt "his shaven head robbed him of his sex appeal."

Ted Healy, Moe, Larry, and Curly were spotted by an MGM talent scout, and they went to Hollywood to appear in *Turn Back the Clock*, a comedy from a Ben Hecht story about a man who gets to live his life over again. They made several other features, but the stooges grew restless serving as Healy's comic foils. In 1934 the act broke up; the stooges, first as Howard, Fine, and Howard, then as the Three Stooges, began making short films at Columbia. (Ted Healy was killed in a nightclub brawl in 1937.) The two-reelers were enormously successful. In fact, their third, *Men in Black*, a parody of Clark Gable's *Men in White*, was nominated for an Academy Award as best short of 1934. In nearly two hundred shorts, with such titles as *Three Missing Links* (1938), *All the World's a Stooge* (1941), and *Idiots Deluxe* (1945), the Three Stooges created a body of work that earned them their fame and established their characters as pop-culture paradigms: Moe the bully who pushed through life ordering "Outta my way, ya knuckleheads!" (and whose bowl haircut not only augured the Beatles' but has recently resurfaced as a fashionable favorite for tots); Larry the hapless middle man with a prototypical Isro hairdo (see "Afros," p. 4); and Curly the chrome-domed divine idiot, known for his hysterical holler of "Wooo-wooo-wooo-wooo!" and conspiratorial yelp of "Nyuk-nyuk-nyuk."

Tragedy struck the Three Stooges in 1945 when Curly suffered a series of strokes. At first he and his partners assumed his mental fog and physical sluggishness were hangover symptoms due to heavy drinking, which Larry later said was a result of Curly's shame about his shaved head (he always wore a hat in public). During the filming of *Half-Wits' Holiday* in 1946, he suffered a major stroke, and now his disability was unmistakable, described in these baleful terms by *The Three Stooges Scrapbook:* "No longer could he fall on the floor and spin like a top. His high-pitched squeal of a voice had become a hoarse croak. He couldn't even muster up enough strength to do his ever-popular 'Wooo-woooo-wooo.' " Curly was forced to retire, and his role in the trio was reclaimed by Shemp; "Woooo-woooo-woooo" gave way to Shemp's own high-pitched "Heep-heep-heep." Despite a doctors'-orders diet of boiled rice and apples, Curly went downhill. In 1952, while filming *He Cooked His Goose*, Moe was called to transfer a completely vegetative Curly to the Baldy View Sanitarium in San Gabriel, California, where he died at the age of forty-eight—his hair long and wavy once again.

While most Three Stooges aficionados prefer the Moe-Larry-Curly team, there is no denying the contribution of Shemp, who mugged his way through seventy-seven short films and helped lift the Three Stooges to their greatest popularity ever, winning the Motion Picture Exhibitors' Laurel Award for the top-grossing short films nearly every year from 1950 to 1955. However, tragedy struck once again: Shemp had a heart attack and died in 1955. Joe Besser became the third Stooge (the only one to defend himself against Moe's relentless beatings); then he was replaced in 1958 by Joe DeRita, known as Curly-Joe.

The Three Stooges almost vanished in the late 1950s, when the market for short theatrical films evaporated, but soon after their Columbia shorts started running on TV in January 1958, a whole new generation discovered them. They went on to make seven feature-length films, starting with *Have Rocket, Will Travel* (1959) and including *Snow White and the Three Stooges* (1961), which the imaginative Frank Tashlin was originally scheduled to direct (but didn't), and *The Three Stooges Meet Hercules* (1962), which connoisseurs consider their best feature-length work. A plan to start a chain of franchised restaurants— specializing in Stoogeburgers, served in plastic buckets—failed, and by the end of the 1960s their career was winding down for good.

After Larry had a stroke in 1970, an aging Moe asked Emil Sitka to take Larry's place alongside him and Curly-Joe for a final movie, to be called *Make Love Not War*, about the Three Stooges' madcap adventures in a World War II concentration camp, but it was never made. Moe died of cancer in 1975, and Larry, who also died in 1975, is said to have had a merry time convalescing from his stroke at the Motion Picture Country House, where he participated each year in the Wheelchair Parade, for which patients festively decorated their chairs and put on costumes. In 1973 he won the "Most Original" award when he rode in the parade wearing diapers, with rouged lips and a girlish bow in his hair, and waving a half-gallon bottle of vodka with a nipple on top.

TOILET BOWL CLEANER (AUTOMATIC)

Imagine if you shrunk to minuscule proportions, maybe two or three inches from head to toe. Where would you go swimming? In the toilet, perhaps? Hold that notion, and then envision a baked potato topped with sour cream. Now, with those two images in mind, consider the unique intellect of Al Eisen, the inventor of 2000 Flushes automatic toilet bowl cleaner. Those are precisely the two thoughts that inspired him.

Mr. Eisen used to hate cleaning the toilet at his house. It was number two on his list of most-hated household chores (after oven cleaning), but he did it, because his wife refused to. One day in 1977, while lounging around a neighborhood swimming pool, idly gazing at the clear blue water, he wondered if chlorine, which keeps pools germ-free, might be the way to banish ring-around-the-toilet-bowl forever. If the water could be infused with chlorine, it would make the toi-

let practically self-cleaning, like a swimming pool: No more scrubbing! Some time later, Mr. Eisen sat down to dinner and looked at the baked potato on his plate. It was topped with sour cream. Where did the sour cream come from? From a cardboard container. Suppose you took that sour cream container, punched holes in the top, filled it with chlorine, and floated it in the toilet tank? That's exactly what Eisen did, and he never scrubbed another toilet. A new era of perpetually clean porcelain bowls had dawned.

Flush Co. was formed, and Al Eisen, who had formerly made his living as a marketing executive, appeared in his own television ads selling 2000 Flushes, waving four fingers in the air and telling viewers that if they put a canister of 2000 Flushes in their tanks they wouldn't have to scrub for four full months. A year after its introduction, 2000 Flushes was the number-one brand of toilet cleaner in the land. Al Eisen had invented something Americans needed. There has been lots of competition over the years, including TV advertisements that feature singing toilets and miniature men rowing boats around inside the tank, but Mr. Eisen is not impressed. "They laugh at these things because they don't know how to deal with the subject," he said. "We're serious about it."

Serious indeed. Since Flush Co. was bought in 1983 by Block Drug Company of New Jersey (maker of Polident and Dentu-Creme), Eisen spends his time with a team of scientists in a state-of-the-art toilet laboratory equipped with seventy-six bowls that are computer-flushed to simulate use pat-

Al Eisen with test toilets

terns typical of the average home: "morning rush," "nighttime lull," and "two-week vacation." He has improved on the original formula by adding detergent to the time-release chlorine formula, packaging it as cubes and in canisters, and designing it to tint the toilet's water blue or green.

Here are some tips about toilet bowl cleaning, courtesy of Mr. Eisen:

- The harder the water, the bigger your soap scum and toilet bowl cleaning problems.
- Be sure to clean the exterior of your toilet bowl, top and bottom, thoroughly.
- To keep the bowl clean while on vacation: Before you leave, flush once, brush the bowl thoroughly, flush again, and place a piece of plastic wrap over the bowl to prevent evaporation and mineral and rust rings.

MR. TRAILER

Wally Byam invented Airstream trailers—those gleaming aluminum dirigibles on wheels that roam highways in search of Jellystone Park and beyond. Not only did he design the archetypal land yacht, but he encouraged thousands of followers to buy one and join in the fun, and he personally led countless expeditions to places no wide load had ever gone before. From the Yucatán to Addis Ababa, from the bluegrass of Kentucky to the dusty plains of northern Kenya, Wally Byam blazed trails for footloose families, freewheeling senior citizens, and all who yearned to travel but didn't want to be away from their own comfortable bed, their collection of hi-fi records, and their favorite casseroles and bundt cake pans. Known among his friends and to generations of caravaners who followed in his mighty tire ruts as "Mr. Trailer," he was one of the modern pioneers of the open road. After him came Jack Kerouac and Ken Kesey, those fidgety hipsters who took to the highway (in vehicles without trailers) searching for life's meaning, but before *On the Road* and the Acid Test bus, Mr. Trailer —a square and proud of it—was out there experiencing his own special kind of ram-

blin' rapture, with a forty-foot Airstream hitched to the bumper of his car.

Nowadays, trailering is a common way for folks to travel, and it's hardly more adventurous than taking an elevator, but when Wally Byam shoved off in 1951 at the head of the first trailer caravan in history, it was a real challenge. He had hauled many a trailer around America since starting to design them in the 1920s, always traveling on his own, but in the postwar years better roads were being built, and Wally and fellow trailerites were growing eager to see more of the world. Inspired by a newspaper story about a man who drove his Jeep all the way to Panama (even though the Pan American Highway wasn't yet fully paved), Wally gathered together sixty-three Airstreams (and a few other brands of trailer) and headed south. The brave pathfinders who piloted them were, in his words, "people from all walks of life, including an army general, a navy admiral, doctors, bankers, teachers, farmers, businessmen of all kinds —mostly retired."

The enthusiastic wayfarers arrayed their rigs outside the El Rancho Grande Trailer Park in El Paso, Texas, and at the head of the procession, Wally leaned out of his car window and called back "Let's roll!" The cry echoed from car to car, everybody honked his horn, and within minutes, as they crossed the International Bridge over the Rio Grande, they were met by crowds of Mexicans shouting *"Saludos, amigos!"* In Chihuahua, Durango, Zacatecas, and Guadalajara, everything was hunky-dory. The caravaners admired the quaint ways of the natives, drank tequila, and bought cheap antiques. But south of Mexico City, the going got tough. Trailers became mired in muddy bogs and broke axles in rocky streams; eventually some drivers had to cannibalize each other's cars and trailers for parts so they could keep moving. Ladies in the group objected to army-type latrines, so they used chamber pots, which were kept outside the trailers, but one night all the pots were stolen. On trails trod only by mules, they hauled their forty-foot behemoths ever further south; they had to boil water to make it potable; their electric iceboxes burnt out the generators, and provisions spoiled. At the end of the journey (they had gotten as far as Managua, Nicaragua), only fourteen trailers remained, and Wally Byam had lost twenty-seven pounds. Was he discouraged? Did the danger and risk dissuade him from continuing? Nosiree, Bob! Wally Byam was a man who ate risk and danger for break-

fast, and that is why, as America's caravaning pioneer, he is the one man in history entitled to the *nom de guerre* "Mr. Trailer."

That first Mexican adventure taught Wally Byam the necessity of utmost organization. And organize he did! His celebrated expeditions during the 1950s—to Mexico again, through Europe, all around America and Canada, and from Capetown to Cairo— were systematized like a well-trained, fast-moving military force, but with all the comforts of home. The men and women of a Wally Byam caravan—sometimes five hundred Airstreams long—included at least one medical doctor and a team of nurses, a spiritual committee to arrange nondenominational services at each camp, a musician or musical troupe to serenade after supper, a Golden Rule Committee to settle all disputes (noisy dogs, unruly children), a social committee to orchestrate potluck suppers and to welcome newcomers who joined the group along the way, a scout to speed up ahead and find a campsite, and two caboose drivers—one to make sure the sanitation committee cleaned up the vacated campground, another to assist any trailer that broke down along the way. In addition, Byam believed that a well-equipped caravan ought to include a postmaster, an entertainment committee for nightly slide shows and square dances, and a dry cleaner. Of course there was a parking committee; it was customary for caravans to find a field where they could arrange themselves in great concentric circles, like a wagon train. The ultrasocial nature of a trailerists' campgrounds (as well as the adventure of highway travel) was the source of great fun in Vincente Minnelli's *The Long, Long Trailer* (1954), starring Lucille Ball and Desi Arnaz as newlyweds who set off on their honeymoon pulling a forty-footer.

Born in Oregon, Wally Byam was himself the descendant of pioneers, which helps explain his passion. He saw trailering as a whole new way of life, especially suited to retired people. What he liked about it most was freedom, or as he put it, the Four Freedoms:

Freedom from Arrangements: No reservations, schedules, taxis, tips. You can relax and enjoy your travels to the full. If a construction area temporarily blocks your road, so what? Go back into your trailer and brew up a cup of coffee, a pot of tea, or take a snooze.

Freedom from the Problems of Age: When the novelty of retirement wears off, there's too much time to kill, too many hours with nothing to do. In caravans, you meet new people continuously, you relax and have fun.

Freedom to Know: Average tourists never really have an opportunity to get to know a country or its people, but if you go trailering through it, you will meet people in their homes and they will meet you in yours.

Freedom for Fun: When you travel by trailer you relax and "lose yourself" mentally. I wish I had "before and after" pictures of caravaners. They start out uncertain and uneasy, with a vague, lustreless look in their eyes. Well, you should see these people after they go caravaning! You hardly recognize them as the same people. They're tanned and interested in life, walk with a springy step, have a whole new batch of friends, and have taken a whole new lease on life.

But it wasn't only for selfish reasons that Wally Byam advocated trailering. To Wally, going places in his trailer was a way of feeling part of the family of man. To join a Wally Byam Caravan was to become a goodwill ambassador on wheels, to get to know the world and be a better human being because of it. "If we look beneath the differences in culture, we usually find that people are pretty much the same all over the world," he observed. "One of the big advantages of trailering is that it gives us so many opportunities to get to know people of other countries well enough to get beyond superficial first impressions."

Reading his accounts of those trailblazing journeys in the books he wrote at the end of the 1950s, *Trailer Travel: The New Way to Adventurous Living* and *Fifth Avenue on Wheels*, it is easy to understand his enthusiasm for the wandering life. There was no obstacle too great to cross, no location too remote for Wally Byam Caravans to reach. And what a photo album Wally put together! There's the caravan parked in the bush of Uganda, where the witch doctor did a ceremonial dance to herald the Americans' arrival. There's Mont-Saint-Michel, visible behind a parade of big, shiny Cadillacs pulling Airstreams. There's veteran caravaner Allene Halbritter in her kitchen, baking cookies in the Ethiopian desert. And look: caravaners joining Tyroleans doing a slap dance, and making ham and eggs for Prince Raymond della Torre y Tasso at Trieste, and getting open-air haircuts at the end of the day, and feeding pigeons at St. Mark's Square. Most impressive is the concluding picture in *Trailer Travel*, one Wally calls "End of the Trail"—twenty-nine Airstreams (out of forty-one that started in South Africa) drawn together in tight formation at the conclusion of a twelve-thousand-mile trip through eleven countries of the Dark Continent, across the desert of Sudan, and into Egypt. Visible above the tops of the gleaming trailers is the Great Pyramid of Cheops. Is this really the end of the trail? Don't you believe it! Next stop: the Holy Land. It won't be an easy trip, Wally knows that, but that's what will make it fun. He wrote:

For in the final analysis the real measure of living is in seeking out and meeting challenges. What point is there, really, in always doing what is easiest? Every one of us could be sitting home in front of the TV set watching films of Mexico, Africa, and Europe. But there is no substitute for experiencing a thing firsthand. We've *earned* our way to the vistas of Arlberg Pass, Paracutín, and Mount Stanley. The joy of triumph is in the earning of it.

Wally's motto was "Have trailer, can travel!"

DONALD TRUMP

Donald Trump is the best-known symbol of a moment in history when businessmen were culture heroes, when business was about winning, and when killing your adversary in the marketplace was as admired as winning a ball game.

Trump did not invent his name—he was born with it, in 1946—but in the 1980s it was a perfect fit. Like a trump card, he ranked higher than anything else in play. He was top dog, Mr. Big, "the people's billionaire" (according to the New York *Daily News*), maybe the savior of New York City. He commanded the most lavish yacht on earth; he was proprietor of Trump Tower, the Trump Plaza, Trump Palace, Trump Parc, the Trump Shuttle, Trump Castle, and Trump's Taj Mahal; he was a best-selling author; and he gave his girlfriend "THE BEST SEX I'VE EVER HAD," according to a New York tabloid headline. He even starred in his own MTV video ("Mr. Big Stuff").

He was the man of the hour, a role model, and an actual idol (bodyguards often had to fend off crowds who wanted only to touch his pinstriped garment, as if he were a holy man or Frank Sinatra). He was living proof of the can-do spirit that made America great, which for a weird while in the delirious 1980s appeared to be indistinguishable from cutthroat avarice, greed, arrogance, and self-promotion. In an era known for high-finance flimflam, he created the ultimate smoke-and-mirrors bluff: himself. He made Donald Trump something to believe in. "Trump draws his own reality and lives in it," said one of the financial advisors Trump licked when he bought Resorts International (and kicked Merv Griffin's financial ass) in a 1988 story called "The Art of the Steal" in *Manhattan Inc.* "The funny thing is everyone else seems to buy his version of reality as well." He created his image by buying everything he wanted, then putting his name on everything he bought. He made himself into, in his own words, "the biggest and greatest and the most spectacular."

The specifics of his immensely successful (for a while) deal making are beside the point. What transformed Donald Trump from a businessman into a pop demigod and then the quintessential symbol of everything wrong about the 1980s was the largest public ego since Alexander the Great. He cultivated his conceit, as Muhammad Ali had done, because it was a way to psych out his opponents and get the upper hand. The theory, as he explained it, was that if they believed he was the greatest, then that meant they were weak, and presto-chango, he *was* the greatest! Trump believed this, the public believed it, and bankers believed it. His name was as good as gold because he was master of the most fabulous pyramid scheme ever, using braggadocio and hype to build what looked like a fortune. He expressed his philosophy of business, and of life, in *Trump: The Art of the Deal*, which one of his aides helped make into a bestselling book by ordering his employees to buy thousands of copies, which helped put it on the bestseller list, which convinced other book buyers that it really was a bestseller and that they should buy it, too, thus making it an even greater bestseller: See how perfect his logic was! (He also encouraged rumors he was planning to run for President to goose sales of the book.) Trump wrote, "The worst thing you can possibly do in a deal is seem desperate to make it. That makes the other guy smell blood, and then you're dead." Trump—in those halcyon days—was never desperate. He was confidence incarnate. "Who has done as much as I have?" he asked a *Time* interviewer. "No one has done more in New York than me."

Trump hadn't been born a billionaire. He started with a Brooklyn-Queens real estate business, created by his father, worth a mere $40 million. College friends remember him planning to change the skyline of New York, and he recalled for a 1980 *New York Times* interview that he had first really resolved to be *somebody* when he was eighteen, on November 21, 1964, and he attended the ribbon-cutting ceremony at the Verrazano-Narrows Bridge with his father. Young Donald was appalled that Robert Moses, chairman of the Bridge and Tunnel Authority, forgot to mention the name of the engineer who designed the bridge, Othmar H. Ammann. "I realized then and there something I would never forget: I don't want to be made anybody's sucker." Biographer Jerome Tuccille believed that on that day, Donald Trump vowed to make

sure his name was prominently displayed on everything he built or owned.

Trump went into the family business and started buying Manhattan properties during the dire 1974–75 recession, when it seemed that the city was about to default on its municipal bonds. For a speculator with a vision, it was the greatest fire sale of the century. Trump wangled tax abatements, acquired properties from Penn Central using sweetheart deals with the state's Urban Development Corporation, built the Grand Hyatt where the old Commodore Hotel used to be, and was by 1980 the city's best-known developer. He began to plan his flagship—Trump Tower on Fifth Avenue. It would be a tear-down job: The old Bonwit Teller building was razed and its art deco statuary jackhammered to dust ("aesthetic vandalism!" cried the *New York Times*) to make way for Trump's vision of excellence. The old masonry building was replaced by a skyscraper of bronze glass and gold mirrors that brought a flashy, new-money sensibility to old New York. Trump chronicler Wayne Barrett described the tenants in the upstairs apartments, which sold for millions of dollars, as "Medicaid cheats, coke dealers, mobsters, or those who may have gotten a touch too friendly with mobsters." These tenants' needs were attended to by doormen in dazzling, Prussian-style uniforms, and the six-story atrium featured a million-dollar, near-silent waterfall, a restaurant named Trumpets, and a huge shiny gold *T*-for-Trump sculpture. Trump declared it "the greatest building in New York" and credited himself with "starting a renaissance."

By the mid-1980s, he was really talked about as New York City's salvation: He rebuilt the Central Park Wollman Skating Rink in four months and for $2.1 million in 1986; municipal government had spent $12 million and six years trying to get the job done. (The only sour note came when authorities made him remove the sign that announced the project as TRUMP ICE, INC.) Then, when Mayor Ed Koch pleaded that New York was broke, Trump personally paid for a ticker-tape parade to honor Dennis Conner, winner of the America's Cup. And if it weren't for stubborn environmentalists and local activists who, strangely enough, wanted to defend the neighborhood in which they lived, he might have totally revamped a good chunk of the West Side of New York, with plans to build the tallest building on earth at the heart of a broadcasting complex originally to be known as Television City, but then rechristened Trump City.

Not only was he a success in business; Donald Trump made himself a fashion plate, too, losing his up-from-the-boroughs wardrobe in favor of a trend-setting high-finance look. As Earl Blackwell put it, he "discarded his former attire of matching maroon suits and shoes for more conservative dress." Trump's blue Brioni business suits and red power ties helped define the entrepreneurial look of the decade.

He bought lots of properties, a football team (the New Jersey Generals of the ill-fated U.S. Football League), and planned (but didn't build) a mind-boggling Manhattan skyscraper (actually six interconnected skyscrapers) to be called Trump Castle, to be surrounded by a real moat (no alligators), with limited access over a guarded drawbridge. His most conspicuous acquisition, and the one that marks the peak of his reputation as a wheeler-dealer who could do no wrong, was his purchase of the *Nabila* from Adnan Khashoggi, who was frequently profiled on "Lifestyles of the Rich and Famous" as the world's richest man. The 282-foot, 100-room pleasure boat, complete with a hairdressing salon, a hospital with operating theater, bulletproof sauna,

solid gold bathroom fixtures, eleven guest suites (each named after a precious metal or gemstone), and a satellite communications system with 210 separate phone lines that Khashoggi had used to arrange the international weapons deals that made him so rich, caused traffic jams on the FDR Drive in New York when it cruised up the East River. "It's the queen of the ocean," Trump said proudly when he acquired it for $29 million in 1988 (and paid another $8.5 million to refit it). On the occasion of the maiden voyage of the newly christened *Trump Princess, Newsweek* called its owner "the world's most buoyant billionaire."

He didn't just make a lot of money or put his name on everything he bought or erected. He liked to think of what he did as "collecting trophies." He told *New York* magazine, "I look at things for the art sake and the beauty sake and for the deal sake," explaining that conspicuous spending for fabulous things added glitter and glamour to the Trump empire, and the glamour gave him all that much more leverage to buy more. He bought what he called "one of the greatest properties in the United States," Mar-A-Lago, the 118-room Palm Beach mansion once owned by Marjorie Merriwether Post ($15 million). For traveling between his properties, he picked up the finest non-military helicopter in the world, a Puma ($2 million), and his own Boeing 727 ($8 million), as well as Khashoggi's yacht. He bought three casinos in Atlantic City (about $220 million), the Eastern Shuttle ($365 million), and what he called the "ultimate trophy," the Plaza Hotel in New York ($400 million). Of course, he didn't pull these sums out of his pocket or write a check or charge it to his bankcard. He acquired everything using credit, junk bonds, and fantastic leveraged financing that seemed— for him and him alone—endlessly available.

At the peak of his career, in 1988, his estimated net worth was $1.7 billion.

In 1990, two years after the *Trump Princess* set sail, an executive in the Trump organization said, "If we had two more years of the 1980s, he'd have been okay." But Donald Trump was not okay anymore. Suddenly, within the course of six months in 1989, he was the one who was getting trumped. As the financial delirium of the decade began to wind down, times got hard, credit dried up, and people came to look not at Donald Trump's trophies but at the spectacular debts he had incurred to possess them. In 1990 his net worth was estimated at *negative* $295 million, and the press that had helped create his image was now taking pleasure in knocking the wind from his sails. As good a story as he was when he was a flamboyant empire-builder with a Midas touch, he was a much juicier subject as a vainglorious blowhard getting his comeuppance. All the envy and admiration easily turned to gloating as one Trump venture after another went bust amidst flurries of bankruptcy negotiation; then came the ultimate embarrassment: His bankers put him on a personal spending allowance of $375,000 per month. The glee about his humiliation was fairly palpable, for there is no loser who inspires more delight than an arrogant one. "How many trophies might he have to sell?" one story asked. "The widespread public perception," *Esquire* noted, is "that he is doomed." In *Trump: The Deals and the Downfall*, Wayne Barrett wrote, "Opposing Donald became New York chic."

None of the financial setbacks would have been all that newsworthy had they not been accompanied by a salacious new twist to the tale of Trump: his appallingly public personal life. Prior to the collapse of his empire, Trump and his wife, Ivana, a former model from Czechoslovakia, were a golden couple, described by *Time* as "a pair of pos-

turing peacocks before an adoring press, [their] marriage a pageant of celebrity appearances surpassing even the vulgarities on 'Lifestyles of the Rich and Famous.'" The pair even had plastic surgery *à deux*— new breasts and a resculpted face for her, liposuction and hair transplants for him. But Donald (or as thick-accented Ivana called him, "*the* Donald") had a serious love affair in 1989 with lovely spokesmodel Marla Maples (whom Ivana called "Moolah"), and the press, especially the tabloid press, went wild. THEY MET IN CHURCH, said one headline, referring to Donald and Marla's illicit rendezvous at Sunday services; SIMPLY MARLA-VOUS, announced one article, in which Donald rated Marla's talents as a paramour "better than a 10."

The divorce, the settlement, the breakup of Donald and Marla, the coming-back-together of Donald and Marla, the quarter-million-dollar, 7.5 carat "friendship ring" Donald gave Marla (and that she threw at him, along with her shoe, in anger one night in 1991 in the lobby of a Washington hotel): The pageant is never-ending. Now that the Donald-Ivana story is old news, although revived in Ivana's "literary debut" in 1992, a roman à clef titled *For Love Alone*—itself an incredible pop-culture curiosity, and the Donald-Marla story is yawningly familiar, what remains newsworthy is Donald Trump the celebrity freak—as seen in stories that dote not on his success or failure as a businessman, nor even on his prowess as a lover, but on how many chocolate bars he eats, his wicked temper, his plastic surgery, his "Elvis Presley jowls" (*Esquire*), and what he wore to a boxing match.

"Couldn't he see what all of his shameless self-promotion was setting him up for?" Jonathan Alter asked in a 1990 *Newsweek* article about the glee felt over his misfortunes. The story described him as "a parody of late 20th century capitalism . . . not tragedy but farce." There is a kind of poetic justice to the evolution of Donald Trump's image from pitiless deal-maker to cash-poor object of derision. It is a morality play about degradation and disgrace, with elements of sexual mortification reminiscent of *The Blue Angel* and of hubris as in *Citizen Kane*, but most of all it is a merciless cautionary tale about the power and perils of modern celebrity. Donald Trump made himself a famous public figure because he relished the prestige it gave him, but like Frankenstein's monster, his masterpiece—the Trump ego—seems to have taken on a life of its own. His image today is less as an orchestrator of publicity than as a publicity addict out of control—always in need of a fix, even if it's dirty or it doesn't really do him any good. Now he says he hates the press of which he was once so enamored (and which was so enamored of him). The media are "the most corrupt people I've ever seen," he declared late in 1991 . . . during an appearance on a television talk show.

"THE TWILIGHT ZONE"

Airplane pilots know "the twilight zone" as a strange, sometimes disorienting loss of aeronautical certainty they experience when a descending aircraft gets so near the runway that the horizon vanishes. The loss of perspective creates an abrupt sense of imbalance that many television viewers know, too—not from piloting an airplane but from traveling to "another dimension, a dimension not only of sight and sound but of mind; a journey into a wondrous land whose boundaries are that of the imagination. That's the signpost up ahead—your next stop, the Twilight Zone!"

These introductory words were accompanied by the most seductively eerie theme music in television history. Written by Marius Constant, a French avant-garde composer, the rhythmic prelude was performed on a synthesizer that made the shrill rush of the opening notes sound like a haywire heartbeat plucked out on tightly drawn strings. Then came frantic bongo drums and urgent horns, all over a surreal visual mon-

Rod Serling

tage of hypnotic whirling spirals and bizarre cosmic images. Thus began a weekly journey into "The Twilight Zone" on Friday nights between October 1959 and September 1964. (In fact, the precise opening sequence changed during the show's run: The images ranged from shattering glass and flying robots to floating graffiti of $E = mc^2$, and the words sometimes referred to "a dimension as vast as space and timeless as infinity" and "the middle ground between light and shadow, science and superstition.")

Although it never cracked into the top-twenty-rated shows, "The Twilight Zone" was a cult favorite in its original run and has gained fans and followers in syndication ever since, inspiring a big-budget movie in 1983 and a modernized, full-color, hour-long TV show in 1985 (with theme music by the Grateful Dead), as well as innumerable parodies in every popular medium. None of the spin-offs has come close to recapturing the low-budget, black-and-white magic of the original series, which remains a high-water mark of television creativity.

It was a rare half hour (a full hour for several weeks in 1963) that rejoiced in being different. Unlike the ritualized westerns that ruled the TV ratings when it debuted ("Gunsmoke," "Wagon Train," "Have Gun, Will Travel") and the silly shenanigans of "The Beverly Hillbillies," which was number one when it finally went off the air, "The Twilight Zone" was a show that aimed to challenge, provoke, trick, surprise, and always leave viewers thinking about what they had seen. An anthology series featuring a different cast of top-notch actors each week, it was a treasure trove of ingenious screen writing by Charles Beaumont, Richard Matheson, and, of course, writer and executive producer Rod Serling. Their tales ranged from horrific science fiction to cautionary parables about good and evil to elegiac fantasies, but the one thing that could be counted on in every episode was a plot twist in which the show's perspective shifted cleverly to create disquieting and disarming new meanings to the action.

One of the best-remembered such twists occurred in a show written by Rod Serling (based on a story by Damon Knight) about space aliens who land and make friends with the people of earth by saying that their goal is to bring peace to mankind. They offer to cart loads of terrestrials back to their home planet, seemingly for friendship visits. Earthlings are especially delighted when the title of a book the obliging aliens leave behind is deciphered as *To Serve Man* (the name of this episode), but at the end of the half hour, as a spacecraft filled with happy humans is about to take off, one of the book's translators tries in vain to stop the supposed sightseeing tour: She has discovered that *To Serve Man* is a cookbook. Another simple and haunting reversal happened in "The Midnight Sun" (written by Serling), in which a delirious woman (Lois Nettleton) sweats copiously and tries to face doomsday as the earth, thrown out of orbit, plummets towards the achingly bright sun. Finally, after freakish scenes in which thermometers burst and paint melts off the pictures on her walls, she collapses from the heat. Then she wakes to realize, with great relief, it was all a dream: It is snowing outside, and it is night. "Isn't it wonderful to have darkness and coolness?" she reflects to her landlady. But the landlady knows better: The earth has indeed been thrown out of orbit, but in reality it is heading away from the sun into a frozen apocalypse. A few other famous such twists include:

- "The Invaders": A lonely old woman (Agnes Moorehead) finds a small flying saucer in her attic from which emerge two tiny, space-suited aliens. They harass her with a ray gun, so she beats one to death, then smashes the saucer to smithereens. As the alien inside dies, he radios back to his planet to warn them to never again send a ship to this land of giants. In the final shot, the writing on the flying saucer is revealed to say "U.S. Air Force—Space Probe No. 1." (Written by Richard Matheson.)

- "A Nice Place to Visit": A gambler (Larry Blyden) wakes up after being shot to death to meet Pip, his guide (Sebastian Cabot), who takes him into an afterlife that seems like heaven because everything happens exactly as he wants it to: He wins each time he gambles; every beautiful woman falls in love with him. The lack of jeopardy drives this gambling man crazy, so he pleads with Pip to send him to "the other place." Pip laughs and informs him, "This *is* the other place!" (Written by Charles Beaumont.)

- "Will the Real Martian Please Stand Up": Police fail to discover which of seven bus passengers stranded in a diner is the alien from outer space. They give up their hunt; the bus proceeds but crashes. A lone surviving passenger returns to the diner to drink coffee and light his cigarette, using all three of his arms, revealing to the diner chef that he is the man from Mars—advance scout of an invading army. The chef smiles knowingly and removes his cap, revealing a third eye in the middle of his forehead: *He* is from Venus, and his people have intercepted the Martians. (Written by Rod Serling.)

- "Time Enough at Last": A bookish, bespectacled bank clerk (Burgess Meredith) is frustrated because his job and his nagging wife don't allow him enough time to read. One lunch hour when he sneaks into the bank vault with a book, there is a devastating war outside. He emerges from the vault and discovers, to his horror, that he is the last man on earth. But his eyes light up when he spots the library, with stacks of books that haven't been destroyed. With delight, he sits down among reading matter enough to last him the rest of his life . . . but then his glasses slip off his face and shatter, leaving him alive and with all the time in the world, but unable to read a word. (Written by Rod Serling, based on a short story by Lynn Venable.)

- "The Eye of the Beholder": A woman lies in a hospital bed, her face swathed in bandages, praying and hoping that plastic surgery will correct her hideous deformity and make her look normal. The bandages are removed; she is a vision of idealized Hollywood beauty: blond, blue-eyed, symmetrical, and well-nigh perfect. (Although actress Maxine Stewart played the woman under bandages, when her face was revealed the part was taken over by Donna Douglas, who would soon become Elly May Clampett on "The Beverly Hillbillies.") The doctors, whose faces have been obscured by shadows during the whole show, recoil in horror when they see her all-American physiognomy: The operation has been a failure! At last the doctors' faces are revealed: They are ugly, piglike beings . . . but they are the norm. (Written by Rod Serling.)

Not all the twists that made "The Twilight Zone" so much fun were fantastic and otherworldly. Although there were hordes of Martians and spooks and outlandish goings-on in the run of 151 episodes (eighty-nine of which were written by Rod Serling), many stories were surprising in the way they teased delicate emotion, whimsy, and sometimes sharp satire out of their implausible situations. In "Walking Distance," a world-weary advertising executive (Gig Young) miraculously returns to his childhood hometown, trying futilely to catch up with himself as a boy, but does wind up rediscovering joy in life; in "In Praise of Pip" a gangster (Jack Klugman) learns his soldier son is dying in the war in Vietnam (a strangely ominous plot device for 1963, when there was no official war yet being waged) and makes a deal with God to exchange his worthless life for his son's—atonement for being an irresponsible father; in "The Bard" William Shakespeare appears in the present and writes a television play —which gets hilariously mangled by censors, sponsors, and a Method actor (Burt Reynolds) who mumbles and scratches himself in the manner of early Marlon Brando.

Food for thought was what "The Twilight Zone" was all about. Frequently, the thoughts provoked were about social and political issues such as conformity (as in "The Eye of the Beholder") and intolerance. The best-remembered message show, and one that demonstrates how much more important good writing was than special effects, is Serling's own "The Monsters Are Due on Maple Street," in which inexplicable electricity outages cause the residents of Maple Street to panic and become convinced that one among them is an invader and a traitor. They argue, fight, and transform from peaceable suburbanites into a terrifying lynch mob of bloodthirsty monsters, and finally they begin to kill one another. At the end of the show the camera pulls back to reveal a couple of calm, fairly ordinary-looking spacemen who have fiddled with the electricity and are encouraged by the earthlings' resultant behavior. "See how easy it is to cause humans to destroy themselves?" they say. As was his signature at the end of every episode, Rod Serling offered a spoken coda to provide perspective on what has transpired:

> The tools of conquest do not necessarily come with bombs and explosions and fallout. There are weapons that are simply thoughts, attitudes, prejudices—to be found only in the minds of men. For the record, prejudices can kill and suspicion can destroy, and a thoughtless, frightened search for a scapegoat has a fallout all its own—for the children, and the children yet unborn. And the pity of it is that these things cannot be confined to the Twilight Zone.

Rod Serling's presence as part of each episode, not only at the end in a voice-over but always at the beginning, in a walk-on after a few minutes of introductory action, gave "The Twilight Zone" a week-to-week consistency and also a rare (for a TV series) sense of a single artistic personality at work shaping the show. He always addressed the audience directly and contemplatively—"Submitted for your approval" were often the words he used to begin describing the situation when he appeared after the prologue—and he took a sophisticated storyteller's pleasure in his dual role as creator and commentator. His wry, curiously cerebral manner is one of those aspects of the program (along with its theme music) that have helped make "The Twilight Zone" a pop-culture icon bigger than merely a well-remembered show. Like Alfred Hitchcock of "Alfred Hitchcock Presents," Rod Serling is one of TV's quintessential dramatic hosts. The image of him, smoldering cigarette between his fingers, brow furrowed with fascination and perplexity, as he emerges from behind a piece of furniture or from an adjoining room, or in limbo at the end of a camera pan away from the establishing action, has become an almost universally known signal that something astonishing, offbeat, and intellectually challenging is about to transpire.

Serling had a distinguished career as a television writer before "The Twilight Zone," winning six Emmy awards for such highly charged (and scrupulously realistic) stories as "Patterns" (1955) for "Kraft Television Theater" and "Requiem for a Heavyweight" (1956) for "Playhouse 90." He was one of television's golden boys in its golden age of live drama, and he was known for teleplays that took on such issues as the failed Hungarian revolution of 1956 ("The Dark Side of the Earth," 1957) and prejudice (in "Noon on Doomsday," about a small town of bigots that acquits a Jew killer). But by the end of the 1950s, live television drama was a dying form, and Serling had become frustrated because of creative interference. "Noon on Doomsday," for example, had to be rewritten to suit the network's innocuous standards: The word "lynch" couldn't be used because executives were worried it would offend southern viewers, and one character wasn't allowed to kill himself because an insurance company that sponsored the show sold policies that didn't cover suicide.

When the highly esteemed Mr. Serling announced his intention to devote himself to "The Twilight Zone," some critics and commentators were shocked. "You've given up writing anything important for television, right?" Mike Wallace asked him just before the show premiered in 1959. For Wallace, as

for so many upholders of approved middle-brow standards, science fiction was a second-rate form, certainly not as important as the realistic social dramas by which Serling had made his reputation. But what Serling, and soon his viewers, understood was that science fiction provided extraordinary opportunities to tell myths and parables with impact that bare realism simply does not allow (and that censors would prohibit). Moreover, the show's gleeful plunge into fantasy created for generations of viewers a set of modern fairy tales that, as much as anything ever regularly broadcast on the networks, showed the potential of television as a truly wondrous medium whose boundaries were only those of its creators' imagination.

"TWIN PEAKS"

David Lynch has had a long and well-appreciated career, but for nearly a year after he co-created the television series "Twin Peaks" and directed its stunning introductory episode in the spring of 1990, he was a culture god of a magnitude few artists ever know.

He began as a cinéaste at the Pennsylvania Academy of Fine Arts, where he made an endless loop film that showed six heads vomiting, then bursting into flames. His talents so impressed the American Film Institute that they helped sponsor his first feature-length movie, *Eraserhead* (1978), a midnight-movie hit about a huge-haired zombie, his spastic spouse, and the mutant child they keep in a bureau drawer. Lynch then directed *The Elephant Man* (1980), about the famous hideously deformed

man's search for love and acceptance; *Dune* (1984), a sci-fi movie no one (including Lynch) liked; and *Blue Velvet* (1986), about sadomasochism, castration, drugs, and voyeurism.

It was said, after the failure of *Dune* and the succès d'estime of *Blue Velvet*, that Lynch was a "cult director," meaning that while a very small group of people liked his work a whole lot, and it was respected by some critics, his sensibility was too esoteric to find a big audience. But in 1990, with the premiere of "Twin Peaks" on ABC-TV, David Lynch (and his co-creator, Mark Frost, formerly of TV's "Hill Street Blues") found about as big an audience as anyone ever gets: one-third of the television viewing public. Lynch made the cover of *Time* magazine, which declared him a "gee-whiz ge-

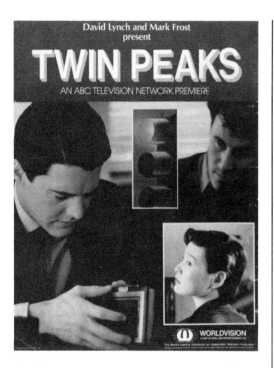

David Lynch and Mark Frost
present

TWIN PEAKS
AN ABC TELEVISION NETWORK PREMIERE

WORLDVISION
A UNIT OF SPELLING ENTERTAINMENT INC.
The World's Leading Distributor for Independent Television Producers

nius," and he was the focus of nearly an entire issue of *People* filled with stories about his show. The *New York Times* ran an editorial suggesting to readers that if there was a popular restaurant where they were having trouble making reservations, they should try nine o'clock on a Thursday night—because everyone who was anyone would be home watching "Twin Peaks." Grocery stores all over the country reported a run on donuts every Thursday, as viewers prepared to eat these symbolic "Twin Peaks" pastries right along with the characters in David Lynch's wacky imaginary world.

The mania for "Twin Peaks" can be traced back to September 1989, when *Connoisseur* magazine ran a cover story announcing that "Twin Peaks," which was going to debut as a two-hour made-for-TV movie the following April, would change the nature of the medium. Across the nation, TV critics—who so seldom get a chance to

haul out the really inflated adjectives—augured greatness for months in advance, and sure enough, the first episode was the most-watched TV movie of the year. Within only weeks, FBI agent Dale Cooper's (Kyle MacLachlan) investigation of the murder of Laura Palmer in the northwestern town of Twin Peaks, told in drawn-out serial form that created more mysteries than it ever solved, became a prime-time obsession unparalleled since the shooting of J.R. Ewing on "Dallas" (see p. 121). It seemed that a large number of Americans were sitting at home wide-eyed and slack-jawed on Thursday (then Saturday) nights as David Lynch's delightfully bughouse show surged forth from the not-so-boobish tube week after week like some brilliant, demented, and hypnotic puzzle—unpredictable, indecipherable, and somehow very outlaw-hip in the kinky way it subverted TV clichés and small-town-America clichés all at once.

Here is a random assortment of a few of the uncanny characters and things fans liked about it:

- *Nadine Hurley* (Wendy Robie): the woman with the eye patch, who was obsessed with perfecting silent runners for curtains.
- *The dancing (and singing) dwarf* (Michael J. Anderson) made his appearance in a dream Dale Cooper had in the second episode; when he talked, he talked backwards, but with subtitles.
- *Saddle shoes* were worn by Audrey Horne (Sherilyn Fenn), the teenage vixen who tried to seduce Agent Cooper.
- *Synthesizer music:* Ominous sounds devised by Angelo Badalamenti helped create the phantasmagoric mood.
- *Cherry pie* was Agent Cooper's favorite food, washed down with what he liked to call "damn good coffee" or "a cup of joe."
- *The Log Lady* (Catherine Coulson): She never went anywhere without her piece of Ponderosa pine, with which she frequently carried on a dialogue.

All these doted-over details were part of a fabulous dream world that John Leonard of *New York* magazine described as "artifacts of Lynch":

the sinister fluidity, the absurd detail, the shocking relief, the elegant gesture, the deadpan jokes, the painterly pointillism, the bad puns, the erotic violence, the lingering close-up camera, the rampaging of non sequiturs, the underlining and italicizing of emotions, the warping of the light, the appetite for all that's grotesque and quirky, a sense of unconscious dreaming... moon thoughts... sadness... demonic possession.

Then, too, there was the strange, portentous acting, which seemed to make no attempt to simulate the behavior of earthlings. Everyone moved a little too slowly (or too fast), stared too long, lingered with a pregnant pause in the midst of a sentence, or averted his or her attention with inexplicable emotion. The hallucinatory feeling of the proceedings was immeasurably enriched by the casting of so many dimly remembered pop-culture heroes in supporting roles: Peggy Lipton, formerly of "Mod Squad," as proprietress of the Double R Diner; Michael Ontkean, once star of "The Rookies," as Twin Peaks' sheriff, Harry S. Truman (named not for the President but for an old hermit who died when Mount Saint Helens blew); Richard Beymer, long-ago star of the movie *West Side Story*, as the town's greedy landowner; Russ Tamblyn, also a *West Side Story* alumnus, as Dr. Jacobs, the psychiatrist with cotton swabs in his ears and a collection of vulgar neckties; Piper Laurie, whose career had been revived by her appearance as the mother in *Carrie*, as Catherine Martell, half-owner of the sawmill. As in a dream, they were all familiar... but a little hard to place.

In the beginning, critics could not say enough wonderful things about this show. It was different, it was provocative, it was an opportunity to write about prime-time television as if it had the intellectual depth of a novel or a serious play. "Just this side of a godsend," announced the Washington *Post;* "*Peyton Place* meets *Naked Lunch*," said John Leonard; "The first TV masterpiece of the '90s," said the Dallas *Morning News. Time* called the show "a soap opera with strychnine" and declared it to be welcome proof "that an eccentric artist can toil in American TV without compromising his vision." For anyone who had ever had a college course in literature that taught about symbols and surrealism, "Twin Peaks" was a bonanza of things to analyze. There was something in it for everyone: *The Nation* said it ripped the lid off Reagan economics, while the totemic foodstuff of the show—donuts—made the cover of *Gourmet* magazine.

At the same time "Twin Peaks" mania mounted during the first season and through the summer of 1990, a really peculiar thing happened: The audience eroded fast. Nearly every succeeding episode attracted fewer viewers than the one before. And at Halloween, when tens of thousands of American children dressed in saddle shoes like Audrey Horne or slicked back their hair like Agent Cooper, the audience of the show was down to half of what it had been six months earlier. Part of the problem might have been that David Lynch's core audience—his cult—was abandoning the show because it had gotten so trendy. Robert J. Thompson, a professor of communications at the State University of New York at Cortland, told the *New York Times*, "The look of the show defined hipness for a while. But once you see your thirteen-year-old sister wearing the clothes, it's over." In fact, Bloomingdale's opened a "Twin

Peaks" department in August to sell lumberjack fashions patterned after characters in the show; in Seattle, Gray Line tours offered sightseers the opportunity to take a charter bus trip past the real-life model for the Double R Diner. "Twin Peaks" simply got too well-known to seem hip anymore.

But it wasn't just the critics' frenzied adulation and an overdose of hype that terminated the "Twin Peaks" phenomenon. A distinct pattern was noticed as the audience shrank: The first to tune out in droves were women over thirty-five, the group known to have been the staunchest fans of earlier, conventional prime-time soap operas. The reason wasn't hard to determine: "Twin Peaks," like all of David Lynch's movies, was filled with scenes of women being abused and wounded, some of them for no apparent reason other than for their disturbing effect—like the rape-torture victim introduced in the first episode then forgotten. In addition to a recurrent theme of wife beating and too many morgue and murder scenes, the show was unpleasantly riddled with glimmers of adolescent-boy humor, such as the title itself, which the *New York Times* referred to as "a male joke about women's breasts," and one particularly crude moment when Ben Horne and his brother Jerry apparently compared the taste of Brie cheese to the taste of a vagina. (We say "apparently" because their conversation, carried on with full mouths, was garbled—but only enough to sneak past censors.) There were many moments such as these when David Lynch's vaunted talent for disturbing an audience seemed less like art than the behavior of an odious little boy saying naughty words or waving dead frogs and spiders in your face to make you flinch or turn away.

Much of the original excitement about "Twin Peaks" had been abetted and embellished by the offbeat personality of Lynch himself. Journalists relished noting that the co-creator of the weirdest, most subversive show ever on television had been an Eagle Scout and drank a milk shake every day for six years and still ate cheese sandwiches for lunch, and was normal as huckleberry pie! For interviews, Lynch played the role of all-American boy with great aplomb: naive, curious, full of energy, bright-eyed, and ever optimistic. However, for many newcomers to the haywire world of David Lynch who wanted to believe in his ingenuousness, a few episodes of "Twin Peaks" quickly disabused them of their faith. Given the grotesque sensibility of the show, his naiveté could seem downright obstinate, and his relentless curiosity too often led towards things that were unhealthy and disturbing. *Newsweek* reported that he once asked a friend to send him her uterus when she went into the hospital for a hysterectomy: "He's fascinated by human organs." Lurking not too far below the ethereal mood and decorative flourishes, among all the cute conceits like the donuts and Cooper's little hand-held Micromac tape recorder, was this simple fact: "Twin Peaks" was extremely repulsive.

The combination of faux naiveté and real perversity eventually proved deadly. By the fall, station breaks were being announced by a cloying voice asking viewers to "stay tuned for more coffee and donuts." The weekly episodes (most of which were *not* directed by Lynch but did ape his style) grew ever more recondite—not merely implausible but annoyingly veiled. Space aliens arrived in Twin Peaks on October 6. But the coup de grace came on November 10—the episode viewers had been anticipating since the premiere in the spring, and the one time ratings went up instead of down: the solution, advertisements promised, to the mystery of "Who killed Laura Palmer?" After much throat-clearing and many false starts, however, the answer didn't come; audiences were asked, once again, to wait till next week. By the time the truth was revealed, on November 17, "Twin Peaks" had lost its fair-weather friends, and when it turned out that the killer was an incubus named Bob (Frank Silva) who inhabited the body of Laura Palmer's father (Ray Wise), a lot of people once enamored of the amusingly quirky show threw up their hands in despair.

"A riddle wrapped in a mystery inside an enigma" is how William Grimes described its nature in the *New York Times*. John Leonard called it "merely moody" and wrote that " 'Twin Peaks' has nothing at all in its pretty little head except to desire to please." The only people who remained pleased by the show's blithe disregard of storytelling conventions were hardcore devotees. (They had formed the Citizens Outraged at the Offing of Peaks—COOP for short—in February when it looked like the series' days were numbered.) Ordinary viewers, who might have been seduced in the beginning by the alleged mystery, felt they were getting hoodwinked when Agent Cooper realized who the murderer was in a dream, but then forgot the name when he woke up, or when he got shot in the chest at the end of one episode and miraculously brushed off the effects of the bullet in the next one (thanks to a bulletproof vest). Cooper also had an ability to be psychic at those times when the plot needed an extra twist of abnormality.

"Twin Peaks" did not change television, as its early champions had predicted. When it went off the air in the spring of 1991, it was the lowest-rated network show of the week, and few people lamented its passing. It felt like a happening that had happened —all the way and then some—and there was little sense, even among most people who had liked it, that great things were left undone. As for its legacy, there wasn't much. The art of "Twin Peaks," such as it was, was too easily rendered as facile artiness to have any real meaning. This could be seen not only in the "Twin Peaks" episodes Lynch didn't direct but also in the execrable Lynch-produced TV series "American Chronicles," for which ordinary documentary films were weirded up by the addition of "Twin Peaks"–like eerie music and the copious use of slow-motion effects. Even Lynch's own *Wild At Heart* (1991), a theatrical film widely expected to be a big hit because of the buzz generated by "Twin Peaks," was a conspicuous commercial failure, scorned by many critics as a mere assemblage of now all-too-familiar Lynchian mannerisms; and the feature film version of "Twin Peaks" was a flop when it premiered at Cannes in 1992.

Co-creator Mark Frost had anticipated the show's demise almost as soon as it became a national sensation in the spring. He saw America as a voracious monster, hungry for new things, and he worried that "Twin Peaks" was simply the bonbon of the moment. "The pace of culture is accelerating all the time in this country," Frost told John Leonard. "Trends and fads. Too much attention is dangerous. Maybe they'll digest us too quickly, spit us out." Note, please, the alimentary logic of Frost's metaphor. He didn't expect anyone to spit out the show after merely tasting it. That would be too ordinary. On the other hand, spewing it out after digesting it would be consistent with the spirit that made "Twin Peaks" such a shock when it splattered onto the network schedule in 1990.

THE TWIST

"I'm almost like Einstein creating atomic power," said Chubby Checker, the man who taught the world how to twist. "Whatever dances came after the twist, it all started here."

It was indeed an A-bomb when it erupted in 1960, and it didn't only affect the way kids danced. The twist set the pace for a decade. It was ecstatic, it was risqué, and it was like nothing that had come before. To twist was to break the rules, not only of ballroom dancing but of etiquette itself. Ten years before, you might have been arrested for lewd behavior if you were caught wiggling your ass in public the way twisters were doing in 1960. It wasn't just pixilated teenagers who were doing it—the twist was a symbol of youth that everyone wanted a piece of. It incited Americans (and significant numbers of people all over the earth) to let themselves go, and go wild; it was the first big portent that the 1960s were going to be a reckless and unruly time.

Its exact origin is hard to pin down. Some contemporary reports say that the dance was discovered in Florida by Hank Ballard, who became known in the mid-1950s as the lead singer of the Midnighters. Ballard had gained a measure of notoriety with his "Annie" records, rhythm-and-blues novelty songs that went from "Work with Me Annie" ("work" supposedly meant "have sex," although Ballard protested it meant "dance") to "Annie Had a Baby" ("she can't work no more") to "Sexy Ways" and "Annie's Aunt Fannie." These records confirmed adults' worst fears about rock music being licentious, a point that seemed to be made even beyond the lyrics when Ballard issued his famous ruttish call in each of the songs, "eee-yah!" His records got good air-

play on some R&B stations, but among almost all Top 40 deejays they were taboo. Ballard is believed to have seen teens in Tampa doing a variation of a group dance called the Madison in which they alternately lifted each foot off the ground and swung their arms back and forth, all the while sticking out their butts and shaking them. This supposedly inspired him to write a song based on the motion, which he named "The Twist" and recorded as the B side of his 1959 breakout hit, "Teardrops on Your Letter." Ballard later claimed that the hip-swinging step was actually invented in 1958 by the Midnighters for their stage act, which was based on precision choreography: All four performers stood in a line and twisted as they sang. In their book *60s!* John and Gordon Javna suggest that Ballard's song may actually have predated the dance, and that it was actually Chubby Checker's little brother Spencer who invented it so Chubby would have something to do while he sang the song.

Chubby Checker became the prime player in this story when Dick Clark, host of "American Bandstand" (see p. 15), decided he liked "The Twist" enough to want to showcase it. He considered bringing

Hank Ballard on the air, but somehow that didn't work out, possibly because he was leery of Ballard's reputation for singing sexually suggestive songs. Clark knew a local Philadelphia singer named Ernest Evans (rechristened "Chubby Checker" by Clark's wife, who thought he resembled Fats Domino), who had a gift for imitating pop stars. Evans, who was nineteen and had worked for a while plucking chickens, had done a song in 1958 called "The Class," in which he mimicked Elvis, the Chipmunks, the Coasters, and Fats Domino, which Clark had sent out that year as a Christmas gift to friends. As Chubby Checker, Evans recorded an exact cover version of Hank Ballard's "The Twist," including even his "eee-yah!"; after he performed it and gave twist lessons on Clark's show it shot to number one on the *Billboard* pop chart (September 1960). Twisting became the biggest teenage fad since the beginning of rock and roll.

It got so popular so fast because it didn't have any rigid rules, and it could be done to almost any song with a good beat. There were no elaborate steps to learn like in dance class, and most important, you hardly had to coordinate your moves with a partner. It was a dance that allowed everyone to do what so many people in the 1960s were yearning to do: *their own thing.* *Time*'s story about the phenomenal success of the dance offered this instructive how-to: "Dancers scarcely ever touch each other or move their feet. Everything else, however, moves. The upper body sways forward and backward and the hips and shoulders twirl erotically while the arms thrust in, out, up, and down with piston-like motions of a baffled birdkeeper fighting off a flock of attacking blue jays." Because you didn't touch your partner, a room full of twisters had a tribal feel about it, and more than one analyst of the fad observed that the basic move-

ments of the dance harkened back to such venerable Afro-American steps as the shimmy and the black bottom, which in turn derived from African dances in which performers move down towards the earth, rather than dances in the European tradition, which tend to send dancers upwards. In his book *Disco* (1978) Albert Goldman observed that the essence of the twist was rotating buttocks. The thrill of wiggling one's ass, Goldman announced, "is exactly the same as the thrill of sexual liberation. With the twist, America learned how to 'get down.'"

There had been other teen dances that enjoyed the notoriety of the twist, including one scandalous one called the gator, a kind of reptilian mating ritual especially popular at keg parties in the Southeast. But the twist turned out to be a phenomenon of a whole other order of magnitude. Instead of staying a rude teenage fad, like Elvis and blue jeans and duck's-ass hairdos had been in the 1950s, the twist got respectable! It broke out of the teen ghetto, and what's most amazing is that it took rock and roll with it. Once viewed as strictly kid stuff, rock and roll's corybantic gyrations were soon considered fun (if not totally decorous) among adults. The solid-citizen activity once known as "social dancing" (consisting of the fox-trot, the waltz, and the lindy, and done by most average Americans only on formal occasions) had been nuked nearly out of existence. In its place came what *Variety* called a "form of shakes."

Less than two years after Chubby Checker introduced it on "American Bandstand," twist bands were playing for the amusement of customers at New York's ultra-swank Four Seasons restaurant and patrons of $100-a-plate dinners at the Metropolitan Museum of Art. Jackie Kennedy was said to have been caught twisting at a discothèque near the family compound in

Palm Beach (an apparently erroneous report for which AP later publicly apologized), and Liz Taylor and Richard Burton were seen twisting as they courted in the fashionable night spots of Rome. Lester Lanin and his high tone orchestra made an album called *Twistin' in High Society*, which instructed twisters to "crook their elbows, bend forward as if suddenly seized with acute appendicitis, and move the hips and shoulders in opposite directions." The liner notes also inform listeners that swells all over the world have come to know the new dance as *il torceménto, la torsion,* or *la torcedura.*

The twist's ascendance from crass to class happened in a roundabout way, starting when Chubby Checker's record found its way to Chez Régine, a Paris discothèque with a fashionable clientele. Mme Régine taught her jet-set customers to twist. When they came to New York at the beginning of the fall social season in 1961 and went slumming at the Peppermint Lounge, a midtown beatnik "flesh spa" (according to *Time*), they joined the regular déclassé denizens, who were still doing the twist from the year before. And they twisted, too. It was a moment that has been described as "a date that will go down in history as the birthday of discothèque social dances." *The Official Guide to Disco Dance Steps* called it "the greatest change in dance of the decade—perhaps in dance of the century."

In October 1961 gossip columnist Cholly Knickerbocker (Igor Cassini) wrote an item in his "Smart Set" column about what fun it was to go to the Peppermint Lounge and enjoy the sight of Colonel Serge Obolensky, Zsa Zsa Gabor, and various dukes and duchesses twisting their booties alongside "sailors, GIs, and young folks in sweaters and tight pants." Almost overnight the twist became the height of chic, and the Peppermint Lounge was the place to go—not for gawky

Dick Clark teens but for that strange, shiftless class of trend setters then known as the Beautiful People. "Society and show folk biggies mingle with beatniks," gasped Louis Sobol of the New York *Journal-American.* Cholly Knickerbocker (who had coined the term "jet set" to refer to modern café society [see p. 251]) wrote that it had become so much the "in" place that "now it's tougher to get a table at the P.L. than at El Morocco." Although Chubby Checker's "The Twist" had been off the charts for months, Ed Sullivan invited him to perform the song (and dance) on his Sunday-night television show. He did, and "The Twist" started selling like crazy all over again.

The scene on the dance floor at the Peppermint Lounge was so frantic that *The New Yorker* ran a "Talk of the Town" story about it in October from which all syntactic articles and pronouns were stripped away:

> Place always jammed. Huge line outside. Portals closely guarded. Finally made it last night, after hour's wait. Exhilarating experience! Feel ten years younger. Hit Peppermint close to midnight, in blue mood. Inside, found pandemonium. Dance floor packed and popping. Was battered by wild swinging of hips and elbows. . . . Garb of twisters seems to run gamut. Some couples in evening dress, others in T shirts and blue jeans. Young. Old. Businessmen. Crew Cuts. Beatniks.

Less breathlessly, *Time* inventoried

> bashful aristocrats . . . a vacant-faced girl in black pants, long black hair, and black glasses . . . a sweet-faced, sweet suited Miss (Vassar? Smith?) . . . her clean cut boyfriend (Yale? Princeton?) . . . a lad in a pinstriped suit . . . a mascara-splotched hoyden in a dress tighter than wallpaper . . . a Negro with ball-bearing hips. . . . They grimaced and they groveled, they

ground and they groaned in the dim light till they were spent.

In January 1962, *two* twist records battled for the number-one spot on the *Billboard* chart: Chubby Checker's original (for a second time) and "Peppermint Twist (Part 1)" by Joey Dee and the Starliters, who were the Peppermint Lounge's house band. In April, Clint Eastwood (then a TV cowboy) made a guest appearance on television's "Mr. Ed," during which he twisted with America's favorite talking horse. By 1962 the twist had become a phenomenon bigger than a dance or a hit record, bigger even than café society or the jet set or Mr. Ed. Doing the twist had become a way for people at almost every level of society to advertise that they were modern. Its democratic popularity was a signal that a new era had arrived—an era in which many adults learned to take their behavioral cues from kids instead of the other way around. Rock music, mod fashions, long hair, even psychedelic drugs and free sex followed the path of the twist up from infamy to widespread acceptance in the 1960s. That path, from antiestablishment irreverence into the pop mainstream, and from juvenile fad to big business, became a common one, and is still a fundamental means of cultural transmission. *Variety* headlined, NEW TWIST IN CAFE SOCIETY: ADULTS NOW DIG JUVES' NEW BEAT, declaring that "the youngsters of America have assumed the entertainment initiative."

Chiropractors were said to be getting rich treating twist-induced sprains, and Chubby Checker was hired by Thom McAn to help design (and endorse) a candy-apple-red, zip-up Twister shoe. Dozens of new dances were invented overnight in hopes of repeating the triumph of the twist. Along came the swim, the frug, the hully gully, the boogaloo, the hitchhike, the hucklebuck (a Chubby Checker specialty), the mouse (by Soupy Sales), the monkey, the watusi, the pony, and the jerk. John Youmans, chairman of the phys ed department at Temple University, bravely tried to catalogue all the variants of posttwist dance mania in his 1969 book *Social Dance*, published by the Goodyear (Rubber) Publishing Company. But Youmans grieved that lack of standardization made precision impossible: "The jerk as danced in West Los Angeles appears to be an entirely different social dance from that rendered by dancers in Los Angeles's Watts district." Furthermore, "the frug, as danced in Manhattan, closely resembles the watusi as danced in Hollywood." Despite these daunting obstacles to an accurate classification of the shaggy dog, the slop, and the funky chicken, Mr. Youmans did offer this summary insight about the floodgates opened by the twist: "These social dances are a revolt against tradition and the restrictions of authority; resulting movements are expressions of youthful desires for freedom."

VALLEY GIRLS

In the smog northwest of Hollywood there is a valley. In this valley there are malls, and in these malls rove adolescent girls who come to shop for fashionable clothes, to get their nails decorated and hair permed, and to otherwise impress their peers. So it is, so it shall forever be, and so it has been at least since the California suburbs boomed in the 1970s. In the summer of 1982, the San Fernando Valley had a moment in the sun.

Like teenage girls everywhere, those who cruised the Galleria in Encino, which according to *The Totally Awesome Val Guide* of 1982 "has more beauty salons and hair removal places than like any other place on the planet," spoke jargon. One of their number, a fourteen-year-old named Moon Unit Zappa, paid attention to what she heard in the mall, at school, at parties and bar mitzvahs. Her father, Frank Zappa, once leader of the Mothers of Invention and professional rock weirdo, was amused by her imitation of her friends. He took Moon into a recording studio and they made a record called "Valley Girl." He sang a chorus—"Okay, fine, fer sure, fer sure"—that framed what *Newsweek* called "a word-perfect portrait of the ultimate Valley girl," delivered by his daughter in the language known as Val-speak (derived mostly from surfer jargon). She bubbled and gushed in the singsong whine of the mall rat in which the speaker always seems, like, dumbstruck and makes statements sound like questions? The lyrics were about such issues as finding jeans tight enough, wearing a retainer, Pac-Man, and her "space cadet" mom, and they introduced listeners to such Valley-girl words as "grody" (disgusting, from grotesque) and "tubular" (excellent,

THE TOTALLY AWESOME VAL GUIDE...

"... I'm a Val, you know. [ ] urr. Like I dunno, It's like s-o [ ] ally awesome to be a total V [ ] , Ferr shurrr ... It's lik [ ] bitchen to like spend d [ ] ks like the Galleria, you kn [ ] t's s-o-o-o-o tubular and ev [ ] ... You know, like ferr shu [ ] ike without my makeup it's [ ] ty, grody to the max, barf ou [ ] err shurrr. Like I talk on t[ ] hor [ ] .."

... Ferr Shurrr!!!

By Jodie Ann Posserello
as told to
Sue Black

originally used to describe a great wave) and the typically verge-of-nausea expressions "gag me with a spoon" and "barf me out."

Moon Unit said she recorded the song merely to amuse her family and her friends, but Valley girls and the way they talked became *the* pet fad of the summer of 1982, eclipsing even Deely Bobbers (a pair of springy antennae for the head with colored balls at the end that boinged as the wearer walked). It didn't only happen in California, because even though the mother of all valleys was there, nearly every suburb in America had a mall and girls who cruised it, buying things and talking their unique kind of trash. "Vals are everywhere," Moon Unit said. By the fall, there was at least one Valley girl in a TV sitcom (the irritating Tracy Nelson character in "Square Pegs"); the following year Martha Coolidge directed the movie *Valley Girl*, starring Deborah Foreman and Nicolas Cage, described in one account as *"Romeo and Juliet* at the shopping mall" (sample dialogue: "Like, he's got the bod but his brains are bad news"); and Valspeak quickly became a widely accepted badge of the brainless, trendy, acquisitive culture of the adolescent middle class.

Here are a few essential Val-speak terms, as catalogued by *The Totally Awesome Val Guide:*

- *bitchen* [alt. *bitchin'*]: "Probably the best thing you can say about something. Encino is *bitchen* and so are some miniskirts and guys and stuff."
- *fer sure!:* "The first words a Valley baby learns to speak."
- *I'm sure:* "Indicates that you can't believe what you just heard. Vals have an intense feeling for the ironic."
- *like:* "The Hamburger Helper of Valley conversation. Goes hand in hand with 'Y'know?'."
- *to the max:* "What you might as well try to do everything to."

- *way:* "A very important word because it exaggerates and emphasizes, which is a key function of any Valley conversation. 'That dude is *way* totally bitchen, fer sure.' "

Vacuous as they seemed, Valley girls captured people's fancy because they were the first group since the trucker-CB radio craze of the mid-seventies (see p. 86) to invent not only a zesty new vocabulary but an attitude to match—blasé, rude, unabashed, and relentlessly egotistical. As a fad, they vanished quickly, but the stick-your-tongue-out-and-wiggle style they epitomized has never gone away. Three years after Valley Girl Summer, *Newsweek* reported that Vals had undergone some changes. Ruffled blouses, miniskirts, costume jewelry, and shaggy hair had become totally uncool. Their old role models, including Brooke Shields and Jamie Lee Curtis, had matured too much and were passé. They now had a new pioneer of insolent materialism to follow. "She just has everything like the typical dream girl," said a sixteen-year-old Valley girl in 1985. "I admire her because she's so popular and pretty." The Valley girls' idol, and the lasting manifestation of their style, was Madonna.

ANDY WARHOL

A ndy Warhol made a simple and stunning contribution to pop culture: He invented instant celebrity. Despite his stature as an important artist who helped bring the word "pop" into the modern vernacular in the 1960s, he is best remembered and most often quoted for a prediction he made in a catalogue for an exhibition of his

work in Stockholm in 1968: "In the future, everyone will be world-famous for fifteen minutes."

Nobody understood the ephemeral nature of modern celebrity better than he. He spent his life magnifying clichés to the heights of glamour and renown. He became famous by making everything around him

Sculpture portraying Andy Warhol. Displayed in a Santa Fe art gallery, 1992

into a glittering firmament of overnight fashion—created by the stroke of his brush, his camera or tape recorder, or just his word that it was so. From Campbell's soup cans and Brillo boxes to a whole galaxy of drag queens, pill poppers, and street beauties who joined his entourage in the early days, anyone and anything could be famous in his world. Fifteen minutes was the perfect amount of time, because Andy, like generations who have come after him, had a television-segment-length attention span.

In the early 1960s, when he left his career as a fashion illustrator to silk-screen big, brilliant paintings of money, Coke bottles, Elvis, and Liz Taylor, he knocked the art world for a loop. He was hugely successful, and the avant-garde man of the moment. But he was unlike Willem de Kooning, Franz Kline, and other trend-setting abstract expressionists of the 1950s, who had hung around the Cedar Tavern in Greenwich Village wearing work shirts, drinking whiskey and espresso, talking about love and life, and then going back to their paint-splattered studios to wrestle with their genius. Warhol was a new kind of artist whose work was cool and modern, mass-produced quickly and unfeelingly, like a typical American product. He rented space on East Forty-seventh Street, covered the walls with silver foil, and called it his Factory. It was at the Factory that he manufactured art and also fame.

Andy Warhol's fascination with products and factories and even his democratic view of stardom reveal his own blue-collar roots. He was born in Pittsburgh to Eastern European immigrant parents, and his earliest memories were of smokestacks and of weary workers returning home from steel and aluminum processing plants. How fitting that as an artist he would grow up to run his own Factory whose product was freshly minted, disposable celebrity. Like many smart marketers of new products, Warhol gave his goods a hyperbolic name: His entourage, who starred in his underground movies and became an ever-present cortège wherever he went, weren't just stars; he called them "superstars." It is a term that has since become part of pop culture's language.

Superstardom was a charismatic idea, especially in a country that tends to operate on the "olive" principle: small ones labeled large and large ones called jumbo, colossal, and even supercolossal. By the 1960s most Americans no longer shopped in stores, but in supermarkets (see p. 491); mighty nations had become superpowers; and our biggest national holiday would soon become the Super Bowl (see p. 485). Andy Warhol's first superstar was a plump girl from Brooklyn named Naomi Levine, whom he cast in a 1963 experimental 16mm movie called *Tar-*

zan and Jane Revisited . . . Sort Of. After her there were Viva, Baby Jane Holzer, Brigid Berlin, Ingrid Superstar, Ultra Violet, Candy Darling, and International Velvet—just some of the motley cast of characters who made their way to Warhol's Factory, performed in the movies that followed, and became part of the Factory scene. Few of them had any noteworthy talents, but they were ANDY WARHOL SUPERSTARS, and so they shimmered with pop prestige and became glamorous icons not only of Andy's world but of the 1960s.

In *Holy Terror*, a memoir of his life as editor of Andy Warhol's *Interview* magazine, Bob Colacello writes that Warhol never went anywhere without the famous people he had, in a sense, created. If you invited Andy to a party in the 1960s, you could expect to also get his "Superstar of the Year"—Edie Sedgwick, or whoever was in favor at the time—as well as the Velvet Underground rock band with a theatrical group called the Exploding Plastic Inevitable, which staged happenings featuring light shows and dances with bullwhips. Traveling en masse was a great way for the shy artist to make himself feel wildly popular and also keep a safe distance from an annoying public and press, who would often ask him such uncool questions as "What is art?" and "Are you a put-on?"

The notion of transforming everyday people into superstars was Warhol's most purely pop invention. By his logic, all that was required to be famous was the right attitude. Fat girls, fey boys—even pimply skinned, balding, wig-wearing, eyeglassed sorts like Warhol himself—could rise to star status in this alternative society of Beautiful People. And yet stardom was silly and contrived and was to be properly viewed with a great dose of irony. Warhol claimed that he craved fame unbounded. "I want to be Matisse," he once said. "I want

to be as famous as the Queen of England."

Ironic celebrity was a revolutionary idea, and one that has stayed around for three decades. It shows up time and again on David Letterman's late-night TV show, which often features such real people as dry cleaners, certified public accountants, or manufacturers of rubber dog poop, invited to share the stage and the spotlight of fame with Cher and to be spectacularly average. The Warhol legacy can be seen in the character of a weird guy like Larry "Bud" Melman, who has no discernible talent for doing anything, and it has also helped explain such instant celebrities as Jessica Hahn, Sukhreet Gabel, and Edith Fore, the lady from the commercial who has fallen and can't get up. Similarly, *Spy* magazine remains passionate about its own average guy, a fellow named Walter Monheit who, like Larry "Bud" Melman, seems to do little but amusingly exist.

As Warhol grew older, richer, and more paranoid (based in part on very real terror from a near-assassination in 1970 by a shunned minor superstar named Valerie Solanas), his love of fame took him further up the social ladder. He began to court, and was in turn courted by, the truly rich and well known. No longer content with the conceptual celebrities of his own making and his status as an avant-garde artist, Warhol left behind the underground counterculture of the 1960s and became what Earl Blackwell called the supreme "jet-set pet" of the 1970s, as socially connected as Truman Capote. Fame was his Holy Grail; the more (as he liked to put it) "up there" someone was, the harder he worked to get close. In part, his effort was a strategy to make more money: Andy Warhol was a shrewd businessman, and by the 1970s his work as an artist was mostly acquiring commissions for portraits of the very rich who liked to be enshrined in the Warhol canon along with such real stars as Marilyn, Elvis, Marlon, and Liz. As a kind of nouveau society court portraitist, Warhol cultivated clients at Studio 54 and at uptown parties virtually every night of the year. His friends were now no longer engaging street people and beautiful misfits but Bianca Jagger, Halston, Jerry Zipkin, Diana Vreeland, the Shah of Iran, Imelda Marcos, Nan Kempner, and São Schlumberger. After Warhol died in 1987, Bob Colacello recalled that the American press treated his passing as though it were Elsa Maxwell who was departed, lamenting that nightlife would never be the same without him.

By the time he went, at age fifty-nine, from unexplained complications after a gall bladder operation, Andy Warhol had come a long, long way from his poor Pennsylvania roots. Eight days before he died at New York Hospital, he lay in bed at home, sick with stomach pains, and watched a tape of a new MTV television show: "Andy Warhol's 15 Minutes." The room where he reposed, like the rest of his elegant house on Manhattan's Upper East Side, was as tasteful and as rarefied as a classical art museum. Valuable antique furniture, old masters on the wall, sacred icons, and rare bibelots had long ago replaced the blaring rock music and vulgar silver decor of his Factory, just as his retinue of faux superstars had been exchanged for a social circle that was the cream of the exclusive haut monde. But in the public's mind, and certainly to viewers of the youthful and newly minted MTV, Andy Warhol's name still symbolized American pop at its simplest: quick and sly as a wink, audacious, and with opportunity for one and all.

WAYFARER SUNGLASSES

Since sunglasses were popularized by movie stars in the 1920s and 1930s as a pseudo-disguise (no one is fooled, but shades eliminate eye contact and thus make their wearer seem unapproachable), they have been a symbol of glamour and coolness. Wayfarers, designed by Ray Stegeman of Bausch and Lomb in 1952 with big plastic frames, extra-dark lenses, and sturdy temples ("for the masculine look," according to early ads), have become the coolest of all. They were originally favored by California lifeguards and government secret agents (in the movies, but also real secret service men protecting the President), and no Hollywood juvenile delinquent was complete without them. They were pretty much forgotten in the sixties and seventies—an era

of sleek metal frames, dramatic oversized lenses, and such pert "fashionable" designs as Pixies, Pucks, Matadors, Mustangs (named after the car), and Seven-O-Sevens (designed to look like the Boeing jet). Foster Grant became the best-known sunglass maker in the sixties with its "Sunglasses of the Stars" ad campaign, which showed celebrities in "cheaters" (as hipsters call sunglasses) and asked "Isn't that Robert Goulet [or whoever] behind those Foster Grants?"

By this time, Wayfarers, with their thick plastic frames (in black or mock tortoise) and cumbersome pre-space-age styling, had begun to look quite passé.

In 1981, Dan Aykroyd and John Belushi chose Wayfarers as part of their so-square-it's-hip Blues Brothers ensemble. It was a time of classic rock-and-roll revival, and the "rediscovery" of Roy Orbison, who had made Wayfarers his trademark since 1963, and it was becoming chic to wear outmoded clothes (Hawaiian shirts, billowy pleated pants, appliqué poodle skirts, clunky wing-tip shoes). Wayfarers, with their faded-fifties glamour aura, quickly became the eyewear of choice among wannabe hipsters. After Tom Cruise wore them in *Risky Business* and Don Johnson in TV's "Miami Vice," sales boomed to nearly two million pairs per year by the end of the decade (up from eighteen thousand in 1981).

The extravagant success of Wayfarers has helped make retro styles the last word in glasses. Even pointy harlequin frames, originally a brand-name advertised in 1943 as being "so gay and debonair they give your very spirits a lift!" but then consigned to the purgatory of housecoat-and-slippers ensembles, have returned as rakish spectacle horseplay. Aviator glasses, designed for the Army Air Corps in the twenties and made into an icon of armed swagger by General Douglas MacArthur and highway patrolmen from coast to coast, have become, in *Esquire*'s words, "the most imitated sunglasses in the world." And Baloramas, another Bausch and Lomb design from the fifties, with the misterioso wraparound look once favored by "beatniks, jazzbos, potheads, and proto-punks," according to *The Catalogue of Cool* (as well as by Jackie during her Onassis years), are back and more popular than ever "as a new crop of customers cruises for cool in the ruins of ages past."

Long a sign of glamour, sunglasses were recently accused of being a fashion accessory favored by the emotionally disturbed, including people who suffer anxiety, phobia, and psychosis. Dr. Michael Terman, director of the light therapy unit at the New York State Psychiatric Institute, said that wearing them expresses "a certain escapism and a desire to reduce interactions that depend on eye contact." Not only do they signal emotional instability, Dr. Terman suggested, they can actually trigger it by cutting light exposure, which can encourage depression.

JOHN WAYNE

John Wayne, who weighed thirteen pounds when he was born on May 26, 1907, in Winterset, Iowa, was the movies' most powerful and popular embodiment of masculinity. He personified all the qualities that were once considered admirable and good about the male sex: He was six-foot-four and broad as a horse, with a craggy face and heavy-lidded mastiff eyes, strong and generally silent but with an authoritative, resonating voice that *Life* magazine once described as sounding "like someone sandpapering the strings of a bass fiddle." Beyond his majestic physical presence, John Wayne created an image of heroism in his movies that stood for generations of Americans (and movie fans around the world) as America's brightest beacon of moral purpose, gallantry, and honor.

His dauntless screen personality has often been caricatured (even by himself as patch-eyed Rooster Cogburn in *True Grit*), and it is not uncommon to see "John Wayne" invoked as a symbol of the ugly side of machismo and of a crude belligerence in the American character. But in fact, his movie roles are more complex than that, and the best of them are delicate portrayals of admirable, interesting, and even enigmatic men: agonizingly ethical (*Rio Grande*), gentle-tempered (*The Long Voyage Home*), able to bend (*The Quiet Man*), troubled by physical frailties (*El Dorado*), tortured by self-doubt (*The High and the Mighty*), and with a fine comic sense of their own swagger (*Rio Bravo*). Molly Haskell has pointed out that John Wayne is just about the only big male movie star who has actually played characters who *make friends* with women in movies (Claire Tre-

vor in *Stagecoach*, Jennifer O'Neill in *Rio Lobo*, Lauren Bacall in *The Shootist*). Although often shy and ungainly in their presence, he talks to women and listens to them the way movie tough guys (Humphrey Bogart) and skirt chasers (Errol Flynn) almost never did. Furthermore, his great on-screen romances have tended to be with women his own age (Maureen O'Hara, Patricia Neal, Katharine Hepburn), seldom with vapid cupcakes from younger generations. In even some of his most brutish roles, John Wayne's iron will is tempered by a capacity for love that belies the common exaggeration of his persona as a macho bully—as when he makes peace with Montgomery Clift at the end of *Red River* (1948), or, most dramatically, in *The Searchers* (1956), where, after twelve years of obsessive hatred of Indians, he finds the object of his search (Natalie Wood), who has virtually been made into an Indian by her captors, and embraces her. The expression on Wayne's face at the moment when he is about to pick her up and hug her is an emotional catharsis with few equals in any film.

Wayne never got a lot of respect from critics as an actor; his one Oscar, for *True Grit* in 1969, seemed more a Lifetime Achievement Award, given to him by the Motion Picture Academy for what was one of the most atypical performances of his career—a broad, indelicate burlesque of all the cowboy roles he had played in earlier decades. Such parody was not what made John Wayne great as a film actor; his genius on screen was his directness, which was in fact a matter of subtle elements—the way his hooded eyes flashed anger, laughed, and sometimes welled with tears (which never actually fell); the fine modulation of his gravel voice; a posture that conveyed moral fortitude tempered by modesty; an agile forcefulness that inspired director John Ford to say that he "moved like a dancer"; and a way with his hands—when twirling a six-gun, stroking a medal (as in *She Wore a Yellow Ribbon* [1949]), rubbing down a horse, or running his fingers through a woman's hair—that expressed the utmost mettle as well as sensitivity. None of these are the kind of overwrought qualities for which actors tend to win glowing notices: Wayne never cried, screamed, had fits, or transformed himself in a tour de force of histrionic art. You could always count on him to be himself—which is why audiences loved him.

He is often remembered for a line he said: "I don't act—I react." But he later added, "Reacting is a form of acting, and damned hard work." Recalling one of the formative moments of his craft, while working for director John Ford, he said that Ford told him, "You're going to get a lot of scenes during your life. They're going to seem corny to you. Play 'em. Play 'em to the hilt. If it's *East Lynne*, play it. You'll get by with it, but if you start trying to play with your tongue in your cheek and getting cute, you'll lose sight of yourself and the scene will be lost."

Wayne was discovered by John Ford in 1928 when Ford was making *Mother Machree* and Wayne had been hired as an off-screen wrangler to herd geese on Mother Machree's farm. He graduated to prop man, stunt man, then bit player, and when director Raoul Walsh needed a young, handsome, rugged-looking cowboy type to star in *The Big Trail* (1930), Ford suggested he try Wayne. At the time, he was still going by his given name, Marion Morrison, but he was known as "Duke" (a moniker he gave himself as a boy—after his pet Airedale—because he so disliked having a "girl's name"). "Duke Morrison" was discarded, however, and John Ford told him to pick the name of someone in American history he really liked, so he chose Mad Anthony Wayne, the Revolutionary War general. When they decided that "Tony Wayne" sounded too Italian, they settled on "John Wayne."

The Big Trail was a huge-budget epic shot in Fox Grandeur (a 70mm wide-screen process), and it put John Wayne on the map as a featured player, but it was a flop. Wayne's next two starring movies were duds, too: *Girls Demand Excitement* (a 1931 musical) and *Three Girls Lost* (a comedy, also 1931). So he went back to playing small roles, mostly in low-budget westerns, until John Ford cast him—against the wishes of the studio, which now considered him a grade-B actor—as the Ringo Kid in *Stagecoach* (1939).

Westerns were pretty much dead in Hollywood in the 1930s; they were thought of strictly as B pictures, for juveniles and hicks. But John Ford believed that "Stage to Lordsburg," a story by Ernest Haycox that appeared in *Collier's* magazine in 1937, had bigger potential. Set in the New Mexico territory during an Apache uprising, it was a rich character study about a group of people who are thrown together on a stagecoach in harm's way. Included among them was an outlaw named Malpais Bill (changed to the Ringo Kid for the movie)—a role Ford believed would be perfect for John Wayne, who had become a drinking and fishing buddy. The first Ford film to be made in Monument Valley (which Wayne claimed to have discovered on a Sunday drive while filming an earlier western on location in Arizona), *Stagecoach* was indeed a success: *Newsweek* called it "a rare screen masterpiece," and just about every review praised its visual beauty. But hardly anybody mentioned John Wayne's performance. As biographer Maurice Zolotow, author of *Shooting Star*, noted, "He was already making his work look too easy." Only C. A. Lejeune, a British critic, singled out Wayne, describing him as "a great film actor with a haunting face." *Stagecoach* revived the western as an A-picture genre and—despite most critics' indifference—made John Wayne into an A-picture star. Audiences—men and women—were mesmerized by him from the moment of his first, breathtaking appearance in the movie, where he stops the stagecoach by standing in the road twirling a Winchester repeating rifle as the camera trucks into a close-up.

Wayne's work in John Ford movies was one of the great collaborations in Hollywood history. Ford's noble vision of the American experience, in such films as *Fort Apache* (1948) and *The Man Who Shot Liberty Valance* (1962), provided Wayne an epic setting in which he established himself as a folk hero bigger than a movie star. He became an embodiment of the history he portrayed, and more than one observer has looked back on his career and likened him to a large section of Mount Rushmore. The America that John Ford envisioned and John Wayne personified was a country built by heroes—soldiers, pioneers, homesteaders, brave men and women with physical courage and spiritual resolve—but Wayne's role in it was frequently as a character who didn't quite fit. He was never a gung-ho "Indian fighter," not even in the cavalry movies; on the contrary, in *She Wore a Yellow Ribbon*, his heroic deed at the end is to avert an Indian war, and in *Fort Apache* he argues against a fight. His crazed hatred of Indians in *The Searchers* eats away at his soul and ensures his loneliness. His heroic passion for naval aviation in *The Wings of Eagles* (1957) destroys his home life. In *The Man Who Shot Liberty Valance* he watches helplessly as history passes him by. Each of these roles was a complex performance, rich with ambiguity, in which John Wayne created a character who was unwaveringly moral but wracked by demons and ulti-mately without a safe and contented place for himself in the world.

John Ford movies established the archetype, and other good directors played off it. Howard Hawks cast Wayne in *Red River* as a ruthless and monomaniacal leader of a cattle drive—the hero of the film, but with an iron will that verges on sadism in his dealings with his employees and an adopted son (played by Montgomery Clift). It was a fantastic role for Wayne, who brought his character to the edge of insanity but held the reins without a jot of leading-man self-indulgence. This lean tour de force as an actor helped audiences (and even critics) realize that there was something more to John Wayne than a tall-in-the saddle cowpoke hero. Similarly, when he was cast by Otto Preminger in *In Harm's Way* (1965) in what could have been a familiar war-movie role as a naval commander, Wayne soared—not so much in the combat scenes but in the romantic interludes with Patricia Neal and the tense interplay with Brandon de Wilde (as his estranged son). Even Preminger was amazed at his effortless ability to convey character, and said that he had rarely worked with a movie star who was so instinctively on target in his movements and expressions, actions and reactions in front of the camera.

It isn't easy to separate the man and the movie star when talking about John Wayne, and that's the way he liked it. "There are some parts I won't play—anybody dishonest or cruel or mean for no reason," he said in 1969, just a year before turning down the role of Dirty Harry (see p. 141). When *Life* did a cover story about him and Dustin Hoffman in 1969 titled "Dusty and the Duke: A Choice of Heroes," they described him as a real, old-fashioned westerner, out of a California tradition "compounded of sun, sea, gracious dark women and men who like to fish, shoot, and vote to the right. [His] politics come as naturally to him as the way he sits on a horse—there are few liberals in cowboy movies."

For John Wayne, there could be no corrupt or dishonorable heroes in cowboy movies, either. His very best roles, especially in westerns, are the ones in which the mythical cowboy's code of honor is challenged, and he suffers for his righteousness, but is never less than ethical: *Red River*, *The Searchers*, *The Man Who Shot Liberty Valance*. For *The Shootist* (1976), his appropriately elegiac final film, about a gunfighter dying of cancer, he insisted the script be cleaned up of its profanity and also that it be rewritten so that the young punk (played by Ron Howard) learns something good and decent, and throws away his gun, at the end. Ironically, in the movies John Wayne himself directed, *The Alamo* (1960) and *The Green Berets* (1968), the characters he plays are some of the least interesting in his career, because the roles are too easy for him. He is so squeaky clean and morally unchallenged, he's a bore.

For two decades, starting in 1949 (after *Red River*, *Fort Apache*, and *She Wore a Yellow Ribbon*), John Wayne was the biggest box-office draw on earth. He remained at the top of the Q polls (the celebrity Americans like most) until his death in 1979, but in the 1960s his politics polarized his fans. Like Jane Fonda (with whom he has nothing else whatsoever in common), John Wayne believed that it was his duty to speak out about the wrongs he saw around him. He had done so for years, becoming a well-known Commie hater in the witch-hunting 1950s, but no one seemed to be bothered by his right-wing beliefs until the war in Vietnam split the country into doves and hawks. Wayne was a hawk, and although everyone in Hollywood told him he was crazy to want to make a movie about an unpopular war, he felt it was his obligation to support his country. After visiting American soldiers in Vietnam, he said, "I owe it to them," and spent his own money directing and starring in *The Green Berets* (1968). It was not a good movie. Unlike the Apaches and Comanches he fought reluctantly in cavalry epics, the Vietcong were made into cartoon enemies, and John Wayne, playing Major Kirby, was a stiff. If the westerns had expressed a certain patriotic ideology (shot through with the ambiguities of history), *The Green Berets* was unshaded propaganda. It was slaughtered by critics. Renata Adler declared it "a film so unspeakable, so stupid, so rotten and false in every detail that it passes through being funny, through being camp, through everything, and becomes an invitation to grieve, not for our soldiers or for Vietnam, but for what has happened to the fantasy-making apparatus in the country. It is vile and insane. On top of that, it is dull." Bad as it may have been, *The Green Berets* showed Vietnam as a nice, old-fashioned war with good guys you could like and bad guys you could loathe, and there were enough Americans who needed that kind of moral support that it was a big box-office hit, earning its eight-million-dollar production cost in three months.

Wayne was convinced that all the treacherous critics were part of a liberal conspiracy who would give a bad review to anything that supported the war effort. He told Roger Ebert, "That little clique back there in the East has taken great personal satisfaction in reviewing my politics instead of my pictures. And they've drawn up a caricature of me." Alas, he was right. *The Green Berets*, if it did nothing else, helped solidify the image of John Wayne as a superpatriotic, cement-headed palooka. As happened to Jane Fonda, the Duke's heavy-handed politics blinded many people to the elegance of his art. Vincent Canby of the *New York Times* wrote that he never thought he could take John Wayne seriously again.

John Wayne redeemed himself, but only by playing a clown. A year after *The Green Berets*, *True Grit* was chosen by Vincent Canby as one of the ten best films of 1969. Critics relished seeing John Wayne poke fun at his ever-honorable screen image, especially after the sanctimony of *The Green Berets*. Even if *The Green Berets* had been a better movie, Wayne's time playing an intrepid hero on a manly mission was gone. He was old, and movies had changed, too: The earnestness that had made him such a standard bearer of virtue for so many years was out of fashion by the late 1960s, when America had become much more interested in screen rebels, brutes, midnight cowboys, and easy riders. Rooster Cogburn, the lead character in *True Grit*, gave John Wayne an opportunity to join the 1960s cinematic gallery of wonderful misfits. Cogburn was fat, wore an eye patch, and cursed out loud. Wayne described him as "an old, sloppy-looking, disreputable one-eyed son-of-a-bitch who used every trick, fair or foul, to get his man." When he picked up his Academy Award for the role, he joked, "If I'd known what I know now, I'd have put a patch on my eye thirty-five years ago."

Wayne continued to make movies, including a sequel to *True Grit*, *Rooster Cogburn* (1975), in which he co-starred with Katharine Hepburn. He died in 1979 of cancer, from which he had first suffered in 1965, when he had a lung removed. Joan Didion had interviewed him back then for the *Saturday Evening Post*, headlining her story "I Licked the Big C" and writing that she delighted in thinking of her girlhood hero "reducing those outlaw cells to the level of any other outlaws."

After his death in 1979, President Jimmy Carter eulogized him: "In an age of few heroes, he was the genuine article. But he was more than a hero; he was a symbol of many of the qualities that made America great. The ruggedness, the tough independence, the sense of personal courage—on screen and off—reflected the best of our national character." John Wayne had wanted his headstone to read *"Feo, Fuerte, y Formal"* —Ugly, Strong, and Dignified—but he was buried in Newport Beach in an unmarked grave because his family was worried about body snatchers. After his death, Congress minted a medal to honor him, the eighty-fourth such medal in the history of the United States. It showed Monument Valley on one side; on the other side was his portrait (as Davy Crockett in *The Alamo*) with the inscription, "John Wayne, American."

WEIGHT WATCHERS

In 1961, when Jean Nidetch was a two-hundred-plus-pound bowling-alley baby-sitter in a size 44 dress, she went on a diet supervised by the New York City Department of Health Obesity Clinic. The diet worked, but more slowly than it was supposed to, because Mrs. Nidetch couldn't stop herself from cheating. Every week she snuck cookies—two packages of Mallomars at a time—but she was so embarrassed by her transgression that she didn't admit what she had done to the nurse at her clinic. Instead, one afternoon she called six overweight friends and invited them to her Long Island apartment, supposedly to tell them about her wonderful new way of losing weight but really to get the forbidden Mallomars off her chest. The women liked hearing about the weight-reduction plan—a high-protein regimen conceived by Dr. Norman Jolliffe in the 1930s and known as the Prudential Diet—but more than that, they liked confessing their gastronomic sins to each other. One said she hid peanuts behind the asparagus cans in the cupboard; another crept down to the refrigerator late at night. "All overweight people have this tremendous desire to talk," Mrs. Nidetch observed.

Each of the fat friends took home a copy of the diet, and the next week, when they met again, they brought three more fat friends—newcomers who listened to the veterans talk about the tribulations of their first week of the new regime. The group grew, and they all chipped in and bought a medical scale for weekly weigh-ins. Soon there were forty of them, and they were meeting in the cellar of Mrs. Nidetch's apartment building, to which each brought her own folding chair. Word spread across Long Island, and soon Jean Nidetch found

herself speaking to strangers who had been inspired by her group to get together to help each other lose weight. In May 1963 she formed Weight Watchers and began charging two dollars to attend a meeting. Before anyone had ever heard the term "support group" (and well before obsessive dieting became fashionable), the members of Weight Watchers were sharing anxieties about forbidden donuts and revealing the secret hiding places for their emergency stash of candy bars. A branch opened in Rhode Island, and by the end of the sixties there were some ninety Weight Watchers franchises in America, England, Australia, and Israel.

Calling it "Alcoholics Anonymous for the overweight," *Business Week* marveled in 1967 about the many ways Weight Watchers was making money, which soon included a cookbook, packaged nonfat milk and low-calorie sugar, food scales, whole frozen meals, and summer camps for obese girls. Two years later *Look* magazine wrote about "Weight Watcher weddings, where reduced brides and grooms thank her [Nidetch] for making it possible," and said that people were clamoring for franchises around the world, "including undernourished India." In 1979 Nidetch and her business partner, Albert Lippert, sold Weight Watchers to Heinz for a hundred million dollars. Today, with three-quarters of all American women and half of all American men believing they are too fat, Weight Watchers has annual sales of $1.6 billion. An estimated fifteen million people have enrolled since 1963.

The basic principles of the fifty-year-old Prudential Diet are still in place, which means that you can eat plenty (of "legal" foods) and don't have to count calories, but Weight Watchers doesn't like to call what their customers do "dieting." It is a *program* that includes "the personal choice food plan," behavior-modification counseling called "challenges and choices," weekly meetings (including confidential weigh-ins) for group support, and an exercise plan. The regular assemblies remain the core of the program and are available in weekly group sessions that are frequently like big revival meetings or in an "At Work" program during lunch hours. There are also more exclusive get-togethers known as the "Inner Circle," for those willing to pay extra for the privilege of sharing their interesting weight-loss adventures in a more intimate setting.

CHARLES WHITMAN

To the end, Charles Whitman was meticulous and considerate. When the twenty-five-year-old architectural engineering student went up to the observation deck of the tower at the University of Texas in Austin on August 1, 1966, in order to shoot as many people on the ground as he could see, he packed a Bowie knife, a machete, and a hatchet; three rifles, two pistols, a sawed-off shotgun, and seven hundred rounds of ammo; and also a family-size can of Spam, a jar of fruit cocktail, an alarm clock, a roll of pink toilet paper, and a green plastic spray bottle of Mennen deodorant. There was so much equipment that he stopped at a rental store on his way to the tower and rented a dolly to carry everything, which he had packed neatly in a footlocker. Before he went to the tower, he stabbed his wife and covered her remains with a sheet. He wrote a note explaining that he loved his wife very much, but thought it was necessary to eliminate her because he wanted to spare her the embar-

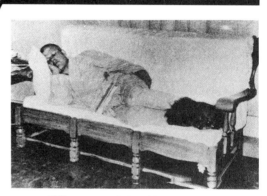

Whitman rests before his murder spree

rassment she no doubt would feel if she were alive when the news went out that he was a homicidal maniac.

After ninety-six minutes of shooting from the twenty-seven-story tower, Whitman was stopped by police, who, having failed to dislodge him with their own sharpshooters and with a light plane (which Whitman repelled with small arms fire), stormed the observation deck and shot him to death. He had murdered thirteen pedestrians plus an unborn baby (not counting his wife and his mother, whom he had also killed before going up to the tower) and had wounded thirty-one. No one had ever slaughtered so many innocent people, and although a man named Howard Unruh had shot thirteen on the streets of Camden, New Jersey, in 1949, Mr. Unruh had been an obvious lunatic who kept a long hate list of all the slights and insults he had suffered and found reason for his rampage in the Bible. Charles Whitman, on the other hand, had been a model citizen; he had been an Eagle Scout, an altar boy, an honorably discharged Marine, an A student. He was tall, well groomed, crewcut, and always polite. Charles Whitman was the all-American mass murderer.

In the last quarter-century, Whitman and his crimes have become an enduring symbol of utterly unexpected frenzy, and also of the abnormality that can lurk beneath a surface of sanity. In movies from Peter Bogdanovich's thriller *Targets* (1968), about a well-groomed psychopath who shoots from inside the screen of a drive-in movie, to Ron Howard's comedy *Parenthood* (1990), in which Steve Martin imagines his ultimate humiliation as a father—his son in a tower with a rifle—the image of the psycho sniper has been one of pop culture's favorite ways to show incomprehensible madness.

Even Charles Whitman couldn't figure himself out. In March 1966 he went to the university psychiatrist because he believed there was something wrong. He was having bad headaches and said that "intense efforts" were required to control his temper. The psychiatrist described him as "oozing with hostility" and took down only one direct quote from the session: "I am thinking about going up on the tower with a deer rifle and start shooting people." Four months later, on July 31, the night before he did what he said he feared he would do, he left this note to whom it may concern:

I don't quite understand what is compelling me to type this note. I've been having fears and violent impulses. I've had some tremendous headaches. I am prepared to die. After my death, I wish an autopsy on me to be performed to see if there's any mental disorders.... 12:00 a.m.—Mother already dead. 3 o'clock—both dead.

Charles Whitman may have had trouble accounting for his savage impulses, but there were others ready with an explanation. By the fall of 1966, America was beginning to polarize: counterculture vs. the establishment, peaceniks vs. hawks, longhairs vs. crewcuts. Charles Whitman was a perfect representative of the establishment America that a lot of disaffected people were opposed to. No one (other than some underground newspapers and the extreme left) said that *all* model citizens were actually berserk criminals, but Charles Whitman was for normal people what Charles Manson would later be for hippies—an unwelcome example of how their lifestyle could be perverted. In *The New Republic*, Robert Coles took the opportunity to write a story called "America Amok" and noted the parallel between Charles Whitman's killings and "a man who wants to be governor of California [Ronald Reagan] and is said to have suggested that North Vietnam be 'turned into a parking lot.' "

Editorial writers wrung their hands over what Charles Whitman's "orgasm of death and destruction" said about Americans and our propensity for violence, and—as happens whenever a mass murderer starts shooting—many used it as an opportunity to plead for stricter gun-control legislation. Always, the focus returned to Whitman himself, who was so nice and apparently uncomplicated that it seemed impossible to make any blame stick to him. And if he was not to blame, then it must be society.

Late in August, however, *U.S. News & World Report* came to society's defense, arguing that Charles Whitman "was no all-American boy"—that in fact he had been "mean as hell." A closer look at this square-jawed paragon revealed that he had been a compulsive gambler, had beaten his wife, had been court-martialed in the Marines for threatening assault. His best friend, Larry Fuess, said he believed that Whitman had been "goaded by self-discipline," and told reporters that although he was superficially cool and appeared to be in control of himself, he perspired gallons of sweat "even on the coldest days" and compulsively chewed his nails to the quick. When Fuess and his wife, Elaine, visited Charles Whitman on the evening before his murder binge, they found him alone at his typewriter. He told them he was writing a letter to a friend. Later, they realized he was writing his suicide and murder note. That night, Fuess noticed that Whitman seemed unusually calm; for the first time since they had met, he wasn't sweating or biting his fingernails. Elaine Fuess later remarked, "Even when he looked perfectly normal, he gave you this feeling of trying to control himself."

Charles Whitman's own theory about his mental disorders—that their cause might be found in an autopsy—at first seemed to be borne out when a neuropathologist found a tumor the size of a pecan (in the shell) growing in his brain. (Kinky Friedman sang a song about him that featured the line "There was a rumor he had a tumor.") However, doctors judged that it was highly unlikely that Whitman's tumor, which was benign and had not yet damaged any motor or sensory pathways, could have caused either his severe headaches or his murderous urges. They said the actions were entirely psychological in origin, the result of "very well concealed extreme hostility which finally matured to the point where he felt he had to act it out." An article about Charles Whitman's autopsy in *Science News* was headlined "TUMOR FOUND INNOCENT."

SLIM WHITMAN

In 1980 Ottis Dewey (Slim) Whitman went double platinum—that's two million records sold. He did this without a single sale in a record store and without any radio airplay, and despite the fact that he was unknown. It happened because Suffolk Marketing of Smithtown, New York, which had previously had good luck selling albums by Jim Nabors and Guy Lombardo through the mail, leased a bunch of Mr. Whitman's old tapes—songs he had recorded in the fifties, sixties, and seventies—and advertised the collection on television.

A new era in direct-response television marketing had begun. Buy-now ads had been successful since the sixties, starting with Ronco's Veg-O-Matic and continuing with such products as the Miracle Paint Roller and Ginsu knives (see "But Wait, There's More!," p. 74), and K-Tel International had sold untold numbers of rollicking Frankie Yankovic polka records through TV offers. But Slim Whitman was something altogether different, with an appeal that transcended country music and intrigued all manner of television viewers. His ads, which generally ran late at night, showed a

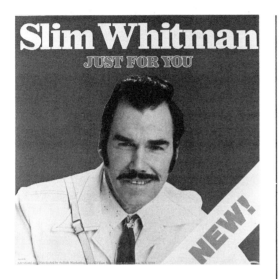

weatherbeaten middle-aged man in a western suit and neckerchief, casually strumming an acoustic guitar and lip-synching the words and yodeling the chorus to "Red River Valley." They were unusually low-key and amiable advertisements for their time slots, which were more typically occupied by hysterical sales pitches for Steam-A-Way irons and insane stereo deals. "Even the announcer touting the record sounds like a good guy," *The New Yorker* noted in a "Talk of the Town" article in November titled "Whitmania."

Once Slim Whitman had made his impression on television, he went on tour across America and played to sellout crowds. He appeared on "The Tonight Show." His next album, *Songs I Love to Sing*, went platinum, too—and this time it got its share of attention from country music radio disc jockeys. Thirty-two years after he had been discovered by Colonel Tom Parker (yes, Elvis's colonel) while singing live on a Tampa radio station, Slim Whitman was a superstar . . . for the second time.

Early in his career he had toured the South singing such country music standards as "Cattle Call" and "Blue Moon of Kentucky" (he topped the bill at Elvis Presley's first concert). He did well but never went national. In the mid-fifties, Slim (who in fact is pretty beefy, but got his name from RCA because they thought it sounded friendly) went to England and became an overnight success for the first time. "I was one of the first singers of this kind of music to go over there," he said. "I guess they liked the whole singin'-cowboy image. But they didn't know too much about country-and-western music, so when they asked me what it was, I said, 'I'm it.'" He wasn't merely successful; Slim Whitman became one of England's all-time most popular performers. His song "Rose Marie" held the number-one spot on British pop charts for eleven straight weeks in 1955—an achievement never bettered by anyone, not even by the Beatles.

He had sold over fifty-five million records before his TV resurrection in 1980, but except for the most devoted country music fans, few Americans knew who he was. "My career was very dormant in the seventies," he said. By the end of 1980, everybody with a television knew him, and it seemed as if half the nation was humming or singing along with such inspiring Whitman standards as "Vaya Con Dios" and "Indian Love Call."

In the wake of Whitmania have come dozens of non-prime-time ads featuring the works of unknown, forgotten, overlooked, and just plain strange musicians whose records are *not available in stores!* Suffolk next introduced Boxcar Willie, "the Singing Hobo," whose first public appearance was on television's "The Gong Show" and whose success (he sold a million albums practically overnight) was explained by a company executive as "bizarre, which makes for good shtick." Then came Frank Patterson, the Irish tenor, who sold three million "It's a Long Way to Tipperary"s in 1983; Nana

Mouskouri, a shy, bespectacled Greek lady who has sold more than thirty million copies of songs ranging from "Ave Maria" to a cover version of Dolly Parton's "Here You Come Again"; Zamfir (see p. 576), "Prince of the Pan Flute," whose "hauntingly beautiful" melodies sold over twenty million; and Whistling Whittaker, a Kenyan biochemist/balladeer, also hauntingly beautiful, who tooted and trilled his way into American television viewers' hearts and earned some two hundred gold, silver, and platinum records. Mr. Whittaker, who seems to have dropped whistling from his special TV record offers, now goes by the name Roger, and was seen only last year on a public television special concert for which he dressed in clown clothes, including makeup and teensy-weensy dunce cap, and crooned his mournful interpretations of "Green, Green Grass of Home," "Oh, My Papa," and "Send in the Clowns."

HANK WILLIAMS

Like Elvis Presley and Marilyn Monroe, Hank Williams has had a much nicer time as a dead person than he had when he was alive. He is today venerated as the King of Country Music, the first to break away from hillbilly charts into mass appeal, and there is hardly a soul in the recording business who doesn't speak about him with awe, respect, and admiration. However, most of those who knew Hank Williams before his corpse was found lying in the backseat of a powder-blue Cadillac on December 31, 1952, were not so rapt with blandishments. Prior to his death, he was nothing but trouble. He drank too much, he caroused with floozies, he took morphine (originally for a bad back), and he knocked himself out with chloral hydrate, which was supposed to help him stop drinking. Sometimes he was so smashed he forgot performances; there were occasions when he did show up on stage that he couldn't stand straight, let alone sing. Audiences heckled and threw things at him, and he hollered back until someone dragged him off to where he could numb himself into oblivion again. In quick succession in 1952, his first wife kicked him out of his mansion and he was fired from the Grand Ole Opry. When he died—of a "heart attack," according to the official death certificate—he was twenty-nine years old.

Hank and Hank Jr.

Only a little more than three years before, on June 11, 1949, Hank Williams had made Grand Ole Opry history when he appeared for the first time, on a Saturday night, and the audience demanded six straight encores of the same song, by then his trademark, "Lovesick Blues." Since arriving in Nashville in 1946, he had become the biggest draw in country music, but while he sailed to the top of the charts and gained a nationwide reputation, he was falling apart fast. Indeed, his very public disintegration was in some ways what made him popular. No doubt about it, there were fans who had a morbid curiosity to see Hank Williams go to pieces: In October 1952, when he was drinking heavily and had finally been shut out by an abashed music industry in Nashville, he married the same woman three times, twice before New Orleans audiences who paid between seventy-five cents and a dollar fifty to watch. It was a pitiful occasion, a last grasp for publicity at the end of his career, and no one from the music business came to be with him.

Such excruciating events are what Hank Williams's legend—as well as his music—is made of. Few artists have told about misery, loneliness, and rejection as nakedly as he did in such songs as "Ramblin' Man," "Why Don't You Love Me?," "Moaning the Blues," "Cold, Cold Heart," and "Your Cheatin' Heart" (the last one reportedly inspired by his first wife's philandering). If ever there was a living demonstration that country music is white man's blues, Hank Williams's music and career were it. Perhaps even more important than what he did as an artist, Williams established the self-destructive, maudlin, mournful rules of life that so many country music singers in his wake have followed.

He lived every tear of the suffering he sang about. Born poor in Alabama, always frail and painfully shy, he first learned music from a black street entertainer named Tee-tot, and by the age of fifteen he was singing in small-town taverns with a backup group called the Drifting Cowboys; he was already an alcoholic. In 1943, while performing with the Hadacol Caravan (which sold a murky brown cure-all with a high-proof moonshine kick), he met a nineteen-year-old girl named Audrey Sheppard, whom he married the following year in Andalusia, Alabama, in a ceremony performed by a gas station attendant who was also a justice of the peace. Audrey had ambition, and it was she who convinced him to go to Nashville and sign the contract with Acuff-Rose records that started his quick rise to stardom. After she divorced him in 1952 (and got custody of Hank, Jr., as well as half of all future record royalties), Hank took up with Billie Jean Jones Eshlimar, a nineteen-year-old he had met before getting fired from the Grand Ole Opry. It was his marriage to Billie Jean that Hank did twice for fans (a matinee and an evening performance) in October 1952, attracting 28,000 spectators and netting a handsome $30,000.

Hank Williams's death did not end the tortuous public disgrace that had simultaneously gilded and ruined his career. At the funeral there were two widows, side by side —Audrey and Billie Jean—and in the months that followed, both of them fought ferociously to be known as Mrs. Hank Williams. Audrey had ten years of marriage in her favor, as well as Hank, Jr., and she also claimed the rather important technicality that when Billie Jean had married Hank, only two months before he died, she was still married to a first husband. Billie Jean was paid $30,000 to forfeit her interest in the estate, and Audrey quickly went on tour across the United States, billing herself as "the One and Only Mrs. Hank Williams, the girl for whom the late, great Hank Williams wrote his famous songs, who is heard on

MGM label with Hank singing his favorite hymns, who appeared on stage with Hank [and] who, singing the songs Hank Williams made famous, recently completed a successful Canadian tour." Billie Jean sued, forcing Audrey to change her name on marquees from "Mrs. Hank Williams" to "Audrey (Mrs. Hank) Williams." Billie Jean then married Johnny Horton, whose big hit "The Battle of New Orleans" came out in 1959, a year before he was killed in a car crash. She married one more time before 1968, when, as Billie Jean Eshlimar Williams Horton Berlin, she filed a million-dollar lawsuit against MGM for its movie biography of Hank Williams, *Your Cheating Heart* (starring George Hamilton!), for which Audrey had been "technical advisor." The movie, Billie Jean complained, depicted Audrey as Hank's one and only love and had turned his marriage to Billie Jean into a shabby fling with what the book *Nashville Babylon* described as a "hillbilly harlot." After many court decisions and appeals, in October 1975 Audrey was stripped of her share of all of Hank's royalties, which were given to Billie Jean, who lived happily ever after.

Audrey Williams, Hank's first wife, was defeated and broke. After she sold some of Hank's things, she had her home seized by the Internal Revenue Service; finally, she retreated to bed and reportedly started taking massive amounts of sleeping pills and shrank to eighty-five pounds. Audrey Williams died late in 1975, at age fifty-two, not of a "heart attack" like Hank but of "natural causes." When she was buried, the officiating minister sang a Hank Williams classic at the coffin as her corpse was lowered into the ground: "Hey, Good Lookin'."

As for Hank Williams himself, his career was born again once he wasn't around to mess things up. Twenty thousand people attended his funeral in Montgomery, Alabama, where they wept at the sight of him lying in his open casket, which got carried in a procession from his mother's rooming house to the Municipal Auditorium to the cemetery. Roy Acuff, Red Foley, Ernest Tubb, and Little Jimmy Dickens all cried and sang Hank's "I Saw the Light." And in the year after his death, Hank Williams records sold more copies than in any year when he was alive.

WOLFMAN JACK

S ome disc jockeys become more famous than the hits they play, so beloved by their listeners that records get phased out altogether to allow them to talk trash for hours. From Murray the K and Alan Freed to Don Imus and Howard Stern, a handful of radio jocks have created a companion sensibility for rock and roll. Their personalities, like rock at its best, are forever young, audacious, and irreverent. The

most famous of them all is the Wolfman—Wolfman Jack, known for his beard and big-brimmed black hat but most of all for his foghorn growl and lycanthropic wails.

The golden age of hepcat deejays was the 1950s, before the spread of the Top 40 concept made so many of them obsolete. Even before there was rock and roll, occasional late-night rhythm-and-blues programs on stations in the South and Southwest were

hosted by black men and women who added a measure of verbal zest to the show, although *Ebony* magazine reported that of the some three thousand disc jockeys on the air in 1947, exactly sixteen of them were African-Americans. Probably the best-known of them was Lavada Durst of Texas, who hosted R&B shows on KVET in Austin from the mid-1940s to the 1960s. Durst, known to listeners as the one and only Dr. Hepcat, thrilled his audience with vocal pyrotechnics so extravagant that he once published a guide called *The Jives of Dr. Hepcat* to help listeners understand what he was saying. In his book *The Pied Pipers of Rock and Roll* Wes Smith offers this sample of Dr. Hepcat language to describe how he would get a job, avoid the police, earn money, straighten his hair, buy some shoes, drive along the street, and make time with a pretty woman: "If I had a pony to ride, I'd domino the nabbers, cop some presidents, gas my moss, and maybe get togged with some beastly ground smashers. Then I'd mellow to puff down the stroll where I'd

motivate my piecechopper onto a fly delosis."

To distinguish their rock-and-roll programs from the standard pop and jazz shows, which almost always featured hosts with measured, mellifluous voices, many early rock deejays developed a flashy patter delivered in a jivey voice like Dr. Hepcat's. John R. Richbourg of Nashville, Douglas ("Great Googa Mooga," host of "Jocko's Rocket Ship") Henderson of Baltimore, and Alan Freed of Cleveland (then New York) were among the best known of the early white rock jocks who sounded black, but Wes Smith writes that by the mid to late 1950s, the airwaves in every American city featured such characters as "the Jet Pilot of Jive," "Daddy-O Hot Rod," "Poppa Stoppa," and even a female "Dizzy Lizzy" or two.

The Wolfman started life as Robert Weston Smith in Brooklyn, where he grew up in the early 1950s speaking street lingo and listening to a transoceanic radio his father bought him in hopes of diverting the boy from mischief on the street. Smith's radio could pick up "Hound Dog" Lorenz of Buffalo, "Jocko" Henderson, even Hoss Allen from Nashville, and Alan Freed, who moved to New York in 1954 and called himself the Moon Dog. Smith wanted to be a radio disc jockey, so he tried to get the attention of the Moon Dog by hanging around a rock-and-roll jubilee show Freed was hosting in Brooklyn in 1955. When that didn't work, Smith went to Nashville and learned from the smooth-talking John Richbourg (known as John R) how to cue records, work the console, and drop the needle on a record in the right place.

Smith bounced from station to station, assuming different show names, playing different formats. In 1960 he found his true self in the Mexican town of Via Cuncio, nine miles south of Del Rio, Texas, at what was known as a border station. XERF was beyond the reach of the FCC, immune to regulation, and empowered with a globe-girdling 250,000 watts. Bill Smith went on the air at seven; he played country tunes and Spanish music; he sold half hours to preachers with miracle cures; then round about midnight, when the moon rose high in the sky, he changed. He howled. He growled. He became the Wolfman. Riding a signal that tore through the night and simply overpowered any puny legal broadcasts in his path, the Wolfman told his listeners to "get nekkid!" or "squeeze my knobs!"; he spun the kind of funky rock and rhythm platters he liked best; and he became known to long-haul truckers, small-town kids listening under cover to their transistor radios, low riders out cruising, and neckers parked on lovers' lanes all over North America. According to Bill Crawford and Gene Fowler in *Border Radio*, "Wolfman and his cohorts pitched sex pills, diet pills, record packages, even Wolfman roach clips, guaranteed to make the intrepid insects easier to handle." The Wolfman was an outlaw voice in the night—invisible, untouchable, and with all the taboo thrill of rock and roll when rock and roll belonged to the iconoclasts.

The fun of the show had a lot to do with wondering exactly who or what the Wolfman was. It didn't help matters that when he appeared in public he wore a paste-on goatee, a cheap black wig, and liberal amounts of pancake makeup in a swarthy shade. As weird as he looked, he acted even odder. Away from the anonymity of the radio microphone, he was painfully shy; at rock-and-roll stage shows he hosted, he would introduce each act, then quickly run for a hidden bucket where he could vomit violently from stage fright. Wes Smith describes one occasion when the Wolfman made a personal appearance at a college in Kansas City: He arrived for the stage show

in a limousine, outfitted with a lupine wig, long fake fingernails, and prosthetic rubber cheeks, his path prepared as he walked by two midgets and two half-nude dancing girls strewing rose petals.

The Wolfman lost his border-station venue in 1970, and his raunchy reputation made him persona non grata in all major American markets, but his star rose again in 1973 when director George Lucas, who as a teenager had been a faithful listener of the Wolfman, cast him to play himself in *American Graffiti*. The movie showcased not only the Wolfman but also, briefly, the man behind the Wolfman, a sympathetic human that no one had known named Bob Smith. Lucas's ode to the shared experience that cruising and radio listening used to be made the Wolfman more famous than he had ever been.

Suddenly everyone wanted a piece of him. He hosted "The Midnight Special" on television, and in 1974 he was recruited by station WNBC in New York to do battle with the reigning king of the morning jocks, "Cousin" Bruce Morrow. It's hard to say who won that war, because the Wolfman was too antsy to stay in one place for long; after eight weeks on WNBC, and no clear victor in the ratings, he headed back to California. Like a tumbleweed, he seemed to pick up some of almost everything he brushed against. He hosted a religious show that featured gospel-styled soft rock; he did road tours and commercials; he appeared on television in "Battlestar Galactica," "The Odd Couple," and "Wonder Woman." He pitched Clearasil acne cream, bathing suits, and stereos. He endorsed burgers by McDonald's, Hardee's, and Arby's. He was enlisted in the advertising campaign for John Landis's *An American Werewolf in London*. He also developed a heavy cocaine habit that almost lost him his devoted wife, Lucy Lamb. As Wes Smith put it, "She married

Bob Smith [in 1961], but Wolfman Jack kept showing up in her bed."

Today the Wolfman and Lucy Lamb live on a plantation in North Carolina. He still hosts rock concerts, makes commercials, and puts on shows for corporate sponsors. Once a mystery to listeners, since *American Grafitti* he has become probably the only disc jockey whose looks are as recognizable as his voice. He is a character from another era, when rock and roll was a hep-cat's gas. He was a hustler, a huckster, a fast talker who created a crazy theater of the mind by sending forth the Wolfman into parked cars and highballing trucks and darkened dens at night and enticing the great web of listeners to share the strange ecstasy of the airwave's ether: "Lay yo' hands onna radio right now," he used to cry out, "an' *feeeel meee!*"

WOODSTOCK

E ven before it began on the weekend of August 15–17, 1969, Woodstock the concert had taken on symbolic meaning and become Woodstock Nation, suggesting a new alignment of citizens, somehow significantly different from the old American nation. In retrospect, the notion seems at least a little grandiose, but the attitudes and beliefs that came together at that summer gathering in upstate New York still have towering resonance. Woodstock is perhaps the best-known single event in the cultural history of the baby boom. When it happened, it seemed like the culmination of the 1960s, and for many it still retains an almost hallowed aura. It became the subject of an Academy Award-winning documentary movie (*Woodstock*) that more than any fiction film or other documentary captured the youth movement as youth wanted to be seen and is still considered a "cult classic," more than twenty years after its 1970 release; it inspired a Joni Mitchell song and the name of a bird in the "Peanuts" cartoon (which in turn inspired Whoopi Goldberg to get a Woodstock tattoo); and its anniversary has been marked every ten years (so far) by outpourings of nostalgia and remembrance in the press, and a reassessment of whether or not the postwar generation is living up to its exalted ideals.

Being at Woodstock was, in the words of a guy named Zodiac, from Ken Kesey's farm in Oregon, "like being one molecule in a big organism. There was a whole bunch of stuff that you had no control over or nothin'. You were just there." Being there wasn't even required to feel part of Woodstock Nation, that glorious convergence of nude bodies, psychedelic drugs, and sense of do-your-own-thing liberation that made concert-goers so ecstatic. To be at Woodstock, or merely to feel that Woodstock was your kind of happening, was to cast your lot with all that was new and fresh and full of life.

The Woodstock Music and Art Fair had originally been planned as nothing more than a great big rock concert that was to take place in Wallkill, New York. The citizens of Wallkill, however, got cold feet when they realized how big the fair was going to be, so after tickets were printed, the organizers, Woodstock Ventures, Inc., were forced to move the event to the nearby

bration of peace (in opposition to the war in Vietnam), and that is the way it has been eulogized. And yet Woodstock had all the bellicose determination of a torchlight political rally. Many of the four hundred thousand knights errant who made the trek to the farmland of upstate New York felt like soldiers in a people's guerrilla force: volunteers from every politically correct walk of life in the Age of Aquarius, including communalists from around the nation, potheads, acid freaks, campus revolutionaries, hip professors, swinging nuns, hippies, Yippies, and Merry Pranksters. They were a motley bunch (although mostly white and middle-class), and they shared some important things: marijuana, rock music, and long hair; they wanted the U.S. out of Vietnam; they were against Nixon, the army, and everyone else who stood for the old way of life. Most important of all the things they shared was a veneration of youth. Youth came to Woodstock to stage a jamboree celebrating its symbolic freedom from the old, straight world.

The primary attraction, of course, was the lineup of heavyweight musicians, although even they were ultimately overshadowed by the monumentality of the event itself. Performers included Jimi Hendrix and the Electric Sky Church; Blood, Sweat and Tears; Joan Baez; the Jefferson Airplane; the Who; Ravi Shankar; Melanie; Joe Cocker; Carlos Santana (who called the event "a coming together of all the tribes"); Crosby, Stills, Nash and Young, and Country Joe and the Fish, who roused the crowd when they led a "F-U-C-K" cheer ("Gimme an F . . .") as part of "The I-Feel-Like-I'm-Fixin'-to-Die Rag."

Woodstock felt less like a concert than a battlefield: tents, army-style mess, makeshift first-aid facilities for casualties (mostly from the notorious bad acid tabs that made people freak out with uncontrollable trem-

town of Bethel. (Today, original Woodstock tickets are worth big bucks to collectors of 1960s memorabilia.) The organizers ran a wrathful advertisement in hundreds of newspapers in the eastern United States, explaining the change of venue: "The whole idea of the festival is to bring you three days of peace and music. Not three days of dirty looks and cold shoulders." The ad promised legal action against "these *concerned* citizens of Wallkill," and showed a caricature of two ugly, hostile hicks with guns raised and ready. All through the summer of 1969, the idea of the forthcoming concert served as a lightning rod for an anxious and oddly angry love generation that felt itself at the barricades against an intolerant America.

That was the strange thing about the Woodstock festival. It was billed as a cele-

ors). Jimi Hendrix even played "The Star-Spangled Banner"—while humping his guitar and making it sound like an exploding bomb. There were hip MPs, in the form of the Hog Farm commune, who were airlifted in from New Mexico, merrily boasting that they used nothing worse than seltzer bottles and cream pies as their weapons. For those bands of ragged crusaders who journeyed to this farm to take their stand with their brothers and sisters, an exciting siege mentality reigned.

In his book *Woodstock Nation*, Abbie Hoffman wrote: "God, how can you capture the feeling of being with 400,000 people and everyone being stoned on something? Were we pilgrims or lemmings? Was this really the beginning of a new civilization or the symptom of a dying one? Were we establishing a liberated zone or entering a detention camp? Like dig it baby." A few months later, when he was on trial for conspiracy to riot at the previous summer's Democratic convention, he insisted to the court that he was a citizen not of the U.S.A. but of Woodstock nation, "a nation of alienated young people." "In what state is Woodstock?" asked the judge. "It is in the state of mind," Hoffman answered, "in the mind of myself and my brothers and sisters. It is a conspiracy."

The very unyouthful *New York Times* called Woodstock "a nightmare of mud and stagnation"; even Abbie Hoffman had some doubts about the downside of the event: "three people getting killed, a few thousand injuries, lack of food and water and hundreds of bum trips," as well as the Woodstock Venture fat cats getting rich by co-opting the movement.

Undaunted by such mundane realities, the myth of victory about that weekend was invincible. On August 18, when the festival was disbanding into acres of rubble that resembled a field where a pitched battle had been fought, the "CBS Evening News" lauded what it called the "outpouring of young people struggling to survive" and spoke about "old-fashioned kindness and caring...harmony and good humor." And that is how Woodstock is remembered: as a great feast of love. It was everybody helping one another: cooperation instead of competition; coping with the mud and the rain; beautiful people having sex; women (two of them) giving birth; and nobody getting hassled by authorities. The festival had captured a piece of upstate New York and the attention of the world by presenting Woodstock Nation as a virtuous and inexorable legion whose good vibes could not be stopped.

YELLOW RIBBONS

If the United States gets into another war soon, it is very likely that the Beatles' "Yesterday" will be deposed as the most-recorded song (over twenty-five hundred cover versions) of the rock era. Hot on its heels at number two is "Tie a Yellow Ribbon Round the Ole Oak Tree," which began life as the best-selling single of 1973. Its popularity soared once again in 1980 when fifty-six Americans were held hostage in Iran, then another time during the Persian Gulf War. Most of the rage for the song, at

least by 1991, was a by-product of another, even more ubiquitous phenomenon: the display of yellow ribbons on tree trunks, front doors, car antennae, mailboxes, whole buildings, and lapels.

People display yellow ribbons as a sign that they want someone to come back home, safe. Unlike star-spangled banners flapping in the wind, which in the words of Russell Banks, writing in the *New York Times*, "express a Super Bowl mentality [and] our collective desire to kick collective butt," yellow ribbons have no military bearing. "Early on in the Gulf crisis, I decided I liked them," Banks wrote, explaining that he believed they signified that America's troops were stationed in a foreign land against their will. Once the shooting in the Persian Gulf started on January 16, however, the subtlety of that symbolism (supporting the troops but not what they were doing) evaporated, and yellow ribbons became, for many people, symbols of support for the war—frequently displayed alongside American flags.

It has long been a custom for the wives of fighting men to keep a piece of their men's colors when they were away at battle. During the Civil War, Union soldiers wore yellow neckerchiefs, and their wives and sweethearts took to wearing yellow ribbons in their hair as a way of feeling close to them and praying for their safe return. It was a tradition carried on in the Indian wars by cavalrymen's wives, as seen in the John Ford movie *She Wore a Yellow Ribbon* (and sung about in a song by the same name), but yellow ribbons had pretty much vanished from popular culture by the time of the Vietnam War.

In 1971 an old man from Georgia, incarcerated in New York for four years on a bad check rap, got out of prison and headed back home on the bus. He told his fellow passengers that before he was released he had written to his wife and told her he was finally returning, and she could dump him if she didn't want him anymore, but if she still loved him, she should tie a yellow handkerchief to the old oak tree in the middle of their hometown, Brunswick, Georgia. By the time the bus approached Brunswick, every passenger knew about the man's gamble, and—according to Pete Hamill, who originally wrote the story in the New York *Post*—they were "up out of their seats, screaming and shouting and crying. The tree was covered with yellow handkerchiefs, twenty of them, thirty of them, maybe hundreds, a tree that stood like a banner of welcome, blowing and billowing in the wind, turned into a gorgeous yellow blur by the passing bus."

Irwin Levine and L. Russell Brown read about the incident and wrote it as a happy-ending ballad called "Tie a Yellow Ribbon Round the Ole Oak Tree." (Pete Hamill speculated that the songwriters changed the handkerchief in the original story to a ribbon "because you can't find anything to rhyme with handkerchief.") Pop singer Tony Orlando didn't much like the song when Telma Hopkins and Joyce Wilson (a duo known as Dawn) proposed they record it together. "I thought it was corny," he said. He and Dawn were ready to break up as an act, anyway: Following their chart-topping success with "Knock Three Times" in 1971, they had gone nowhere. Still, after hearing it, Orlando recalled, "I found it was stuck in my head, I kept singing it around the house. Against my will." It turned out to be a monster number-one hit. It revived the flagging career of Tony Orlando and Dawn and led to a CBS-TV prime-time series for them in 1974. Thereafter, it became Tony Orlando's signature song.

Among the many fans of the song was Penne Laingen, of Bethesda, Maryland. Mrs. Laingen's husband was one of the Americans taken hostage by Iranian students in 1979, and when she saw news reports that showed angry Americans throwing dog food at Iranians in the United States, she was awfully upset. "I didn't want us behaving that way," she recalled. Searching for a dignified way to remind people that her husband was a captive, she thought of Tony Orlando's feel-good song. She began a campaign to tie yellow ribbons around trees, and by the time the hostages were released after 444 days in captivity, in January 1981, there were yellow ribbons knotted onto things all over America.

Almost as soon as American troops started getting shipped to the Persian Gulf in the fall of 1990, yellow ribbons started appearing everywhere again. A month into the war, C. M. Offray and Sons, a New Jersey ribbon-maker, reported having sold over thirty million yards of yellow ribbon— over ten times their normal production. Florists, gift stores, supermarkets, scout troops, and clubs all wanted ribbon to tie into bows and festoon the nation. Businesses began to announce great sales by hanging up yellow bunting; some gave away lengths of free ribbon with every purchase (we got eight yards with our McMuffin when we breakfasted at a McDonald's in Nebraska City, Nebraska on July 4, 1991). The Los Angeles *Times* told about a local crafts store that had run out of ribbon and was cutting yellow tablecloths to meet demand, and at Los Feliz Doggery, a pet-grooming salon, every customer was sent home with a yellow ribbon tied around its collar or to its ear.

In Brunswick, Georgia, the old oak tree was still standing in 1991—sheathed in a single huge yellow ribbon. "Yellow ribbons have shown the world that this country is indeed united," Tony Orlando observed during the Gulf War, taking pains to explain that he didn't want to sound self-promotional. "This is America's story, not my story," he said, calling yellow ribbons "the unifying strand that connects everyone—a coalition of the heart."

YUPPIES

Can you remember when yuppies were amusing? That's before they became annoying, then detestable, and now, annoying all over again because they have turned into nearly everybody's favorite all-purpose whipping boy. Towards the end of the 1980s, it grew very tedious (not to mention morally repugnant) to hear about yuppies and their spoiled, materialistic life all the time, but what is even more irritating today is to hear yuppies invoked whenever anybody wants to say something bad about the Reagan years. Because no one ever proudly declared himself to be one, they form an easy, risk-free target whenever a sanctimonious moralist, TV movie-of-the-week screenwriter, commentator, or politician wants to vilify hedonism and greed. No one will really be offended if you wear a T-shirt that says DIE, YUPPIE SCUM! on it, because the word "yuppie" is almost guaranteed to generate a knee-jerk response: They're vile! To call someone a yuppie in 1992 is only a little bit nicer than calling him or her a criminal, and certainly the same as calling him or her an asshole.

Few synthesized concepts of class and status have acquired so much purely moral (or, we should say, immoral) resonance. The word "yuppie" was first uttered some time in the late 1970s, echoing such earlier charismatic lifestyles as hippies (see p. 212), Yippies, and preppies (see p. 400). At first, it implied no value or judgment, it was simply a demographic acronym for "young urban professional," and its earliest use in

print is credited to Bob Greene in a March 1983 newspaper column. By the time Greene used it, "yuppie" already had elitist undertones, but also a certain ambivalent appeal. Yuppies were the people that all advertisers wanted to reach, characterized by *Time* in a review of *The Yuppie Handbook* in 1984 as "fast trackers now united under a sassy name and invited to smile along at their own trendiness." They were the ones who, following Malcolm Forbes's dictum "He who dies with the most toys wins," had figured out a new way to enjoy life: by treating themselves to all kinds of good stuff. And hey, they asked, why not? They worked very, very hard, so they figured they deserved it. When *Business Week* analyzed the newest lifestyle configuration in 1984, which they called the YAP (for "young aspiring professional"; also "pay" spelled backwards), the editors said that YAPs were "fast becoming the emblem of the 1980s. In fact, you might even be a YAP yourself." What an amusing notion! Hot on the heels of the hugely popular preppy trend, which peaked in 1982, yuppies appeared to be the latest example of the baby boomers' never-ending aptitude for popping up in yet another merry guise.

No one knows exactly who originally coined the word, but when it first got extremely popular in 1984, it had lots of competition, including YAP, Y.P. (young professional), Y.E. (young elite), Yo-Pro, and yumpie (young upwardly mobile professional). *The Young Aspiring Professional's Fast Track Handbook* (1984) explained what they were: "twenty-five to forty years old, well educated, well motivated, well dressed, and well exercised. [They] don't hold jobs, they enjoy *careers*. Frenetic travel, overtime hours (without pay, since you are a *professional*), and a constant search for contacts (networking; a.k.a. touching base) go with the territory." The

Charlie Sheen as a Yuppie in Oliver Stone's film *Wall Street*

YAP motto, the *Handbook* advised, expressed the fast-track view of life: *"Veni, vidi, priorificavi"*—I came, I saw, I prioritized.

Yumpies were essentially the same thing, described by *Time*, which used the term in a March 1984 article about the upwardly mobile professionals who were presidential candidate Gary Hart's constituency, as the latest incarnation of the generational energy first let loose in the 1960s. They were characterized as baby boomers who were still skeptical about the establishment, but who had lived through the Me Decade and had "shed idealism for pragmatism, and liberalism for moderation." *Time* noticed that "many Yumpies seem more interested in making money for themselves than in redistributing it to the poor."

Yaps, yumpies, yuppies: The latter name finally prevailed, perhaps because it sounded most like a cheer, which seemed appropriate for these hard-charging players in the game of life. But whatever they were labeled, they were a purposeful bunch: self-indulgent, success-oriented, fashionable, and—thanks to abundant credit and their ruthless, type-A work ethic—prosperous. Almost nobody boasted that he or she was a yuppie; it always seemed to be someone else who daydreamed about a new Filofax organizer or spent hours obsessing about the implications of leather vs. faux leather seats in a new German sports sedan (as did Albert Brooks in his yuppie pilgrim parody, *Lost in America* [1985]). But even if no one laid claim to being one, during the reign of Reagan (whom the *Wall Street Journal* once called "the most aged yuppie") wanting it all wasn't yet considered extremely shameful. A lot of thirtysomething citizens longed to wear Rolex watches, drive Beamers (BMWs), carry Gucci briefcases, outfit themselves in Ralph Lauren clothes, brunch under ceiling fans on goat cheese or sushi or anything doused with raspberry vinaigrette, and work out on Nautilus equipment at the gym. Perhaps it was a little embarrassing to be so insatiate and worldly, but what was wrong, these tireless yuppies asked, with wanting to possess the best things in life, and working hard to get them?

These are some of the essential elements of the yuppie lifestyle, as it was posited in the early 1980s:

- a brick-walled industrial loft or townhouse in a neighborhood recently rescued from urban blight (Many yuppies actually commuted from suburbia, but they didn't brag about it.)
- for wearing to work, pinstriped suits and yellow power ties and suspenders for men; business suits with running shoes for women; Walkmen, squash rackets, and a copy of the *Wall Street Journal* for both of them. For weekend leisure wear, including brunch, designer jogging clothes were acceptable for both sexes
- a fetish for New American cuisine, including all noniceberg lettuces and anything mesquite-grilled; also a preference for designer water—Perrier and beyond—and any well-packaged luxury variant of a cheap foodstuff, such as Dove Bars instead of Fudgsicles, ten-dollar-a-pound coffee instead of Maxwell House, Sichuan food instead of egg foo young
- a state-of-the-art butcher-block-and-stainless-steel kitchen with every conceivable gadget, including digital timers, a pasta maker, a gelato machine, and a suite of Krups stuff to grind coffee beans and brew cappuccino
- an herb garden in the kitchen window (for making pesto and gathering tarragon for salad dressing), but no marijuana allowed —too hippie!
- an Akita dog named Chevre or Kiwi
- a German or Swedish car; a Jeep or Land Rover for suburbanites or for trips into the country

- a large collection of mail-order catalogs, including Williams-Sonoma, Eddie Bauer, the Sharper Image, J. Peterman
- a yearly income of at least twice one's age in thousands
- nagging self-doubt about the value of all of one's achievements and possessions.

One of the appealing things about the yuppie idea was how democratic it was—a real relief from the preppymania that had run rampant in the first few years of the decade. Even though anyone could *pretend* to be a preppie, true prepdom required breeding and genealogy, which couldn't be faked. Marissa Piesman, co-author of *The Yuppie Handbook*, explained to *People* magazine, "Yuppie is more an achieved state while preppy is an inherited state." To be a yuppie required only the willingness to work hard and go into serious debt obtaining the proper turbo-charged, anthracite-gray sports coupe, a condo in an upscale neighborhood, and membership in an exclusive health club.

At a time when acronymania was rampant, the yuppie label, applied to all things avaricious and trendy, was soon supplemented by "buppie" (black urban professional), "guppie" (gay urban professional), "huppie" (Hispanic urban professional), "juppie" (Japanese urban professional), "puppie" (pregnant urban professional), "muppie" (medical urban professional), and "dink" (double income, no kids).

In 1985, after the cover of 1984's final *Newsweek* announced "The Year of the Yuppie," a Roper Poll found that 60 percent of all adult Americans knew what one was. The same poll, however, showed that a vast majority of people who had been questioned thought yuppies were "overly concerned with themselves." Even earlier, in the days before the Democratic convention of 1984, Gary Hart was already trying to distance himself from the label, which had been thrown at him by his opponents for its untoward connotations of snobbery and luxe. From the time Bob Greene first wrote about them, yuppies were simply too selfish to be role models, and too acquisitive to fit the nonprofit image required of all political candidates.

Because they were so ripe for parody, yuppies made appearances in many of the decade's situation comedies: Young Alex Keaton (Michael J. Fox) yearned to be one in "Family Ties" (Fox then grew up to play a sort of mutant one in the movie of Jay McInerney's hyper-yuppie book *Bright Lights, Big City*); Angela Bower (Judith Light) was such a fast-track mom in "Who's the Boss" that she needed to hire a live-in housekeeper (Tony Danza) so she could spend her day touching base and networking; Frazier Crane (Kelsey Grammer) joined the cast of "Cheers" in 1984 and gradually developed, with his wife, Lilith (Bebe Neuwirth), into a prime-time pillar of yuppiedom, complete with a BMW and a taste for pretentious food. The most fully realized yuppie on TV was Michael Harris (Peter Scolari), who also came to the small screen in the great Yup Year of 1984 as the producer of Dick Loudon's (Bob Newhart) television talk show on "Newhart." Michael was an exquisite caricature—materialistic, amoral, superficial, and so full of drive to succeed that he verged on dementia. And as the yuppie ideal was scorned in the later 1980s, so was Michael. Fired from his executive position, he became a common shoe salesman—supreme humiliation for a yuppie—and eventually went hilariously insane (he was later redeemed).

"Yuppies have become a bore," the *Wall Street Journal* announced in 1987, the year of the big stock market crash. Whatever currency the concept retained into the last years of the decade was eradicated by the simple facts and figures of an economic downturn. Somehow, it wasn't so much fun anymore to worry about which professional kitchen range had the better flame pattern when the real issue was how to pay the rent. At the same time, yuppie idols were falling in disgrace: Wall Street brokerage scandals, the collapse of the junk bond market, the humiliation of Donald Trump (see p. 529), the ignominy of corporate raiders like Ivan Boesky and Carl Icahn all signaled the definitive end of an era when predatory business practices were a strategy to be admired. Make no mistake: Boesky, Trump, Michael Milken, et al. were no yuppies, but they had been men that yuppies wanted to emulate. No more. The look of corporate upward mobility, which was the original mark of the energetic yuppie, became not only morally wrong but—even worse for many of them—socially embarrassing.

Gil Schwartz expressed his mortification in a very funny column for *New York* magazine in which he confessed, in hushed and worried tones, that he actually enjoyed goat cheese and sun-dried tomatoes, and he couldn't turn off "thirtysomething" (p. 518) when it came on TV, and he drank Pellegrino water and designer beer from Lapland: all stereotypical yuppie behavior. He yearned to order a certain sleeveless sweater from the Eddie Bauer catalog, and he found himself obsessing about real estate values, and to fall asleep, he counted Range Rovers jumping over a fence. "Why fight it?" he finally sighed in his article, which was titled "The Last American Yuppie."

In April 1991 *Time* printed what it suggested just might be the very last story on yuppies, after approximately 22,000 such stories, many of which, since 1986, had proclaimed the death of yuppiedom. But slippery as real yuppies may have been, the concept has proven to be rock steady. Even though it is virtually impossible to find anyone who admits to being one, or to *ever* having been one, the discredited yuppie value system is too useful for self-righteous people who need a greedy foe to rail against. And so they live, if only in our moral imagination; *Time*'s writer, Walter Shapiro, wondered if, even after five years of being declared dead by the press, yuppies might not fill the void in our culture's value system for years to come. "One can imagine the horror movie," he joked: *"Nightmare at the Brie Counter, Part 12: Die Again, Yuppie Scum."*

Funny as the *Time* story was, it was also absolutely right. Yuppies are definitely not dead, at least not yet, according to *The New Republic*, which ran an article a few years ago about what it called "the last yuppie status symbol"—a designer cemetery plot. "Yuppies have seen the future, and it is death," author Michael Specter wrote. "Successful young people with little else to worry about have become the driving force of the growing multibillion-dollar death business. They are out there hustling for the 'right' cemetery plot in much the same way they have scoured the nation for the most sophisticated cabernets, the most authentic Italian espresso machines, and the best Aprica strollers." Specter quoted one urban professional, not so young anymore, who explained his logic in acquiring a choice parcel of burial ground on a very desirable Long Island knoll: "If you struggle all your life to get good jobs and the best apartments and to send your children to Harvard, why the hell should you want to spend three thousand years lying under a highway in Queens?"

ZAMFIR

Zamfir is the world's best-known—the world's *only* known—Pan flutist. A one-named phenomenon like Hildegarde and Tinkerbelle, he was famous in his native Romania, then throughout Eastern Europe, before anyone in North America had ever heard of him, but he made a giant reputation in the United States and Canada starting in the mid-1980s when he was featured in wee-hour advertisements for his records (available *exclusively* via special TV offers). The ads show him tooting out plaintive tunes such as "Memory" (from *Cats*) and "Plaisir d'Amour" on a bamboo instrument that resembles a hand-held set of miniaturized church organ pipes. As he produces his fragile melodies, an announcer proclaims him "master of the Pan flute" and describes his sound as "hauntingly beautiful." His talent has proven to be so haunting that Zamfir has joined the elite likes of Slim Whitman, Roger Whittaker, Nana Mous-

kouri, and Frank Patterson (see p. 560) as one of what the *Star* calls "the reigning royalty of mail-order superstars."

Young Gheorghe Zamfir first picked up a Pan flute only because Romania was suffering a severe accordion-teacher shortage when he was a boy. The accordion had been his original chosen instrument, and as a teen coming of age on a vineyard in the village of Gaiesti in the 1950s, he demonstrated his abilities squeezing out gypsy ballads and enthusiastic two-steps on the accordion at local weddings. But when he wanted to further his studies at the local music school, there was no one there who knew anything about the instrument. There was, however, a place available in the Pan flute class. Gheorghe enrolled, and his aptitude was immediately apparent. He realized he was born to play the Pan flute.

Not that it was easy for him: "The first time I played the instrument I became dizzy after two minutes," he recalled, describing it like "blowing into a flame." Breath control is all that matters, because the Pan flute has no reeds or keys and finger holes. The player cannot see it as he blows (because it is held dangling down below his chin); and it demands such control and concentration that Zamfir now says he needs to go on a yoga retreat every summer and to engage in transcendental meditation every day to maintain his edge. In a concert, he stands on stage surrounded by four different Pan flutes, each capable of a twenty-octave range, and puffs on them all, ending a performance nearly as wrung-out as Springsteen.

After mastering the pipes of the Pan flute, Zamfir continued his education at the Bucharest Conservatory, graduating with hon-

ors and going on to conduct the 350-musician Romanian Folk Ensemble during its triumphant tour of Bulgaria, the USSR, and Mongolia. His talents as a soloist became known to the western world in the early 1970s when he gave a series of concerts in Paris, and by the end of the decade, his ethereal recording of "The Lonely Shepherd" made him an international phenomenon.

Since he first appeared on American television pitching his recordings, he has sold more than twenty million records, tapes, and CDs and earned thirty-three platinum discs; he has recorded mystical soundtrack music for *The Karate Kid* and *The Karate Kid II;* and his theme for the TV soap opera "Ciao Christiana" made him a matinee idol in Venezuela. The pipes of Pan are probably the world's oldest instrument (they are described in Greek mythology), and there is something so uncommon about them that Zamfir's much-vaunted mastery has made him into an amusing oddball celebrity beyond his ability to play. Johnny Carson has cracked jokes about his ardent flautistry, and he has even been anointed as an au courant celebrity in a guest appearance on "Late Night with David Letterman." He is a curiously pop phenomenon, known as much for his television ads as for his musical abilities, and definitely *better*-known among ordinary TV viewers than he is among devoted music connoisseurs.

Despite the strange nature of his renown, Zamfir is not a famous-for-fifteen-minutes kind of guy. In addition to composing and arranging works for solo flute, Pan flute, and Pan flute with orchestral accompaniment, he devotes himself to training Pan flute disciples. He says that he feels a strong responsibility to teach others because he is one of the few masters of the ancient instrument still alive.

Index